FREDDIE
& ME

FREDDIE
& ME

A Coming of Age (Bohemian) Rhapsody

Mike Dawson

JONATHAN CAPE
LONDON

Published by Jonathan Cape 2008

2 4 6 8 10 9 7 5 3 1

First published in Great Britain in 2008 by
Jonathan Cape
Random House, 20 Vauxhall Bridge Road,
London SW1V 2SA

www.rbooks.co.uk

Addresses for companies within The Random House Group Limited can be found at:
www.randomhouse.co.uk/offices.htm

The Random House Group Limited Reg. No. 954009

A CIP catalogue record for this book is available from the British Library

ISBN 9780224081931

The Random House Group Limited supports The Forest Stewardship
Council (FSC), the leading international forest certification organisation. All our
titles that are printed on Greenpeace approved FSC certified paper carry the FSC logo.
Our paper procurement policy can be found at www.rbooks.co.uk/environment

Printed and bound in Slovenia by MKT Print d.d.

For My Family

This book couldn't have been written without the continued love and support of my wife, Aliza. She is an inspiration, and always makes me believe that great things are possible.

Thank you to my family for a lifetime of nothing but encouragement.

Thanks to my pal Alex Robinson, for many Wednesday nights at Foley's talking about the rewarding world of comics and life in general. To PJ Mark for taking on this book and finding some amazing homes for it, and Yelena Gitlin, Dan Franklin, and Colin Dickerman for helping me to shape this story into its final form.

I am especially grateful to the following friends and family: Chris Radtke, Gary Gretsky, Robert Poole, Kristen Siebecker, Vania Tseng, Tony Consiglio, Jonathan Bennett, Luke Harms, Brandi Kattan, Nancy Tsai, John Kerschbaum, and the Best Family: Marc, Betsy, Micah and Jen.

Very special thanks to Chris Pitzer of AdHouse Books.

Thanks also to: James Boyle, Charles Brownstein, Jeff Cioletti, Alain David, Vito Delsante, Christian Dumais, Serge Ewenczyk, Aaron F. Gonzalez, Dean Haspiel, Brian Jacks, Phil Jackson, Damien Jay, Tom Kaczynski, Charlie LaGreca, Heidi MacDonald, Jeff Manley, Janna Morishima, Alex Ness, Mark Nevins, Mike O'Connor, Annette Rella, Stephen Schwartz, Casey Seijas, Dave Sim, Chris Staros, Alexandria Steppe, Cynthia Stierle, Adam Suerte, Jennifer and Francis Tunney, Brett Warnock, Mike Watanabe, Rich Watson, and Caleb Wright.

And, of course, thanks to Freddie, Brian, Roger, and John.

'I THINK PEOPLE SHOULD JUST LISTEN TO IT,
THINK ABOUT IT, AND THEN MAKE UP THEIR OWN
MINDS AS TO WHAT IT SAYS TO THEM'

Freddie Mercury on *Bohemian Rhapsody*

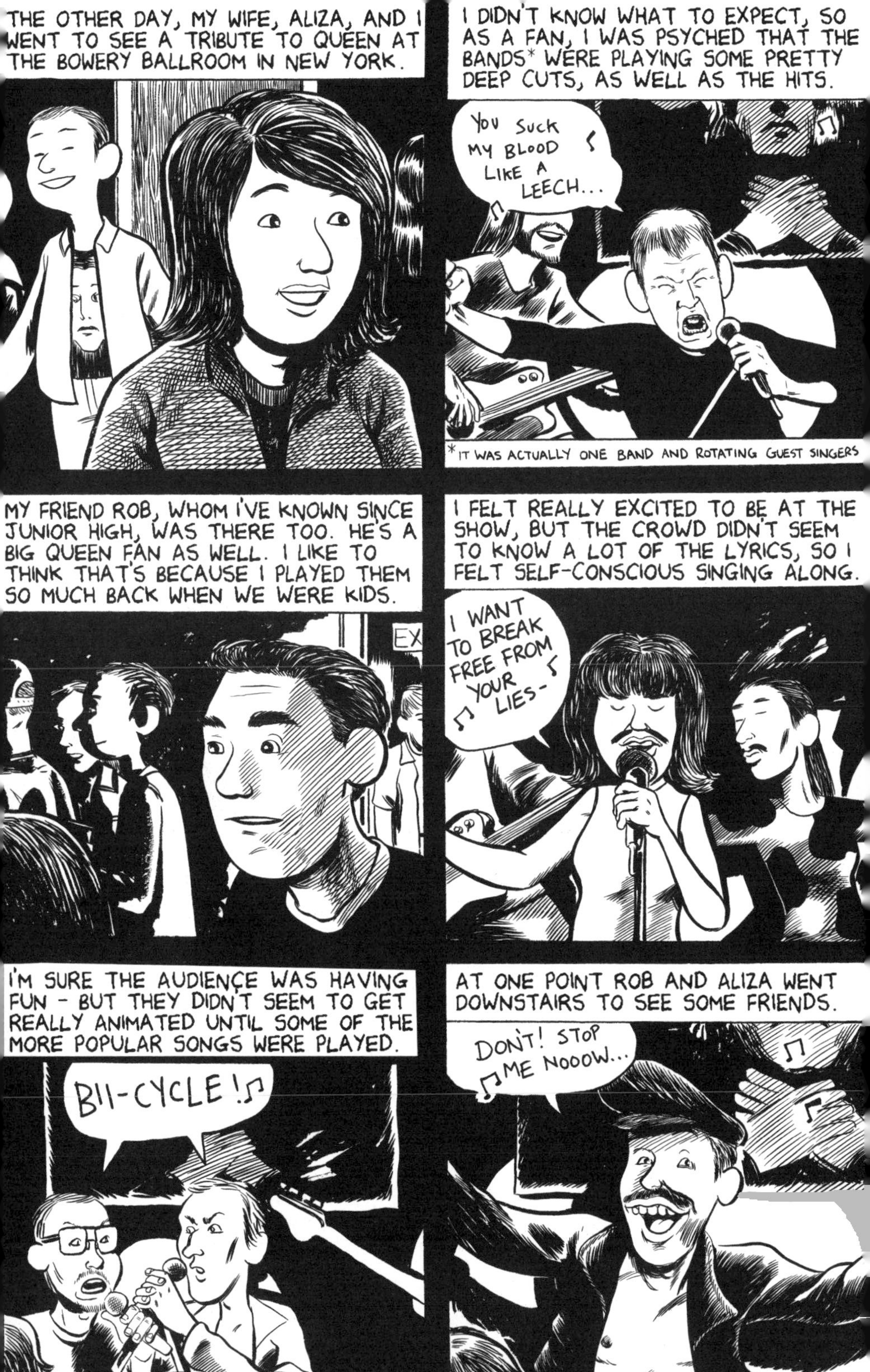
THE OTHER DAY, MY WIFE, ALIZA, AND I WENT TO SEE A TRIBUTE TO QUEEN AT THE BOWERY BALLROOM IN NEW YORK.
I DIDN'T KNOW WHAT TO EXPECT, SO AS A FAN, I WAS PSYCHED THAT THE BANDS* WERE PLAYING SOME PRETTY DEEP CUTS, AS WELL AS THE HITS.
YOU SUCK MY BLOOD LIKE A LEECH...
*IT WAS ACTUALLY ONE BAND AND ROTATING GUEST SINGERS
MY FRIEND ROB, WHOM I'VE KNOWN SINCE JUNIOR HIGH, WAS THERE TOO. HE'S A BIG QUEEN FAN AS WELL. I LIKE TO THINK THAT'S BECAUSE I PLAYED THEM SO MUCH BACK WHEN WE WERE KIDS.
I FELT REALLY EXCITED TO BE AT THE SHOW, BUT THE CROWD DIDN'T SEEM TO KNOW A LOT OF THE LYRICS, SO I FELT SELF-CONSCIOUS SINGING ALONG.
I WANT TO BREAK FREE FROM YOUR LIES-
I'M SURE THE AUDIENCE WAS HAVING FUN - BUT THEY DIDN'T SEEM TO GET REALLY ANIMATED UNTIL SOME OF THE MORE POPULAR SONGS WERE PLAYED.
BII-CYCLE!
AT ONE POINT ROB AND ALIZA WENT DOWNSTAIRS TO SEE SOME FRIENDS.
DON'T! STOP ME NOOOW...

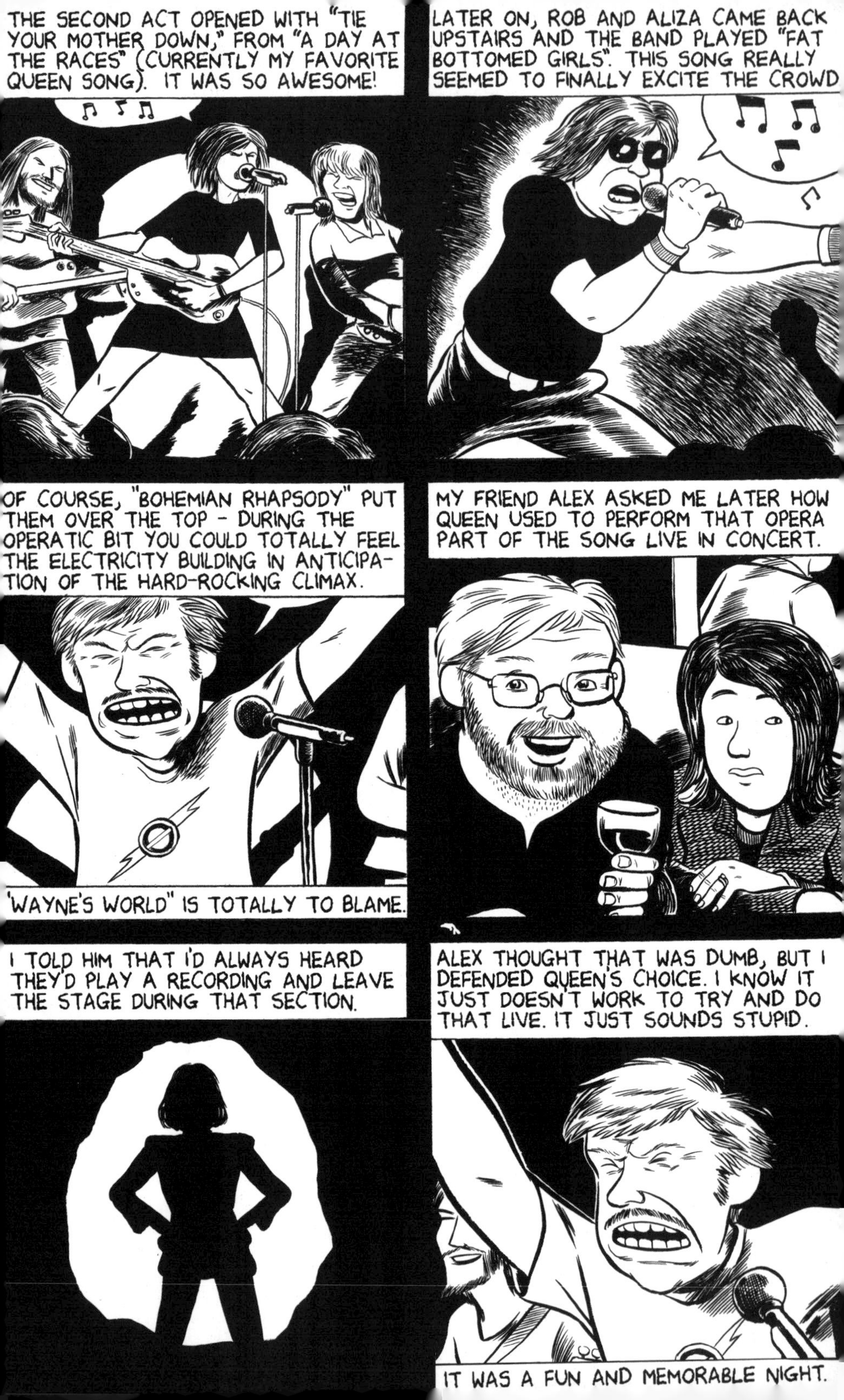
THE SECOND ACT OPENED WITH "TIE YOUR MOTHER DOWN," FROM "A DAY AT THE RACES" (CURRENTLY MY FAVORITE QUEEN SONG). IT WAS SO AWESOME!
LATER ON, ROB AND ALIZA CAME BACK UPSTAIRS AND THE BAND PLAYED "FAT BOTTOMED GIRLS". THIS SONG REALLY SEEMED TO FINALLY EXCITE THE CROWD
OF COURSE, "BOHEMIAN RHAPSODY" PUT THEM OVER THE TOP - DURING THE OPERATIC BIT YOU COULD TOTALLY FEEL THE ELECTRICITY BUILDING IN ANTICIPA-TION OF THE HARD-ROCKING CLIMAX.
"WAYNE'S WORLD" IS TOTALLY TO BLAME.
MY FRIEND ALEX ASKED ME LATER HOW QUEEN USED TO PERFORM THAT OPERA PART OF THE SONG LIVE IN CONCERT.
I TOLD HIM THAT I'D ALWAYS HEARD THEY'D PLAY A RECORDING AND LEAVE THE STAGE DURING THAT SECTION.
ALEX THOUGHT THAT WAS DUMB, BUT I DEFENDED QUEEN'S CHOICE. I KNOW IT JUST DOESN'T WORK TO TRY AND DO THAT LIVE. IT JUST SOUNDS STUPID.
IT WAS A FUN AND MEMORABLE NIGHT.

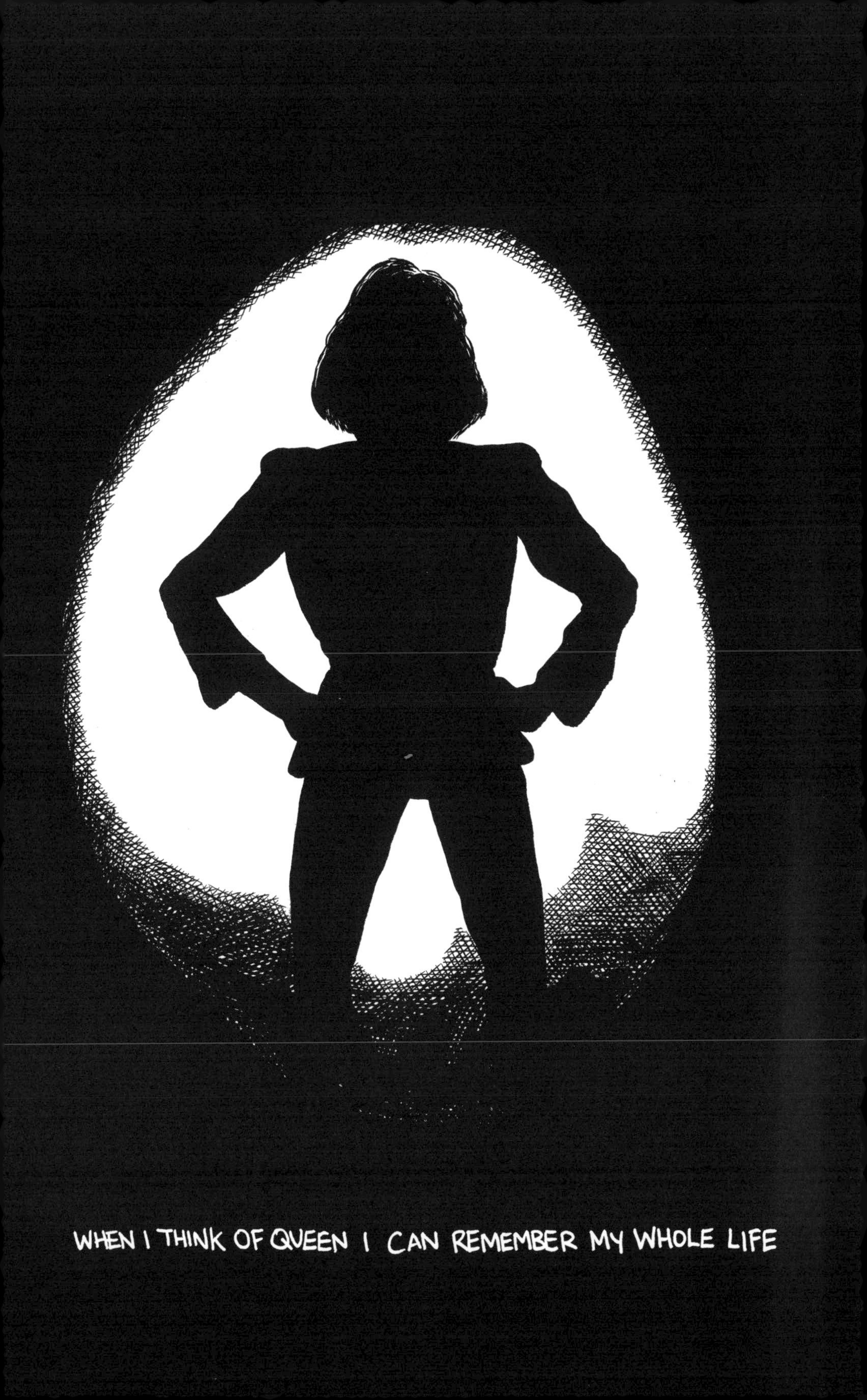
WHEN I THINK OF QUEEN I CAN REMEMBER MY WHOLE LIFE

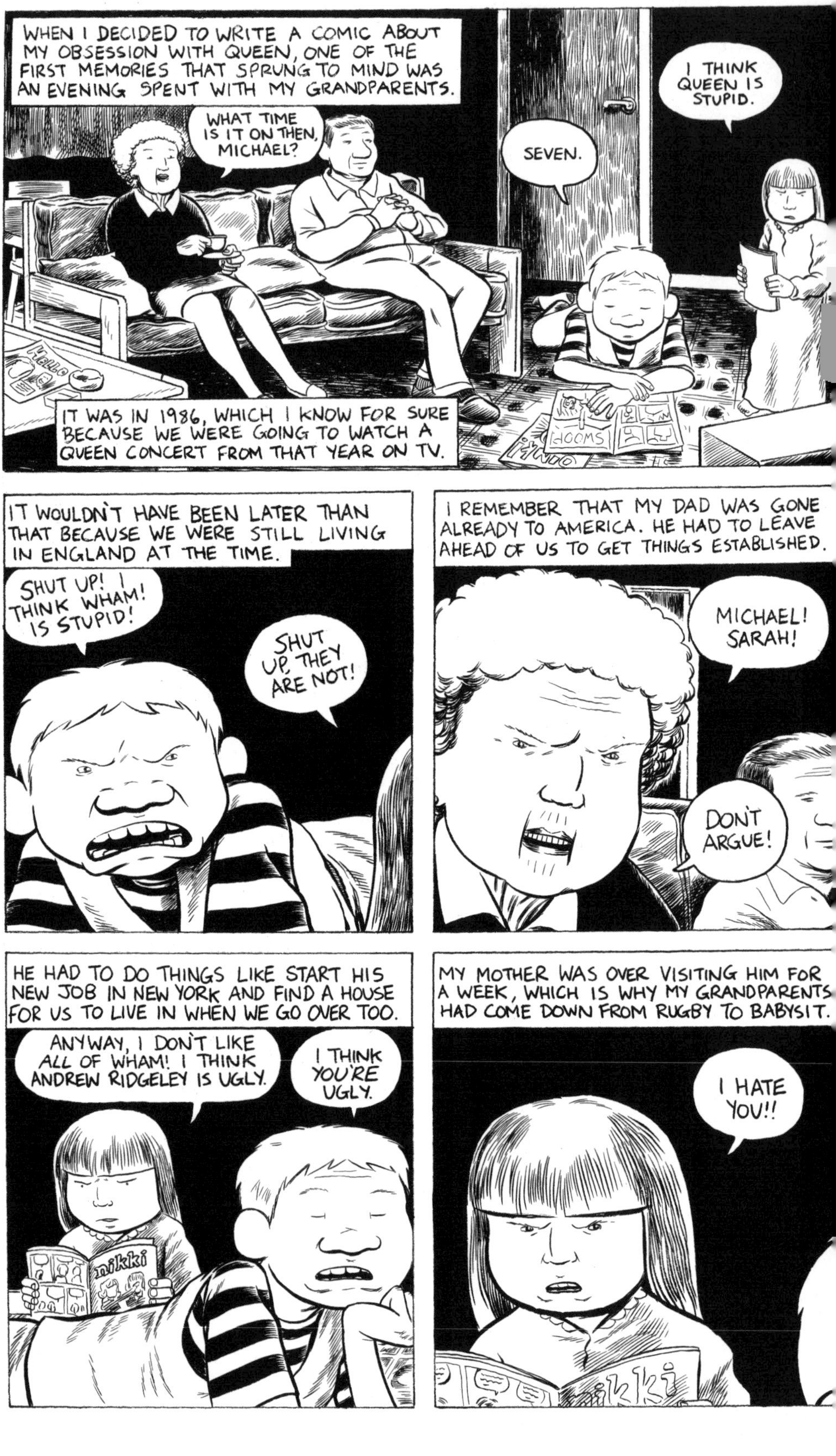
WHEN I DECIDED TO WRITE A COMIC ABOUT MY OBSESSION WITH QUEEN, ONE OF THE FIRST MEMORIES THAT SPRUNG TO MIND WAS AN EVENING SPENT WITH MY GRANDPARENTS.
WHAT TIME IS IT ON THEN, MICHAEL?
SEVEN.
I THINK QUEEN IS STUPID.
IT WAS IN 1986, WHICH I KNOW FOR SURE BECAUSE WE WERE GOING TO WATCH A QUEEN CONCERT FROM THAT YEAR ON TV.
IT WOULDN'T HAVE BEEN LATER THAN THAT BECAUSE WE WERE STILL LIVING IN ENGLAND AT THE TIME.
SHUT UP! I THINK WHAM! IS STUPID!
SHUT UP, THEY ARE NOT!
I REMEMBER THAT MY DAD WAS GONE ALREADY TO AMERICA. HE HAD TO LEAVE AHEAD OF US TO GET THINGS ESTABLISHED.
MICHAEL! SARAH!
DON'T ARGUE!
HE HAD TO DO THINGS LIKE START HIS NEW JOB IN NEW YORK AND FIND A HOUSE FOR US TO LIVE IN WHEN WE GO OVER TOO.
ANYWAY, I DON'T LIKE ALL OF WHAM! I THINK ANDREW RIDGELEY IS UGLY.
I THINK YOU'RE UGLY.
nikki
MY MOTHER WAS OVER VISITING HIM FOR A WEEK, WHICH IS WHY MY GRANDPARENTS HAD COME DOWN FROM RUGBY TO BABYSIT.
I HATE YOU!!

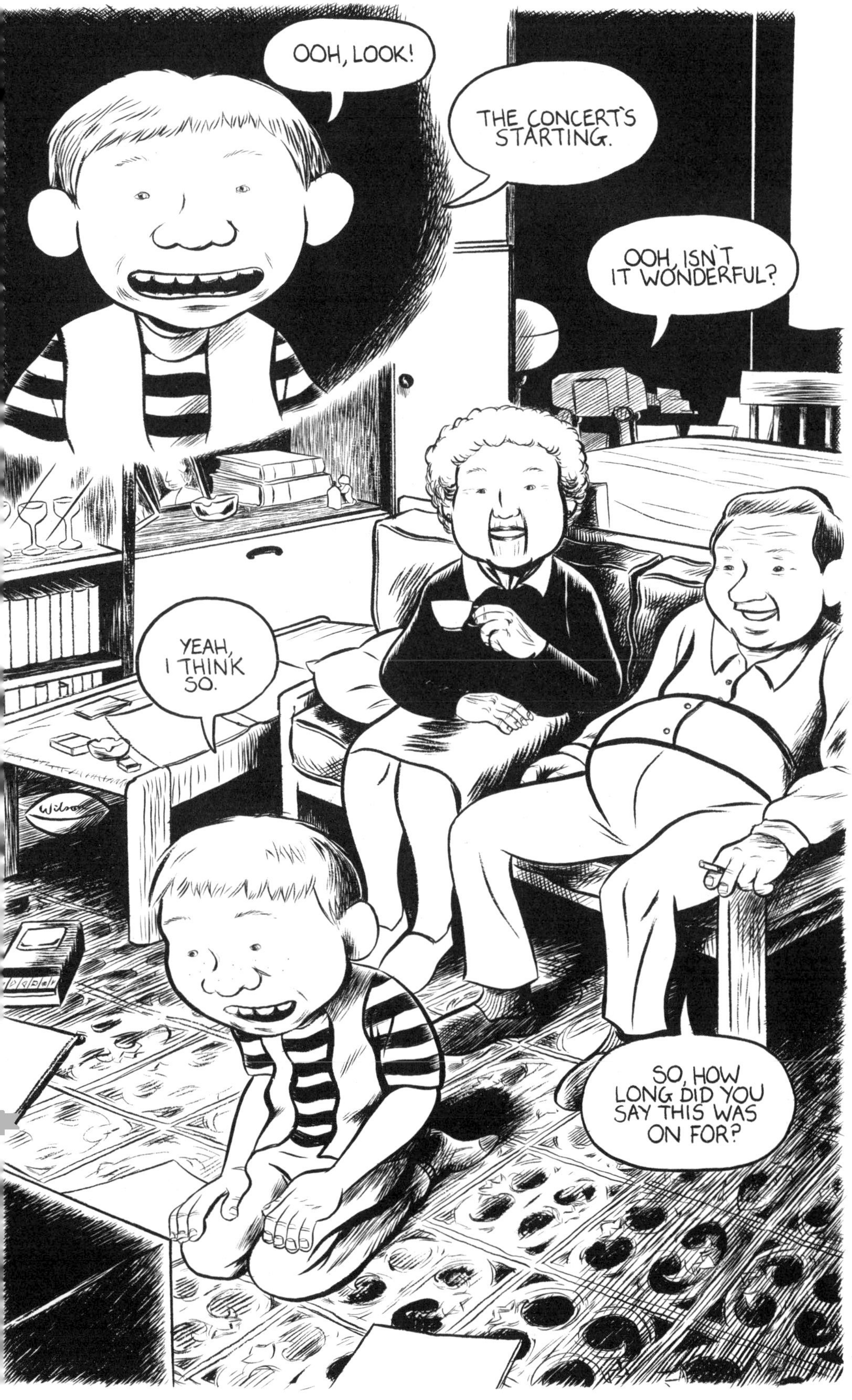
OOH, LOOK!
THE CONCERT'S STARTING.
OOH, ISN'T IT WONDERFUL?
YEAH, I THINK SO.
SO, HOW LONG DID YOU SAY THIS WAS ON FOR?
Wilson

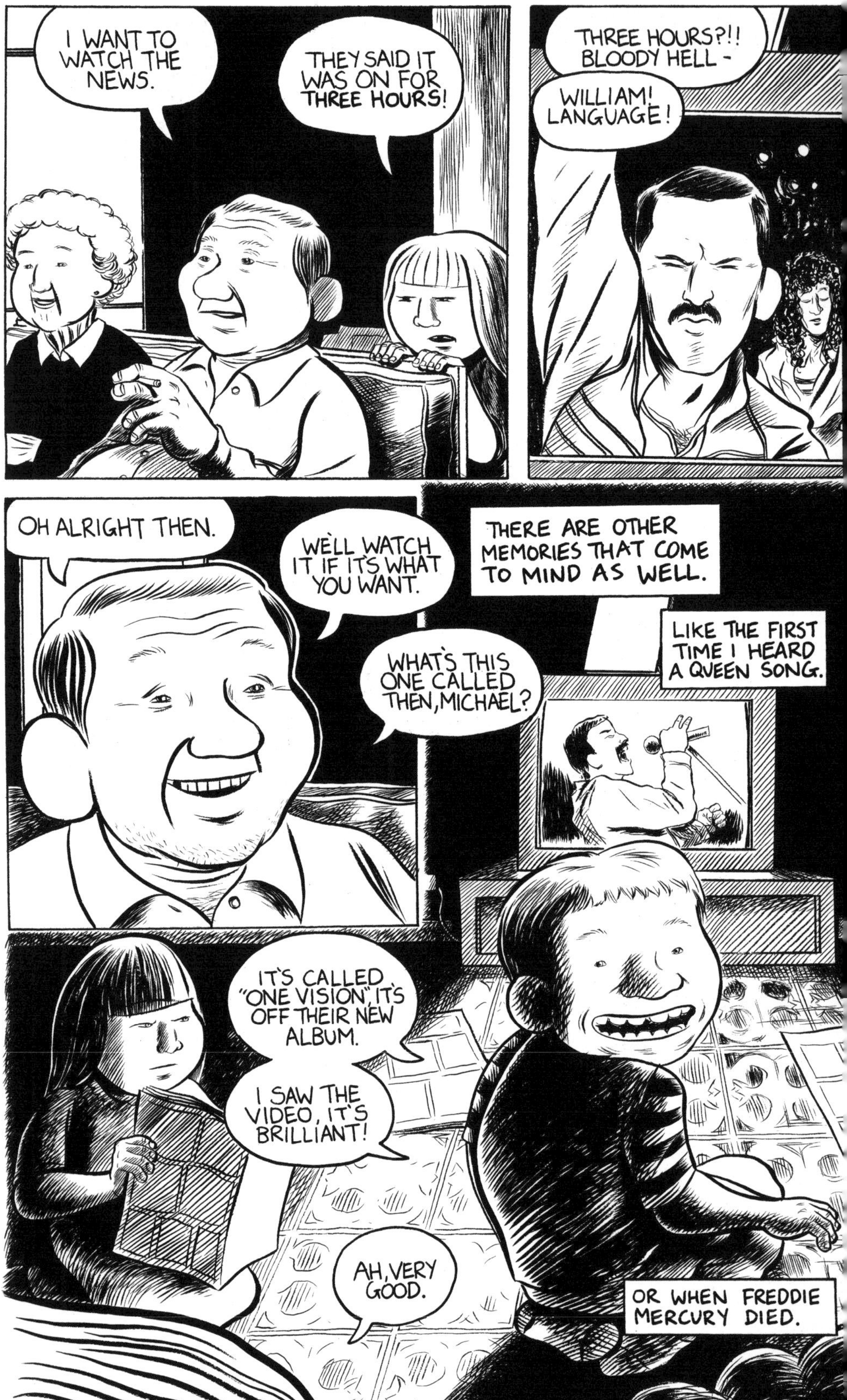
I WANT TO WATCH THE NEWS.
THEY SAID IT WAS ON FOR THREE HOURS!
THREE HOURS?!! BLOODY HELL -
WILLIAM! LANGUAGE!
OH ALRIGHT THEN.
WE'LL WATCH IT IF IT'S WHAT YOU WANT.
THERE ARE OTHER MEMORIES THAT COME TO MIND AS WELL.
LIKE THE FIRST TIME I HEARD A QUEEN SONG.
WHAT'S THIS ONE CALLED THEN, MICHAEL?
IT'S CALLED "ONE VISION", IT'S OFF THEIR NEW ALBUM.
I SAW THE VIDEO, IT'S BRILLIANT!
AH, VERY GOOD.
OR WHEN FREDDIE MERCURY DIED.

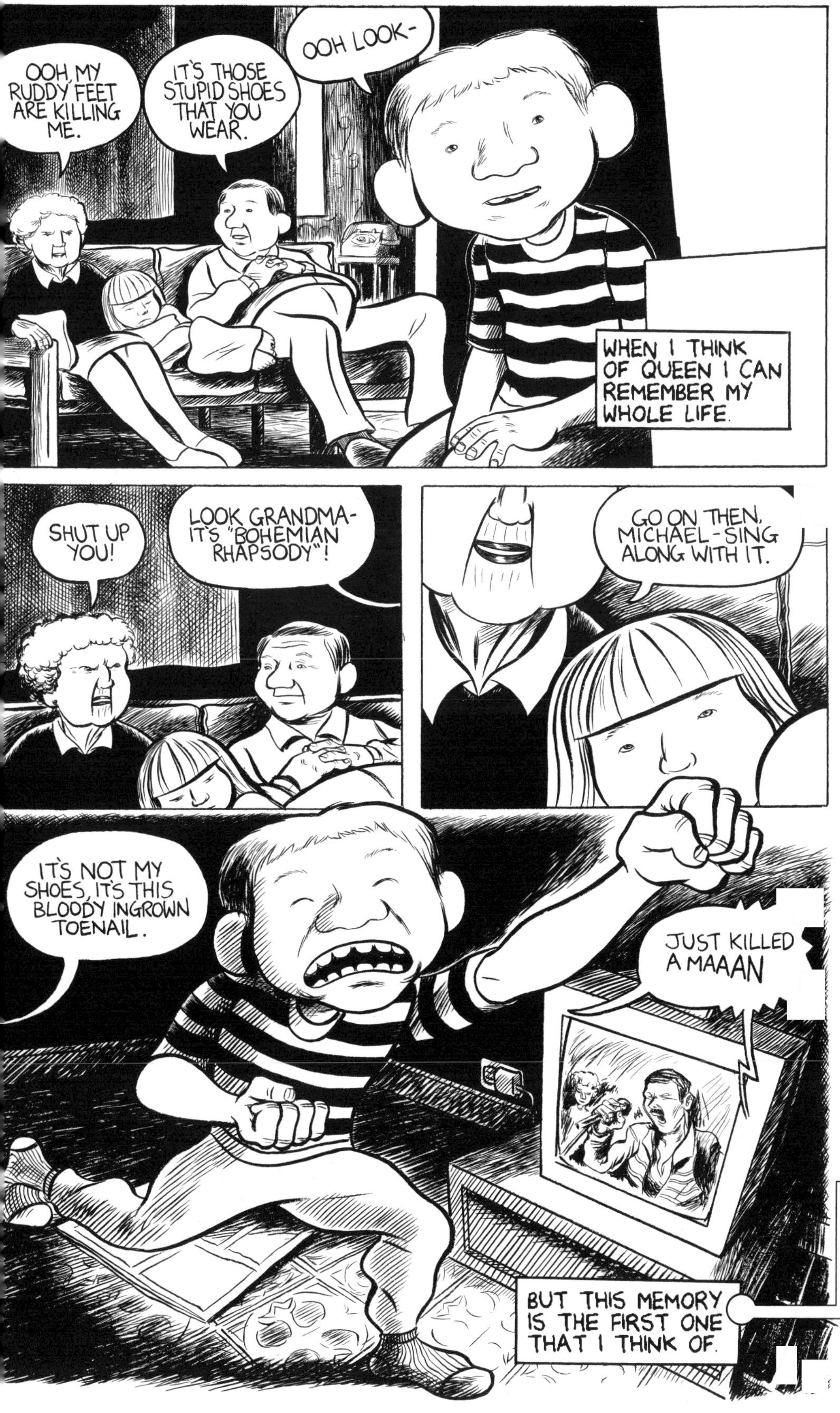

OOH, MY RUDDY FEET ARE KILLING ME.
IT'S THOSE STUPID SHOES THAT YOU WEAR.
OOH LOOK-
WHEN I THINK OF QUEEN I CAN REMEMBER MY WHOLE LIFE.
SHUT UP YOU!
LOOK GRANDMA- IT'S "BOHEMIAN RHAPSODY"!
GO ON THEN, MICHAEL-SING ALONG WITH IT.
IT'S NOT MY SHOES, IT'S THIS BLOODY INGROWN TOENAIL.
JUST KILLED A MAAAN
BUT THIS MEMORY IS THE FIRST ONE THAT I THINK OF.

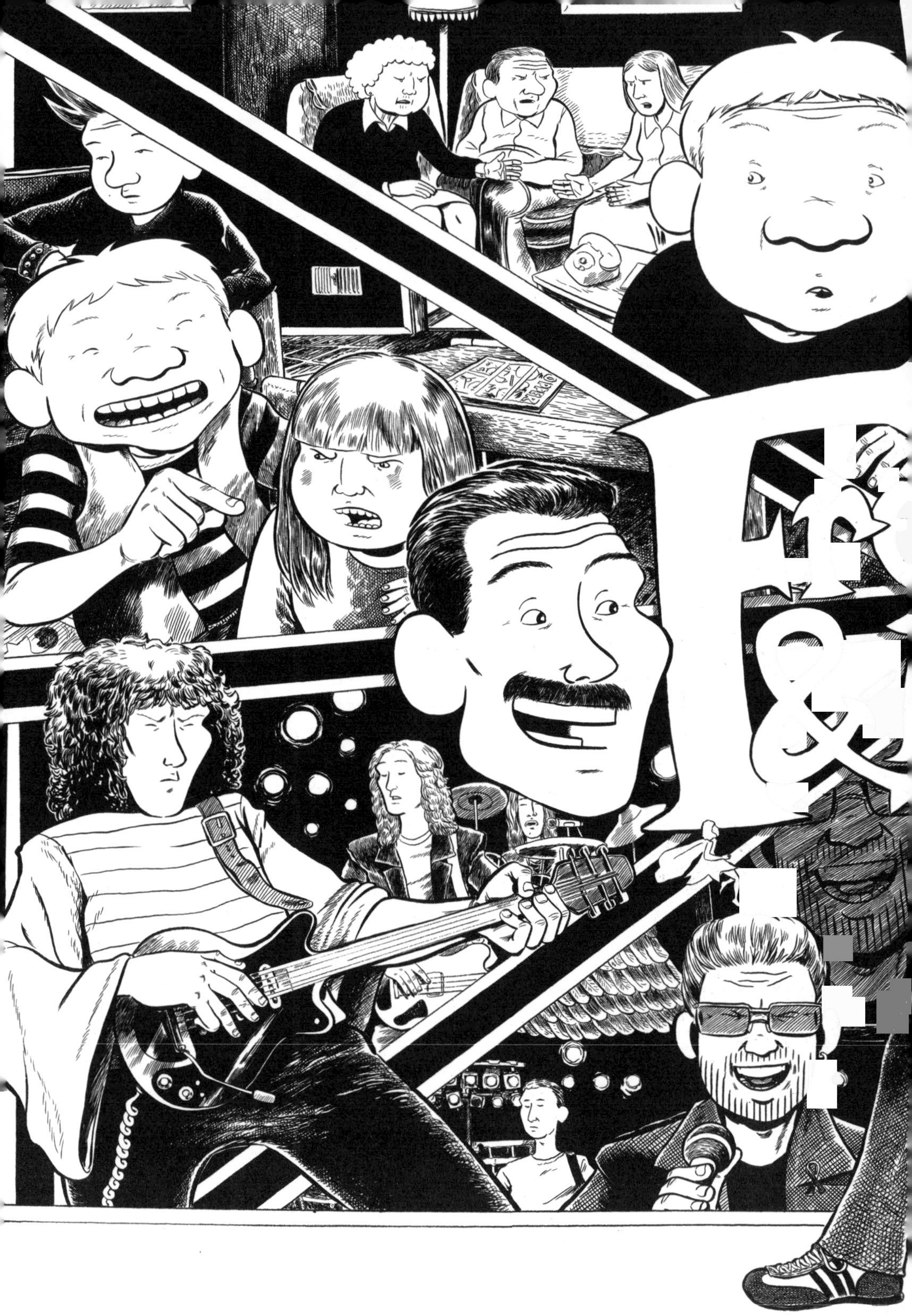

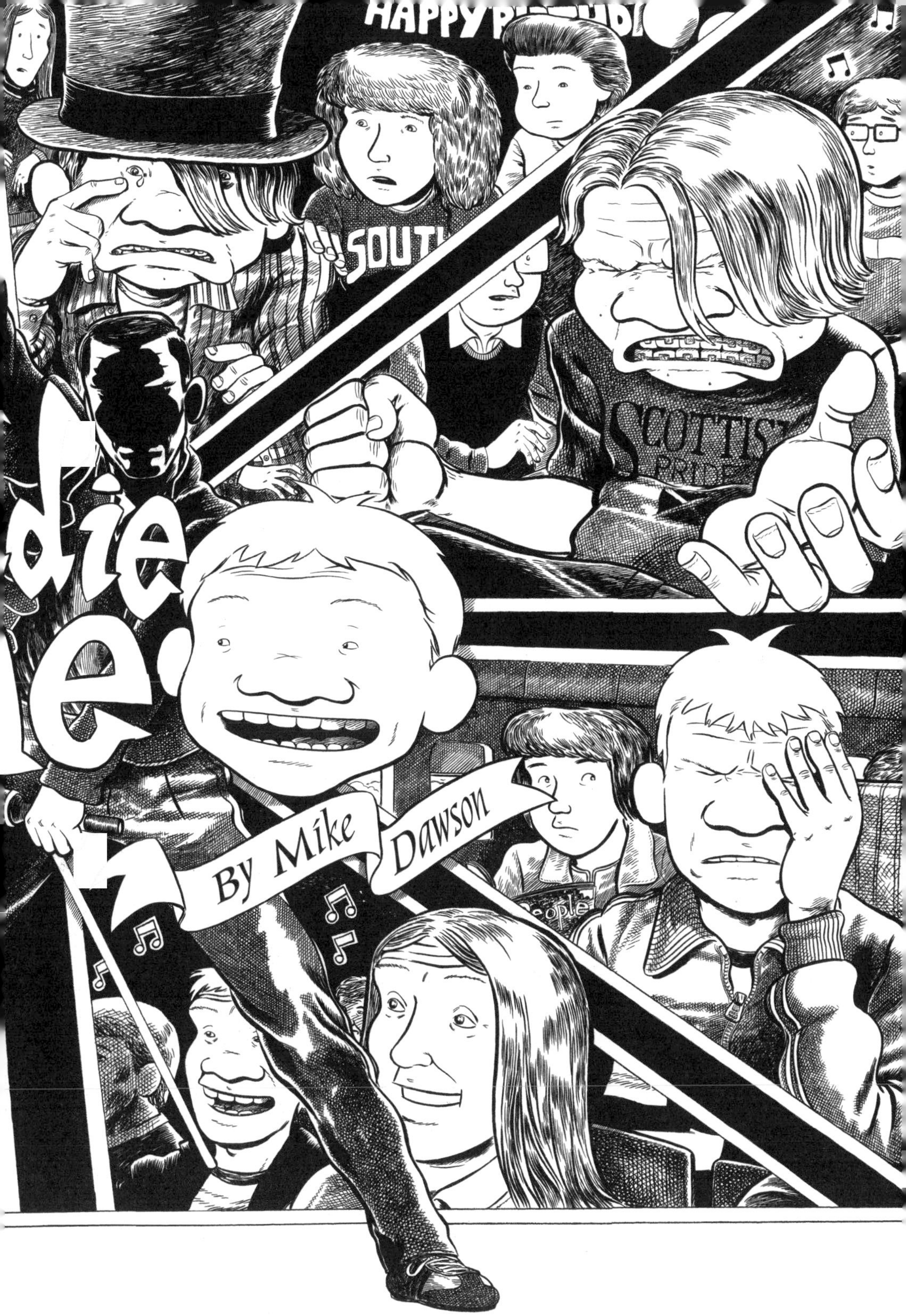

HAPPY BIRTHD
SOUTH
SCOTTISH PRIDE
die
e
By Mike Dawson
People

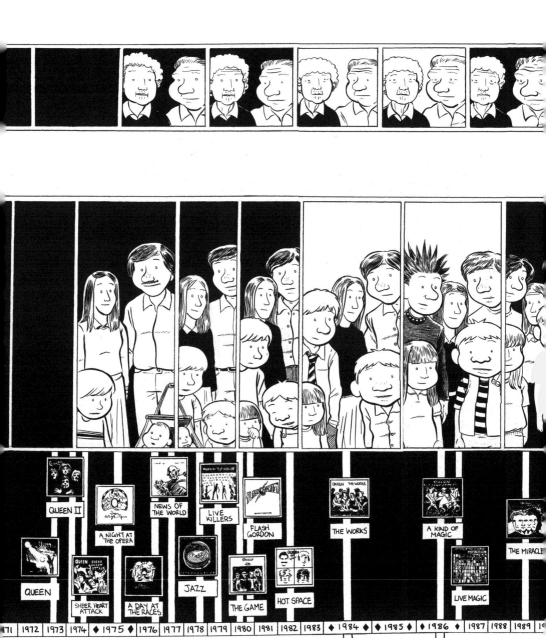

QUEEN II

A NIGHT AT
THE OPERA

NEWS OF
THE WORLD

LIVE
KILLERS

FLASH
GORDON

THE WORKS

A KIND OF
MAGIC

THE MIRACLE

QUEEN

SHEER HEART
ATTACK

A DAY AT
THE RACES

JAZZ

THE GAME

HOT SPACE

LIVE MAGIC

71 | 1972 | 1973 | 1974 | ◆ 1975 ◆ | 1976 | 1977 | 1978 | 1979 | 1980 | 1981 | 1982 | 1983 | ◆ 1984 ◆ | ◆ 1985 ◆ | ◆ 1986 ◆ | 1987 | 1988 | 1989 | 1

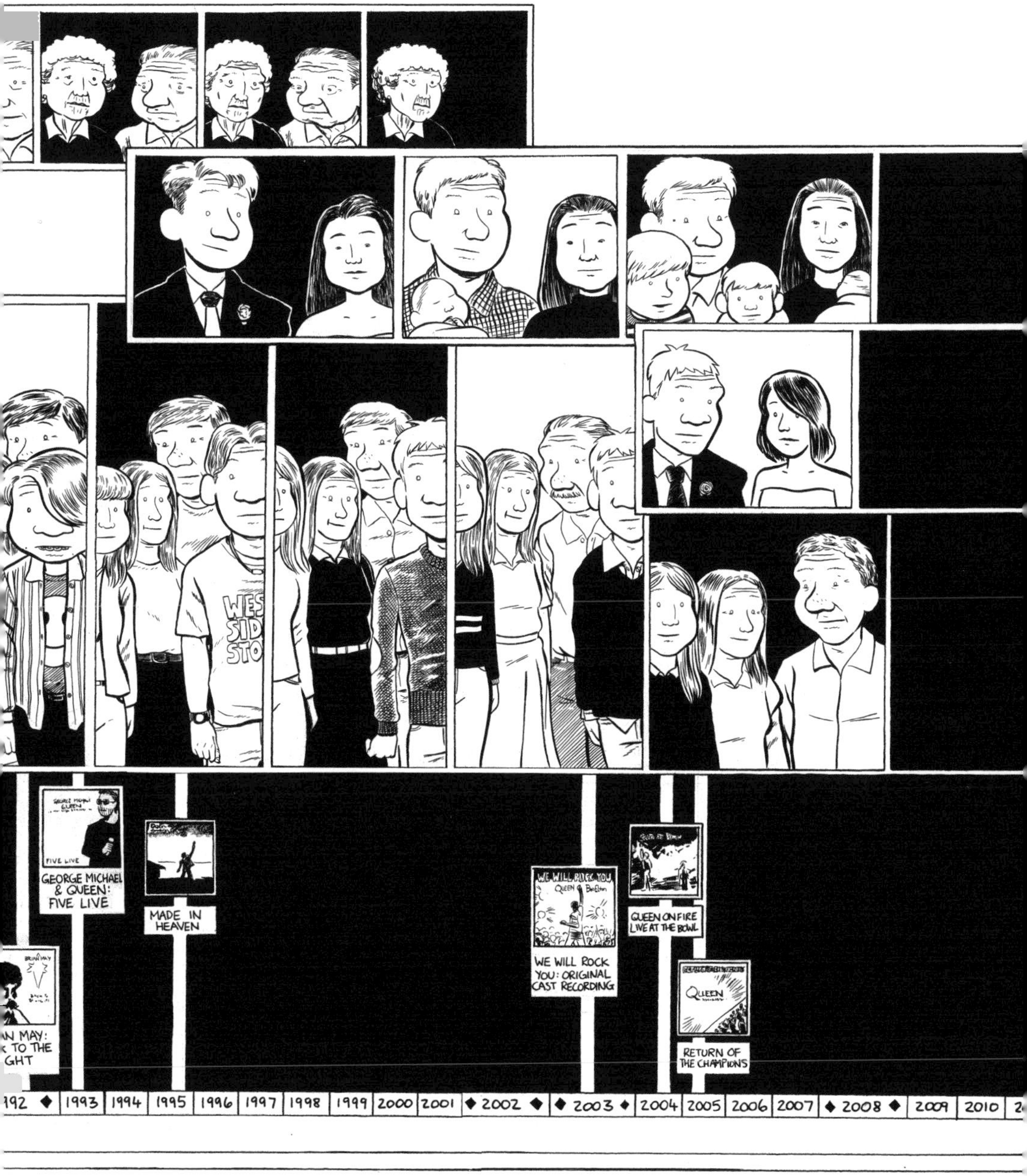

GEORGE MICHAEL & QUEEN: FIVE LIVE
MADE IN HEAVEN
WE WILL ROCK YOU: ORIGINAL CAST RECORDING
QUEEN ON FIRE LIVE AT THE BOWL
RETURN OF THE CHAMPIONS
1993
1994
1995
1996
1997
1998
1999
2000
2001
2002
2003
2004
2005
2006
2007
2008
2009
2010

The Ballad

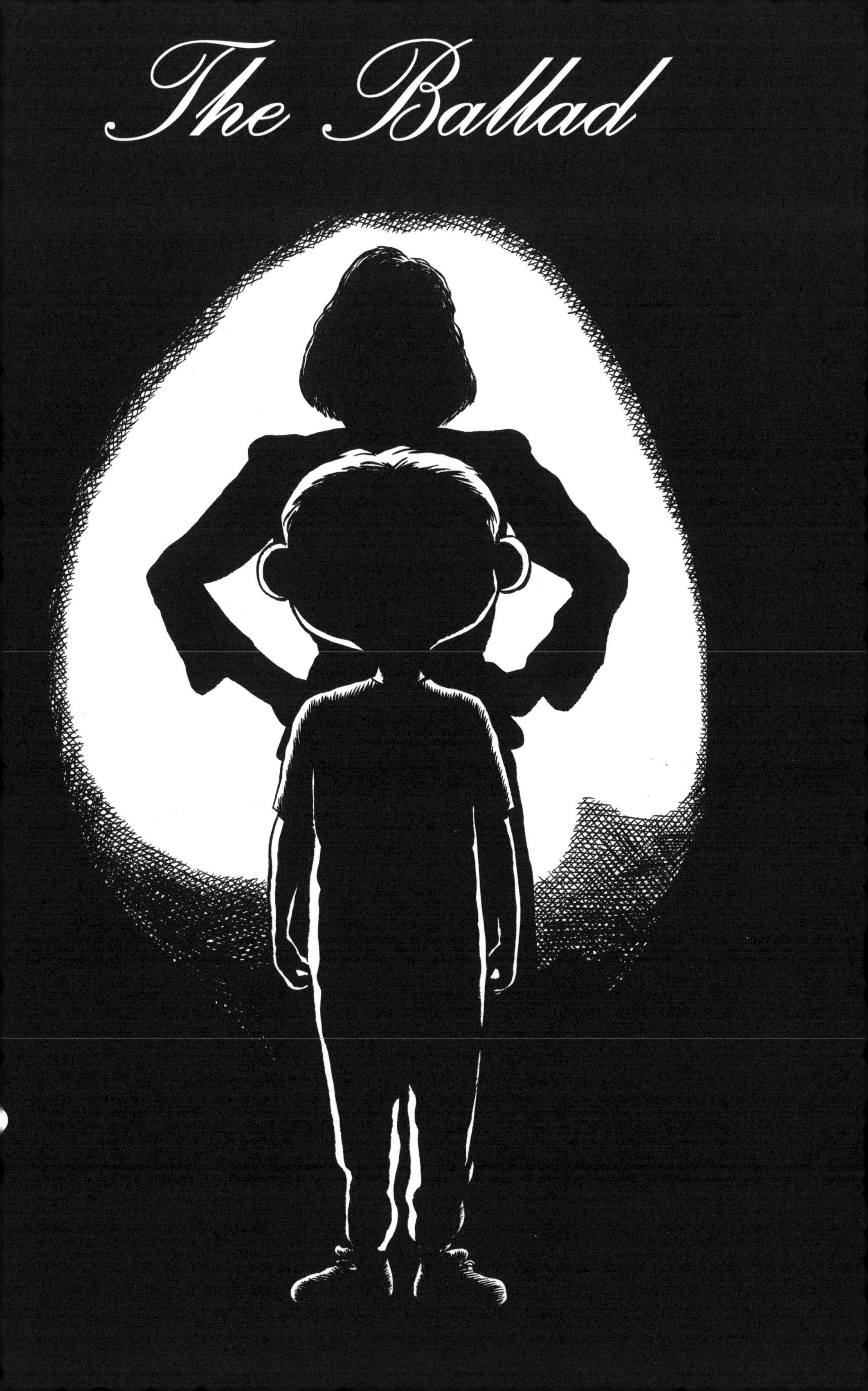

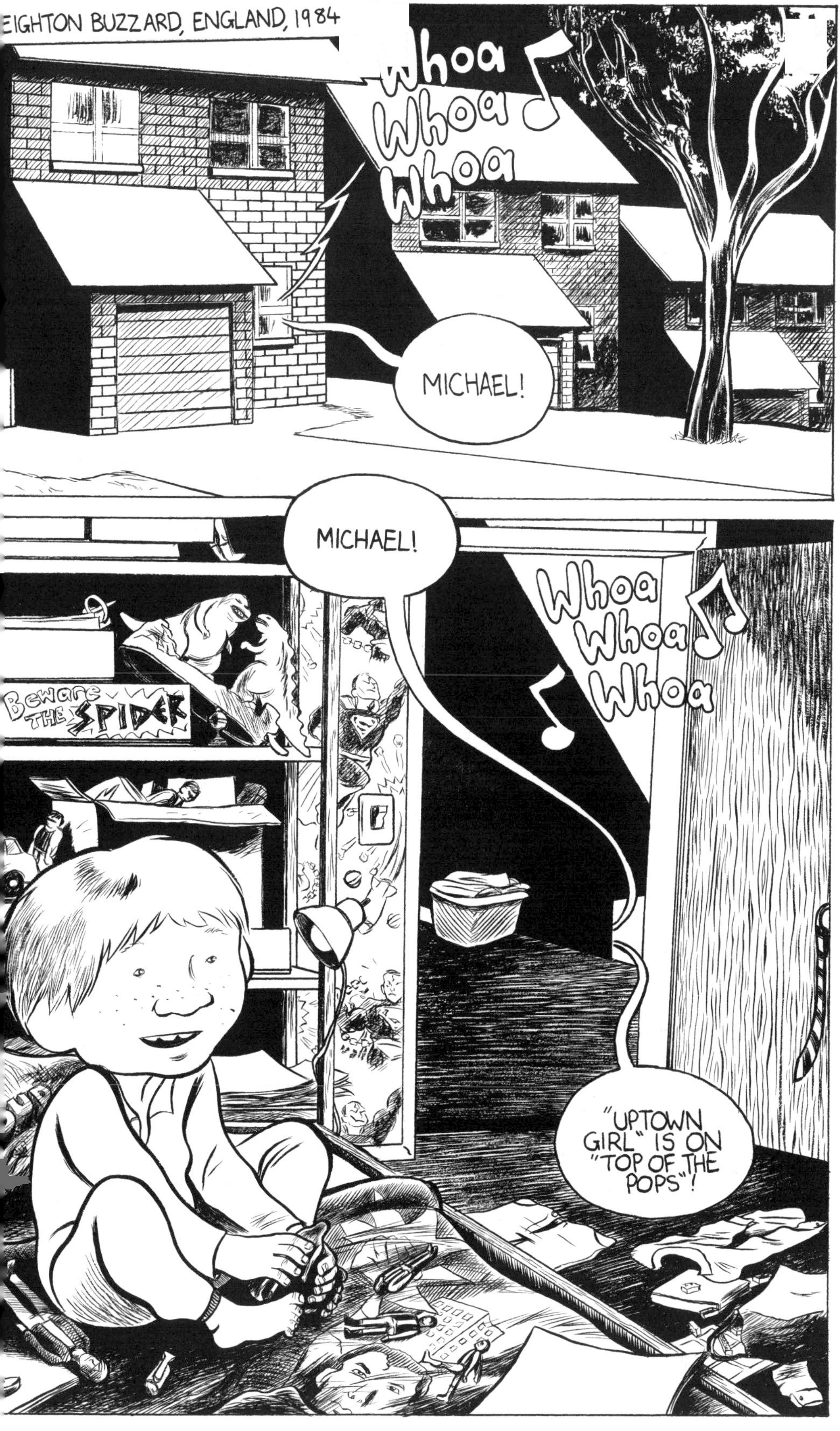
EIGHTON BUZZARD, ENGLAND, 1984
Whoa Whoa Whoa
MICHAEL!
MICHAEL!
Beware THE SPIDER
Whoa Whoa Whoa
"UPTOWN GIRL" IS ON "TOP OF THE POPS"!

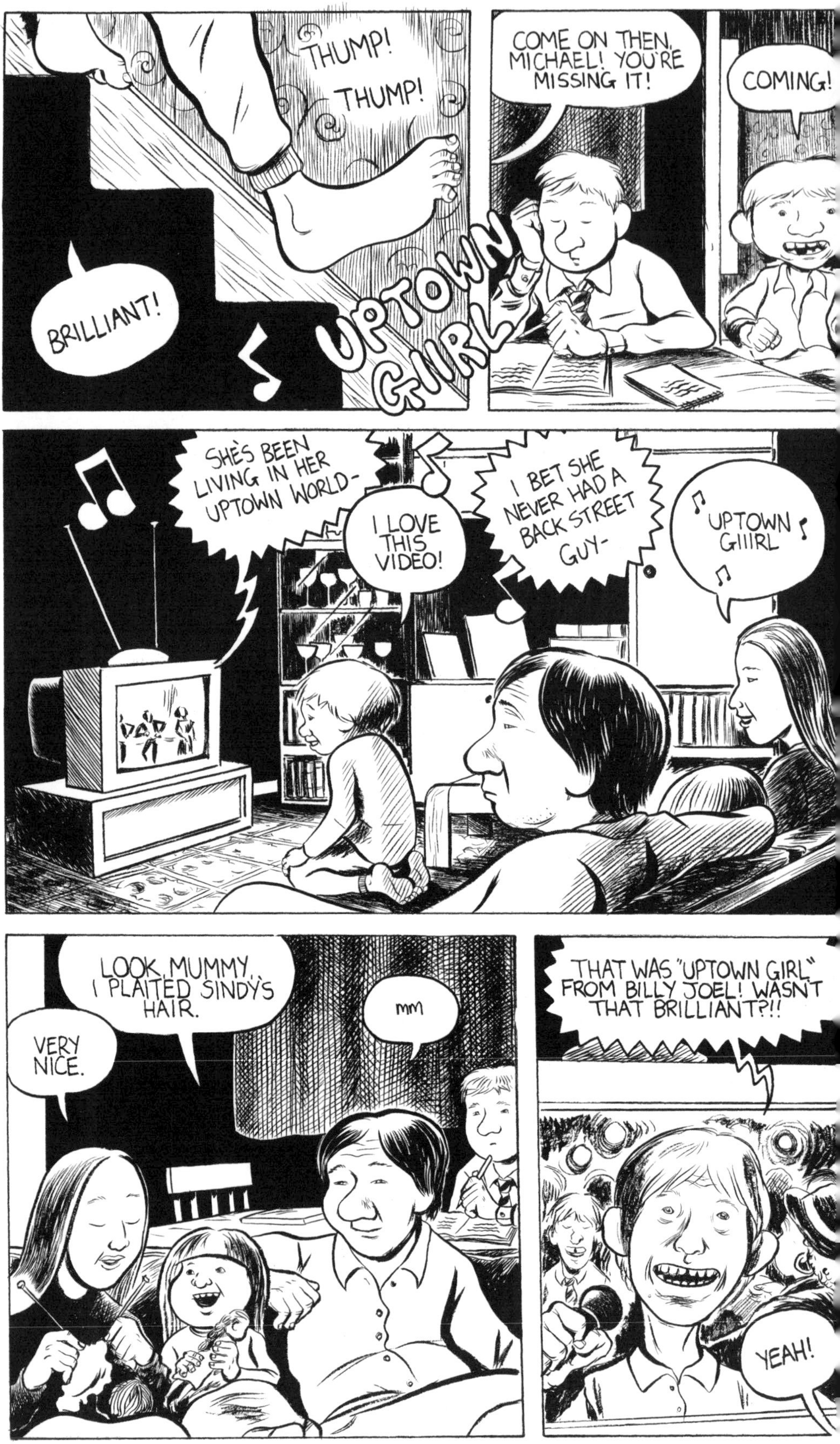
THUMP!
THUMP!
BRILLIANT!
UPTOWN GIRL
COME ON THEN, MICHAEL! YOU'RE MISSING IT!
COMING!
SHE'S BEEN LIVING IN HER UPTOWN WORLD-
I LOVE THIS VIDEO!
I BET SHE NEVER HAD A BACK STREET GUY-
UPTOWN GIIIRL
LOOK, MUMMY, I PLAITED SINDY'S HAIR.
VERY NICE.
mm
THAT WAS "UPTOWN GIRL" FROM BILLY JOEL! WASN'T THAT BRILLIANT?!!
YEAH!

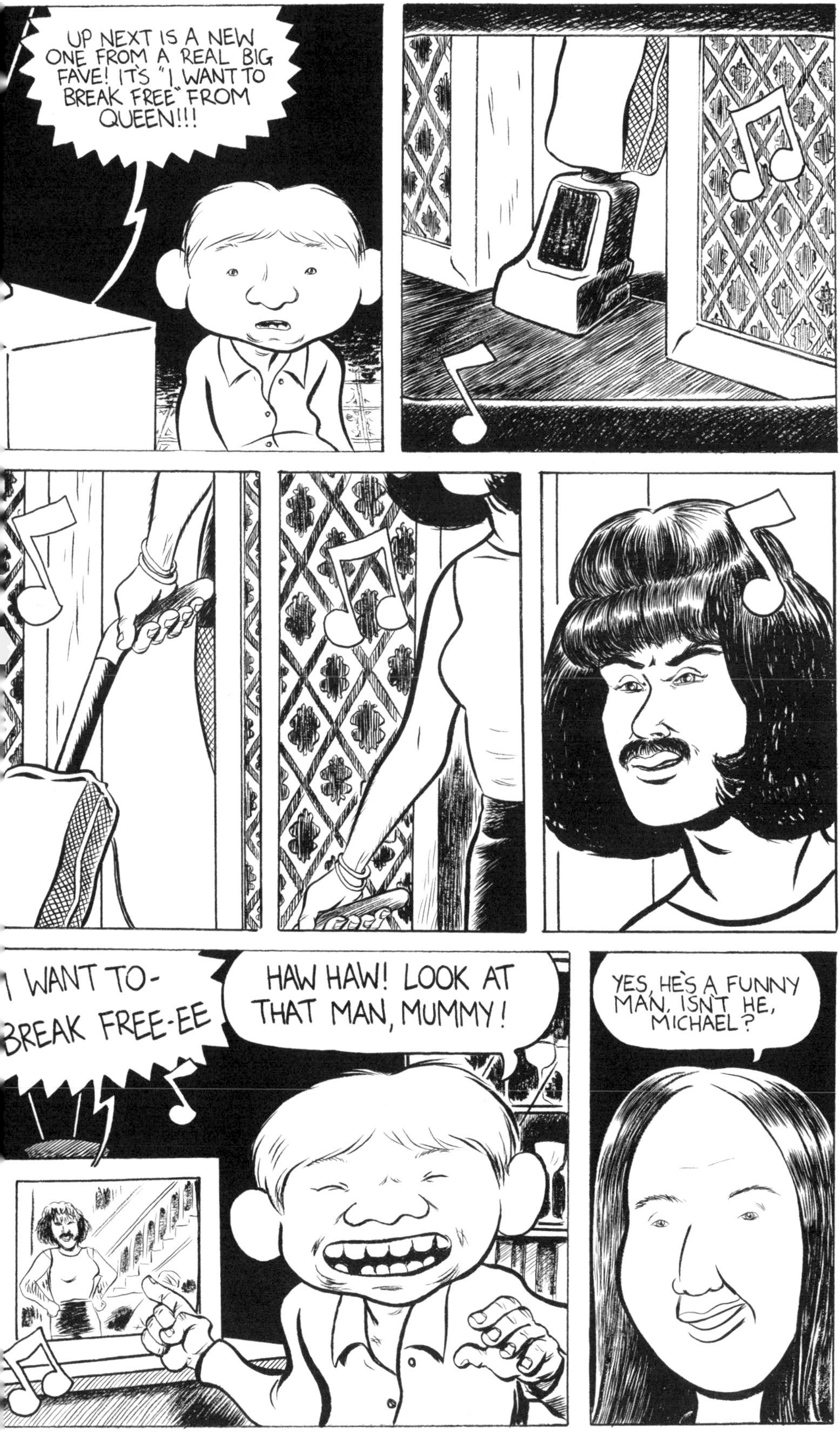
UP NEXT IS A NEW ONE FROM A REAL BIG FAVE! IT'S "I WANT TO BREAK FREE" FROM QUEEN!!!
I WANT TO-BREAK FREE-EE
HAW HAW! LOOK AT THAT MAN, MUMMY!
YES, HE'S A FUNNY MAN, ISN'T HE, MICHAEL?

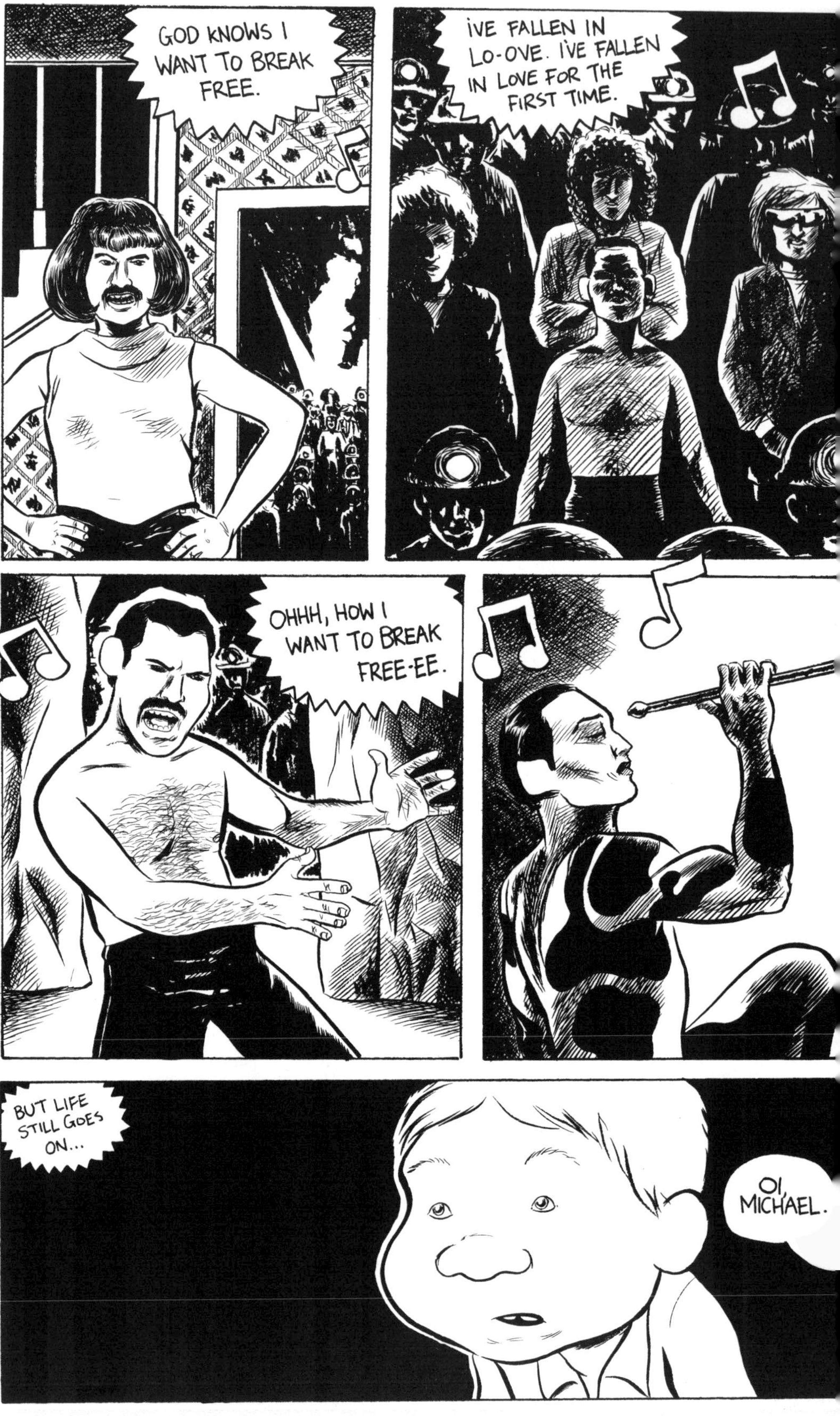
GOD KNOWS I WANT TO BREAK FREE.
I'VE FALLEN IN LO-OVE. I'VE FALLEN IN LOVE FOR THE FIRST TIME.
OHHH, HOW I WANT TO BREAK FREE-EE.
BUT LIFE STILL GOES ON...
OI, MICHAEL.

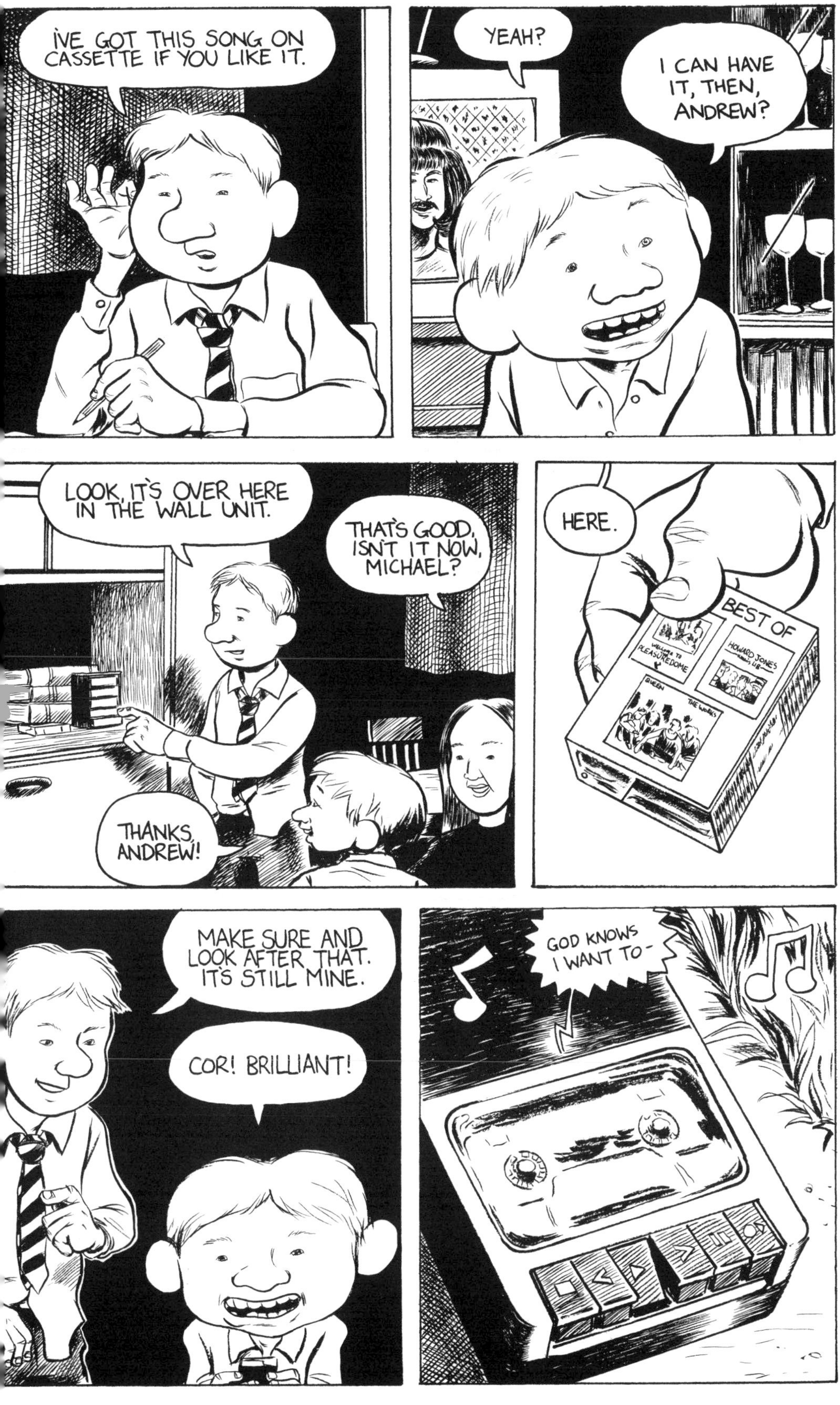
I'VE GOT THIS SONG ON CASSETTE IF YOU LIKE IT.
YEAH?
I CAN HAVE IT, THEN, ANDREW?
LOOK, IT'S OVER HERE IN THE WALL UNIT.
THAT'S GOOD, ISN'T IT NOW, MICHAEL?
THANKS, ANDREW!
HERE.
BEST OF
WELCOME TO PLEASUREDOME
HOWARD JONES
QUEEN THE WORKS
MAKE SURE AND LOOK AFTER THAT. IT'S STILL MINE.
COR! BRILLIANT!
GOD KNOWS I WANT TO-

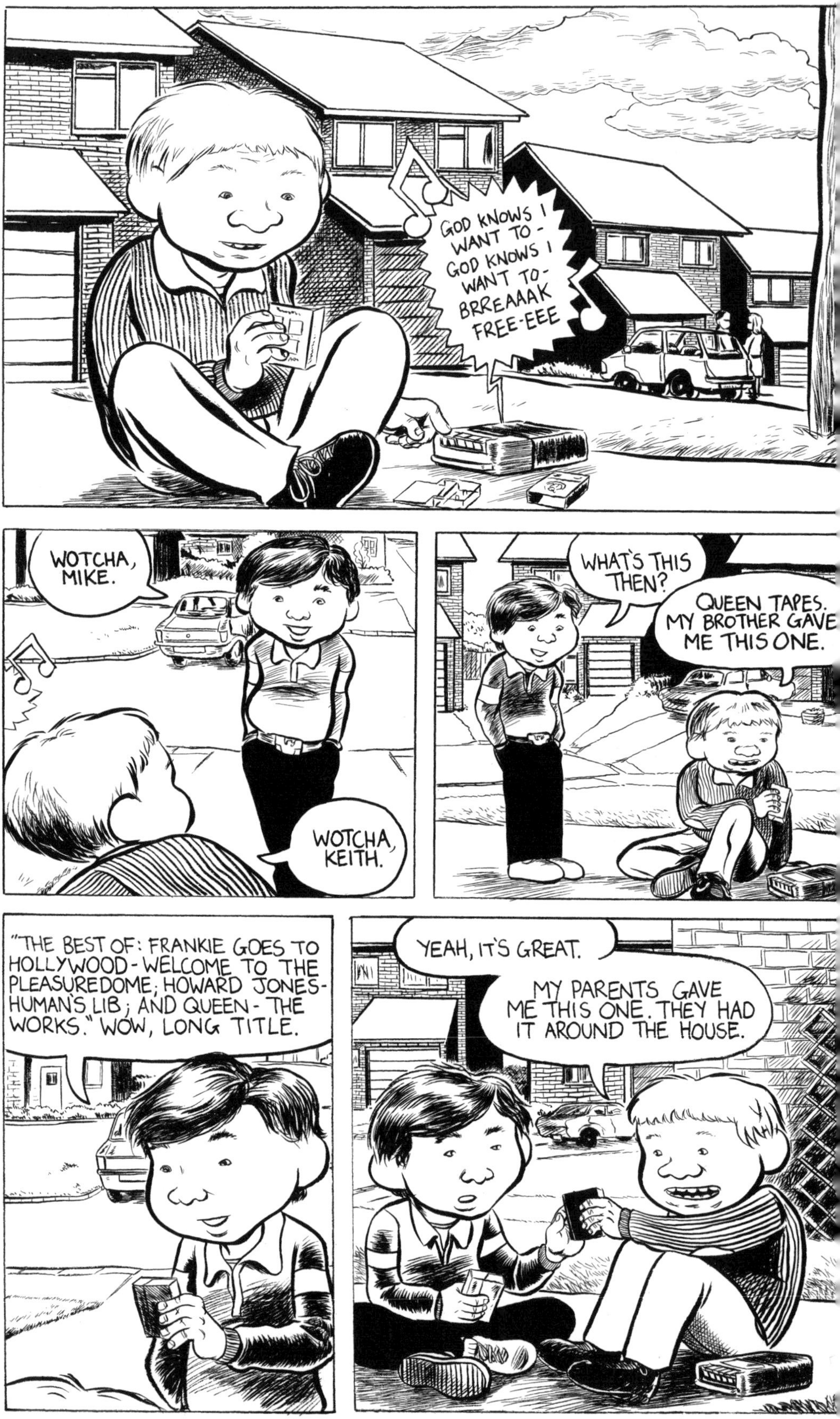
GOD KNOWS I WANT TO - GOD KNOWS I WANT TO - BRREAAAK FREE-EEE
WOTCHA, MIKE.
WOTCHA, KEITH.
WHAT'S THIS THEN?
QUEEN TAPES. MY BROTHER GAVE ME THIS ONE.
"THE BEST OF: FRANKIE GOES TO HOLLYWOOD - WELCOME TO THE PLEASUREDOME; HOWARD JONES - HUMAN'S LIB; AND QUEEN - THE WORKS." WOW, LONG TITLE.
YEAH, IT'S GREAT.
MY PARENTS GAVE ME THIS ONE. THEY HAD IT AROUND THE HOUSE.

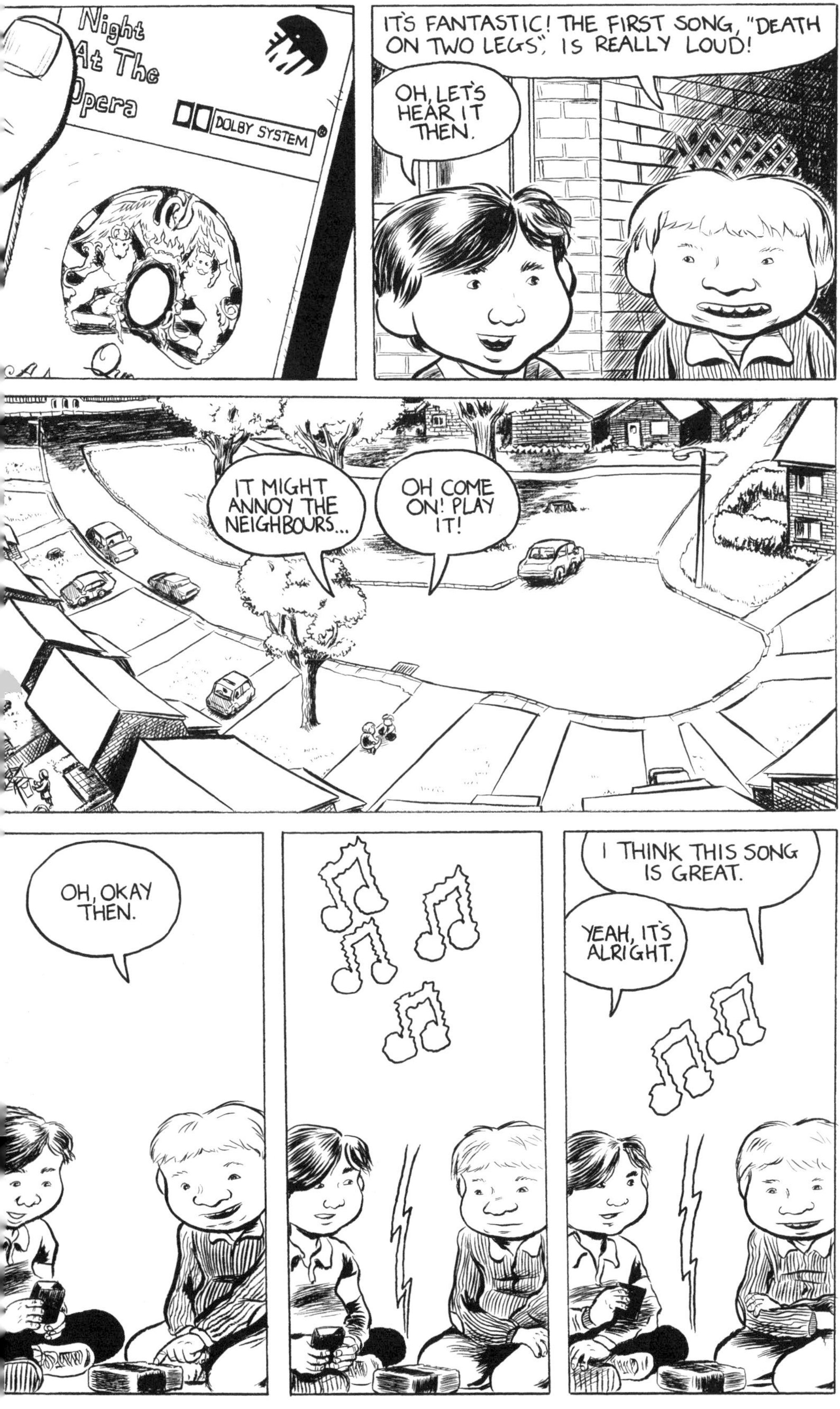
Night At The Opera
DOLBY SYSTEM
IT'S FANTASTIC! THE FIRST SONG, "DEATH ON TWO LEGS", IS REALLY LOUD!
OH, LET'S HEAR IT THEN.
IT MIGHT ANNOY THE NEIGHBOURS...
OH COME ON! PLAY IT!
OH, OKAY THEN.
I THINK THIS SONG IS GREAT.
YEAH, IT'S ALRIGHT.

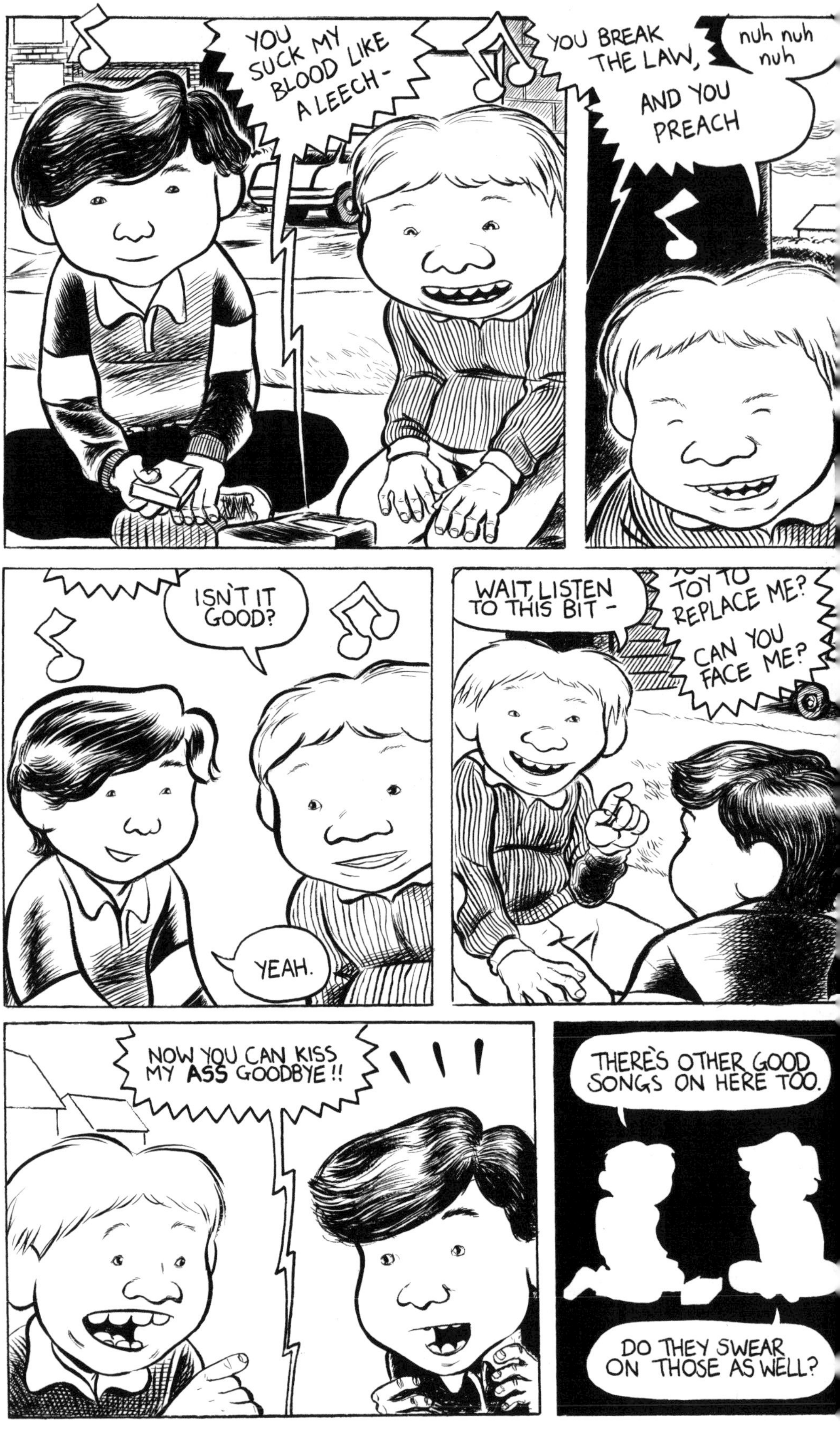
YOU SUCK MY BLOOD LIKE A LEECH -
YOU BREAK THE LAW,
nuh nuh nuh
AND YOU PREACH
ISN'T IT GOOD?
YEAH.
WAIT, LISTEN TO THIS BIT -
TOY TO REPLACE ME?
CAN YOU FACE ME?
NOW YOU CAN KISS MY **ASS** GOODBYE!!
THERE'S OTHER GOOD SONGS ON HERE TOO.
DO THEY SWEAR ON THOSE AS WELL?

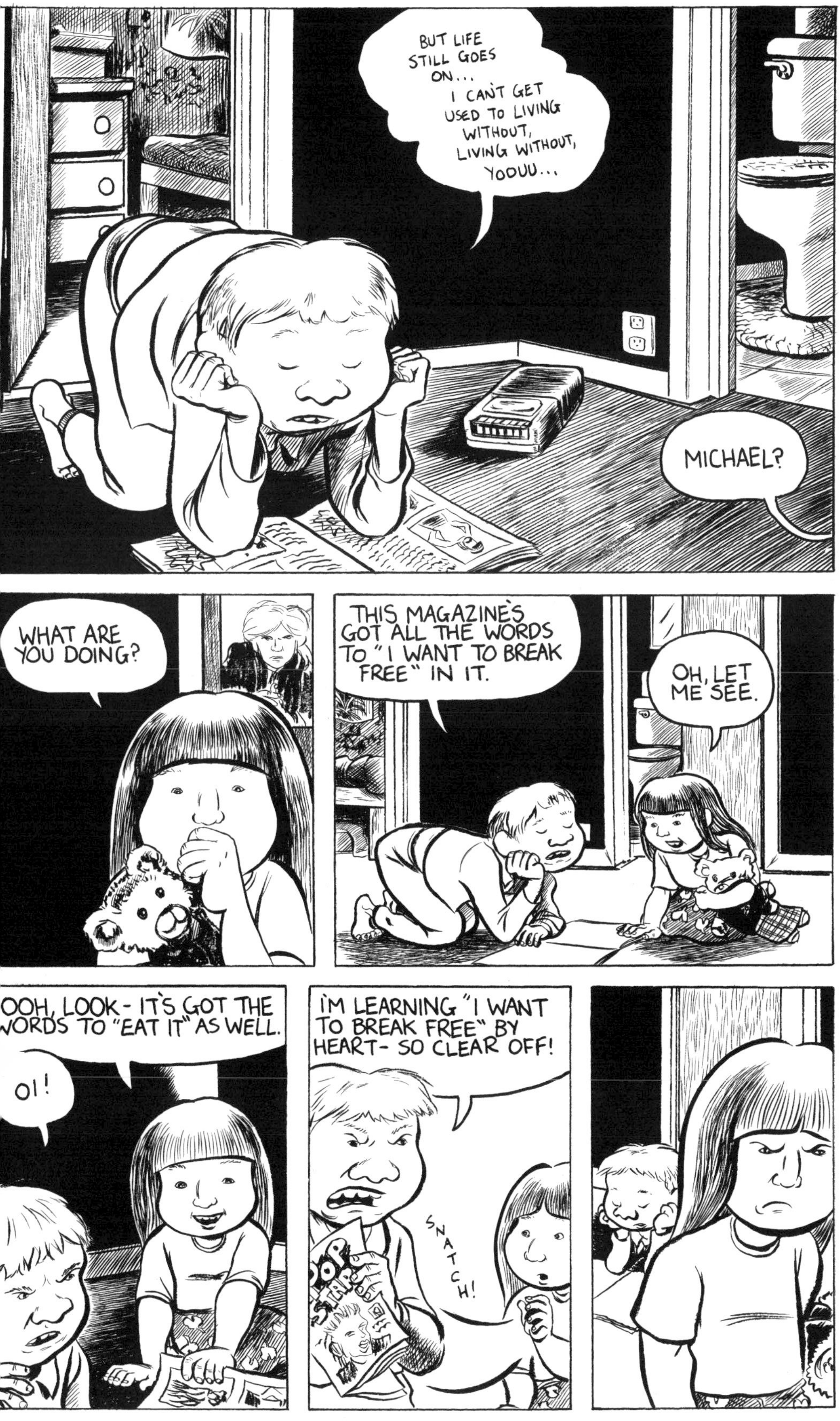
BUT LIFE STILL GOES ON... I CAN'T GET USED TO LIVING WITHOUT, LIVING WITHOUT, YOOUU...
MICHAEL?
WHAT ARE YOU DOING?
THIS MAGAZINE'S GOT ALL THE WORDS TO "I WANT TO BREAK FREE" IN IT.
OH, LET ME SEE.
OOH, LOOK- IT'S GOT THE WORDS TO "EAT IT" AS WELL.
OI!
I'M LEARNING "I WANT TO BREAK FREE" BY HEART- SO CLEAR OFF!
SNATCH!

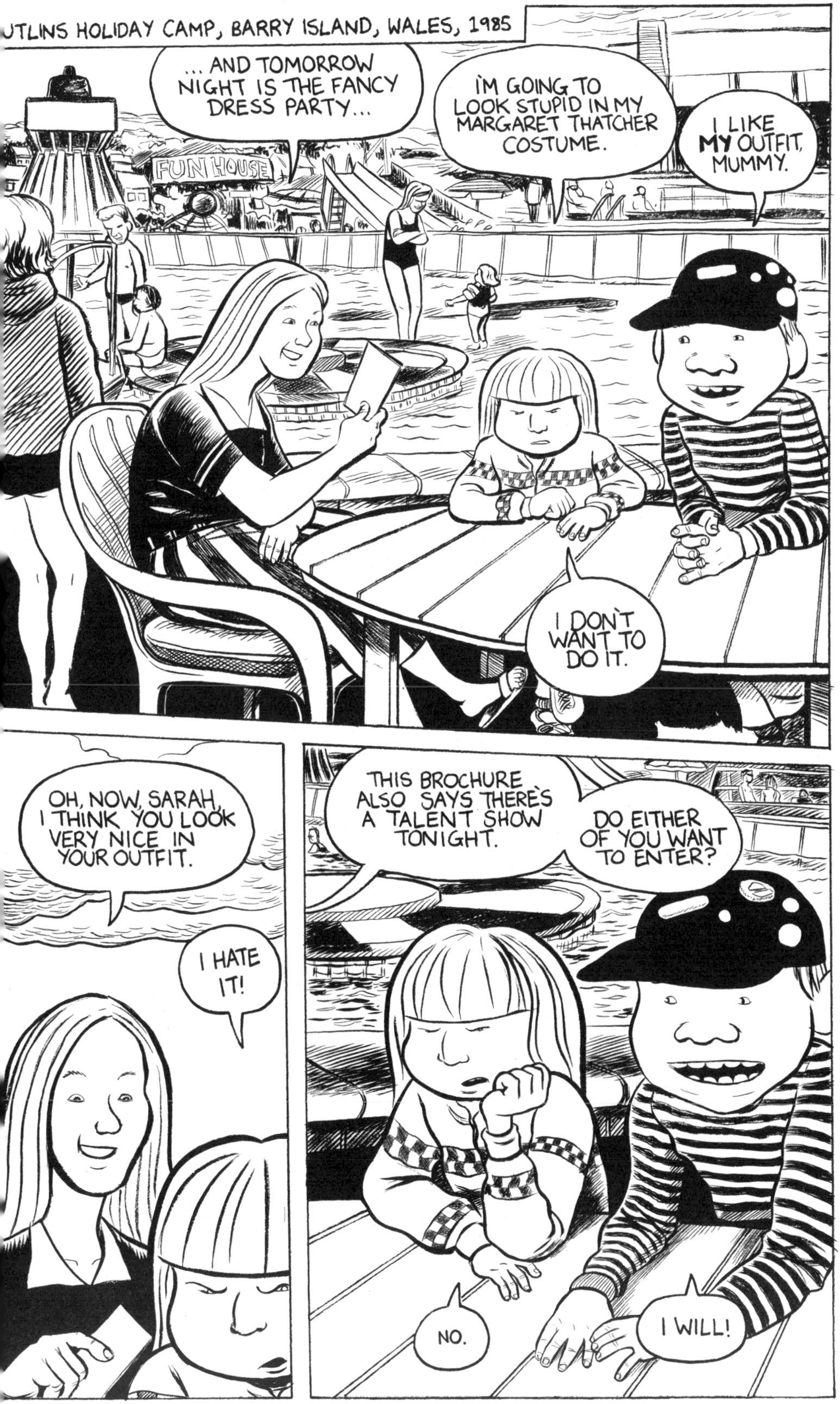
UTLINS HOLIDAY CAMP, BARRY ISLAND, WALES, 1985
FUN HOUSE
... AND TOMORROW NIGHT IS THE FANCY DRESS PARTY...
I'M GOING TO LOOK STUPID IN MY MARGARET THATCHER COSTUME.
I LIKE **MY** OUTFIT, MUMMY.
I DON'T WANT TO DO IT.
OH, NOW, SARAH, I THINK YOU LOOK VERY NICE IN YOUR OUTFIT.
I HATE IT!
THIS BROCHURE ALSO SAYS THERE'S A TALENT SHOW TONIGHT.
DO EITHER OF YOU WANT TO ENTER?
NO.
I WILL!

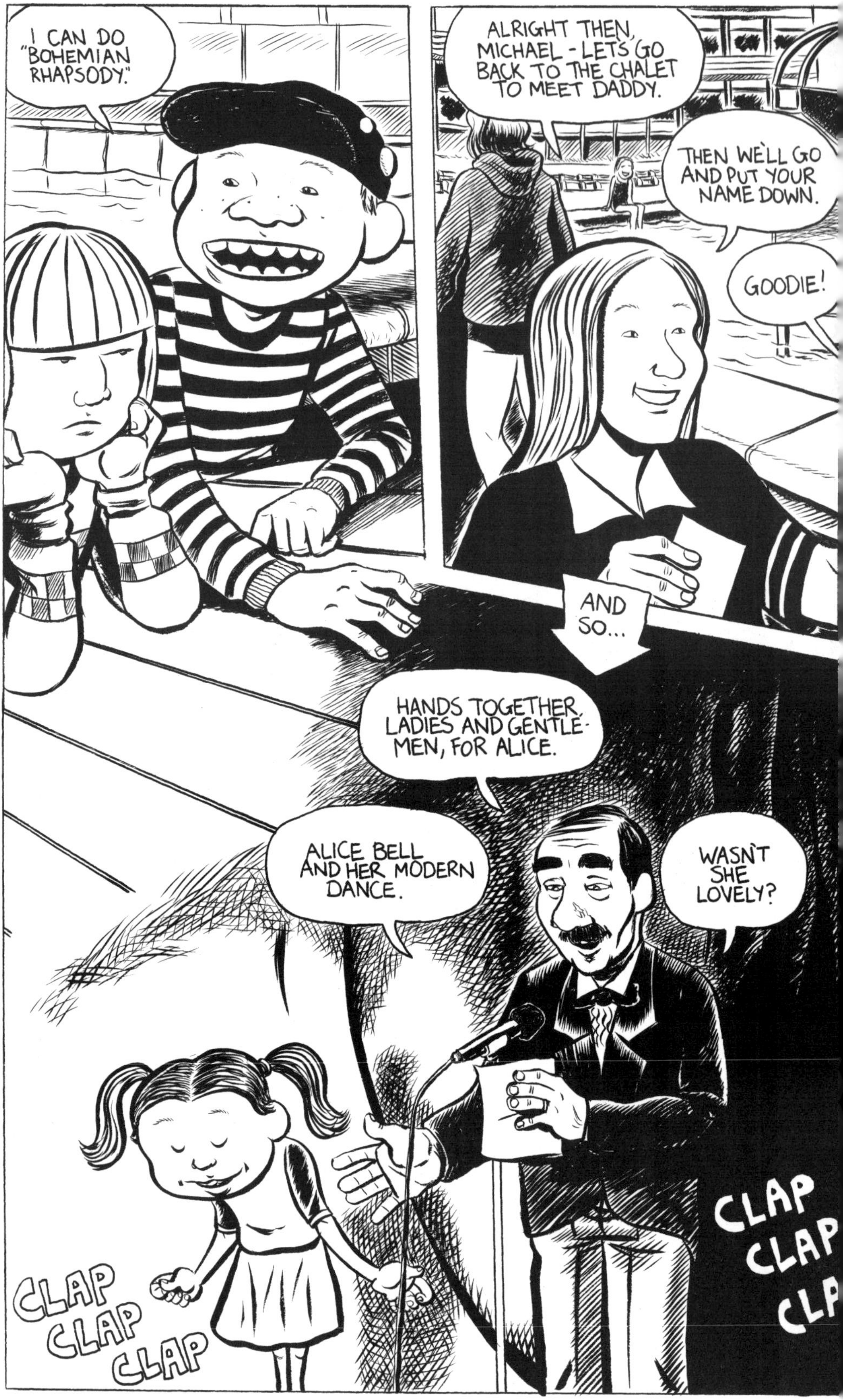
I CAN DO "BOHEMIAN RHAPSODY."
ALRIGHT THEN, MICHAEL - LET'S GO BACK TO THE CHALET TO MEET DADDY.
THEN WE'LL GO AND PUT YOUR NAME DOWN.
GOODIE!
AND SO...
HANDS TOGETHER, LADIES AND GENTLE-MEN, FOR ALICE.
ALICE BELL AND HER MODERN DANCE.
WASN'T SHE LOVELY?
CLAP CLAP CLAP
CLAP CLAP

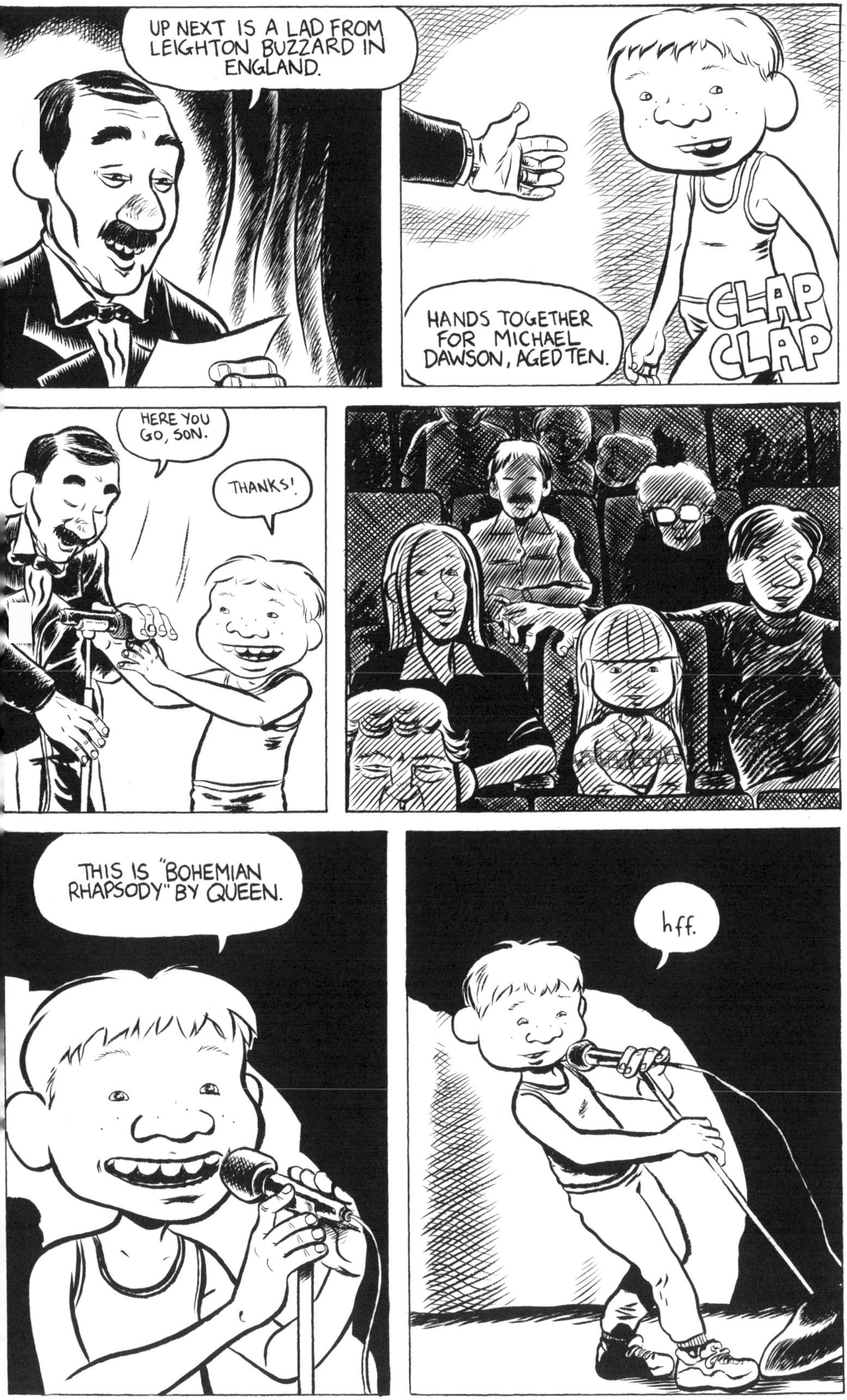
UP NEXT IS A LAD FROM LEIGHTON BUZZARD IN ENGLAND.
HANDS TOGETHER FOR MICHAEL DAWSON, AGED TEN.
CLAP CLAP
HERE YOU GO, SON.
THANKS!
THIS IS "BOHEMIAN RHAPSODY" BY QUEEN.
hff.

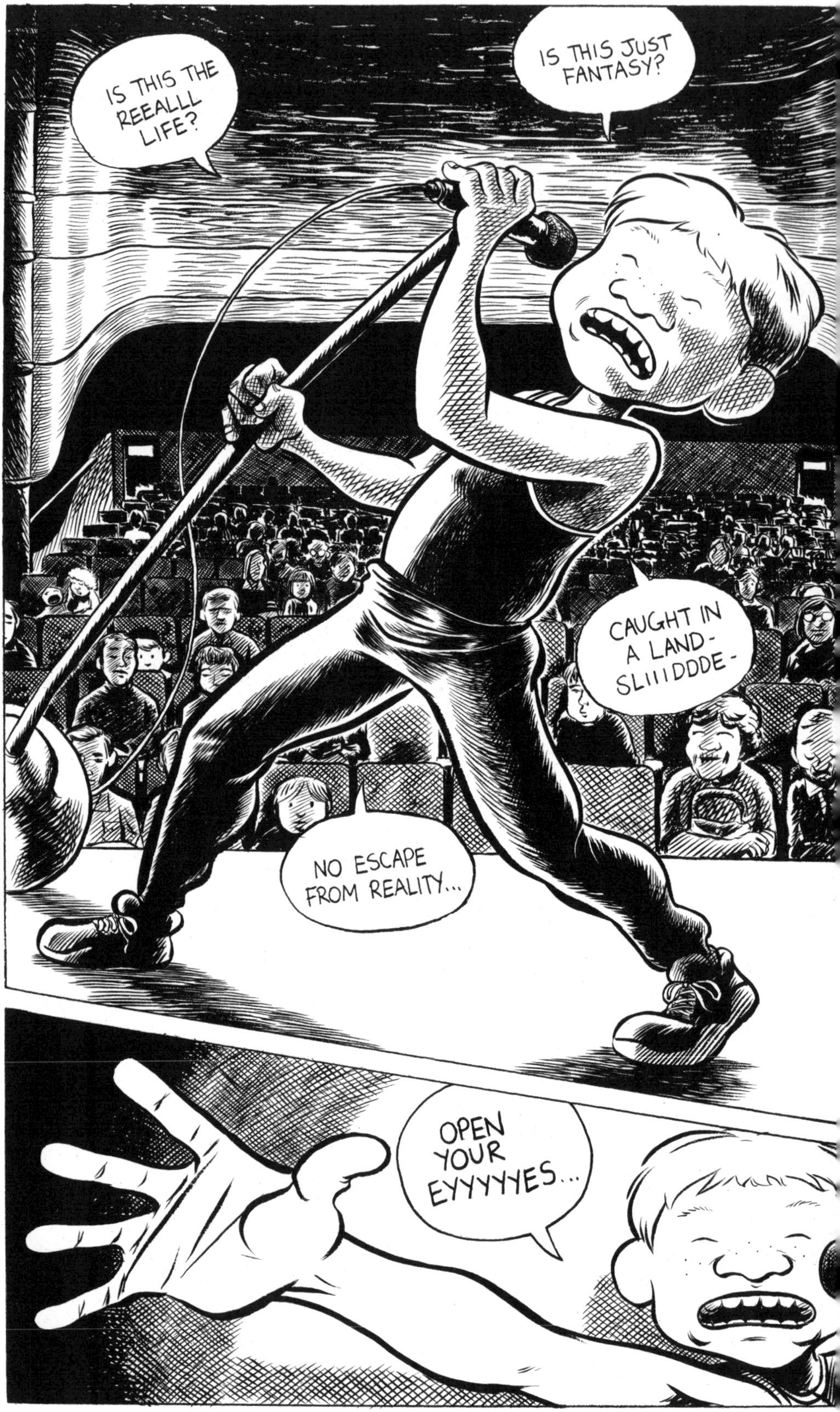
IS THIS THE REEALLL LIFE?
IS THIS JUST FANTASY?
CAUGHT IN A LAND-SLIIIDDDE-
NO ESCAPE FROM REALITY...
OPEN YOUR EYYYYYES...

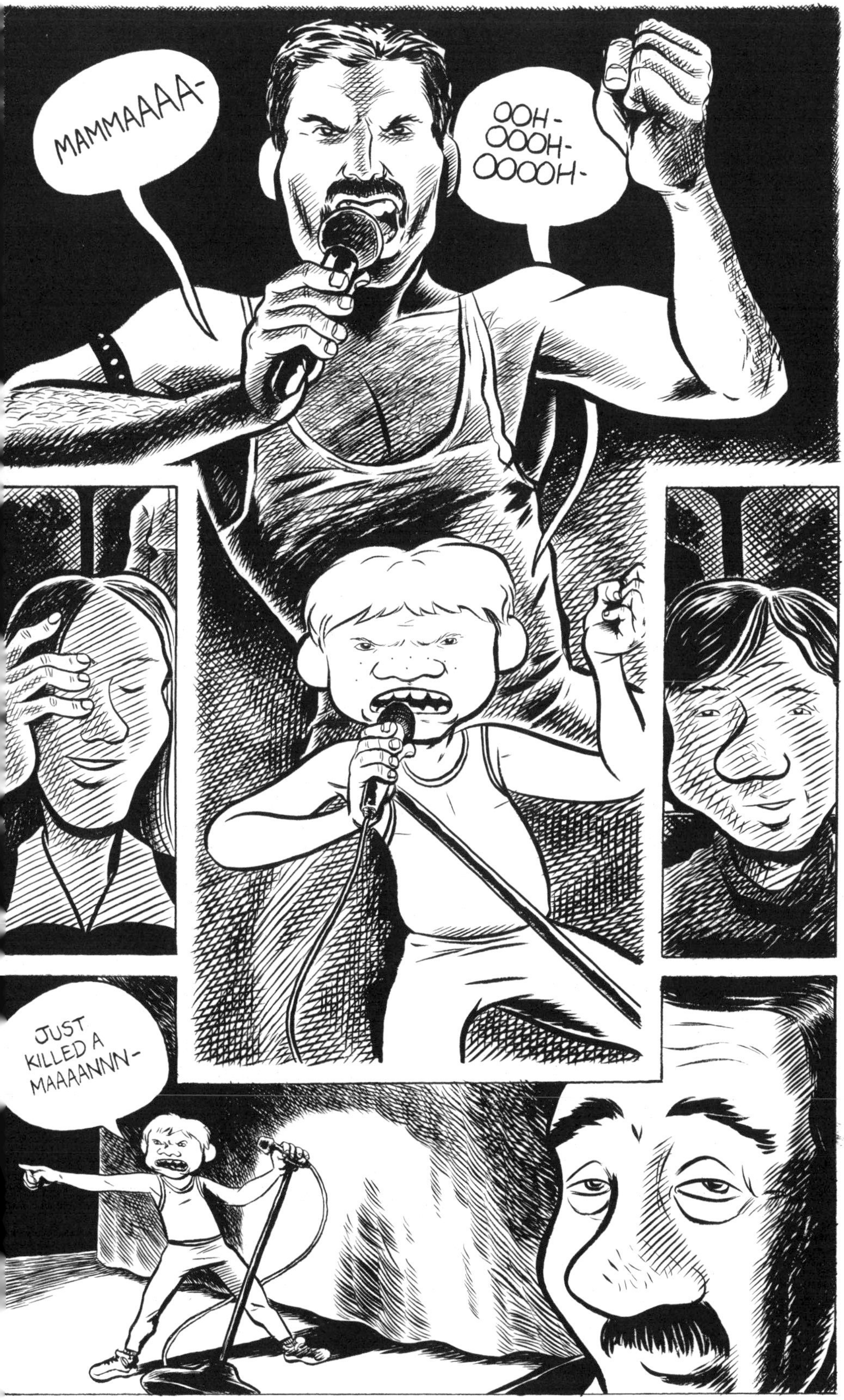
MAMMAAAA-
OOH-
OOOH-
OOOOH-
JUST KILLED A MAAAANNN-

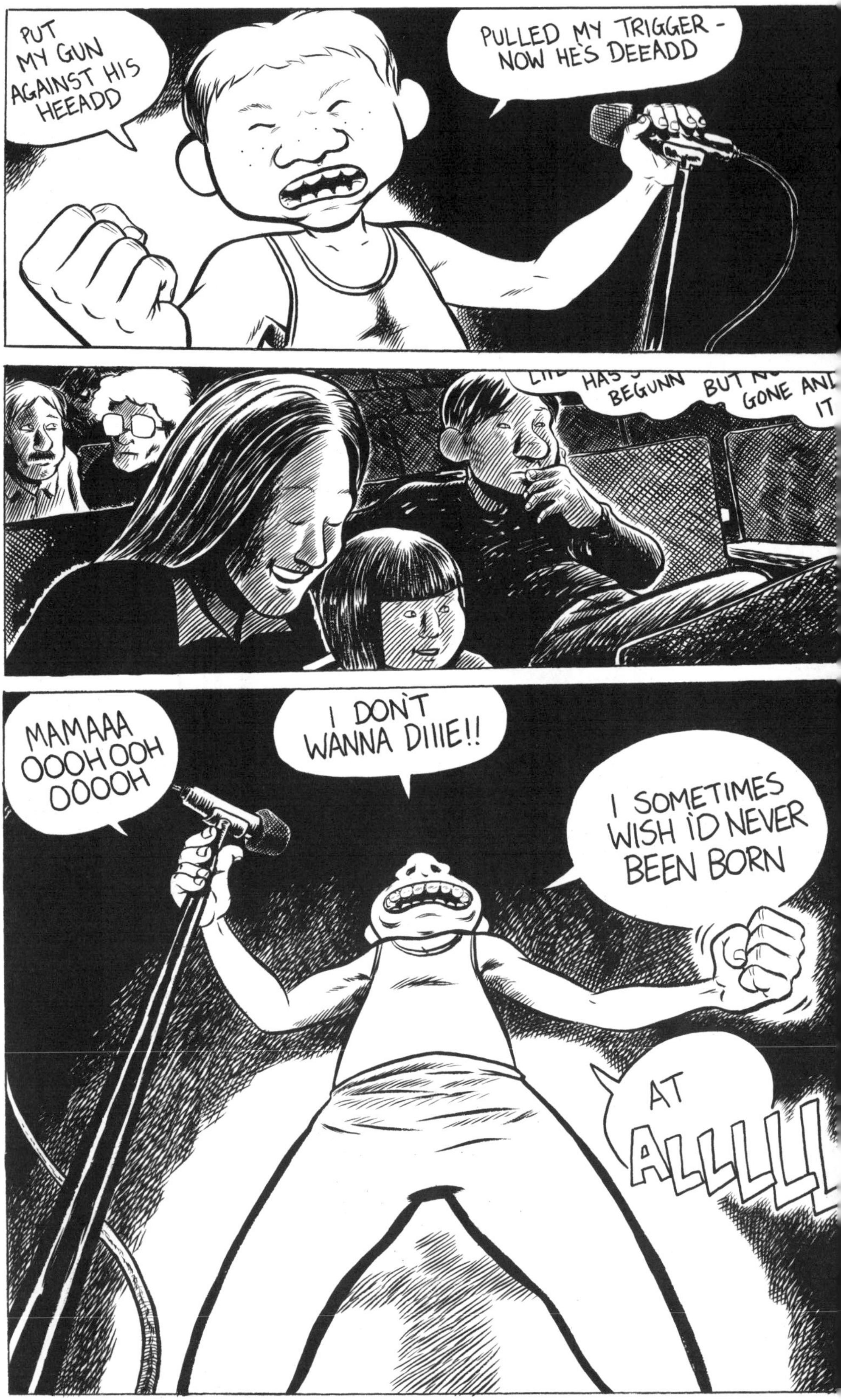
PUT MY GUN AGAINST HIS HEEADD
PULLED MY TRIGGER - NOW HE'S DEEADD
HAS
BEGUNN
GONE
MAMAAA OOOH OOH OOOOH
I DON'T WANNA DIIIE!!
I SOMETIMES WISH I'D NEVER BEEN BORN
AT

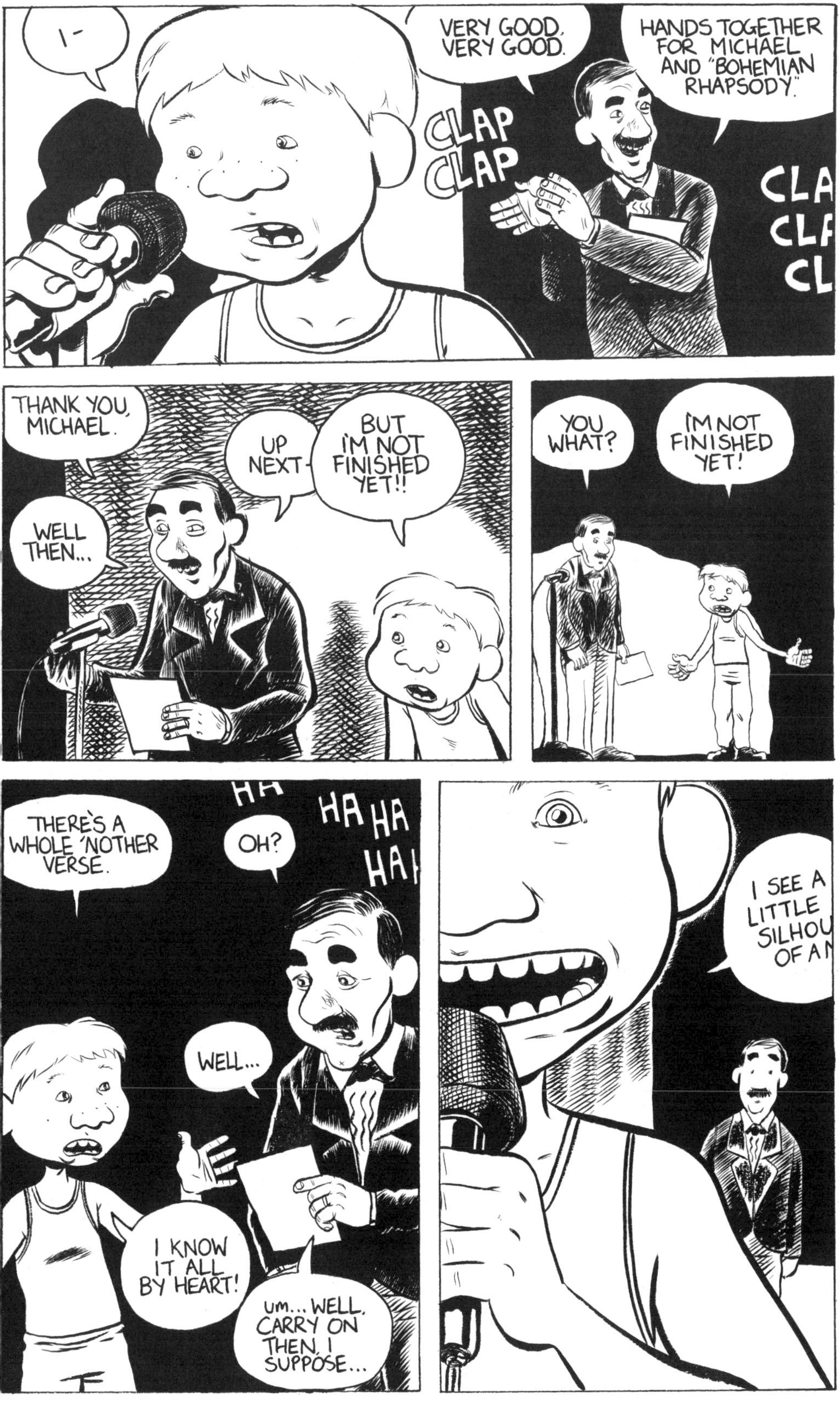
I-
VERY GOOD. VERY GOOD.
HANDS TOGETHER FOR MICHAEL AND "BOHEMIAN RHAPSODY."
CLAP CLAP
CLA CLA CL
THANK YOU, MICHAEL.
WELL THEN...
UP NEXT-
BUT I'M NOT FINISHED YET!!
YOU WHAT?
I'M NOT FINISHED YET!
THERE'S A WHOLE 'NOTHER VERSE.
HA
OH?
HA HA HA
WELL...
I KNOW IT ALL BY HEART!
UM... WELL, CARRY ON THEN, I SUPPOSE...
I SEE A LITTLE SILHOU OF A M

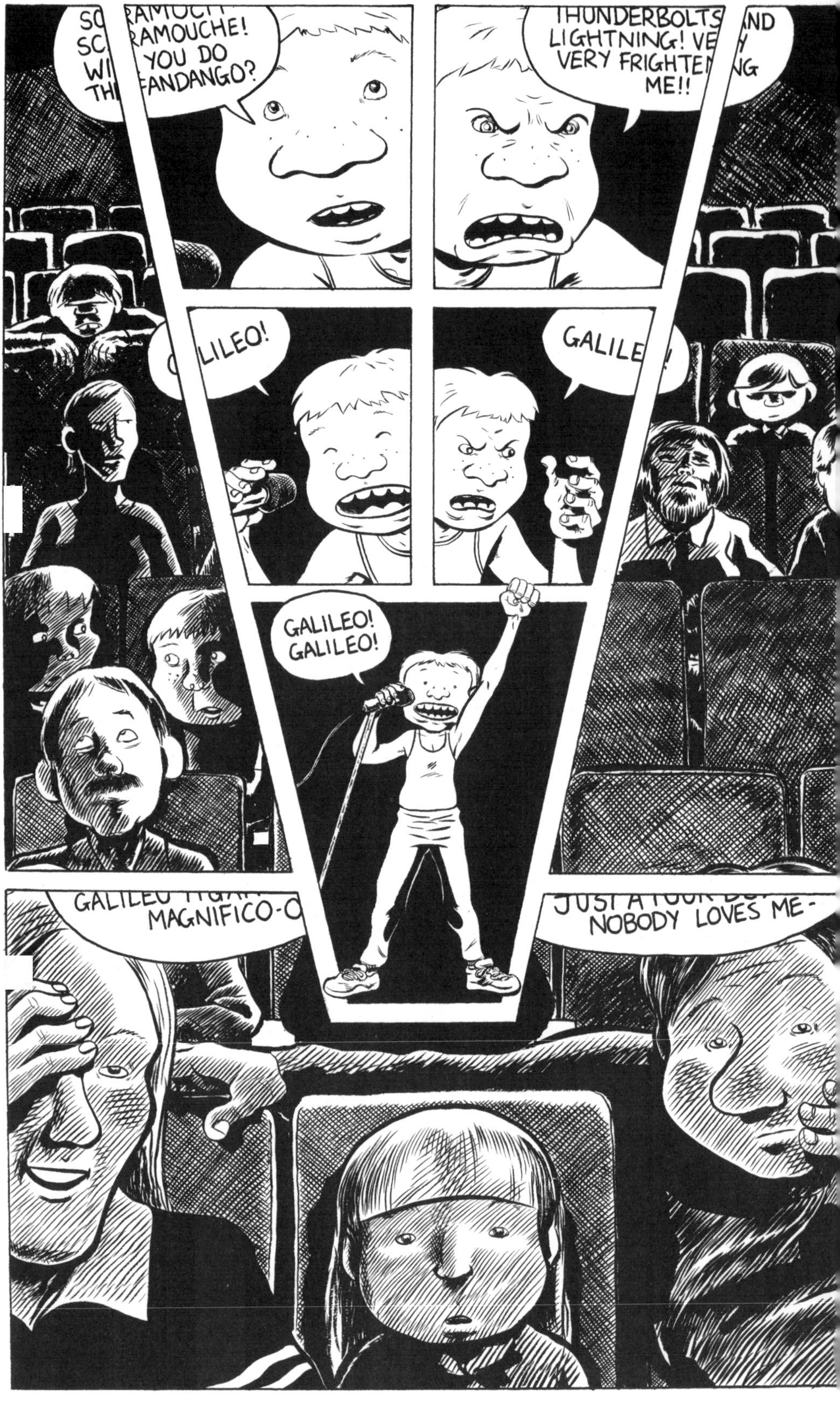
RAMOUCHE! YOU DO FANDANGO?
THUNDERBOLTS ND LIGHTNING! VE VERY FRIGHTE NG ME!!
LILEO!
GALILE
GALILEO! GALILEO!
MAGNIFICO-O
NOBODY LOVES ME-

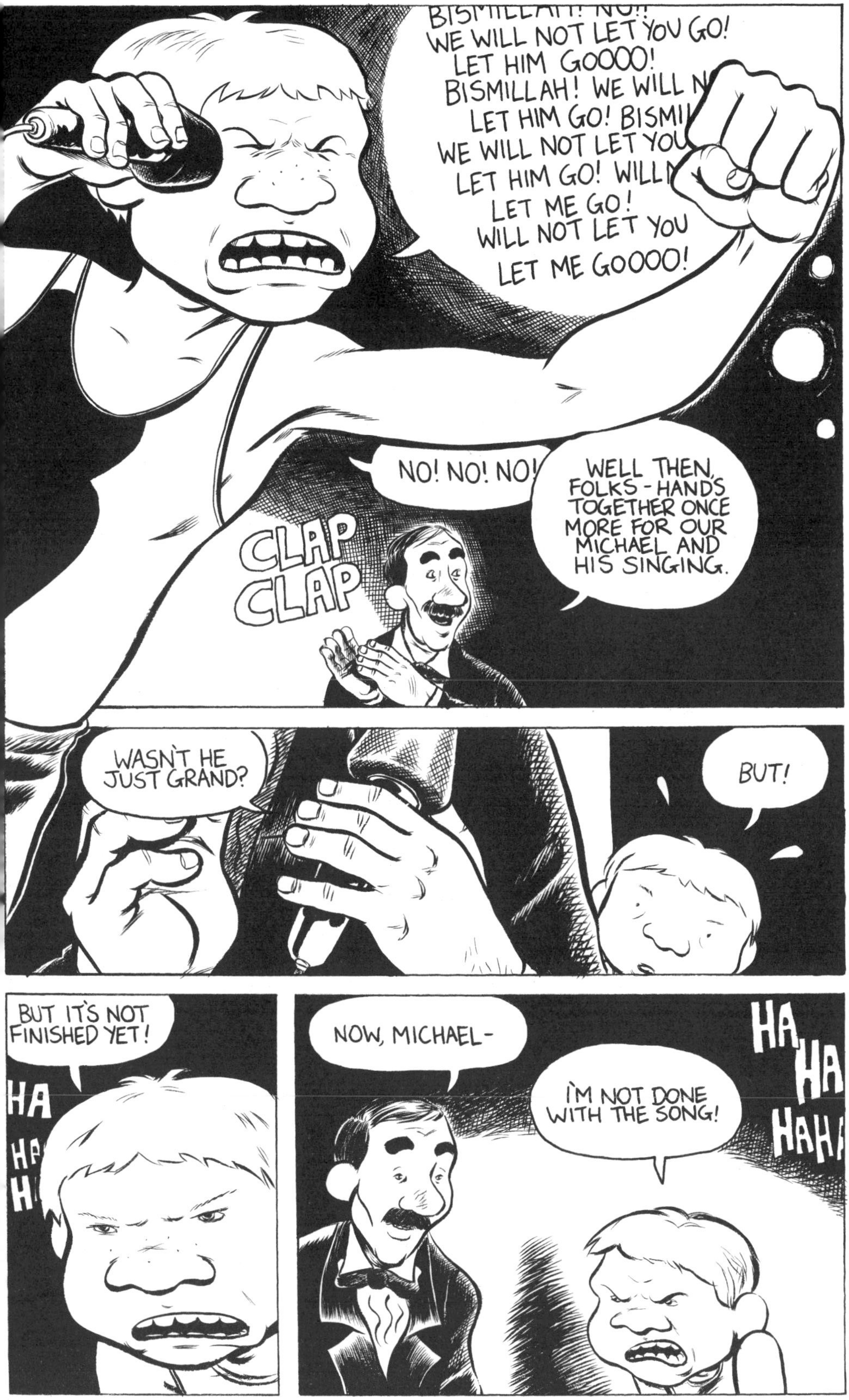
BISMILLAH! NO!!
WE WILL NOT LET YOU GO!
LET HIM GOOOO!
BISMILLAH! WE WILL N
LET HIM GO! BISMIL
WE WILL NOT LET YOU
LET HIM GO! WILL N
LET ME GO!
WILL NOT LET YOU
LET ME GOOOO!
NO! NO! NO!
WELL THEN, FOLKS - HANDS TOGETHER ONCE MORE FOR OUR MICHAEL AND HIS SINGING.
CLAP CLAP
WASN'T HE JUST GRAND?
BUT!
BUT IT'S NOT FINISHED YET!
HA
NOW, MICHAEL-
HA HA HAHA
I'M NOT DONE WITH THE SONG!

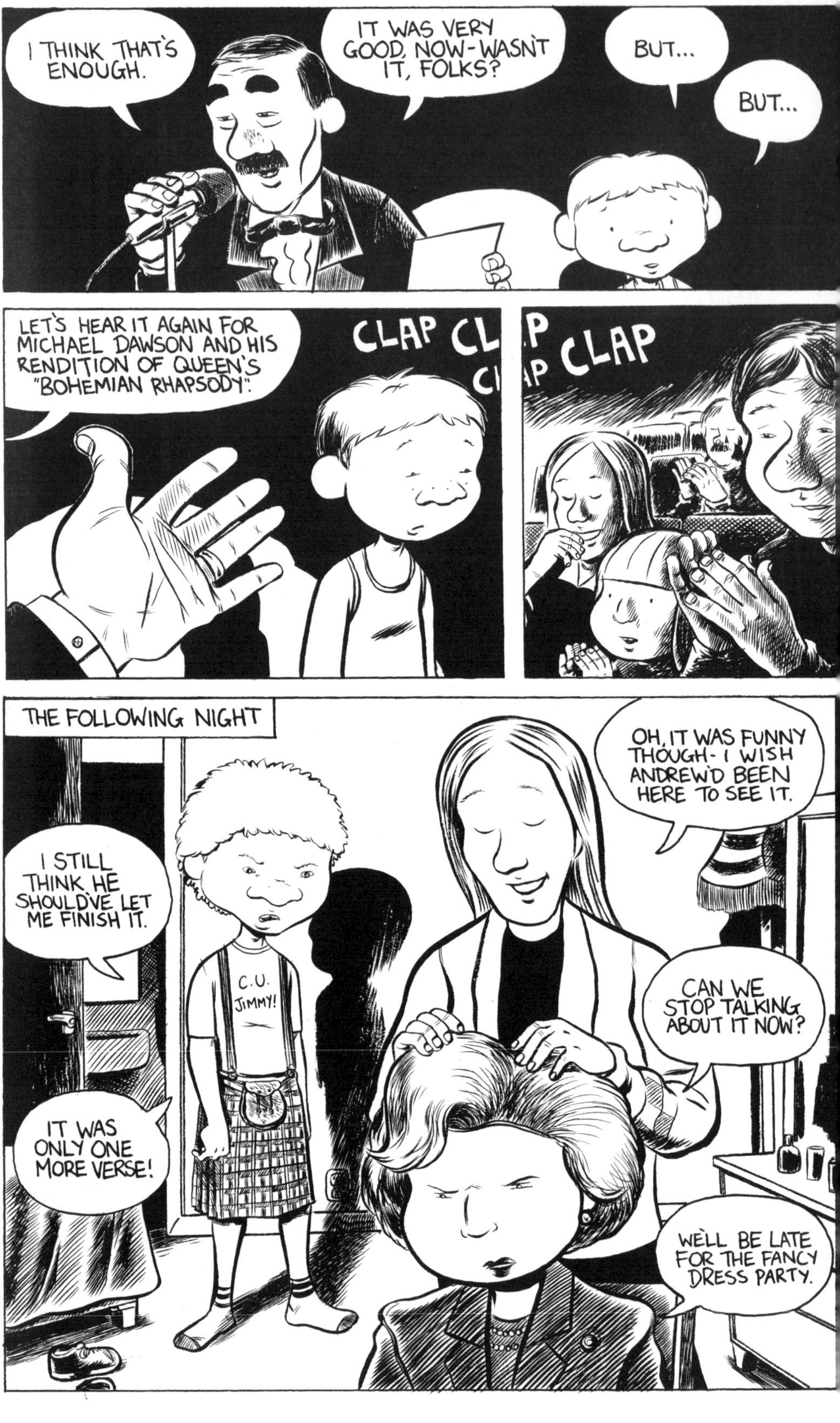
I THINK THAT'S ENOUGH.
IT WAS VERY GOOD, NOW-WASN'T IT, FOLKS?
BUT...
BUT...
LET'S HEAR IT AGAIN FOR MICHAEL DAWSON AND HIS RENDITION OF QUEEN'S "BOHEMIAN RHAPSODY".
CLAP CLAP
CLAP CLAP
THE FOLLOWING NIGHT
OH, IT WAS FUNNY THOUGH- I WISH ANDREW'D BEEN HERE TO SEE IT.
I STILL THINK HE SHOULD'VE LET ME FINISH IT.
C.U. JIMMY!
CAN WE STOP TALKING ABOUT IT NOW?
IT WAS ONLY ONE MORE VERSE!
WE'LL BE LATE FOR THE FANCY DRESS PARTY.

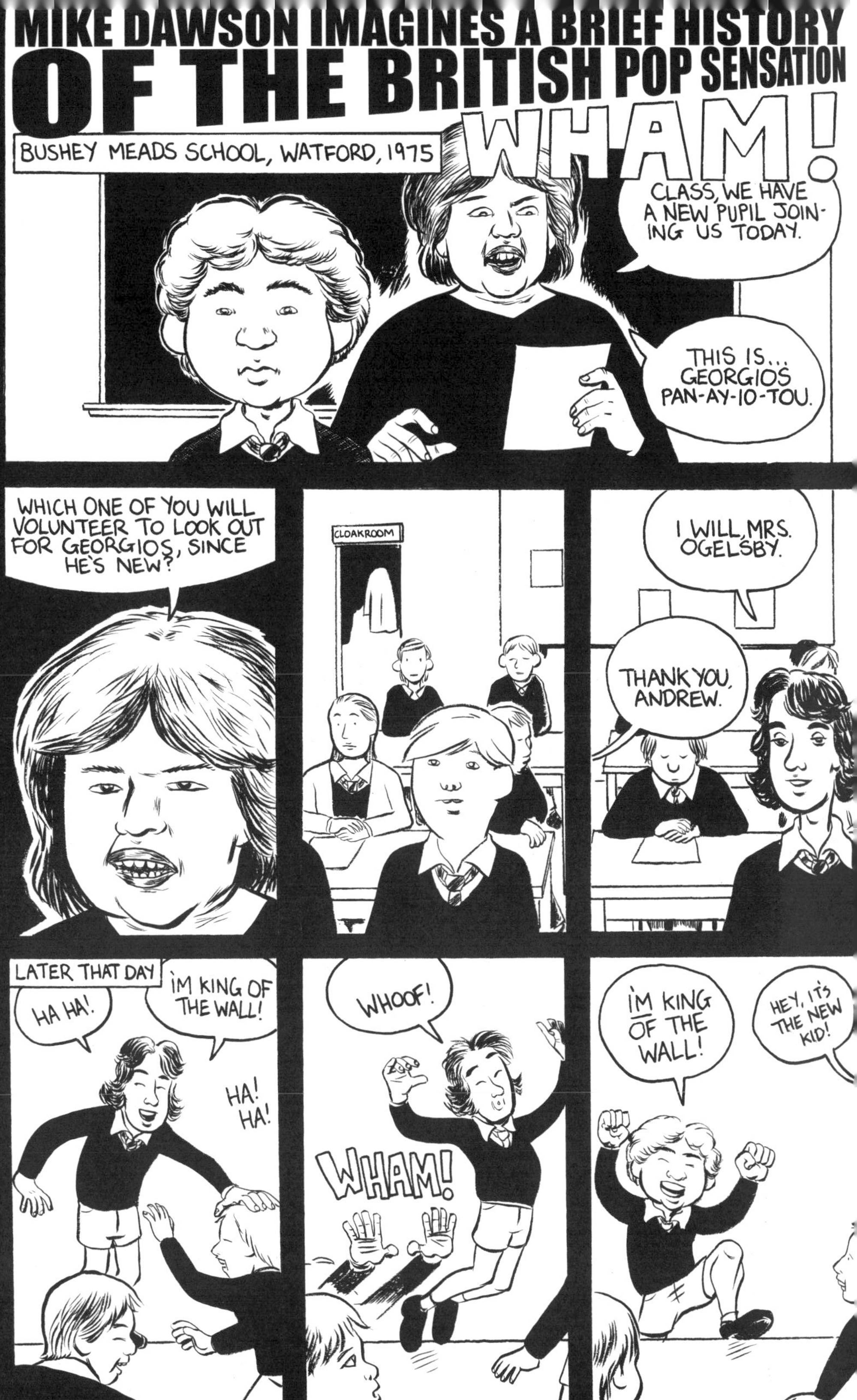
MIKE DAWSON IMAGINES A BRIEF HISTORY OF THE BRITISH POP SENSATION
WHAM!
BUSHEY MEADS SCHOOL, WATFORD, 1975
CLASS, WE HAVE A NEW PUPIL JOINING US TODAY.
THIS IS... GEORGIOS PAN-AY-IO-TOU.
WHICH ONE OF YOU WILL VOLUNTEER TO LOOK OUT FOR GEORGIOS, SINCE HE'S NEW?
CLOAKROOM
I WILL, MRS. OGELSBY.
THANK YOU, ANDREW.
LATER THAT DAY
HA HA!
I'M KING OF THE WALL!
HA! HA!
WHOOF!
WHAM!
I'M KING OF THE WALL!
HEY, IT'S THE NEW KID!

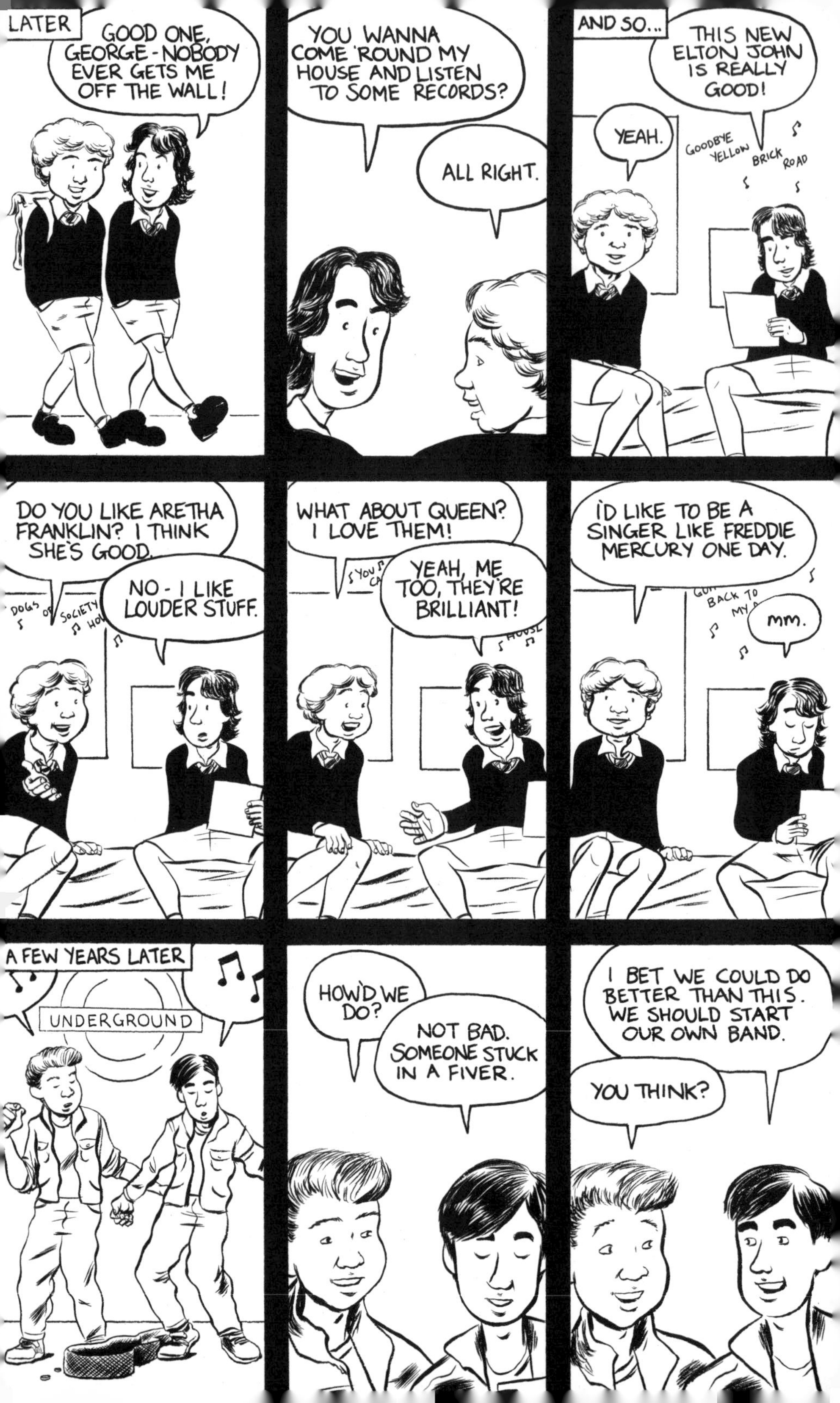
LATER
GOOD ONE, GEORGE - NOBODY EVER GETS ME OFF THE WALL!
YOU WANNA COME 'ROUND MY HOUSE AND LISTEN TO SOME RECORDS?
ALL RIGHT.
AND SO...
THIS NEW ELTON JOHN IS REALLY GOOD!
YEAH.
GOODBYE YELLOW BRICK ROAD
DO YOU LIKE ARETHA FRANKLIN? I THINK SHE'S GOOD.
NO - I LIKE LOUDER STUFF.
WHAT ABOUT QUEEN? I LOVE THEM!
YEAH, ME TOO, THEY'RE BRILLIANT!
I'D LIKE TO BE A SINGER LIKE FREDDIE MERCURY ONE DAY.
MM.
A FEW YEARS LATER
UNDERGROUND
HOW'D WE DO?
NOT BAD. SOMEONE STUCK IN A FIVER.
I BET WE COULD DO BETTER THAN THIS. WE SHOULD START OUR OWN BAND.
YOU THINK?

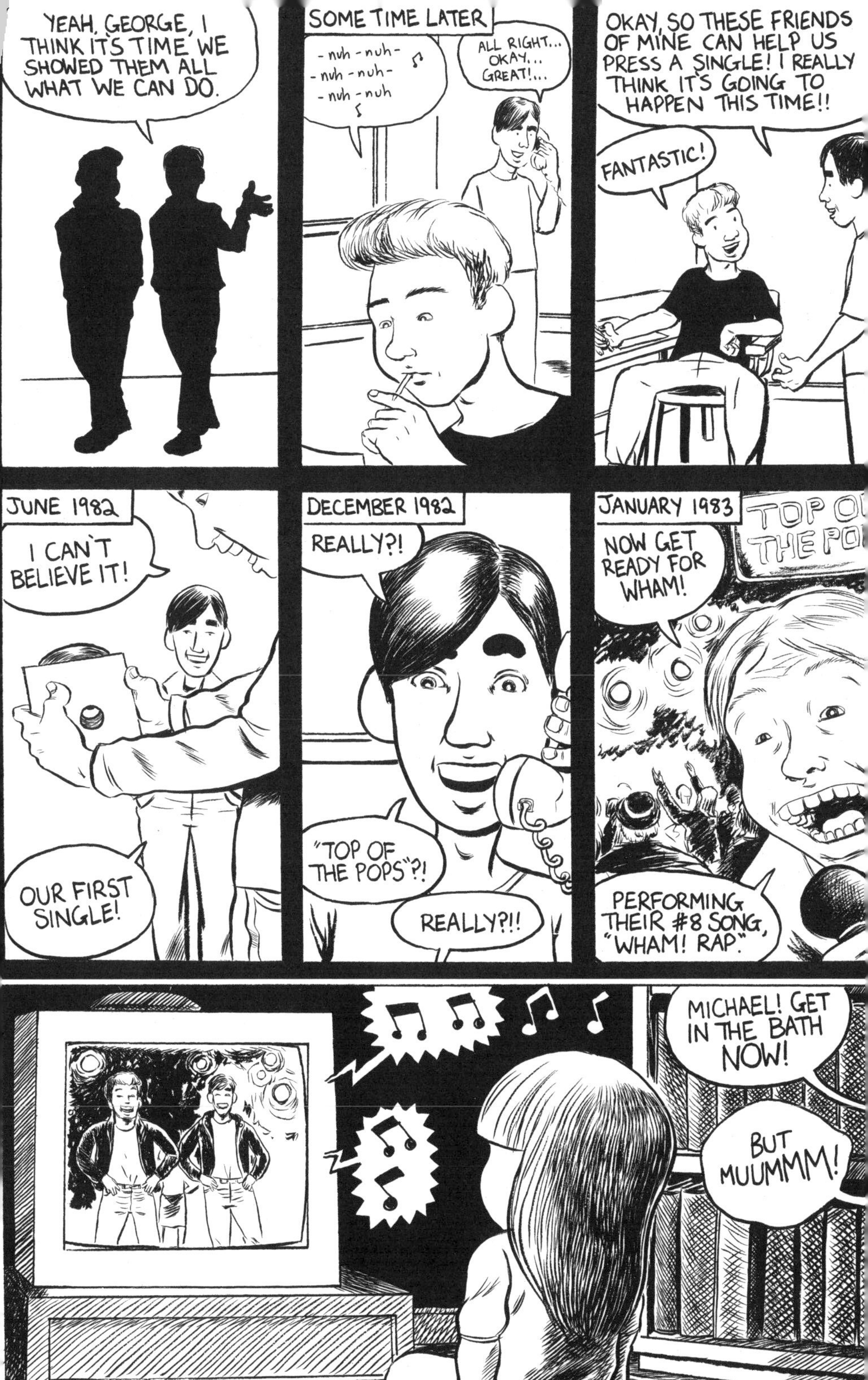

YEAH, GEORGE, I THINK IT'S TIME WE SHOWED THEM ALL WHAT WE CAN DO.
SOME TIME LATER
-nuh-nuh- -nuh-nuh- -nuh-nuh
ALL RIGHT... OKAY... GREAT!...
OKAY, SO THESE FRIENDS OF MINE CAN HELP US PRESS A SINGLE! I REALLY THINK IT'S GOING TO HAPPEN THIS TIME!!
FANTASTIC!
JUNE 1982
I CAN'T BELIEVE IT!
OUR FIRST SINGLE!
DECEMBER 1982
REALLY?!
"TOP OF THE POPS"?!
REALLY?!!
JANUARY 1983
NOW GET READY FOR WHAM!
PERFORMING THEIR #8 SONG, "WHAM! RAP."
MICHAEL! GET IN THE BATH NOW!
BUT MUUMMM!

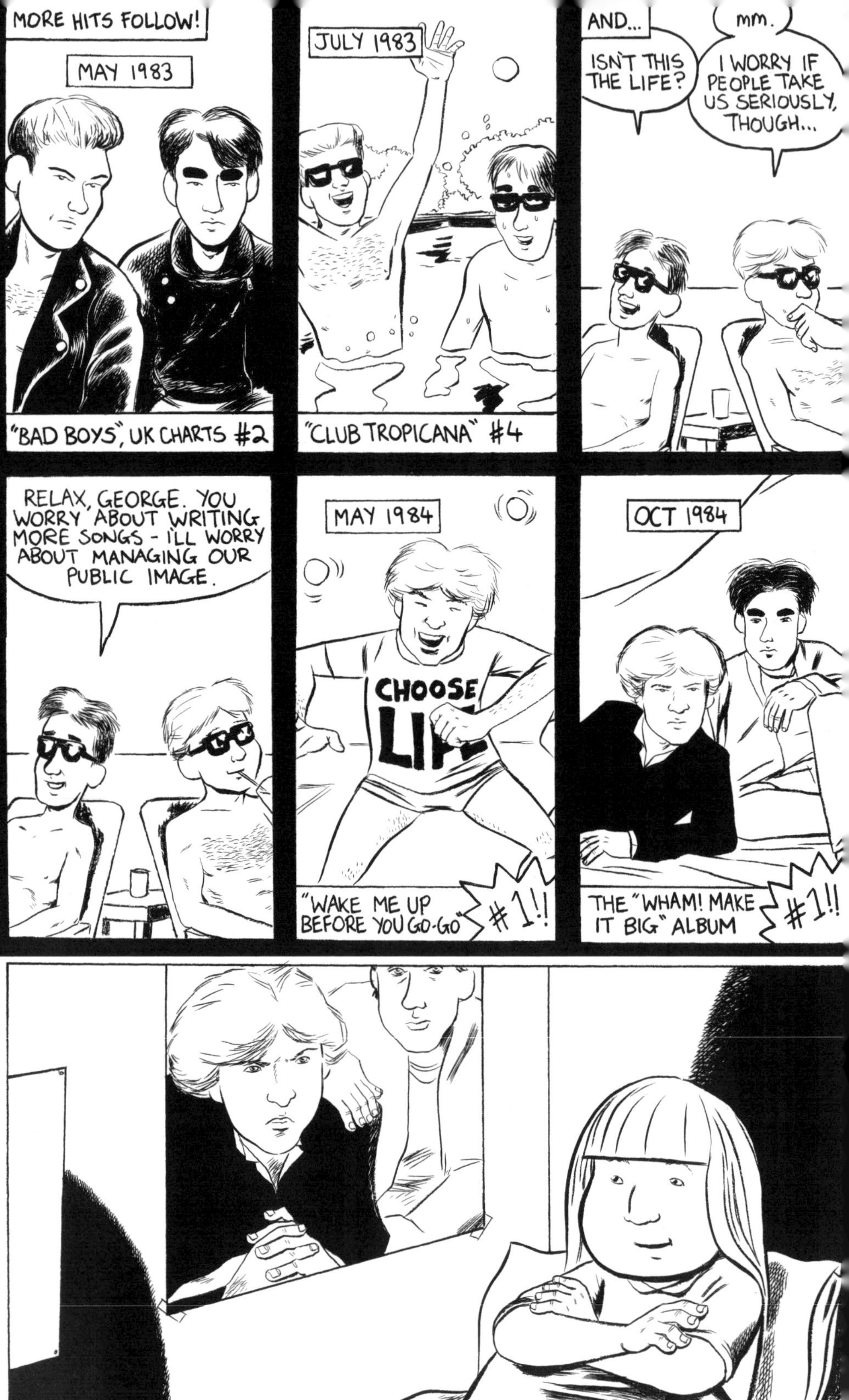
MORE HITS FOLLOW!
MAY 1983
"BAD BOYS", UK CHARTS #2
JULY 1983
"CLUB TROPICANA" #4
AND...
ISN'T THIS THE LIFE?
mm.
I WORRY IF PEOPLE TAKE US SERIOUSLY, THOUGH...
RELAX, GEORGE. YOU WORRY ABOUT WRITING MORE SONGS - I'LL WORRY ABOUT MANAGING OUR PUBLIC IMAGE.
MAY 1984
CHOOSE LIFE
"WAKE ME UP BEFORE YOU GO-GO"
#1!!
OCT 1984
THE "WHAM! MAKE IT BIG" ALBUM
#1!!

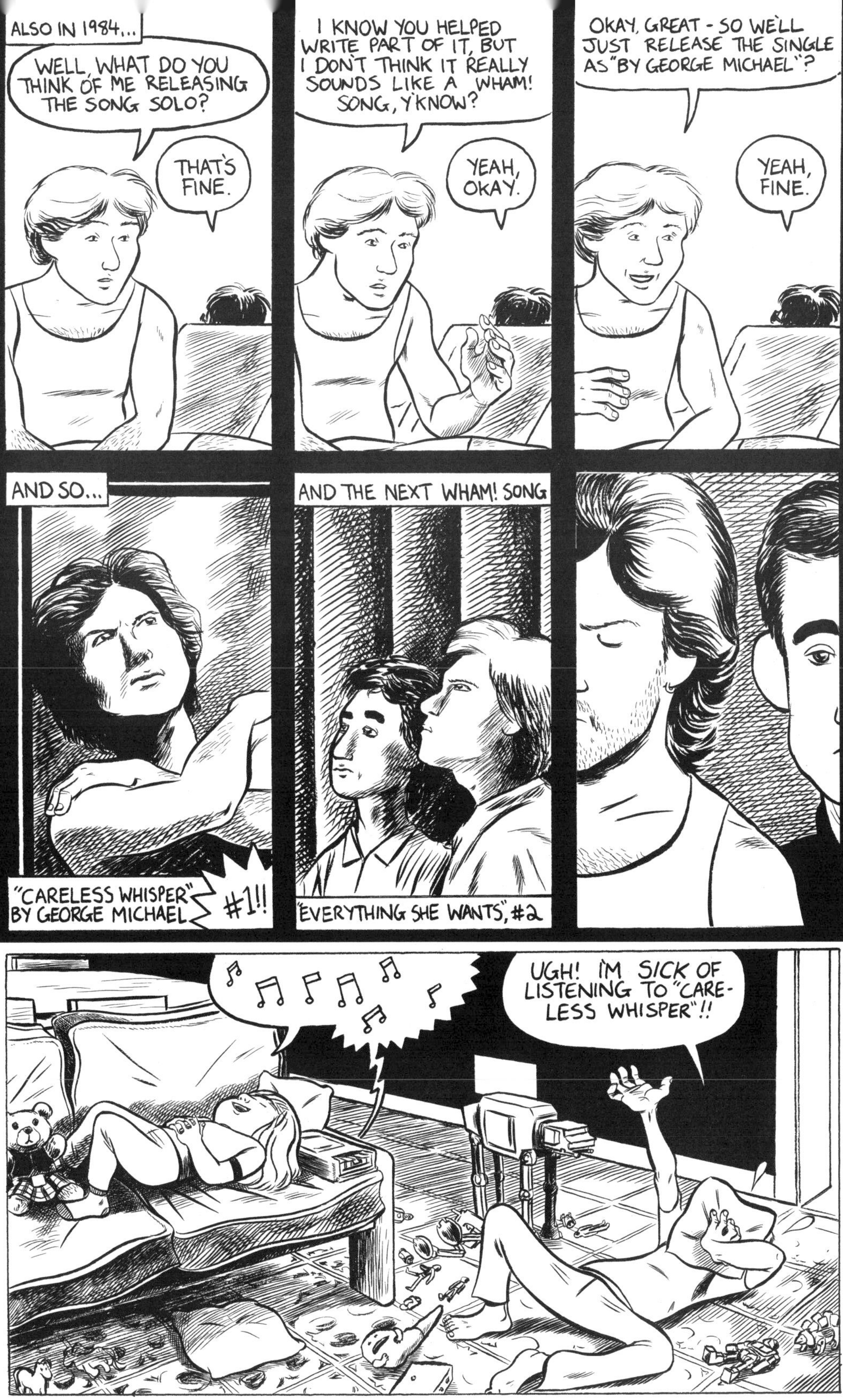
ALSO IN 1984...
WELL, WHAT DO YOU THINK OF ME RELEASING THE SONG SOLO?
THAT'S FINE.
I KNOW YOU HELPED WRITE PART OF IT, BUT I DON'T THINK IT REALLY SOUNDS LIKE A WHAM! SONG, Y'KNOW?
YEAH, OKAY.
OKAY, GREAT - SO WE'LL JUST RELEASE THE SINGLE AS "BY GEORGE MICHAEL"?
YEAH, FINE.
AND SO...
"CARELESS WHISPER" BY GEORGE MICHAEL
#1!!
AND THE NEXT WHAM! SONG
"EVERYTHING SHE WANTS," #2
UGH! I'M SICK OF LISTENING TO "CARE-LESS WHISPER"!!

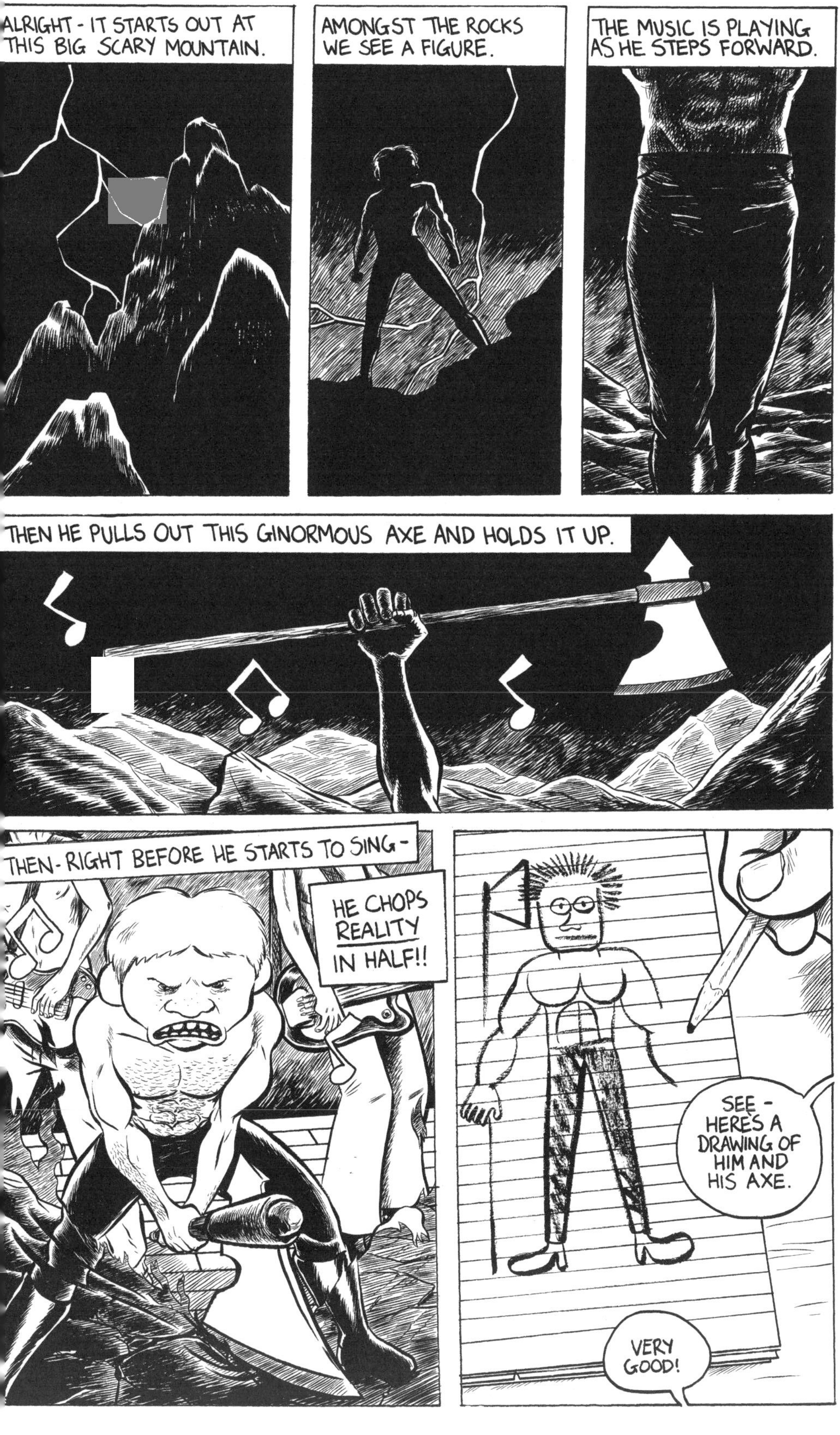
ALRIGHT - IT STARTS OUT AT THIS BIG SCARY MOUNTAIN.
AMONGST THE ROCKS WE SEE A FIGURE.
THE MUSIC IS PLAYING AS HE STEPS FORWARD.
THEN HE PULLS OUT THIS GINORMOUS AXE AND HOLDS IT UP.
THEN - RIGHT BEFORE HE STARTS TO SING -
HE CHOPS REALITY IN HALF!!
SEE - HERE'S A DRAWING OF HIM AND HIS AXE.
VERY GOOD!

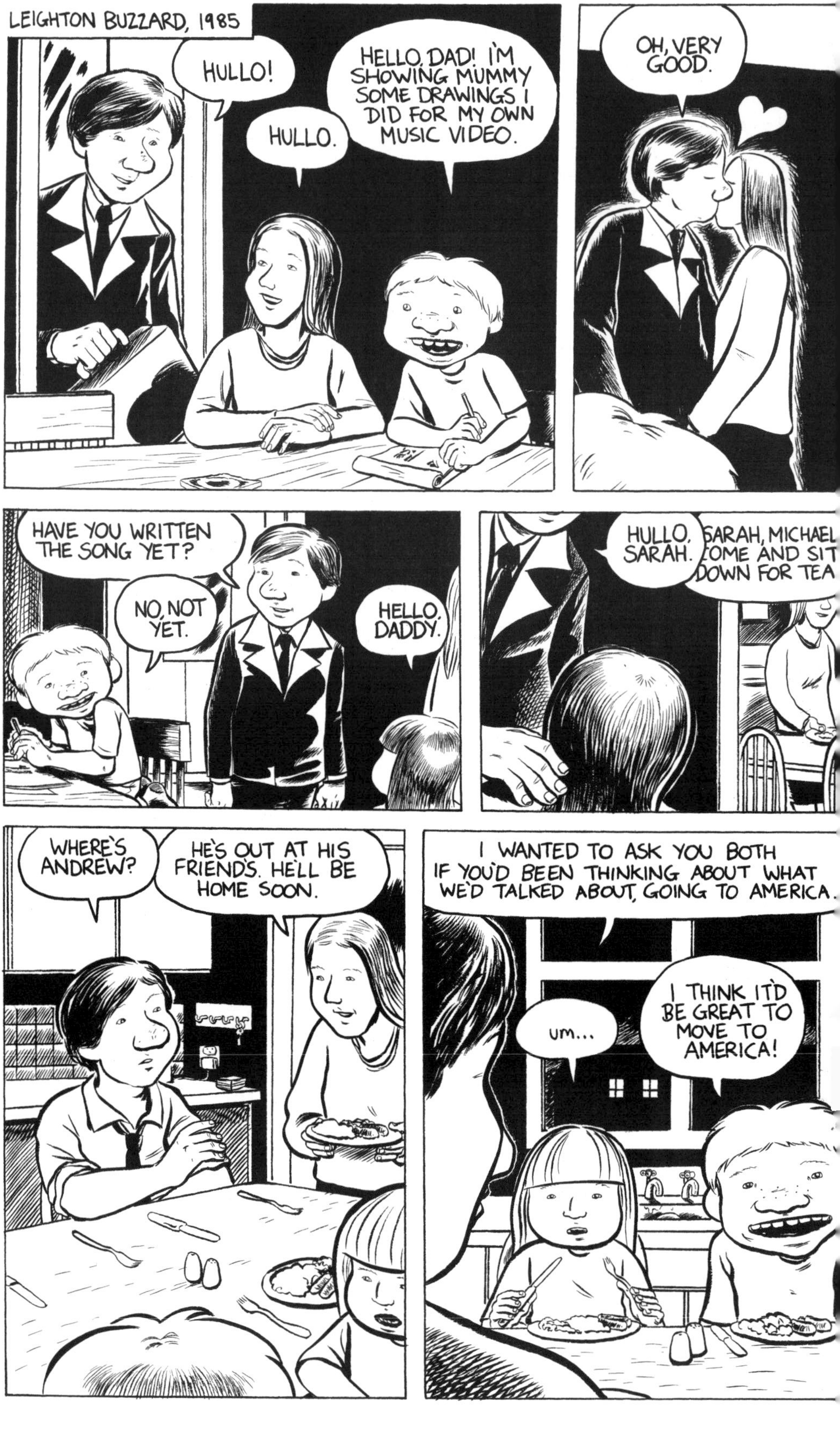
LEIGHTON BUZZARD, 1985
HULLO!
HULLO.
HELLO, DAD! I'M SHOWING MUMMY SOME DRAWINGS I DID FOR MY OWN MUSIC VIDEO.
OH, VERY GOOD.
HAVE YOU WRITTEN THE SONG YET?
NO, NOT YET.
HELLO, DADDY.
HULLO, SARAH.
SARAH, MICHAEL COME AND SIT DOWN FOR TEA
WHERE'S ANDREW?
HE'S OUT AT HIS FRIEND'S. HE'LL BE HOME SOON.
I WANTED TO ASK YOU BOTH IF YOU'D BEEN THINKING ABOUT WHAT WE'D TALKED ABOUT, GOING TO AMERICA.
um...
I THINK IT'D BE GREAT TO MOVE TO AMERICA!

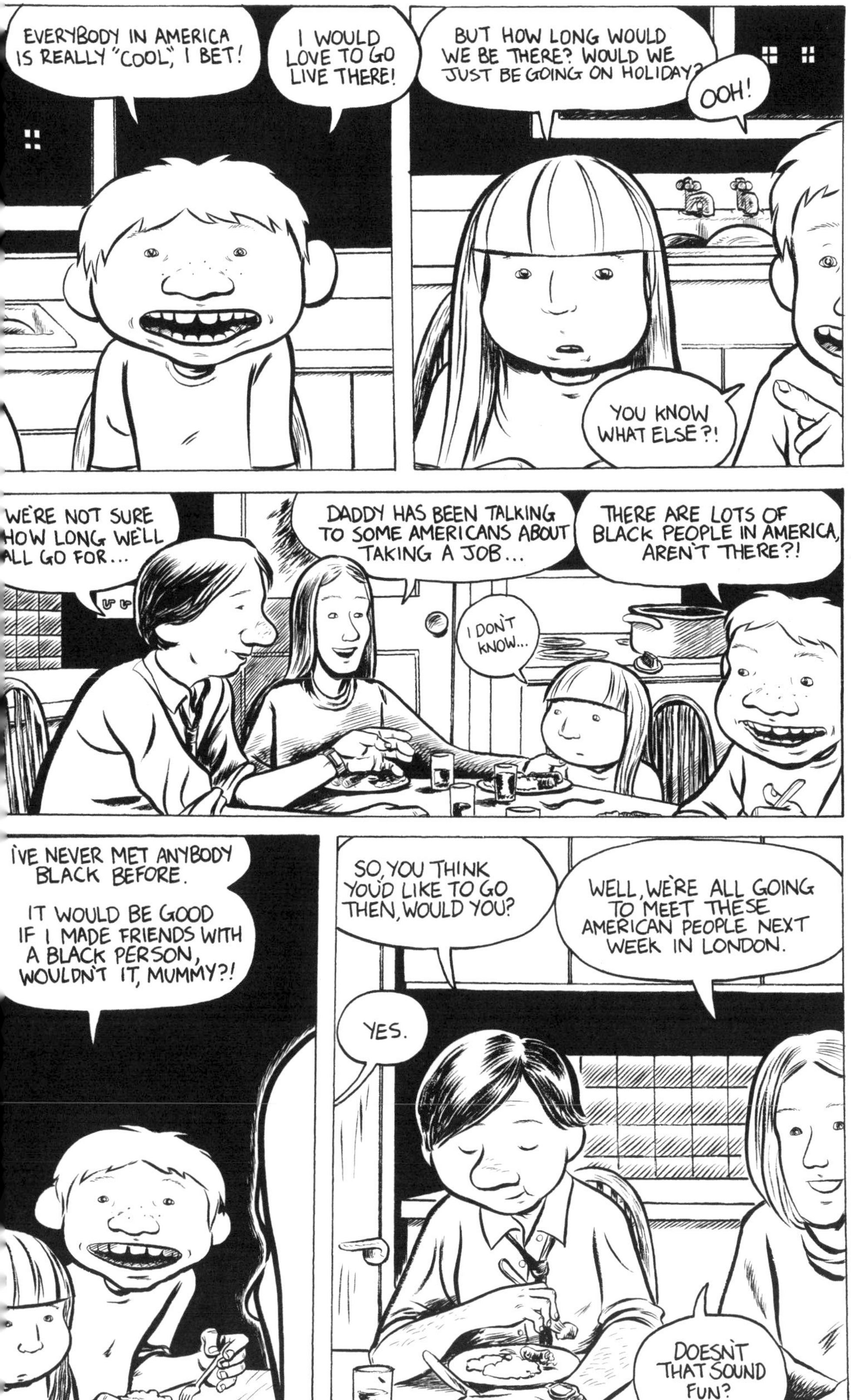
EVERYBODY IN AMERICA IS REALLY "COOL," I BET!
I WOULD LOVE TO GO LIVE THERE!
BUT HOW LONG WOULD WE BE THERE? WOULD WE JUST BE GOING ON HOLIDAY?
OOH!
YOU KNOW WHAT ELSE?!
WE'RE NOT SURE HOW LONG WE'LL ALL GO FOR...
DADDY HAS BEEN TALKING TO SOME AMERICANS ABOUT TAKING A JOB...
I DON'T KNOW...
THERE ARE LOTS OF BLACK PEOPLE IN AMERICA, AREN'T THERE?!
I'VE NEVER MET ANYBODY BLACK BEFORE.
IT WOULD BE GOOD IF I MADE FRIENDS WITH A BLACK PERSON, WOULDN'T IT, MUMMY?!
SO, YOU THINK YOU'D LIKE TO GO THEN, WOULD YOU?
YES.
WELL, WE'RE ALL GOING TO MEET THESE AMERICAN PEOPLE NEXT WEEK IN LONDON.
DOESN'T THAT SOUND FUN?

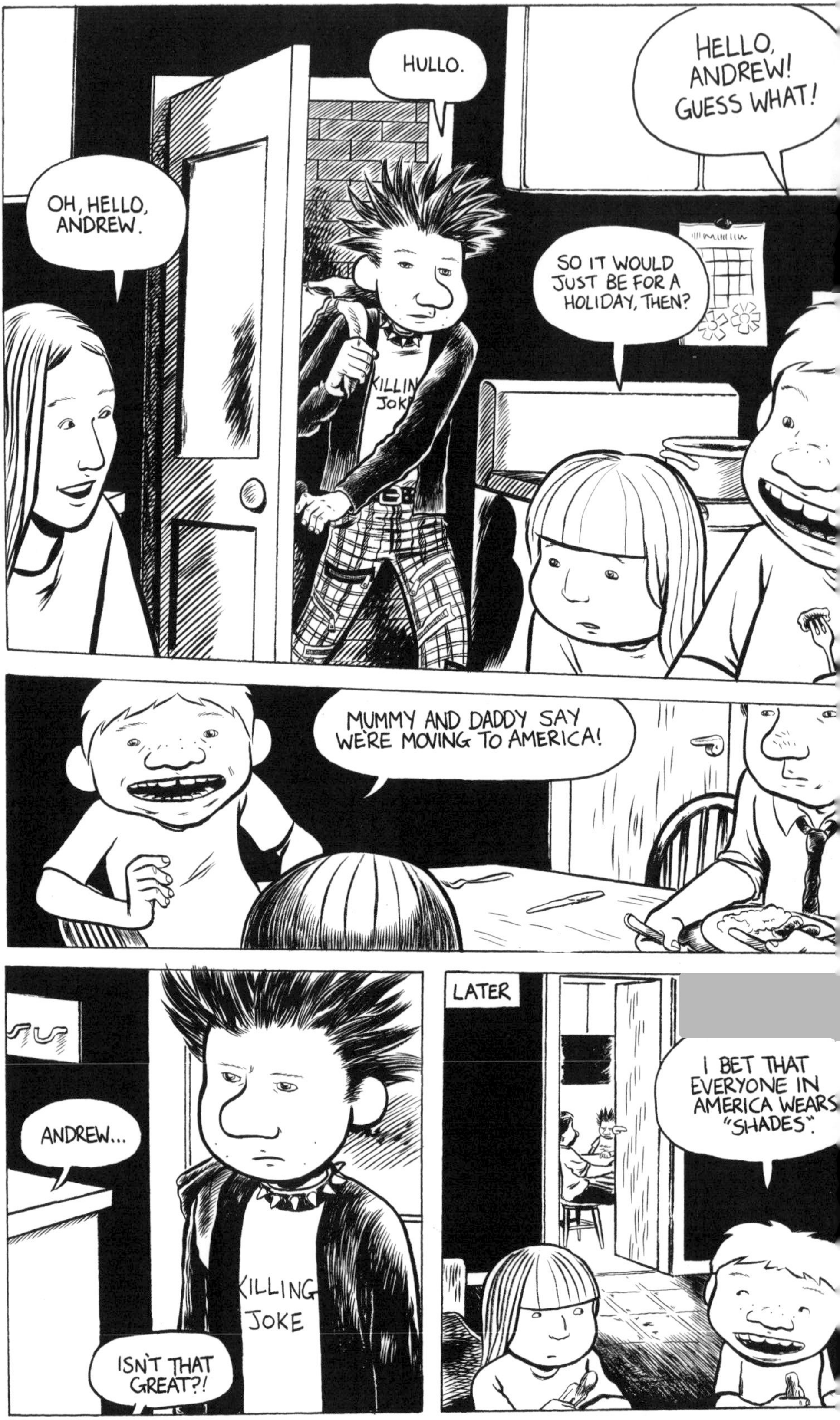
HULLO.
HELLO, ANDREW! GUESS WHAT!
OH, HELLO, ANDREW.
SO IT WOULD JUST BE FOR A HOLIDAY, THEN?
KILLING JOKE
MUMMY AND DADDY SAY WE'RE MOVING TO AMERICA!
ANDREW...
KILLING JOKE
ISN'T THAT GREAT?!
LATER
I BET THAT EVERYONE IN AMERICA WEARS "SHADES".

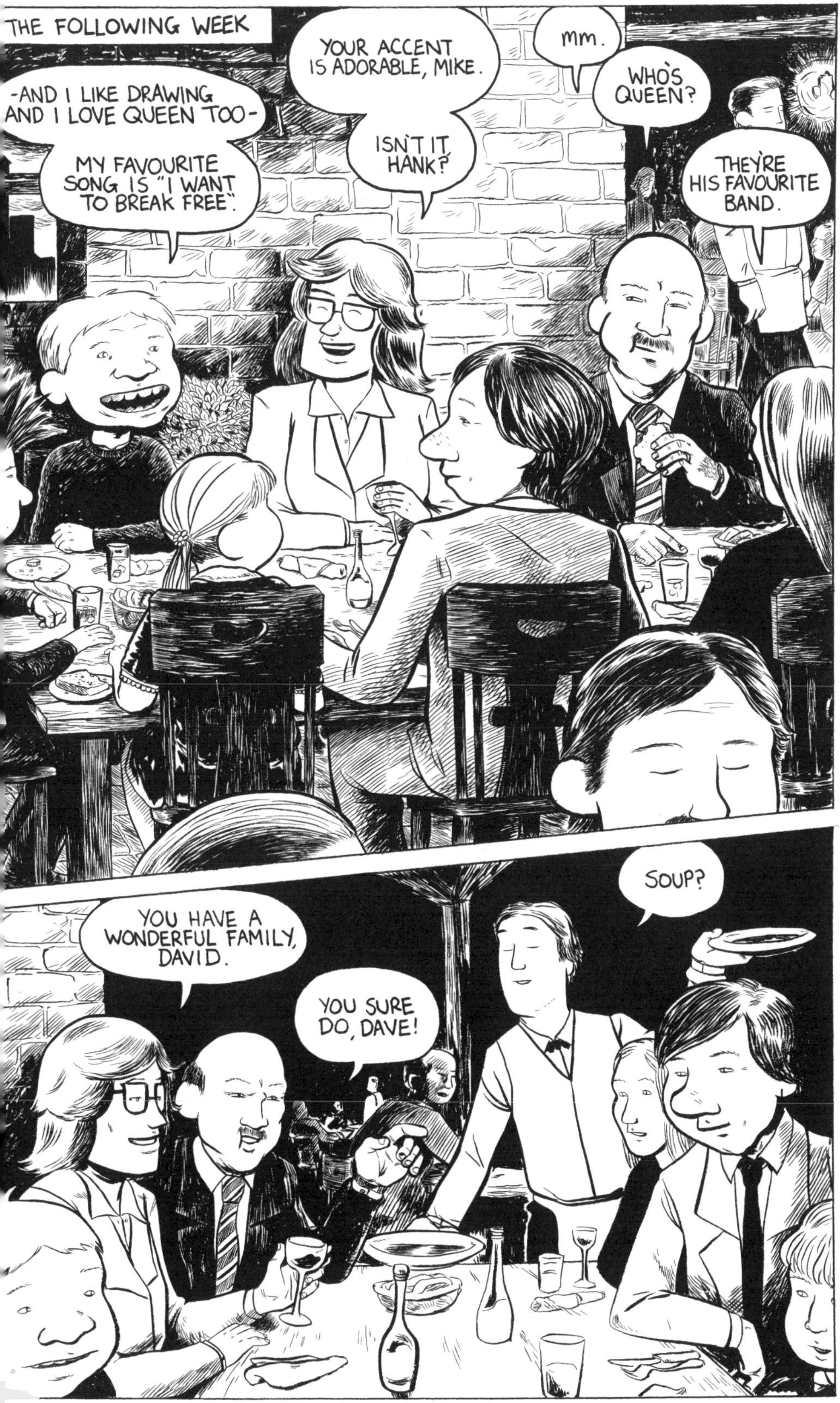
THE FOLLOWING WEEK
-AND I LIKE DRAWING AND I LOVE QUEEN TOO-
MY FAVOURITE SONG IS "I WANT TO BREAK FREE".
YOUR ACCENT IS ADORABLE, MIKE.
ISN'T IT HANK?
mm.
WHO'S QUEEN?
THEY'RE HIS FAVOURITE BAND.
YOU HAVE A WONDERFUL FAMILY, DAVID.
YOU SURE DO, DAVE!
SOUP?

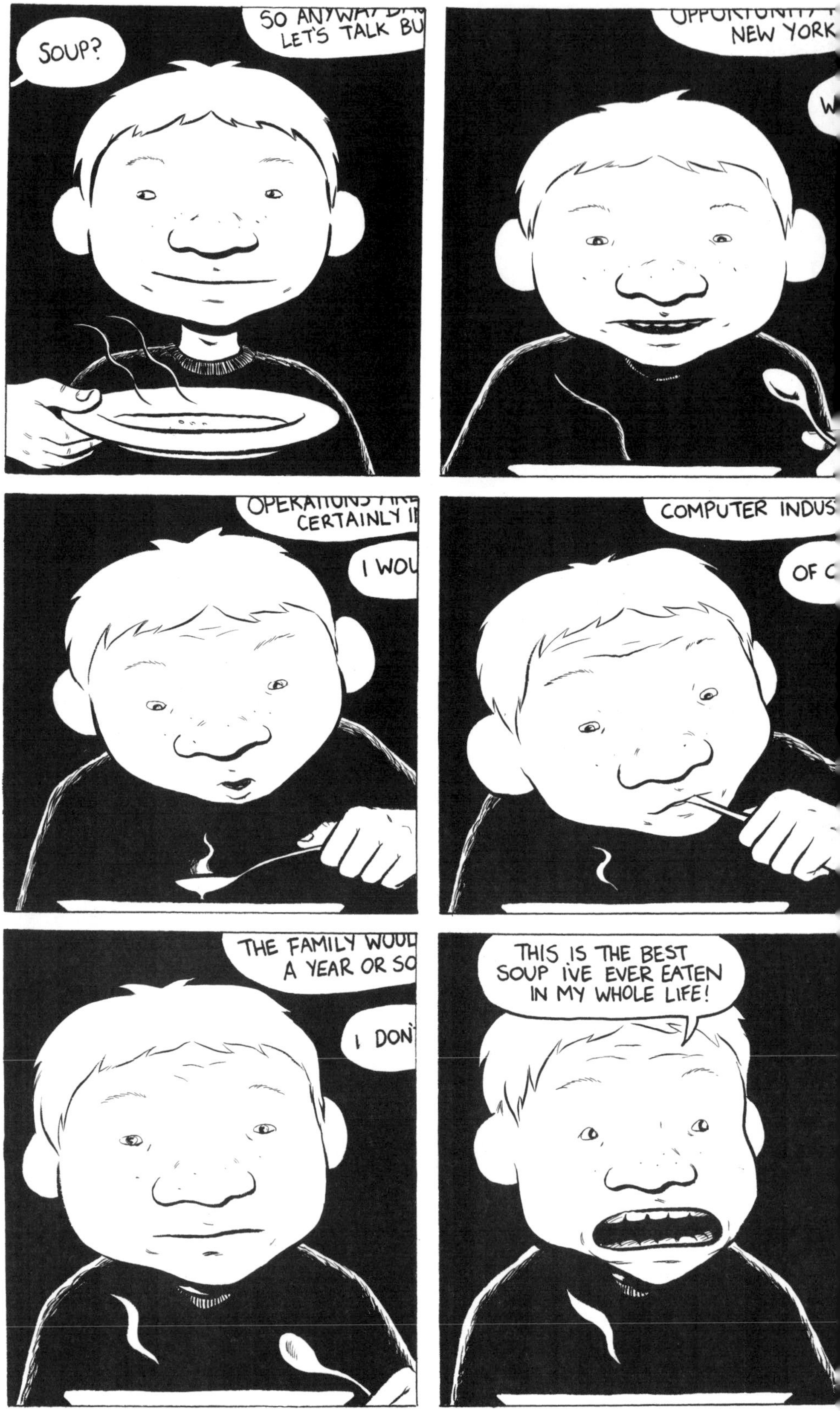
SOUP?
SO ANYWAY
LET'S TALK
NEW YORK
CERTAINLY
COMPUTER
THE FAMILY
A YEAR OR
THIS IS THE BEST SOUP I'VE EVER EATEN IN MY WHOLE LIFE!

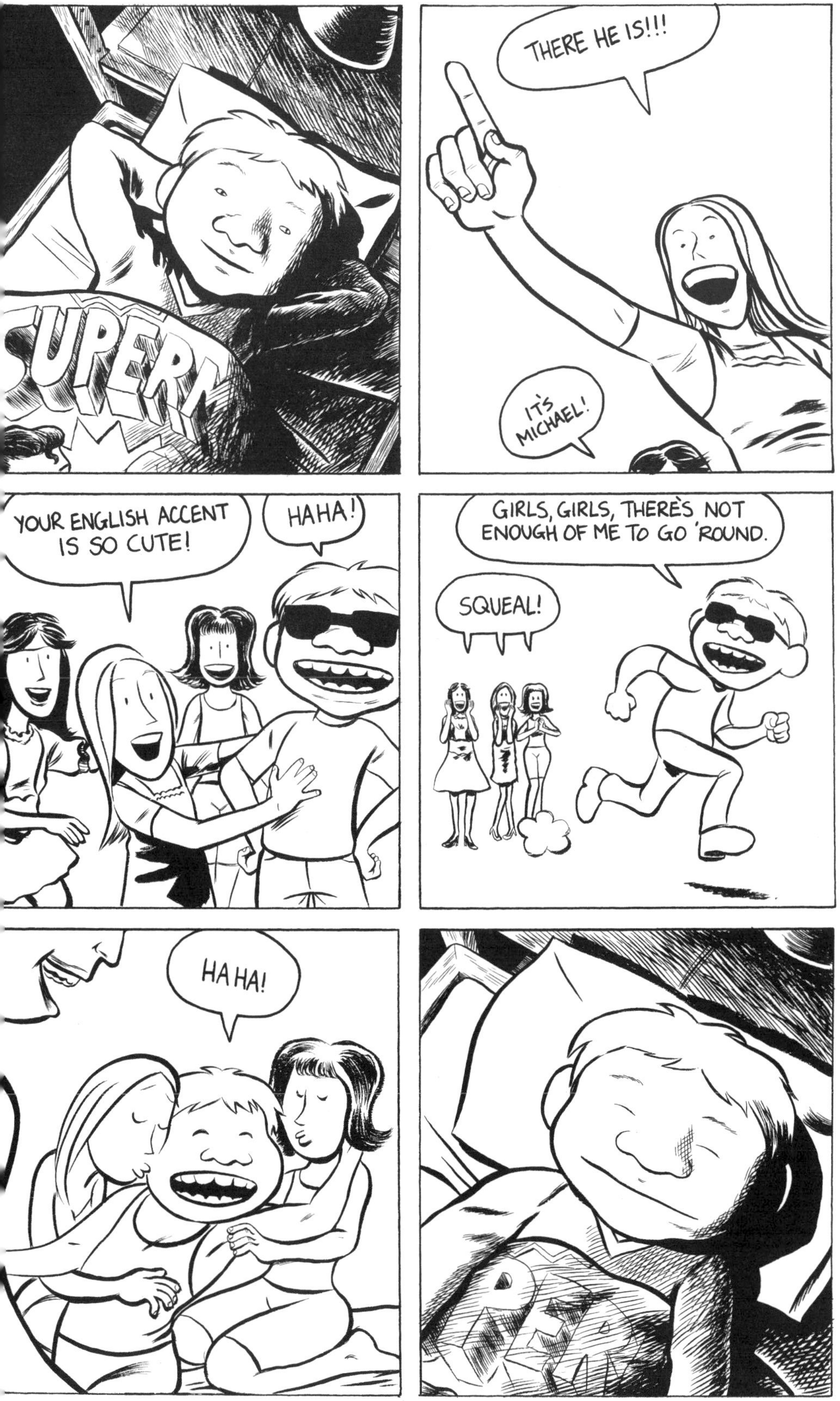
SUPERM
THERE HE IS!!!
IT'S MICHAEL!
YOUR ENGLISH ACCENT IS SO CUTE!
HAHA!
GIRLS, GIRLS, THERE'S NOT ENOUGH OF ME TO GO 'ROUND.
SQUEAL!
HAHA!

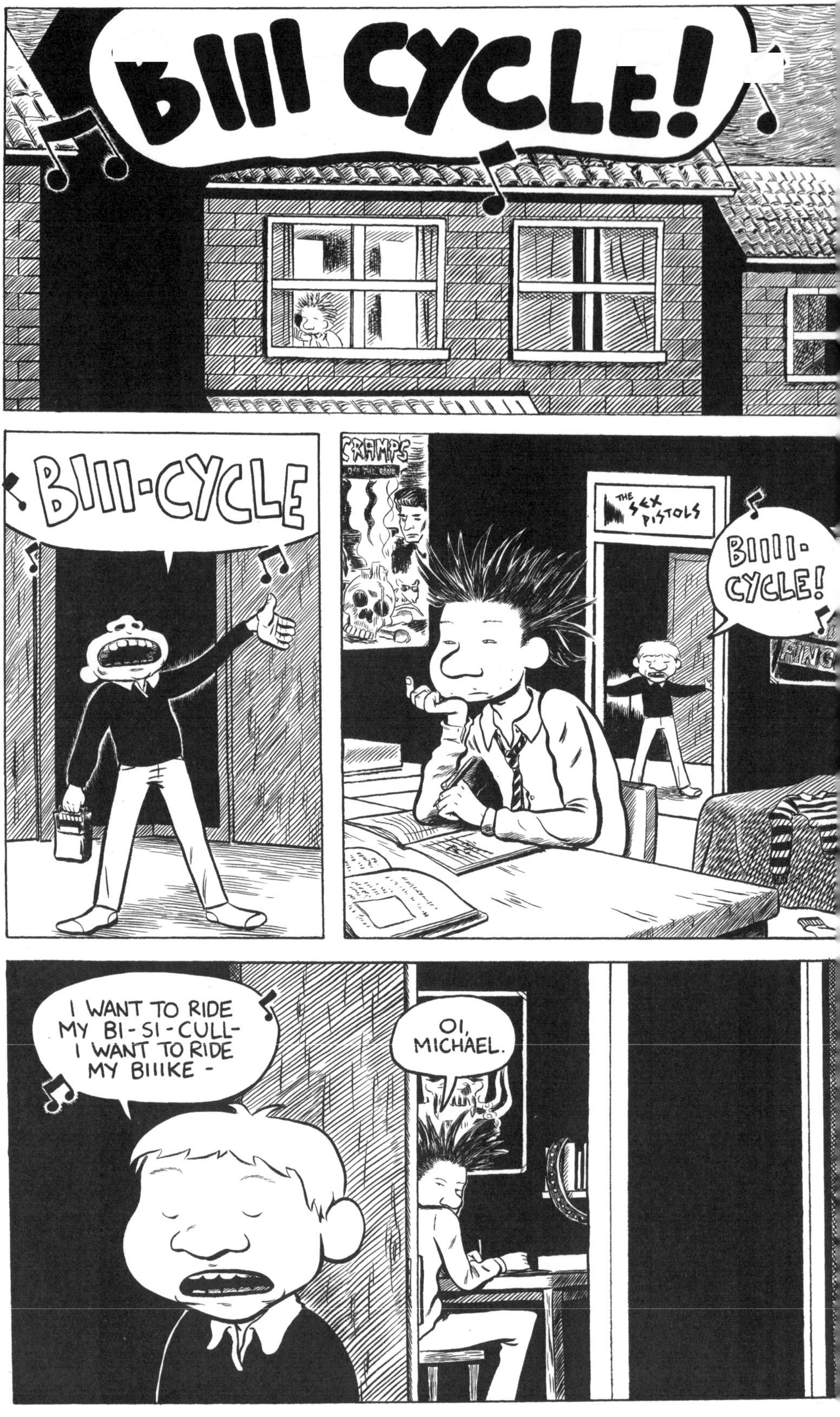
BIII CYCLE!
BIII-CYCLE
CRAMPS
THE SEX PISTOLS
BIIII-CYCLE!
I WANT TO RIDE MY BI-SI-CULL- I WANT TO RIDE MY BIIIKE -
OI, MICHAEL.

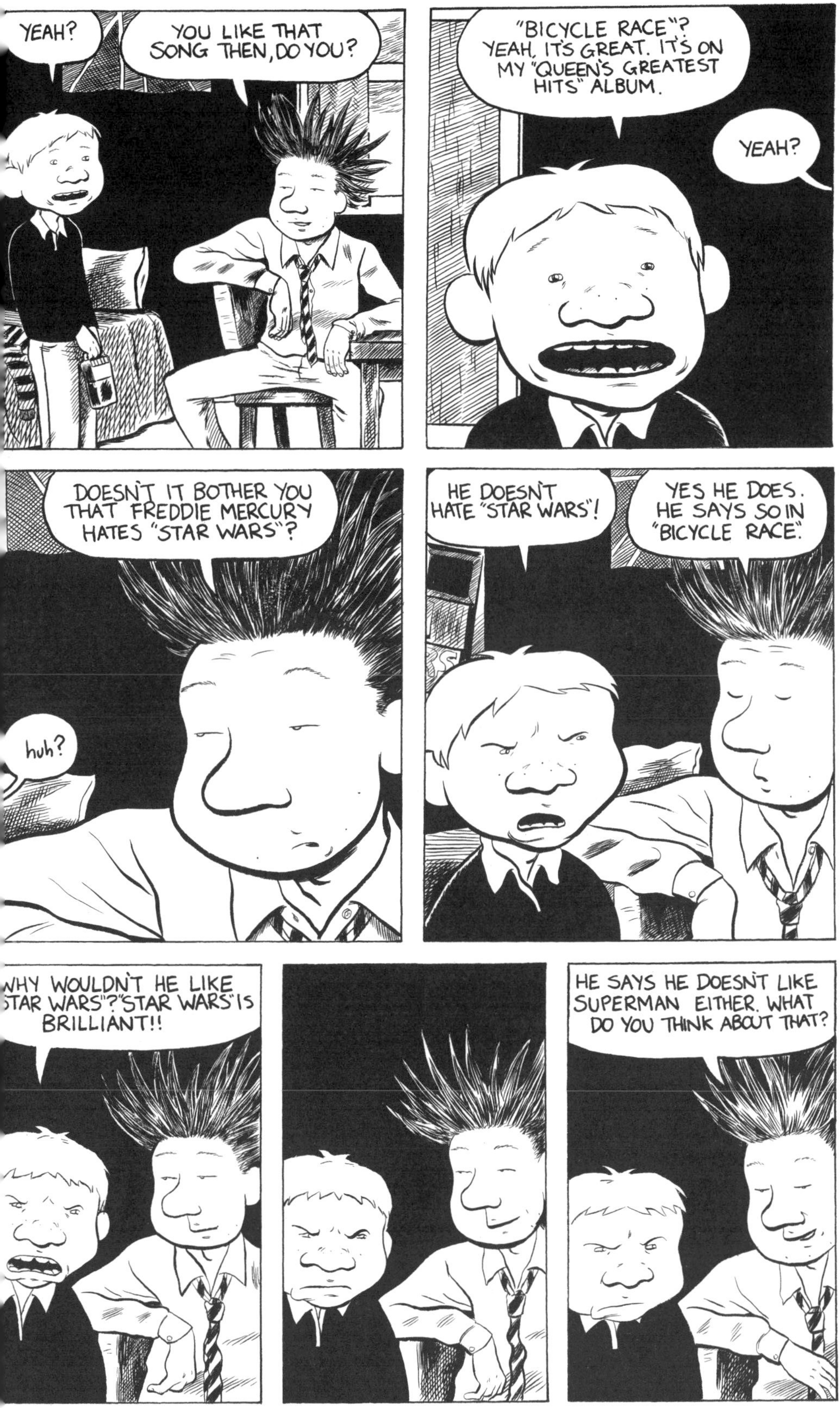
YEAH?
YOU LIKE THAT SONG THEN, DO YOU?
"BICYCLE RACE"? YEAH, IT'S GREAT. IT'S ON MY "QUEEN'S GREATEST HITS" ALBUM.
YEAH?
DOESN'T IT BOTHER YOU THAT FREDDIE MERCURY HATES "STAR WARS"?
huh?
HE DOESN'T HATE "STAR WARS"!
YES HE DOES. HE SAYS SO IN "BICYCLE RACE".
WHY WOULDN'T HE LIKE "STAR WARS"? "STAR WARS" IS BRILLIANT!!
HE SAYS HE DOESN'T LIKE SUPERMAN EITHER. WHAT DO YOU THINK ABOUT THAT?

I DON'T CARE — I THINK HE'S GREAT.

DOESN'T HE HAVE ANOTHER SONG ABOUT HATING "RETURN OF THE JEDI" TOO?

NO!

I THINK HE DOES...

YOU'D BETTER LISTEN CLOSELY...

HE DOES NOT!!

SO, ARE YOU EXCITED ABOUT MOVING TO AMERICA THEN?

TOO-NIIG I'M GO HAV

I DON'T THINK WE'RE GOING.

WE'RE NOT?

THE WORLD I'LL TURN INSIDE

NOPE, I DON'T THINK DAD WANTS TO TAKE THAT JOB ANY MORE.

WHY NOT?

I WAS ALL EXCITED...

TASY SO DON'T STOP ME NOOWWW

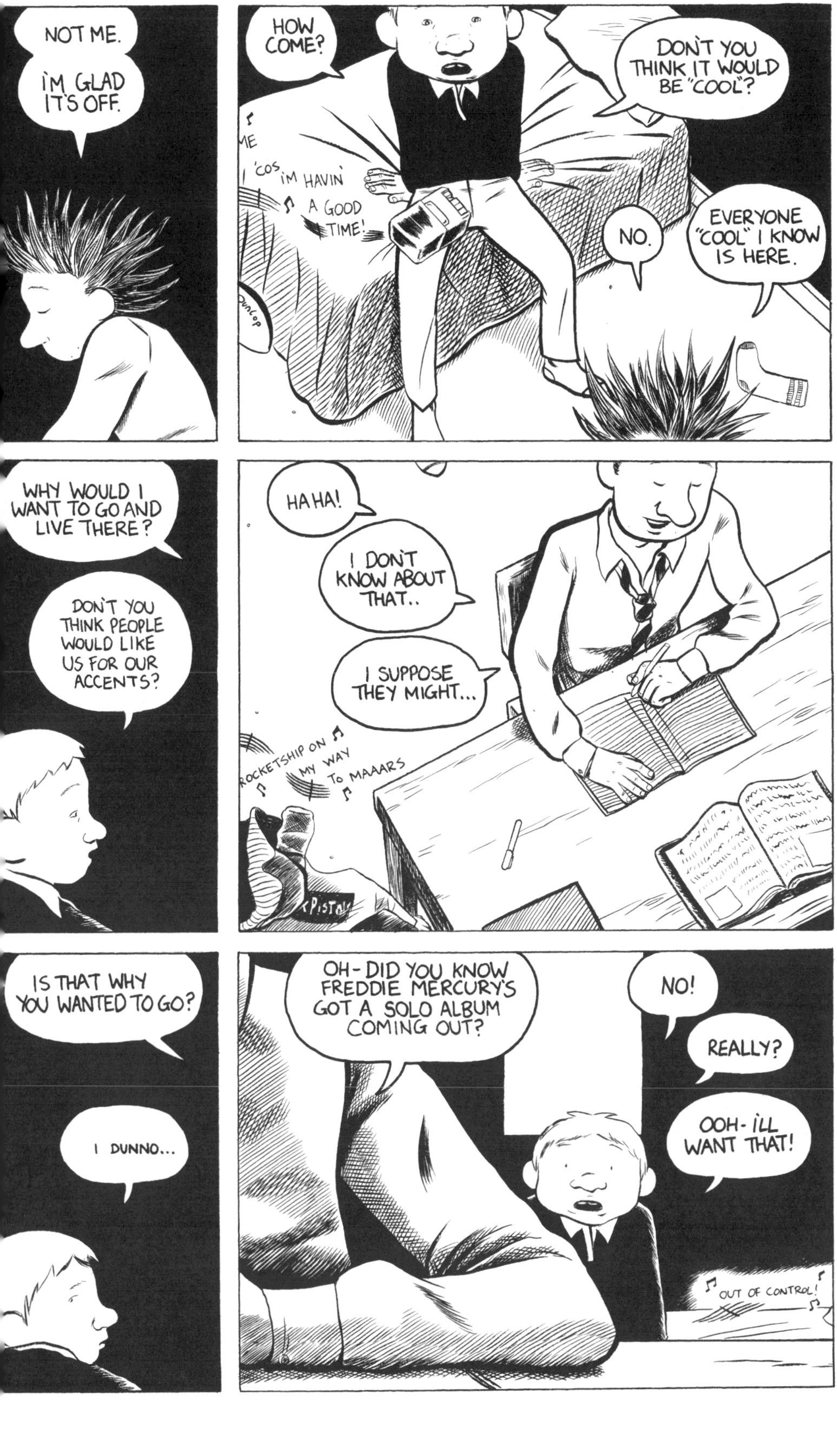
NOT ME.
I'M GLAD IT'S OFF.
HOW COME?
DON'T YOU THINK IT WOULD BE "COOL"?
'COS I'M HAVIN' A GOOD TIME!
NO.
EVERYONE "COOL" I KNOW IS HERE.
WHY WOULD I WANT TO GO AND LIVE THERE?
DON'T YOU THINK PEOPLE WOULD LIKE US FOR OUR ACCENTS?
HA HA!
I DON'T KNOW ABOUT THAT..
I SUPPOSE THEY MIGHT...
ROCKETSHIP ON MY WAY TO MAAARS
IS THAT WHY YOU WANTED TO GO?
I DUNNO...
OH - DID YOU KNOW FREDDIE MERCURY'S GOT A SOLO ALBUM COMING OUT?
NO!
REALLY?
OOH - I'LL WANT THAT!
OUT OF CONTROL!

MIKE DAWSON IMAGINES WHAT IT MIGHT HAVE BEEN LIKE TO WITNESS THE BREAKUP OF THE BRITISH POP PHENOMENON WHAM!

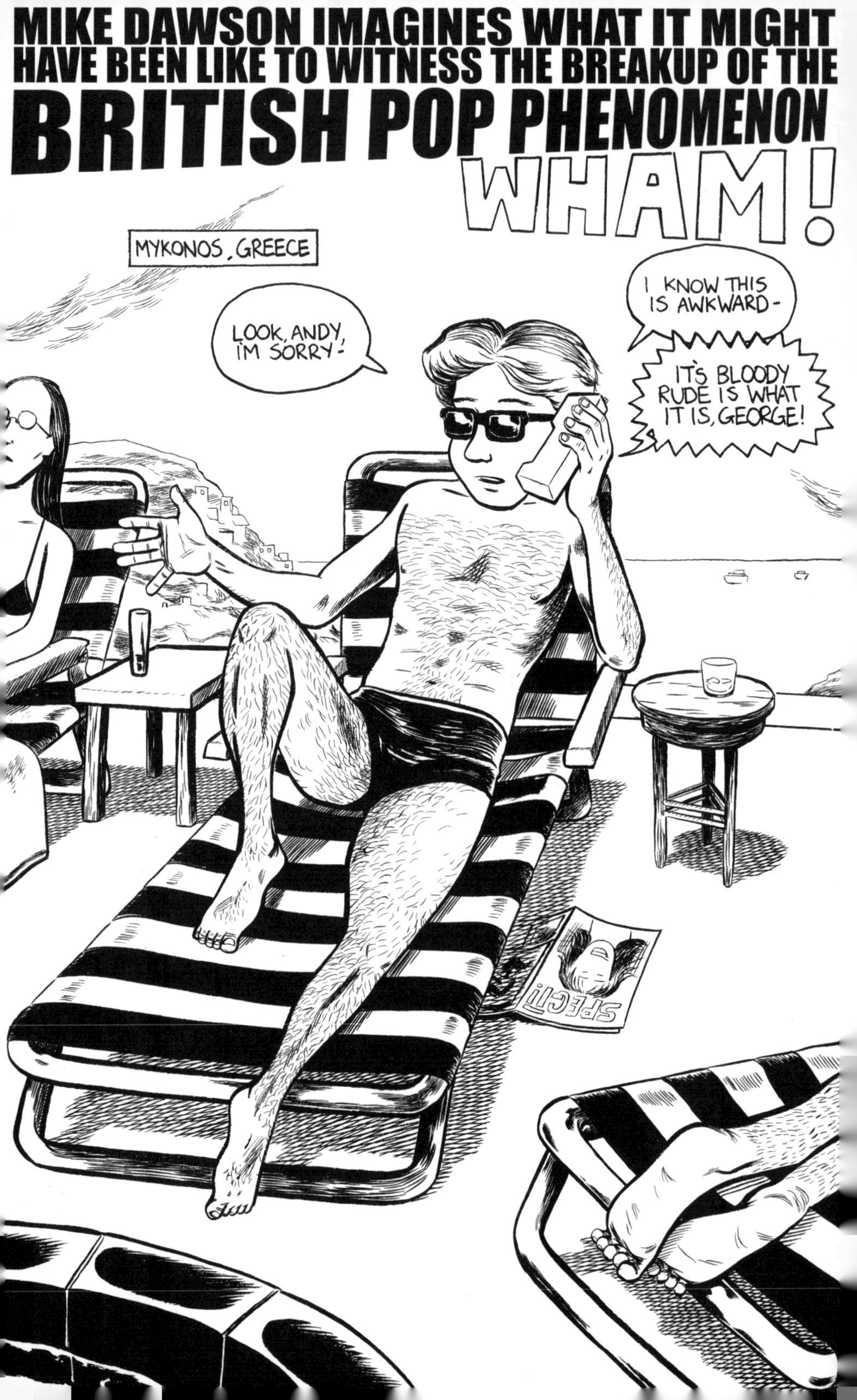
MYKONOS, GREECE
LOOK, ANDY, I'M SORRY!
I KNOW THIS IS AWKWARD-
IT'S BLOODY RUDE IS WHAT IT IS, GEORGE!

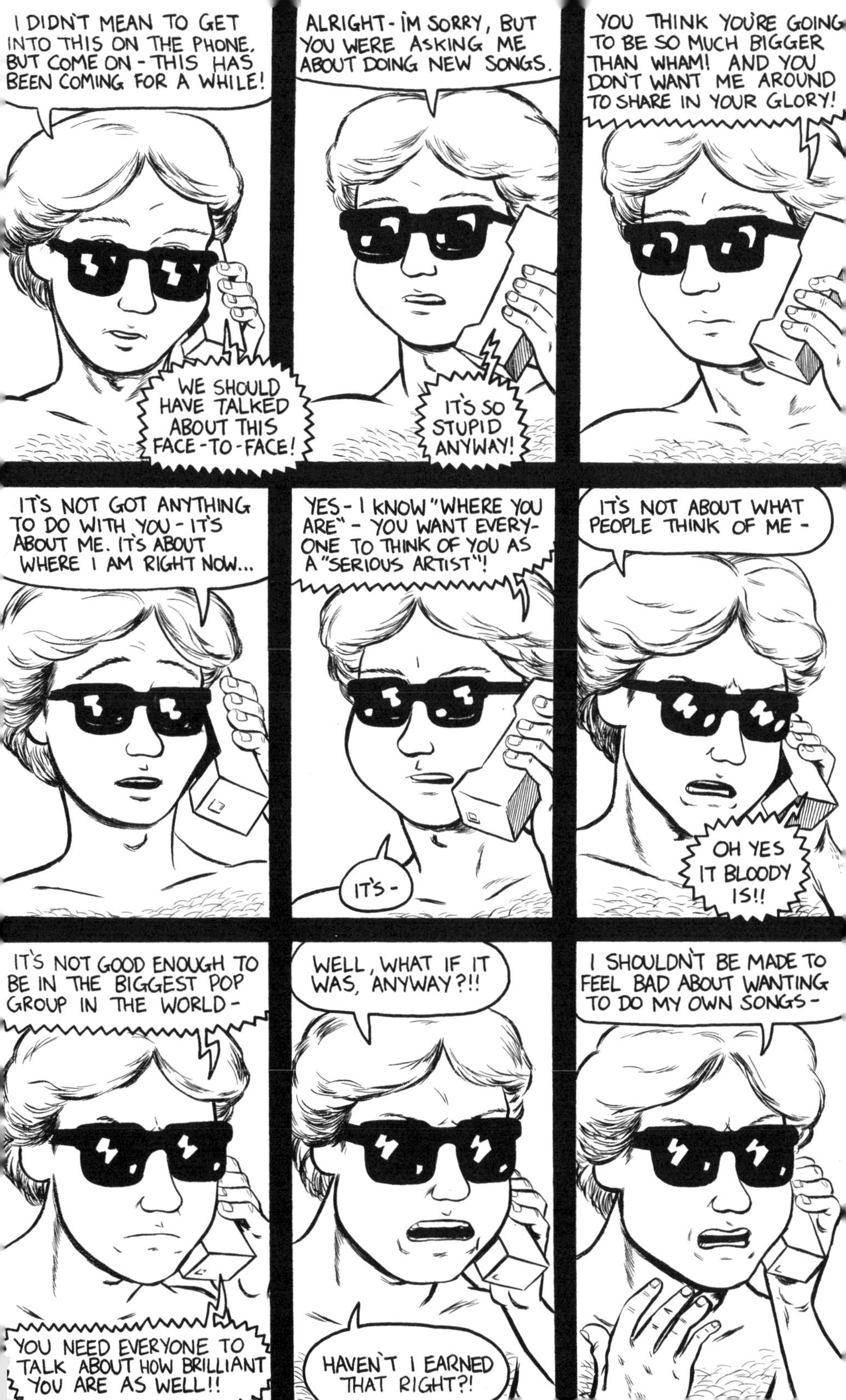
I DIDN'T MEAN TO GET INTO THIS ON THE PHONE, BUT COME ON - THIS HAS BEEN COMING FOR A WHILE!
WE SHOULD HAVE TALKED ABOUT THIS FACE-TO-FACE!
ALRIGHT - I'M SORRY, BUT YOU WERE ASKING ME ABOUT DOING NEW SONGS.
IT'S SO STUPID ANYWAY!
YOU THINK YOU'RE GOING TO BE SO MUCH BIGGER THAN WHAM! AND YOU DON'T WANT ME AROUND TO SHARE IN YOUR GLORY!
IT'S NOT GOT ANYTHING TO DO WITH YOU - IT'S ABOUT ME. IT'S ABOUT WHERE I AM RIGHT NOW...
YES - I KNOW "WHERE YOU ARE" - YOU WANT EVERY-ONE TO THINK OF YOU AS A "SERIOUS ARTIST"!
IT'S -
IT'S NOT ABOUT WHAT PEOPLE THINK OF ME -
OH YES IT BLOODY IS!!
IT'S NOT GOOD ENOUGH TO BE IN THE BIGGEST POP GROUP IN THE WORLD -
YOU NEED EVERYONE TO TALK ABOUT HOW BRILLIANT YOU ARE AS WELL!!
WELL, WHAT IF IT WAS, ANYWAY?!!
HAVEN'T I EARNED THAT RIGHT?!
I SHOULDN'T BE MADE TO FEEL BAD ABOUT WANTING TO DO MY OWN SONGS -

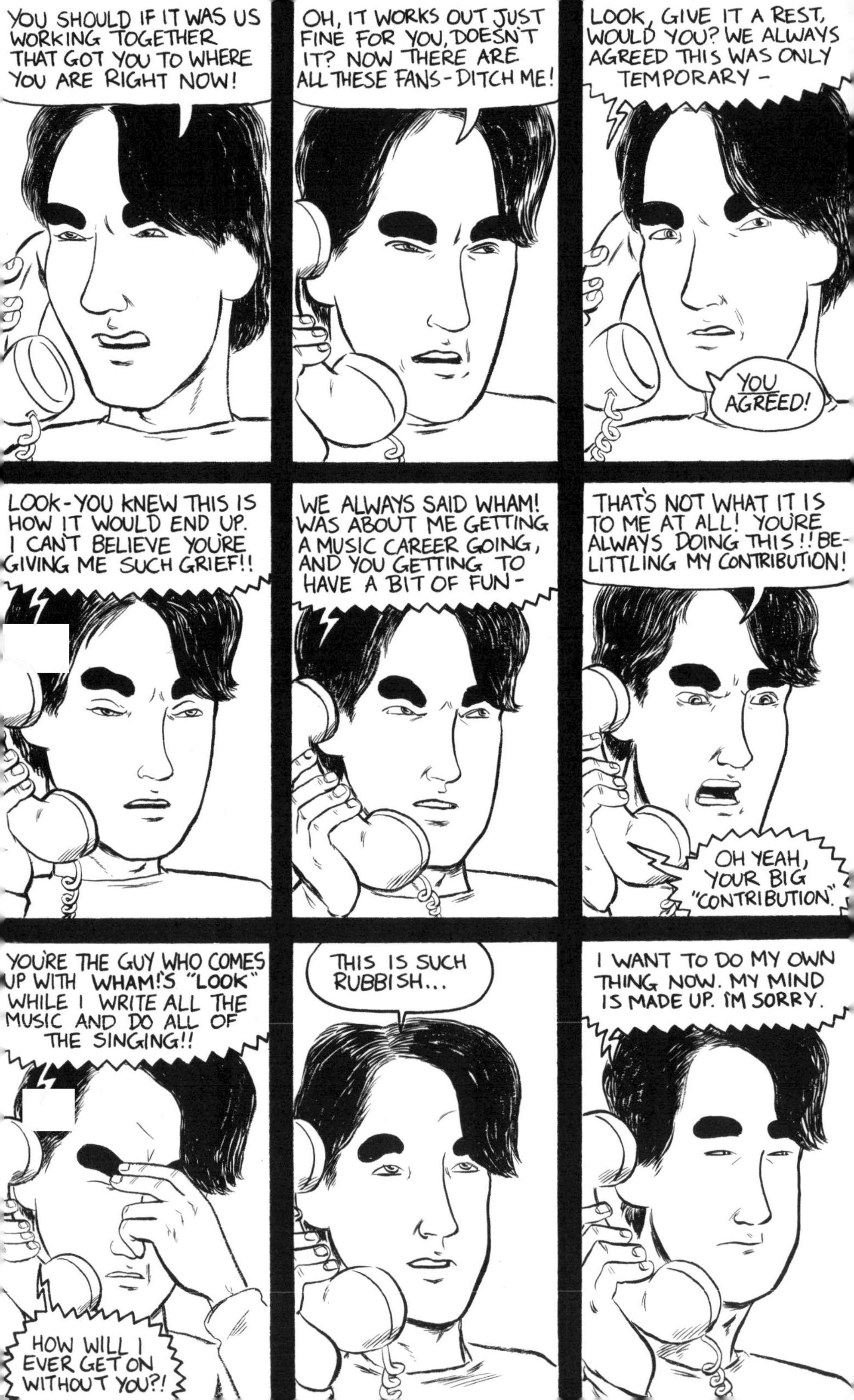
YOU SHOULD IF IT WAS US WORKING TOGETHER THAT GOT YOU TO WHERE YOU ARE RIGHT NOW!
OH, IT WORKS OUT JUST FINE FOR YOU, DOESN'T IT? NOW THERE ARE ALL THESE FANS - DITCH ME!
LOOK, GIVE IT A REST, WOULD YOU? WE ALWAYS AGREED THIS WAS ONLY TEMPORARY -
YOU AGREED!
LOOK - YOU KNEW THIS IS HOW IT WOULD END UP. I CAN'T BELIEVE YOU'RE GIVING ME SUCH GRIEF!!
WE ALWAYS SAID WHAM! WAS ABOUT ME GETTING A MUSIC CAREER GOING, AND YOU GETTING TO HAVE A BIT OF FUN -
THAT'S NOT WHAT IT IS TO ME AT ALL! YOU'RE ALWAYS DOING THIS!! BE-LITTLING MY CONTRIBUTION!
OH YEAH, YOUR BIG "CONTRIBUTION."
YOU'RE THE GUY WHO COMES UP WITH WHAM!'S "LOOK" WHILE I WRITE ALL THE MUSIC AND DO ALL OF THE SINGING!!
HOW WILL I EVER GET ON WITHOUT YOU?!
THIS IS SUCH RUBBISH...
I WANT TO DO MY OWN THING NOW. MY MIND IS MADE UP. I'M SORRY.

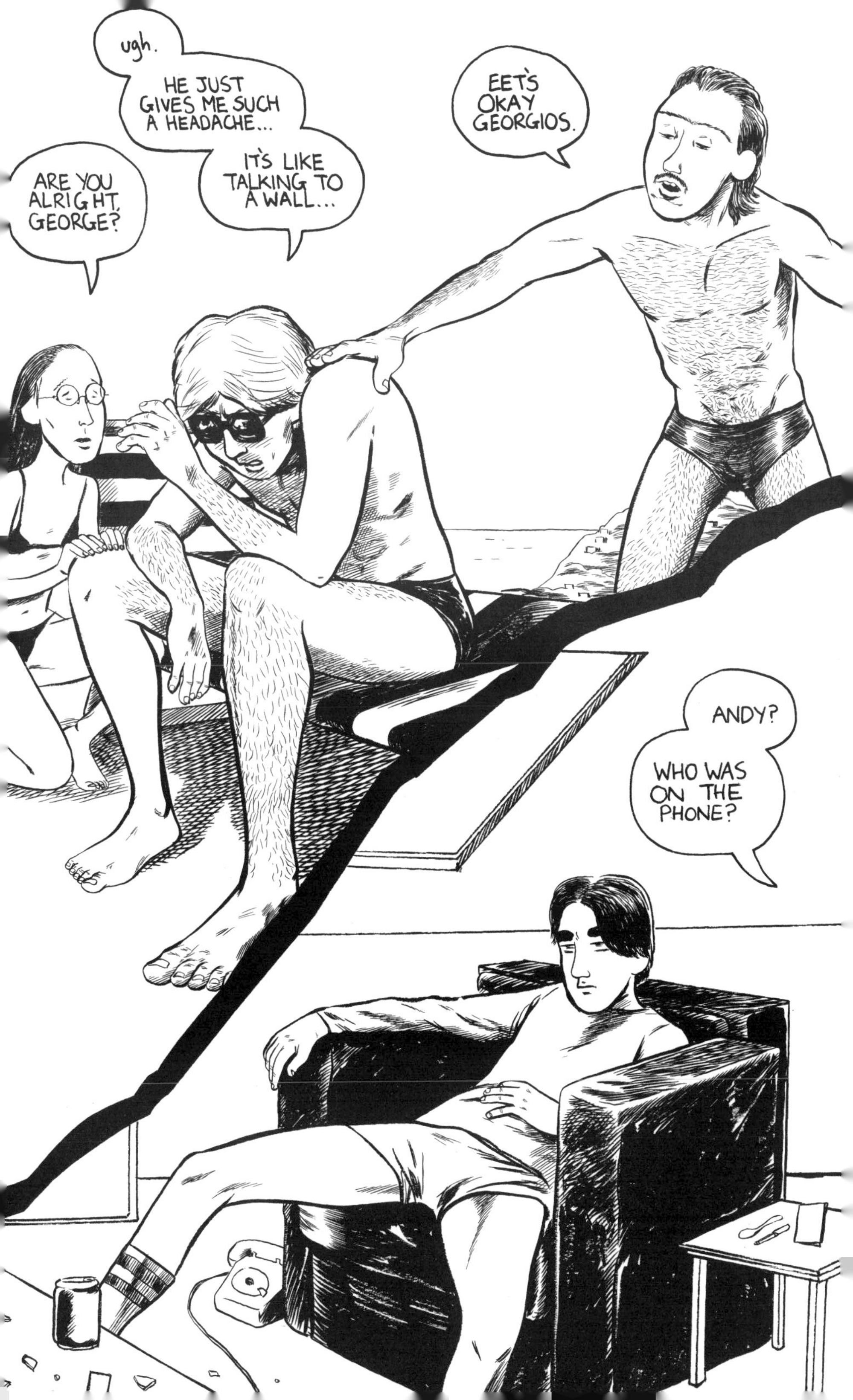
ARE YOU ALRIGHT, GEORGE?
ugh.
HE JUST GIVES ME SUCH A HEADACHE...
IT'S LIKE TALKING TO A WALL...
EET'S OKAY GEORGIOS.
ANDY?
WHO WAS ON THE PHONE?

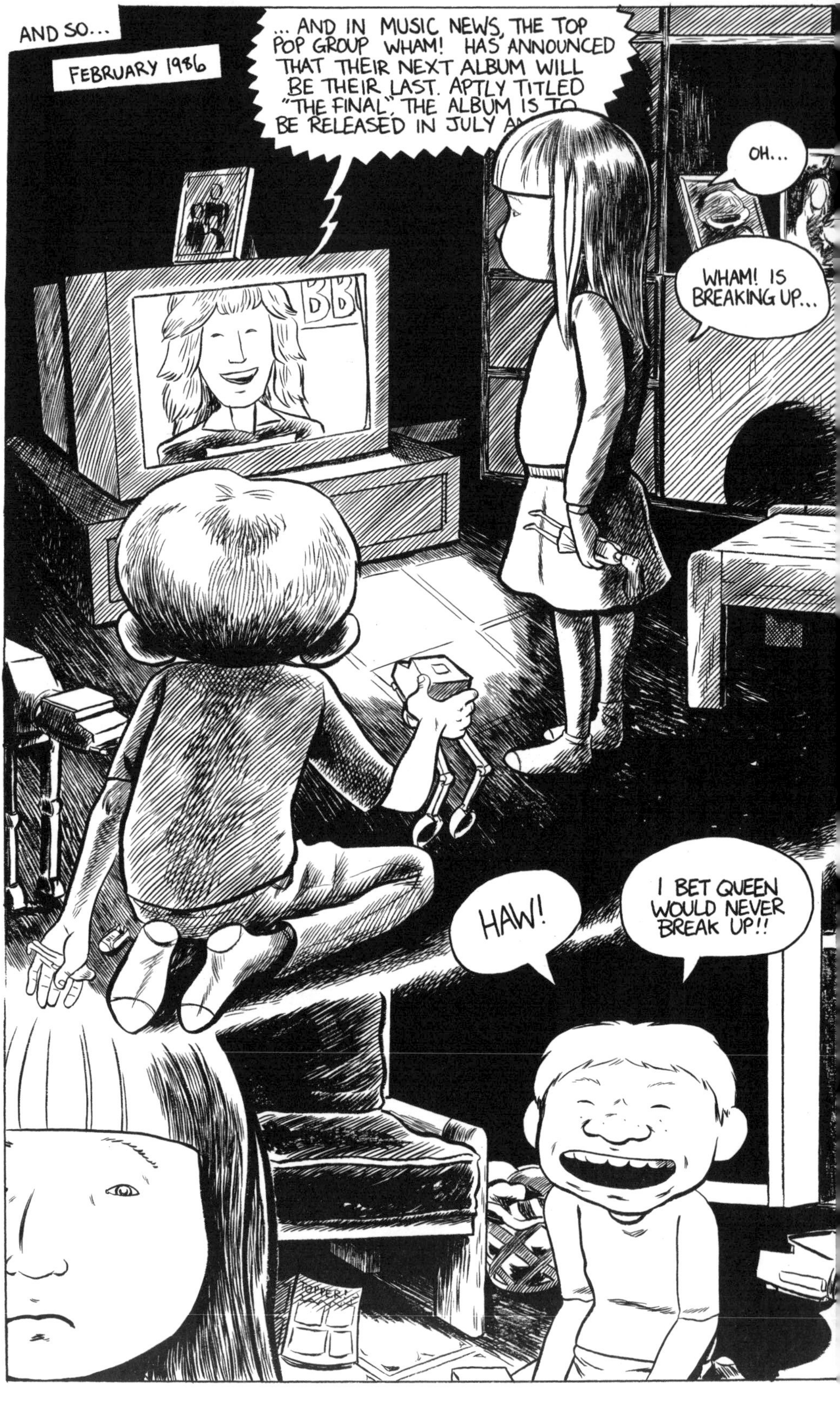
AND SO...
FEBRUARY 1986
... AND IN MUSIC NEWS, THE TOP POP GROUP WHAM! HAS ANNOUNCED THAT THEIR NEXT ALBUM WILL BE THEIR LAST. APTLY TITLED "THE FINAL", THE ALBUM IS TO BE RELEASED IN JULY AN
OH...
WHAM! IS BREAKING UP...
HAW!
I BET QUEEN WOULD NEVER BREAK UP!!

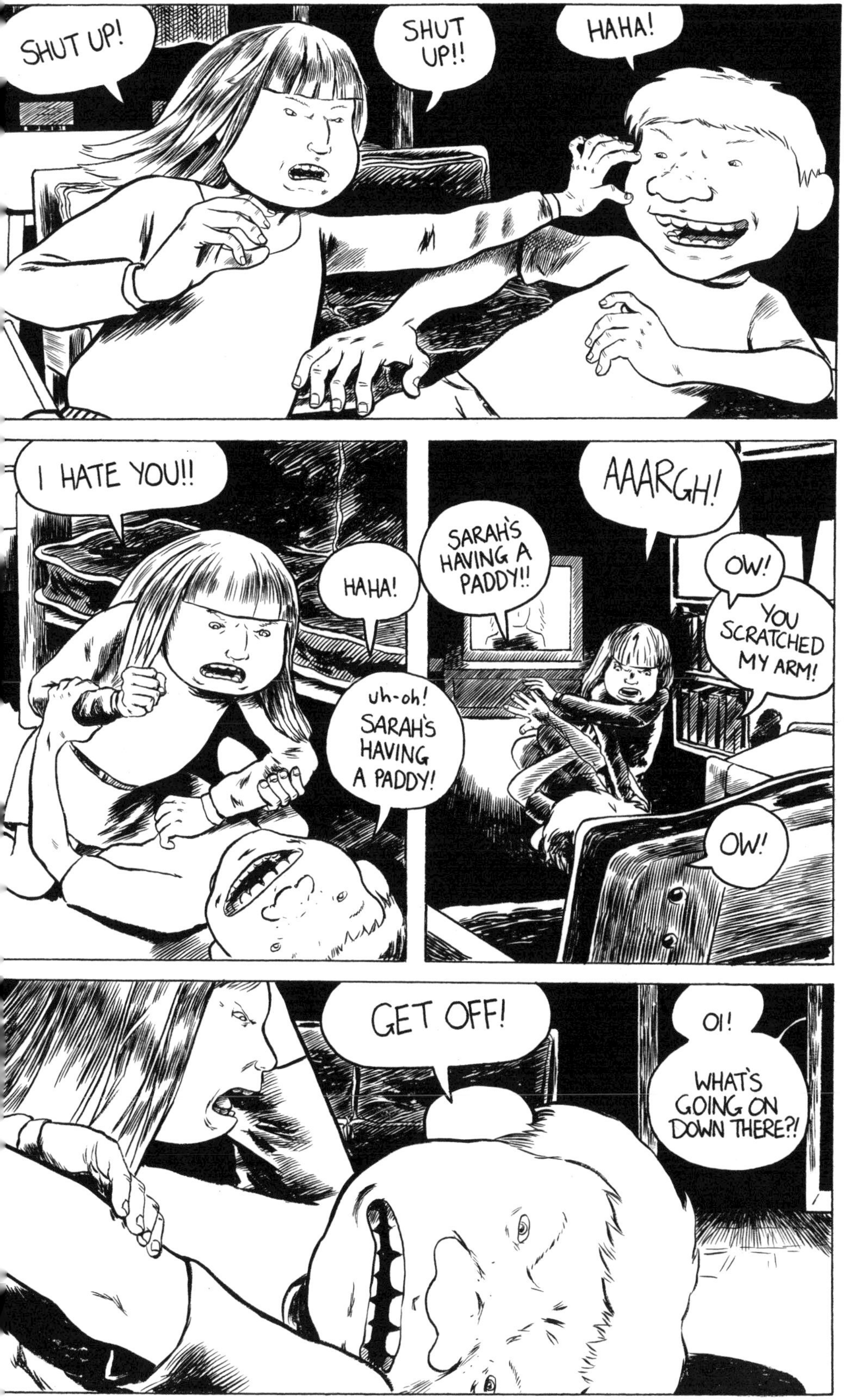
SHUT UP!
SHUT UP!!
HAHA!
I HATE YOU!!
HAHA!
uh-oh! SARAH'S HAVING A PADDY!
AAARGH!
SARAH'S HAVING A PADDY!!
OW!
YOU SCRATCHED MY ARM!
OW!
GET OFF!
OI!
WHAT'S GOING ON DOWN THERE?!

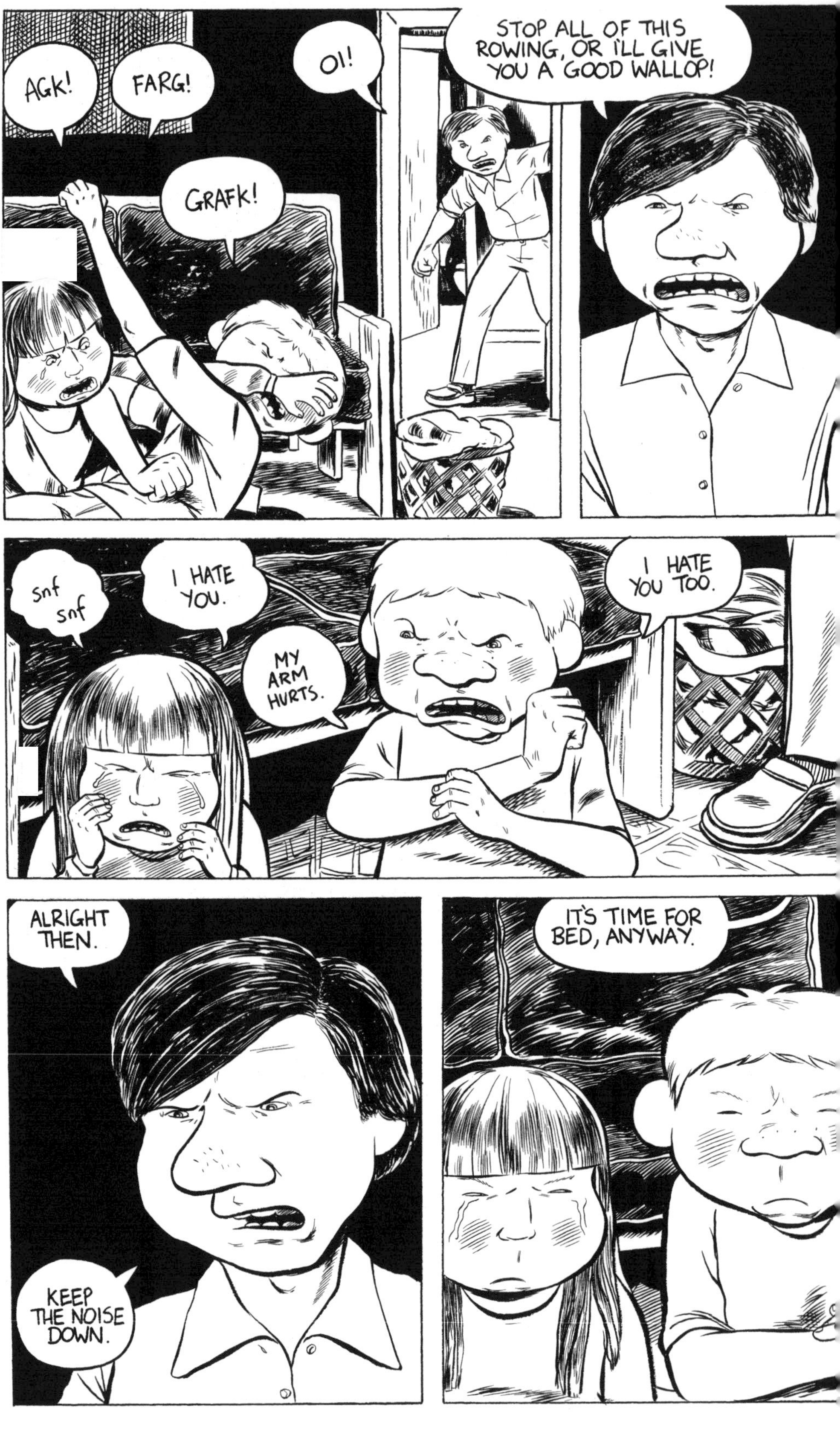
AGK!
FARG!
GRAFK!
OI!
STOP ALL OF THIS ROWING, OR I'LL GIVE YOU A GOOD WALLOP!
snf snf
I HATE YOU.
MY ARM HURTS.
I HATE YOU TOO.
ALRIGHT THEN.
KEEP THE NOISE DOWN.
IT'S TIME FOR BED, ANYWAY.

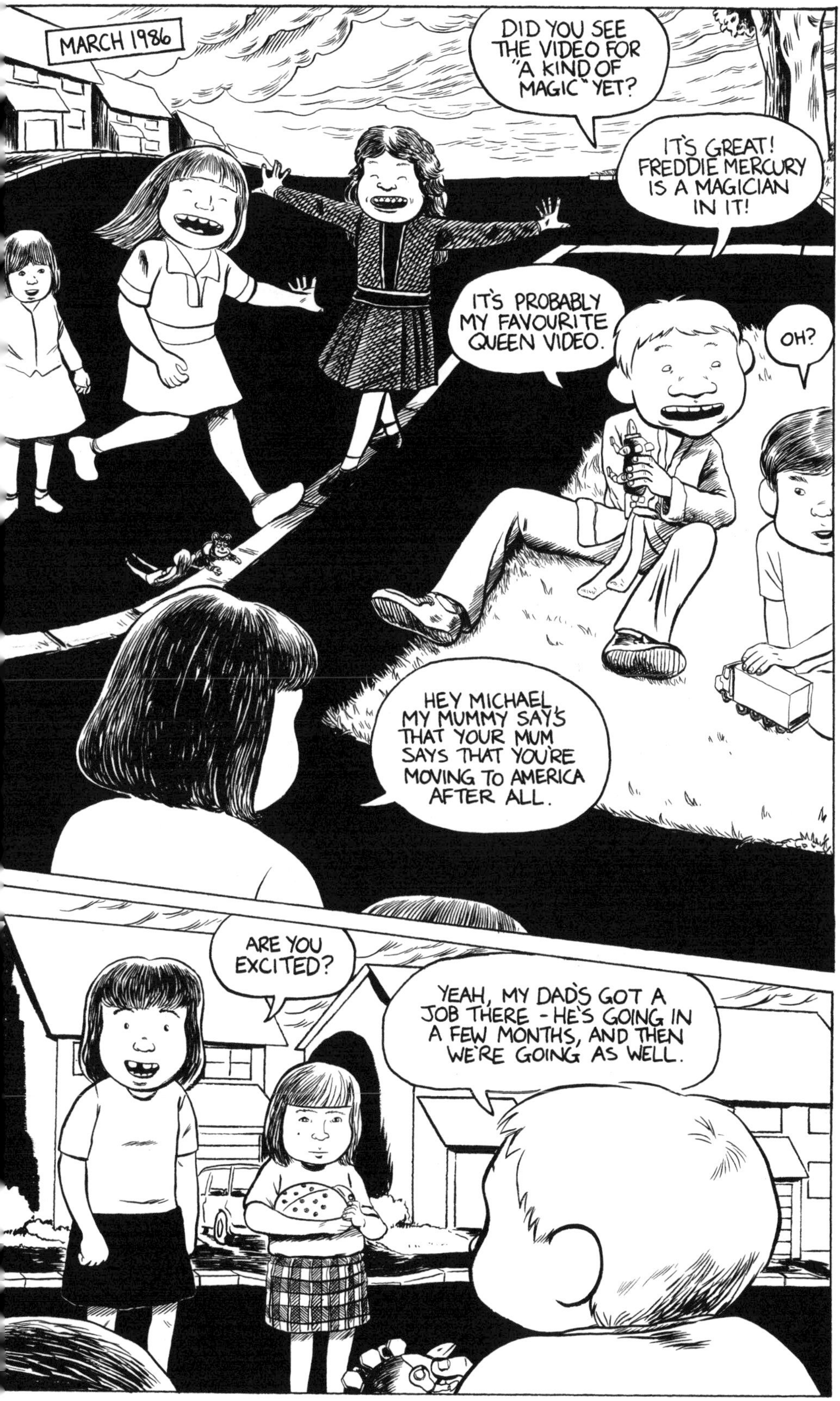

MARCH 1986
DID YOU SEE THE VIDEO FOR "A KIND OF MAGIC" YET?
IT'S GREAT! FREDDIE MERCURY IS A MAGICIAN IN IT!
IT'S PROBABLY MY FAVOURITE QUEEN VIDEO.
OH?
HEY MICHAEL, MY MUMMY SAYS THAT YOUR MUM SAYS THAT YOU'RE MOVING TO AMERICA AFTER ALL.
ARE YOU EXCITED?
YEAH, MY DAD'S GOT A JOB THERE - HE'S GOING IN A FEW MONTHS, AND THEN WE'RE GOING AS WELL.

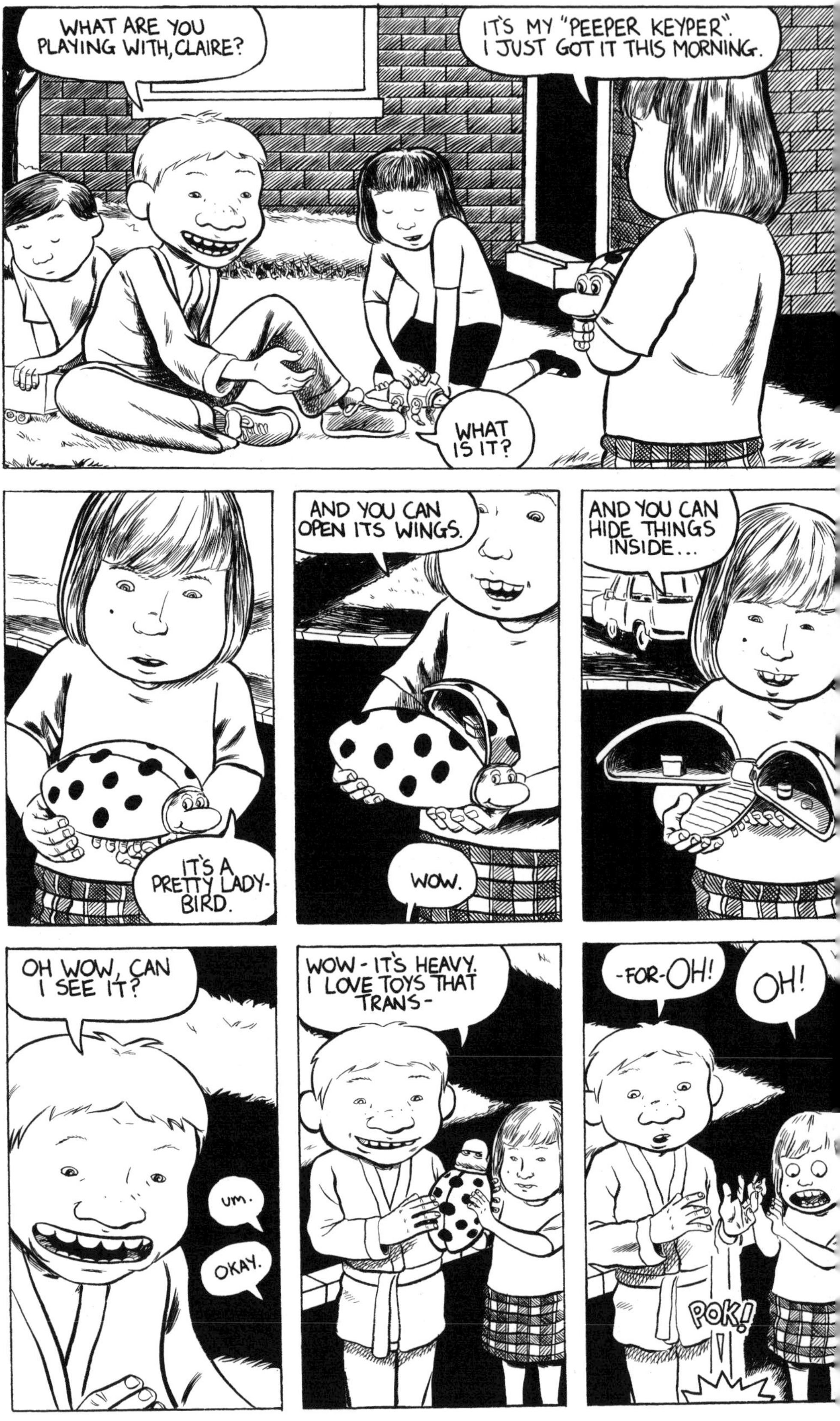
WHAT ARE YOU PLAYING WITH, CLAIRE?
IT'S MY "PEEPER KEYPER". I JUST GOT IT THIS MORNING.
WHAT IS IT?
IT'S A PRETTY LADY-BIRD.
AND YOU CAN OPEN ITS WINGS.
WOW.
AND YOU CAN HIDE THINGS INSIDE...
OH WOW, CAN I SEE IT?
um.
OKAY.
WOW - IT'S HEAVY. I LOVE TOYS THAT TRANS-
-FOR-OH!
OH!
POK!

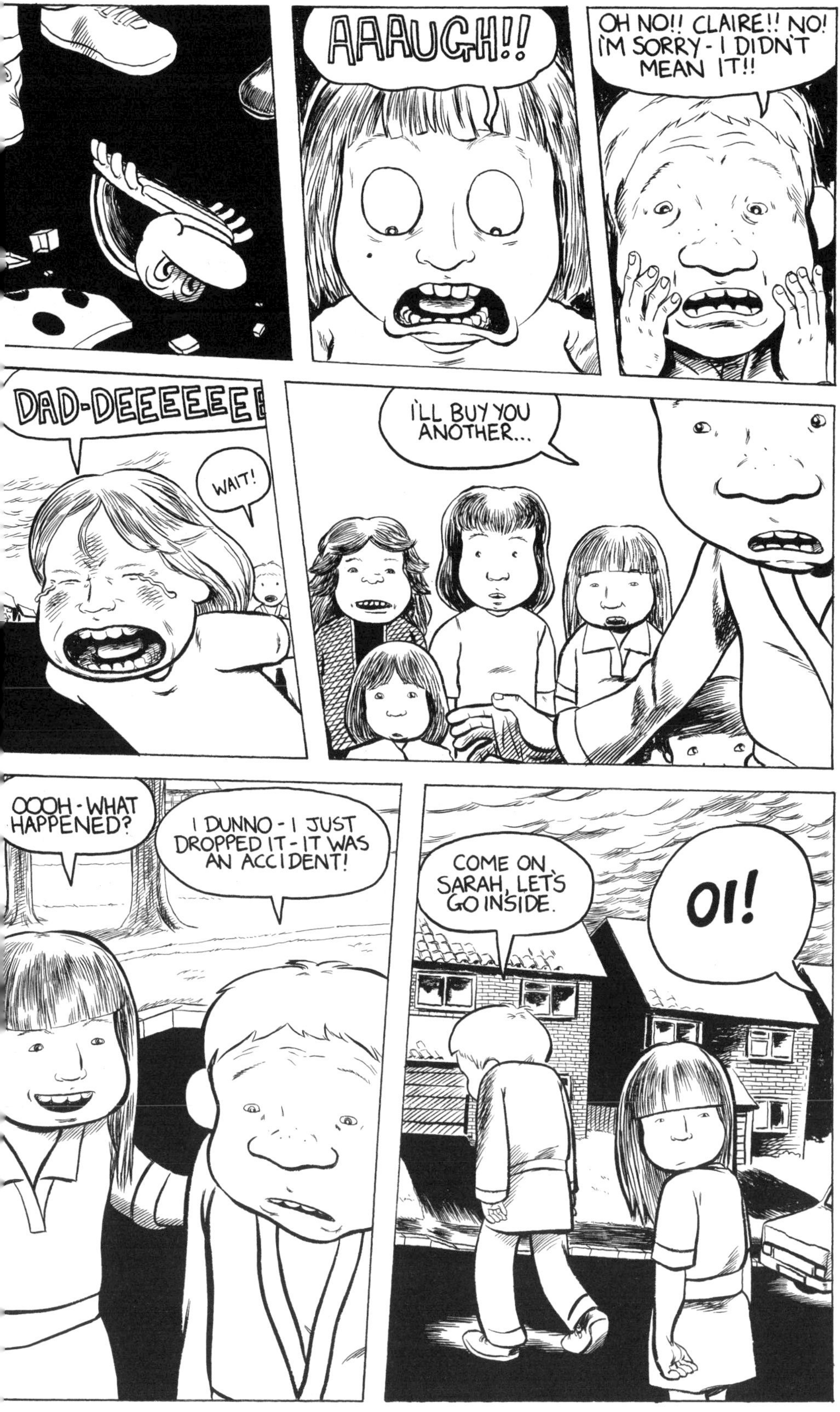
AAAUGH!!
OH NO!! CLAIRE!! NO! I'M SORRY - I DIDN'T MEAN IT!!
DAD-DEEEEEEEE
WAIT!
I'LL BUY YOU ANOTHER...
OOOH - WHAT HAPPENED?
I DUNNO - I JUST DROPPED IT - IT WAS AN ACCIDENT!
COME ON SARAH, LET'S GO INSIDE.
OI!

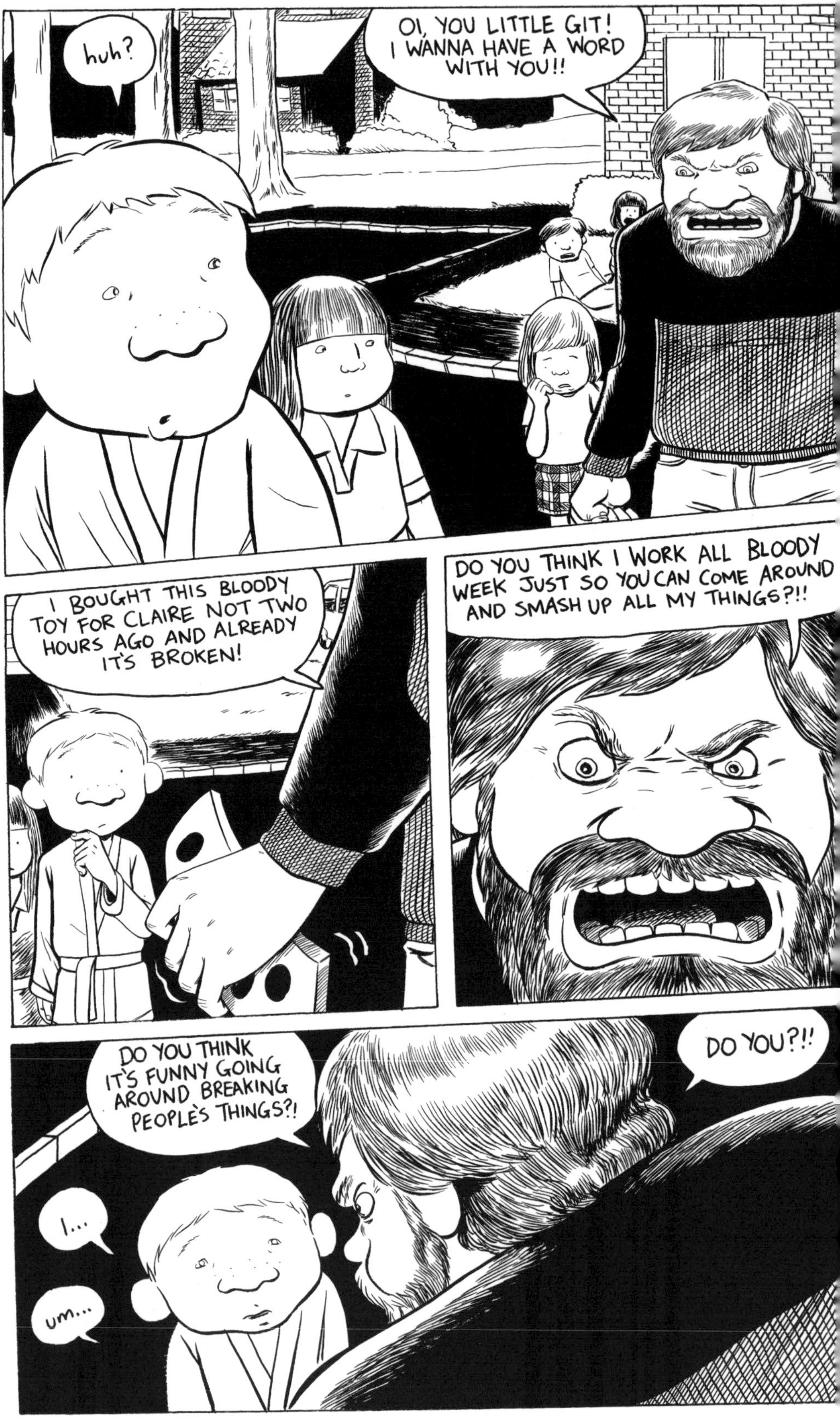
huh?
OI, YOU LITTLE GIT! I WANNA HAVE A WORD WITH YOU!!
I BOUGHT THIS BLOODY TOY FOR CLAIRE NOT TWO HOURS AGO AND ALREADY IT'S BROKEN!
DO YOU THINK I WORK ALL BLOODY WEEK JUST SO YOU CAN COME AROUND AND SMASH UP ALL MY THINGS?!!
DO YOU THINK IT'S FUNNY GOING AROUND BREAKING PEOPLE'S THINGS?!
DO YOU?!!
I...
um...

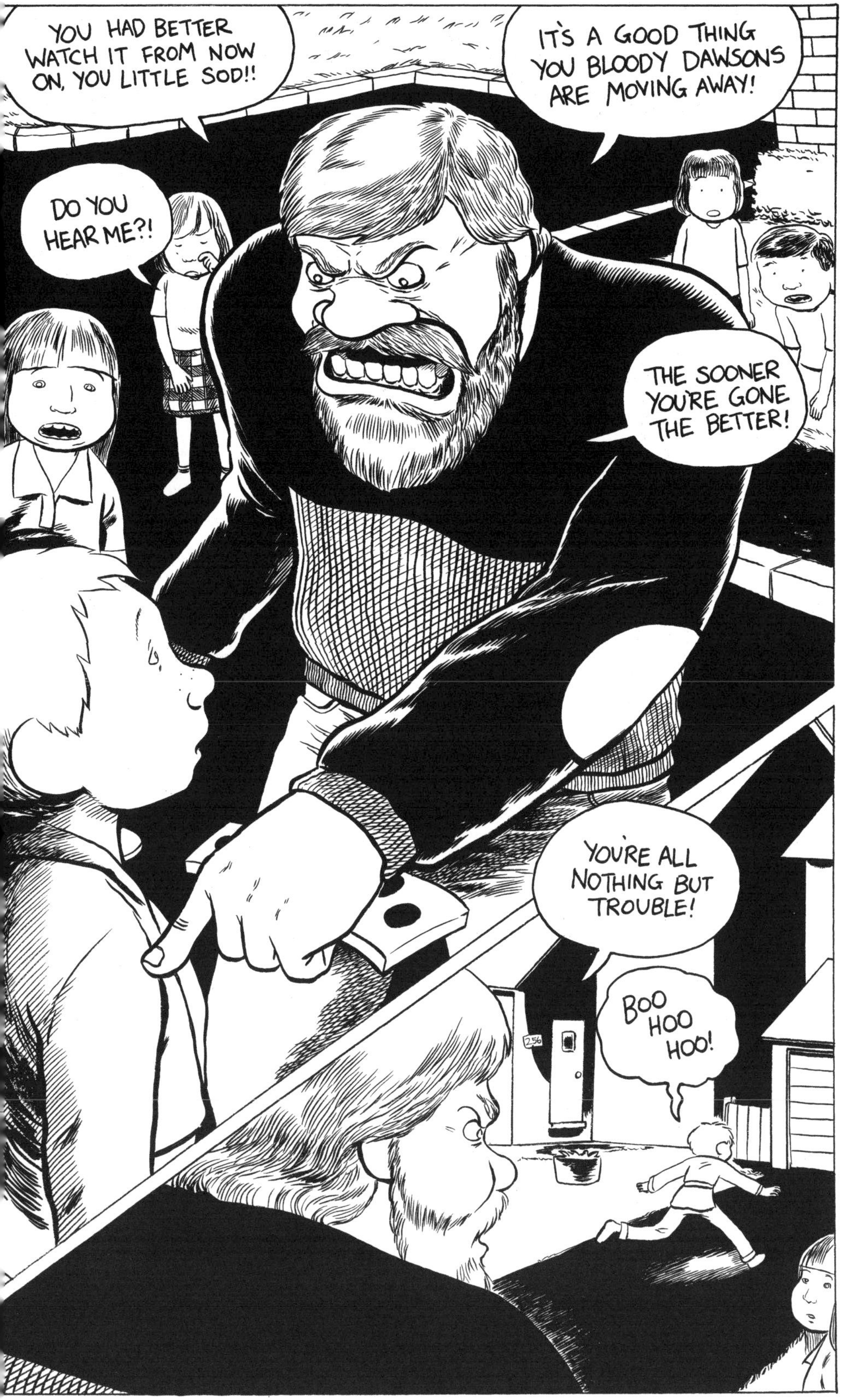
YOU HAD BETTER WATCH IT FROM NOW ON, YOU LITTLE SOD!!
IT'S A GOOD THING YOU BLOODY DAWSONS ARE MOVING AWAY!
DO YOU HEAR ME?!
THE SOONER YOU'RE GONE THE BETTER!
YOU'RE ALL NOTHING BUT TROUBLE!
BOO HOO HOO!
256

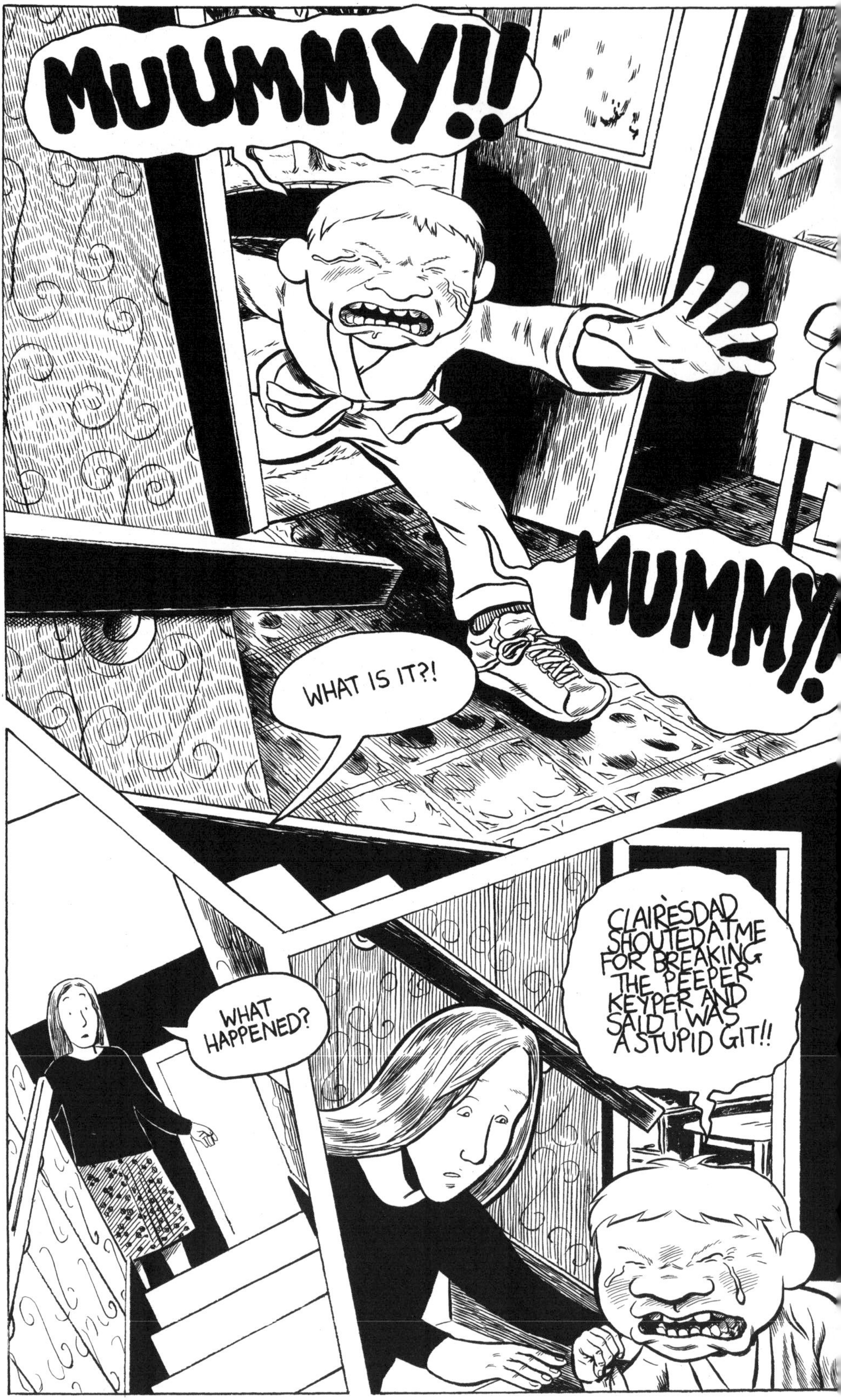
MUUMMY!!
MUMMY!!
WHAT IS IT?!
WHAT HAPPENED?
CLAIRE'SDAD SHOUTEDATME FOR BREAKING THE PEEPER KEYPER AND SAID I WAS A STUPID GIT!!

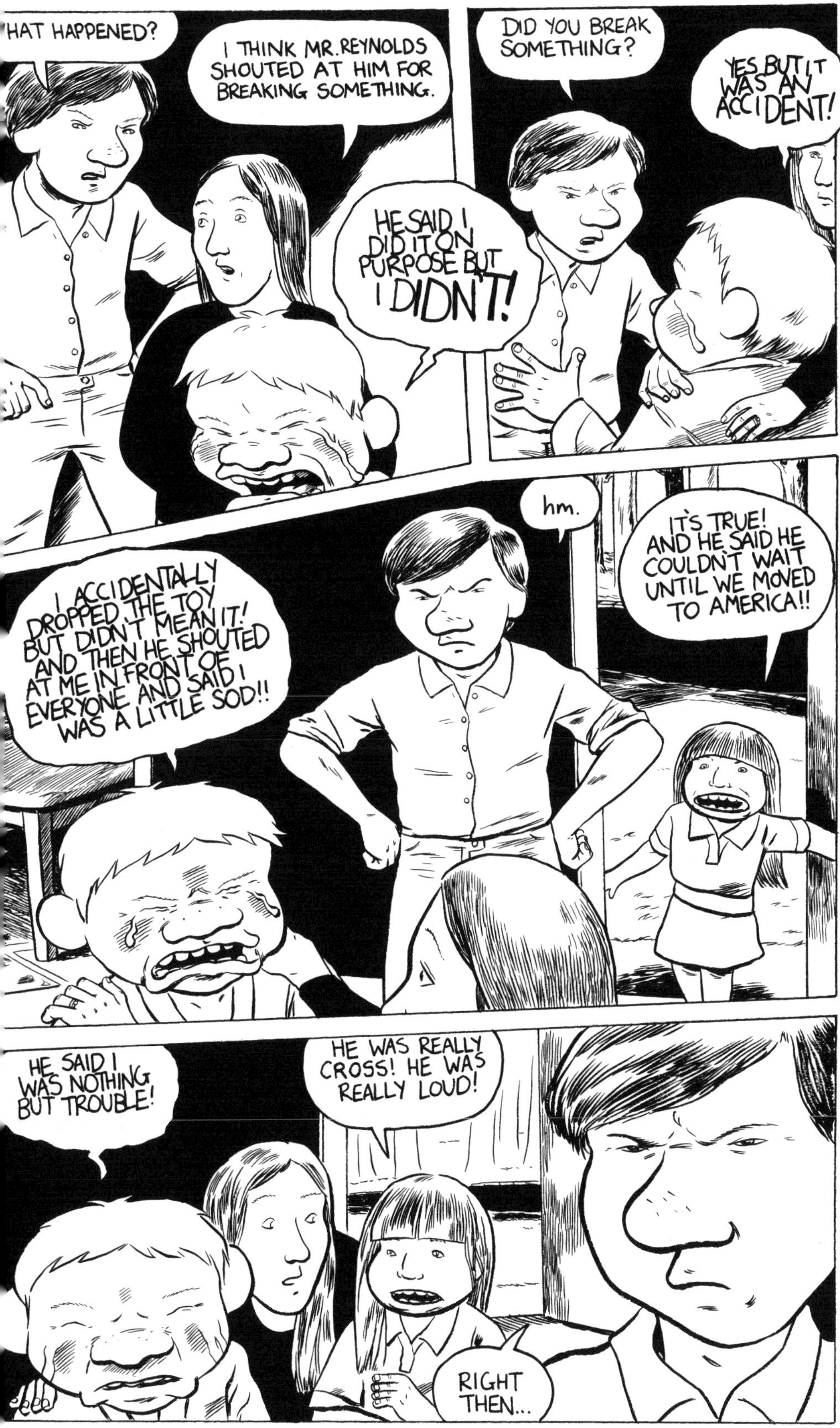
HAT HAPPENED?
I THINK MR. REYNOLDS SHOUTED AT HIM FOR BREAKING SOMETHING.
HE SAID I DID IT ON PURPOSE BUT I DIDN'T!
DID YOU BREAK SOMETHING?
YES BUT IT WAS AN ACCIDENT!
hm.
I ACCIDENTALLY DROPPED THE TOY BUT DIDN'T MEAN IT! AND THEN HE SHOUTED AT ME IN FRONT OF EVERYONE AND SAID I WAS A LITTLE SOD!!
IT'S TRUE! AND HE SAID HE COULDN'T WAIT UNTIL WE MOVED TO AMERICA!!
HE SAID I WAS NOTHING BUT TROUBLE!
HE WAS REALLY CROSS! HE WAS REALLY LOUD!
RIGHT THEN...

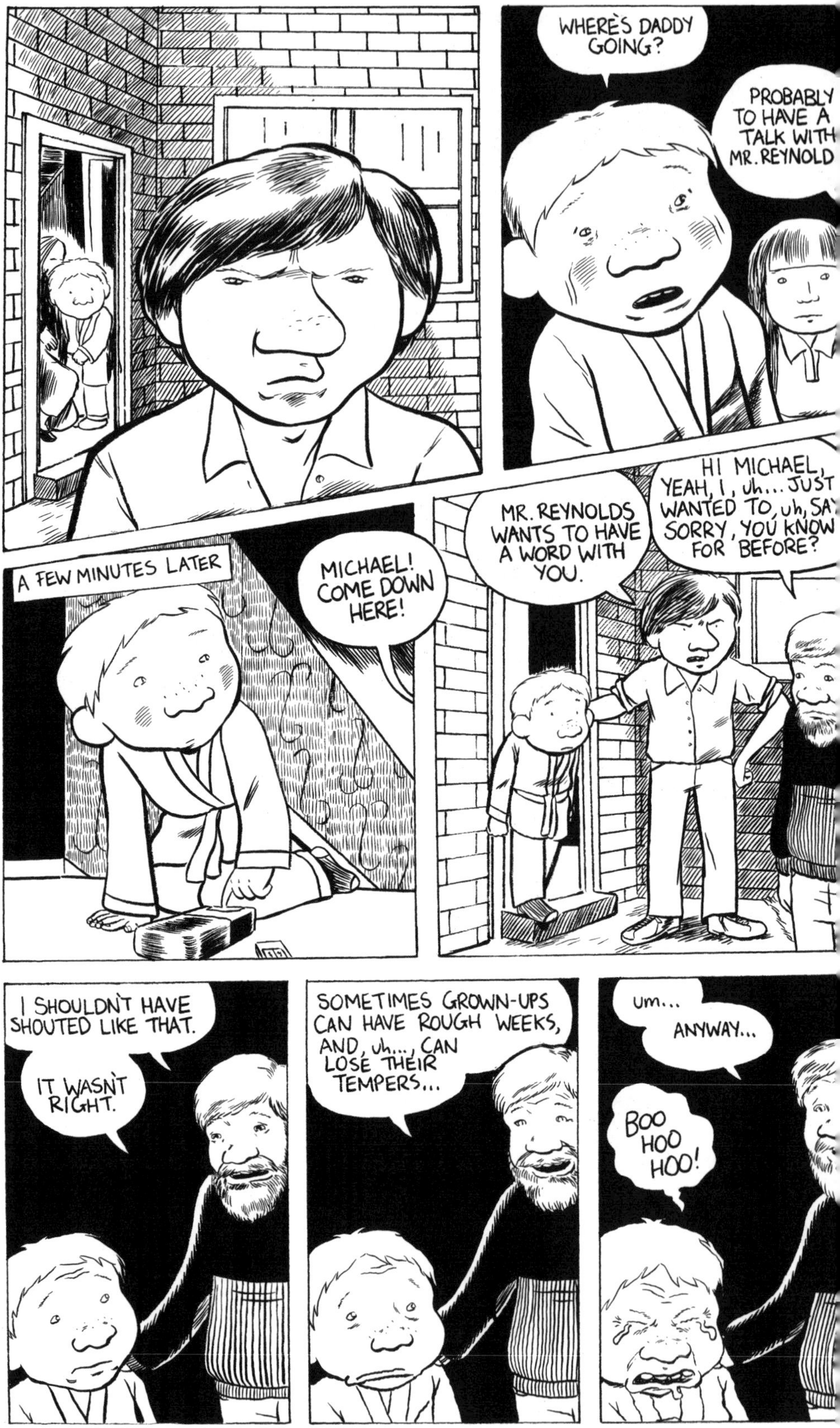
WHERE'S DADDY GOING?
PROBABLY TO HAVE A TALK WITH MR. REYNOLD
A FEW MINUTES LATER
MICHAEL! COME DOWN HERE!
MR. REYNOLDS WANTS TO HAVE A WORD WITH YOU.
HI MICHAEL, YEAH, I, uh... JUST WANTED TO, uh, SA SORRY, YOU KNOW FOR BEFORE?
I SHOULDN'T HAVE SHOUTED LIKE THAT.
IT WASN'T RIGHT.
SOMETIMES GROWN-UPS CAN HAVE ROUGH WEEKS, AND, uh..., CAN LOSE THEIR TEMPERS...
um...
ANYWAY...
BOO HOO HOO!

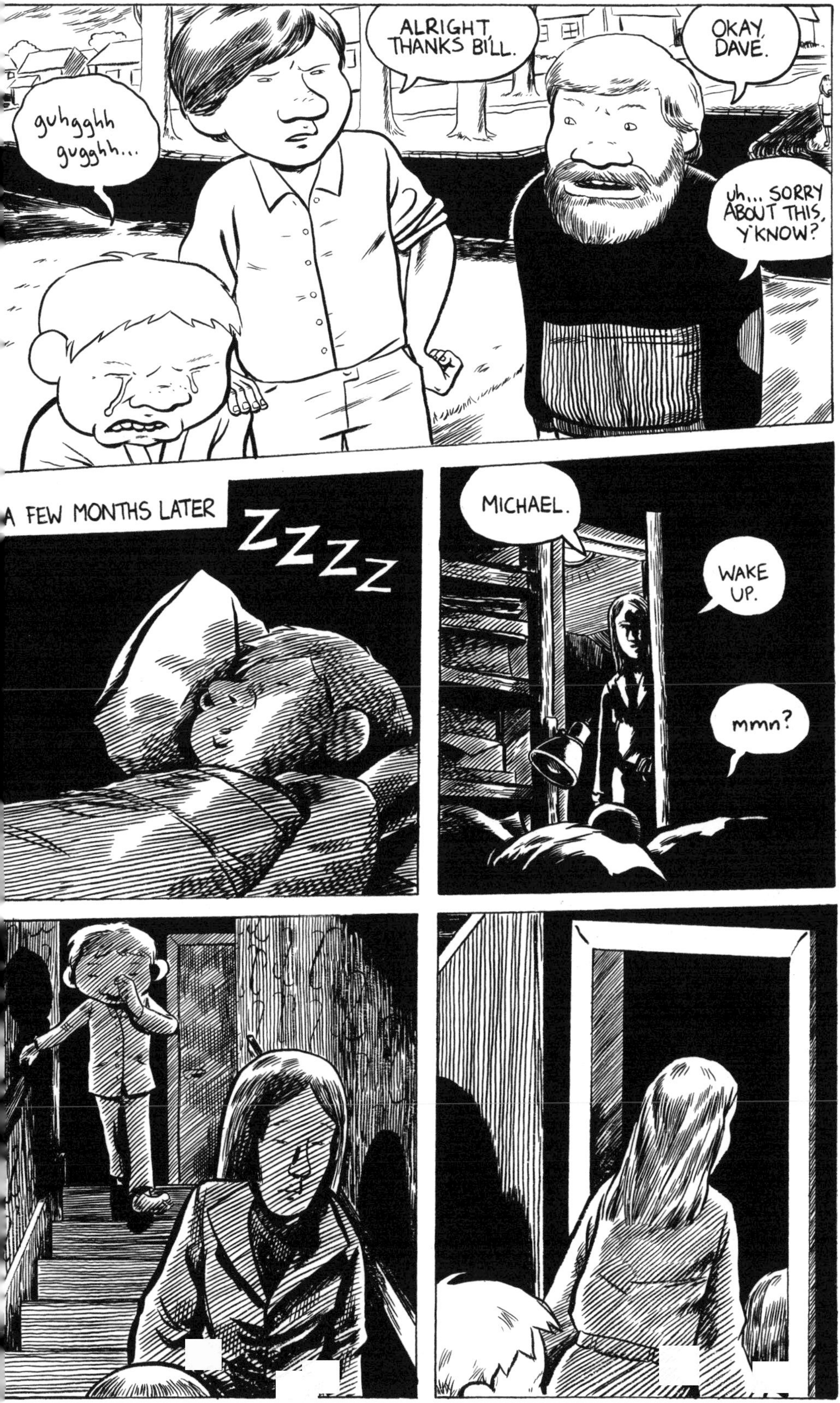
guhgghh gugghh...
ALRIGHT, THANKS BILL.
OKAY, DAVE.
uh... SORRY ABOUT THIS, Y'KNOW?
A FEW MONTHS LATER
ZZZZ
MICHAEL.
WAKE UP.
mmn?

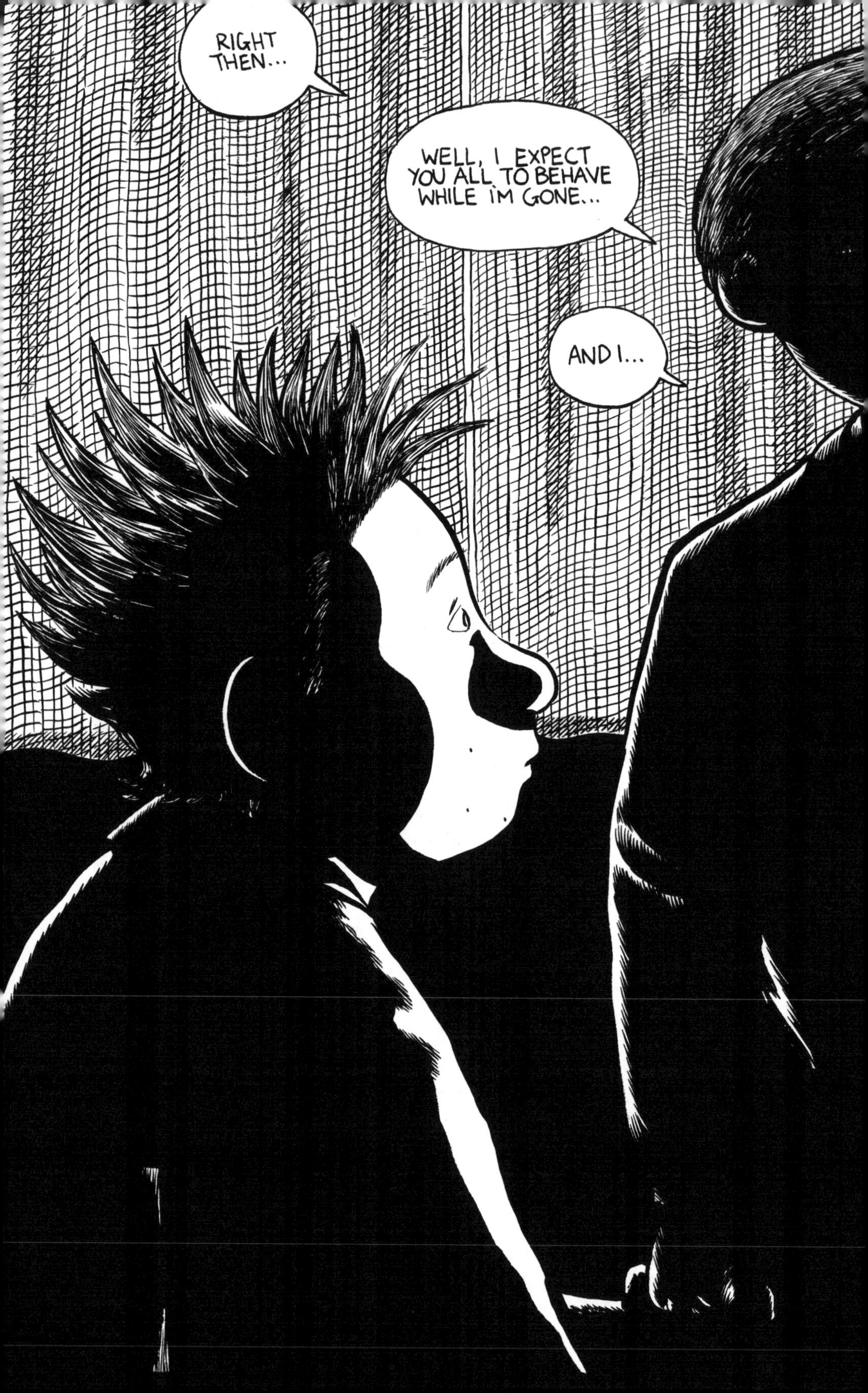
RIGHT THEN...
WELL, I EXPECT YOU ALL TO BEHAVE WHILE I'M GONE...
AND I...

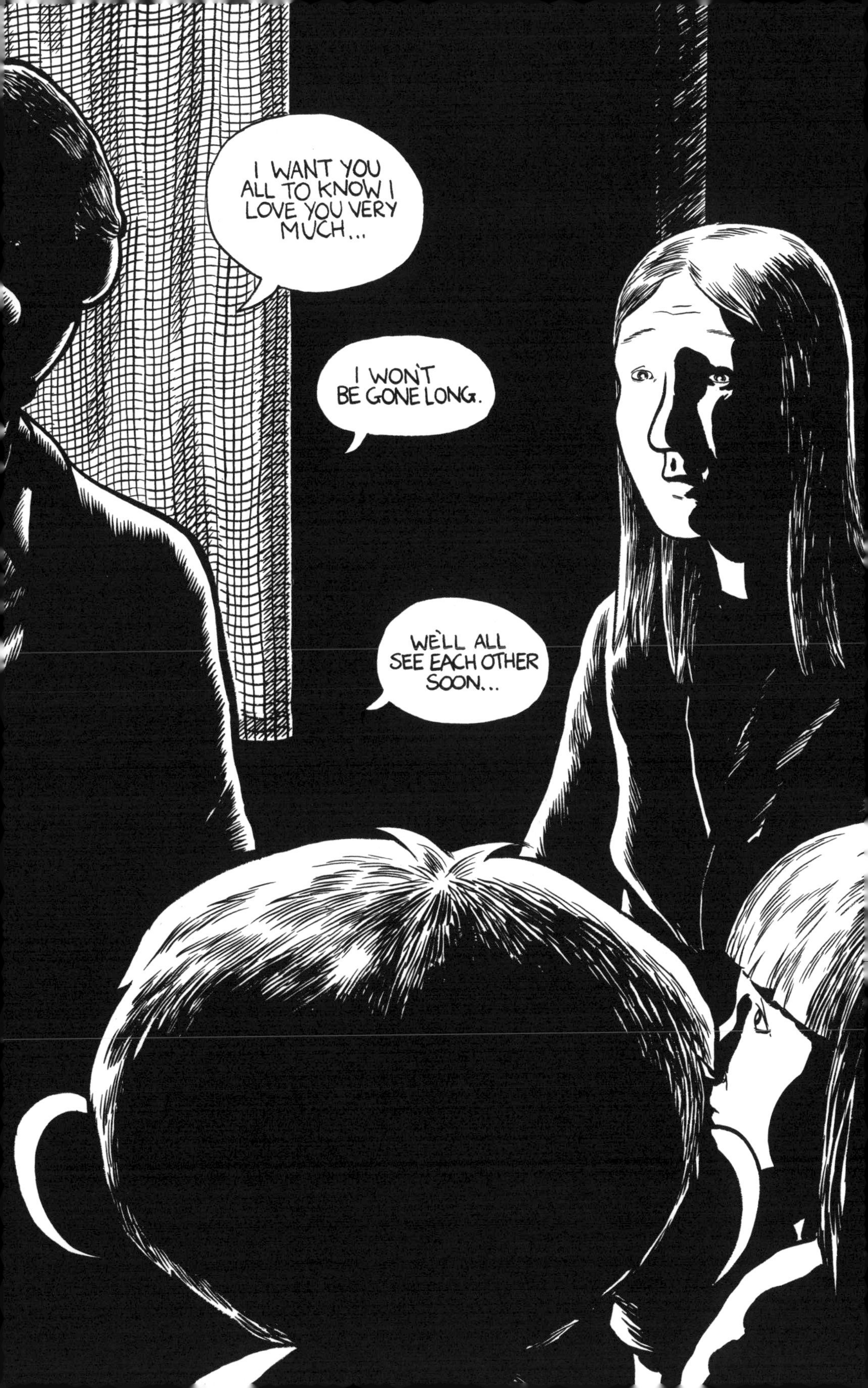
I WANT YOU ALL TO KNOW I LOVE YOU VERY MUCH...
I WON'T BE GONE LONG.
WE'LL ALL SEE EACH OTHER SOON...

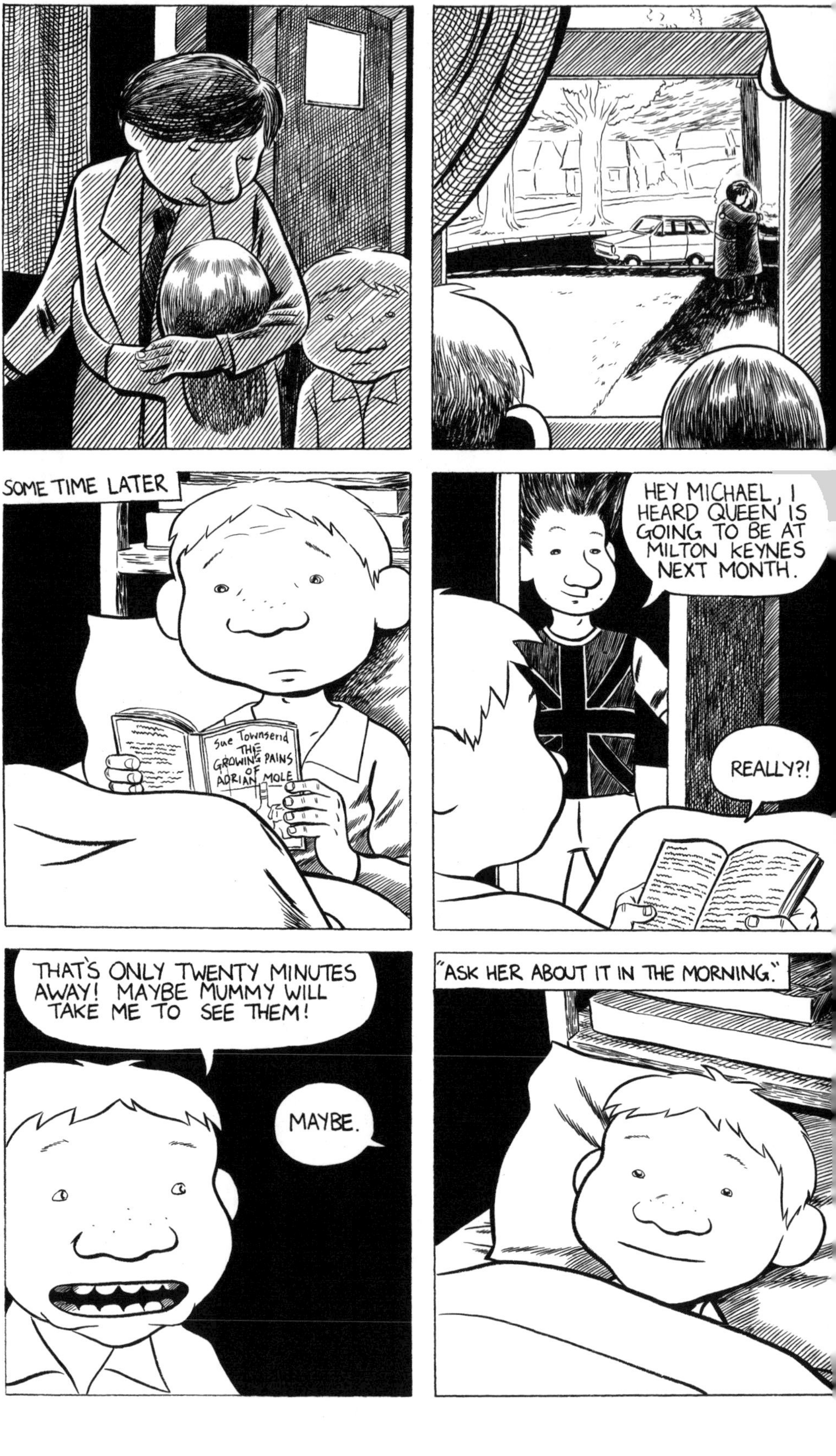
SOME TIME LATER
Sue Townsend THE GROWING PAINS OF ADRIAN MOLE
HEY MICHAEL, I HEARD QUEEN IS GOING TO BE AT MILTON KEYNES NEXT MONTH.
REALLY?!
THAT'S ONLY TWENTY MINUTES AWAY! MAYBE MUMMY WILL TAKE ME TO SEE THEM!
MAYBE.
"ASK HER ABOUT IT IN THE MORNING."

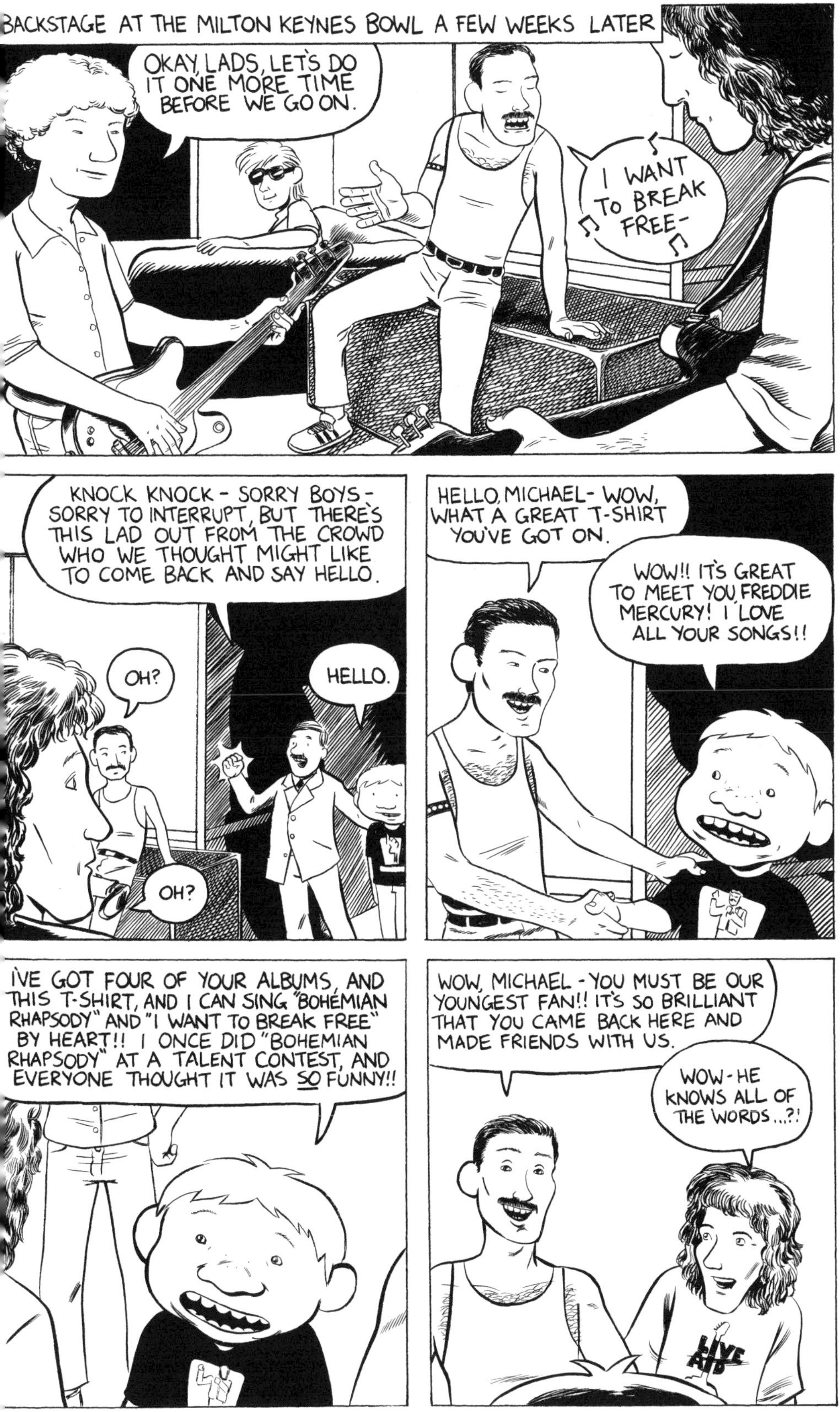
BACKSTAGE AT THE MILTON KEYNES BOWL A FEW WEEKS LATER
OKAY, LADS, LET'S DO IT ONE MORE TIME BEFORE WE GO ON.
I WANT TO BREAK FREE-
KNOCK KNOCK - SORRY BOYS - SORRY TO INTERRUPT, BUT THERE'S THIS LAD OUT FROM THE CROWD WHO WE THOUGHT MIGHT LIKE TO COME BACK AND SAY HELLO.
OH?
HELLO.
OH?
HELLO, MICHAEL- WOW, WHAT A GREAT T-SHIRT YOU'VE GOT ON.
WOW!! IT'S GREAT TO MEET YOU, FREDDIE MERCURY! I LOVE ALL YOUR SONGS!!
I'VE GOT FOUR OF YOUR ALBUMS, AND THIS T-SHIRT, AND I CAN SING "BOHEMIAN RHAPSODY" AND "I WANT TO BREAK FREE" BY HEART!! I ONCE DID "BOHEMIAN RHAPSODY" AT A TALENT CONTEST, AND EVERYONE THOUGHT IT WAS SO FUNNY!!
WOW, MICHAEL - YOU MUST BE OUR YOUNGEST FAN!! IT'S SO BRILLIANT THAT YOU CAME BACK HERE AND MADE FRIENDS WITH US.
WOW - HE KNOWS ALL OF THE WORDS...?!
LIVE AID

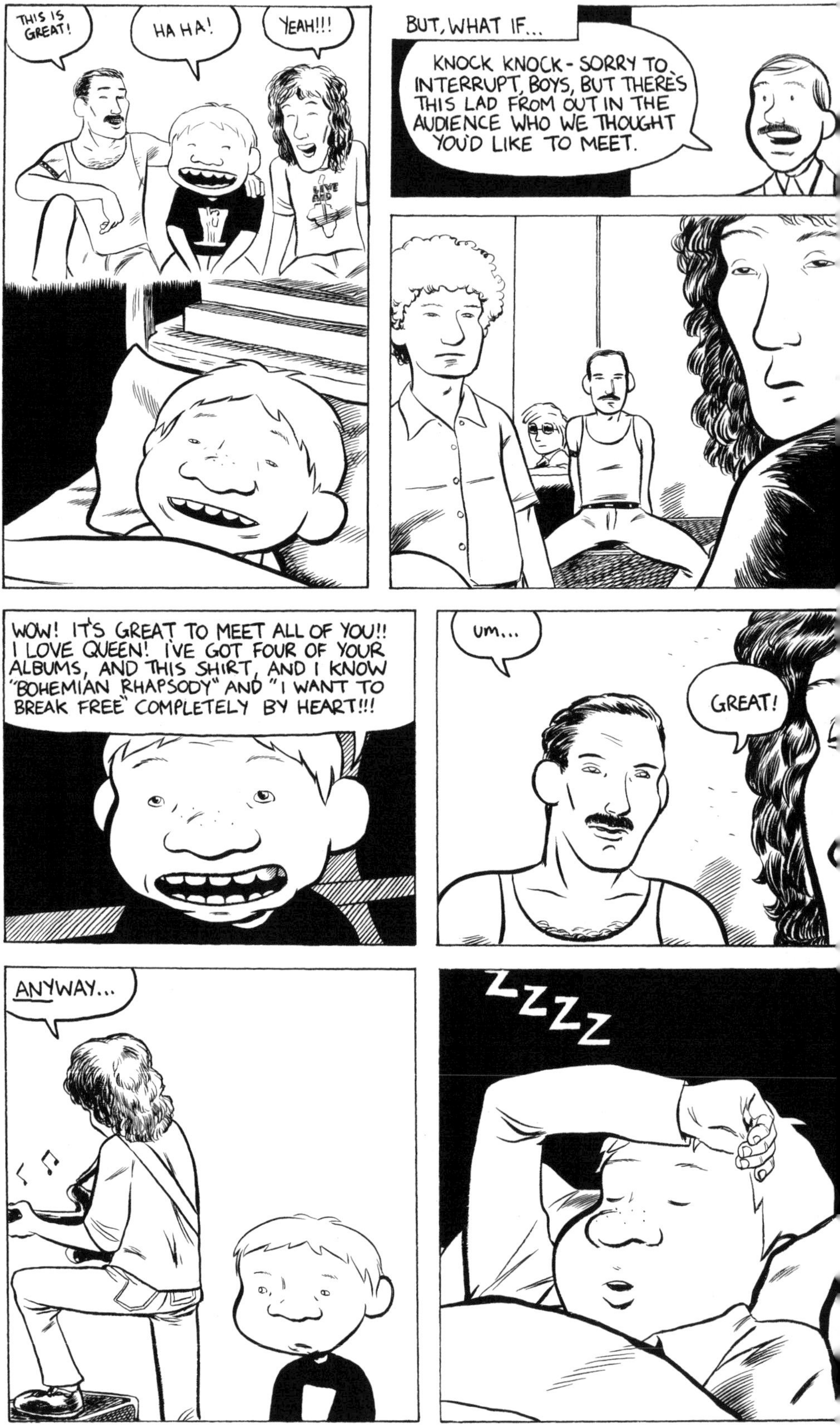
THIS IS GREAT!
HA HA!
YEAH!!!
BUT, WHAT IF...
KNOCK KNOCK - SORRY TO INTERRUPT, BOYS, BUT THERE'S THIS LAD FROM OUT IN THE AUDIENCE WHO WE THOUGHT YOU'D LIKE TO MEET.
WOW! IT'S GREAT TO MEET ALL OF YOU!! I LOVE QUEEN! I'VE GOT FOUR OF YOUR ALBUMS, AND THIS SHIRT, AND I KNOW "BOHEMIAN RHAPSODY" AND "I WANT TO BREAK FREE" COMPLETELY BY HEART!!!
UM...
GREAT!
ANYWAY...
ZZZZ

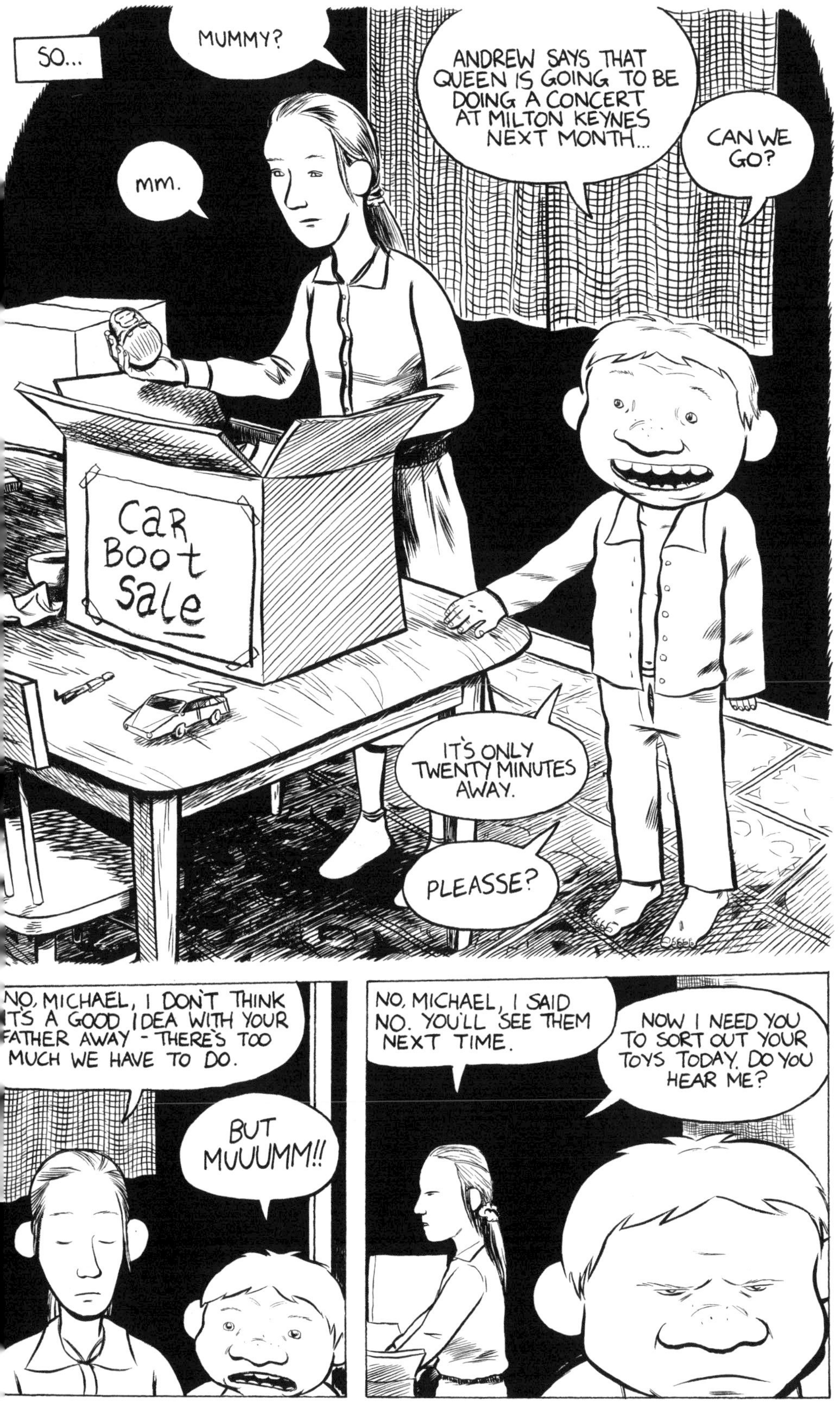
SO...
MUMMY?
mm.
ANDREW SAYS THAT QUEEN IS GOING TO BE DOING A CONCERT AT MILTON KEYNES NEXT MONTH...
CAN WE GO?
Car Boot Sale
IT'S ONLY TWENTY MINUTES AWAY.
PLEASSE?
NO, MICHAEL, I DON'T THINK IT'S A GOOD IDEA WITH YOUR FATHER AWAY - THERE'S TOO MUCH WE HAVE TO DO.
BUT MUUUMM!!
NO, MICHAEL, I SAID NO. YOU'LL SEE THEM NEXT TIME.
NOW I NEED YOU TO SORT OUT YOUR TOYS TODAY. DO YOU HEAR ME?

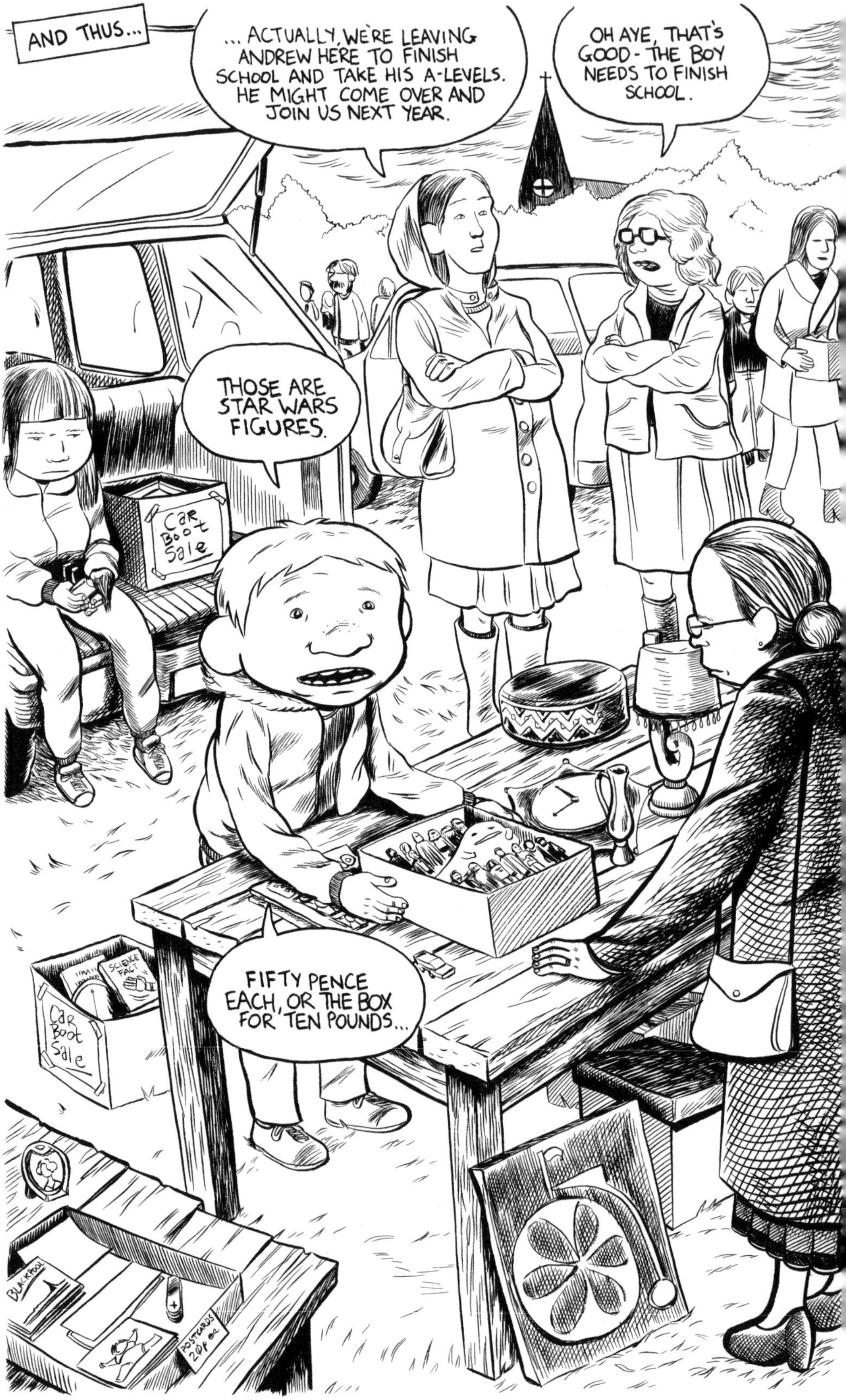
AND THUS...
... ACTUALLY, WE'RE LEAVING ANDREW HERE TO FINISH SCHOOL AND TAKE HIS A-LEVELS. HE MIGHT COME OVER AND JOIN US NEXT YEAR.
OH AYE, THAT'S GOOD - THE BOY NEEDS TO FINISH SCHOOL.
THOSE ARE STAR WARS FIGURES.
Car Boot Sale
FIFTY PENCE EACH, OR THE BOX FOR TEN POUNDS...
SCIENCE FACT
Car Boot Sale
BLACKPOOL
POSTCARDS 20p ea.

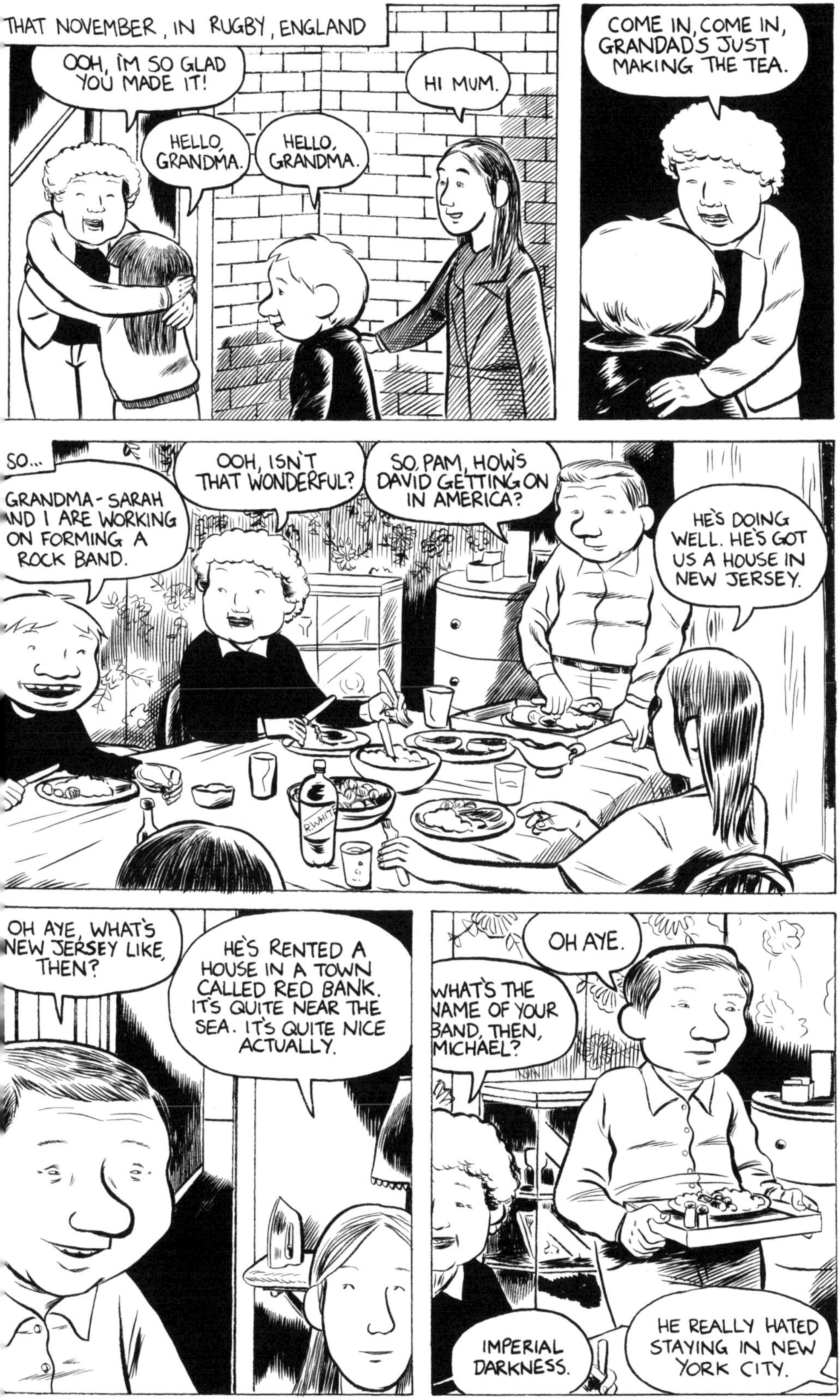
THAT NOVEMBER, IN RUGBY, ENGLAND
OOH, I'M SO GLAD YOU MADE IT!
HELLO, GRANDMA.
HELLO, GRANDMA.
HI MUM.
COME IN, COME IN, GRANDAD'S JUST MAKING THE TEA.
SO...
GRANDMA-SARAH AND I ARE WORKING ON FORMING A ROCK BAND.
OOH, ISN'T THAT WONDERFUL?
SO, PAM, HOW'S DAVID GETTING ON IN AMERICA?
HE'S DOING WELL. HE'S GOT US A HOUSE IN NEW JERSEY.
R. WHITE
OH AYE, WHAT'S NEW JERSEY LIKE, THEN?
HE'S RENTED A HOUSE IN A TOWN CALLED RED BANK. IT'S QUITE NEAR THE SEA. IT'S QUITE NICE ACTUALLY.
OH AYE.
WHAT'S THE NAME OF YOUR BAND, THEN, MICHAEL?
IMPERIAL DARKNESS.
HE REALLY HATED STAYING IN NEW YORK CITY.

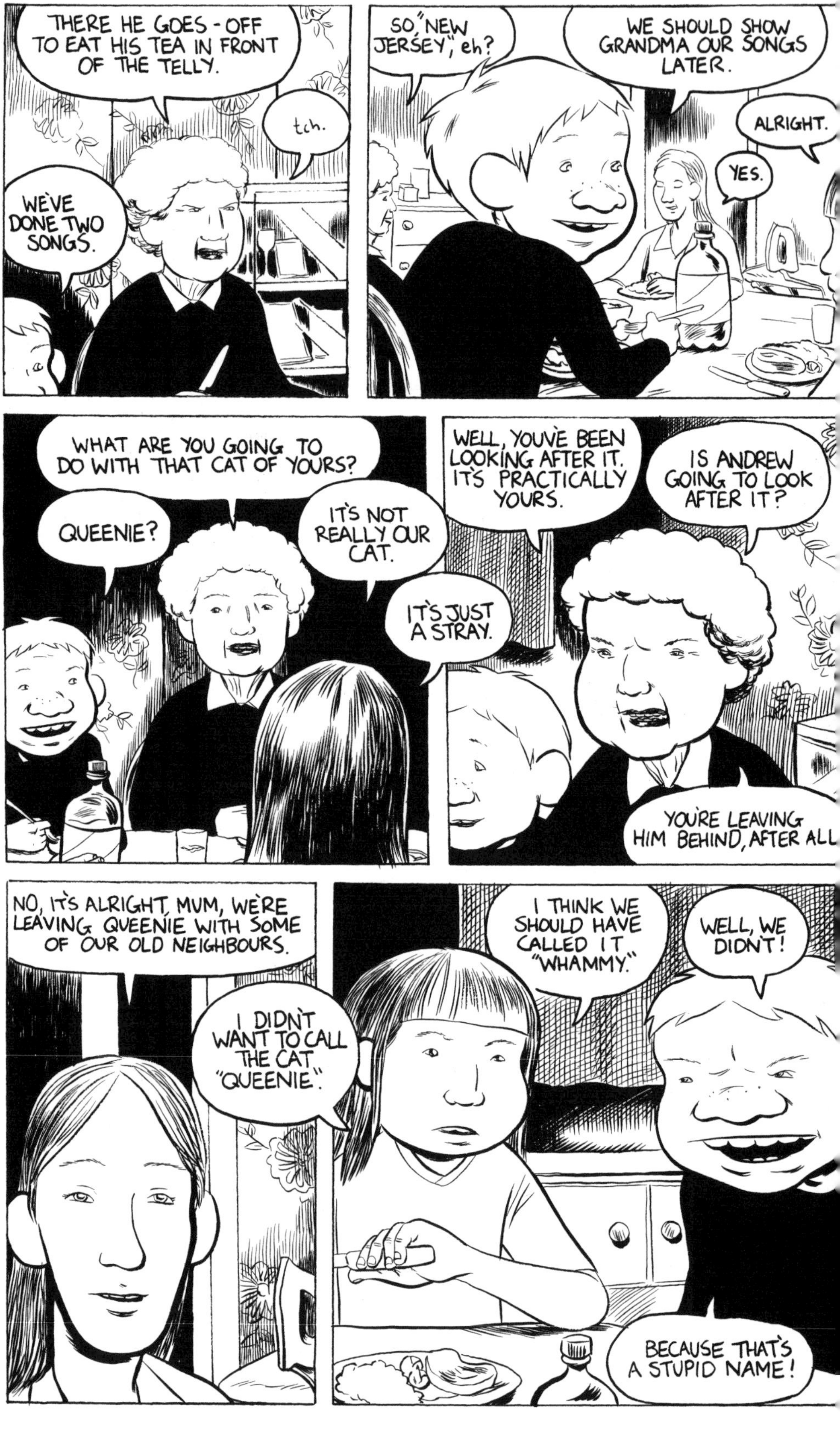
THERE HE GOES - OFF TO EAT HIS TEA IN FRONT OF THE TELLY.
tch.
WE'VE DONE TWO SONGS.
SO, "NEW JERSEY", eh?
WE SHOULD SHOW GRANDMA OUR SONGS LATER.
ALRIGHT.
YES.
WHAT ARE YOU GOING TO DO WITH THAT CAT OF YOURS?
QUEENIE?
IT'S NOT REALLY OUR CAT.
IT'S JUST A STRAY.
WELL, YOU'VE BEEN LOOKING AFTER IT. IT'S PRACTICALLY YOURS.
IS ANDREW GOING TO LOOK AFTER IT?
YOU'RE LEAVING HIM BEHIND, AFTER ALL
NO, IT'S ALRIGHT, MUM, WE'RE LEAVING QUEENIE WITH SOME OF OUR OLD NEIGHBOURS.
I DIDN'T WANT TO CALL THE CAT "QUEENIE".
I THINK WE SHOULD HAVE CALLED IT "WHAMMY."
WELL, WE DIDN'T!
BECAUSE THAT'S A STUPID NAME!

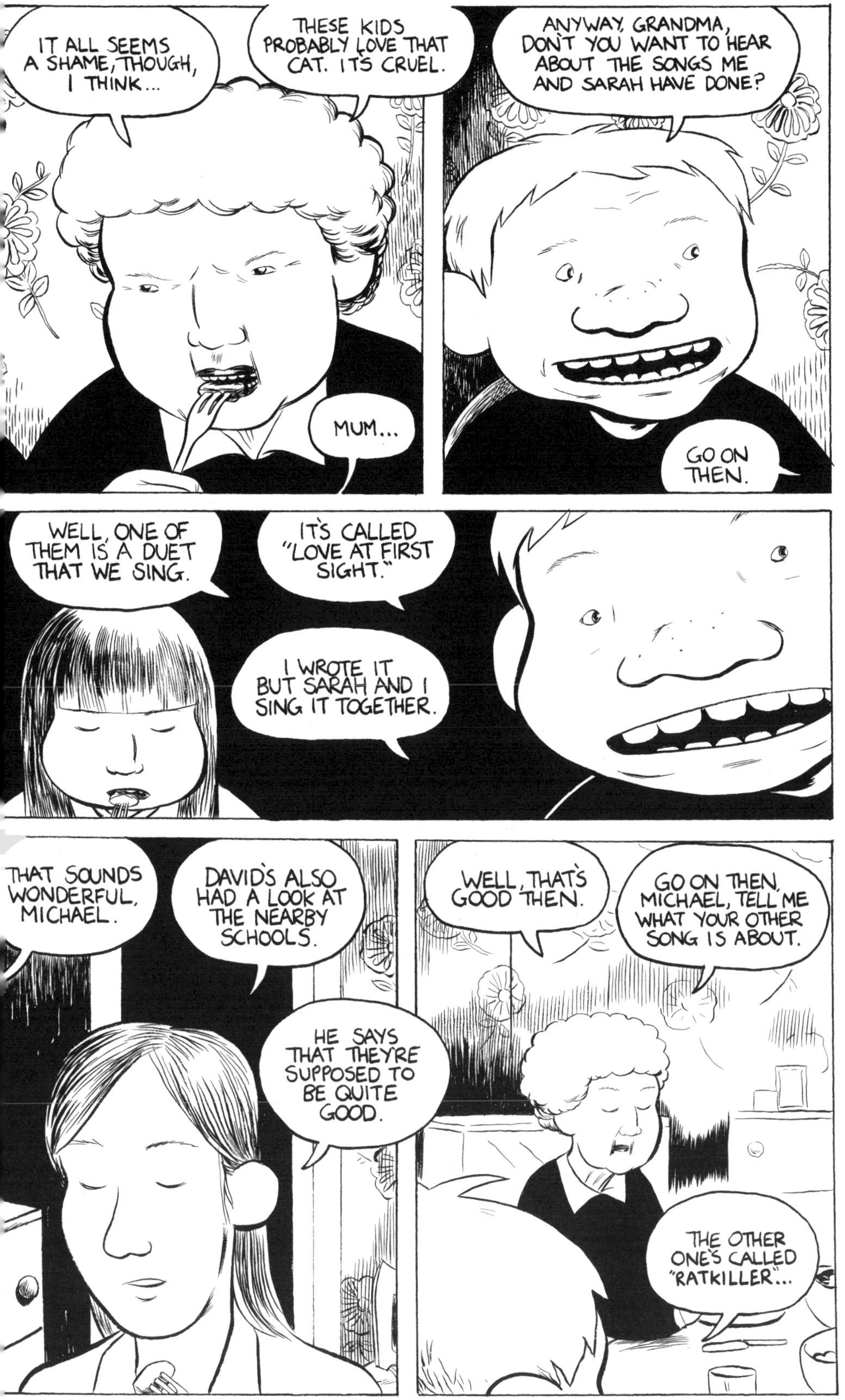
IT ALL SEEMS A SHAME, THOUGH, I THINK...
THESE KIDS PROBABLY LOVE THAT CAT. IT'S CRUEL.
MUM...
ANYWAY, GRANDMA, DON'T YOU WANT TO HEAR ABOUT THE SONGS ME AND SARAH HAVE DONE?
GO ON THEN.
WELL, ONE OF THEM IS A DUET THAT WE SING.
IT'S CALLED "LOVE AT FIRST SIGHT."
I WROTE IT BUT SARAH AND I SING IT TOGETHER.
THAT SOUNDS WONDERFUL, MICHAEL.
DAVID'S ALSO HAD A LOOK AT THE NEARBY SCHOOLS.
HE SAYS THAT THEY'RE SUPPOSED TO BE QUITE GOOD.
WELL, THAT'S GOOD THEN.
GO ON THEN, MICHAEL, TELL ME WHAT YOUR OTHER SONG IS ABOUT.
THE OTHER ONE'S CALLED "RATKILLER"...

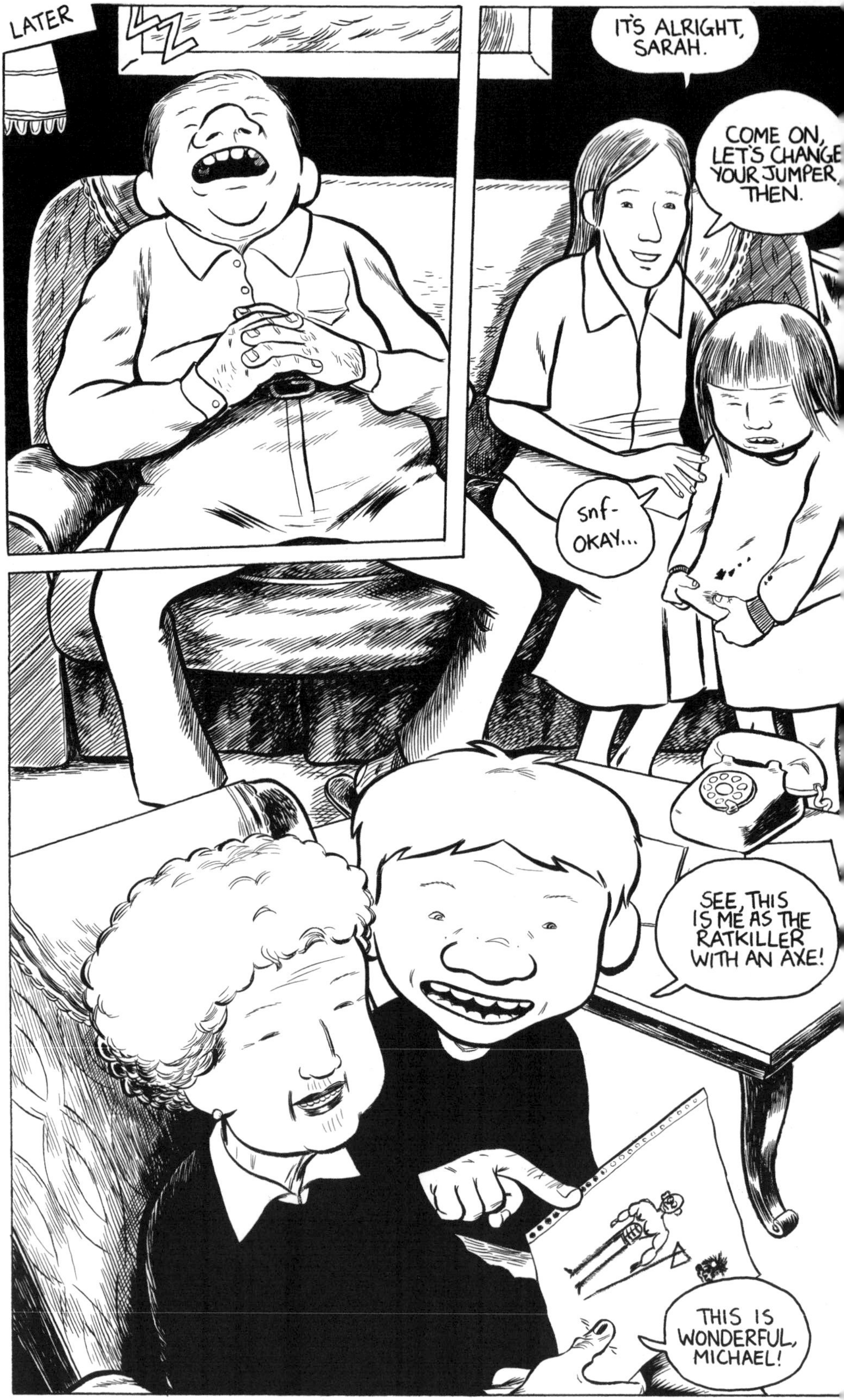
LATER
IT'S ALRIGHT, SARAH.
COME ON, LET'S CHANGE YOUR JUMPER, THEN.
snf- OKAY...
SEE, THIS IS ME AS THE RATKILLER WITH AN AXE!
THIS IS WONDERFUL, MICHAEL!

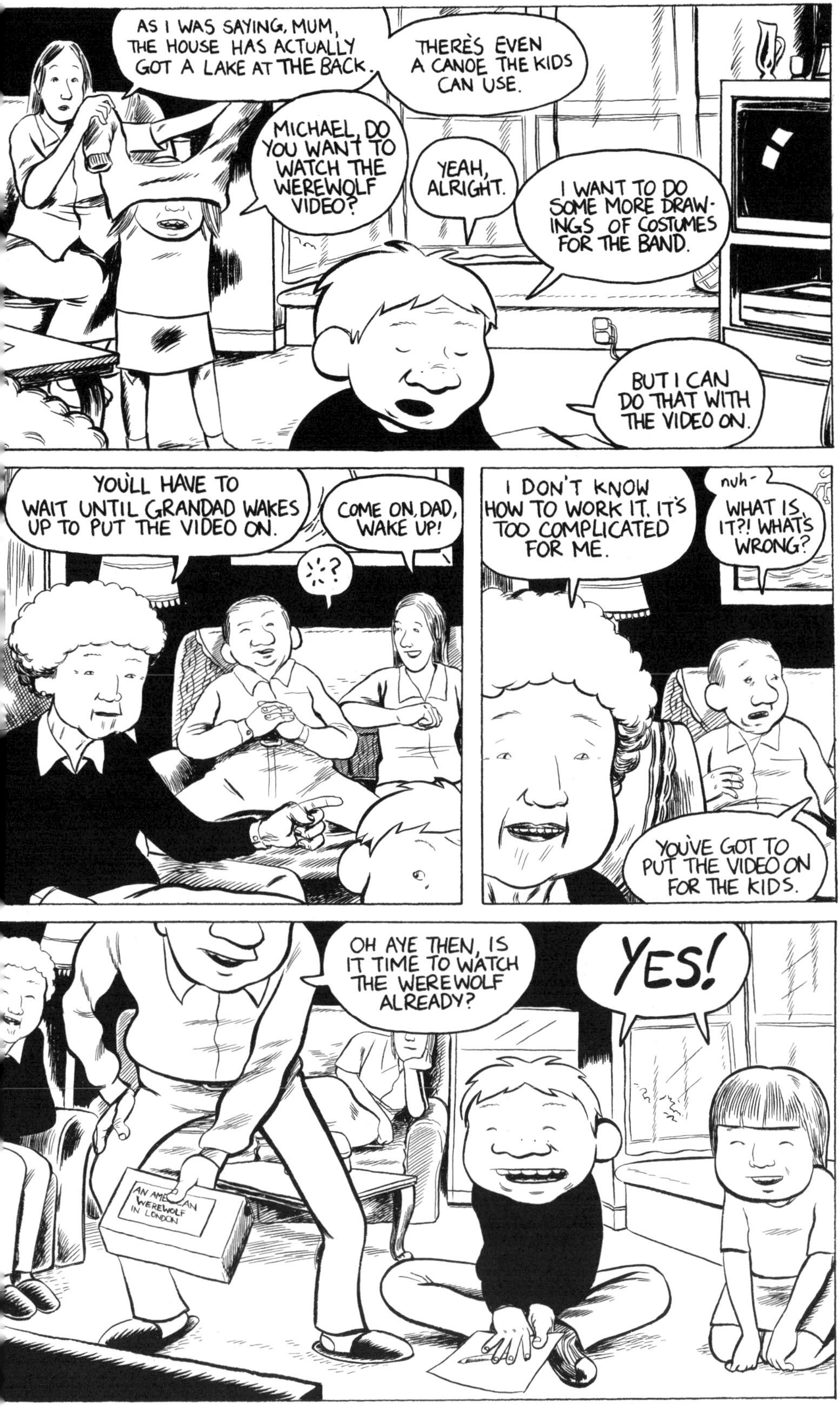
AS I WAS SAYING, MUM, THE HOUSE HAS ACTUALLY GOT A LAKE AT THE BACK.
THERÈS EVEN A CANOE THE KIDS CAN USE.
MICHAEL, DO YOU WANT TO WATCH THE WEREWOLF VIDEO?
YEAH, ALRIGHT.
I WANT TO DO SOME MORE DRAWINGS OF COSTUMES FOR THE BAND.
BUT I CAN DO THAT WITH THE VIDEO ON.
YOU'LL HAVE TO WAIT UNTIL GRANDAD WAKES UP TO PUT THE VIDEO ON.
COME ON, DAD, WAKE UP!
?
I DON'T KNOW HOW TO WORK IT. IT'S TOO COMPLICATED FOR ME.
nuh-
WHAT IS IT?! WHAT'S WRONG?
YOU'VE GOT TO PUT THE VIDEO ON FOR THE KIDS.
OH AYE THEN, IS IT TIME TO WATCH THE WEREWOLF ALREADY?
YES!
AN AMERICAN WEREWOLF IN LONDON

WATCHING IT AGAIN HA HA!

LOVELY SHEEP

BOYS, KEEP OFF THE MOORS...

THE BROONS

WELL, I SHALL MISS THIS— HAVING YOU ALL HERE.

AYE.

I KNOW, BUT WE AREN'T GOING FOREVER.

AND BESIDES—

YO NOT FUN YO

YOU CAN COME AND SEE US IN AMERICA— DO NT TO Y?

I K L

SEE, NOW I'M DRAWING ME FIGHTING A MONSTER.

DON'T KNOW BOUT THAT...

I THINK THIS WOULD MAKE A GREAT VIDEO FOR OUR SONG, SARAH.

OH, COME ON MUM...

SHE MEET ME I ROM

OH

CAN YOU IMAGINE ME AND YOUR FATHER ON A PLANE FOR TEN HOURS? I DON'T THINK SO...

MUM, IT'S ONLY SIX —IT'S NOT THAT BAD—

S ME W

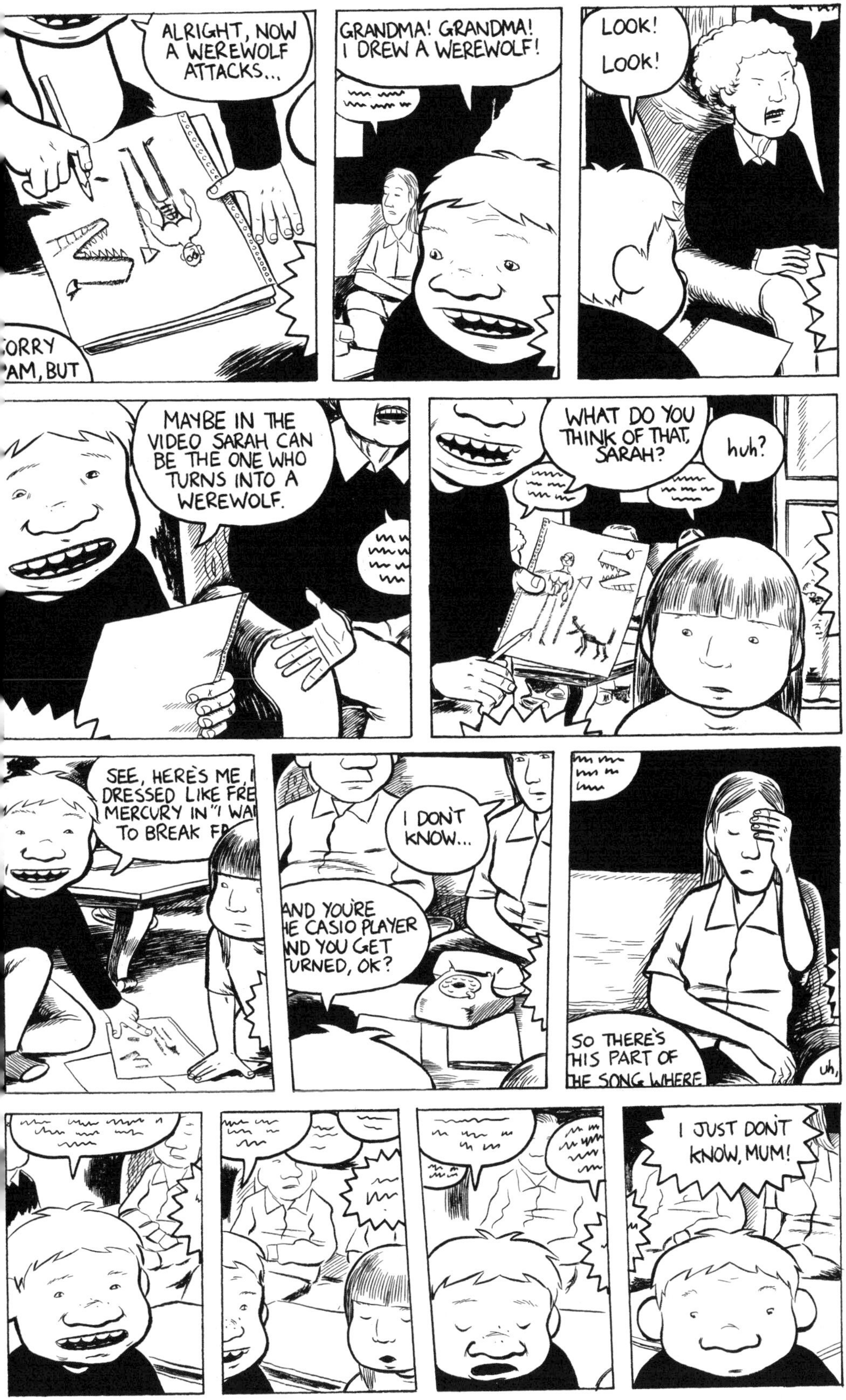
ALRIGHT, NOW A WEREWOLF ATTACKS...
ORRY AM, BUT
GRANDMA! GRANDMA! I DREW A WEREWOLF!
LOOK!
LOOK!
MAYBE IN THE VIDEO SARAH CAN BE THE ONE WHO TURNS INTO A WEREWOLF.
WHAT DO YOU THINK OF THAT, SARAH?
huh?
SEE, HERE'S ME, I DRESSED LIKE FRE MERCURY IN "I WA TO BREAK FR
I DON'T KNOW...
AND YOU'RE HE CASIO PLAYER ND YOU GET TURNED, OK?
SO THERE'S HIS PART OF HE SONG WHERE
uh,
I JUST DON'T KNOW, MUM!

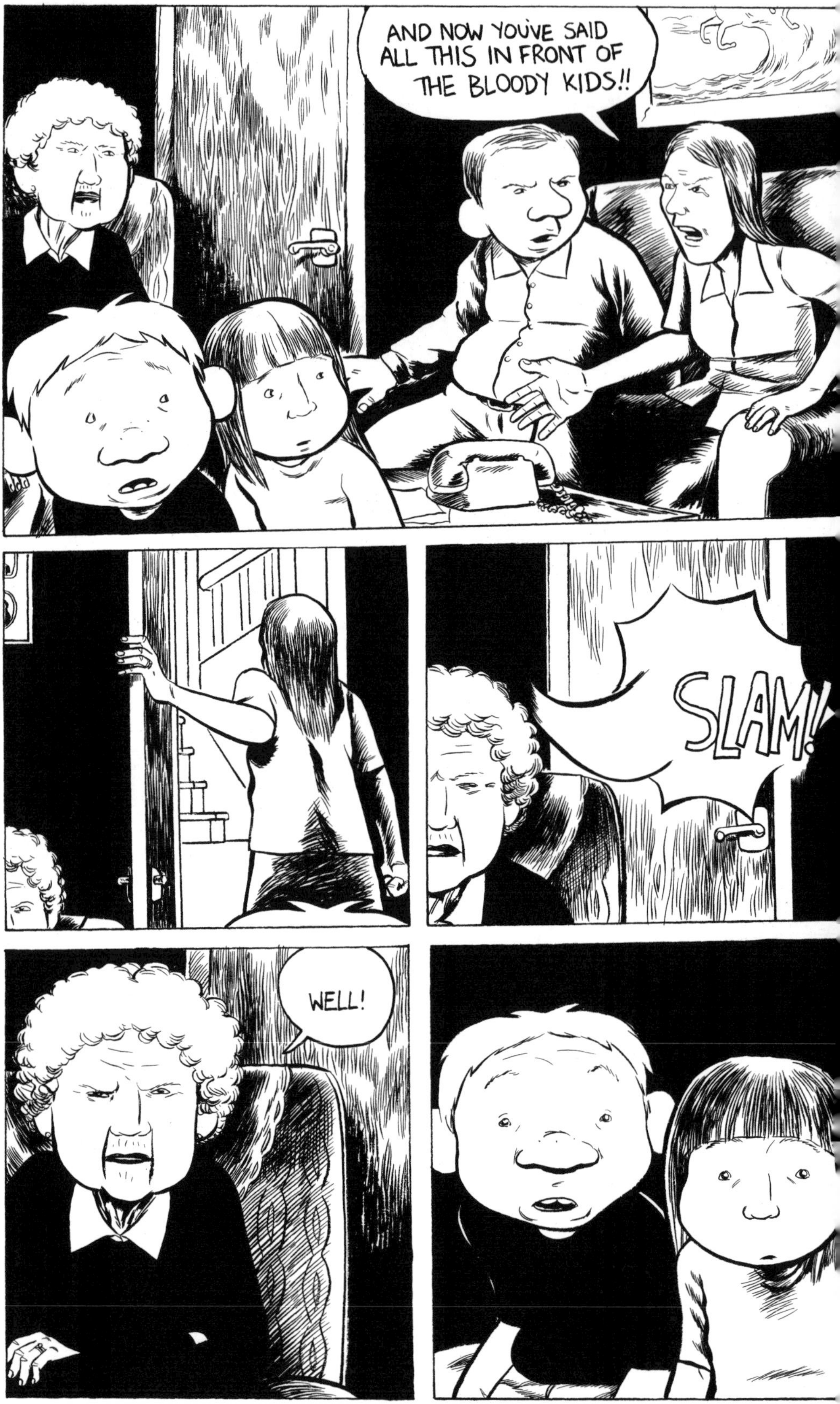
AND NOW YOU'VE SAID ALL THIS IN FRONT OF THE BLOODY KIDS!!
SLAM!
WELL!

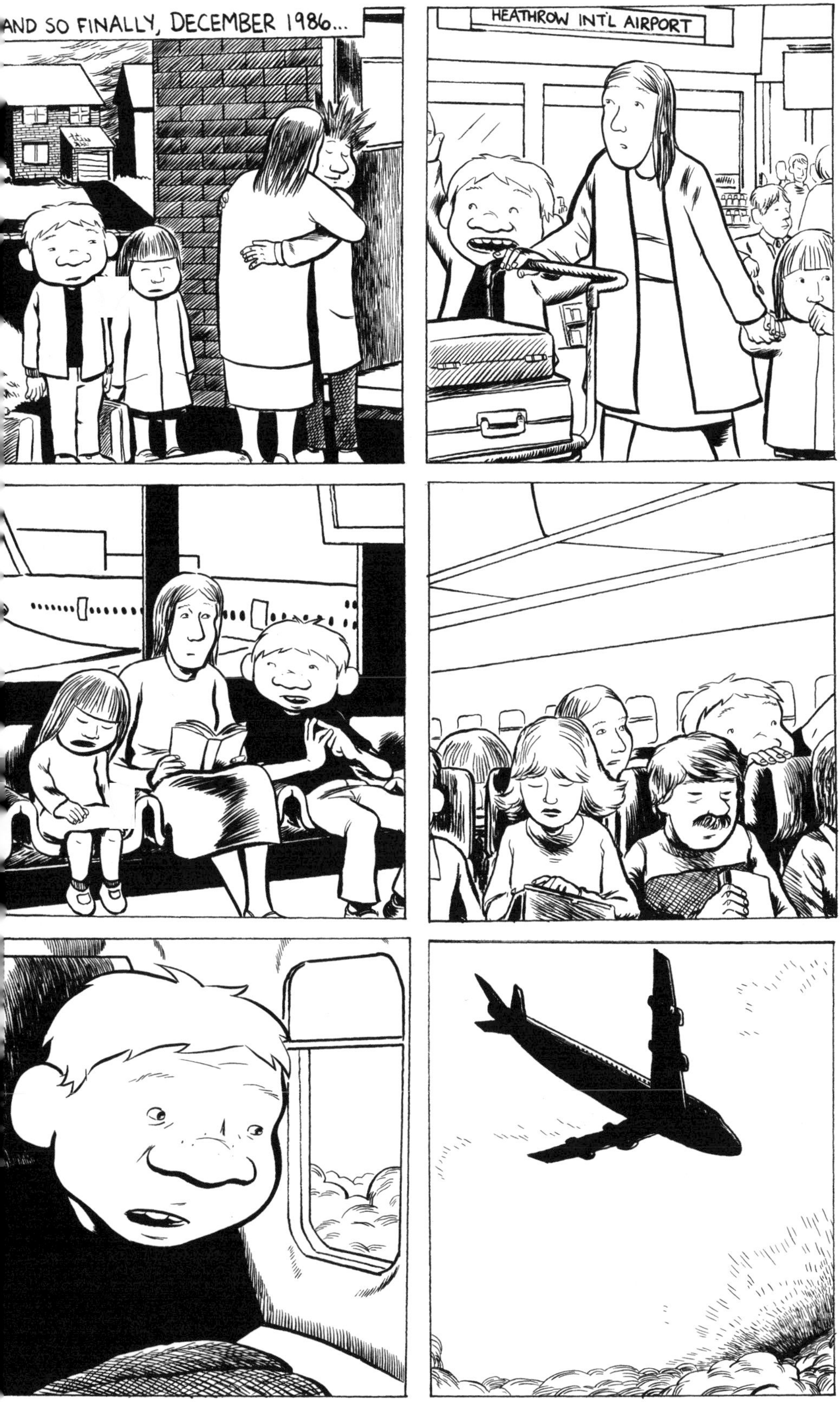
AND SO FINALLY, DECEMBER 1986...
HEATHROW INT'L AIRPORT

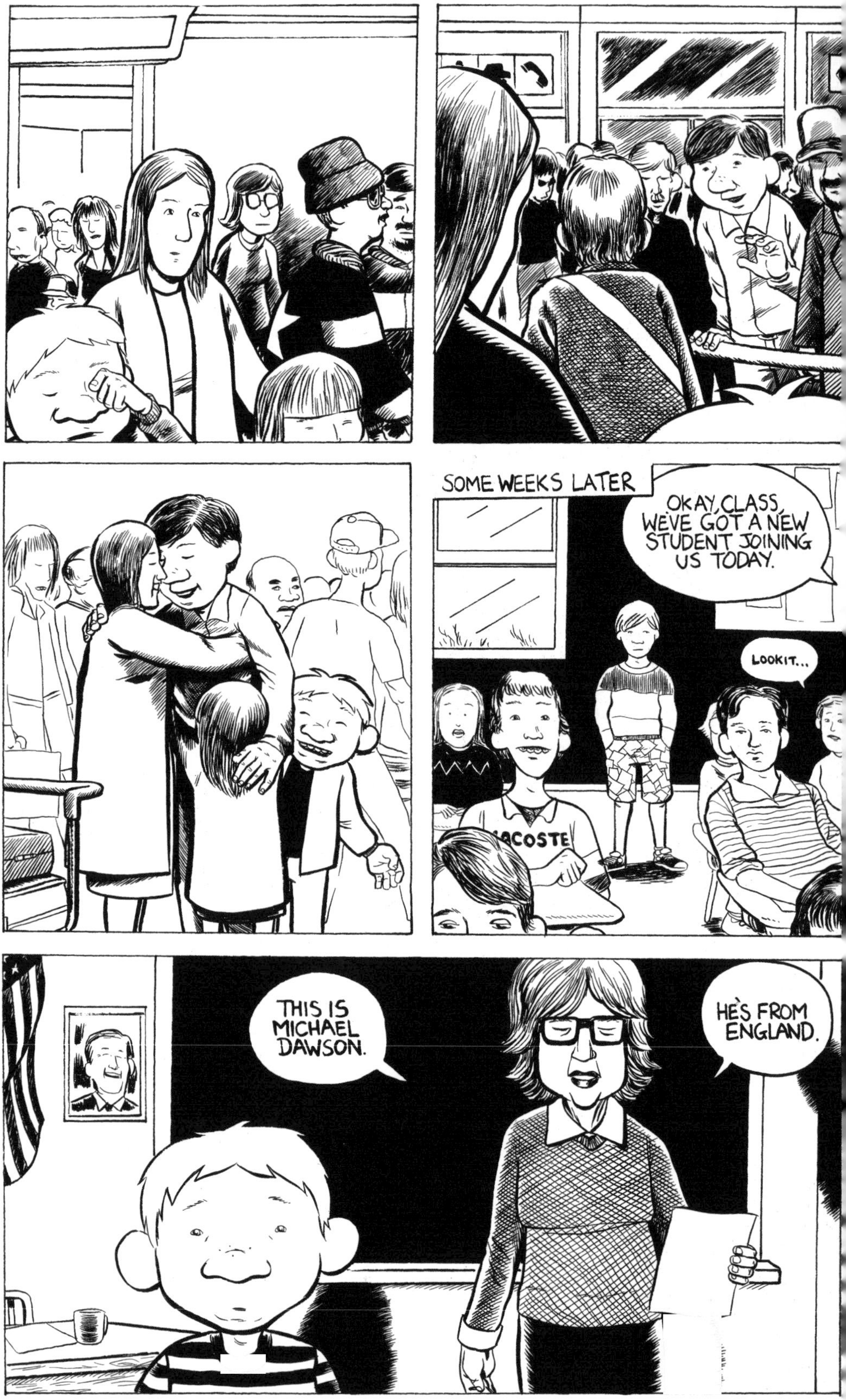
SOME WEEKS LATER
OKAY, CLASS, WE'VE GOT A NEW STUDENT JOINING US TODAY.
LOOKIT...
ACOSTE
THIS IS MICHAEL DAWSON.
HE'S FROM ENGLAND.

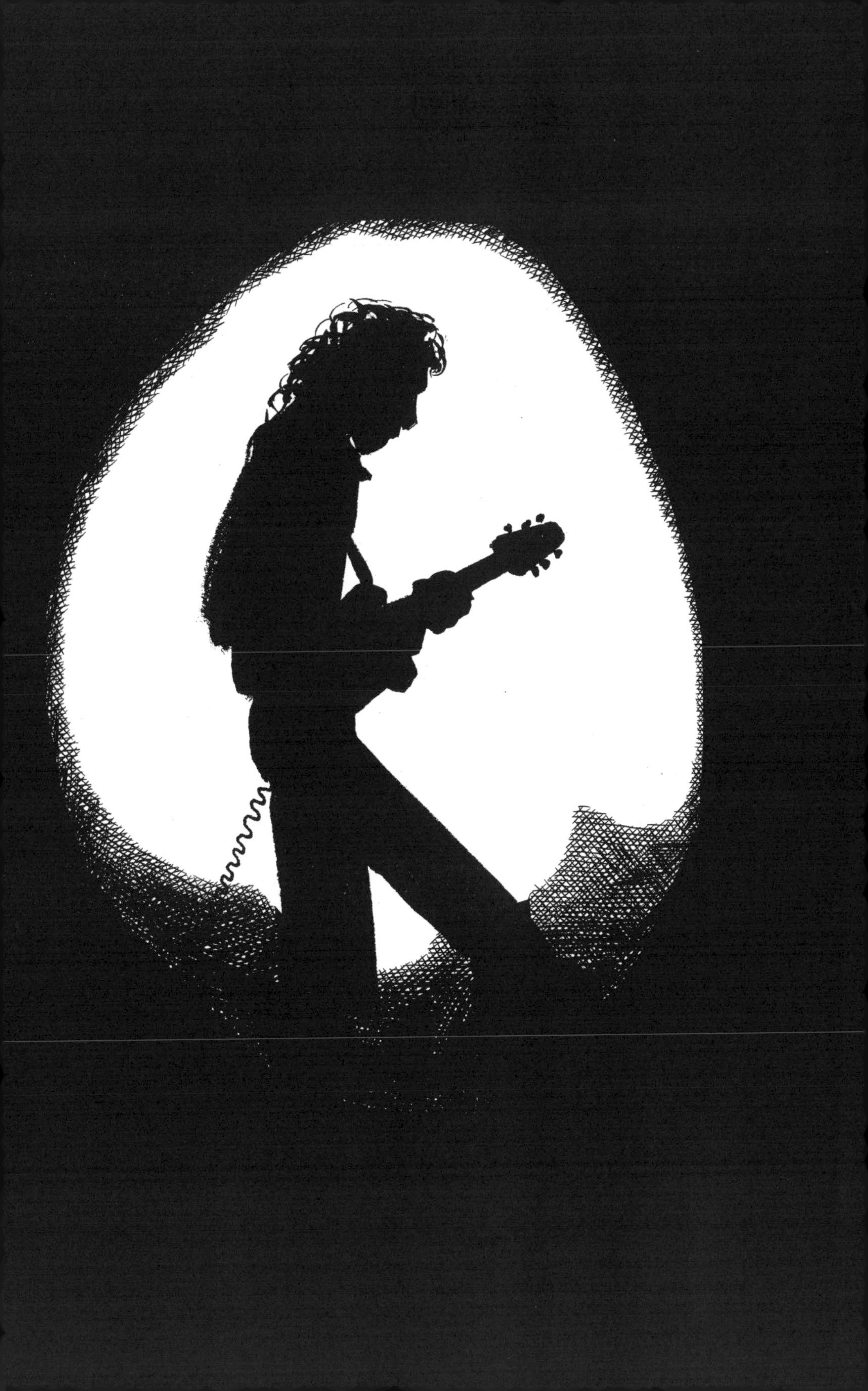

I REMEMBER STANDING IN FRONT OF THE CLASS AND BEING INTRODUCED.

I'M NOT SURE IF I WAS ACTUALLY WEARING A STRIPED SHIRT, THOUGH.

GUITAR

I KNOW I USED TO HAVE A STRIPED SWEATSHIRT. IT WAS BLUE AND WHITE, AND CAME WITH A PAIR OF MATCHING SWEATPANTS AND A HAN SOLO VEST.

I LOVED THIS OUTFIT - FOR SOME ODD REASON I THOUGHT IT MADE ME LOOK LIKE FREDDIE MERCURY FROM QUEEN.

CAN Y FACE ME

SOLO

SO I CAN EASILY IMAGINE MYSELF THINKING THAT THE OUTFIT WOULD BE PERFECT TO WEAR FOR MY FIRST DAY OF SCHOOL IN AMERICA.

BUT TRUTHFULLY I HAVE NO **REAL** MEMORY AT ALL OF WHAT I MIGHT HAVE HAD ON. THE ONLY ACTUAL MEMORY I HAVE IS STANDING UP AT THE FRONT OF A CLASSROOM WHILE A TEACHER EXPLAINED WHO I WAS.

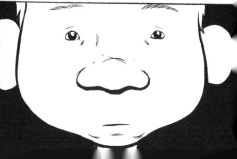

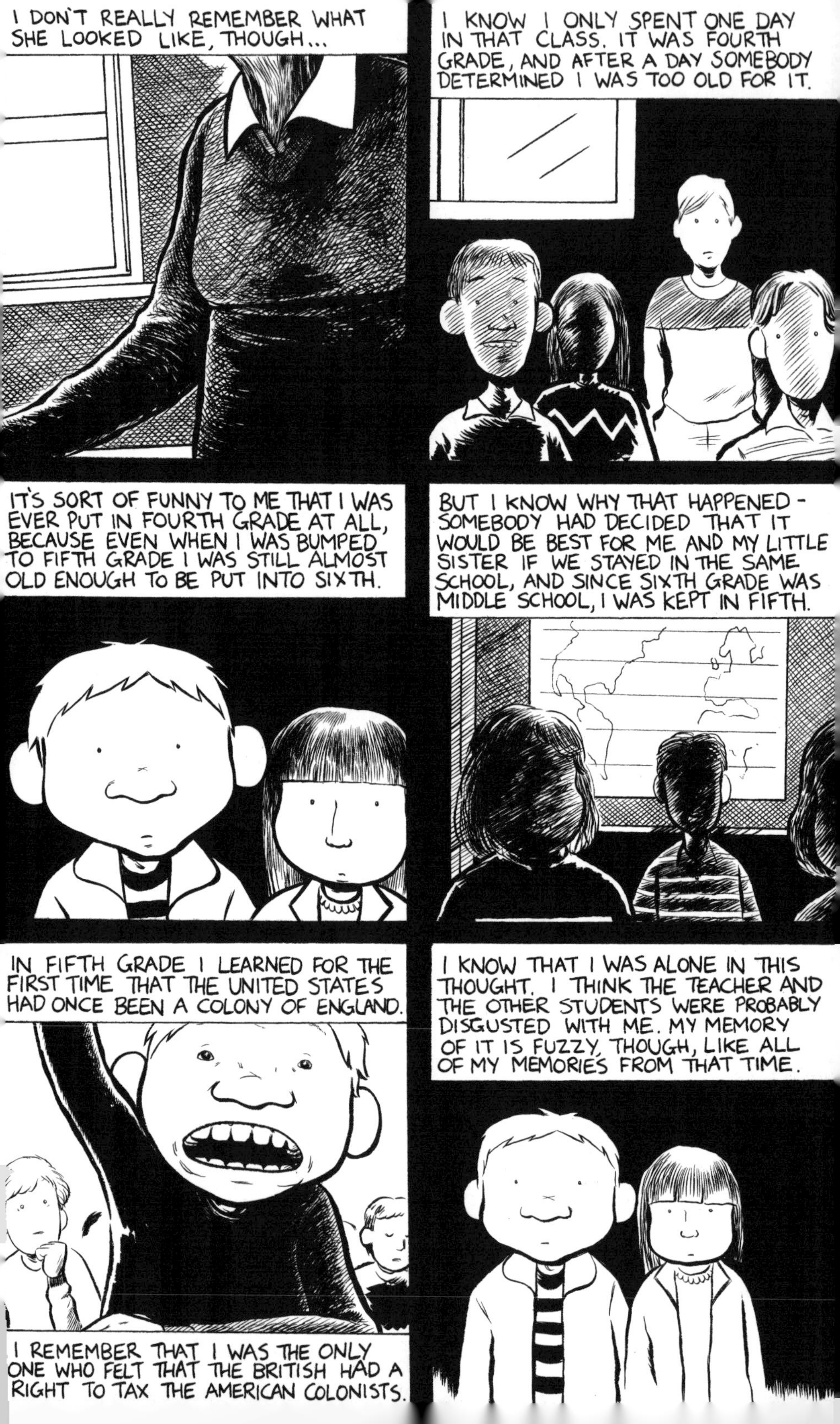
I DON'T REALLY REMEMBER WHAT SHE LOOKED LIKE, THOUGH...
I KNOW I ONLY SPENT ONE DAY IN THAT CLASS. IT WAS FOURTH GRADE, AND AFTER A DAY SOMEBODY DETERMINED I WAS TOO OLD FOR IT.
IT'S SORT OF FUNNY TO ME THAT I WAS EVER PUT IN FOURTH GRADE AT ALL, BECAUSE EVEN WHEN I WAS BUMPED TO FIFTH GRADE I WAS STILL ALMOST OLD ENOUGH TO BE PUT INTO SIXTH.
BUT I KNOW WHY THAT HAPPENED - SOMEBODY HAD DECIDED THAT IT WOULD BE BEST FOR ME AND MY LITTLE SISTER IF WE STAYED IN THE SAME SCHOOL, AND SINCE SIXTH GRADE WAS MIDDLE SCHOOL, I WAS KEPT IN FIFTH.
IN FIFTH GRADE I LEARNED FOR THE FIRST TIME THAT THE UNITED STATES HAD ONCE BEEN A COLONY OF ENGLAND.
I REMEMBER THAT I WAS THE ONLY ONE WHO FELT THAT THE BRITISH HAD A RIGHT TO TAX THE AMERICAN COLONISTS.
I KNOW THAT I WAS ALONE IN THIS THOUGHT. I THINK THE TEACHER AND THE OTHER STUDENTS WERE PROBABLY DISGUSTED WITH ME. MY MEMORY OF IT IS FUZZY, THOUGH, LIKE ALL OF MY MEMORIES FROM THAT TIME.

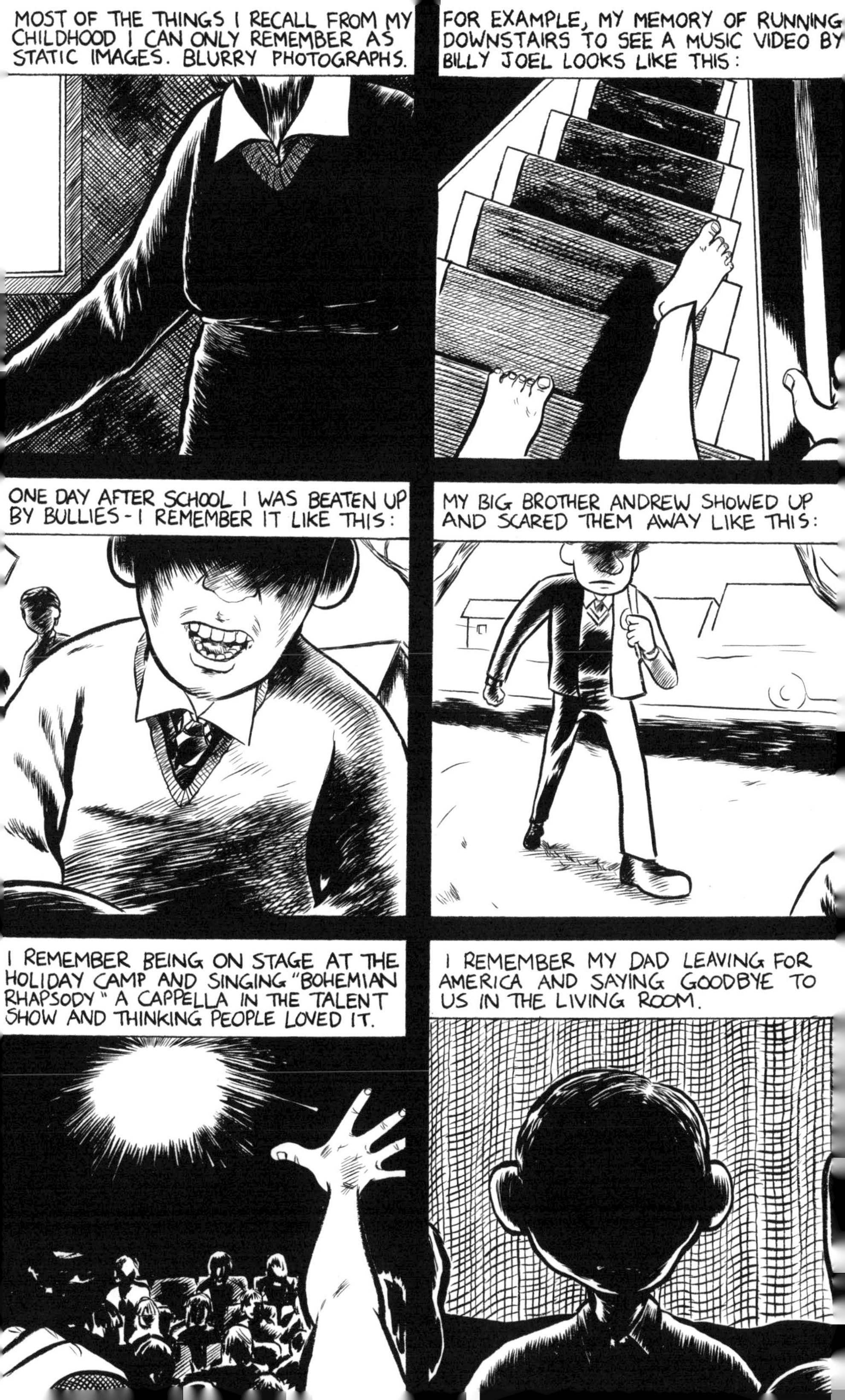
MOST OF THE THINGS I RECALL FROM MY CHILDHOOD I CAN ONLY REMEMBER AS STATIC IMAGES. BLURRY PHOTOGRAPHS.
FOR EXAMPLE, MY MEMORY OF RUNNING DOWNSTAIRS TO SEE A MUSIC VIDEO BY BILLY JOEL LOOKS LIKE THIS:
ONE DAY AFTER SCHOOL I WAS BEATEN UP BY BULLIES - I REMEMBER IT LIKE THIS:
MY BIG BROTHER ANDREW SHOWED UP AND SCARED THEM AWAY LIKE THIS:
I REMEMBER BEING ON STAGE AT THE HOLIDAY CAMP AND SINGING "BOHEMIAN RHAPSODY" A CAPPELLA IN THE TALENT SHOW AND THINKING PEOPLE LOVED IT.
I REMEMBER MY DAD LEAVING FOR AMERICA AND SAYING GOODBYE TO US IN THE LIVING ROOM.

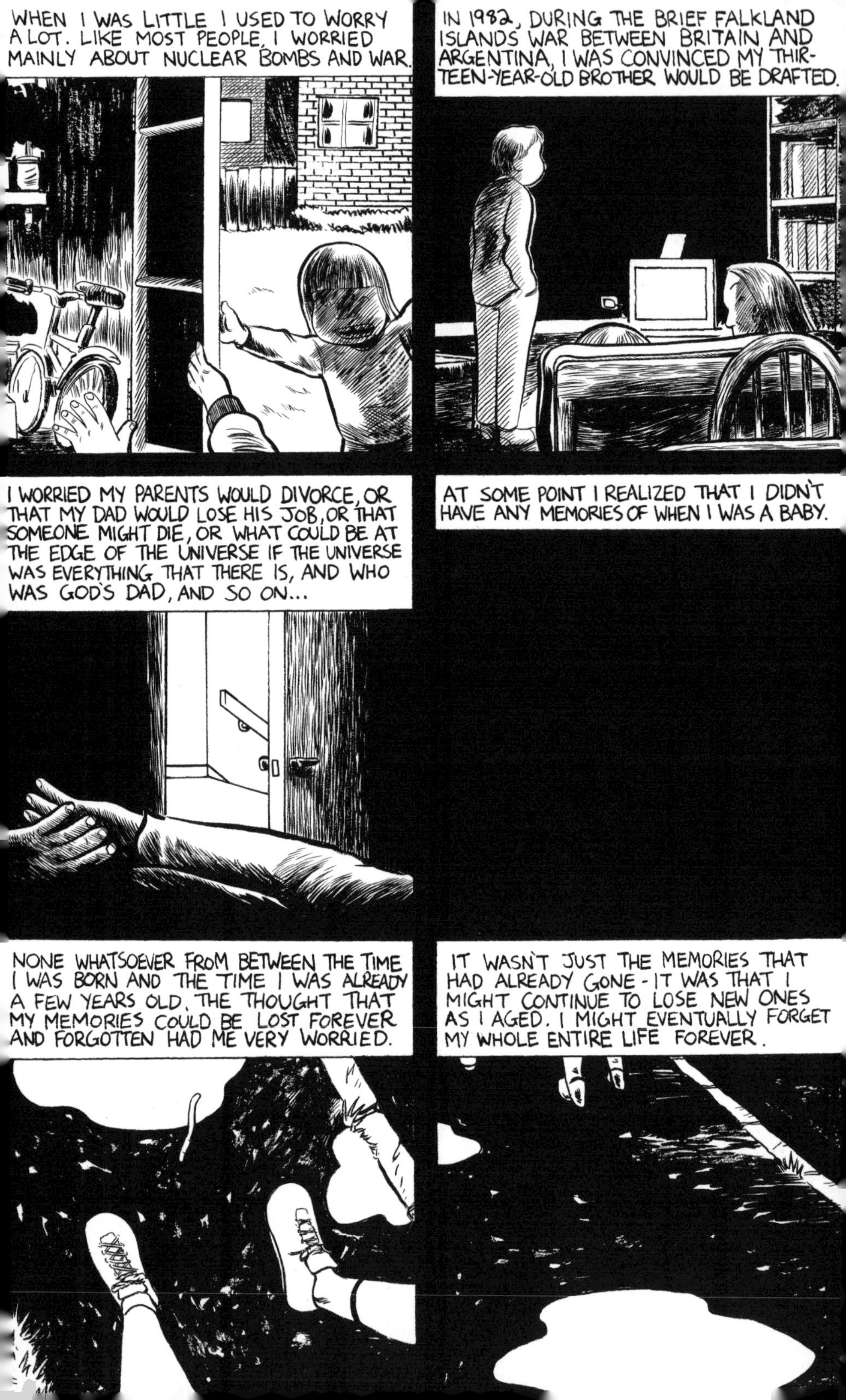
WHEN I WAS LITTLE I USED TO WORRY A LOT. LIKE MOST PEOPLE, I WORRIED MAINLY ABOUT NUCLEAR BOMBS AND WAR.
IN 1982, DURING THE BRIEF FALKLAND ISLANDS WAR BETWEEN BRITAIN AND ARGENTINA, I WAS CONVINCED MY THIRTEEN-YEAR-OLD BROTHER WOULD BE DRAFTED.
I WORRIED MY PARENTS WOULD DIVORCE, OR THAT MY DAD WOULD LOSE HIS JOB, OR THAT SOMEONE MIGHT DIE, OR WHAT COULD BE AT THE EDGE OF THE UNIVERSE IF THE UNIVERSE WAS EVERYTHING THAT THERE IS, AND WHO WAS GOD'S DAD, AND SO ON...
AT SOME POINT I REALIZED THAT I DIDN'T HAVE ANY MEMORIES OF WHEN I WAS A BABY.
NONE WHATSOEVER FROM BETWEEN THE TIME I WAS BORN AND THE TIME I WAS ALREADY A FEW YEARS OLD. THE THOUGHT THAT MY MEMORIES COULD BE LOST FOREVER AND FORGOTTEN HAD ME VERY WORRIED.
IT WASN'T JUST THE MEMORIES THAT HAD ALREADY GONE - IT WAS THAT I MIGHT CONTINUE TO LOSE NEW ONES AS I AGED. I MIGHT EVENTUALLY FORGET MY WHOLE ENTIRE LIFE FOREVER.

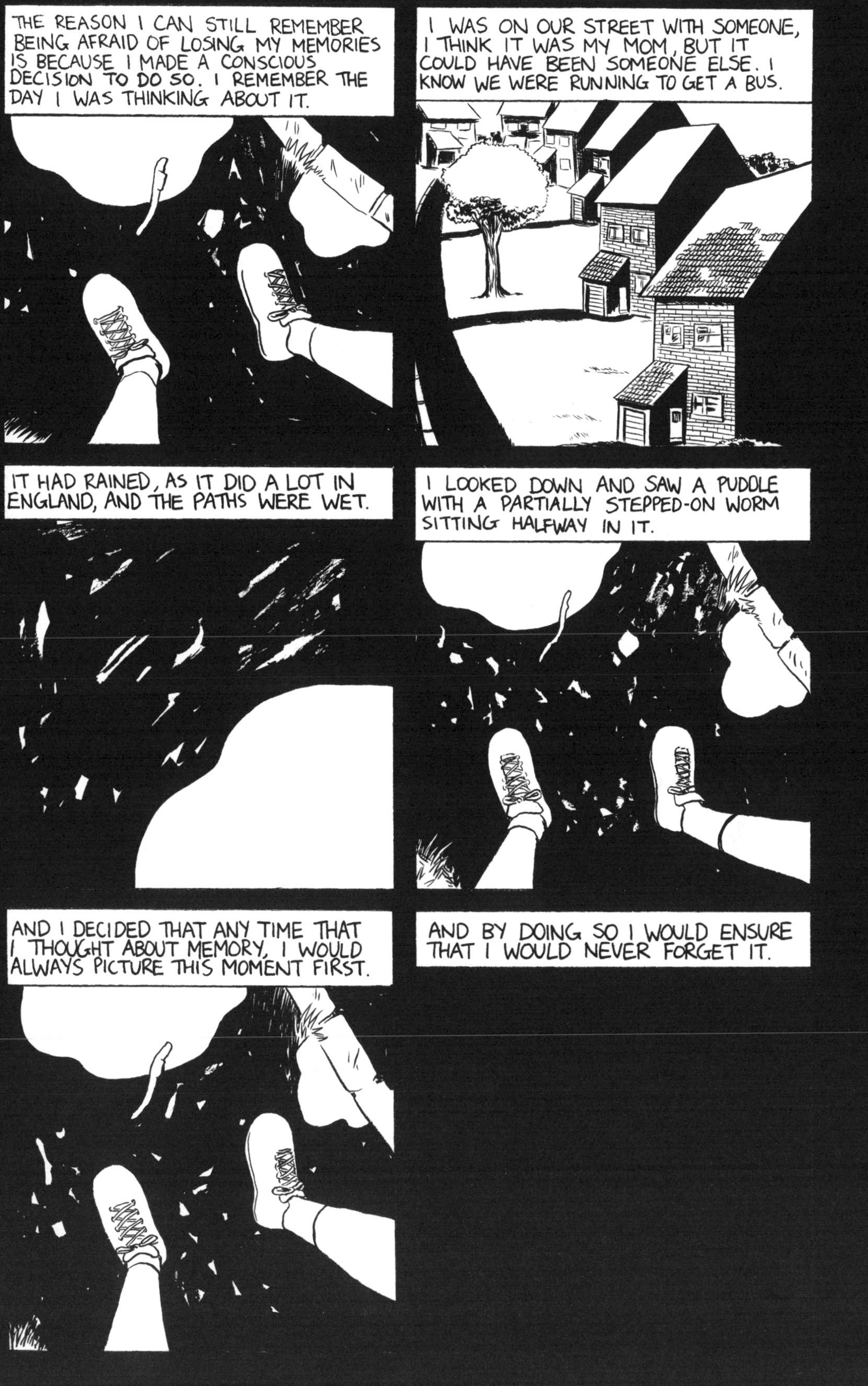

THE REASON I CAN STILL REMEMBER BEING AFRAID OF LOSING MY MEMORIES IS BECAUSE I MADE A CONSCIOUS DECISION TO DO SO. I REMEMBER THE DAY I WAS THINKING ABOUT IT.
I WAS ON OUR STREET WITH SOMEONE, I THINK IT WAS MY MOM, BUT IT COULD HAVE BEEN SOMEONE ELSE. I KNOW WE WERE RUNNING TO GET A BUS.
IT HAD RAINED, AS IT DID A LOT IN ENGLAND, AND THE PATHS WERE WET.
I LOOKED DOWN AND SAW A PUDDLE WITH A PARTIALLY STEPPED-ON WORM SITTING HALFWAY IN IT.
AND I DECIDED THAT ANY TIME THAT I THOUGHT ABOUT MEMORY, I WOULD ALWAYS PICTURE THIS MOMENT FIRST.
AND BY DOING SO I WOULD ENSURE THAT I WOULD NEVER FORGET IT.

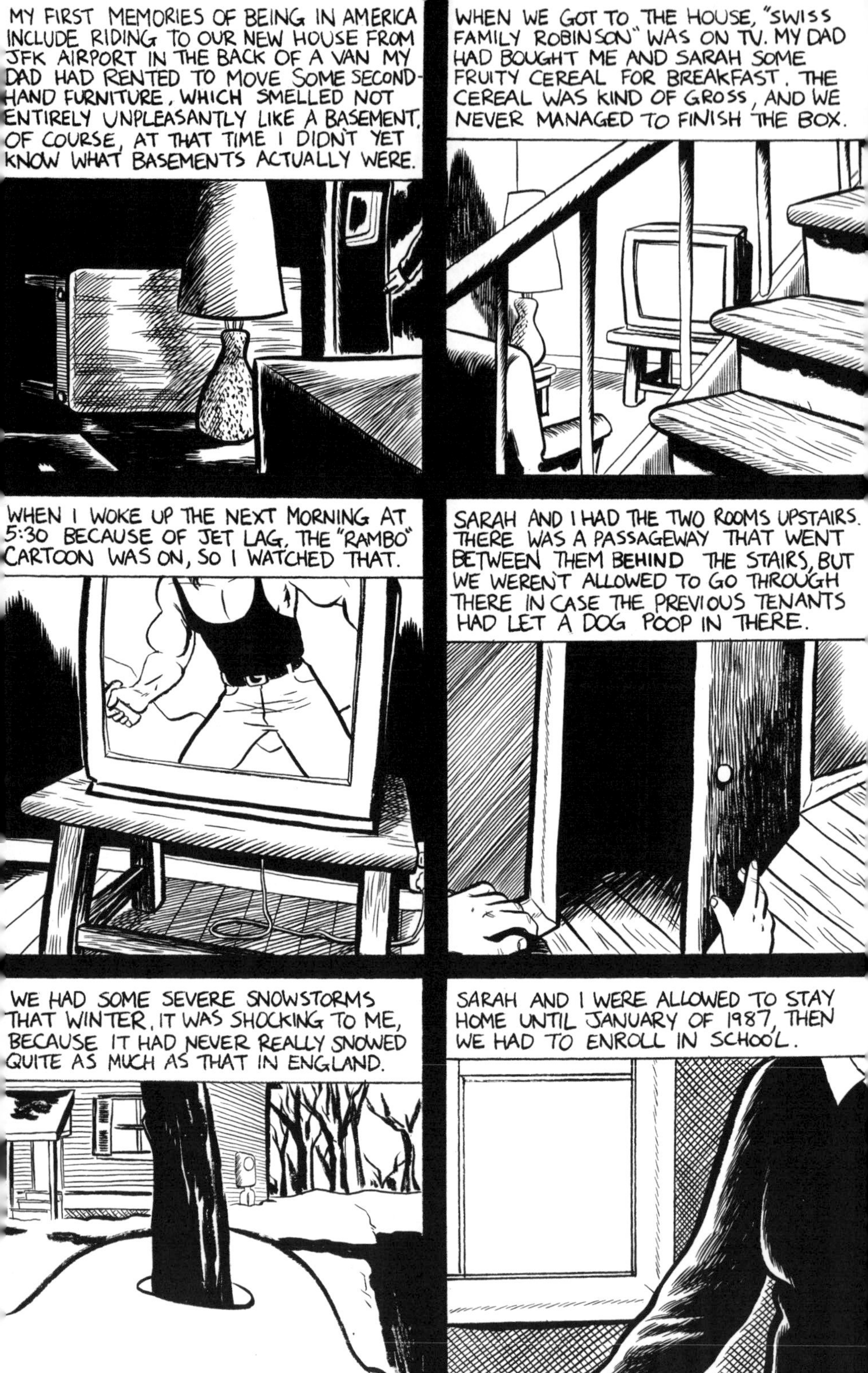
MY FIRST MEMORIES OF BEING IN AMERICA INCLUDE RIDING TO OUR NEW HOUSE FROM JFK AIRPORT IN THE BACK OF A VAN MY DAD HAD RENTED TO MOVE SOME SECOND-HAND FURNITURE, WHICH SMELLED NOT ENTIRELY UNPLEASANTLY LIKE A BASEMENT. OF COURSE, AT THAT TIME I DIDN'T YET KNOW WHAT BASEMENTS ACTUALLY WERE.
WHEN WE GOT TO THE HOUSE, "SWISS FAMILY ROBINSON" WAS ON TV. MY DAD HAD BOUGHT ME AND SARAH SOME FRUITY CEREAL FOR BREAKFAST. THE CEREAL WAS KIND OF GROSS, AND WE NEVER MANAGED TO FINISH THE BOX.
WHEN I WOKE UP THE NEXT MORNING AT 5:30 BECAUSE OF JET LAG, THE "RAMBO" CARTOON WAS ON, SO I WATCHED THAT.
SARAH AND I HAD THE TWO ROOMS UPSTAIRS. THERE WAS A PASSAGEWAY THAT WENT BETWEEN THEM BEHIND THE STAIRS, BUT WE WEREN'T ALLOWED TO GO THROUGH THERE IN CASE THE PREVIOUS TENANTS HAD LET A DOG POOP IN THERE.
WE HAD SOME SEVERE SNOWSTORMS THAT WINTER. IT WAS SHOCKING TO ME, BECAUSE IT HAD NEVER REALLY SNOWED QUITE AS MUCH AS THAT IN ENGLAND.
SARAH AND I WERE ALLOWED TO STAY HOME UNTIL JANUARY OF 1987, THEN WE HAD TO ENROLL IN SCHOOL.

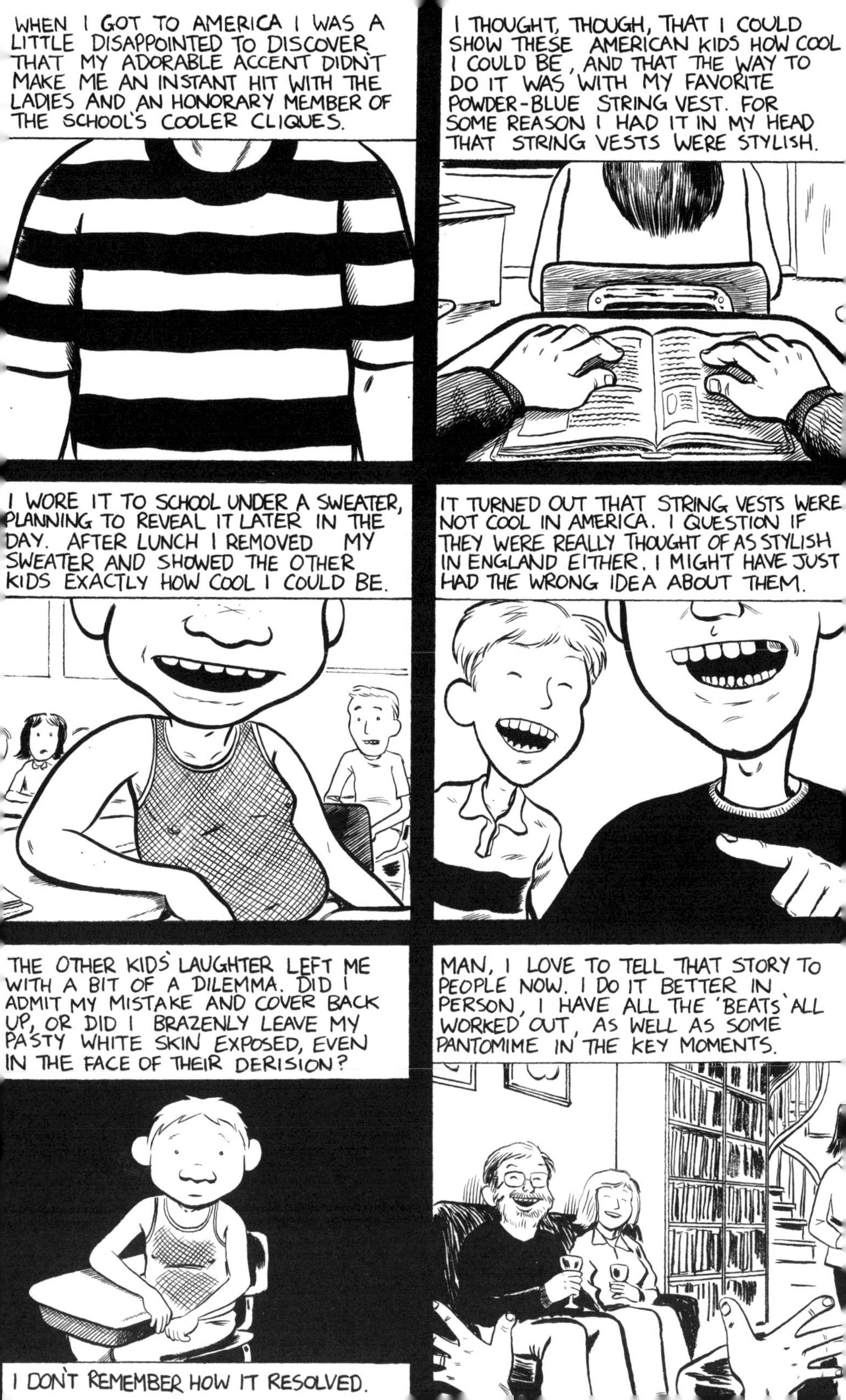
WHEN I GOT TO AMERICA I WAS A LITTLE DISAPPOINTED TO DISCOVER THAT MY ADORABLE ACCENT DIDN'T MAKE ME AN INSTANT HIT WITH THE LADIES AND AN HONORARY MEMBER OF THE SCHOOL'S COOLER CLIQUES.
I THOUGHT, THOUGH, THAT I COULD SHOW THESE AMERICAN KIDS HOW COOL I COULD BE, AND THAT THE WAY TO DO IT WAS WITH MY FAVORITE POWDER-BLUE STRING VEST. FOR SOME REASON I HAD IT IN MY HEAD THAT STRING VESTS WERE STYLISH.
I WORE IT TO SCHOOL UNDER A SWEATER, PLANNING TO REVEAL IT LATER IN THE DAY. AFTER LUNCH I REMOVED MY SWEATER AND SHOWED THE OTHER KIDS EXACTLY HOW COOL I COULD BE.
IT TURNED OUT THAT STRING VESTS WERE NOT COOL IN AMERICA. I QUESTION IF THEY WERE REALLY THOUGHT OF AS STYLISH IN ENGLAND EITHER. I MIGHT HAVE JUST HAD THE WRONG IDEA ABOUT THEM.
THE OTHER KIDS' LAUGHTER LEFT ME WITH A BIT OF A DILEMMA. DID I ADMIT MY MISTAKE AND COVER BACK UP, OR DID I BRAZENLY LEAVE MY PASTY WHITE SKIN EXPOSED, EVEN IN THE FACE OF THEIR DERISION?
I DON'T REMEMBER HOW IT RESOLVED.
MAN, I LOVE TO TELL THAT STORY TO PEOPLE NOW. I DO IT BETTER IN PERSON, I HAVE ALL THE 'BEATS' ALL WORKED OUT, AS WELL AS SOME PANTOMIME IN THE KEY MOMENTS.

I WAS LISTENING TO TALK RADIO THE OTHER DAY WHILE I DREW. THE SHOW WAS ABOUT DIFFERENT PEOPLE'S THEORIES ABOUT WHAT IS A HUMAN SELF, OR WHAT IS IT THAT MAKES ME, ME?

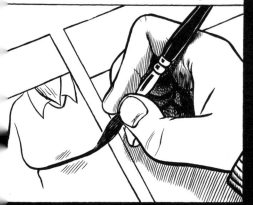

ONE OF THE COMMENTATORS, HIS NAME WAS DAVID BROCK, CONFESSED HIS OWN DISBELIEF IN THE NOTION OF THE SELF AS A SOUL. WHEN ASKED, "THEN WHAT IS IT THAT MAKES YOU, YOU?", HE REPLIED, "THAT I TELL YOU A STORY."

HE WAS SAYING THAT THE THING THAT MAKES US BE US IS THE ONGOING NARRATIVE OF OUR LIFE THAT WE TELL TO OURSELVES. IT MADE ME THINK OF THE MOVIE "FIGHT CLUB," IN WHICH BRAD PITT'S CHARACTER INSISTS THAT "WE'RE NOT OUR JOBS, WE'RE NOT OUR CARS, WE'RE NOT OUR @#☆!! KHAKIS!"

I'VE ALWAYS HAD TO DISAGREE WITH BRAD, BECAUSE, WHILE NOBODY WANTS TO BE THEIR JOBS, THERE'S A LOT OF TRUTH IN THE FACT THAT WE ARE THE SUM OF ALL THE THINGS THAT HAVE HAPPENED TO US. IN SOME RESPECTS WE ARE WHAT WE DO.

EVERYTHING THAT'S HAPPENED TO US MAKES US WHO WE ARE. IF DIFFERENT THINGS HAD HAPPENED WE'D BE SOMEONE ELSE. WE'D HAVE DIFFERENT MEMORIES. DIFFERENT STORIES.

TRYING TO DRAW MEMORIES IS TRICKY, THEY'RE LIKE SOMETHING YOU CAN ONLY SEE IN YOUR PERIPHERAL VISION — THEY SEEM CONCRETE UNTIL YOU TRY TO LOOK DIRECTLY AT THEM IN ORDER TO RECREATE THE PICTURE IN YOUR MIND.

THEN THEY GET ALL FUZZY AND CRUMBLE.

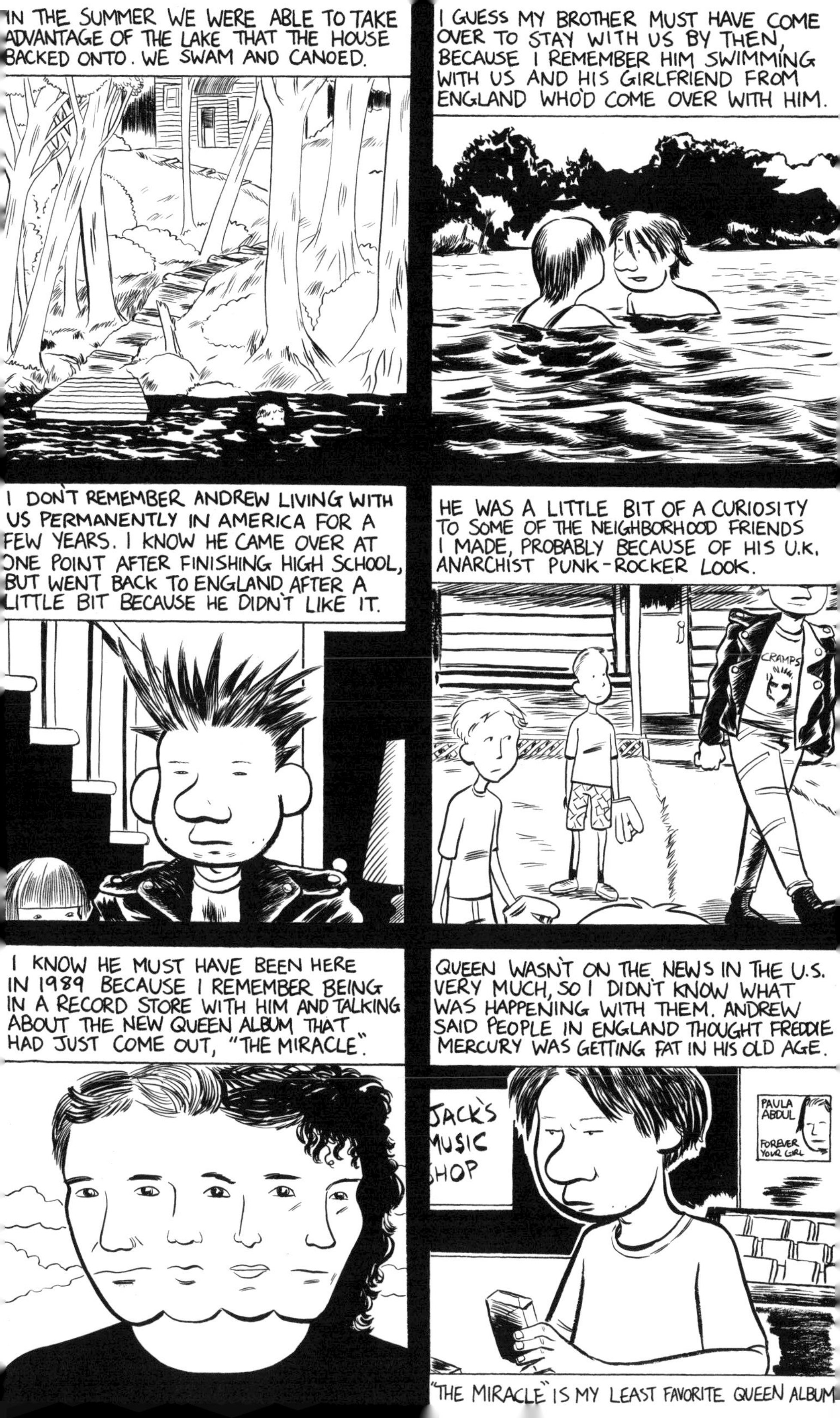
IN THE SUMMER WE WERE ABLE TO TAKE ADVANTAGE OF THE LAKE THAT THE HOUSE BACKED ONTO. WE SWAM AND CANOED.
I GUESS MY BROTHER MUST HAVE COME OVER TO STAY WITH US BY THEN, BECAUSE I REMEMBER HIM SWIMMING WITH US AND HIS GIRLFRIEND FROM ENGLAND WHO'D COME OVER WITH HIM.
I DON'T REMEMBER ANDREW LIVING WITH US PERMANENTLY IN AMERICA FOR A FEW YEARS. I KNOW HE CAME OVER AT ONE POINT AFTER FINISHING HIGH SCHOOL, BUT WENT BACK TO ENGLAND AFTER A LITTLE BIT BECAUSE HE DIDN'T LIKE IT.
HE WAS A LITTLE BIT OF A CURIOSITY TO SOME OF THE NEIGHBORHOOD FRIENDS I MADE, PROBABLY BECAUSE OF HIS U.K. ANARCHIST PUNK-ROCKER LOOK.
CRAMPS
I KNOW HE MUST HAVE BEEN HERE IN 1989 BECAUSE I REMEMBER BEING IN A RECORD STORE WITH HIM AND TALKING ABOUT THE NEW QUEEN ALBUM THAT HAD JUST COME OUT, "THE MIRACLE".
QUEEN WASN'T ON THE NEWS IN THE U.S. VERY MUCH, SO I DIDN'T KNOW WHAT WAS HAPPENING WITH THEM. ANDREW SAID PEOPLE IN ENGLAND THOUGHT FREDDIE MERCURY WAS GETTING FAT IN HIS OLD AGE.
JACK'S
MUSIC
HOP
PAULA ABDUL
FOREVER YOUR GIRL
"THE MIRACLE" IS MY LEAST FAVORITE QUEEN ALBUM

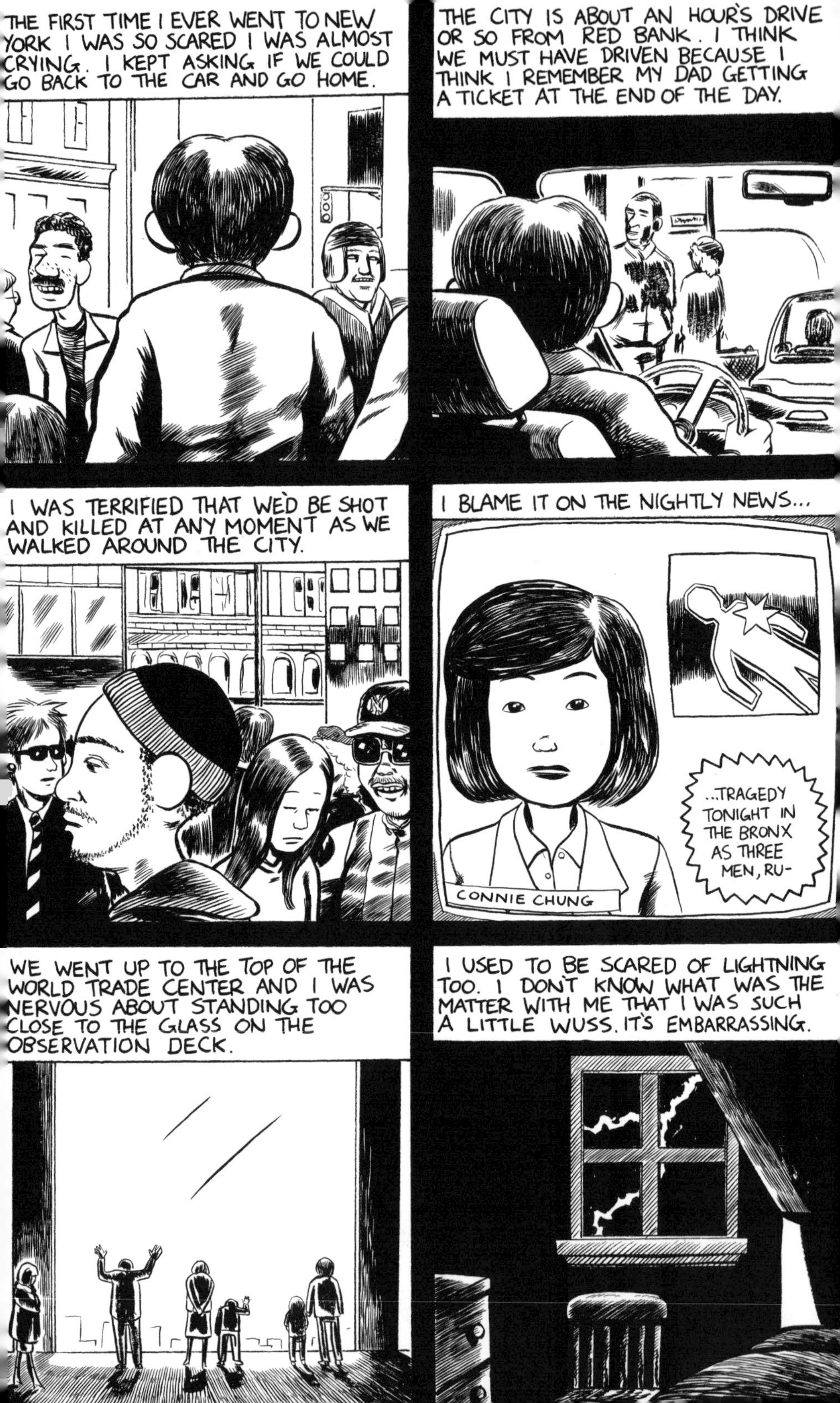
THE FIRST TIME I EVER WENT TO NEW YORK I WAS SO SCARED I WAS ALMOST CRYING. I KEPT ASKING IF WE COULD GO BACK TO THE CAR AND GO HOME.
THE CITY IS ABOUT AN HOUR'S DRIVE OR SO FROM RED BANK. I THINK WE MUST HAVE DRIVEN BECAUSE I THINK I REMEMBER MY DAD GETTING A TICKET AT THE END OF THE DAY.
I WAS TERRIFIED THAT WE'D BE SHOT AND KILLED AT ANY MOMENT AS WE WALKED AROUND THE CITY.
I BLAME IT ON THE NIGHTLY NEWS...
...TRAGEDY TONIGHT IN THE BRONX AS THREE MEN, RU-
CONNIE CHUNG
WE WENT UP TO THE TOP OF THE WORLD TRADE CENTER AND I WAS NERVOUS ABOUT STANDING TOO CLOSE TO THE GLASS ON THE OBSERVATION DECK.
I USED TO BE SCARED OF LIGHTNING TOO. I DON'T KNOW WHAT WAS THE MATTER WITH ME THAT I WAS SUCH A LITTLE WUSS. IT'S EMBARRASSING.

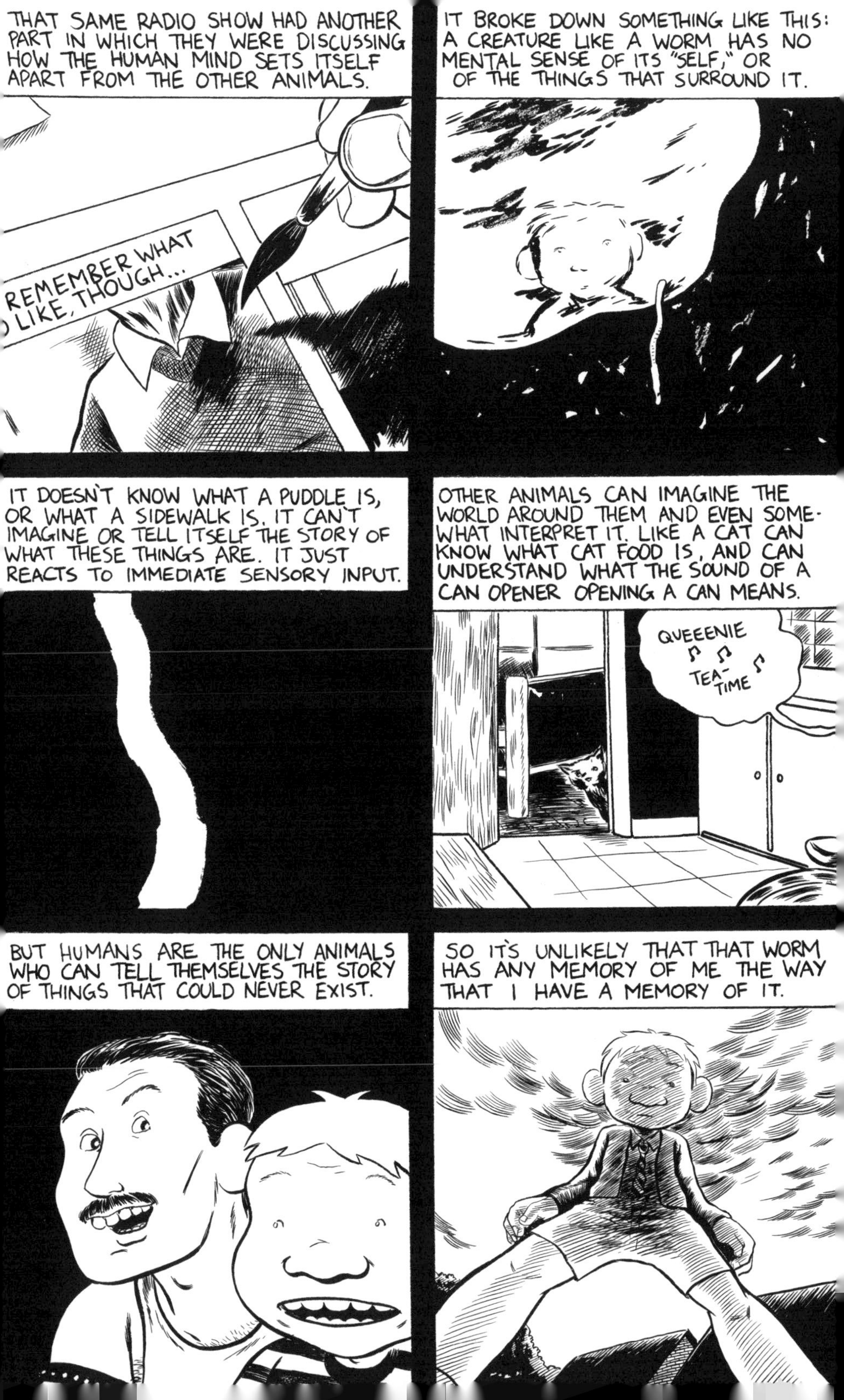
THAT SAME RADIO SHOW HAD ANOTHER PART IN WHICH THEY WERE DISCUSSING HOW THE HUMAN MIND SETS ITSELF APART FROM THE OTHER ANIMALS.
REMEMBER WHAT
LIKE, THOUGH...
IT BROKE DOWN SOMETHING LIKE THIS: A CREATURE LIKE A WORM HAS NO MENTAL SENSE OF ITS "SELF," OR OF THE THINGS THAT SURROUND IT.
IT DOESN'T KNOW WHAT A PUDDLE IS, OR WHAT A SIDEWALK IS. IT CAN'T IMAGINE OR TELL ITSELF THE STORY OF WHAT THESE THINGS ARE. IT JUST REACTS TO IMMEDIATE SENSORY INPUT.
OTHER ANIMALS CAN IMAGINE THE WORLD AROUND THEM AND EVEN SOME-WHAT INTERPRET IT. LIKE A CAT CAN KNOW WHAT CAT FOOD IS, AND CAN UNDERSTAND WHAT THE SOUND OF A CAN OPENER OPENING A CAN MEANS.
QUEEENIE ♪ ♫ TEA-TIME ♪
BUT HUMANS ARE THE ONLY ANIMALS WHO CAN TELL THEMSELVES THE STORY OF THINGS THAT COULD NEVER EXIST.
SO IT'S UNLIKELY THAT THAT WORM HAS ANY MEMORY OF ME THE WAY THAT I HAVE A MEMORY OF IT.

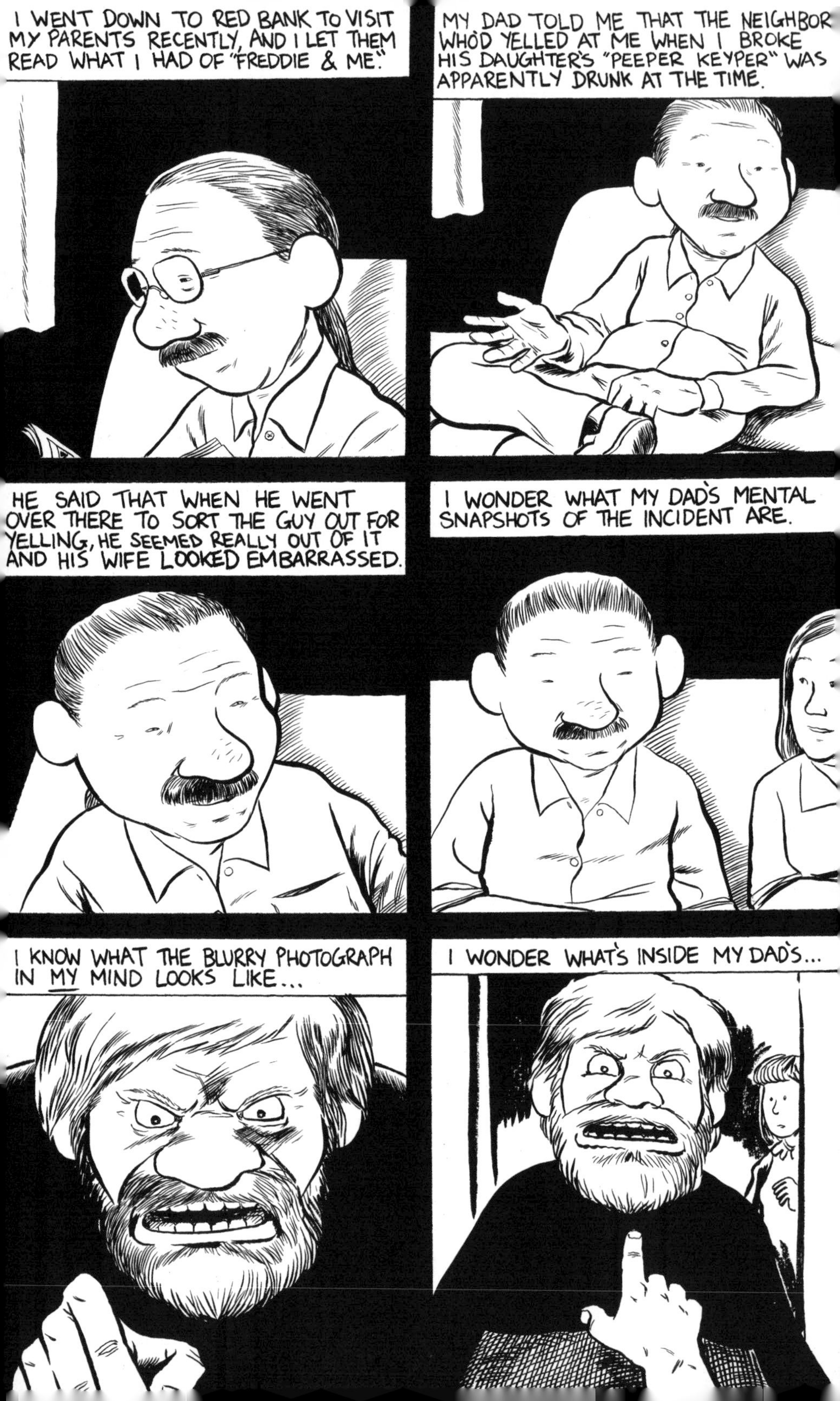
I WENT DOWN TO RED BANK TO VISIT MY PARENTS RECENTLY, AND I LET THEM READ WHAT I HAD OF "FREDDIE & ME."
MY DAD TOLD ME THAT THE NEIGHBOR WHO'D YELLED AT ME WHEN I BROKE HIS DAUGHTER'S "PEEPER KEYPER" WAS APPARENTLY DRUNK AT THE TIME.
HE SAID THAT WHEN HE WENT OVER THERE TO SORT THE GUY OUT FOR YELLING, HE SEEMED REALLY OUT OF IT AND HIS WIFE LOOKED EMBARRASSED.
I WONDER WHAT MY DAD'S MENTAL SNAPSHOTS OF THE INCIDENT ARE.
I KNOW WHAT THE BLURRY PHOTOGRAPH IN MY MIND LOOKS LIKE...
I WONDER WHAT'S INSIDE MY DAD'S...

WHAT'S THE MEMORY THAT THE FOURTH-GRADE TEACHER HAS OF ME COMING INTO HER CLASS FOR A DAY?

DOES MY MOTHER HAVE A SNAPSHOT IN HER MIND OF ME RUNNING DOWNSTAIRS TO SEE QUEEN ON THE TELLY?

THUMP
THUMP
THUMP

DOES THAT BULLY REMEMBER THIS?

ANDREW?

THE AUDIENCE?

DAD?

The Opera

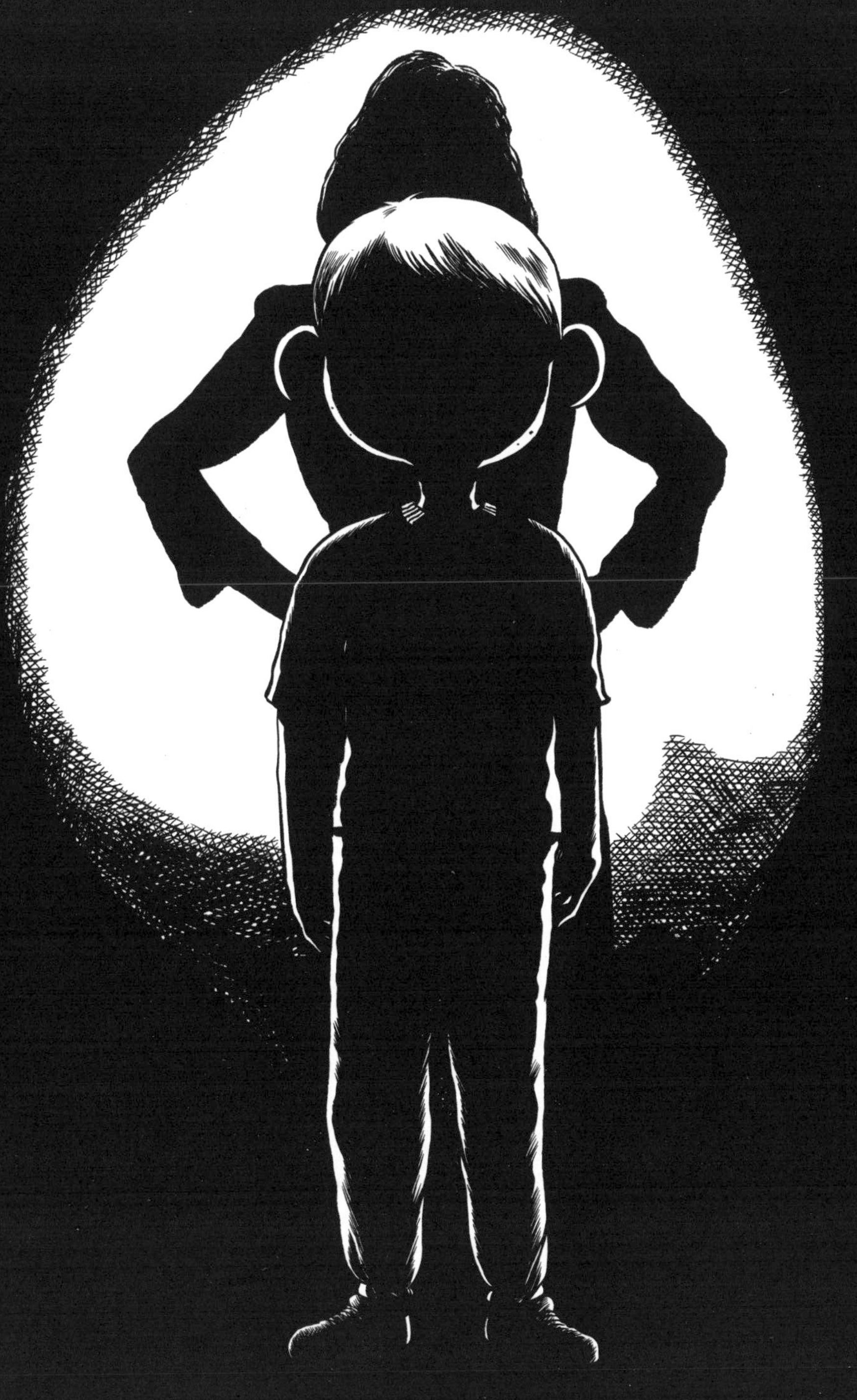

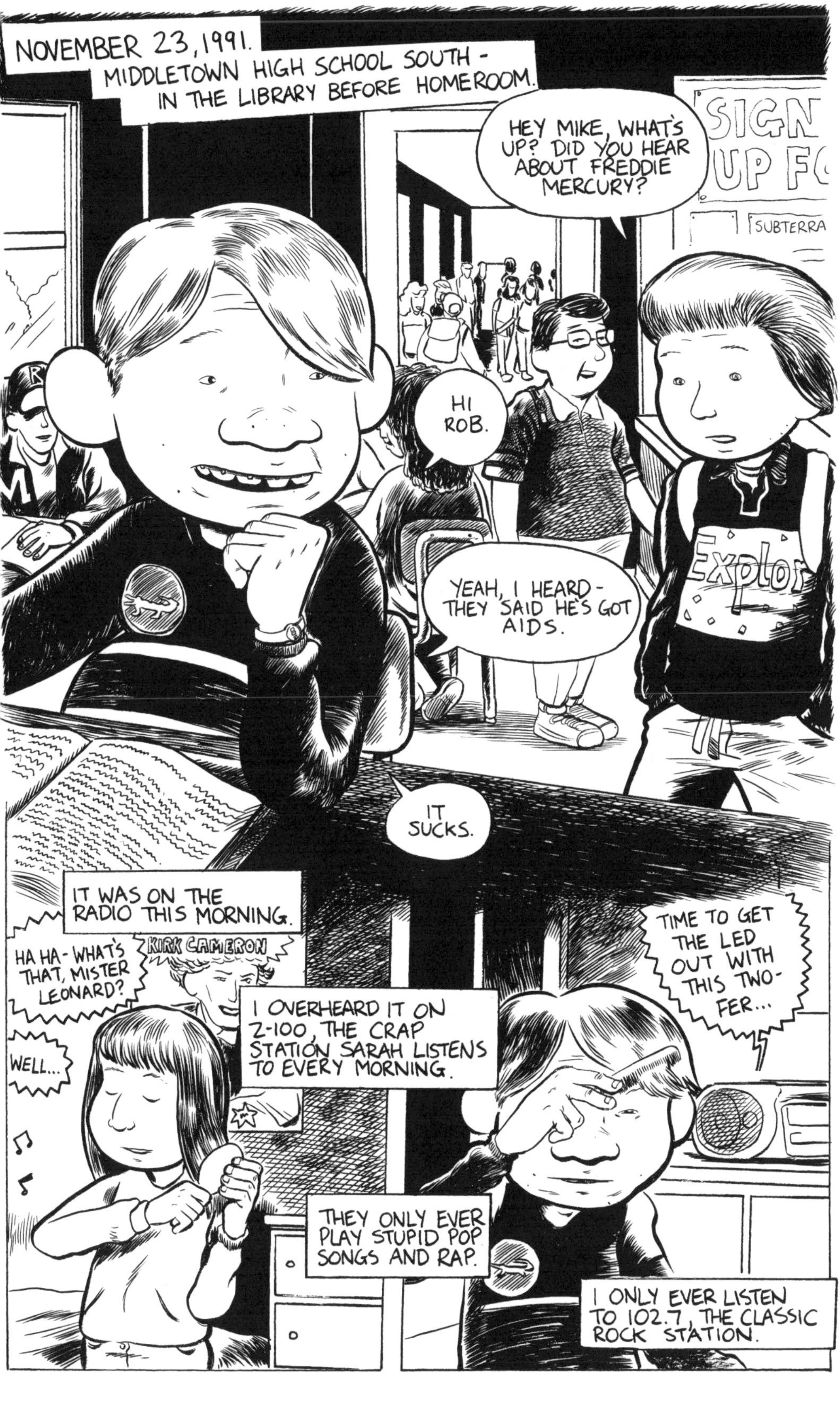
NOVEMBER 23, 1991.
MIDDLETOWN HIGH SCHOOL SOUTH - IN THE LIBRARY BEFORE HOMEROOM.
SIGN UP FO
SUBTERRA
HEY MIKE, WHAT'S UP? DID YOU HEAR ABOUT FREDDIE MERCURY?
HI ROB.
YEAH, I HEARD - THEY SAID HE'S GOT AIDS.
Explor
IT SUCKS.
IT WAS ON THE RADIO THIS MORNING.
HA HA - WHAT'S THAT, MISTER LEONARD?
KIRK CAMERON
WELL...
I OVERHEARD IT ON Z-100, THE CRAP STATION SARAH LISTENS TO EVERY MORNING.
TIME TO GET THE LED OUT WITH THIS TWO-FER...
THEY ONLY EVER PLAY STUPID POP SONGS AND RAP.
I ONLY EVER LISTEN TO 102.7, THE CLASSIC ROCK STATION.

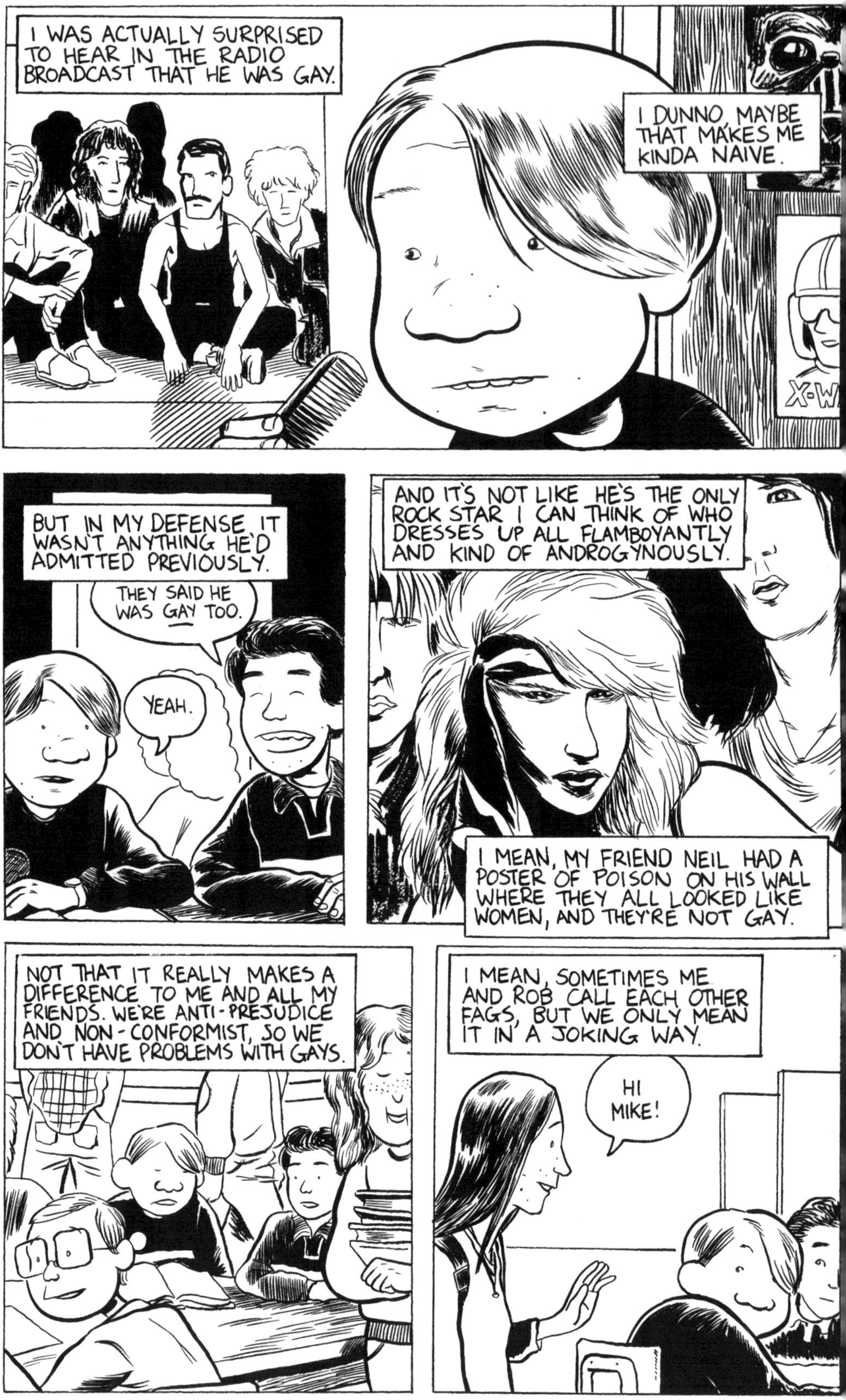
I WAS ACTUALLY SURPRISED TO HEAR IN THE RADIO BROADCAST THAT HE WAS GAY.
I DUNNO, MAYBE THAT MAKES ME KINDA NAIVE.
X-W
BUT IN MY DEFENSE IT WASN'T ANYTHING HE'D ADMITTED PREVIOUSLY.
THEY SAID HE WAS GAY TOO.
YEAH.
AND IT'S NOT LIKE HE'S THE ONLY ROCK STAR I CAN THINK OF WHO DRESSES UP ALL FLAMBOYANTLY AND KIND OF ANDROGYNOUSLY.
I MEAN, MY FRIEND NEIL HAD A POSTER OF POISON ON HIS WALL WHERE THEY ALL LOOKED LIKE WOMEN, AND THEY'RE NOT GAY.
NOT THAT IT REALLY MAKES A DIFFERENCE TO ME AND ALL MY FRIENDS. WE'RE ANTI-PREJUDICE AND NON-CONFORMIST, SO WE DON'T HAVE PROBLEMS WITH GAYS.
I MEAN, SOMETIMES ME AND ROB CALL EACH OTHER FAGS, BUT WE ONLY MEAN IT IN A JOKING WAY.
HI MIKE!

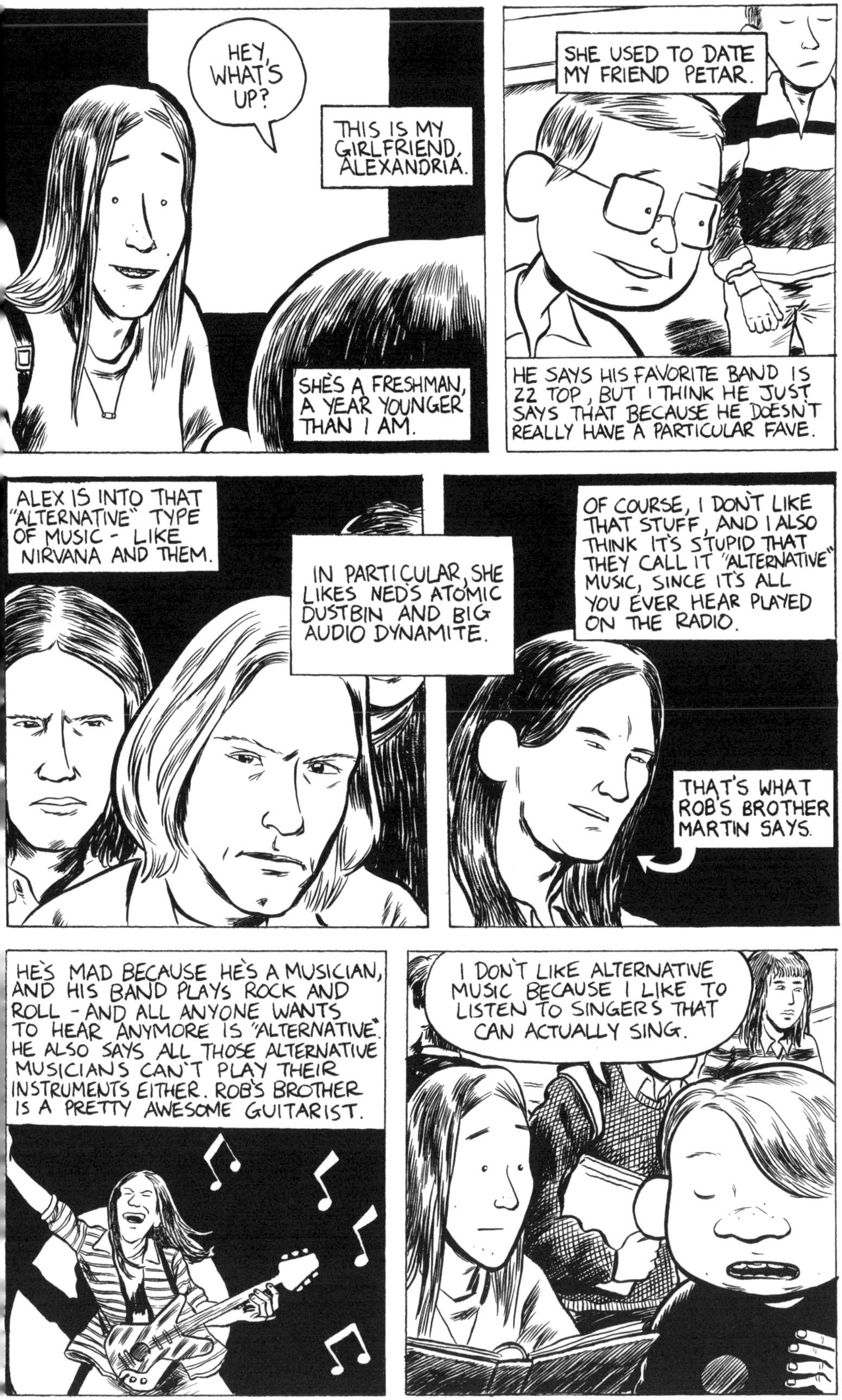
HEY, WHAT'S UP?
THIS IS MY GIRLFRIEND, ALEXANDRIA.
SHE'S A FRESHMAN, A YEAR YOUNGER THAN I AM.
SHE USED TO DATE MY FRIEND PETAR.
HE SAYS HIS FAVORITE BAND IS ZZ TOP, BUT I THINK HE JUST SAYS THAT BECAUSE HE DOESN'T REALLY HAVE A PARTICULAR FAVE.
ALEX IS INTO THAT "ALTERNATIVE" TYPE OF MUSIC - LIKE NIRVANA AND THEM.
IN PARTICULAR, SHE LIKES NED'S ATOMIC DUSTBIN AND BIG AUDIO DYNAMITE.
OF COURSE, I DON'T LIKE THAT STUFF, AND I ALSO THINK IT'S STUPID THAT THEY CALL IT "ALTERNATIVE" MUSIC, SINCE IT'S ALL YOU EVER HEAR PLAYED ON THE RADIO.
THAT'S WHAT ROB'S BROTHER MARTIN SAYS.
HE'S MAD BECAUSE HE'S A MUSICIAN, AND HIS BAND PLAYS ROCK AND ROLL - AND ALL ANYONE WANTS TO HEAR ANYMORE IS "ALTERNATIVE". HE ALSO SAYS ALL THOSE ALTERNATIVE MUSICIANS CAN'T PLAY THEIR INSTRUMENTS EITHER. ROB'S BROTHER IS A PRETTY AWESOME GUITARIST.
I DON'T LIKE ALTERNATIVE MUSIC BECAUSE I LIKE TO LISTEN TO SINGERS THAT CAN ACTUALLY SING.

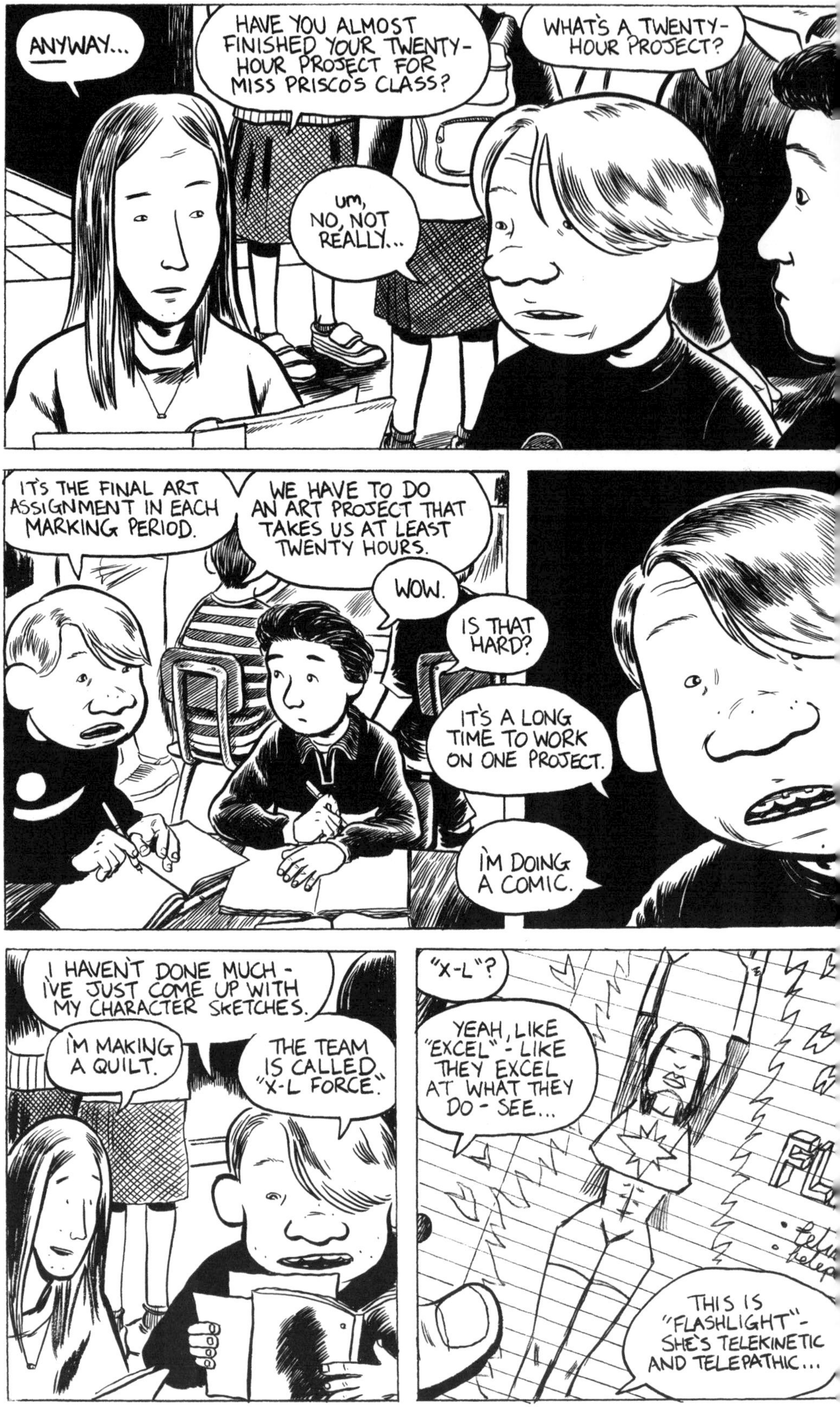
ANYWAY...
HAVE YOU ALMOST FINISHED YOUR TWENTY-HOUR PROJECT FOR MISS PRISCO'S CLASS?
UM, NO, NOT REALLY...
WHAT'S A TWENTY-HOUR PROJECT?
IT'S THE FINAL ART ASSIGNMENT IN EACH MARKING PERIOD.
WE HAVE TO DO AN ART PROJECT THAT TAKES US AT LEAST TWENTY HOURS.
WOW.
IS THAT HARD?
IT'S A LONG TIME TO WORK ON ONE PROJECT.
I'M DOING A COMIC.
I HAVEN'T DONE MUCH - I'VE JUST COME UP WITH MY CHARACTER SKETCHES.
I'M MAKING A QUILT.
THE TEAM IS CALLED "X-L FORCE."
"X-L"?
YEAH, LIKE "EXCEL" - LIKE THEY EXCEL AT WHAT THEY DO - SEE...
THIS IS "FLASHLIGHT" - SHE'S TELEKINETIC AND TELEPATHIC...

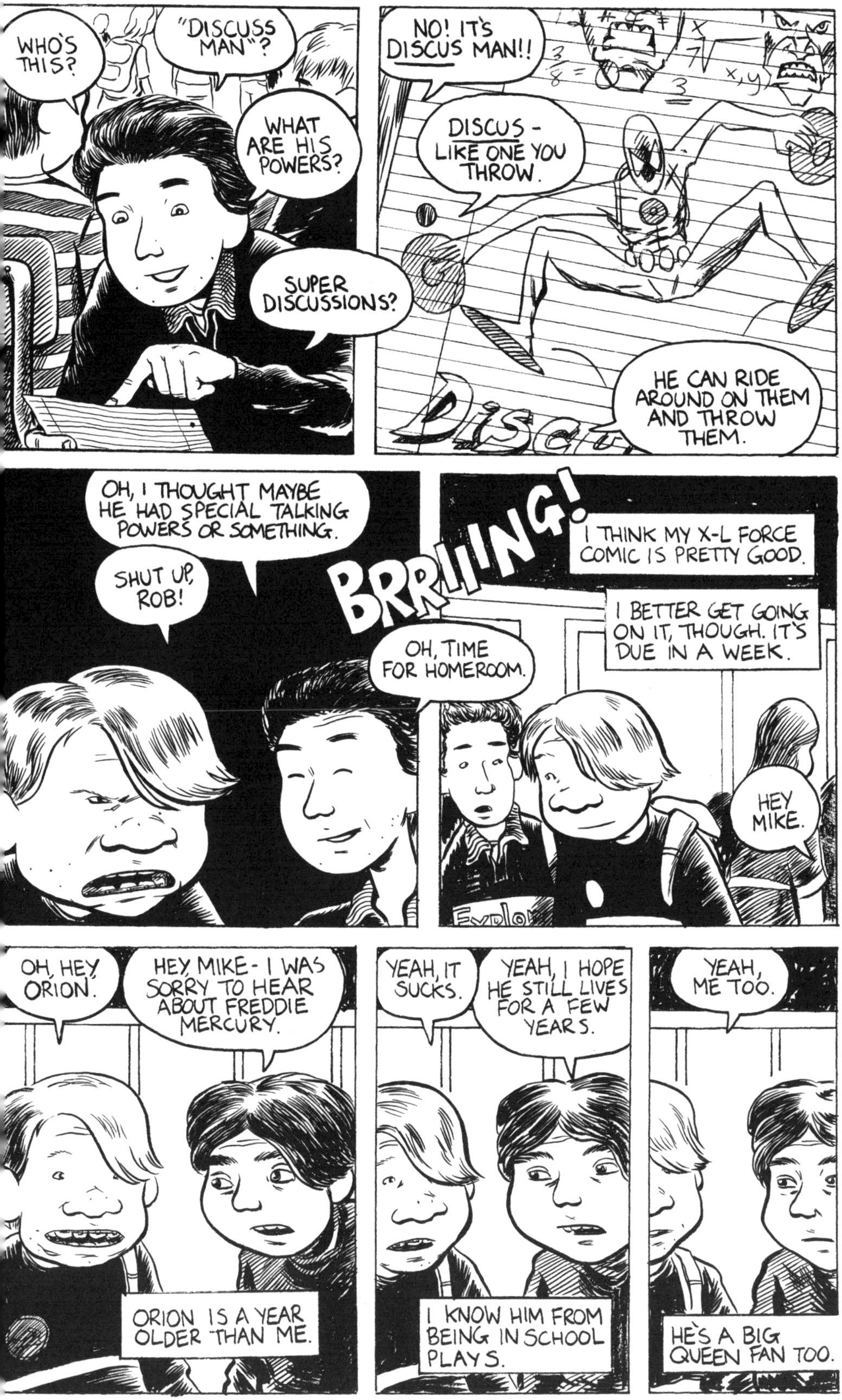
WHO'S THIS?
"DISCUSS MAN"?
WHAT ARE HIS POWERS?
SUPER DISCUSSIONS?
NO! IT'S DISCUS MAN!!
DISCUS - LIKE ONE YOU THROW.
HE CAN RIDE AROUND ON THEM AND THROW THEM.
OH, I THOUGHT MAYBE HE HAD SPECIAL TALKING POWERS OR SOMETHING.
SHUT UP, ROB!
OH, TIME FOR HOMEROOM.
BRRIIING!
I THINK MY X-L FORCE COMIC IS PRETTY GOOD.
I BETTER GET GOING ON IT, THOUGH. IT'S DUE IN A WEEK.
HEY MIKE.
OH, HEY ORION.
HEY, MIKE - I WAS SORRY TO HEAR ABOUT FREDDIE MERCURY.
ORION IS A YEAR OLDER THAN ME.
YEAH, IT SUCKS.
YEAH, I HOPE HE STILL LIVES FOR A FEW YEARS.
I KNOW HIM FROM BEING IN SCHOOL PLAYS.
YEAH, ME TOO.
HE'S A BIG QUEEN FAN TOO.

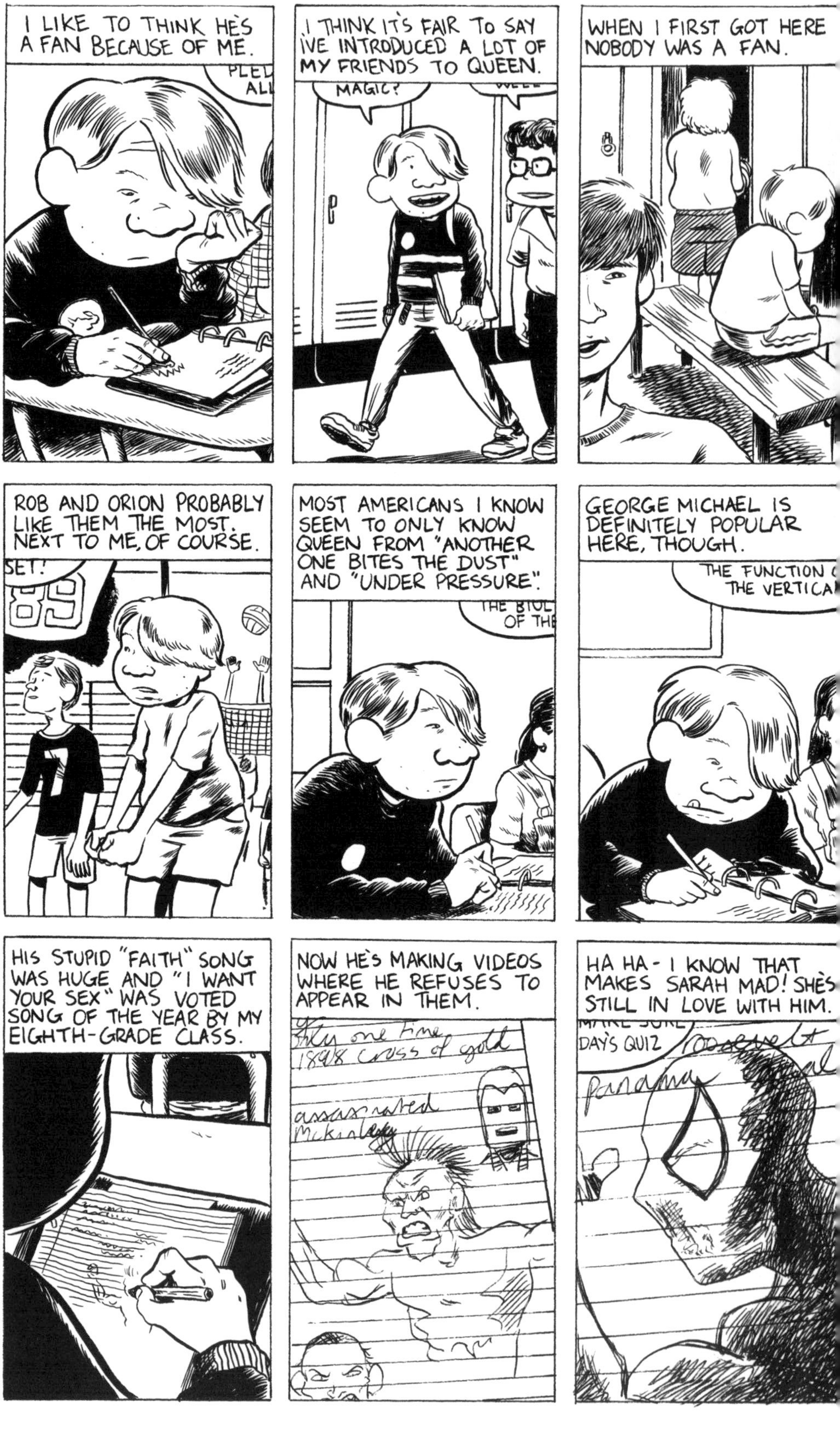
I LIKE TO THINK HE'S A FAN BECAUSE OF ME.
I THINK IT'S FAIR TO SAY I'VE INTRODUCED A LOT OF MY FRIENDS TO QUEEN.
MAGIC?
WHEN I FIRST GOT HERE NOBODY WAS A FAN.
ROB AND ORION PROBABLY LIKE THEM THE MOST. NEXT TO ME, OF COURSE.
SET!
MOST AMERICANS I KNOW SEEM TO ONLY KNOW QUEEN FROM "ANOTHER ONE BITES THE DUST" AND "UNDER PRESSURE".
GEORGE MICHAEL IS DEFINITELY POPULAR HERE, THOUGH.
THE FUNCTION
HIS STUPID "FAITH" SONG WAS HUGE AND "I WANT YOUR SEX" WAS VOTED SONG OF THE YEAR BY MY EIGHTH-GRADE CLASS.
NOW HE'S MAKING VIDEOS WHERE HE REFUSES TO APPEAR IN THEM.
1898 cross of gold
assassinated McKinley
HA HA - I KNOW THAT MAKES SARAH MAD! SHE'S STILL IN LOVE WITH HIM.
DAY'S QUIZ
panama

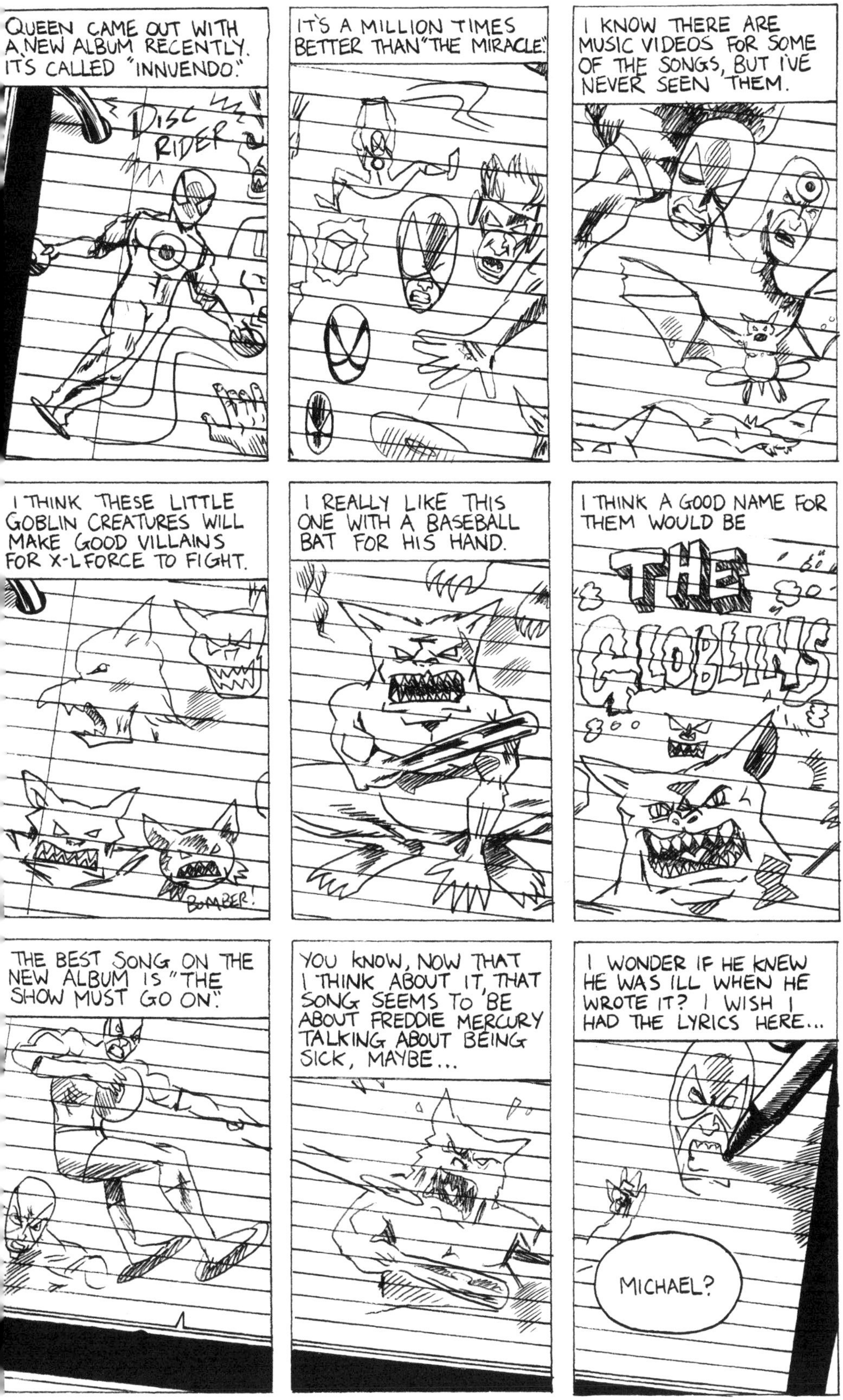
QUEEN CAME OUT WITH A NEW ALBUM RECENTLY. IT'S CALLED "INNUENDO."
DISC RIDER
IT'S A MILLION TIMES BETTER THAN "THE MIRACLE."
I KNOW THERE ARE MUSIC VIDEOS FOR SOME OF THE SONGS, BUT I'VE NEVER SEEN THEM.
I THINK THESE LITTLE GOBLIN CREATURES WILL MAKE GOOD VILLAINS FOR X-L FORCE TO FIGHT.
BOMBER!
I REALLY LIKE THIS ONE WITH A BASEBALL BAT FOR HIS HAND.
I THINK A GOOD NAME FOR THEM WOULD BE
THE GOBLINS
THE BEST SONG ON THE NEW ALBUM IS "THE SHOW MUST GO ON."
YOU KNOW, NOW THAT I THINK ABOUT IT, THAT SONG SEEMS TO BE ABOUT FREDDIE MERCURY TALKING ABOUT BEING SICK, MAYBE...
I WONDER IF HE KNEW HE WAS ILL WHEN HE WROTE IT? I WISH I HAD THE LYRICS HERE...
MICHAEL?

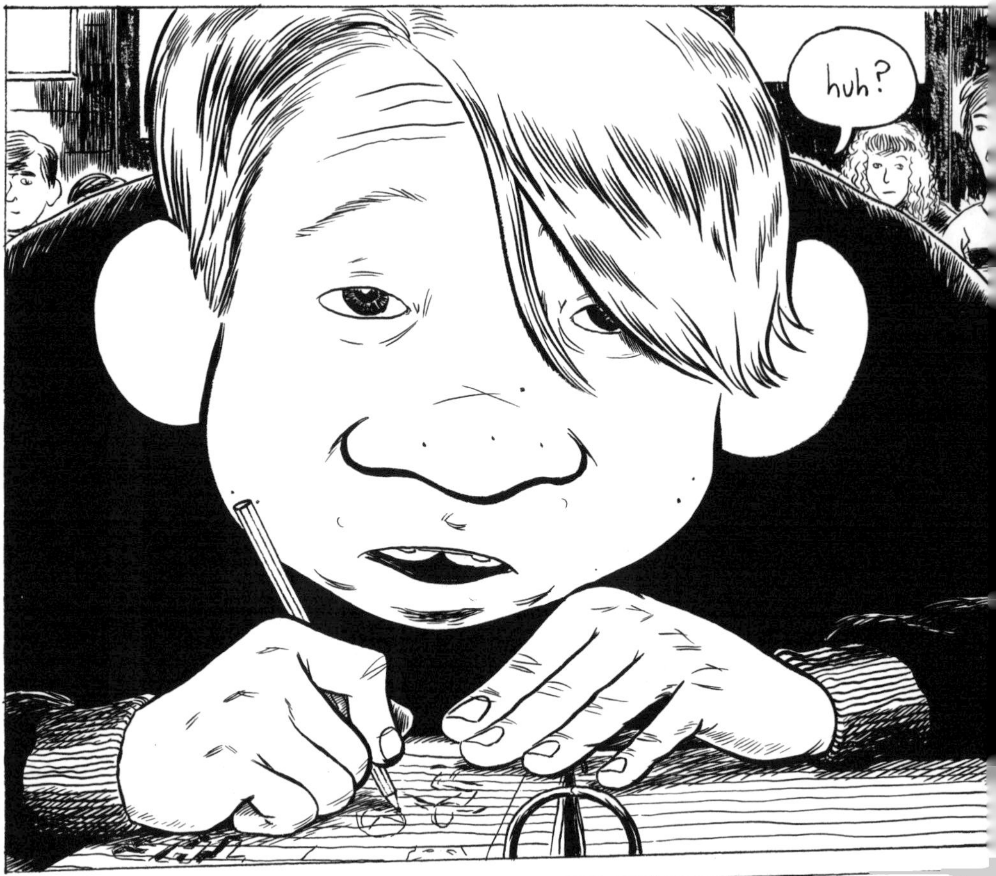
huh?

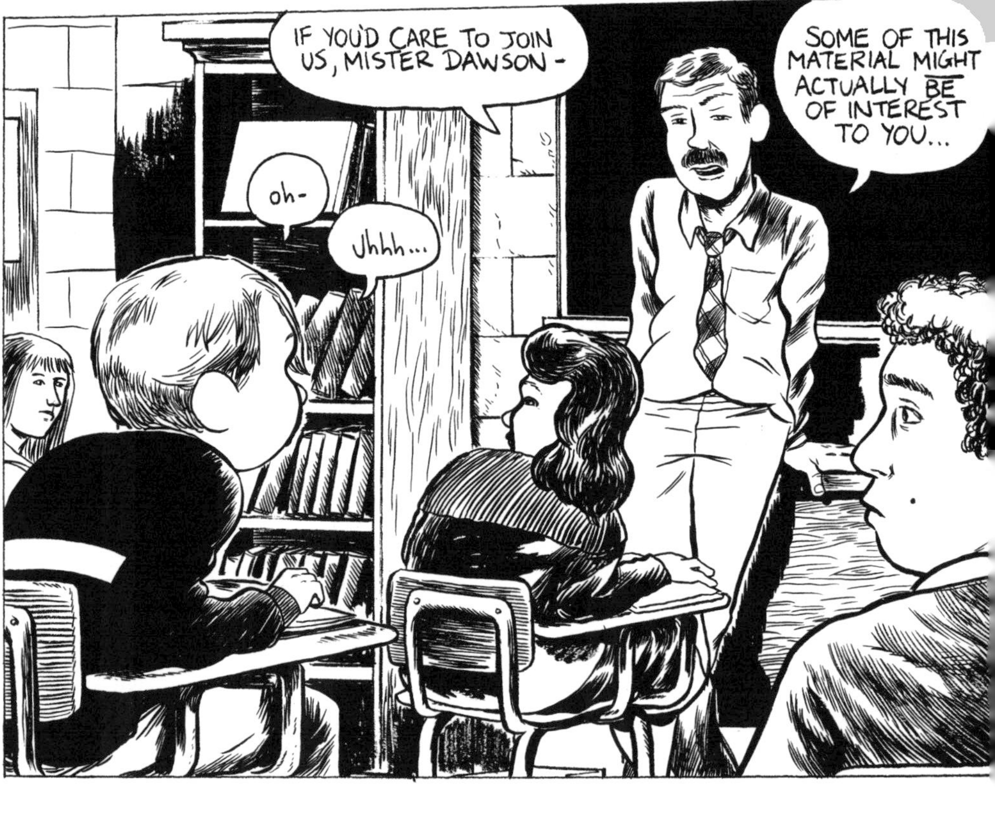
IF YOU'D CARE TO JOIN US, MISTER DAWSON -
oh-
Uhhh...
SOME OF THIS MATERIAL MIGHT ACTUALLY BE OF INTEREST TO YOU...

UM...

SO IT BECAME APPARENT TOWARDS THE END OF THE CENTURY THAT CITIES HAD REPLACED THE COUNTRY-SIDE AS POPULATION CENTERS. PEOPLE ARE JUST POURING IN THERE.

uh...

AND PART OF THIS IS THE "NEW IMMIGRATION."

I DON'T USUALLY GET YELLED AT BY TEACHERS.

it's uh...

HOW EMBARRASSING...

NOBODY SEEMS TO HAVE NOTICED...

TEACHERS DON'T USUALLY GET MAD AT ME FOR MY DRAWING.

UNLESS TO COMPLIMENT ME, THEY DON'T NOTICE.

OKAY, TIME TO PAY ATTENTION.

THEM WERE JEWISH AND IRISH AS WELL AS A

MAYBE MR. McKENZIE DOESN'T LIKE ME AS MUCH AS OTHER TEACHERS DO...

New Immigra

TEACHERS LIKE MISS PRISCO THINK I'M GREAT...

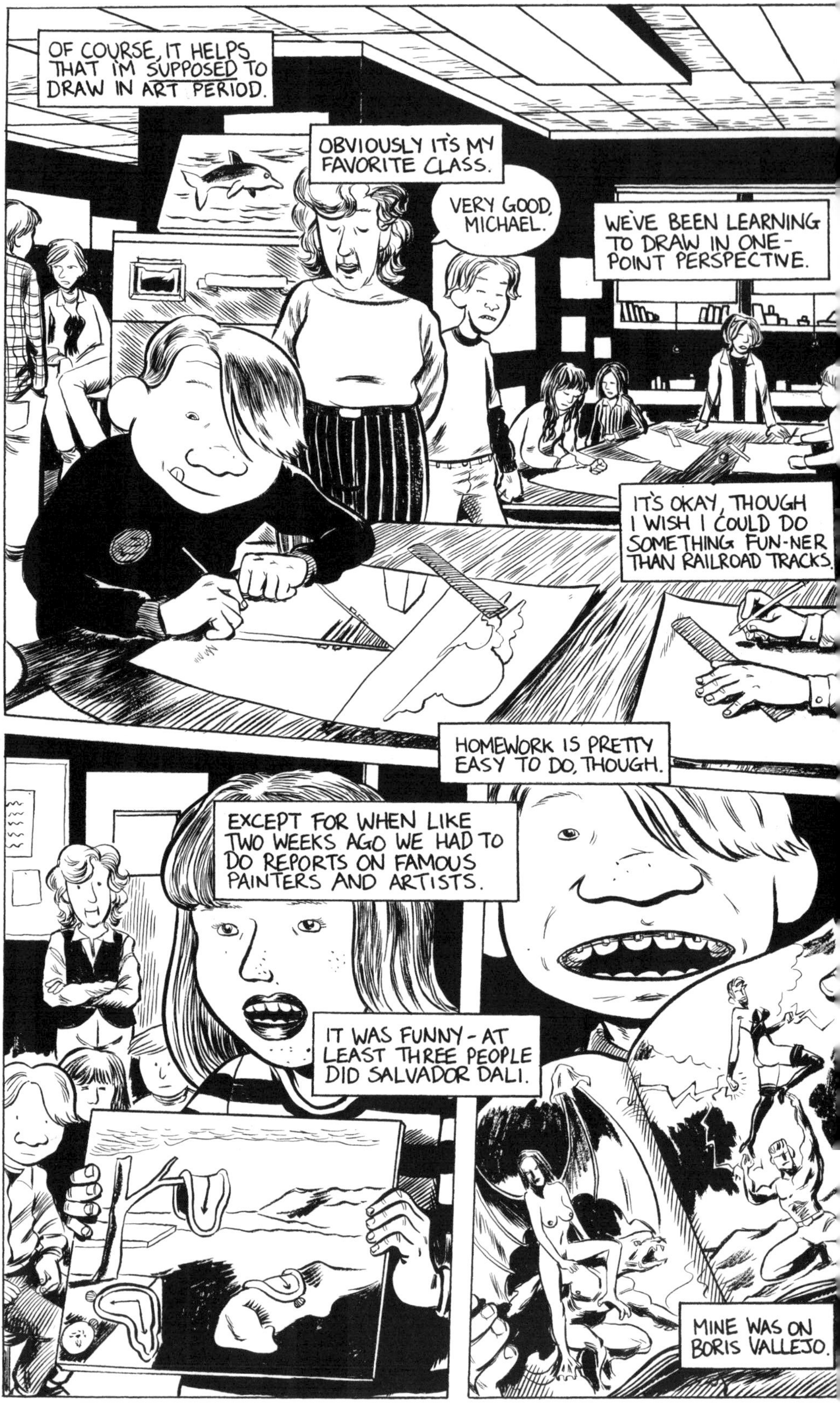
OF COURSE, IT HELPS THAT I'M SUPPOSED TO DRAW IN ART PERIOD.
OBVIOUSLY IT'S MY FAVORITE CLASS.
VERY GOOD, MICHAEL.
WE'VE BEEN LEARNING TO DRAW IN ONE-POINT PERSPECTIVE.
IT'S OKAY, THOUGH I WISH I COULD DO SOMETHING FUN-NER THAN RAILROAD TRACKS.
HOMEWORK IS PRETTY EASY TO DO, THOUGH.
EXCEPT FOR WHEN LIKE TWO WEEKS AGO WE HAD TO DO REPORTS ON FAMOUS PAINTERS AND ARTISTS.
IT WAS FUNNY - AT LEAST THREE PEOPLE DID SALVADOR DALI.
MINE WAS ON BORIS VALLEJO.

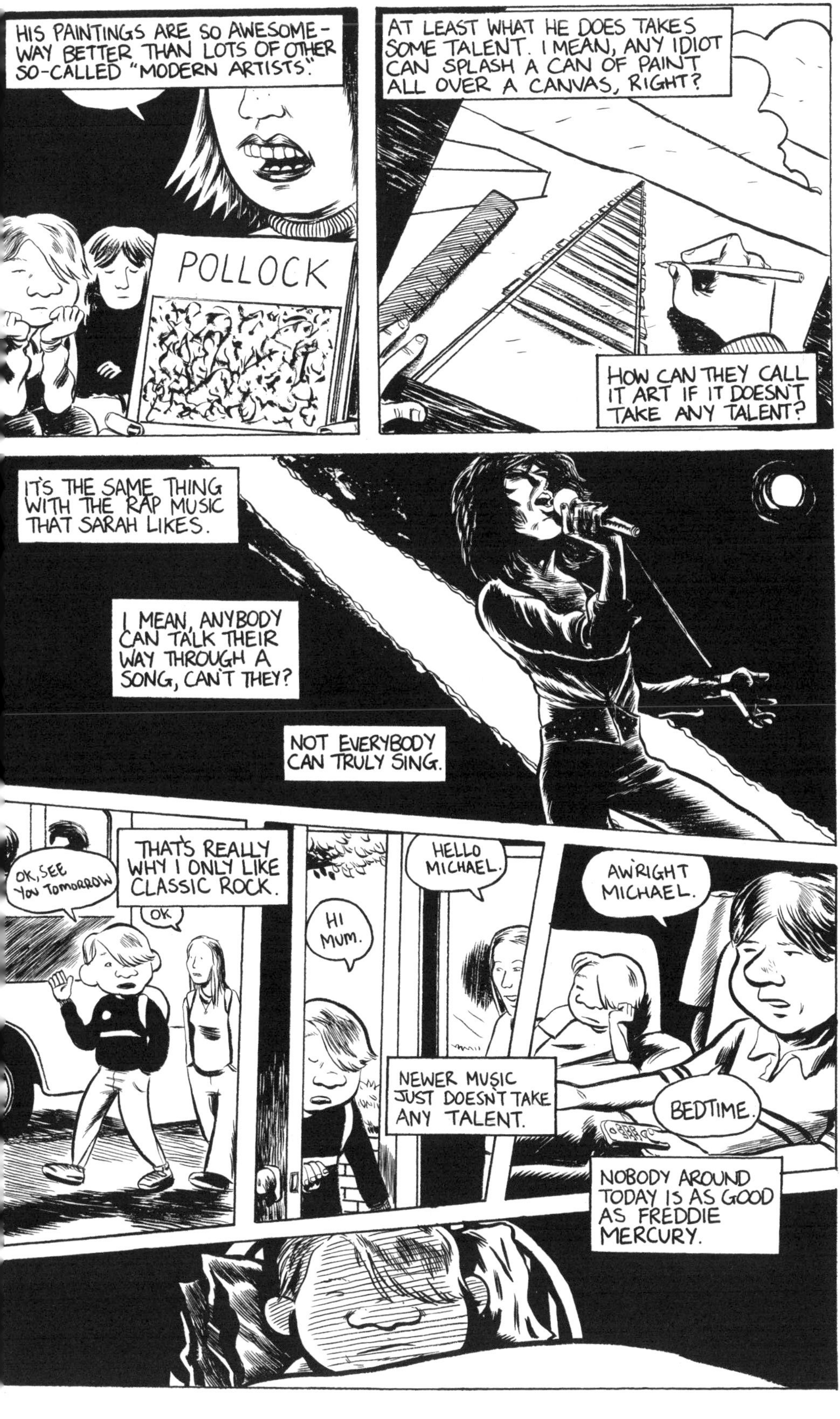

HIS PAINTINGS ARE SO AWESOME - WAY BETTER THAN LOTS OF OTHER SO-CALLED "MODERN ARTISTS".
POLLOCK
AT LEAST WHAT HE DOES TAKES SOME TALENT. I MEAN, ANY IDIOT CAN SPLASH A CAN OF PAINT ALL OVER A CANVAS, RIGHT?
HOW CAN THEY CALL IT ART IF IT DOESN'T TAKE ANY TALENT?
IT'S THE SAME THING WITH THE RAP MUSIC THAT SARAH LIKES.
I MEAN, ANYBODY CAN TALK THEIR WAY THROUGH A SONG, CAN'T THEY?
NOT EVERYBODY CAN TRULY SING.
OK, SEE YOU TOMORROW
THAT'S REALLY WHY I ONLY LIKE CLASSIC ROCK.
OK
HI MUM.
HELLO MICHAEL.
AWRIGHT MICHAEL.
NEWER MUSIC JUST DOESN'T TAKE ANY TALENT.
BEDTIME.
NOBODY AROUND TODAY IS AS GOOD AS FREDDIE MERCURY.

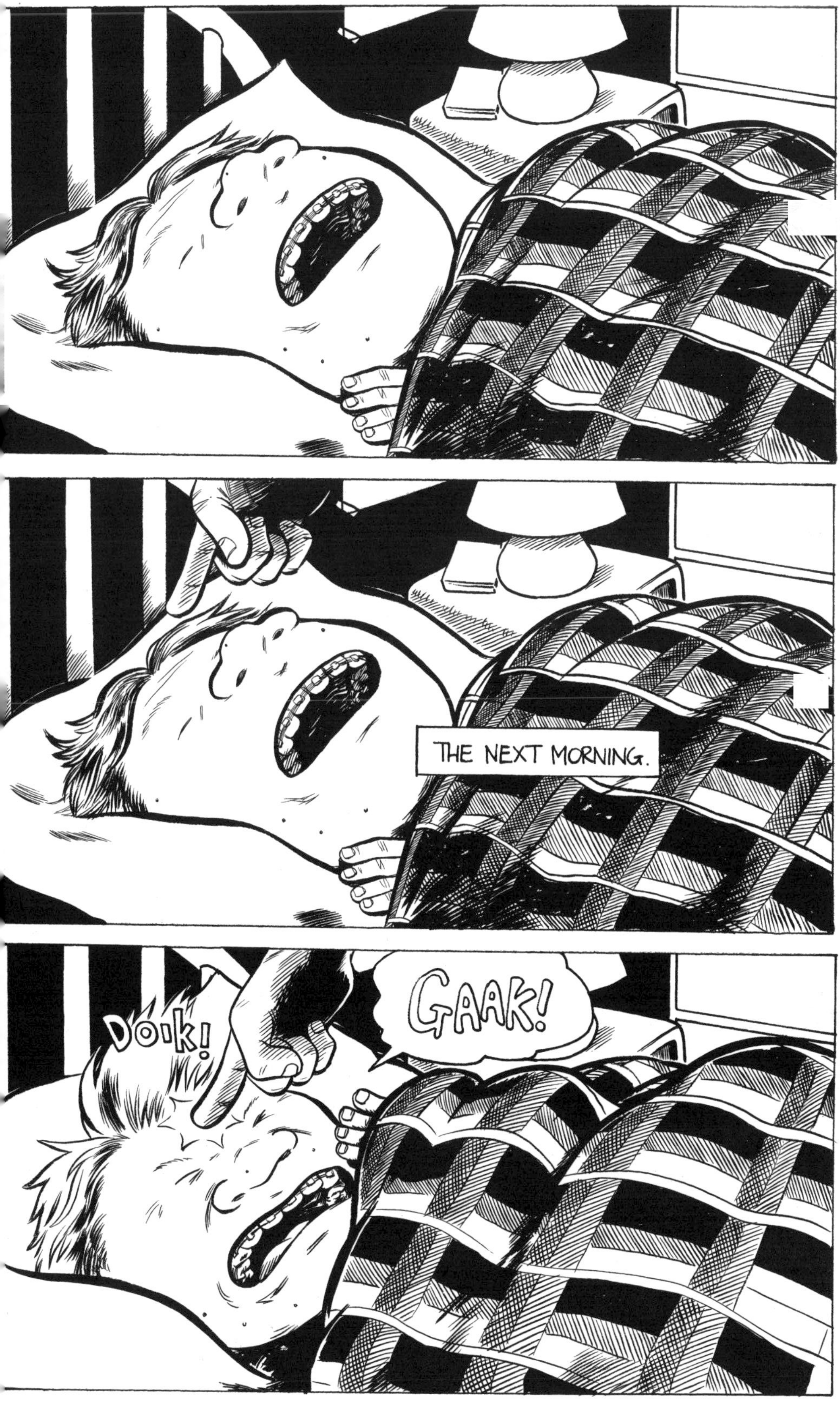
THE NEXT MORNING.
DOIK!
GAAK!

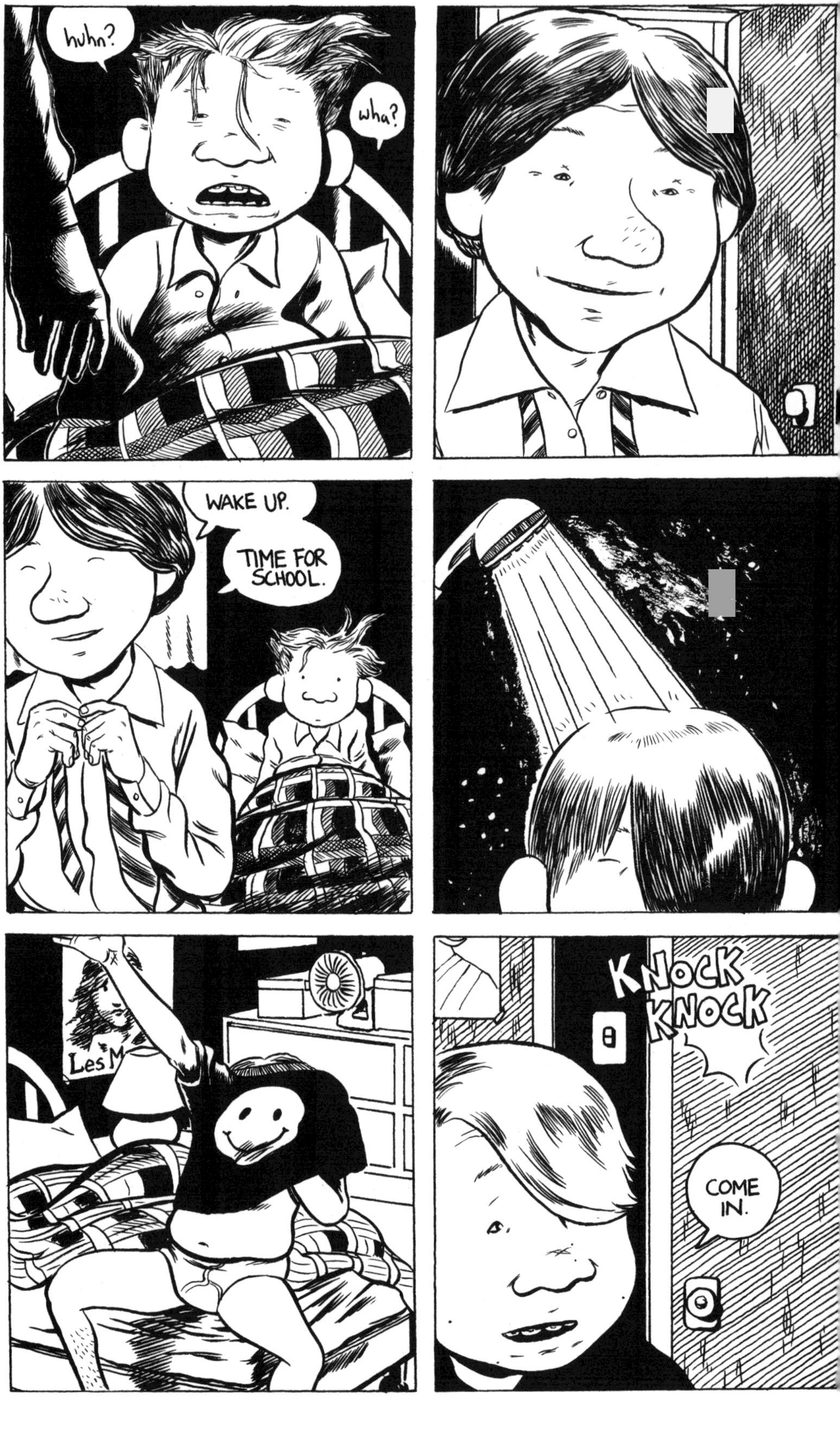
huhn?
wha?
WAKE UP.
TIME FOR SCHOOL.
Les M
KNOCK KNOCK
COME IN.

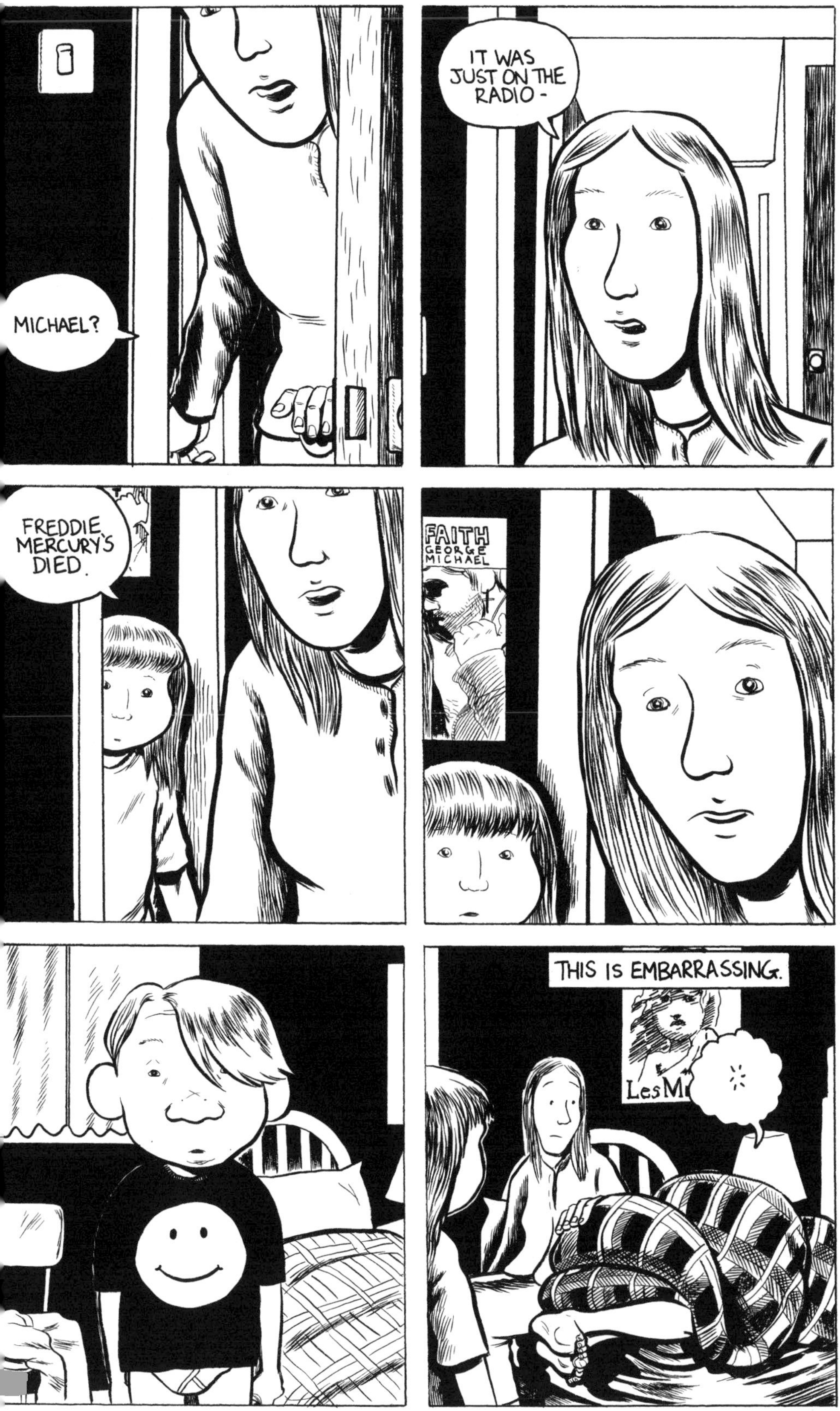
MICHAEL?
IT WAS JUST ON THE RADIO -
FREDDIE MERCURY'S DIED.
FAITH
GEORGE MICHAEL
THIS IS EMBARRASSING.
LesMi

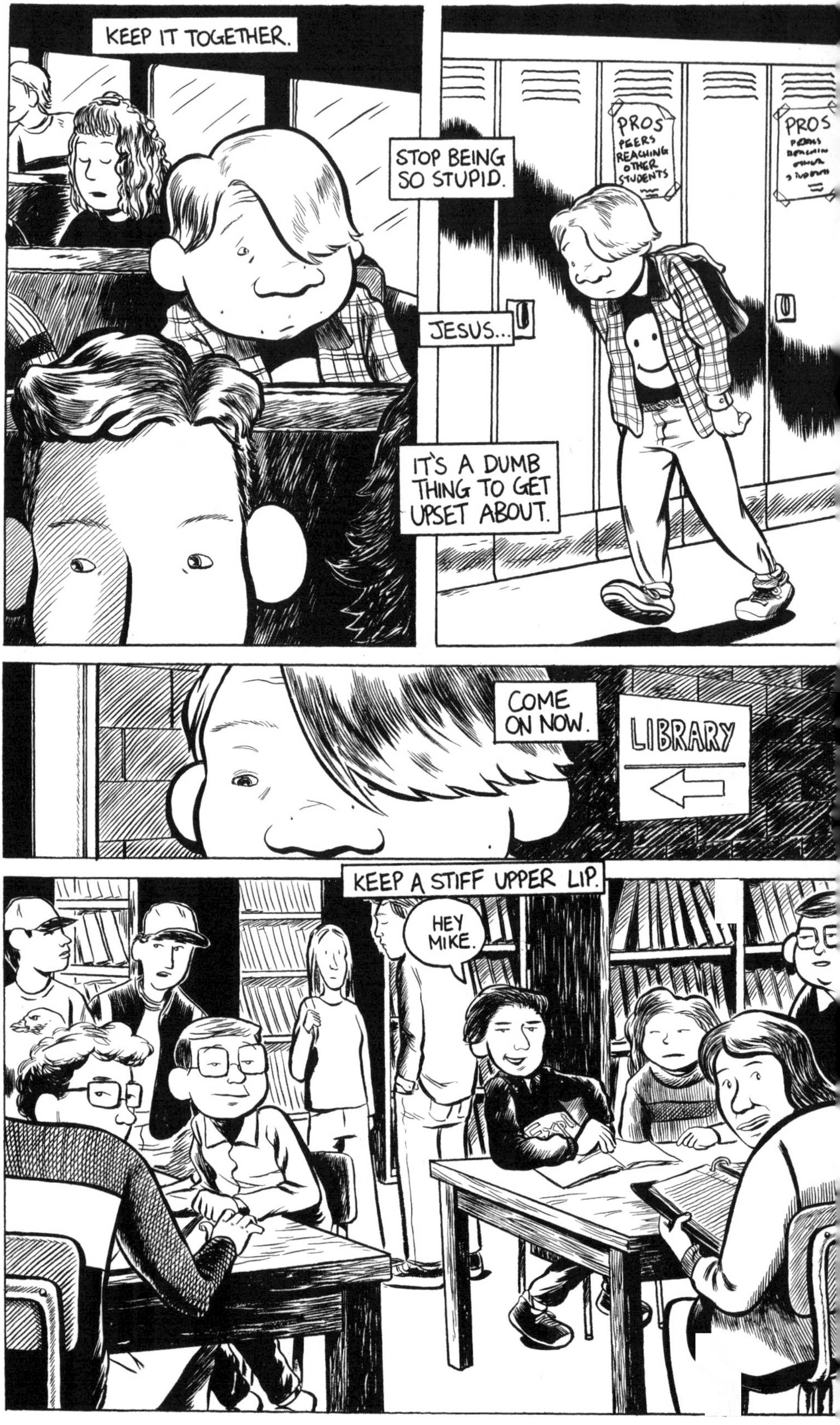

KEEP IT TOGETHER.
STOP BEING SO STUPID.
PROS
PEERS REACHING OTHER STUDENTS
JESUS...
IT'S A DUMB THING TO GET UPSET ABOUT.
COME ON NOW.
LIBRARY
KEEP A STIFF UPPER LIP.
HEY MIKE.

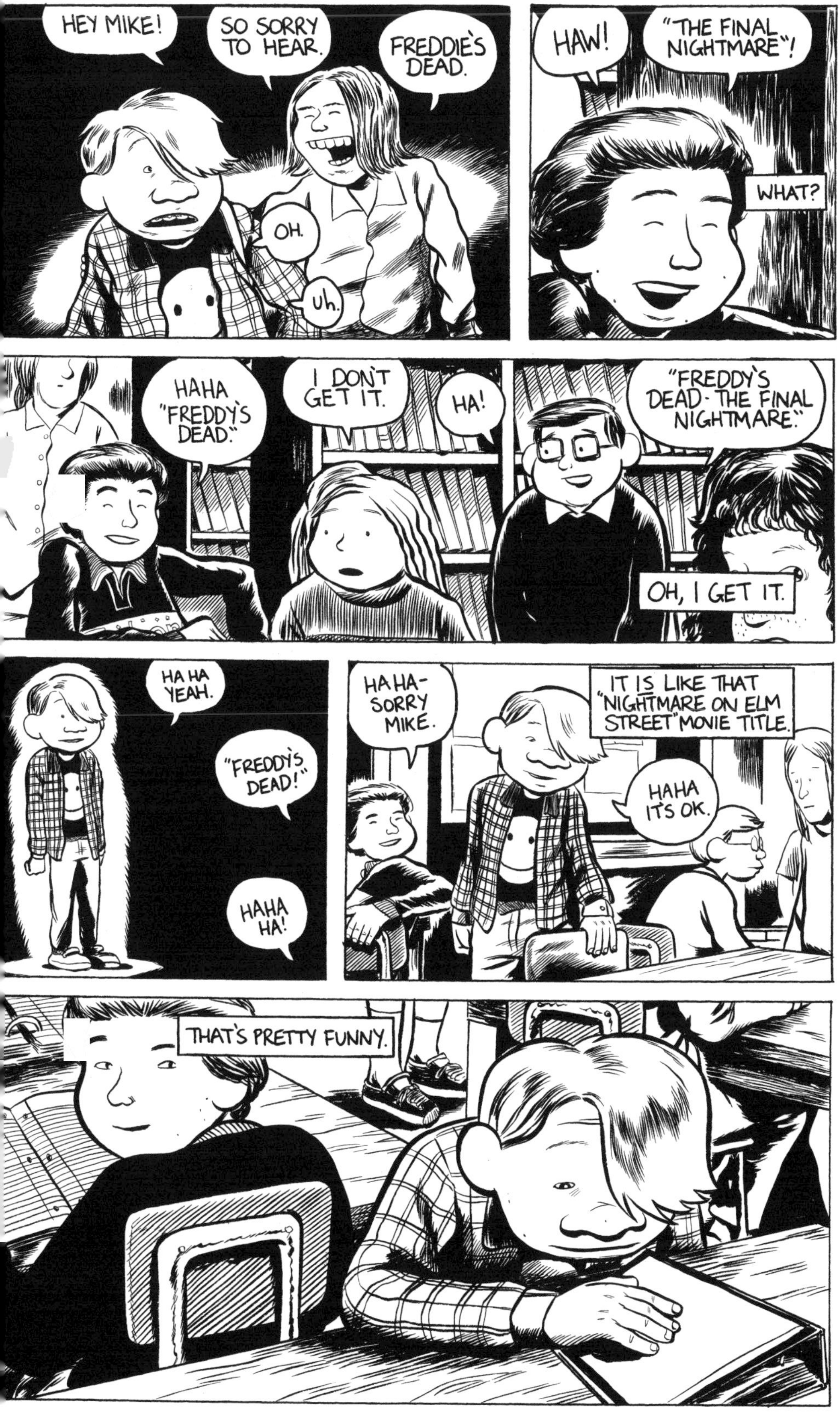
HEY MIKE!
SO SORRY TO HEAR.
FREDDIE'S DEAD.
OH.
Uh.
HAW!
"THE FINAL NIGHTMARE"!
WHAT?
HAHA "FREDDY'S DEAD."
I DON'T GET IT.
HA!
"FREDDY'S DEAD- THE FINAL NIGHTMARE."
OH, I GET IT.
HA HA YEAH.
"FREDDY'S DEAD!"
HAHA HA!
HA HA- SORRY MIKE.
IT IS LIKE THAT "NIGHTMARE ON ELM STREET" MOVIE TITLE.
HAHA IT'S OK.
THAT'S PRETTY FUNNY.

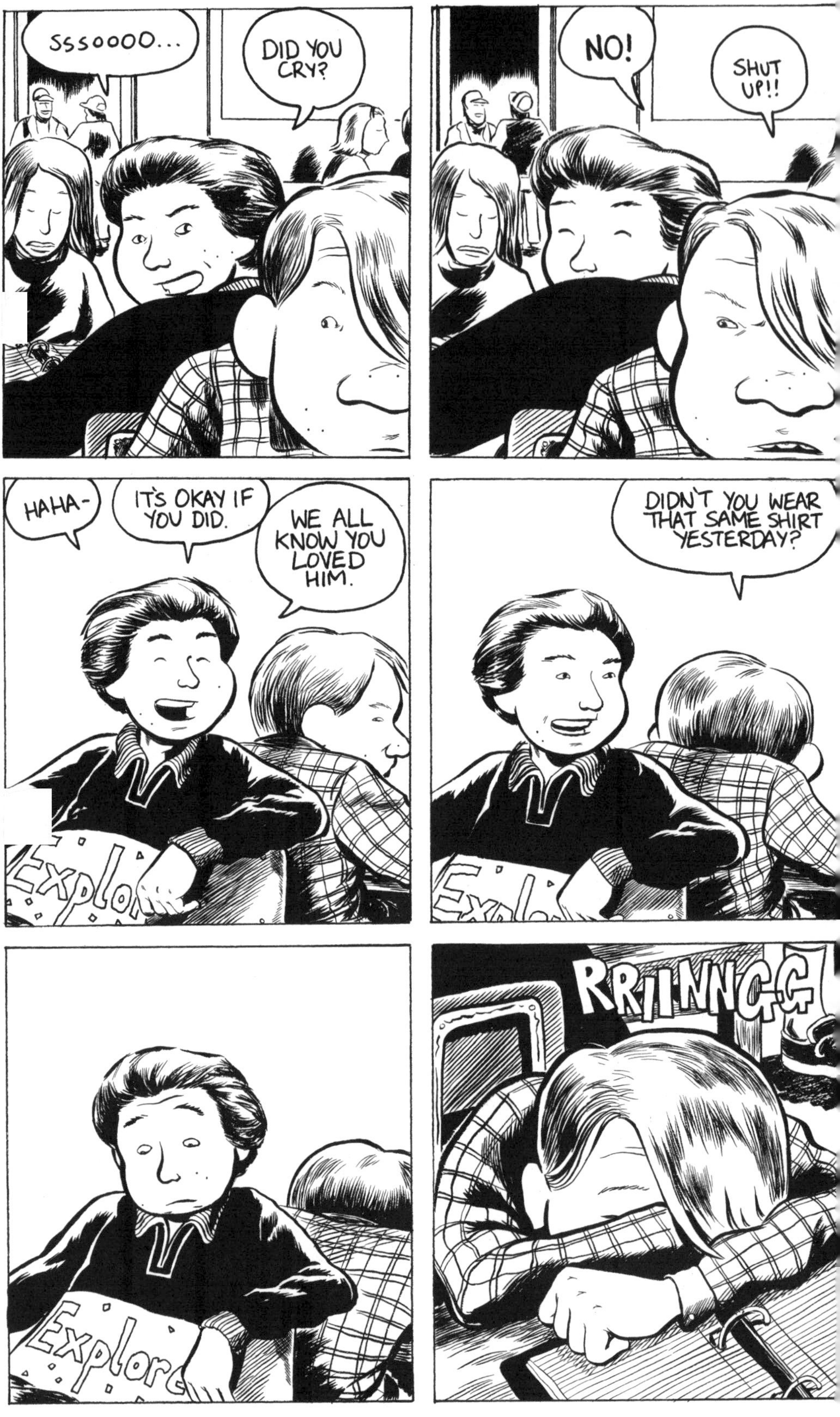
SSSOOOO...
DID YOU CRY?
NO!
SHUT UP!!
HAHA-
IT'S OKAY IF YOU DID.
WE ALL KNOW YOU LOVED HIM.
DIDN'T YOU WEAR THAT SAME SHIRT YESTERDAY?
RRIINNGG

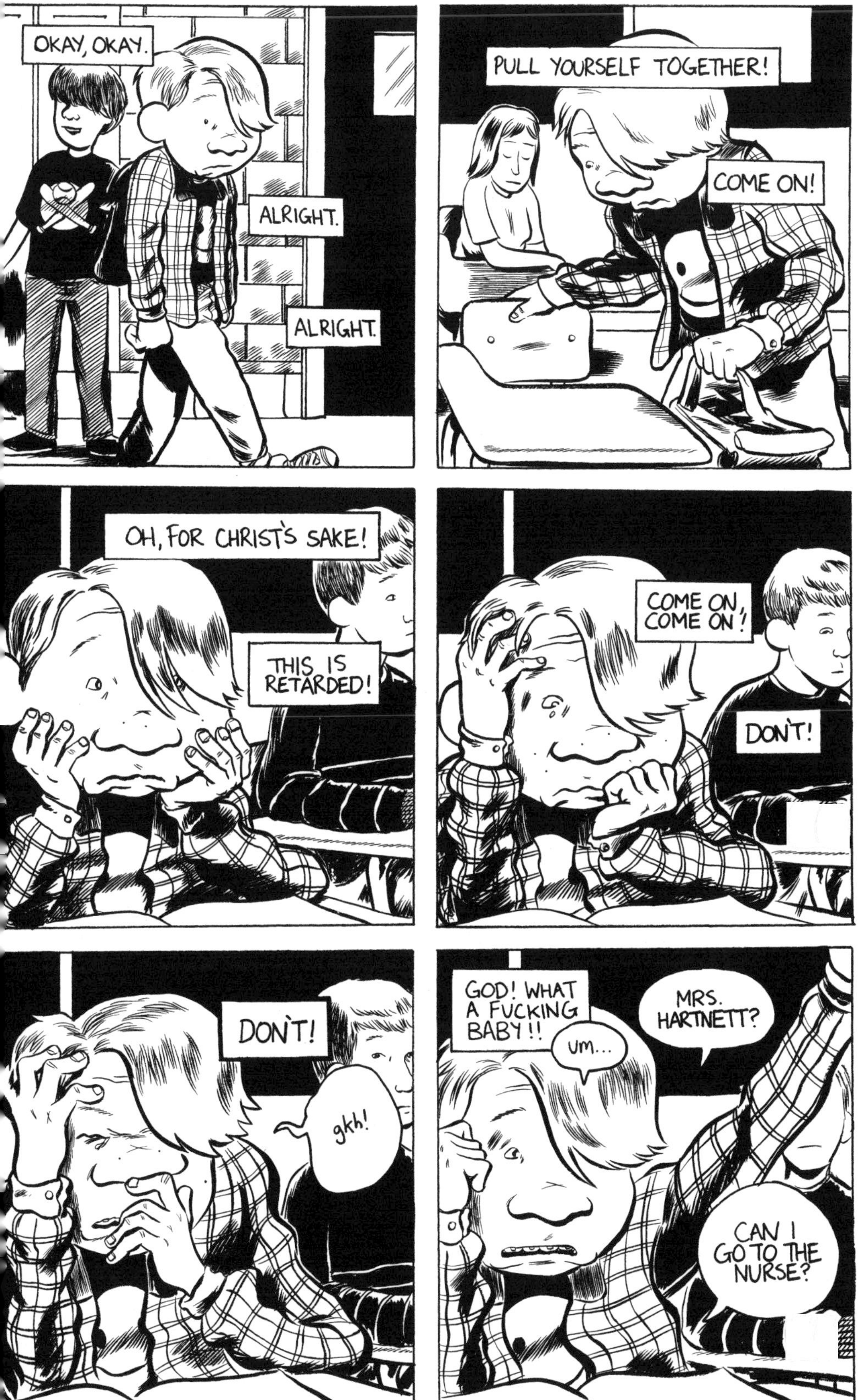

OKAY, OKAY.
ALRIGHT.
ALRIGHT.
PULL YOURSELF TOGETHER!
COME ON!
OH, FOR CHRIST'S SAKE!
THIS IS RETARDED!
COME ON, COME ON!
DON'T!
DON'T!
gkh!
GOD! WHAT A FUCKING BABY!!
um...
MRS. HARTNETT?
CAN I GO TO THE NURSE?

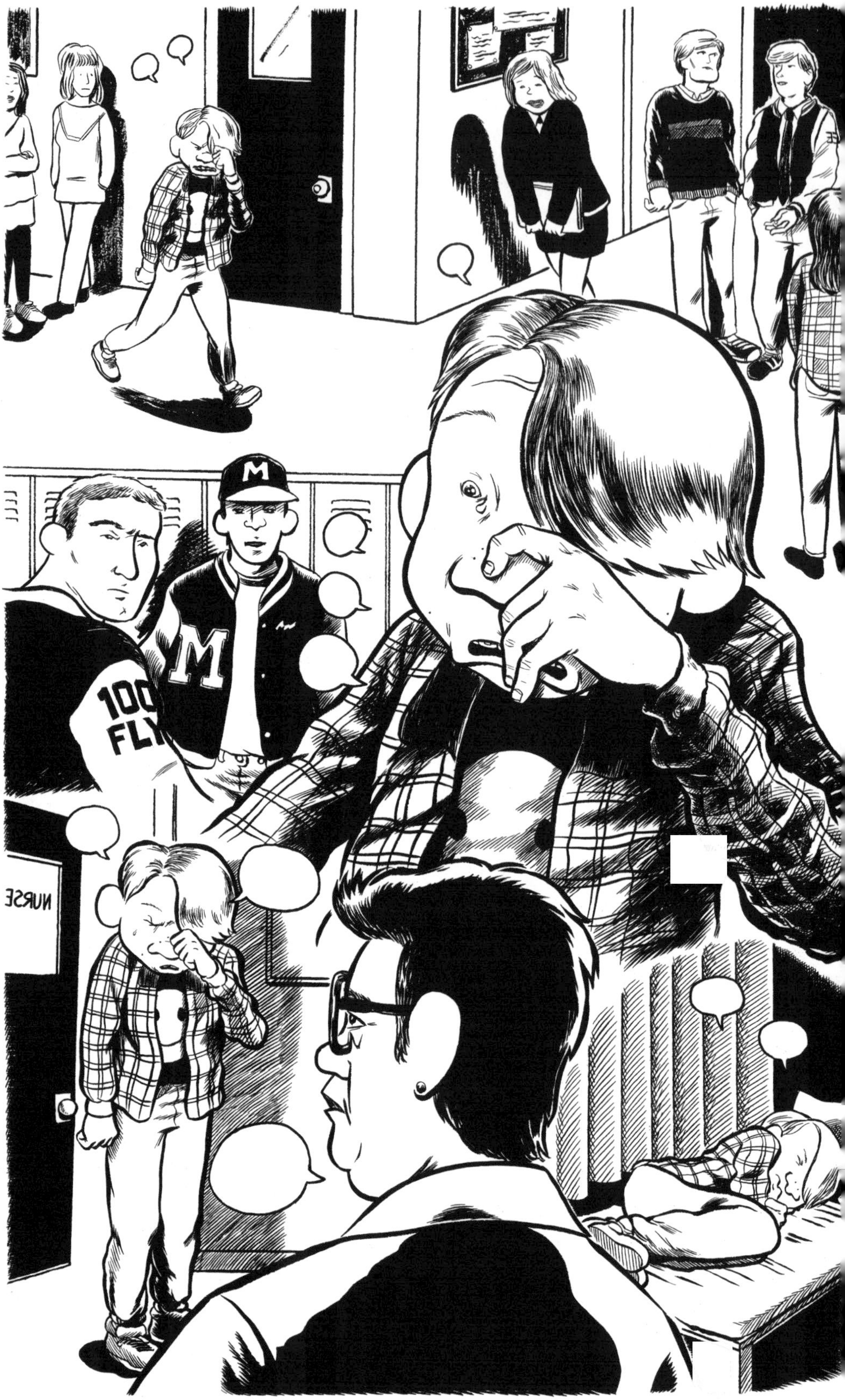
M
M
100 FLY
NURSE

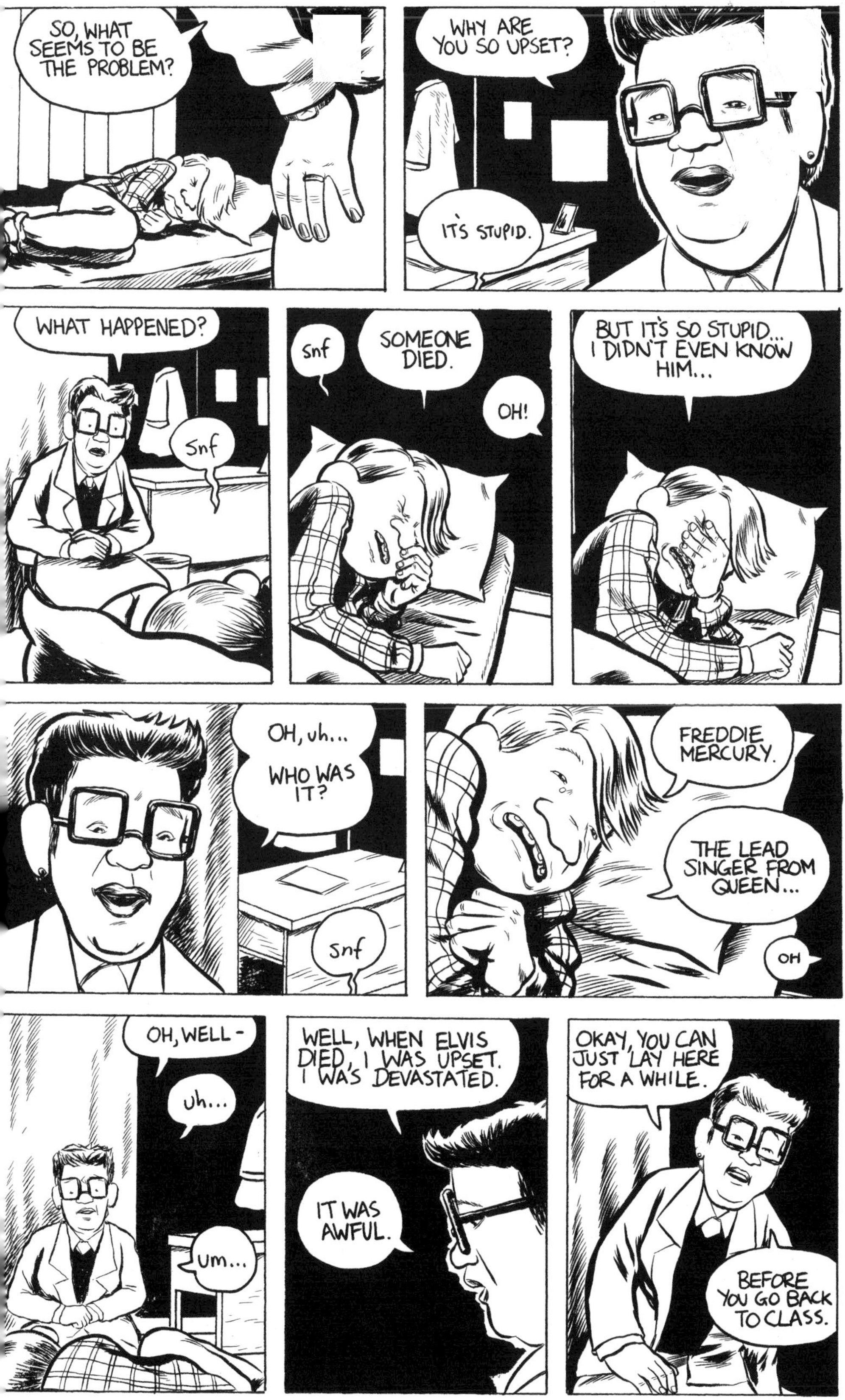
SO, WHAT SEEMS TO BE THE PROBLEM?
WHY ARE YOU SO UPSET?
IT'S STUPID.
WHAT HAPPENED?
Snf
Snf
SOMEONE DIED.
OH!
BUT IT'S SO STUPID... I DIDN'T EVEN KNOW HIM...
OH, uh...
WHO WAS IT?
Snf
FREDDIE MERCURY.
THE LEAD SINGER FROM QUEEN...
OH
OH, WELL-
uh...
um...
WELL, WHEN ELVIS DIED, I WAS UPSET. I WAS DEVASTATED.
IT WAS AWFUL.
OKAY, YOU CAN JUST LAY HERE FOR A WHILE.
BEFORE YOU GO BACK TO CLASS.

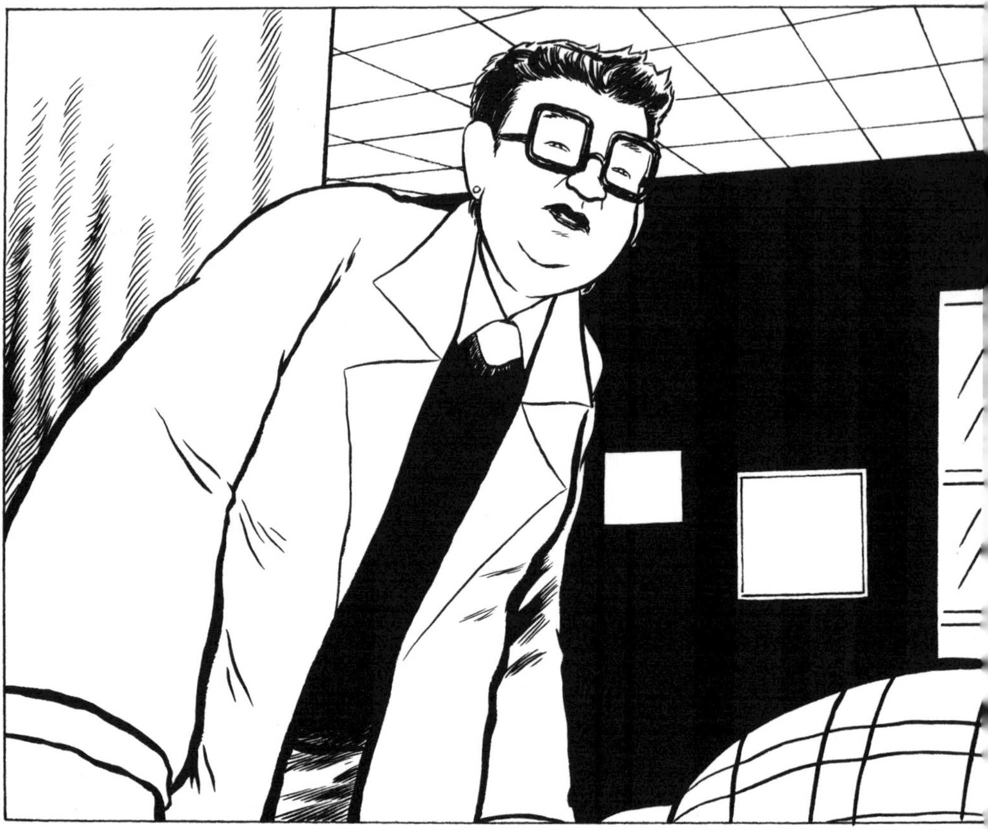

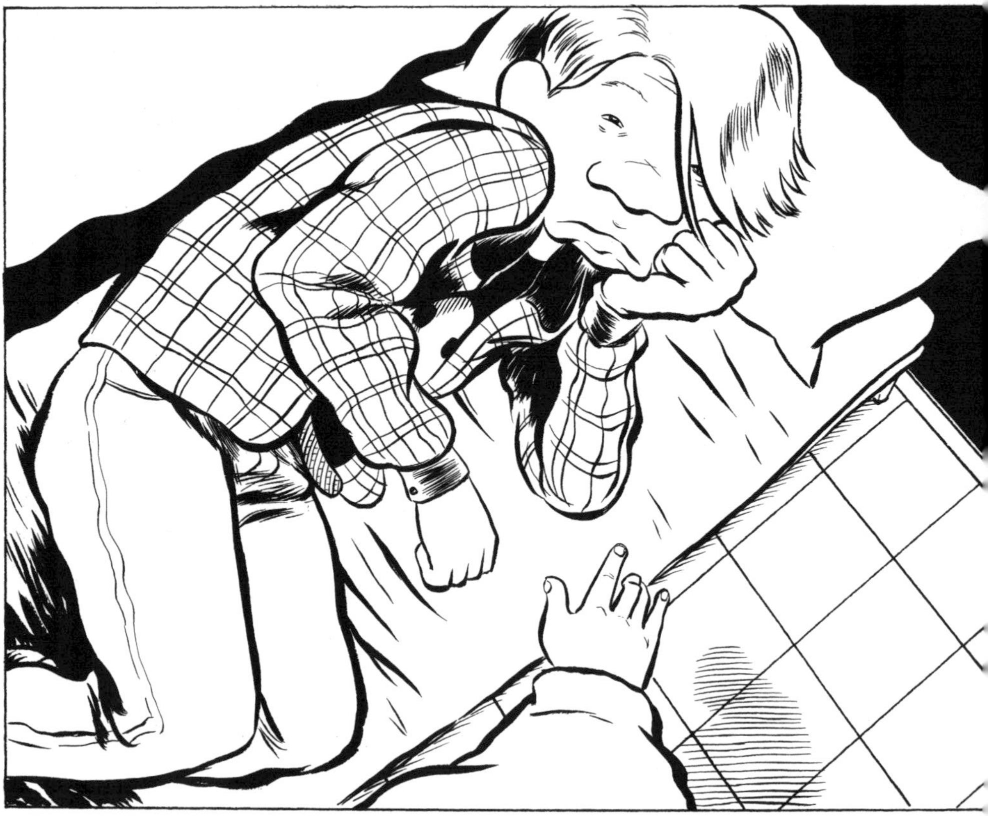

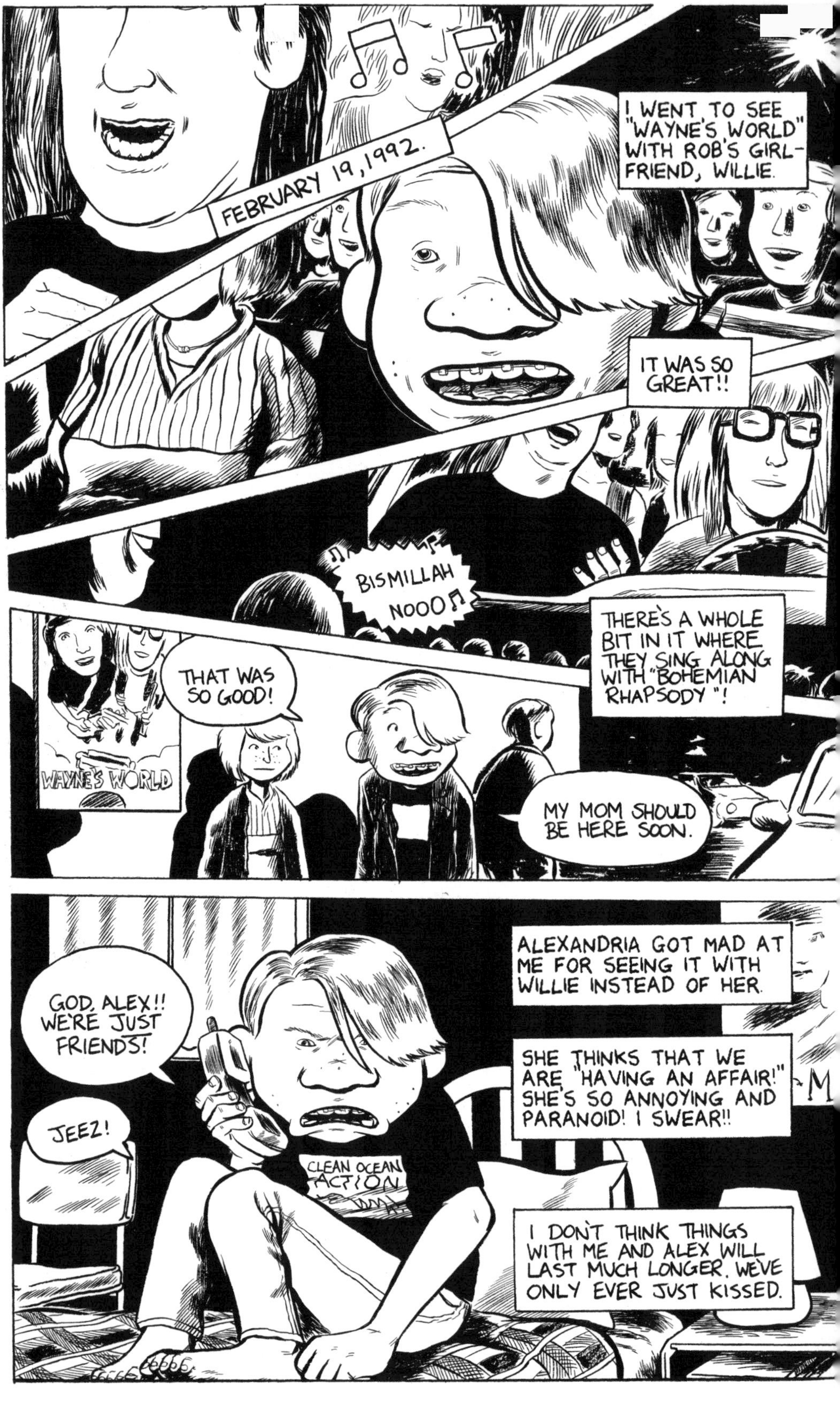

FEBRUARY 19, 1992.
I WENT TO SEE "WAYNE'S WORLD" WITH ROB'S GIRL-FRIEND, WILLIE.
IT WAS SO GREAT!!
BISMILLAH NOOO
THERE'S A WHOLE BIT IN IT WHERE THEY SING ALONG WITH "BOHEMIAN RHAPSODY"!
WAYNE'S WORLD
THAT WAS SO GOOD!
MY MOM SHOULD BE HERE SOON.
ALEXANDRIA GOT MAD AT ME FOR SEEING IT WITH WILLIE INSTEAD OF HER.
GOD, ALEX!! WE'RE JUST FRIENDS!
SHE THINKS THAT WE ARE "HAVING AN AFFAIR!" SHE'S SO ANNOYING AND PARANOID! I SWEAR!!
JEEZ!
CLEAN OCEAN ACTION
I DON'T THINK THINGS WITH ME AND ALEX WILL LAST MUCH LONGER. WE'VE ONLY EVER JUST KISSED.

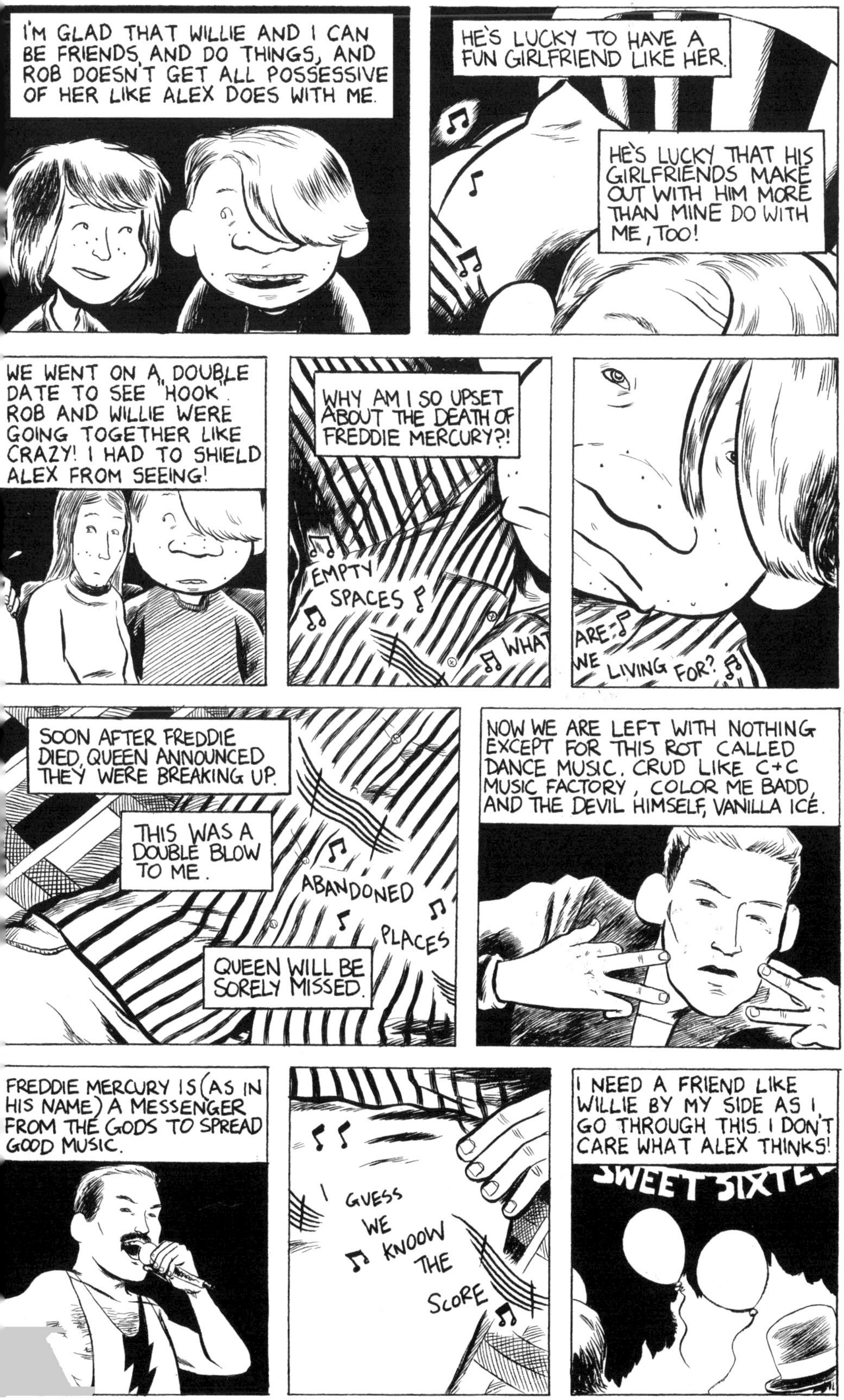
I'M GLAD THAT WILLIE AND I CAN BE FRIENDS, AND DO THINGS, AND ROB DOESN'T GET ALL POSSESSIVE OF HER LIKE ALEX DOES WITH ME.
HE'S LUCKY TO HAVE A FUN GIRLFRIEND LIKE HER.
HE'S LUCKY THAT HIS GIRLFRIENDS MAKE OUT WITH HIM MORE THAN MINE DO WITH ME, TOO!
WE WENT ON A DOUBLE DATE TO SEE "HOOK". ROB AND WILLIE WERE GOING TOGETHER LIKE CRAZY! I HAD TO SHIELD ALEX FROM SEEING!
WHY AM I SO UPSET ABOUT THE DEATH OF FREDDIE MERCURY?!
EMPTY SPACES
WHAT ARE WE LIVING FOR?
SOON AFTER FREDDIE DIED, QUEEN ANNOUNCED THEY WERE BREAKING UP.
THIS WAS A DOUBLE BLOW TO ME.
ABANDONED PLACES
QUEEN WILL BE SORELY MISSED.
NOW WE ARE LEFT WITH NOTHING EXCEPT FOR THIS ROT CALLED DANCE MUSIC. CRUD LIKE C+C MUSIC FACTORY, COLOR ME BADD, AND THE DEVIL HIMSELF, VANILLA ICE.
FREDDIE MERCURY IS (AS IN HIS NAME) A MESSENGER FROM THE GODS TO SPREAD GOOD MUSIC.
I GUESS WE KNOOW THE SCORE
I NEED A FRIEND LIKE WILLIE BY MY SIDE AS I GO THROUGH THIS. I DON'T CARE WHAT ALEX THINKS!
SWEET SIXTE

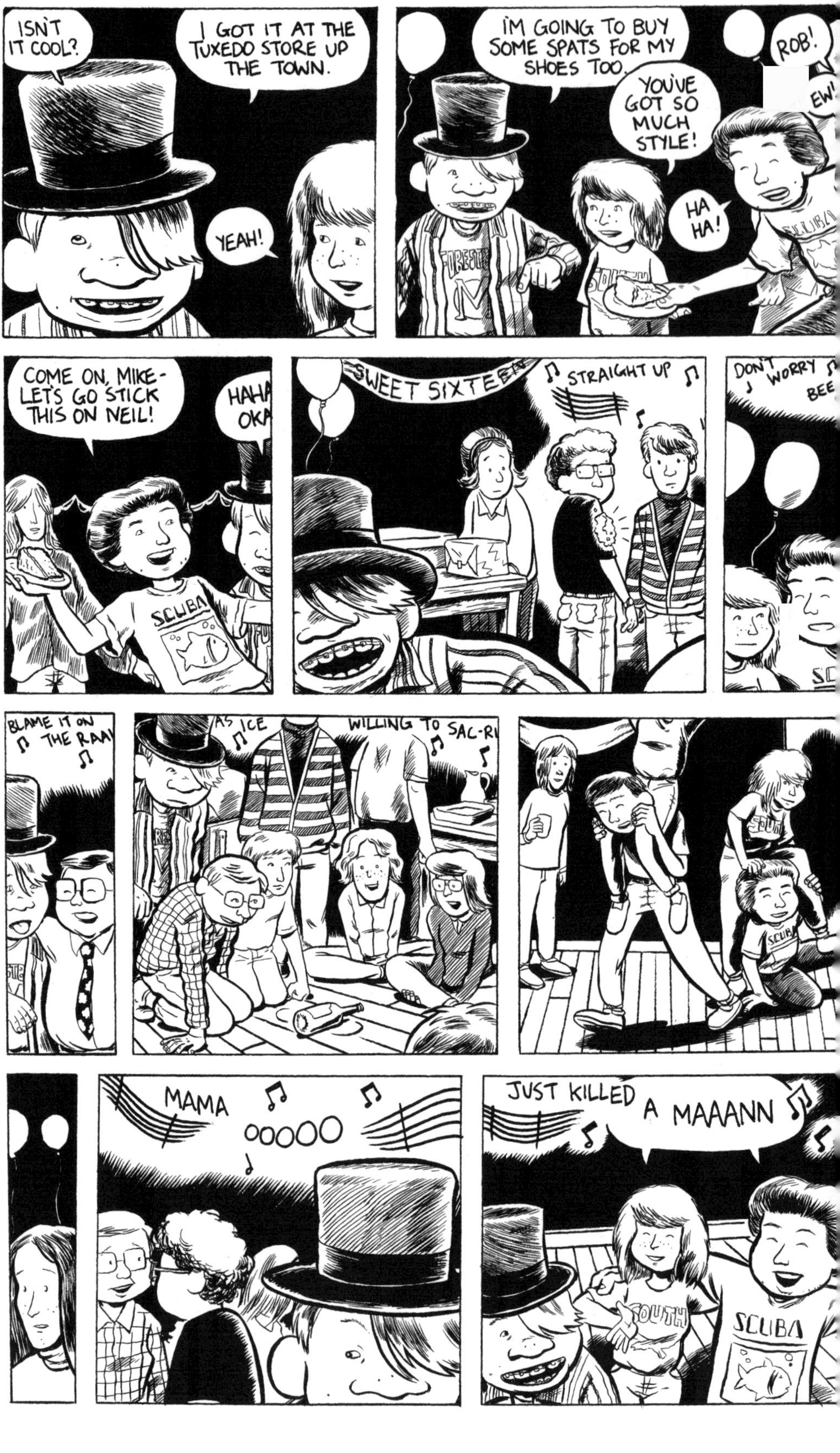
ISN'T IT COOL?
I GOT IT AT THE TUXEDO STORE UP THE TOWN.
YEAH!
I'M GOING TO BUY SOME SPATS FOR MY SHOES TOO.
YOU'VE GOT SO MUCH STYLE!
HA HA!
ROB!
EW!
COME ON, MIKE- LET'S GO STICK THIS ON NEIL!
HAHA OKA
SWEET SIXTEE
STRAIGHT UP
DON'T WORRY BEE
BLAME IT ON THE RAA
AS ICE
WILLING TO SAC-RI
MAMA
OOOOO
JUST KILLED
A MAAANN

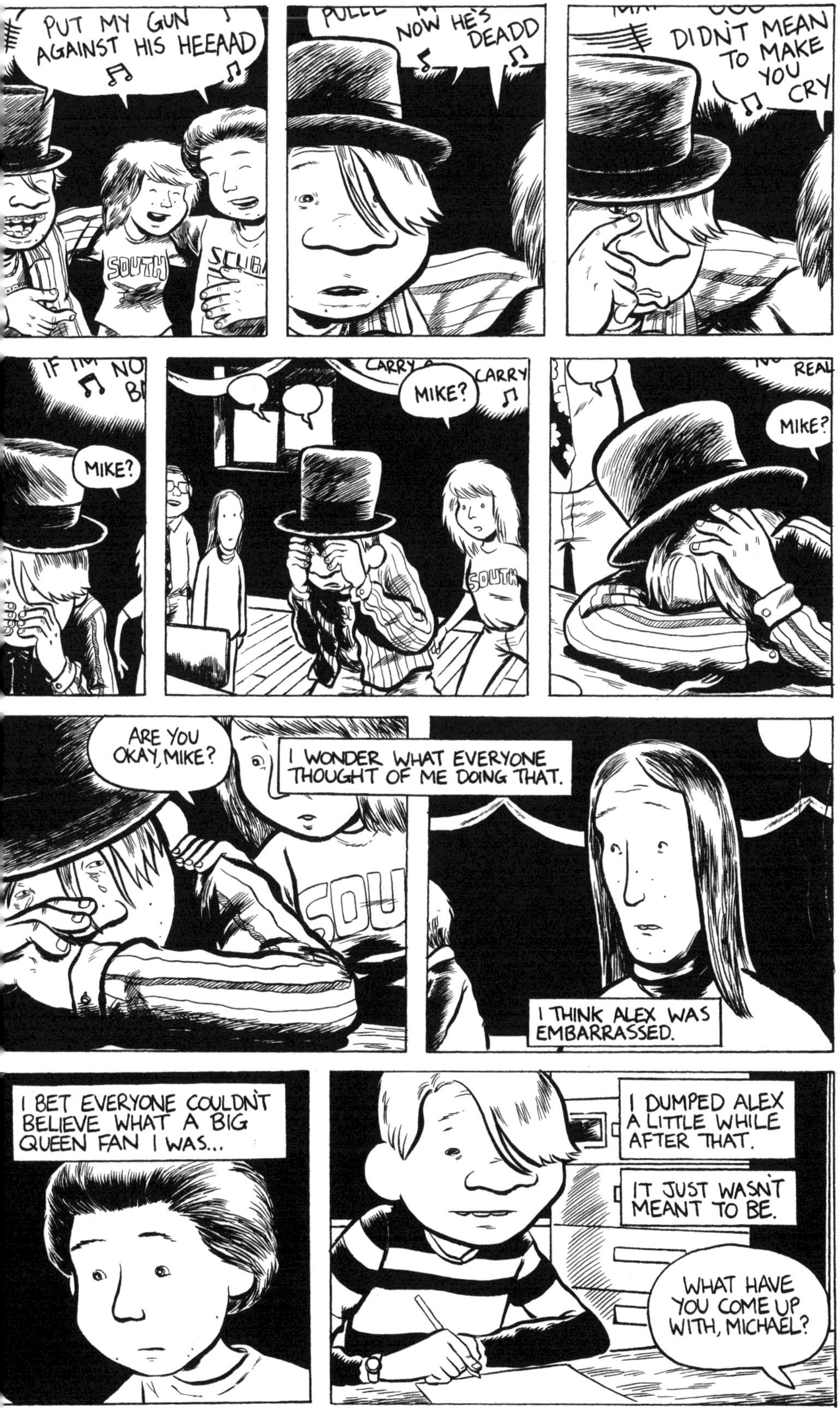
PUT MY GUN AGAINST HIS HEEAAD
NOW HE'S DEADD
DIDN'T MEAN TO MAKE YOU CRY
MIKE?
MIKE?
CARRY
MIKE?
ARE YOU OKAY, MIKE?
I WONDER WHAT EVERYONE THOUGHT OF ME DOING THAT.
I THINK ALEX WAS EMBARRASSED.
I BET EVERYONE COULDN'T BELIEVE WHAT A BIG QUEEN FAN I WAS...
I DUMPED ALEX A LITTLE WHILE AFTER THAT.
IT JUST WASN'T MEANT TO BE.
WHAT HAVE YOU COME UP WITH, MICHAEL?

WHAT HAVE YOU GOT THERE?

MISS PRISCO IS TEACHING US HOW TO DO SILK-SCREENING.

WELL...

IT'S LIKE A TRIBUTE...

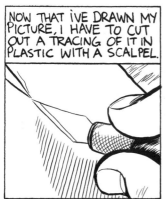

NOW THAT I'VE DRAWN MY PICTURE, I HAVE TO CUT OUT A TRACING OF IT IN PLASTIC WITH A SCALPEL.

IT TAKES A LONG TIME.

IT'S GOING TO BE AWESOME.

NOW THAT I'VE BROKEN UP WITH ALEX, I HAVE TO THINK ABOUT GETTING ANOTHER GIRLFRIEND.

THERE ARE DEFINITELY SOME GIRLS IN SCHOOL THAT I LIKE-LIKE.

I KNOW ROB HAS A BETTER "LOVE LIFE" THAN I DO, BUT I THINK SOME GIRLS THINK I'M CUTE TOO.

I THINK SOME GIRLS THINK I'M FUNNY. I KNOW WILLIE THINKS I'M HILARIOUS. SO I HAVE THAT.

THE OTHER DAY I WAS OVER ROB'S AND HE AND WILLIE WERE MAKING OUT LIKE I WASN'T EVEN THERE.
I WISH HE WOULDN'T BOTHER INVITING ME OVER IF HE'S PLANNING ON HAVING HIS GIRLFRIEND OVER AS WELL.
THE ONLY REASON I'M INVITED HALF THE TIME IS SO HIS PARENTS DON'T THINK HE'S DOING ANYTHING.
I THINK THAT'S SELFISH.
THIS CAME OUT GOOD!
XL
THAT DOES LOOK NICE - IS YOUR SCREEN FOR THE FRONT READY TO GO?
YEAH.
I'M SO EXCITED ABOUT MY TRIBUTE T-SHIRT!
IT'S GOING TO BE SO COOL TO WEAR AROUND SCHOOL NEXT WEEK.
Queen
Freddie Mercury
1946-1991

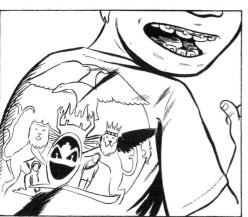

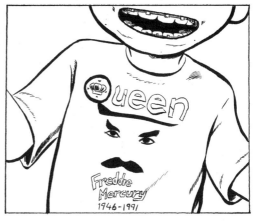

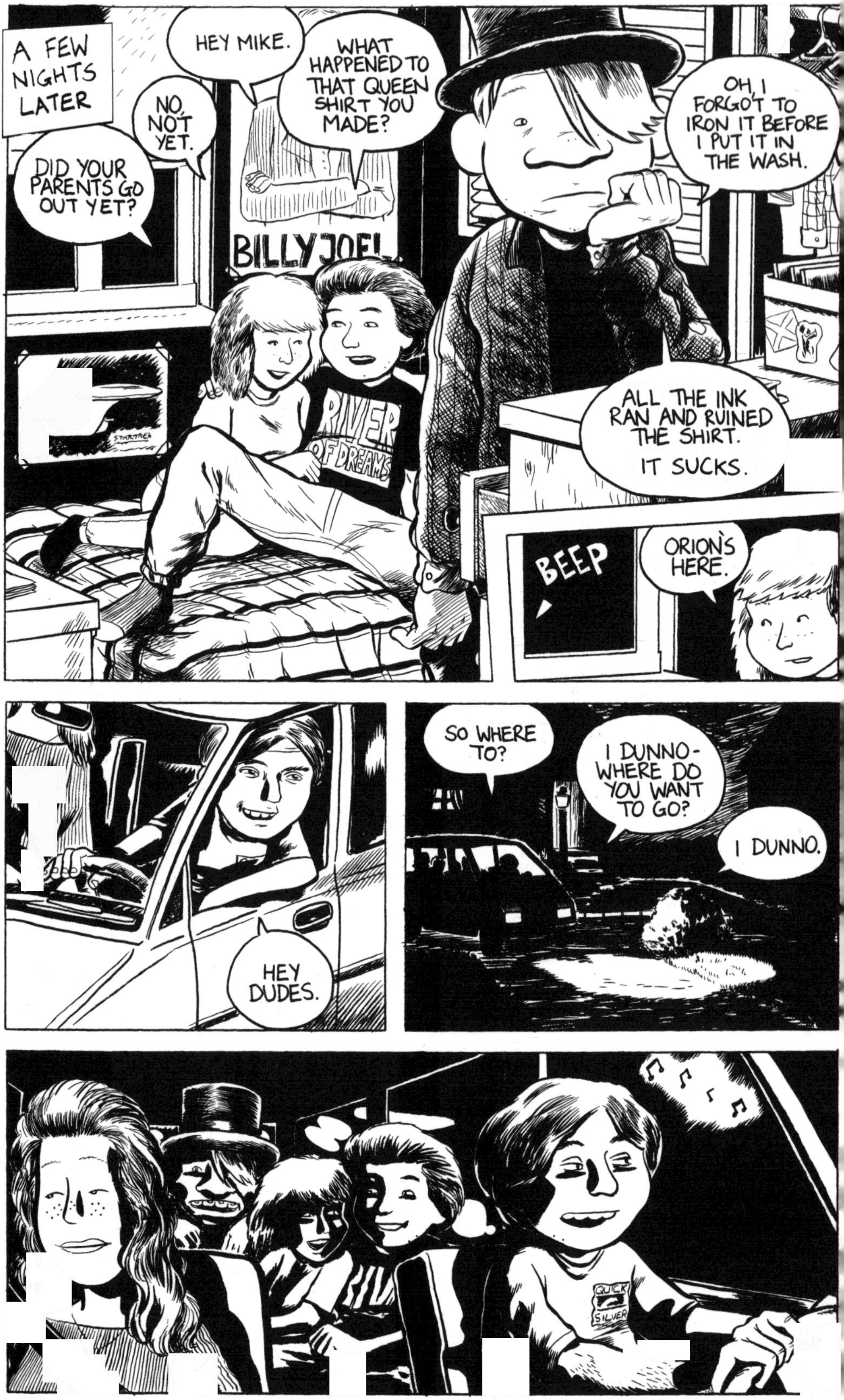
A FEW NIGHTS LATER
DID YOUR PARENTS GO OUT YET?
NO, NOT YET.
HEY MIKE.
WHAT HAPPENED TO THAT QUEEN SHIRT YOU MADE?
BILLY JOEL
OH, I FORGOT TO IRON IT BEFORE I PUT IT IN THE WASH.
RIVER OF DREAMS
ALL THE INK RAN AND RUINED THE SHIRT.
IT SUCKS.
BEEP
ORION'S HERE.
HEY DUDES.
SO WHERE TO?
I DUNNO- WHERE DO YOU WANT TO GO?
I DUNNO.
QUICK SILVER

MAN, I'VE JUST BEEN THINKING — WHAT MR. LYNN SAID IN ENGLISH CLASS — MAYBE IT WOULD BE A GOOD EXPERIENCE TO JUST TAKE OFF FOR A WHILE...

YOU KNOW — JUST GET OUT OF HERE — GO ON THE ROAD...

JUST LIVE A LITTLE, RIGHT?

HEY, IS THAT TAPE OVER?

I BROUGHT THIS QUEEN MIX.

OH COOL.

CASSETTE

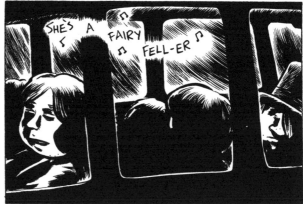

SHE'S A FAIRY FELL-ER

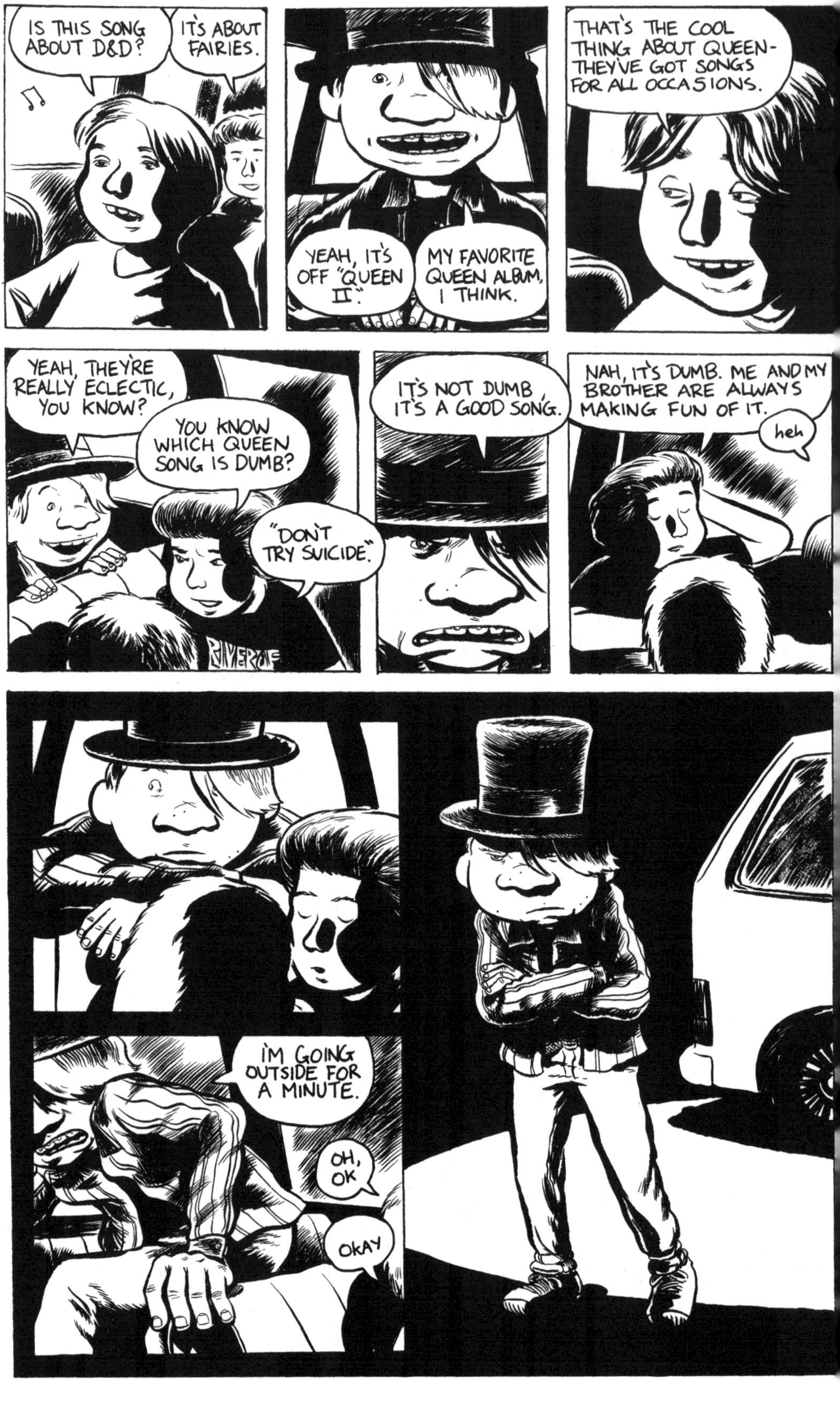
IS THIS SONG ABOUT D&D?
IT'S ABOUT FAIRIES.
YEAH, IT'S OFF "QUEEN II".
MY FAVORITE QUEEN ALBUM, I THINK.
THAT'S THE COOL THING ABOUT QUEEN- THEY'VE GOT SONGS FOR ALL OCCASIONS.
YEAH, THEY'RE REALLY ECLECTIC, YOU KNOW?
YOU KNOW WHICH QUEEN SONG IS DUMB?
"DON'T TRY SUICIDE".
IT'S NOT DUMB, IT'S A GOOD SONG.
NAH, IT'S DUMB. ME AND MY BROTHER ARE ALWAYS MAKING FUN OF IT.
heh
I'M GOING OUTSIDE FOR A MINUTE.
OH, OK
OKAY

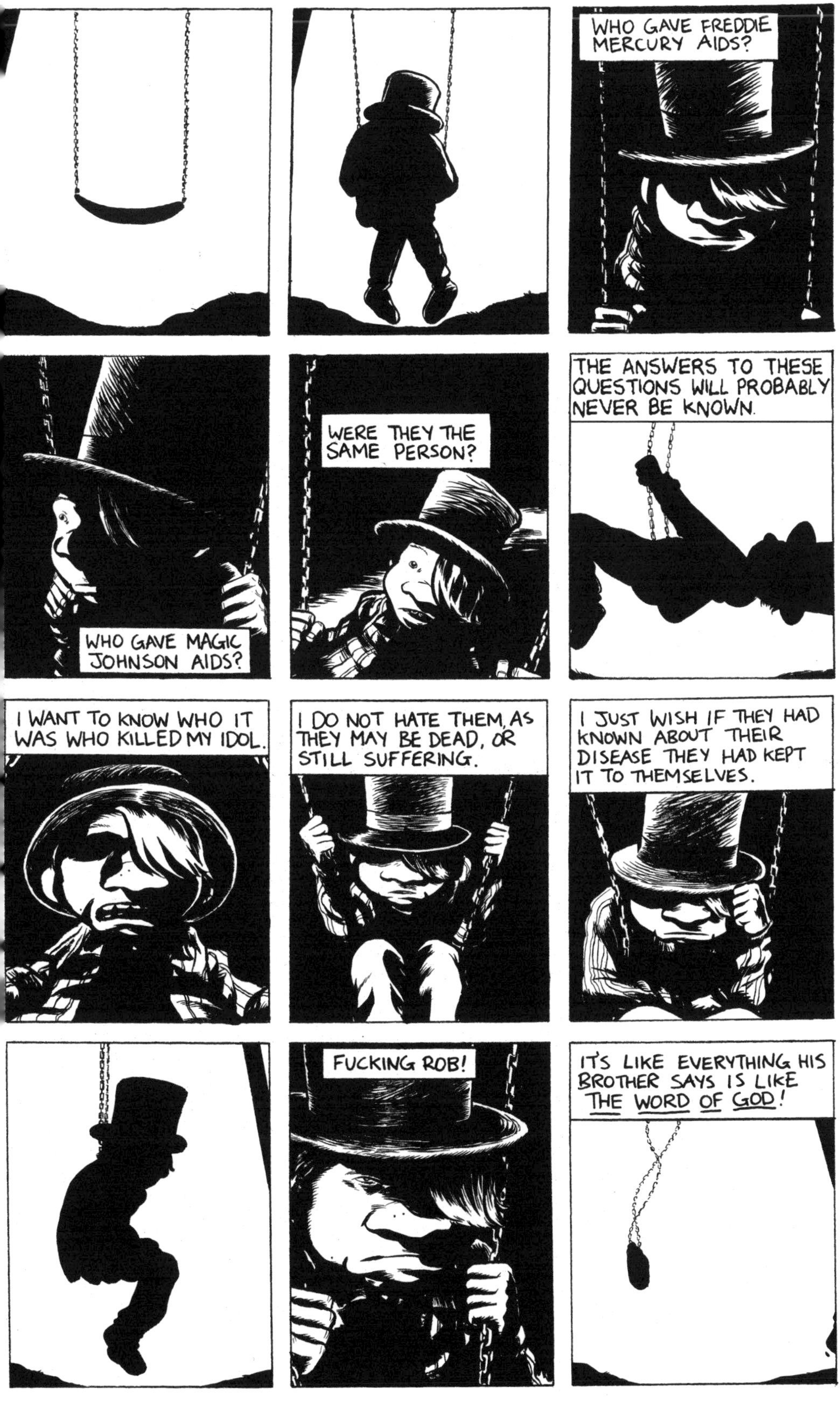
WHO GAVE FREDDIE MERCURY AIDS?
WHO GAVE MAGIC JOHNSON AIDS?
WERE THEY THE SAME PERSON?
THE ANSWERS TO THESE QUESTIONS WILL PROBABLY NEVER BE KNOWN.
I WANT TO KNOW WHO IT WAS WHO KILLED MY IDOL.
I DO NOT HATE THEM, AS THEY MAY BE DEAD, OR STILL SUFFERING.
I JUST WISH IF THEY HAD KNOWN ABOUT THEIR DISEASE THEY HAD KEPT IT TO THEMSELVES.
FUCKING ROB!
IT'S LIKE EVERYTHING HIS BROTHER SAYS IS LIKE THE WORD OF GOD!

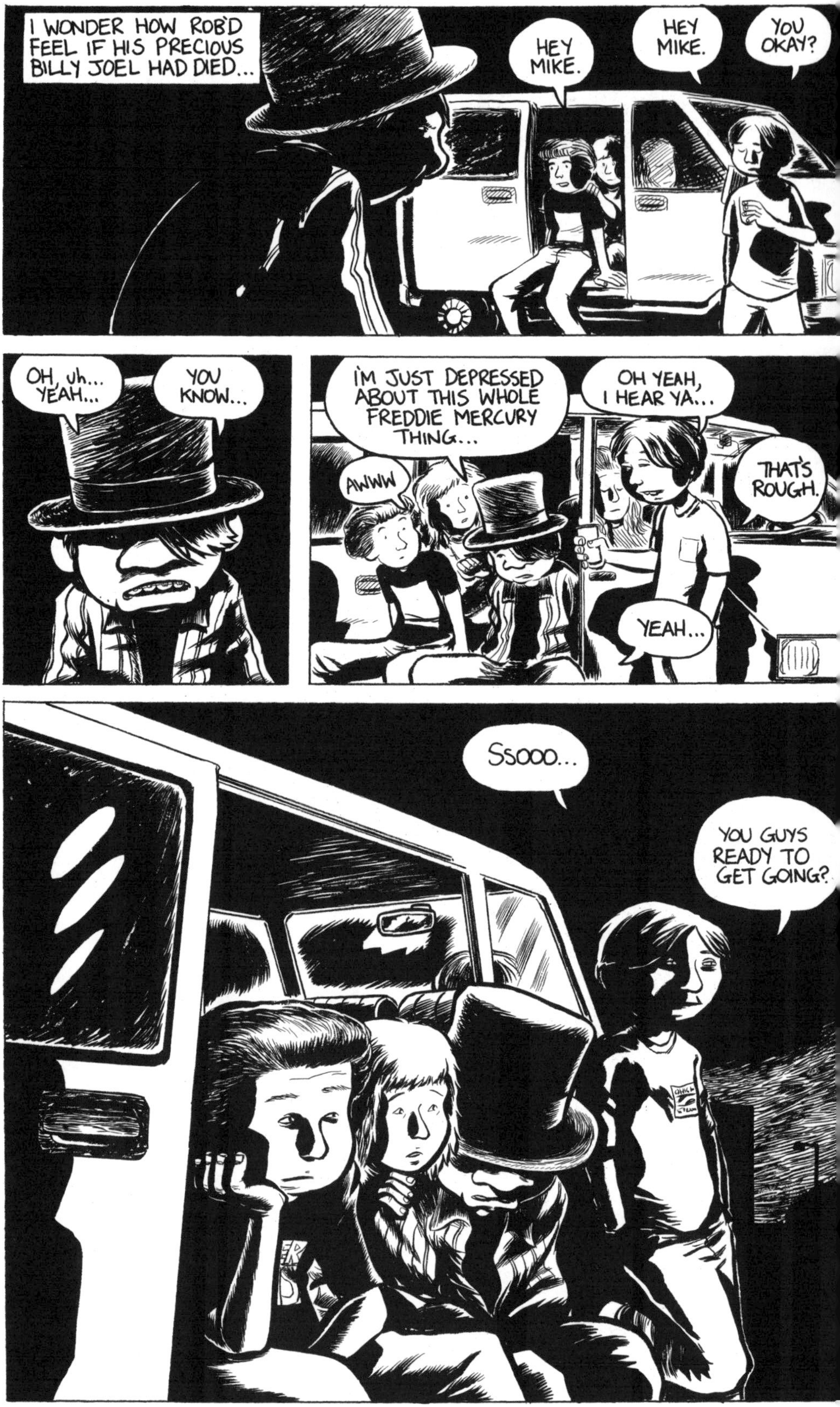
I WONDER HOW ROB'D FEEL IF HIS PRECIOUS BILLY JOEL HAD DIED...
HEY MIKE.
HEY MIKE.
YOU OKAY?
OH, uh... YEAH...
YOU KNOW...
I'M JUST DEPRESSED ABOUT THIS WHOLE FREDDIE MERCURY THING...
OH YEAH, I HEAR YA...
AWWW
THAT'S ROUGH.
YEAH...
Ssooo...
YOU GUYS READY TO GET GOING?

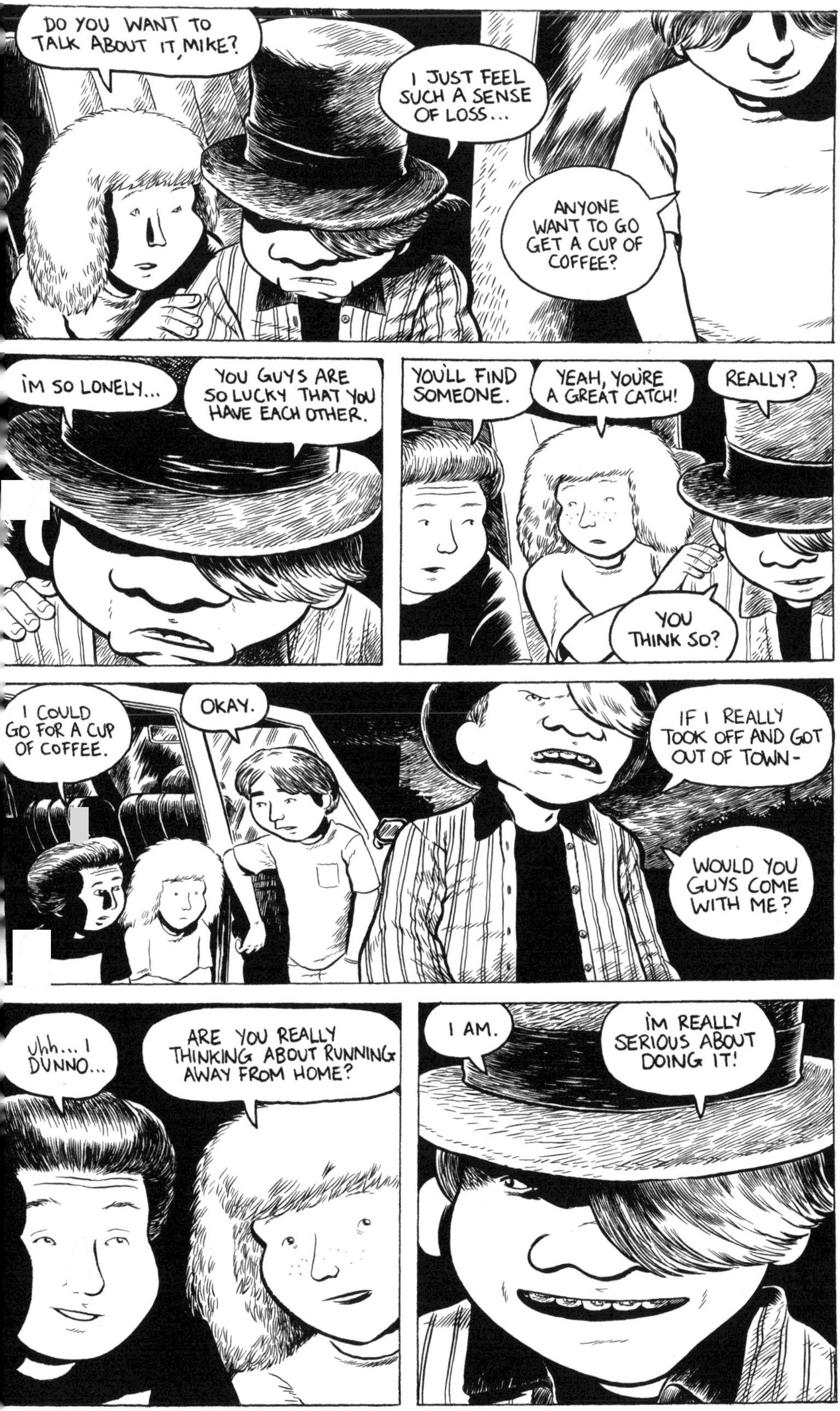
DO YOU WANT TO TALK ABOUT IT, MIKE?
I JUST FEEL SUCH A SENSE OF LOSS...
ANYONE WANT TO GO GET A CUP OF COFFEE?
I'M SO LONELY...
YOU GUYS ARE SO LUCKY THAT YOU HAVE EACH OTHER.
YOU'LL FIND SOMEONE.
YEAH, YOU'RE A GREAT CATCH!
REALLY?
YOU THINK SO?
I COULD GO FOR A CUP OF COFFEE.
OKAY.
IF I REALLY TOOK OFF AND GOT OUT OF TOWN-
WOULD YOU GUYS COME WITH ME?
uhh... I DUNNO...
ARE YOU REALLY THINKING ABOUT RUNNING AWAY FROM HOME?
I AM.
I'M REALLY SERIOUS ABOUT DOING IT!

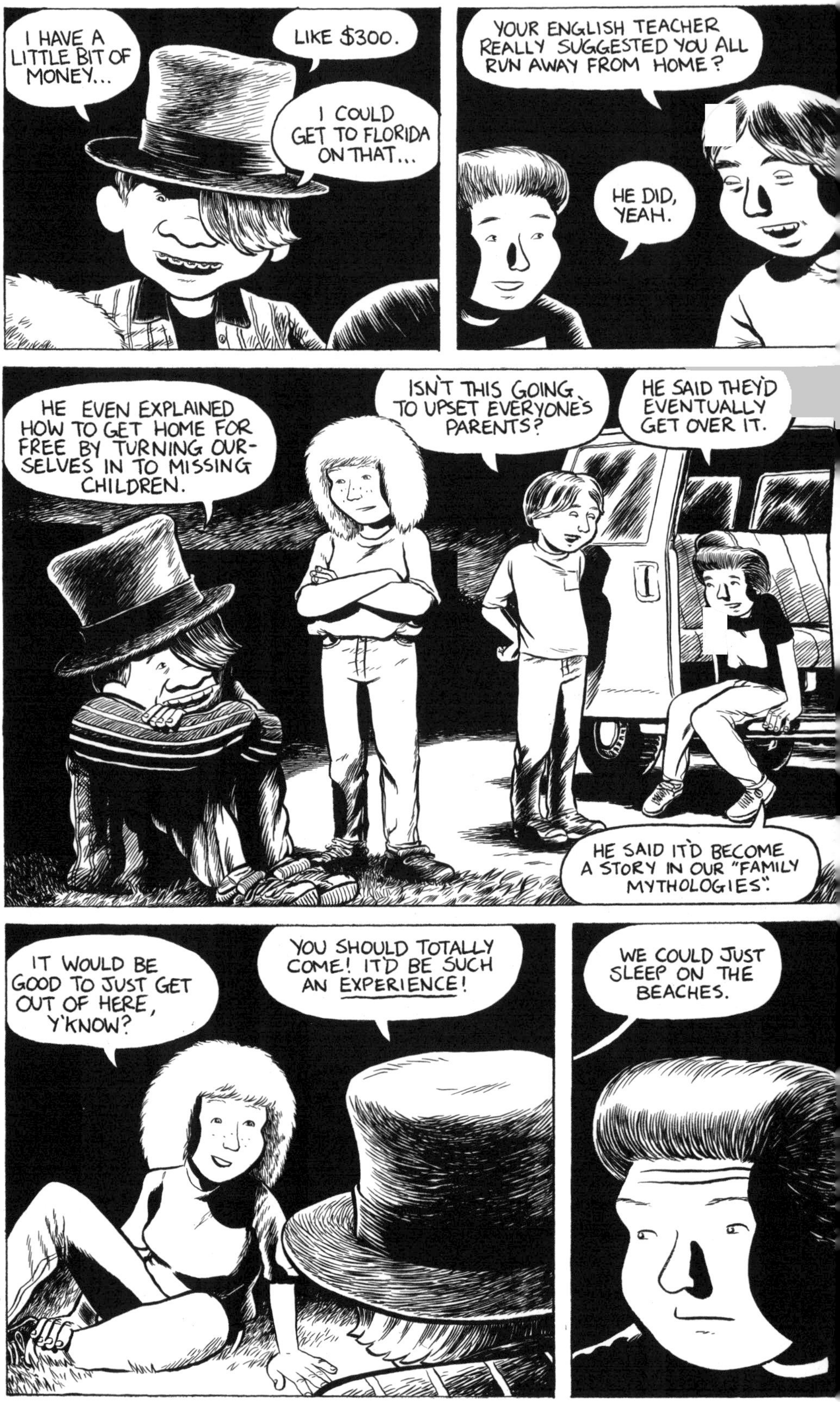
I HAVE A LITTLE BIT OF MONEY...
LIKE $300.
I COULD GET TO FLORIDA ON THAT...
YOUR ENGLISH TEACHER REALLY SUGGESTED YOU ALL RUN AWAY FROM HOME?
HE DID, YEAH.
HE EVEN EXPLAINED HOW TO GET HOME FOR FREE BY TURNING OUR-SELVES IN TO MISSING CHILDREN.
ISN'T THIS GOING TO UPSET EVERYONE'S PARENTS?
HE SAID THEY'D EVENTUALLY GET OVER IT.
HE SAID IT'D BECOME A STORY IN OUR "FAMILY MYTHOLOGIES".
IT WOULD BE GOOD TO JUST GET OUT OF HERE, Y'KNOW?
YOU SHOULD TOTALLY COME! IT'D BE SUCH AN EXPERIENCE!
WE COULD JUST SLEEP ON THE BEACHES.

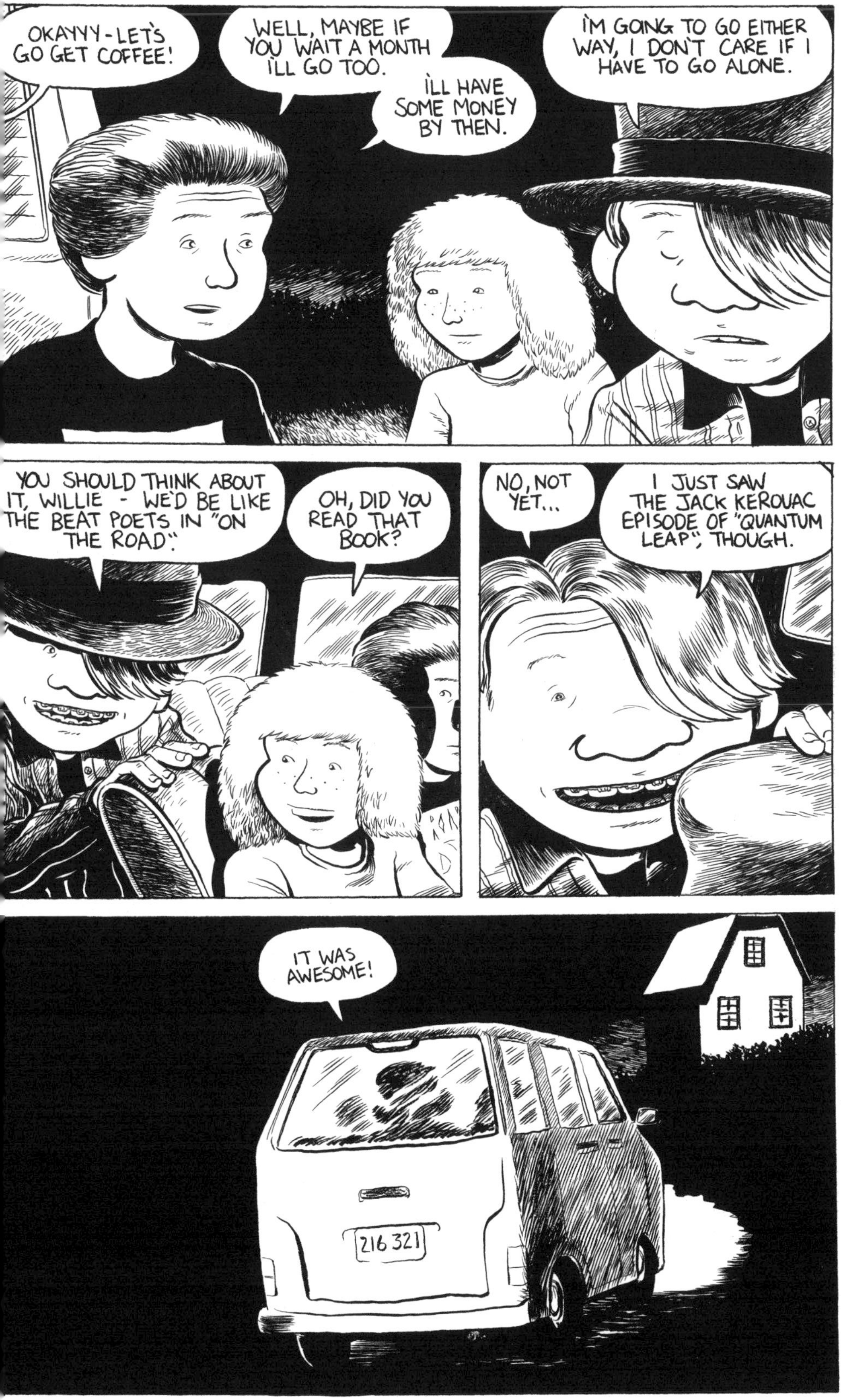
OKAYYY-LET'S GO GET COFFEE!
WELL, MAYBE IF YOU WAIT A MONTH I'LL GO TOO.
I'LL HAVE SOME MONEY BY THEN.
I'M GOING TO GO EITHER WAY, I DON'T CARE IF I HAVE TO GO ALONE.
YOU SHOULD THINK ABOUT IT, WILLIE - WE'D BE LIKE THE BEAT POETS IN "ON THE ROAD".
OH, DID YOU READ THAT BOOK?
NO, NOT YET...
I JUST SAW THE JACK KEROUAC EPISODE OF "QUANTUM LEAP", THOUGH.
IT WAS AWESOME!
216 321

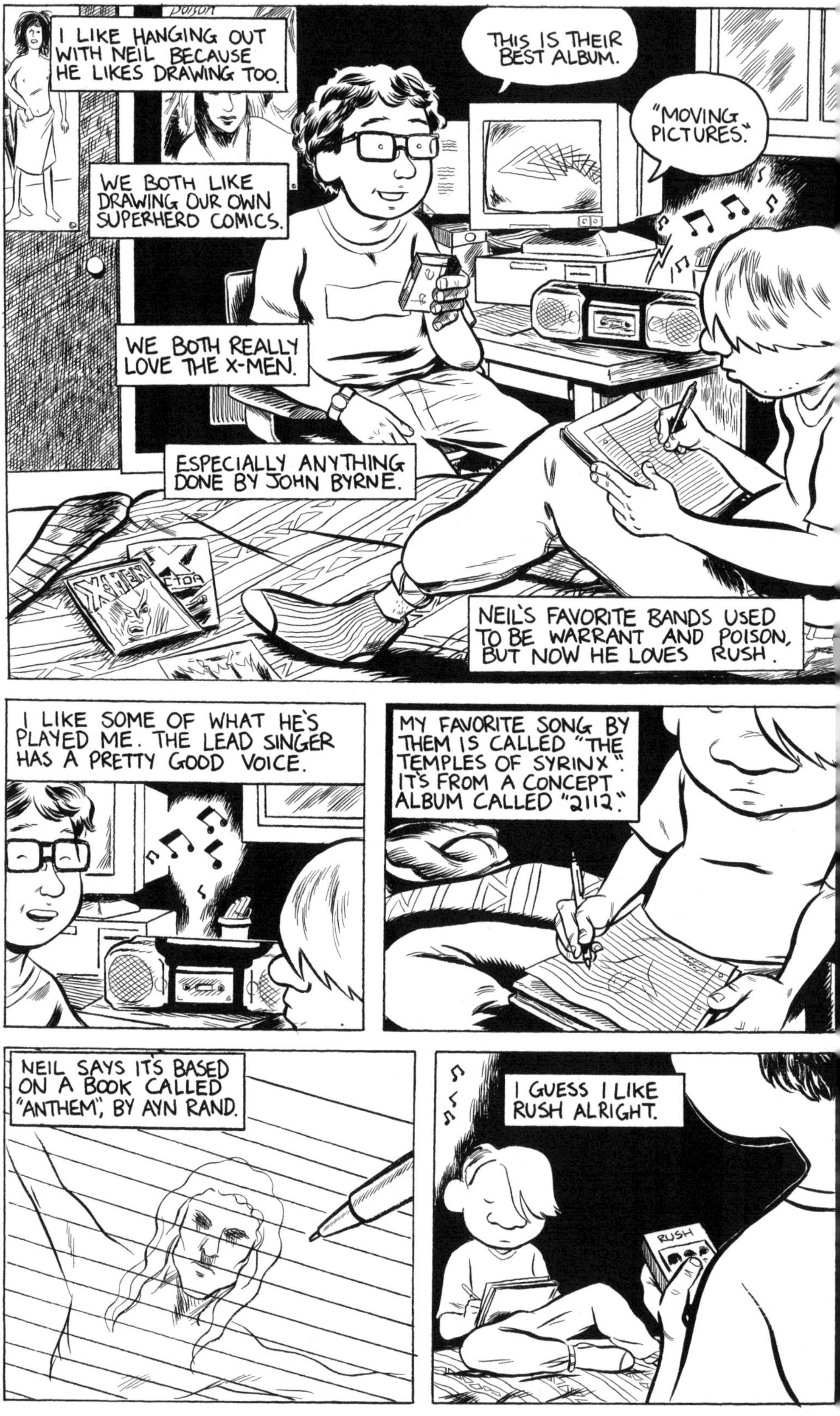
I LIKE HANGING OUT WITH NEIL BECAUSE HE LIKES DRAWING TOO.
THIS IS THEIR BEST ALBUM.
"MOVING PICTURES."
WE BOTH LIKE DRAWING OUR OWN SUPERHERO COMICS.
WE BOTH REALLY LOVE THE X-MEN.
ESPECIALLY ANYTHING DONE BY JOHN BYRNE.
NEIL'S FAVORITE BANDS USED TO BE WARRANT AND POISON, BUT NOW HE LOVES RUSH.
I LIKE SOME OF WHAT HE'S PLAYED ME. THE LEAD SINGER HAS A PRETTY GOOD VOICE.
MY FAVORITE SONG BY THEM IS CALLED "THE TEMPLES OF SYRINX". IT'S FROM A CONCEPT ALBUM CALLED "2112."
NEIL SAYS IT'S BASED ON A BOOK CALLED "ANTHEM", BY AYN RAND.
I GUESS I LIKE RUSH ALRIGHT.
RUSH

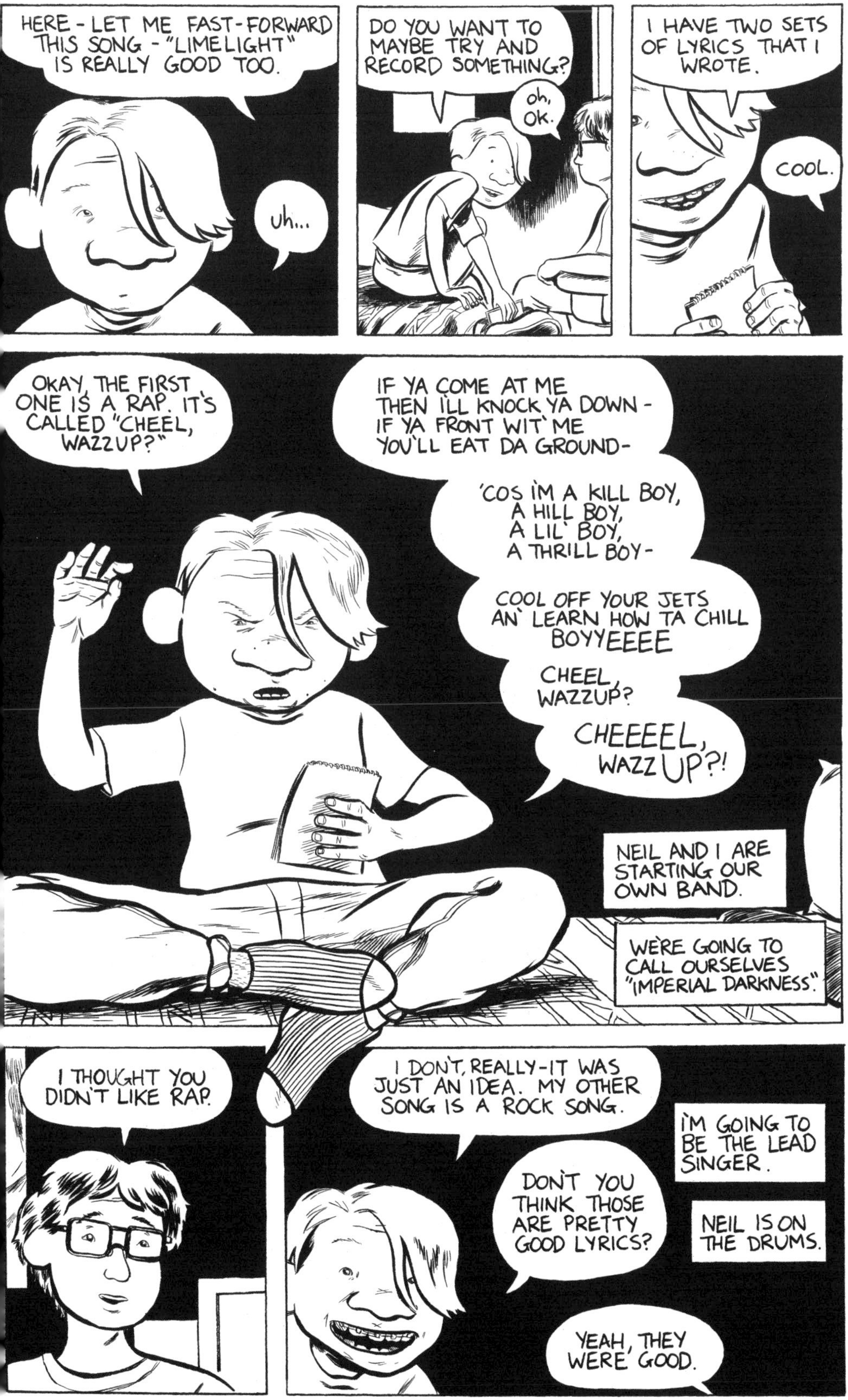

HERE - LET ME FAST-FORWARD THIS SONG - "LIMELIGHT" IS REALLY GOOD TOO.
uh...
DO YOU WANT TO MAYBE TRY AND RECORD SOMETHING?
oh, OK.
I HAVE TWO SETS OF LYRICS THAT I WROTE.
COOL.
OKAY, THE FIRST ONE IS A RAP. IT'S CALLED "CHEEL, WAZZUP?"
IF YA COME AT ME THEN I'LL KNOCK YA DOWN - IF YA FRONT WIT' ME YOU'LL EAT DA GROUND-
'COS I'M A KILL BOY, A HILL BOY, A LIL' BOY, A THRILL BOY-
COOL OFF YOUR JETS AN' LEARN HOW TA CHILL BOYYEEEE
CHEEL, WAZZUP?
CHEEEEL, WAZZ UP?!
NEIL AND I ARE STARTING OUR OWN BAND.
WE'RE GOING TO CALL OURSELVES "IMPERIAL DARKNESS".
I THOUGHT YOU DIDN'T LIKE RAP.
I DON'T, REALLY - IT WAS JUST AN IDEA. MY OTHER SONG IS A ROCK SONG.
I'M GOING TO BE THE LEAD SINGER.
DON'T YOU THINK THOSE ARE PRETTY GOOD LYRICS?
NEIL IS ON THE DRUMS.
YEAH, THEY WERE GOOD.

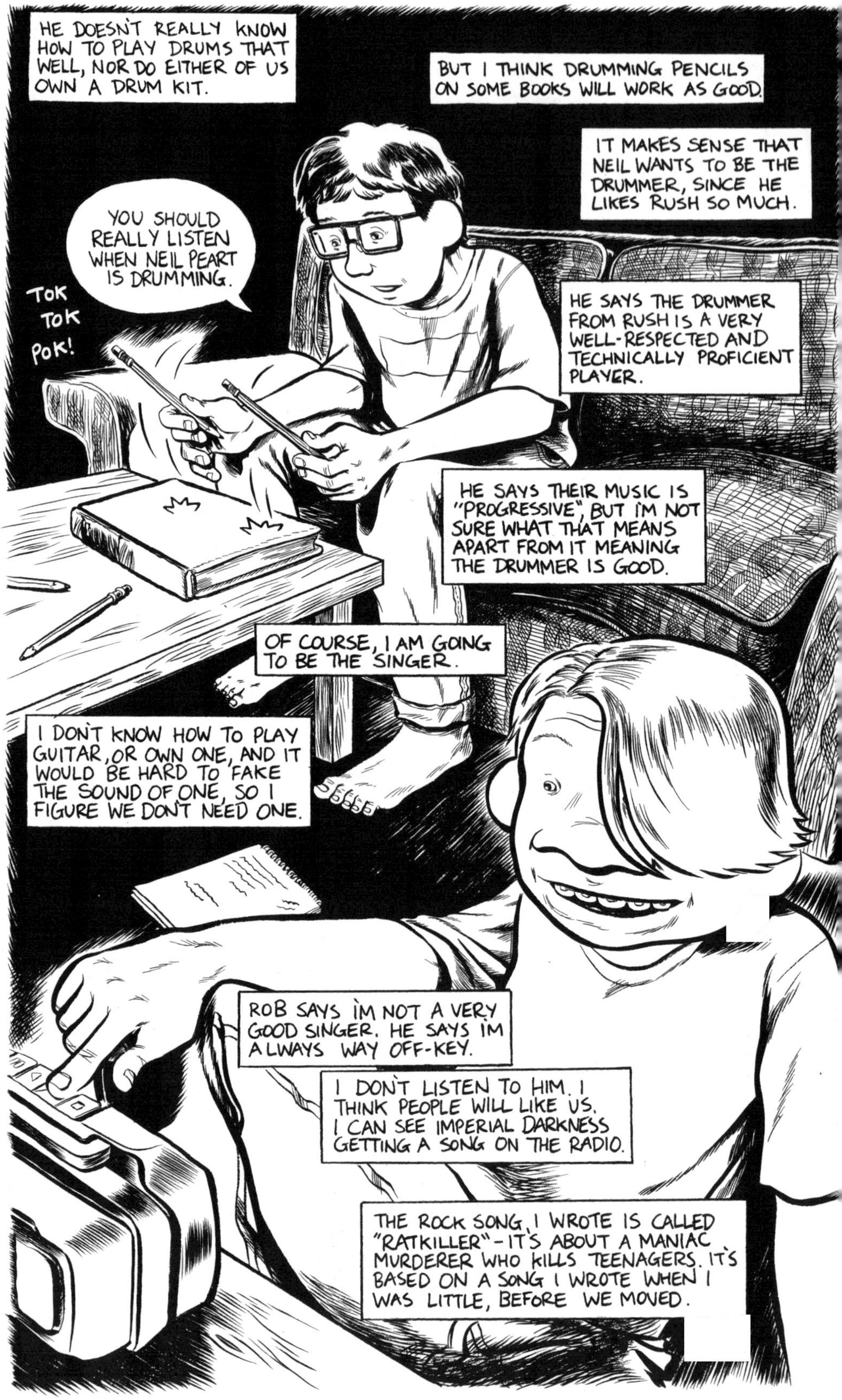
HE DOESN'T REALLY KNOW HOW TO PLAY DRUMS THAT WELL, NOR DO EITHER OF US OWN A DRUM KIT.
BUT I THINK DRUMMING PENCILS ON SOME BOOKS WILL WORK AS GOOD.
IT MAKES SENSE THAT NEIL WANTS TO BE THE DRUMMER, SINCE HE LIKES RUSH SO MUCH.
YOU SHOULD REALLY LISTEN WHEN NEIL PEART IS DRUMMING.
TOK TOK POK!
HE SAYS THE DRUMMER FROM RUSH IS A VERY WELL-RESPECTED AND TECHNICALLY PROFICIENT PLAYER.
HE SAYS THEIR MUSIC IS "PROGRESSIVE", BUT I'M NOT SURE WHAT THAT MEANS APART FROM IT MEANING THE DRUMMER IS GOOD.
OF COURSE, I AM GOING TO BE THE SINGER.
I DON'T KNOW HOW TO PLAY GUITAR, OR OWN ONE, AND IT WOULD BE HARD TO FAKE THE SOUND OF ONE, SO I FIGURE WE DON'T NEED ONE.
ROB SAYS I'M NOT A VERY GOOD SINGER. HE SAYS I'M ALWAYS WAY OFF-KEY.
I DON'T LISTEN TO HIM. I THINK PEOPLE WILL LIKE US. I CAN SEE IMPERIAL DARKNESS GETTING A SONG ON THE RADIO.
THE ROCK SONG I WROTE IS CALLED "RATKILLER" - IT'S ABOUT A MANIAC MURDERER WHO KILLS TEENAGERS. IT'S BASED ON A SONG I WROTE WHEN I WAS LITTLE, BEFORE WE MOVED.

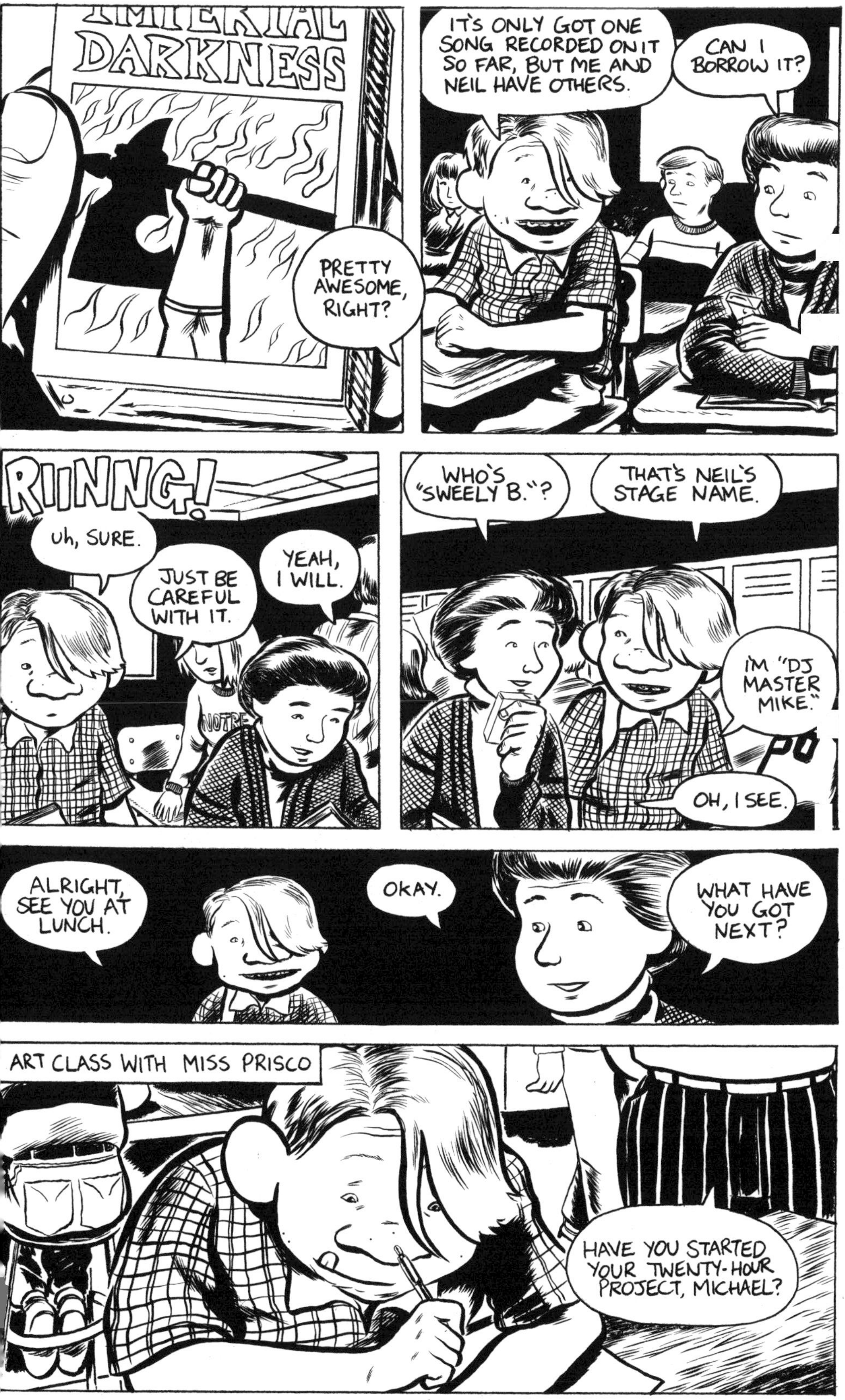
IMPERIAL
DARKNESS
PRETTY AWESOME, RIGHT?
IT'S ONLY GOT ONE SONG RECORDED ON IT SO FAR, BUT ME AND NEIL HAVE OTHERS.
CAN I BORROW IT?
RIINNG!
uh, SURE.
JUST BE CAREFUL WITH IT.
YEAH, I WILL.
NOTRE
WHO'S "SWEELY B."?
THAT'S NEIL'S STAGE NAME.
I'M "DJ MASTER MIKE."
OH, I SEE.
ALRIGHT, SEE YOU AT LUNCH.
OKAY.
WHAT HAVE YOU GOT NEXT?
ART CLASS WITH MISS PRISCO
HAVE YOU STARTED YOUR TWENTY-HOUR PROJECT, MICHAEL?

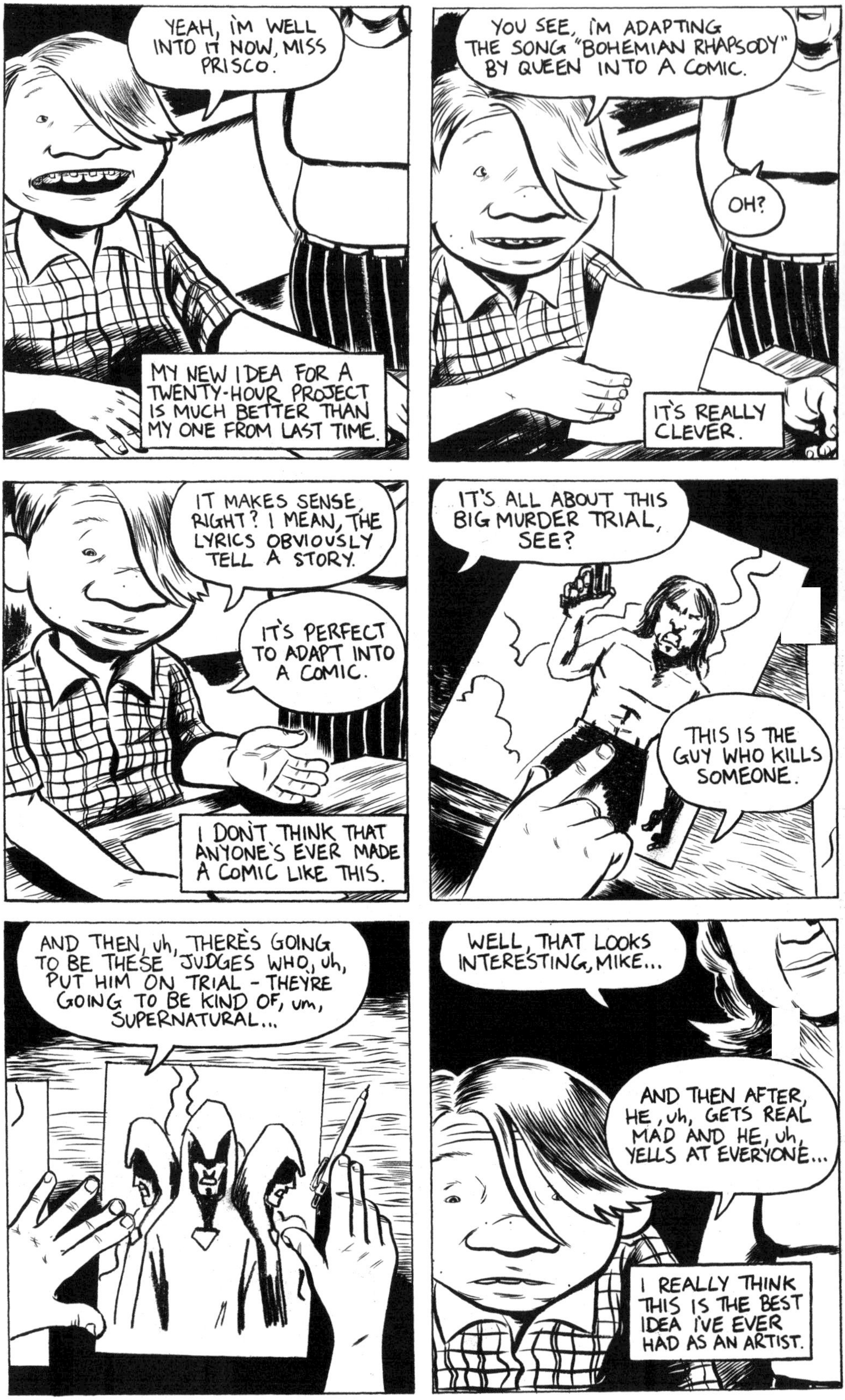
YEAH, I'M WELL INTO IT NOW, MISS PRISCO.
MY NEW IDEA FOR A TWENTY-HOUR PROJECT IS MUCH BETTER THAN MY ONE FROM LAST TIME.
YOU SEE, I'M ADAPTING THE SONG "BOHEMIAN RHAPSODY" BY QUEEN INTO A COMIC.
OH?
IT'S REALLY CLEVER.
IT MAKES SENSE, RIGHT? I MEAN, THE LYRICS OBVIOUSLY TELL A STORY.
IT'S PERFECT TO ADAPT INTO A COMIC.
I DON'T THINK THAT ANYONE'S EVER MADE A COMIC LIKE THIS.
IT'S ALL ABOUT THIS BIG MURDER TRIAL, SEE?
THIS IS THE GUY WHO KILLS SOMEONE.
AND THEN, uh, THERE'S GOING TO BE THESE JUDGES WHO, uh, PUT HIM ON TRIAL - THEY'RE GOING TO BE KIND OF, um, SUPERNATURAL...
WELL, THAT LOOKS INTERESTING, MIKE...
AND THEN AFTER, HE, uh, GETS REAL MAD AND HE, uh, YELLS AT EVERYONE...
I REALLY THINK THIS IS THE BEST IDEA I'VE EVER HAD AS AN ARTIST.

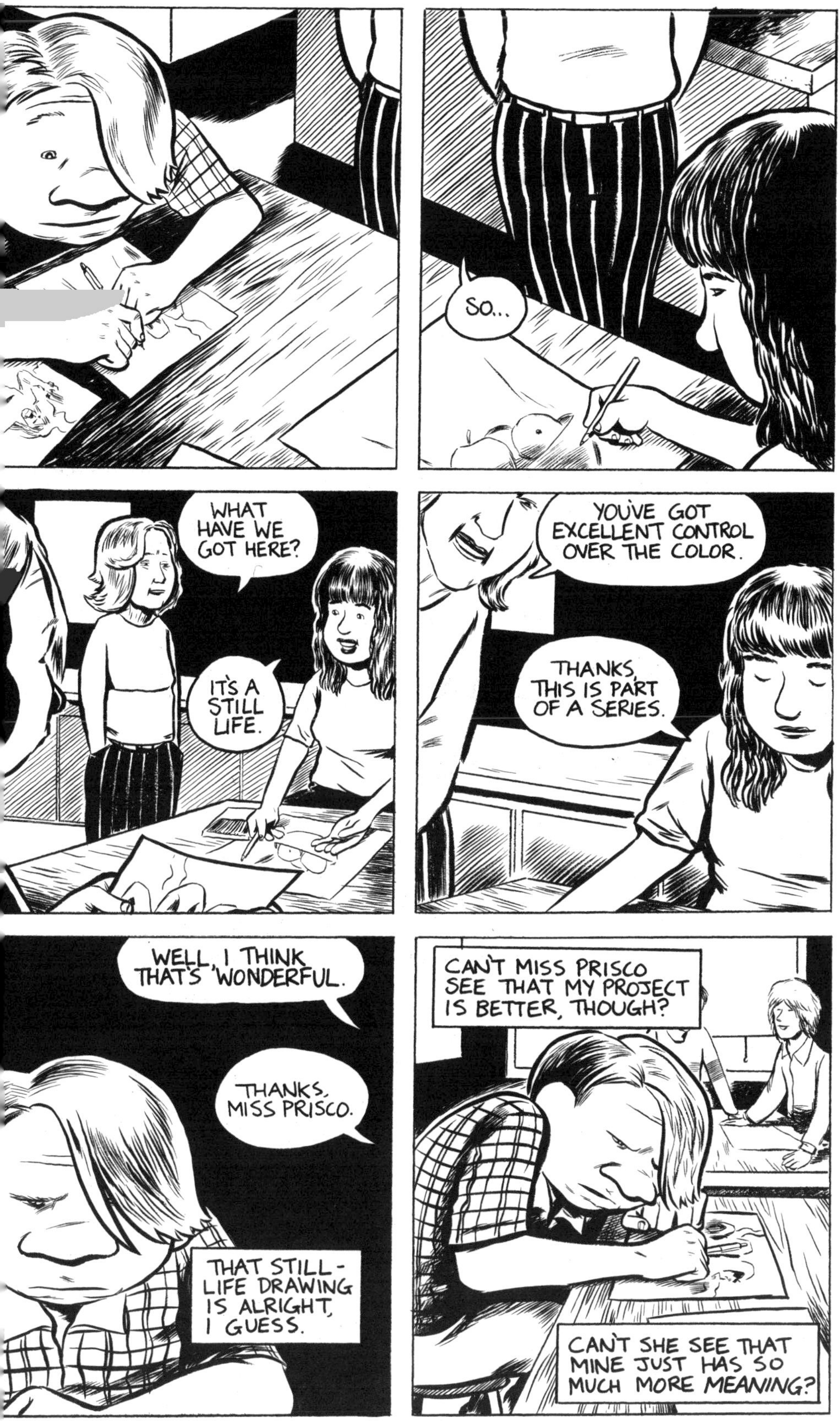
SO...
WHAT HAVE WE GOT HERE?
IT'S A STILL LIFE.
YOU'VE GOT EXCELLENT CONTROL OVER THE COLOR.
THANKS, THIS IS PART OF A SERIES.
WELL, I THINK THAT'S WONDERFUL.
THANKS, MISS PRISCO.
THAT STILL-LIFE DRAWING IS ALRIGHT, I GUESS.
CAN'T MISS PRISCO SEE THAT MY PROJECT IS BETTER, THOUGH?
CAN'T SHE SEE THAT MINE JUST HAS SO MUCH MORE MEANING?

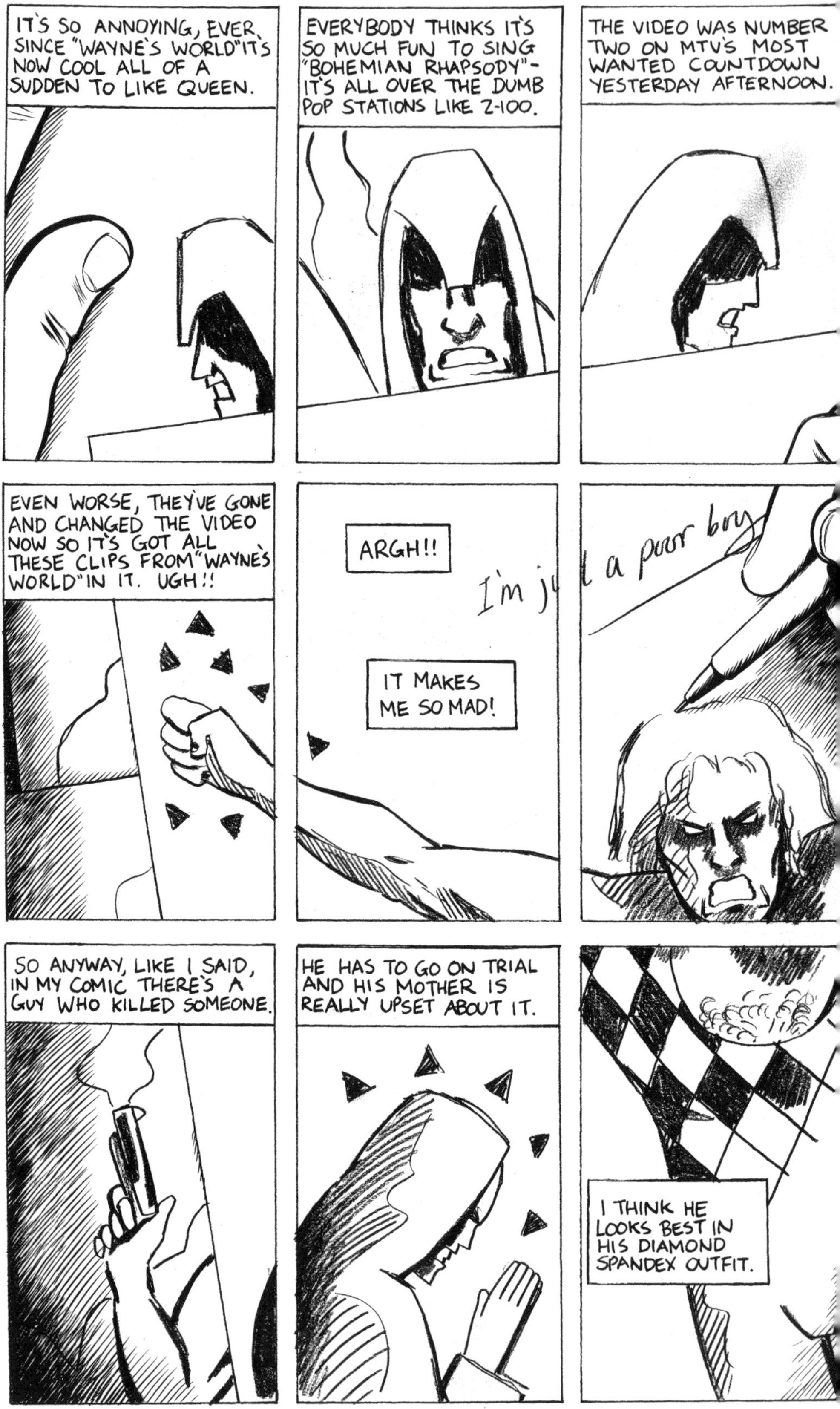
IT'S SO ANNOYING, EVER SINCE "WAYNE'S WORLD" IT'S NOW COOL ALL OF A SUDDEN TO LIKE QUEEN.
EVERYBODY THINKS IT'S SO MUCH FUN TO SING "BOHEMIAN RHAPSODY"- IT'S ALL OVER THE DUMB POP STATIONS LIKE Z-100.
THE VIDEO WAS NUMBER TWO ON MTV'S MOST WANTED COUNTDOWN YESTERDAY AFTERNOON.
EVEN WORSE, THEY'VE GONE AND CHANGED THE VIDEO NOW SO IT'S GOT ALL THESE CLIPS FROM "WAYNE'S WORLD" IN IT. UGH!!
ARGH!!
IT MAKES ME SO MAD!
I'm ju a poor boy
SO ANYWAY, LIKE I SAID, IN MY COMIC THERE'S A GUY WHO KILLED SOMEONE.
HE HAS TO GO ON TRIAL AND HIS MOTHER IS REALLY UPSET ABOUT IT.
I THINK HE LOOKS BEST IN HIS DIAMOND SPANDEX OUTFIT.

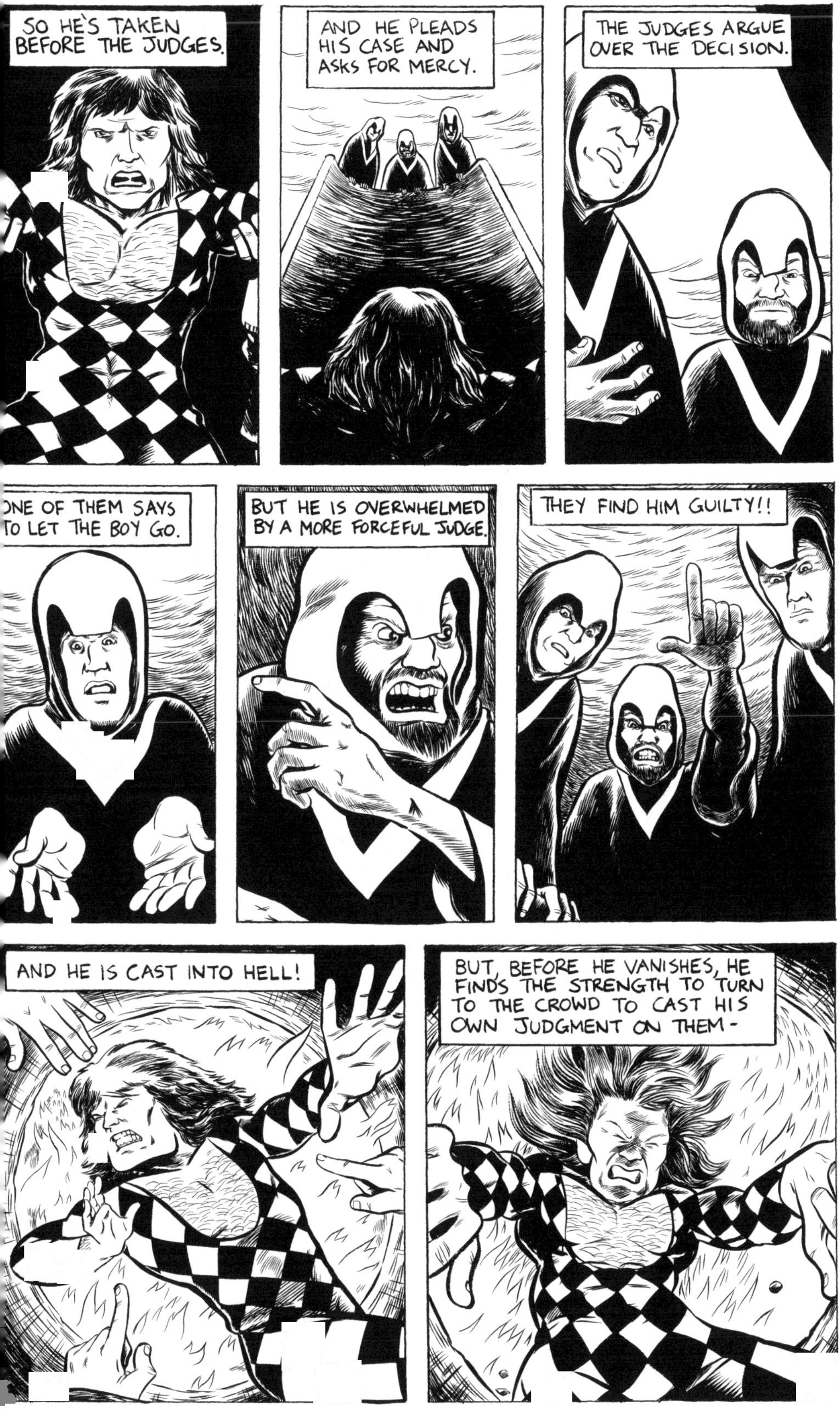
SO HE'S TAKEN BEFORE THE JUDGES.
AND HE PLEADS HIS CASE AND ASKS FOR MERCY.
THE JUDGES ARGUE OVER THE DECISION.
ONE OF THEM SAYS TO LET THE BOY GO.
BUT HE IS OVERWHELMED BY A MORE FORCEFUL JUDGE.
THEY FIND HIM GUILTY!!
AND HE IS CAST INTO HELL!
BUT, BEFORE HE VANISHES, HE FINDS THE STRENGTH TO TURN TO THE CROWD TO CAST HIS OWN JUDGMENT ON THEM -

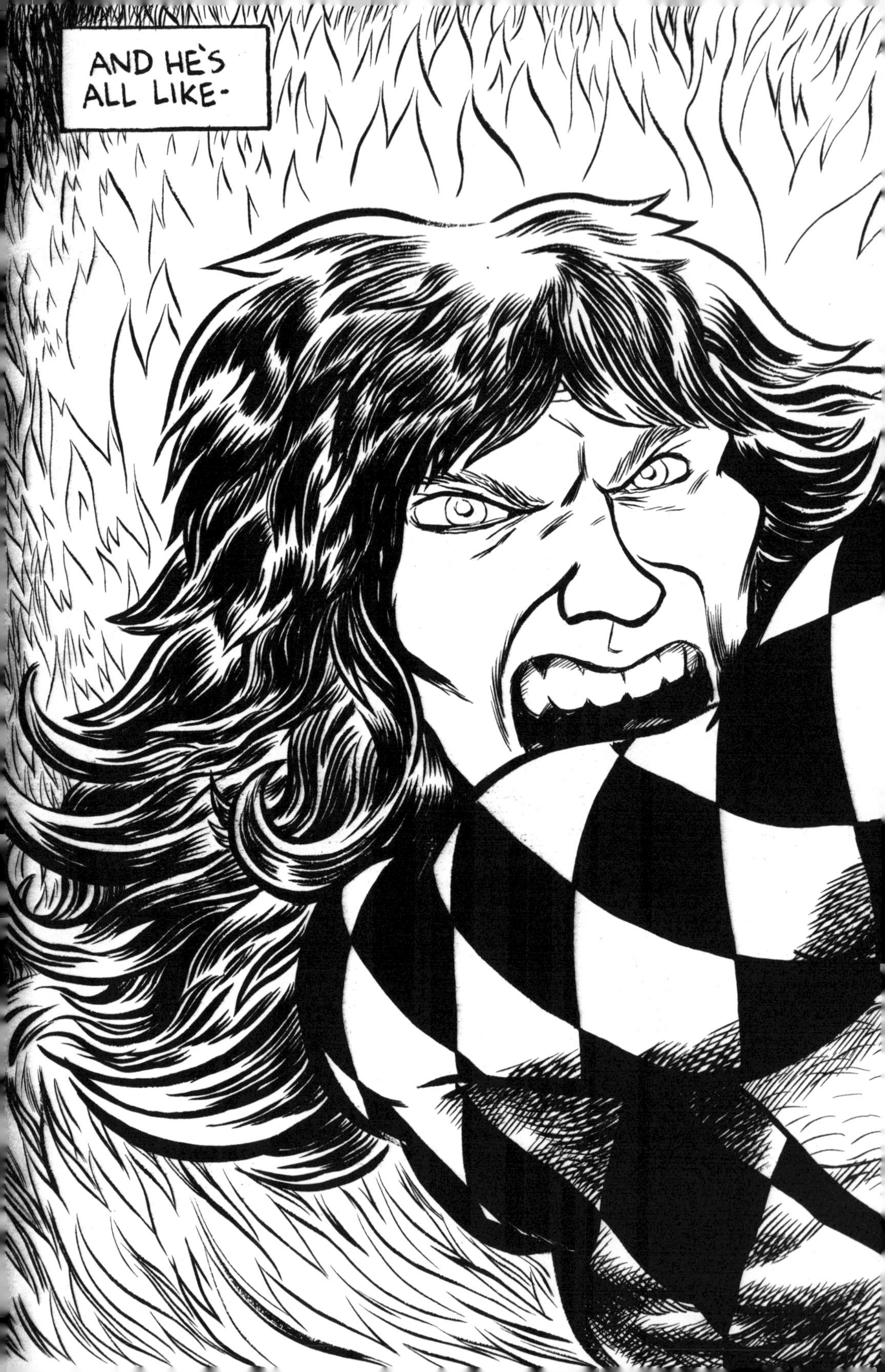
AND HE'S ALL LIKE-

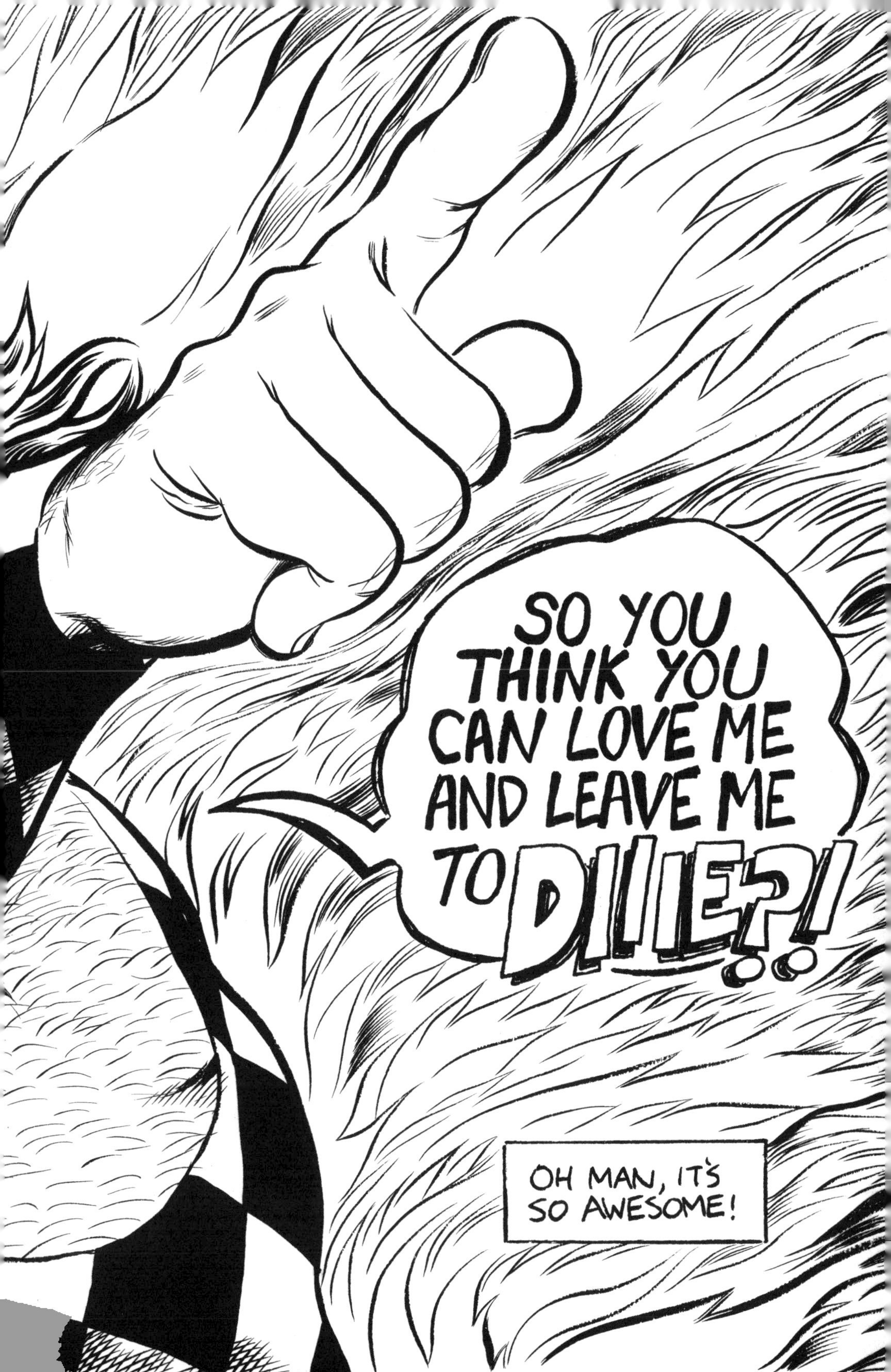
SO YOU THINK YOU CAN LOVE ME AND LEAVE ME TO DIIIE?!
OH MAN, IT'S SO AWESOME!

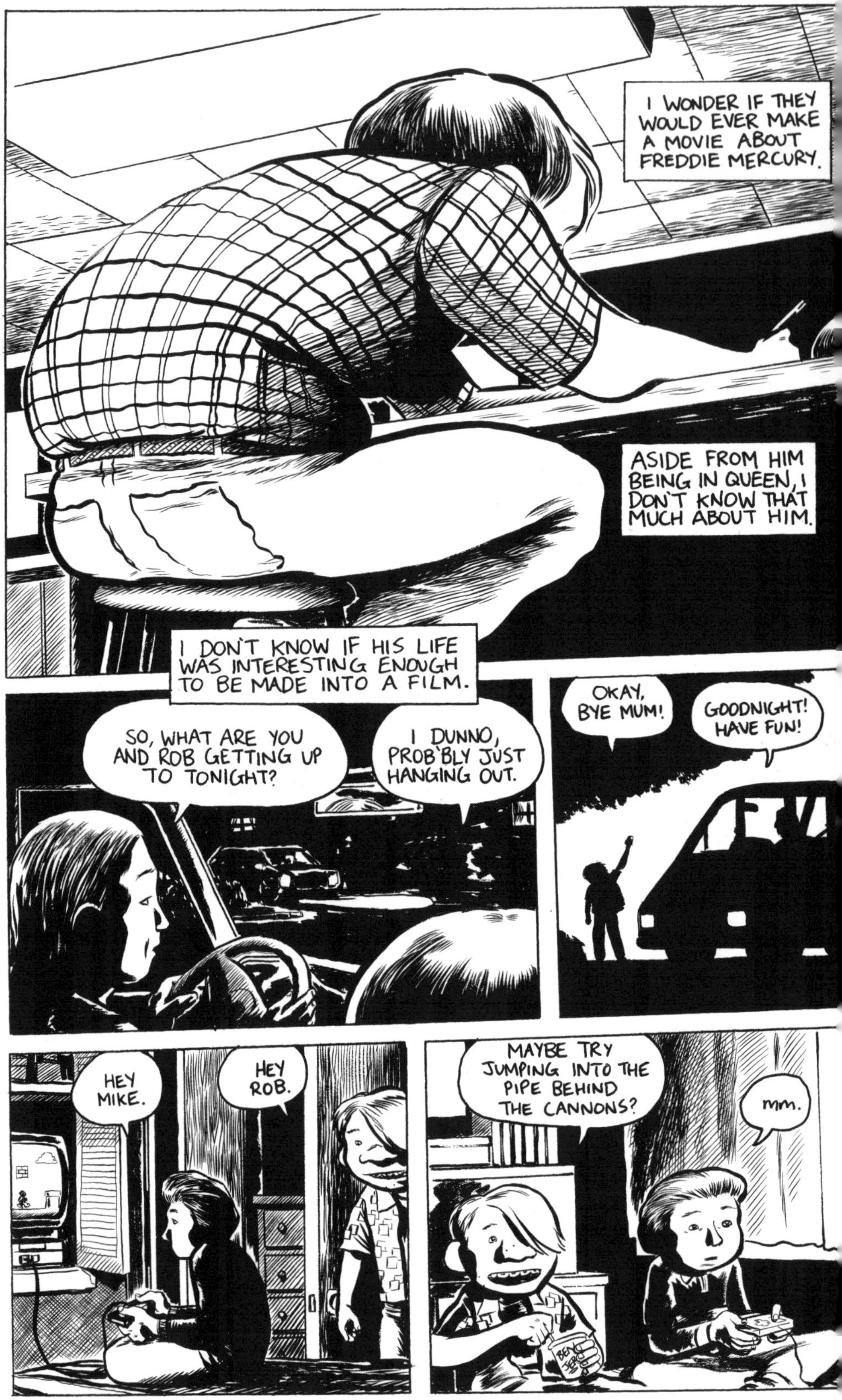
I WONDER IF THEY WOULD EVER MAKE A MOVIE ABOUT FREDDIE MERCURY.
ASIDE FROM HIM BEING IN QUEEN, I DON'T KNOW THAT MUCH ABOUT HIM.
I DON'T KNOW IF HIS LIFE WAS INTERESTING ENOUGH TO BE MADE INTO A FILM.
SO, WHAT ARE YOU AND ROB GETTING UP TO TONIGHT?
I DUNNO, PROB'BLY JUST HANGING OUT.
OKAY, BYE MUM!
GOODNIGHT! HAVE FUN!
HEY MIKE.
HEY ROB.
MAYBE TRY JUMPING INTO THE PIPE BEHIND THE CANNONS?
mm.

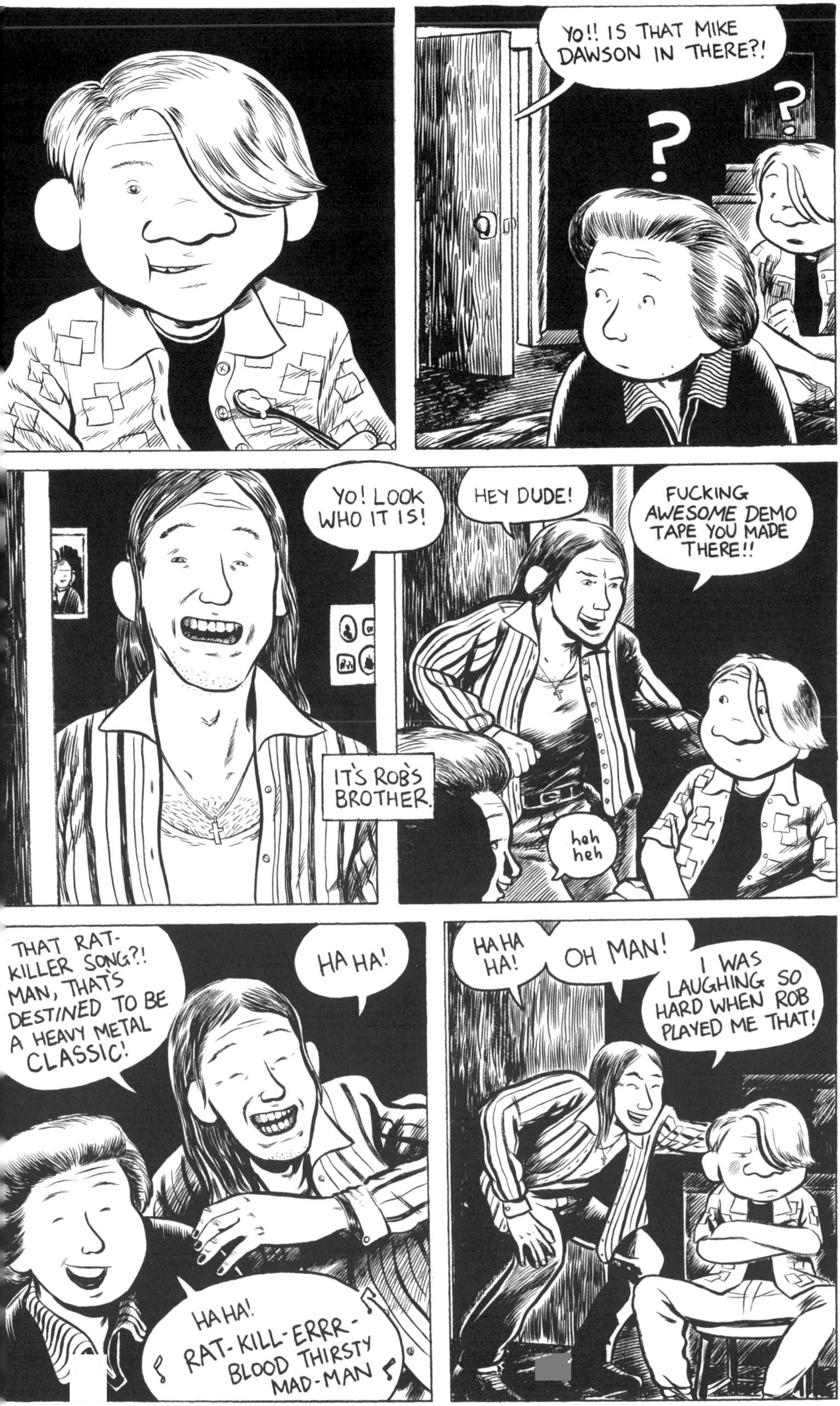
YO!! IS THAT MIKE DAWSON IN THERE?!
?
?
YO! LOOK WHO IT IS!
IT'S ROB'S BROTHER.
HEY DUDE!
FUCKING AWESOME DEMO TAPE YOU MADE THERE!!
heh heh
THAT RAT-KILLER SONG?! MAN, THAT'S DESTINED TO BE A HEAVY METAL CLASSIC!
HA HA!
HA HA! RAT-KILL-ERRR- BLOOD THIRSTY MAD-MAN
HA HA HA!
OH MAN!
I WAS LAUGHING SO HARD WHEN ROB PLAYED ME THAT!

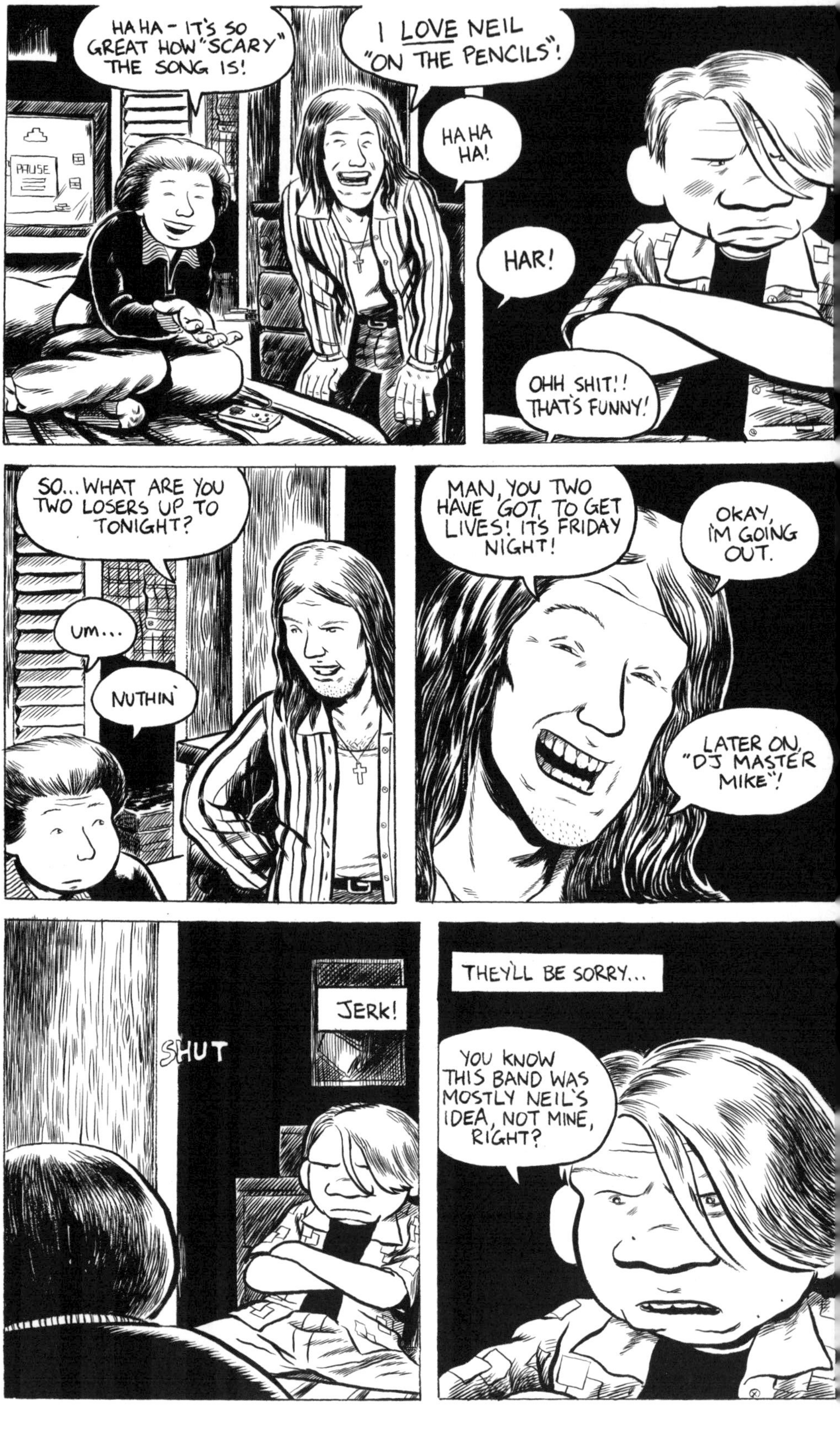
HA HA - IT'S SO GREAT HOW "SCARY" THE SONG IS!
I LOVE NEIL "ON THE PENCILS"!
HA HA HA!
HAR!
OHH SHIT!! THAT'S FUNNY!
SO... WHAT ARE YOU TWO LOSERS UP TO TONIGHT?
UM...
NUTHIN'
MAN, YOU TWO HAVE GOT TO GET LIVES! IT'S FRIDAY NIGHT!
OKAY, I'M GOING OUT.
LATER ON, "DJ MASTER MIKE"!
SHUT
JERK!
THEY'LL BE SORRY...
YOU KNOW THIS BAND WAS MOSTLY NEIL'S IDEA, NOT MINE, RIGHT?

ONCE MORE, AN IMAGINED CONVERSATION BETWEEN TWO OF ROCK'S BIGGEST SUPERSTARS

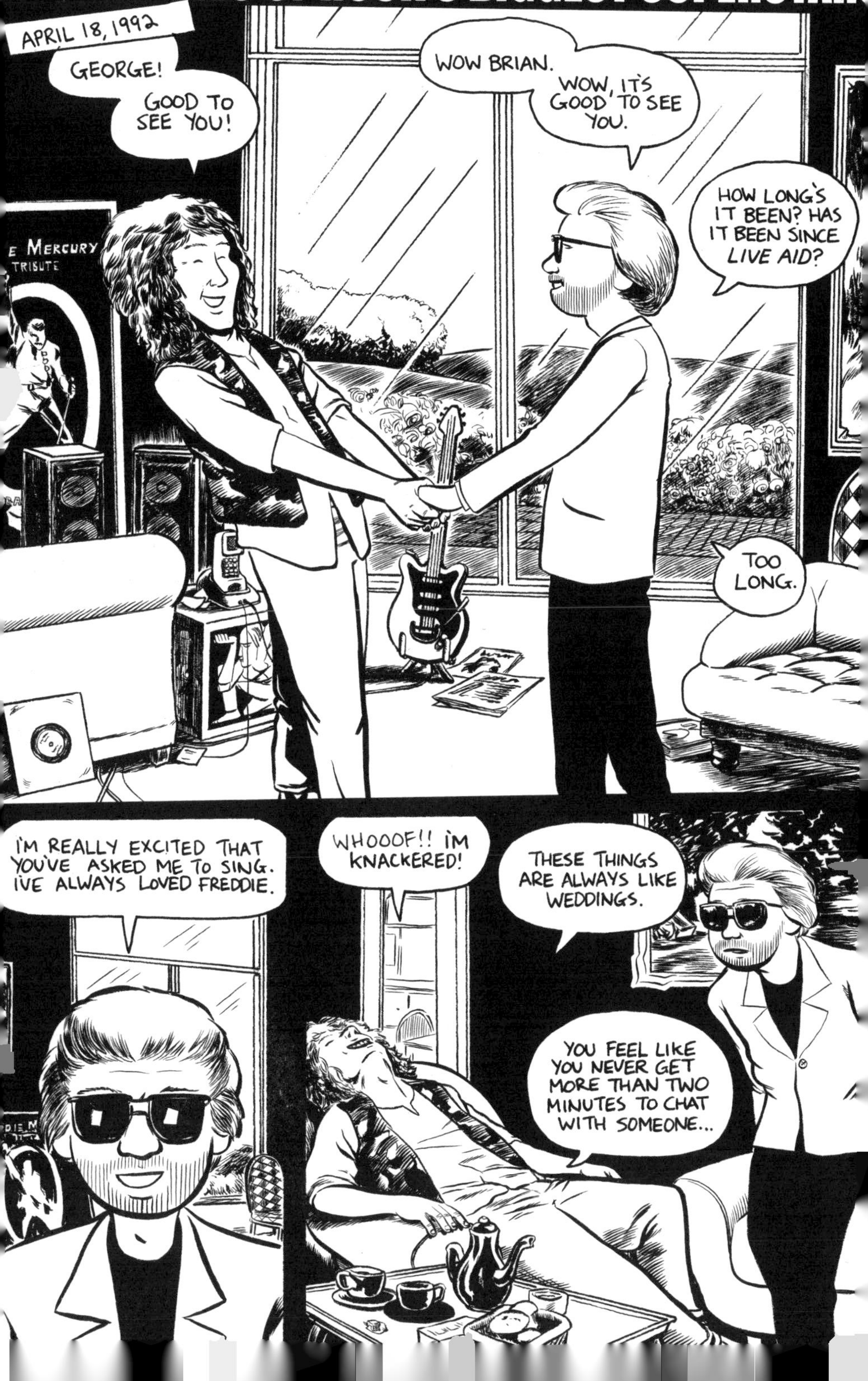
APRIL 18, 1992
GEORGE!
GOOD TO SEE YOU!
WOW BRIAN.
WOW, IT'S GOOD TO SEE YOU.
MERCURY
TRIBUTE
HOW LONG'S IT BEEN? HAS IT BEEN SINCE *LIVE AID*?
TOO LONG.
I'M REALLY EXCITED THAT YOU'VE ASKED ME TO SING. I'VE ALWAYS LOVED FREDDIE.
WHOOOF!! I'M KNACKERED!
THESE THINGS ARE ALWAYS LIKE WEDDINGS.
YOU FEEL LIKE YOU NEVER GET MORE THAN TWO MINUTES TO CHAT WITH SOMEONE...

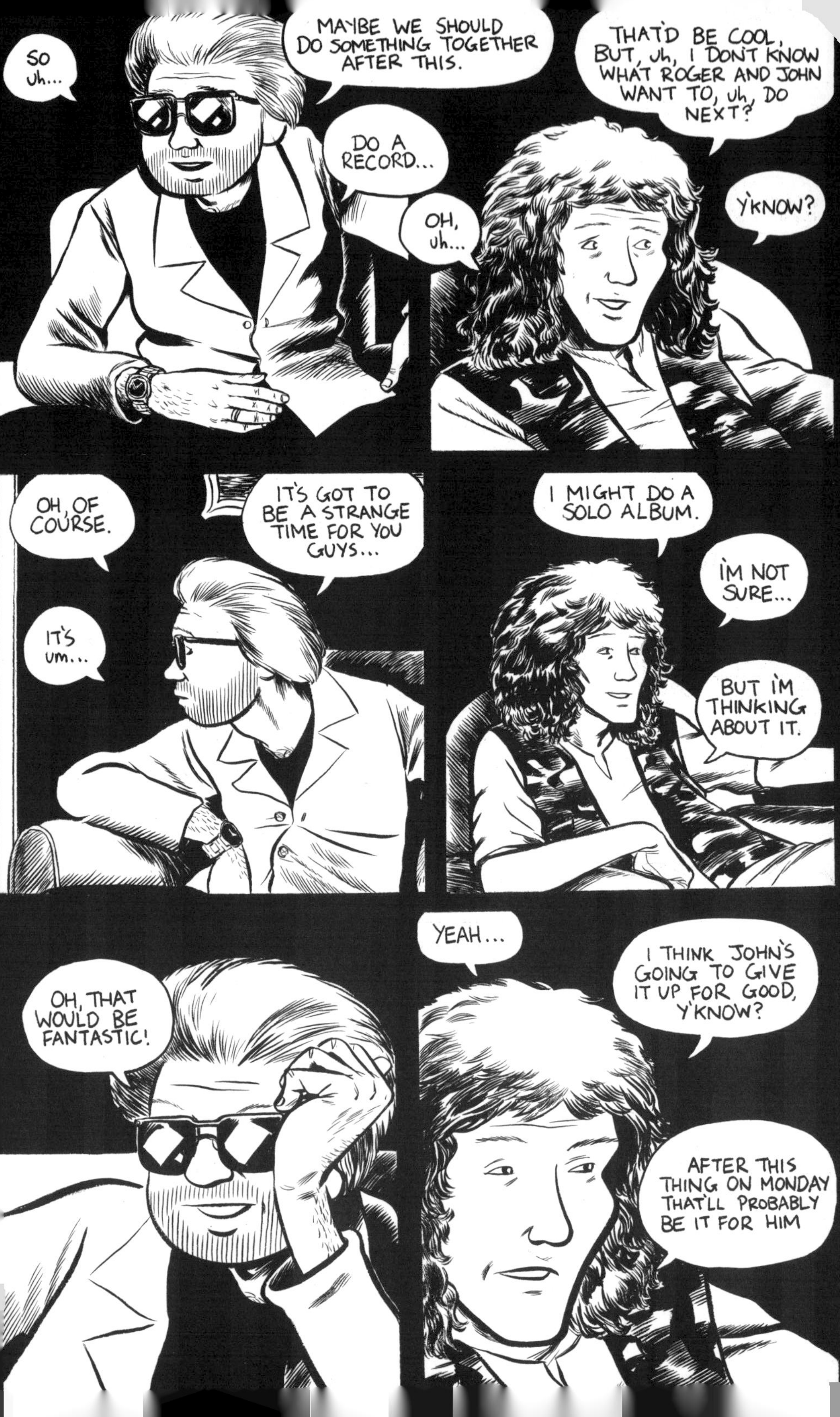
SO uh...
MAYBE WE SHOULD DO SOMETHING TOGETHER AFTER THIS.
THAT'D BE COOL, BUT, uh, I DON'T KNOW WHAT ROGER AND JOHN WANT TO, uh, DO NEXT?
DO A RECORD...
OH, uh...
Y'KNOW?
OH, OF COURSE.
IT'S GOT TO BE A STRANGE TIME FOR YOU GUYS...
IT'S um...
I MIGHT DO A SOLO ALBUM.
I'M NOT SURE...
BUT I'M THINKING ABOUT IT.
OH, THAT WOULD BE FANTASTIC!
YEAH...
I THINK JOHN'S GOING TO GIVE IT UP FOR GOOD, Y'KNOW?
AFTER THIS THING ON MONDAY THAT'LL PROBABLY BE IT FOR HIM

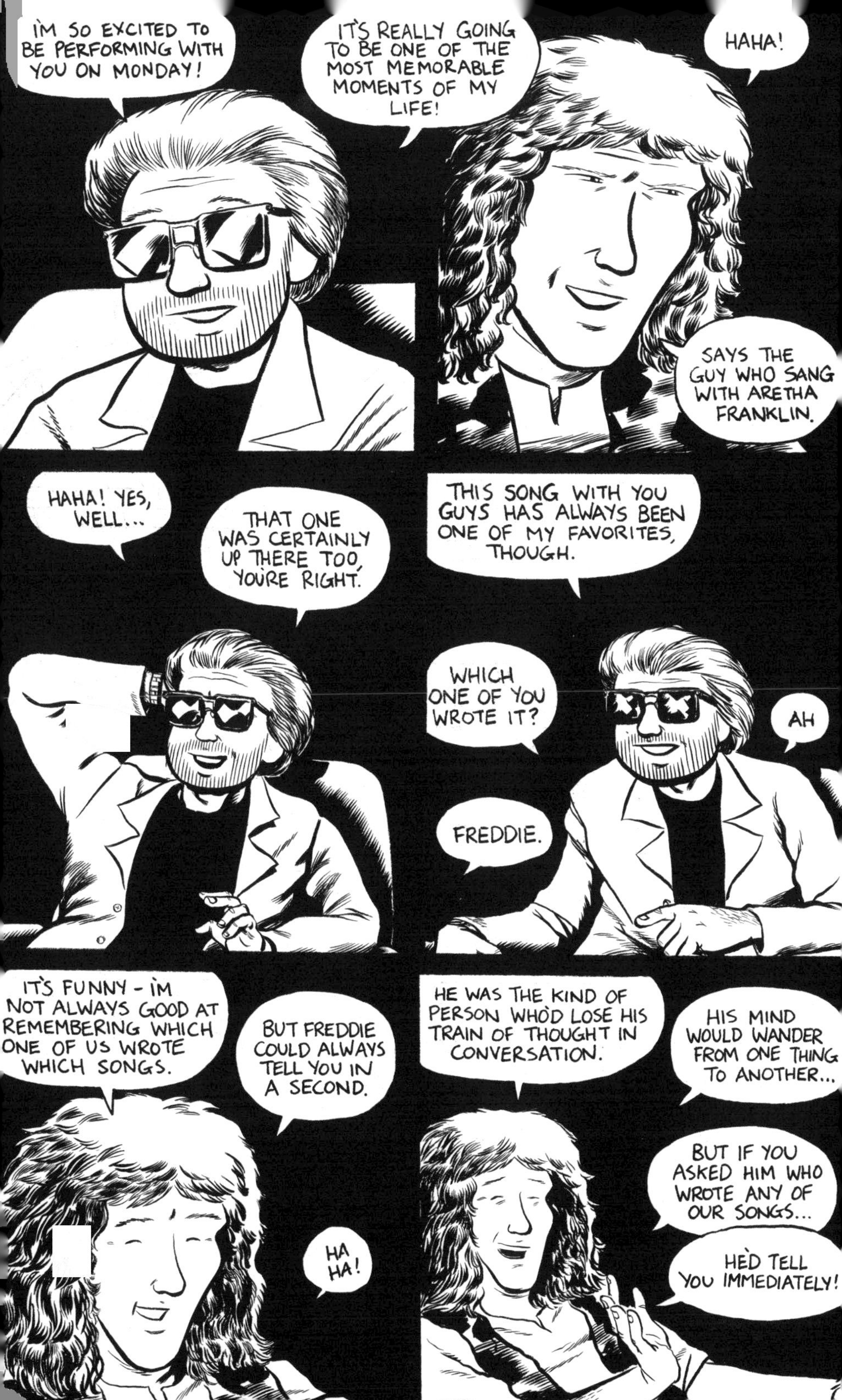
I'M SO EXCITED TO BE PERFORMING WITH YOU ON MONDAY!
IT'S REALLY GOING TO BE ONE OF THE MOST MEMORABLE MOMENTS OF MY LIFE!
HAHA!
SAYS THE GUY WHO SANG WITH ARETHA FRANKLIN.
HAHA! YES, WELL...
THAT ONE WAS CERTAINLY UP THERE TOO, YOU'RE RIGHT.
THIS SONG WITH YOU GUYS HAS ALWAYS BEEN ONE OF MY FAVORITES, THOUGH.
WHICH ONE OF YOU WROTE IT?
AH
FREDDIE.
IT'S FUNNY - I'M NOT ALWAYS GOOD AT REMEMBERING WHICH ONE OF US WROTE WHICH SONGS.
BUT FREDDIE COULD ALWAYS TELL YOU IN A SECOND.
HA HA!
HE WAS THE KIND OF PERSON WHO'D LOSE HIS TRAIN OF THOUGHT IN CONVERSATION.
HIS MIND WOULD WANDER FROM ONE THING TO ANOTHER...
BUT IF YOU ASKED HIM WHO WROTE ANY OF OUR SONGS...
HE'D TELL YOU IMMEDIATELY!

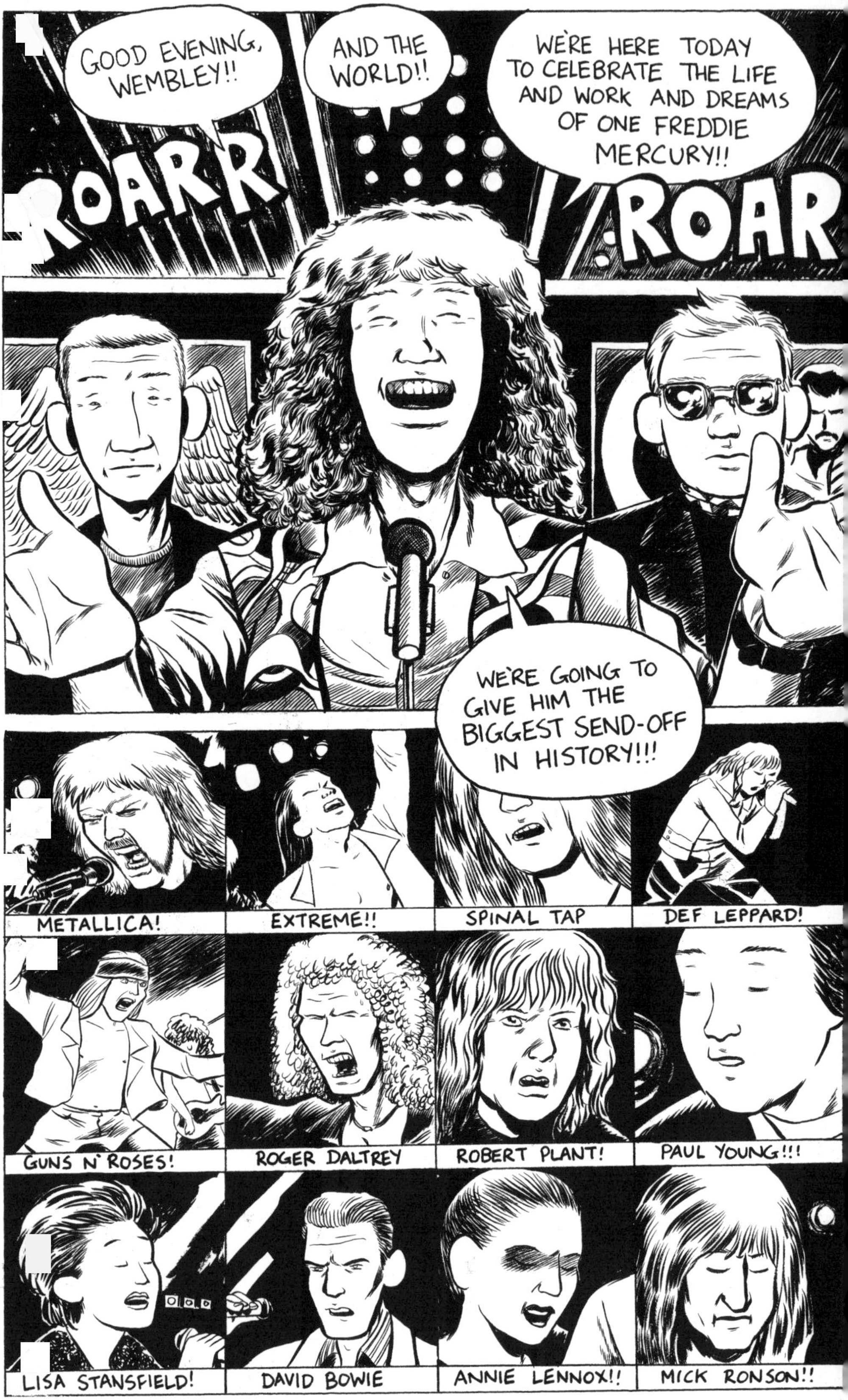
GOOD EVENING, WEMBLEY!!
AND THE WORLD!!
WE'RE HERE TODAY TO CELEBRATE THE LIFE AND WORK AND DREAMS OF ONE FREDDIE MERCURY!!
ROARR
ROAR
WE'RE GOING TO GIVE HIM THE BIGGEST SEND-OFF IN HISTORY!!!
METALLICA!
EXTREME!!
SPINAL TAP
DEF LEPPARD!
GUNS N' ROSES!
ROGER DALTREY
ROBERT PLANT!
PAUL YOUNG!!!
LISA STANSFIELD!
DAVID BOWIE
ANNIE LENNOX!!
MICK RONSON!!

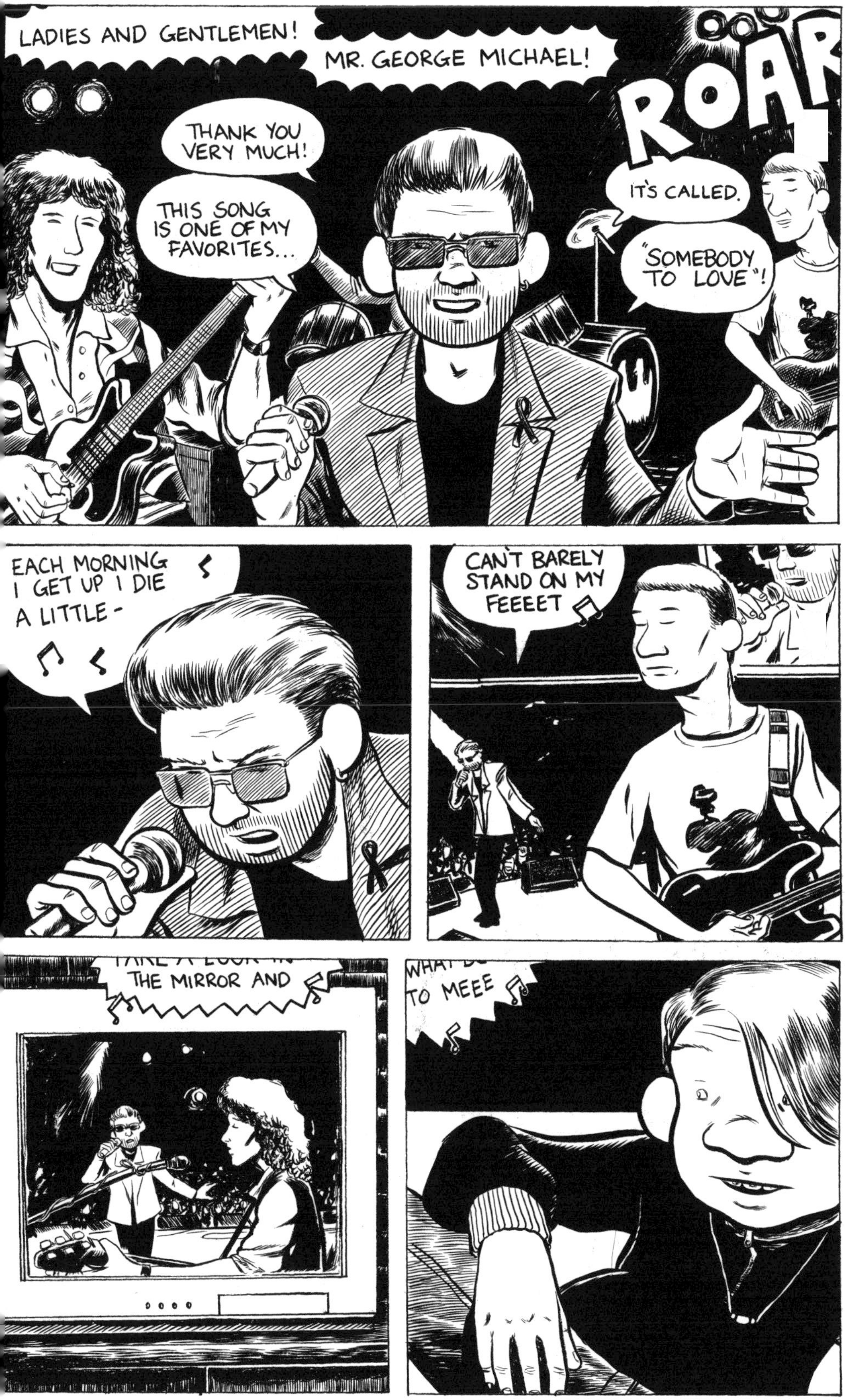
LADIES AND GENTLEMEN!
MR. GEORGE MICHAEL!
ROAR
THANK YOU VERY MUCH!
THIS SONG IS ONE OF MY FAVORITES...
IT'S CALLED.
"SOMEBODY TO LOVE"!
EACH MORNING I GET UP I DIE A LITTLE -
CAN'T BARELY STAND ON MY FEEEET
THE MIRROR AND
TO MEEE

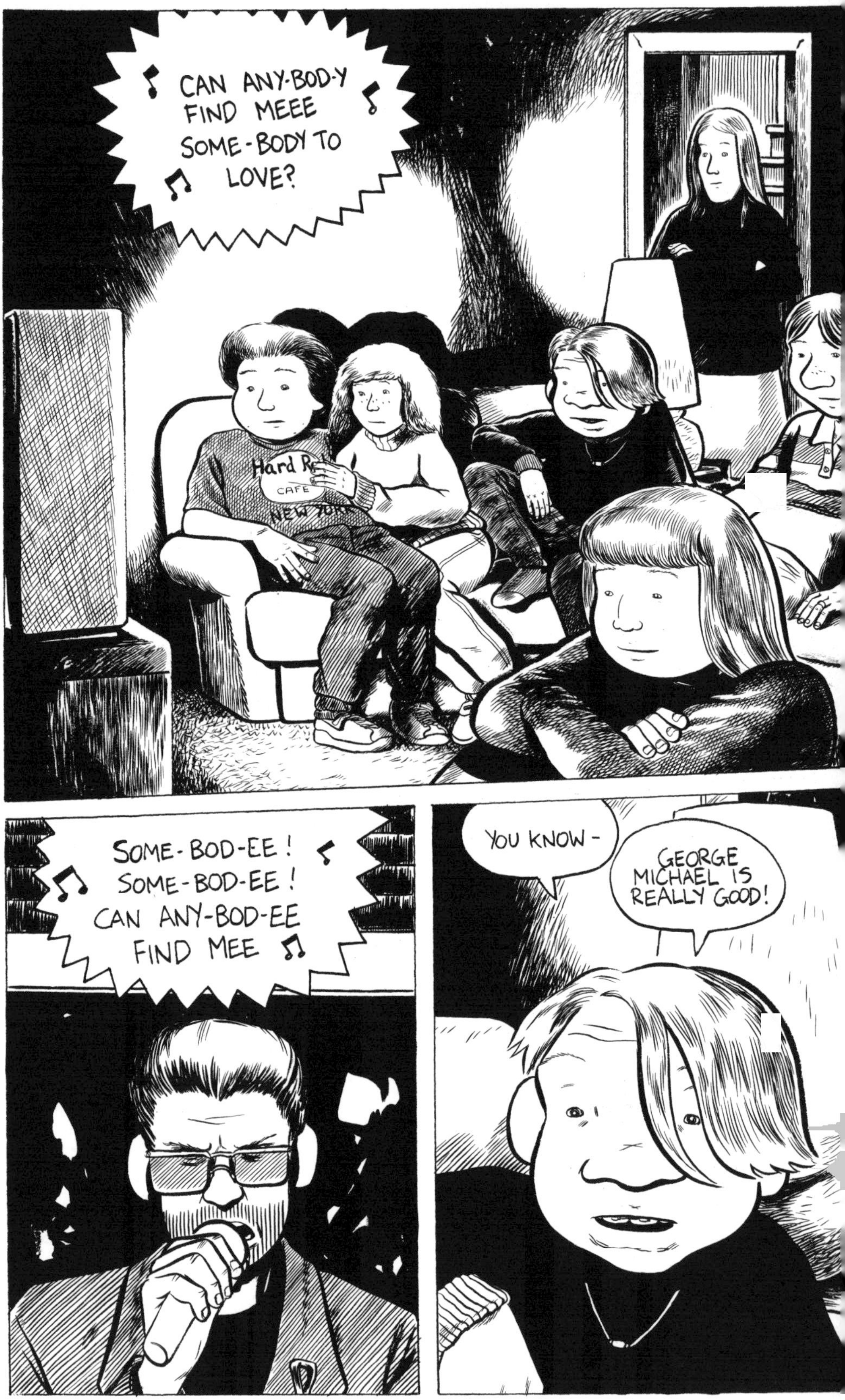
CAN ANY-BOD-Y FIND MEEE SOME-BODY TO LOVE?
Hard Rock CAFE NEW YORK
SOME-BOD-EE! SOME-BOD-EE! CAN ANY-BOD-EE FIND MEE
YOU KNOW -
GEORGE MICHAEL IS REALLY GOOD!

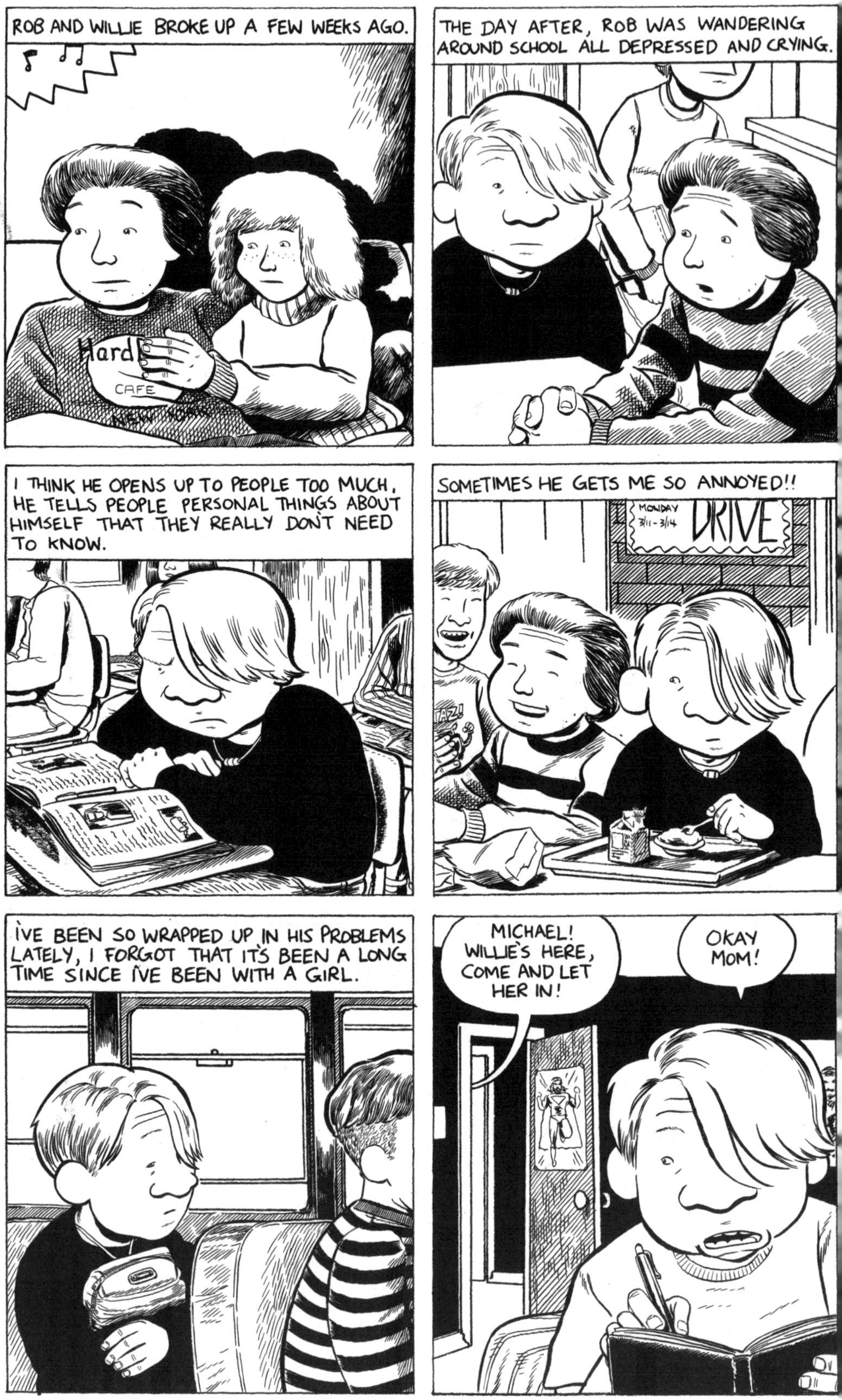
ROB AND WILLIE BROKE UP A FEW WEEKS AGO.
Hard
CAFE
NEW YORK
THE DAY AFTER, ROB WAS WANDERING AROUND SCHOOL ALL DEPRESSED AND CRYING.
I THINK HE OPENS UP TO PEOPLE TOO MUCH, HE TELLS PEOPLE PERSONAL THINGS ABOUT HIMSELF THAT THEY REALLY DON'T NEED TO KNOW.
SOMETIMES HE GETS ME SO ANNOYED!!
MONDAY 3/11 - 3/14
DRIVE
I'VE BEEN SO WRAPPED UP IN HIS PROBLEMS LATELY, I FORGOT THAT IT'S BEEN A LONG TIME SINCE I'VE BEEN WITH A GIRL.
MICHAEL! WILLIE'S HERE, COME AND LET HER IN!
OKAY MOM!

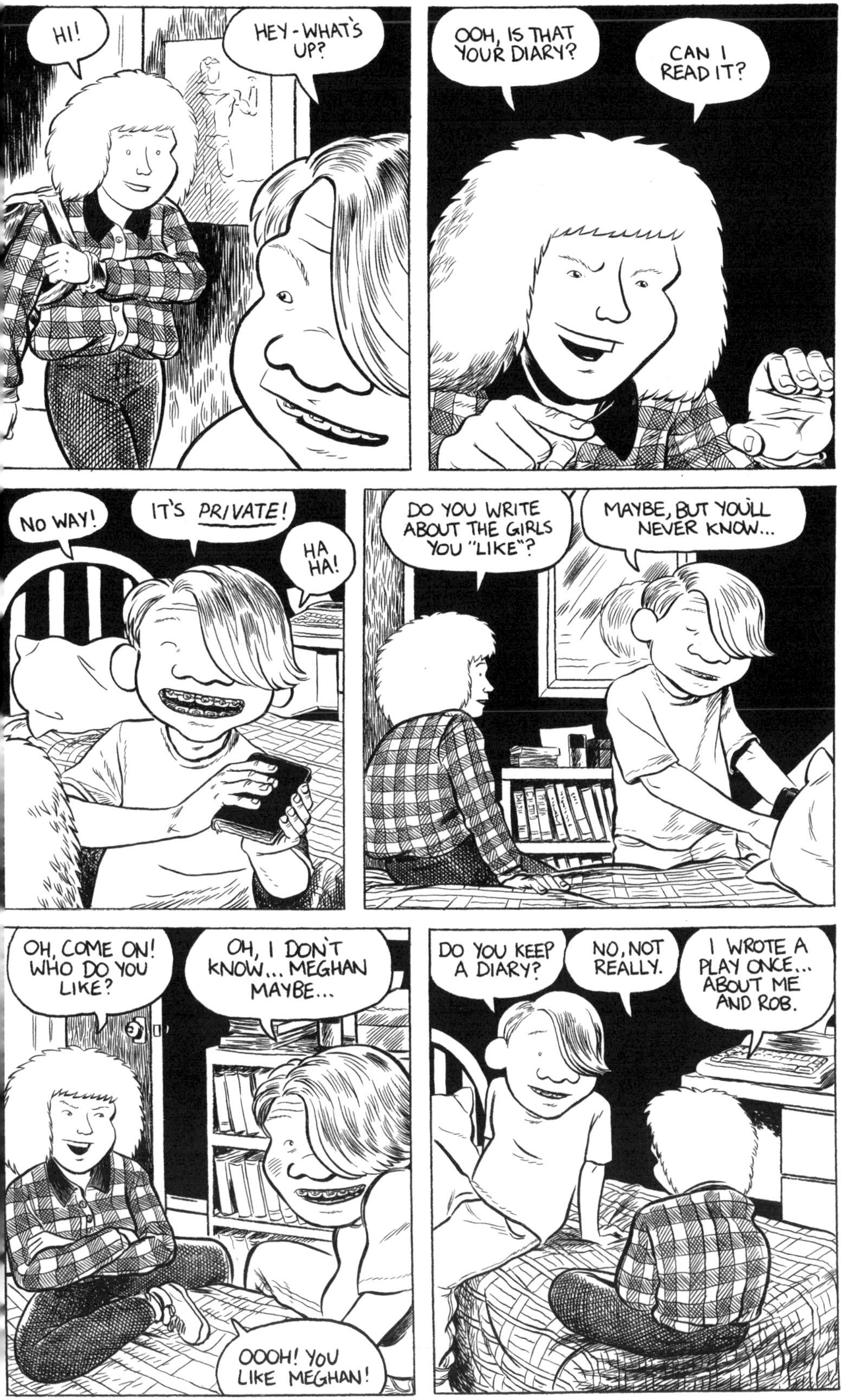
HI!
HEY - WHAT'S UP?
OOH, IS THAT YOUR DIARY?
CAN I READ IT?
NO WAY!
IT'S PRIVATE!
HA HA!
DO YOU WRITE ABOUT THE GIRLS YOU "LIKE"?
MAYBE, BUT YOU'LL NEVER KNOW...
OH, COME ON! WHO DO YOU LIKE?
OH, I DON'T KNOW... MEGHAN MAYBE...
OOOH! YOU LIKE MEGHAN!
DO YOU KEEP A DIARY?
NO, NOT REALLY.
I WROTE A PLAY ONCE... ABOUT ME AND ROB.

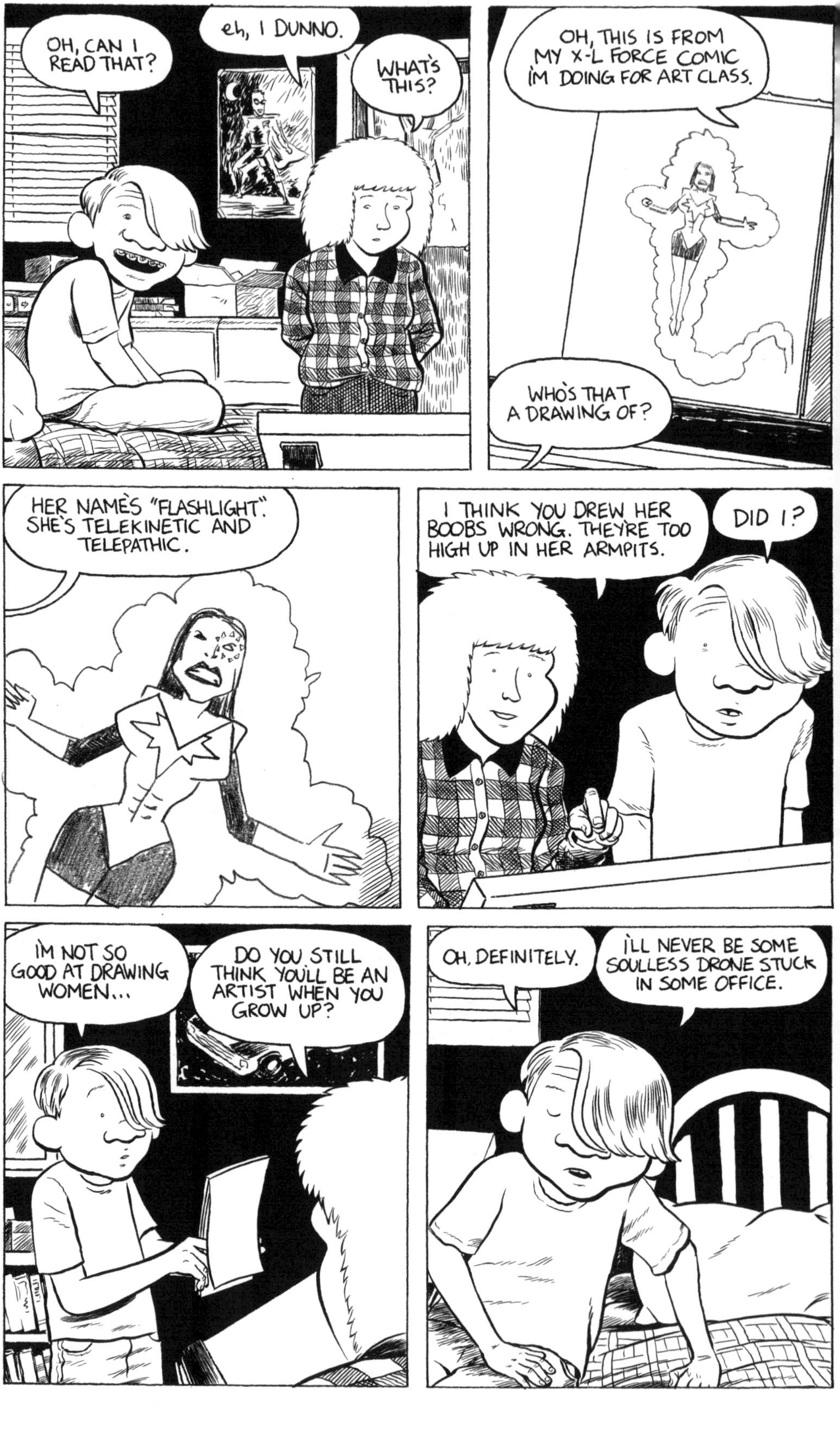
OH, CAN I READ THAT?
eh, I DUNNO.
WHAT'S THIS?
OH, THIS IS FROM MY X-L FORCE COMIC I'M DOING FOR ART CLASS.
WHO'S THAT A DRAWING OF?
HER NAME'S "FLASHLIGHT". SHE'S TELEKINETIC AND TELEPATHIC.
I THINK YOU DREW HER BOOBS WRONG. THEY'RE TOO HIGH UP IN HER ARMPITS.
DID I?
I'M NOT SO GOOD AT DRAWING WOMEN...
DO YOU STILL THINK YOU'LL BE AN ARTIST WHEN YOU GROW UP?
OH, DEFINITELY.
I'LL NEVER BE SOME SOULLESS DRONE STUCK IN SOME OFFICE.

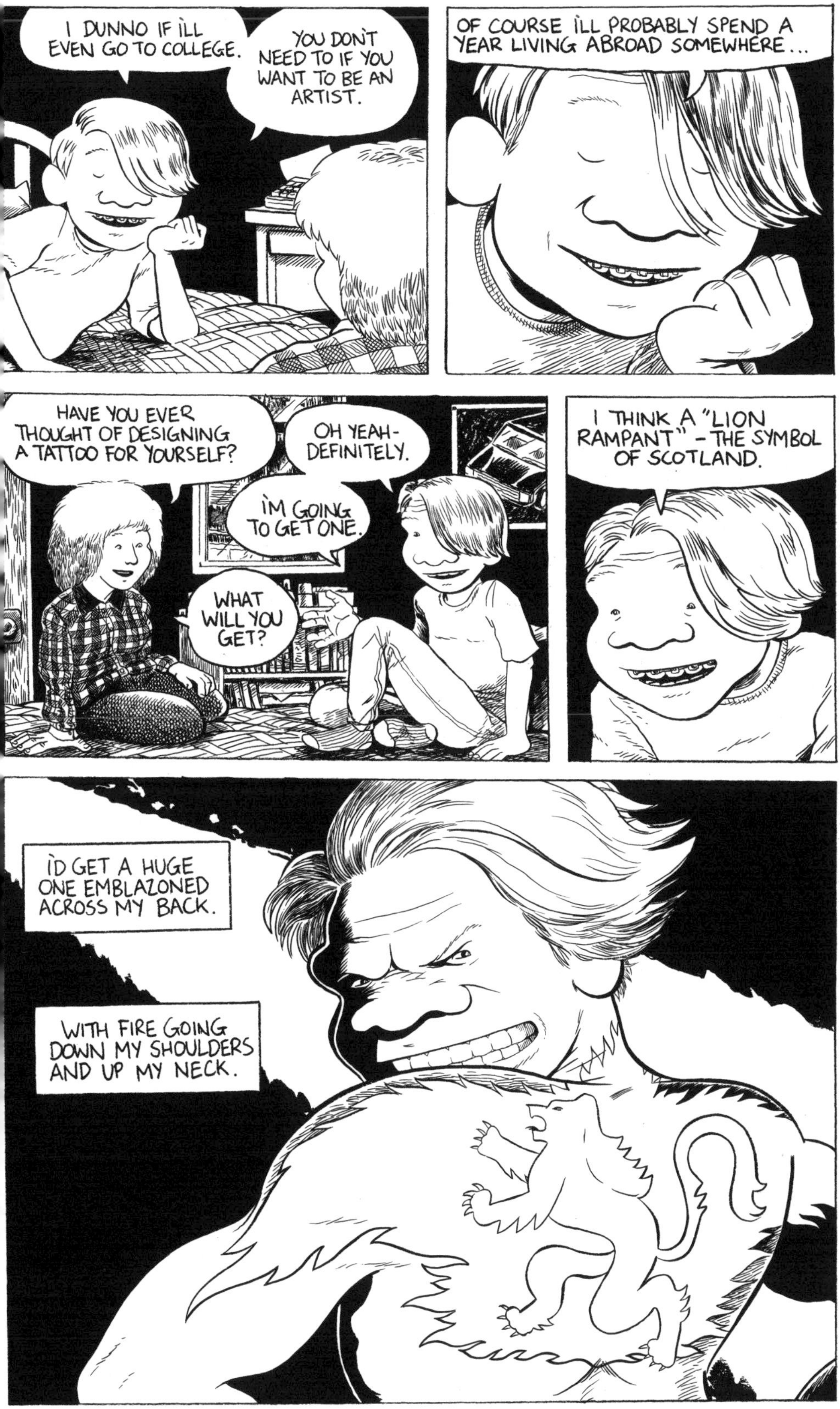
I DUNNO IF I'LL EVEN GO TO COLLEGE.
YOU DON'T NEED TO IF YOU WANT TO BE AN ARTIST.
OF COURSE I'LL PROBABLY SPEND A YEAR LIVING ABROAD SOMEWHERE...
HAVE YOU EVER THOUGHT OF DESIGNING A TATTOO FOR YOURSELF?
OH YEAH- DEFINITELY.
I'M GOING TO GET ONE.
WHAT WILL YOU GET?
I THINK A "LION RAMPANT" - THE SYMBOL OF SCOTLAND.
I'D GET A HUGE ONE EMBLAZONED ACROSS MY BACK.
WITH FIRE GOING DOWN MY SHOULDERS AND UP MY NECK.

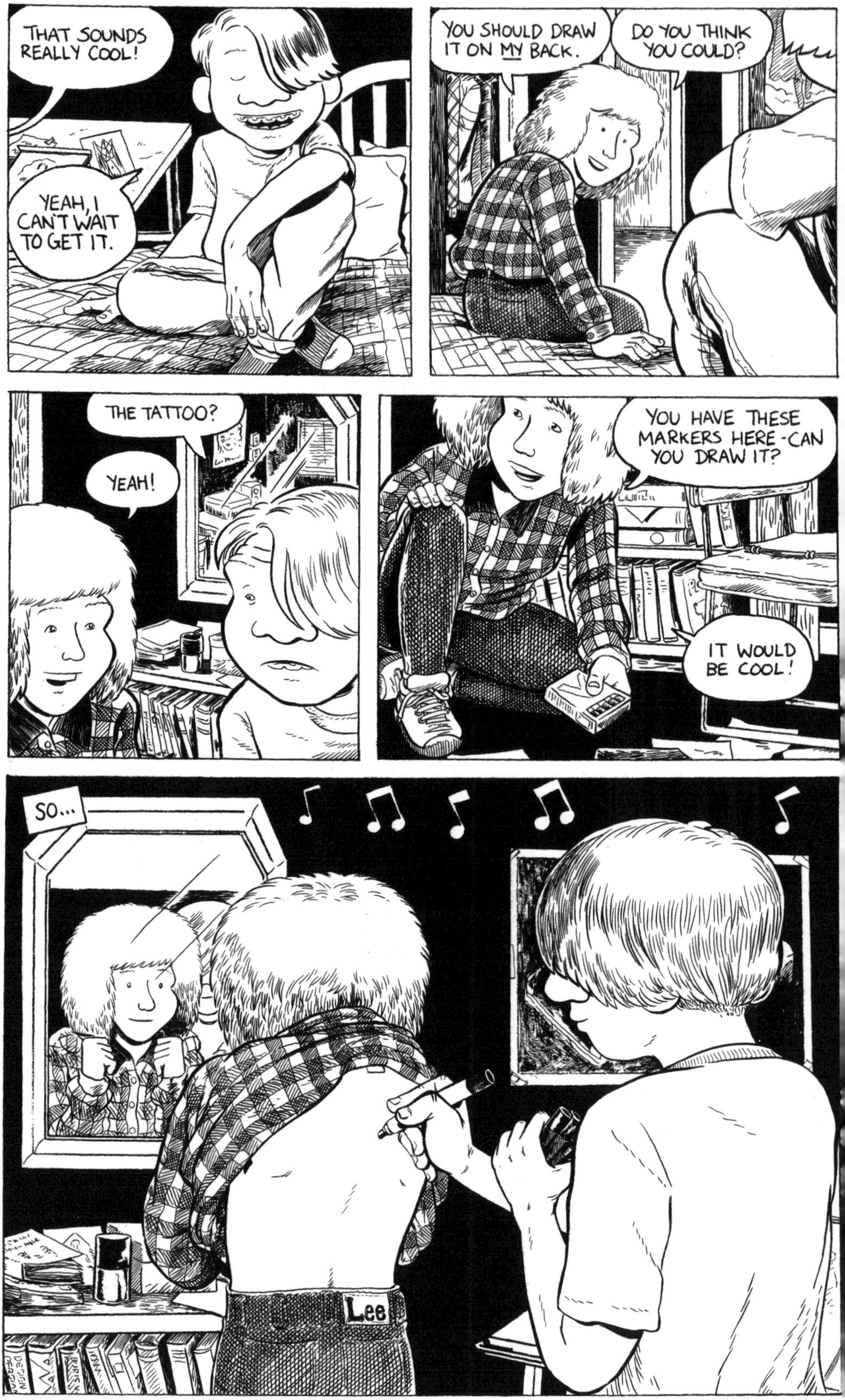
THAT SOUNDS REALLY COOL!
YEAH, I CAN'T WAIT TO GET IT.
YOU SHOULD DRAW IT ON MY BACK.
DO YOU THINK YOU COULD?
THE TATTOO?
YEAH!
YOU HAVE THESE MARKERS HERE - CAN YOU DRAW IT?
IT WOULD BE COOL!
SO...
Lee

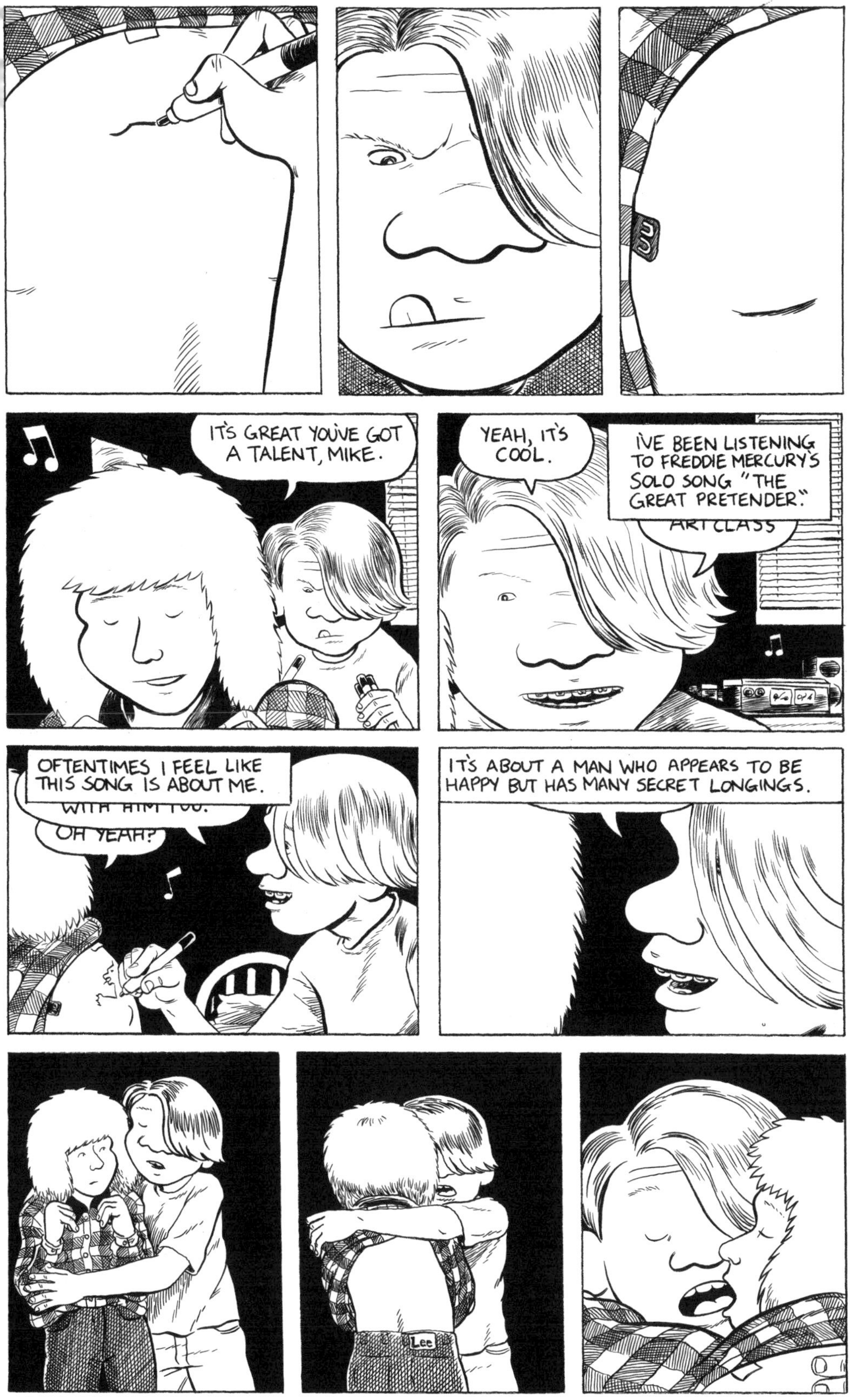
IT'S GREAT YOU'VE GOT A TALENT, MIKE.
YEAH, IT'S COOL.
I'VE BEEN LISTENING TO FREDDIE MERCURY'S SOLO SONG "THE GREAT PRETENDER."
OFTENTIMES I FEEL LIKE THIS SONG IS ABOUT ME.
OH YEAH?
IT'S ABOUT A MAN WHO APPEARS TO BE HAPPY BUT HAS MANY SECRET LONGINGS.
Lee

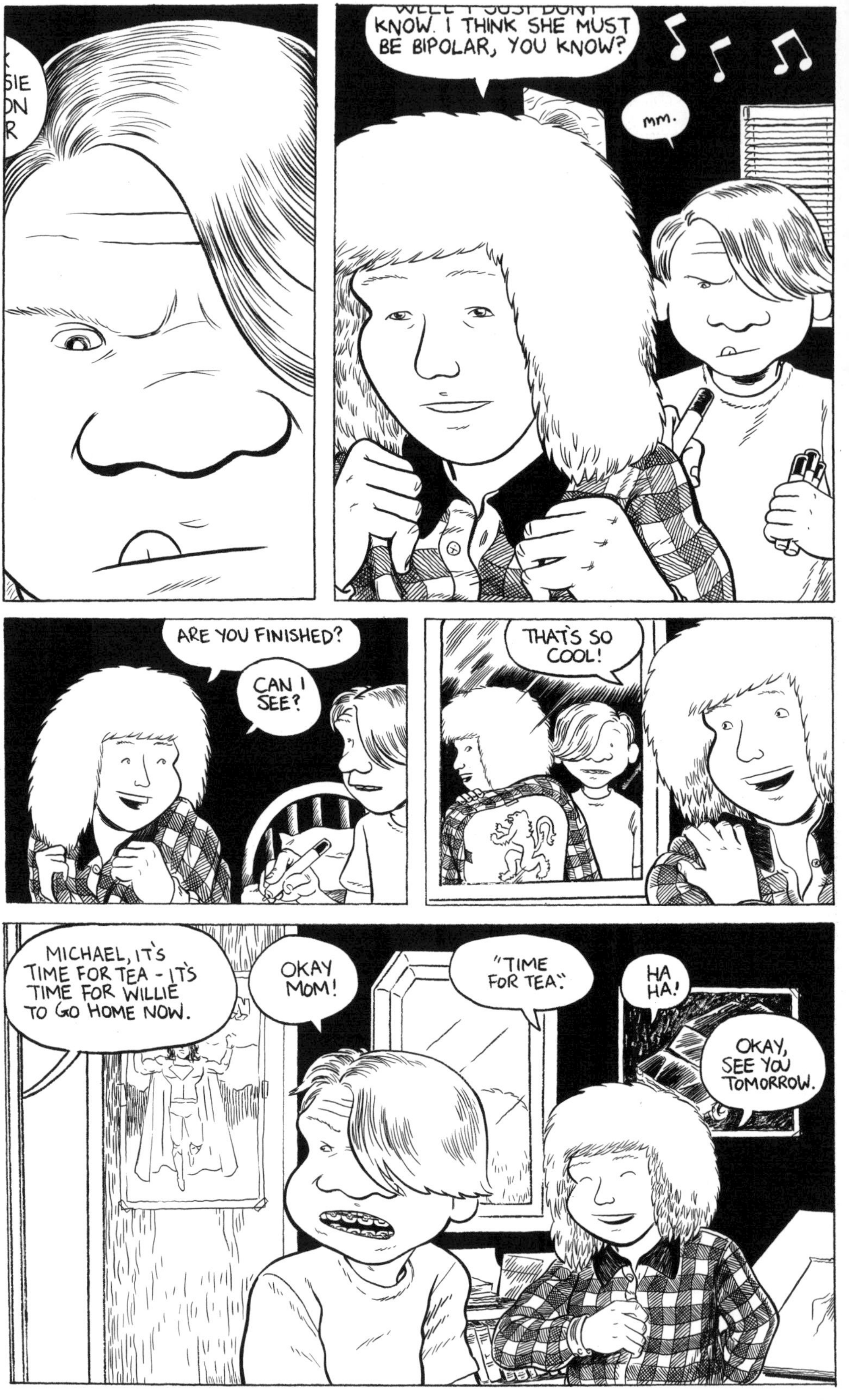
KNOW. I THINK SHE MUST BE BIPOLAR, YOU KNOW?
mm.
ARE YOU FINISHED?
CAN I SEE?
THAT'S SO COOL!
MICHAEL, IT'S TIME FOR TEA - IT'S TIME FOR WILLIE TO GO HOME NOW.
OKAY MOM!
"TIME FOR TEA."
HA HA!
OKAY, SEE YOU TOMORROW.

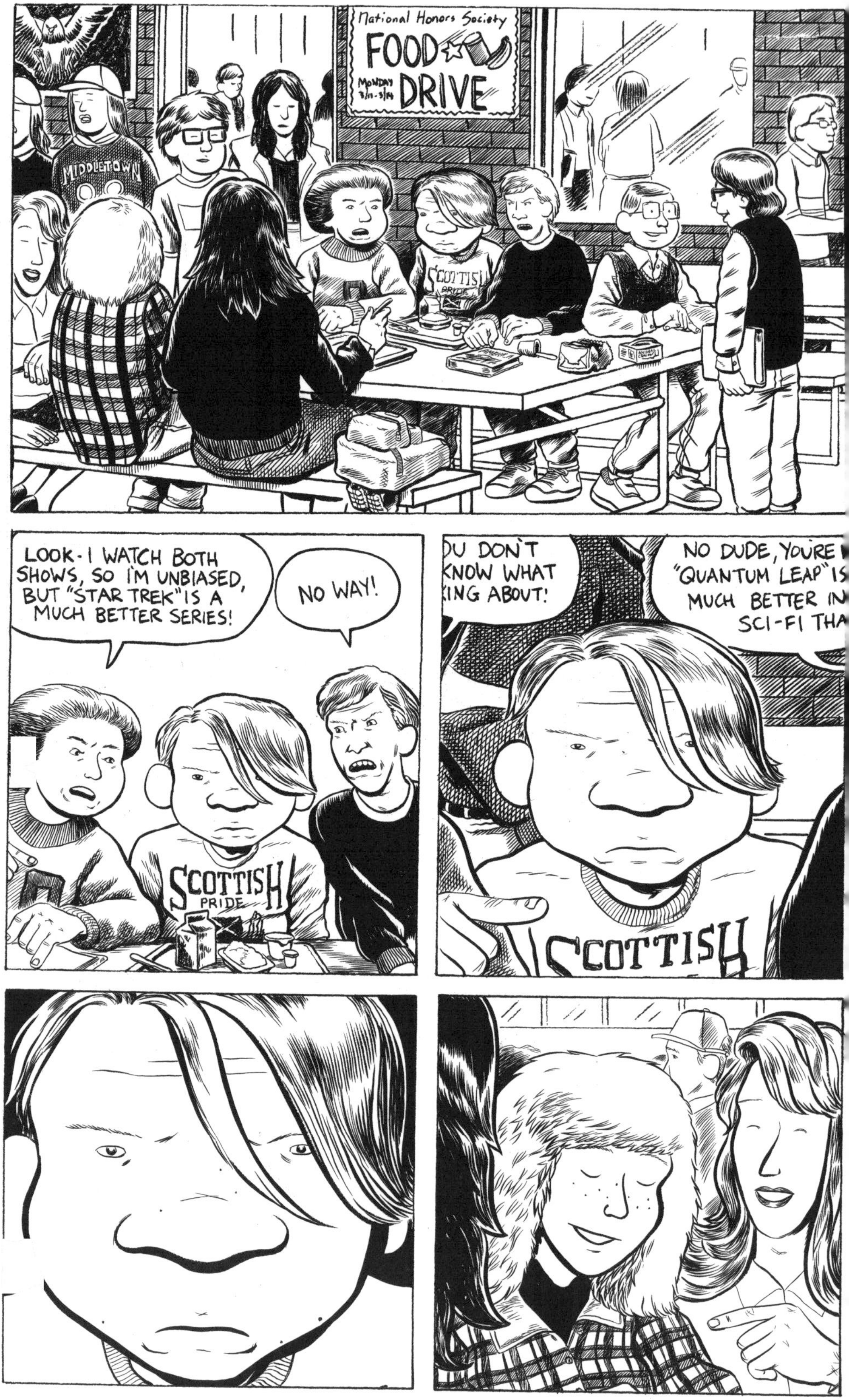
National Honors Society
FOOD DRIVE
MONDAY
MIDDLETOWN
SCOTTISH PRIDE
LOOK - I WATCH BOTH SHOWS, SO I'M UNBIASED, BUT "STAR TREK" IS A MUCH BETTER SERIES!
NO WAY!
SCOTTISH PRIDE
DU DON'T KNOW WHAT ING ABOUT!
NO DUDE, YOU'RE "QUANTUM LEAP" IS MUCH BETTER IN SCI-FI THA
SCOTTISH

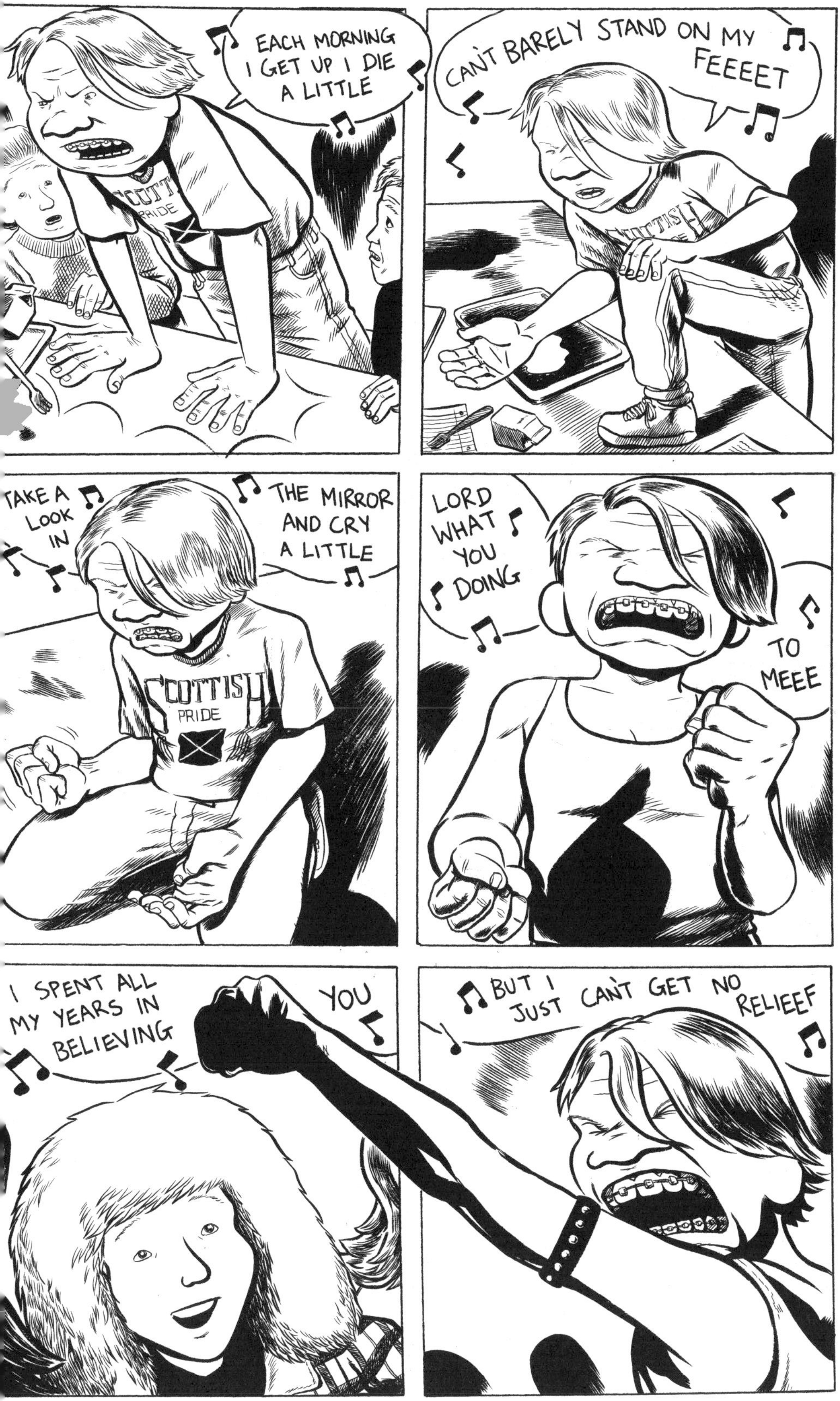
EACH MORNING I GET UP I DIE A LITTLE
SCOTTI PRIDE
CAN'T BARELY STAND ON MY FEEEEET
TAKE A LOOK IN
THE MIRROR AND CRY A LITTLE
SCOTTISH PRIDE
LORD WHAT YOU DOING
TO MEEE
I SPENT ALL MY YEARS IN BELIEVING
YOU
BUT I JUST CAN'T GET NO RELIEEF

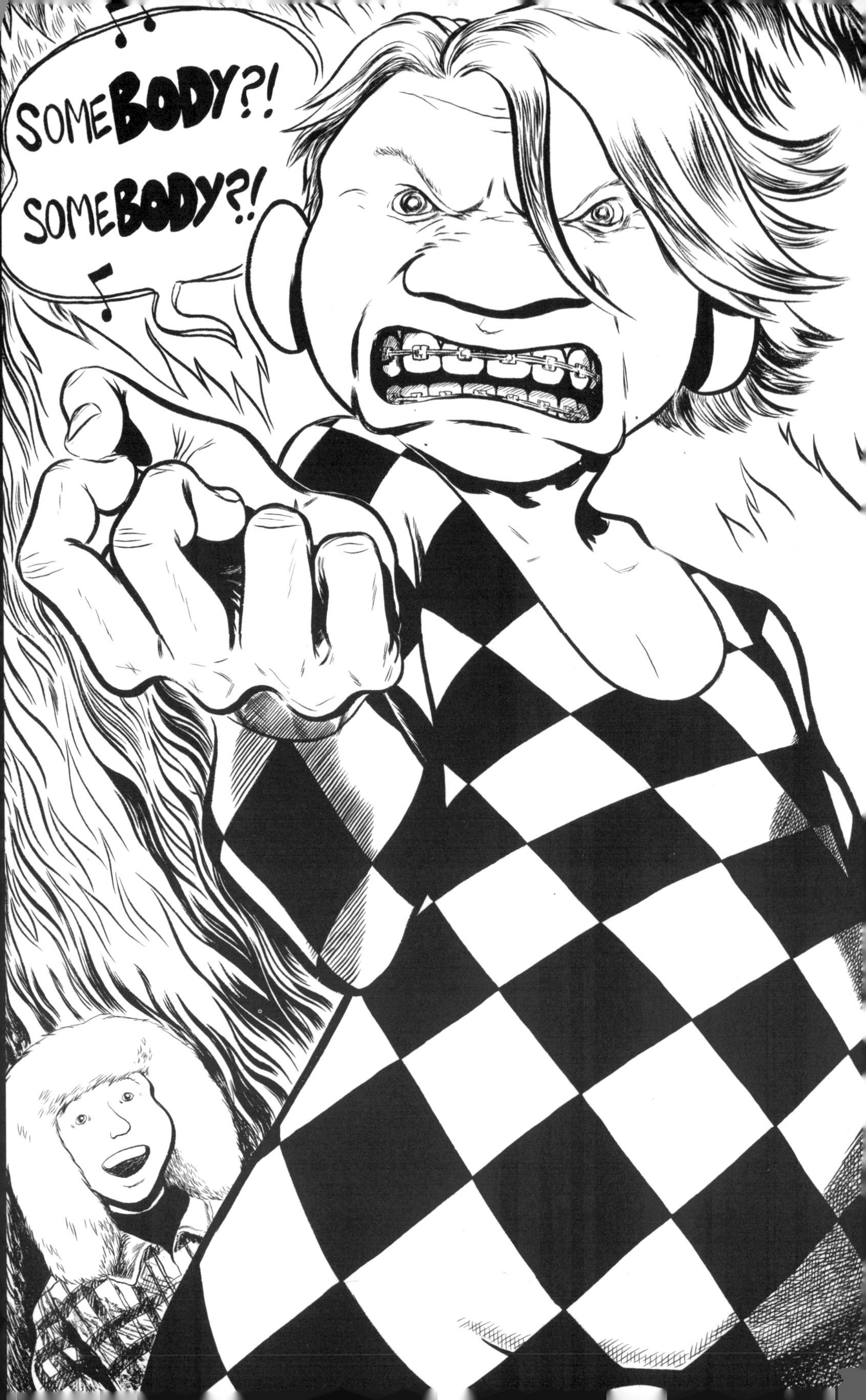
SOMEBODY?! SOMEBODY?!

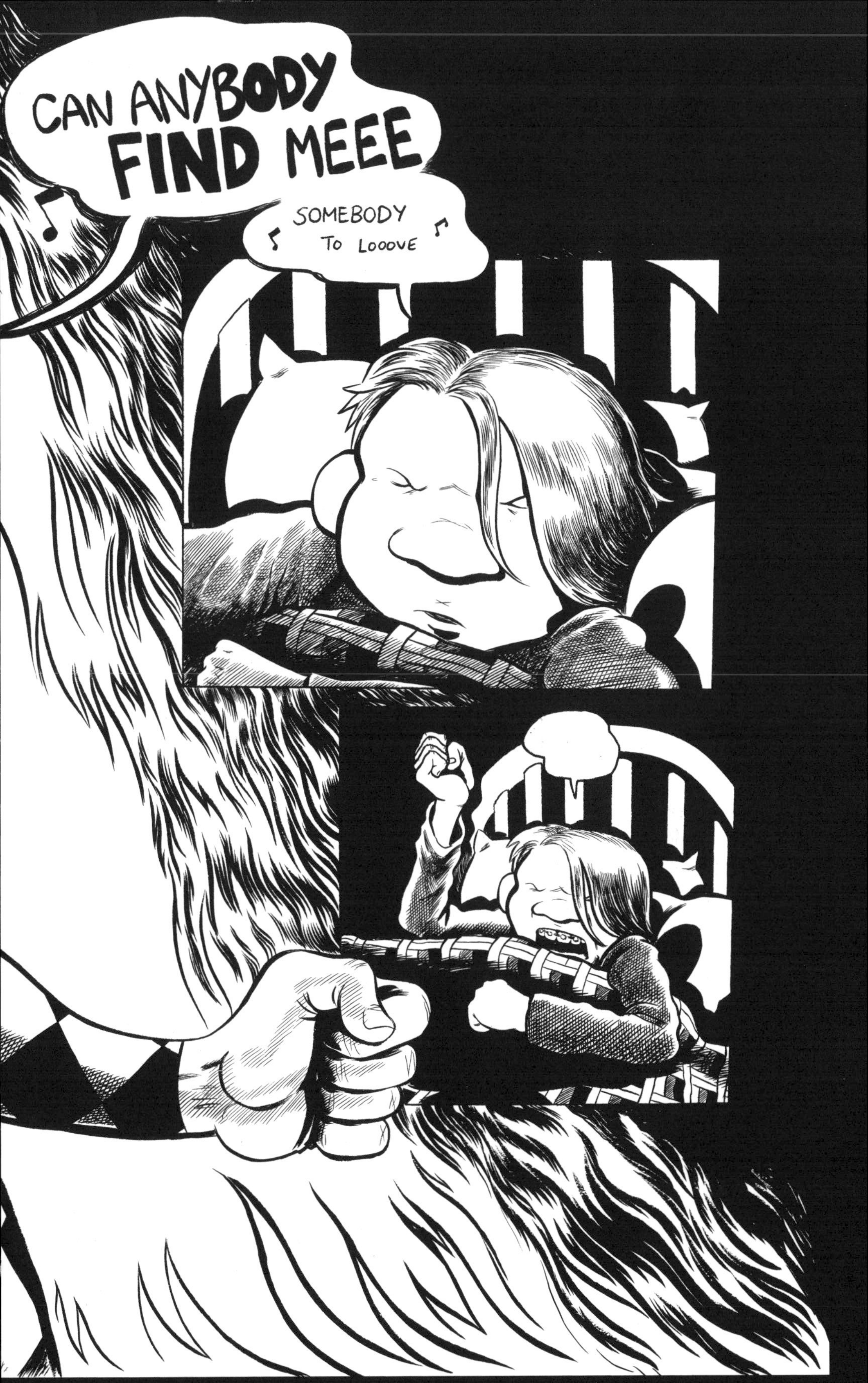
CAN ANYBODY FIND MEEE
SOMEBODY TO LOOOVE

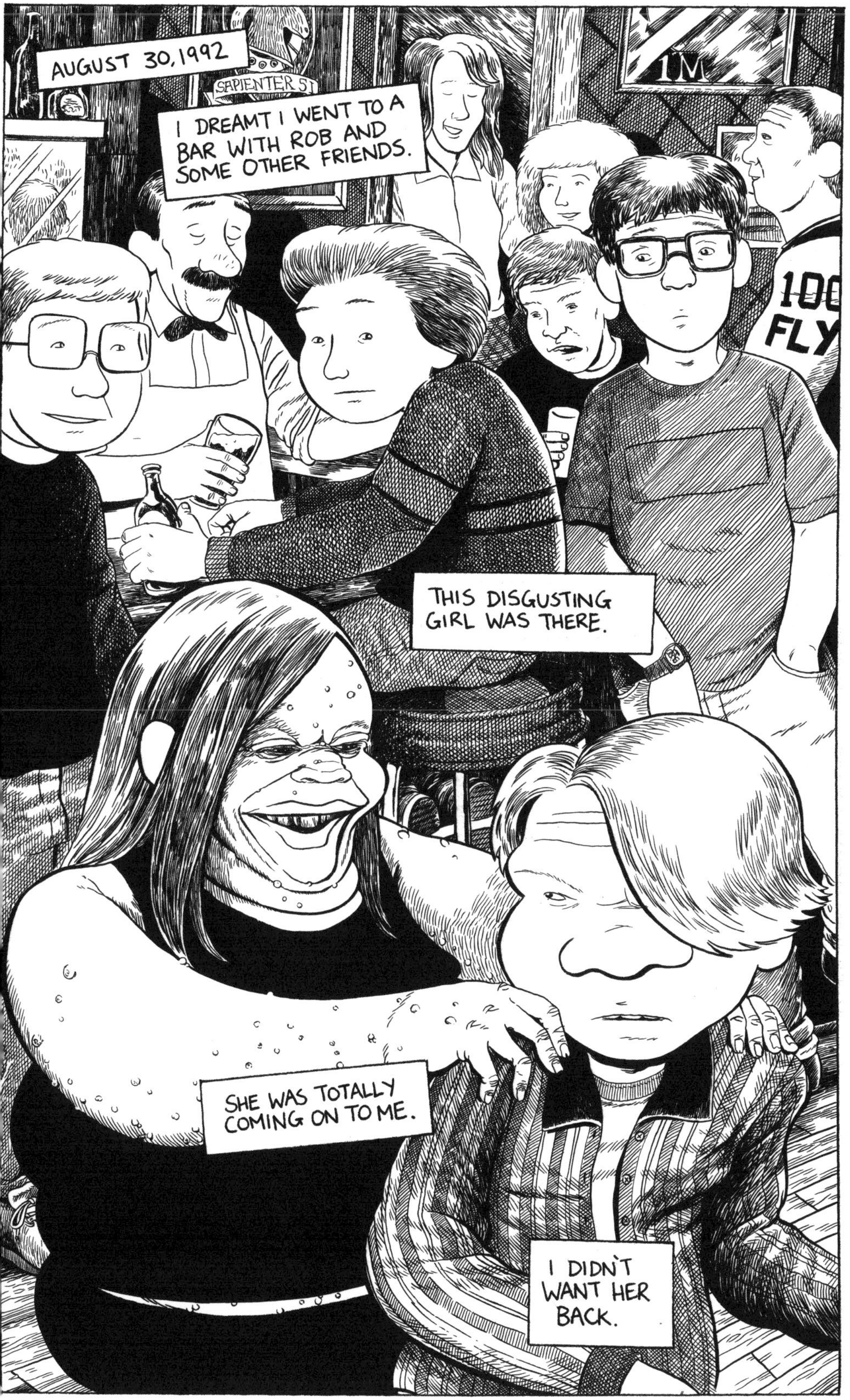
AUGUST 30, 1992
SAPIENTER 51
1M
I DREAMT I WENT TO A BAR WITH ROB AND SOME OTHER FRIENDS.
100 FLY
THIS DISGUSTING GIRL WAS THERE.
SHE WAS TOTALLY COMING ON TO ME.
I DIDN'T WANT HER BACK.

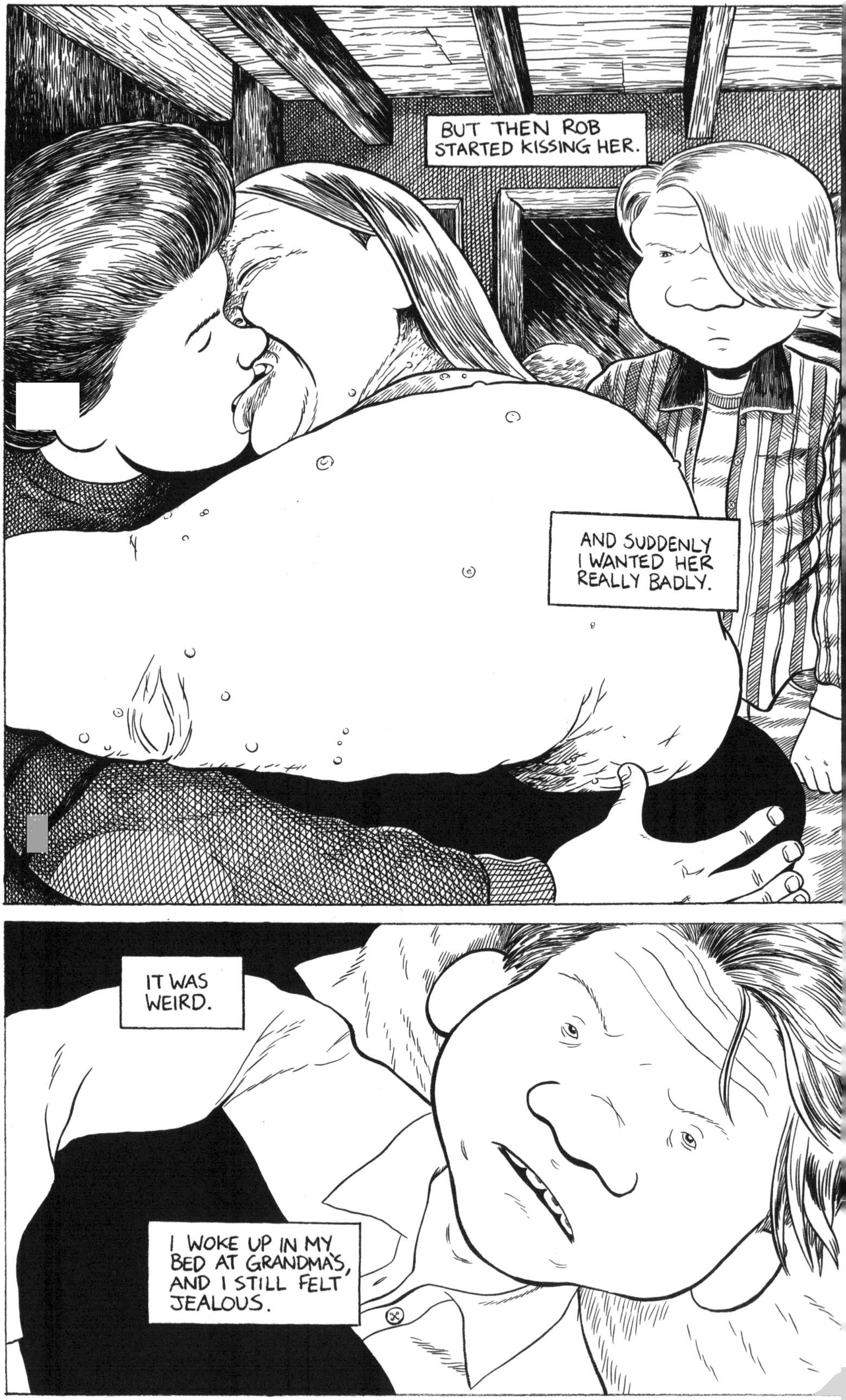
BUT THEN ROB STARTED KISSING HER.
AND SUDDENLY I WANTED HER REALLY BADLY.
IT WAS WEIRD.
I WOKE UP IN MY BED AT GRANDMA'S, AND I STILL FELT JEALOUS.

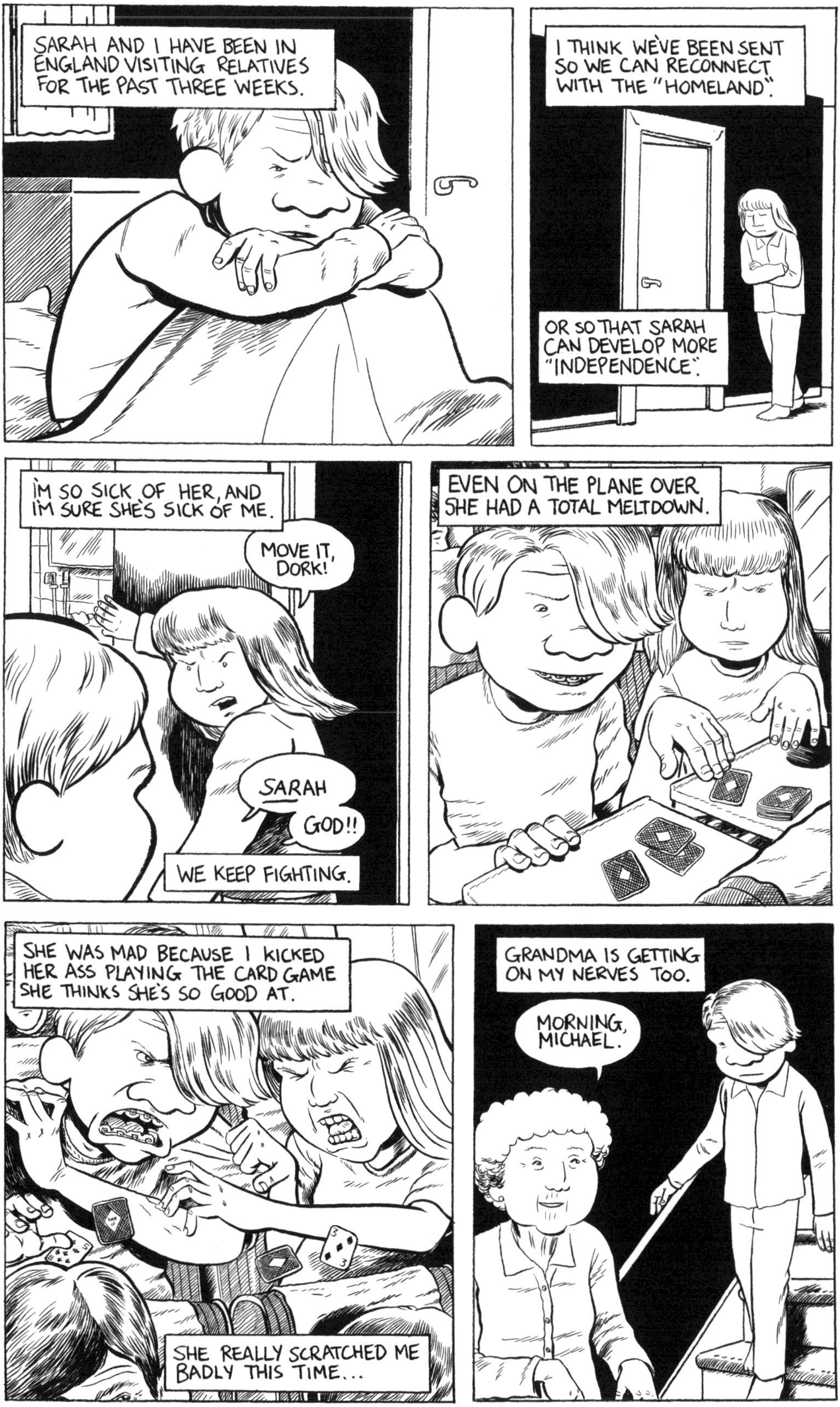
SARAH AND I HAVE BEEN IN ENGLAND VISITING RELATIVES FOR THE PAST THREE WEEKS.
I THINK WE'VE BEEN SENT SO WE CAN RECONNECT WITH THE "HOMELAND".
OR SO THAT SARAH CAN DEVELOP MORE "INDEPENDENCE".
I'M SO SICK OF HER, AND I'M SURE SHE'S SICK OF ME.
MOVE IT, DORK!
SARAH
GOD!!
WE KEEP FIGHTING.
EVEN ON THE PLANE OVER SHE HAD A TOTAL MELTDOWN.
SHE WAS MAD BECAUSE I KICKED HER ASS PLAYING THE CARD GAME SHE THINKS SHE'S SO GOOD AT.
SHE REALLY SCRATCHED ME BADLY THIS TIME...
GRANDMA IS GETTING ON MY NERVES TOO.
MORNING, MICHAEL.

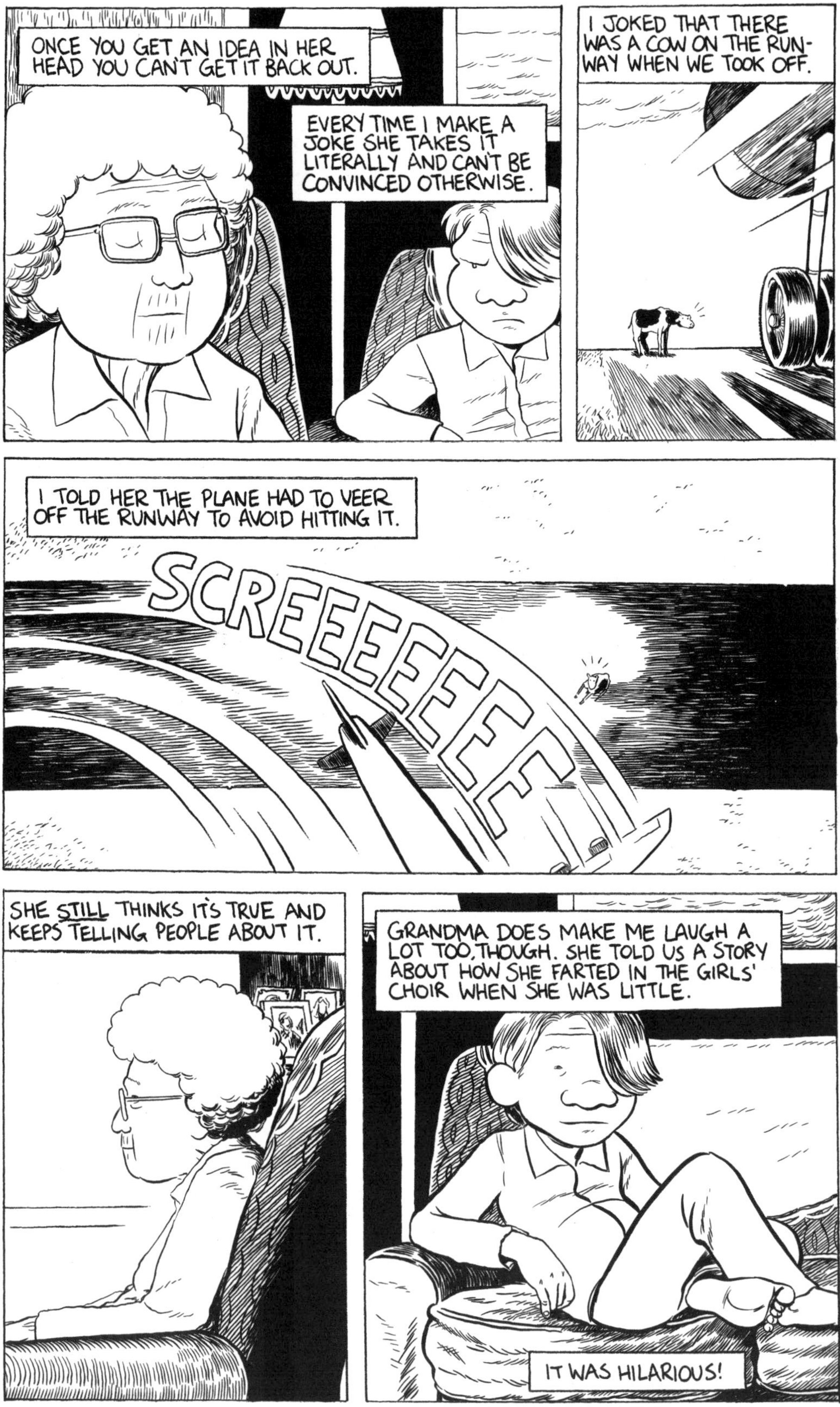
ONCE YOU GET AN IDEA IN HER HEAD YOU CAN'T GET IT BACK OUT.
EVERY TIME I MAKE A JOKE SHE TAKES IT LITERALLY AND CAN'T BE CONVINCED OTHERWISE.
I JOKED THAT THERE WAS A COW ON THE RUNWAY WHEN WE TOOK OFF.
I TOLD HER THE PLANE HAD TO VEER OFF THE RUNWAY TO AVOID HITTING IT.
SCREEEEEEEE
SHE STILL THINKS IT'S TRUE AND KEEPS TELLING PEOPLE ABOUT IT.
GRANDMA DOES MAKE ME LAUGH A LOT TOO, THOUGH. SHE TOLD US A STORY ABOUT HOW SHE FARTED IN THE GIRLS' CHOIR WHEN SHE WAS LITTLE.
IT WAS HILARIOUS!

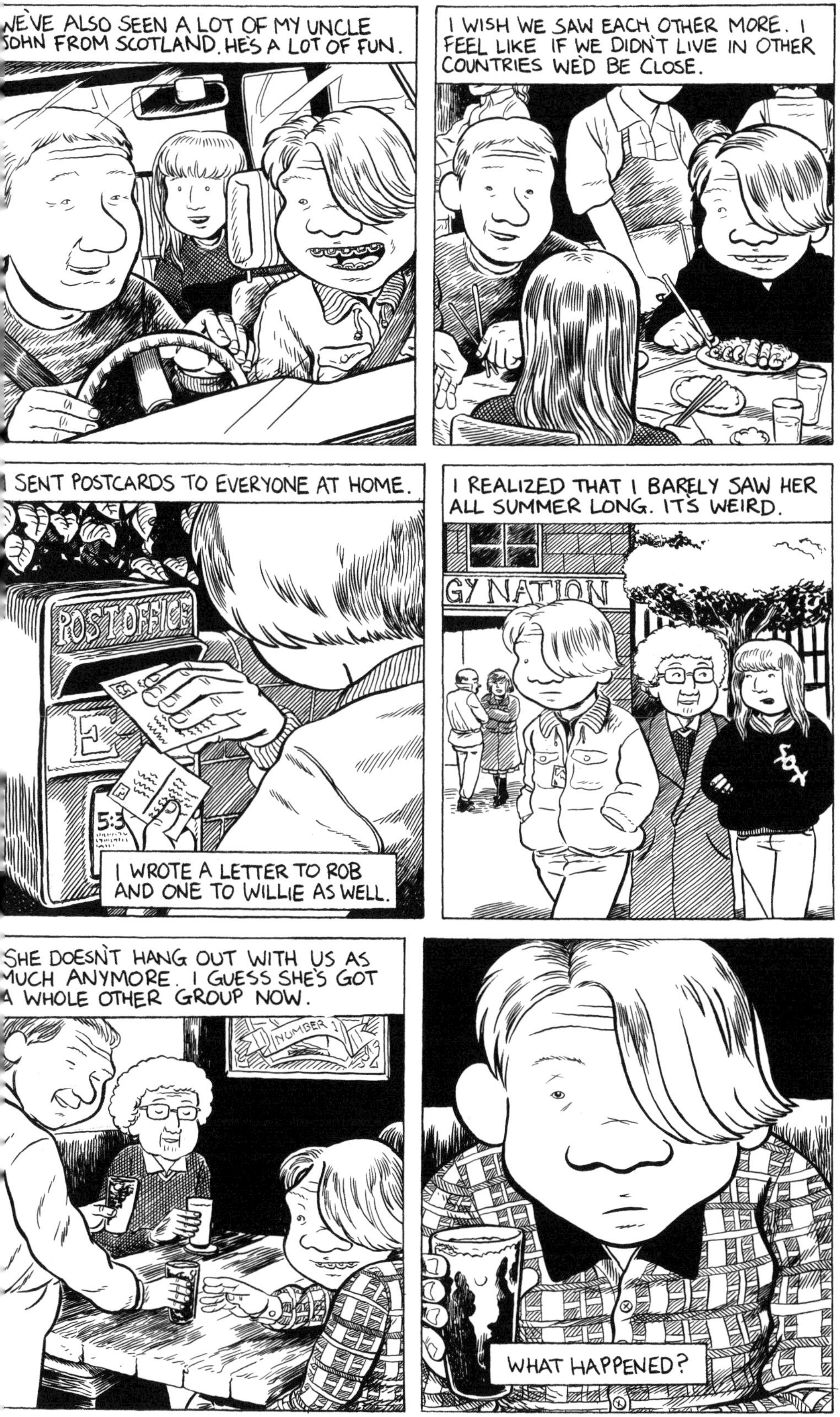
WE'VE ALSO SEEN A LOT OF MY UNCLE JOHN FROM SCOTLAND. HE'S A LOT OF FUN.
I WISH WE SAW EACH OTHER MORE. I FEEL LIKE IF WE DIDN'T LIVE IN OTHER COUNTRIES WE'D BE CLOSE.
I SENT POSTCARDS TO EVERYONE AT HOME.
POST OFFICE
I WROTE A LETTER TO ROB AND ONE TO WILLIE AS WELL.
I REALIZED THAT I BARELY SAW HER ALL SUMMER LONG. IT'S WEIRD.
GY NATION
SHE DOESN'T HANG OUT WITH US AS MUCH ANYMORE. I GUESS SHE'S GOT A WHOLE OTHER GROUP NOW.
NUMBER 1
WHAT HAPPENED?

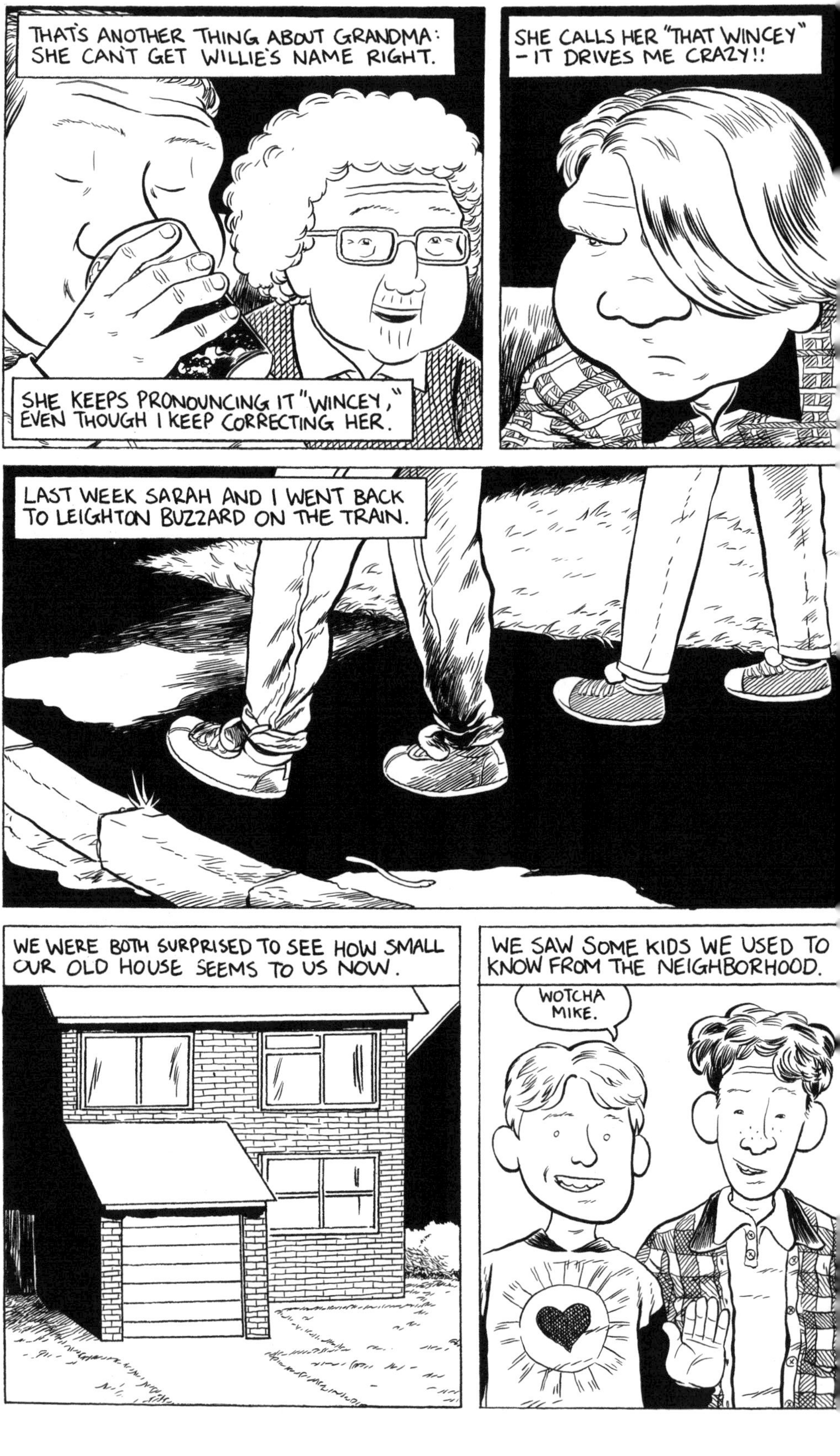
THAT'S ANOTHER THING ABOUT GRANDMA: SHE CAN'T GET WILLIE'S NAME RIGHT.
SHE KEEPS PRONOUNCING IT "WINCEY," EVEN THOUGH I KEEP CORRECTING HER.
SHE CALLS HER "THAT WINCEY" - IT DRIVES ME CRAZY!!
LAST WEEK SARAH AND I WENT BACK TO LEIGHTON BUZZARD ON THE TRAIN.
WE WERE BOTH SURPRISED TO SEE HOW SMALL OUR OLD HOUSE SEEMS TO US NOW.
WE SAW SOME KIDS WE USED TO KNOW FROM THE NEIGHBORHOOD.
WOTCHA MIKE.

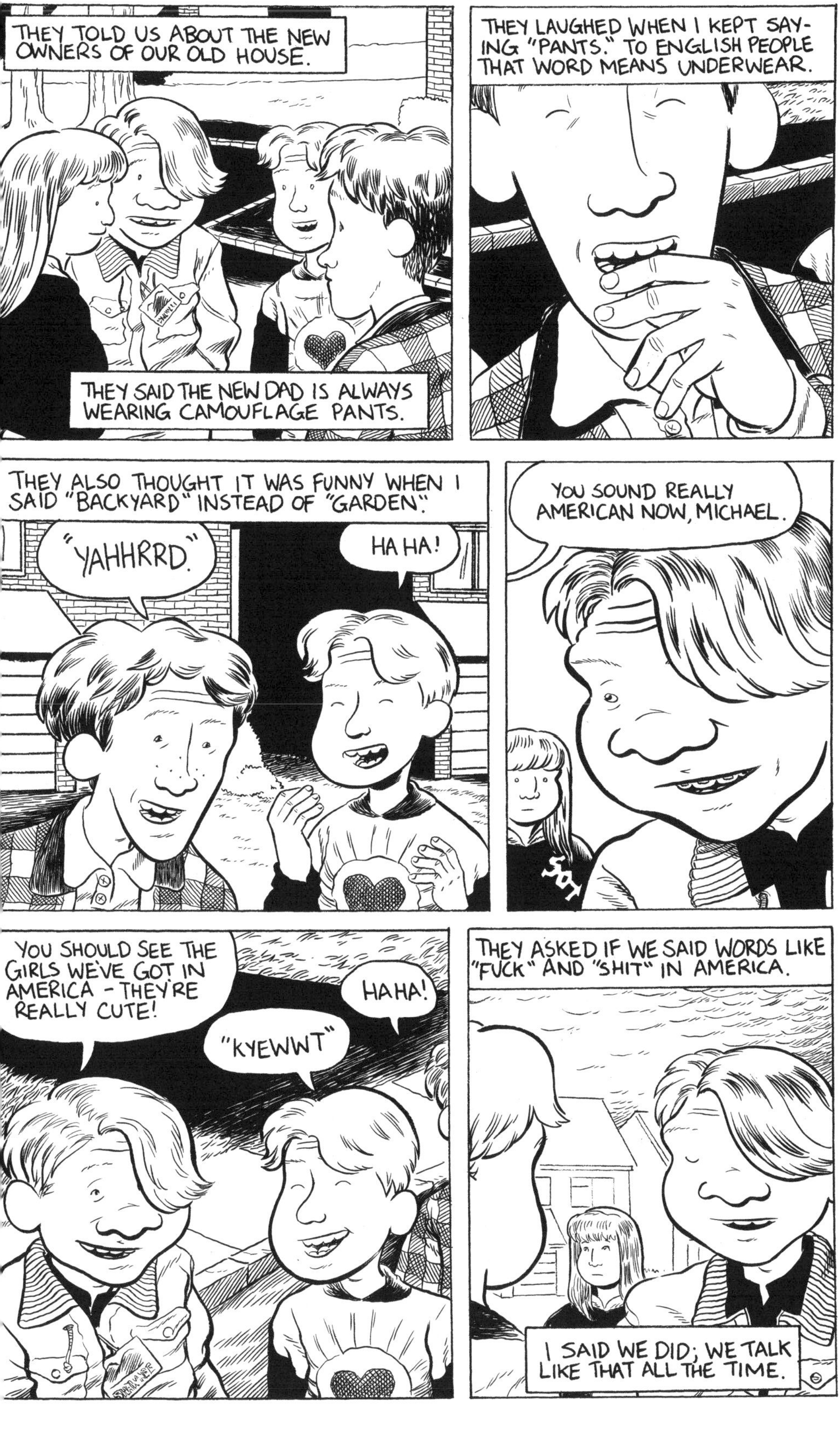
THEY TOLD US ABOUT THE NEW OWNERS OF OUR OLD HOUSE.
THEY SAID THE NEW DAD IS ALWAYS WEARING CAMOUFLAGE PANTS.
THEY LAUGHED WHEN I KEPT SAYING "PANTS." TO ENGLISH PEOPLE THAT WORD MEANS UNDERWEAR.
THEY ALSO THOUGHT IT WAS FUNNY WHEN I SAID "BACKYARD" INSTEAD OF "GARDEN".
"YAHHRRD."
HA HA!
YOU SOUND REALLY AMERICAN NOW, MICHAEL.
YOU SHOULD SEE THE GIRLS WE'VE GOT IN AMERICA - THEY'RE REALLY CUTE!
HA HA!
"KYEWWT"
THEY ASKED IF WE SAID WORDS LIKE "FUCK" AND "SHIT" IN AMERICA.
I SAID WE DID; WE TALK LIKE THAT ALL THE TIME.

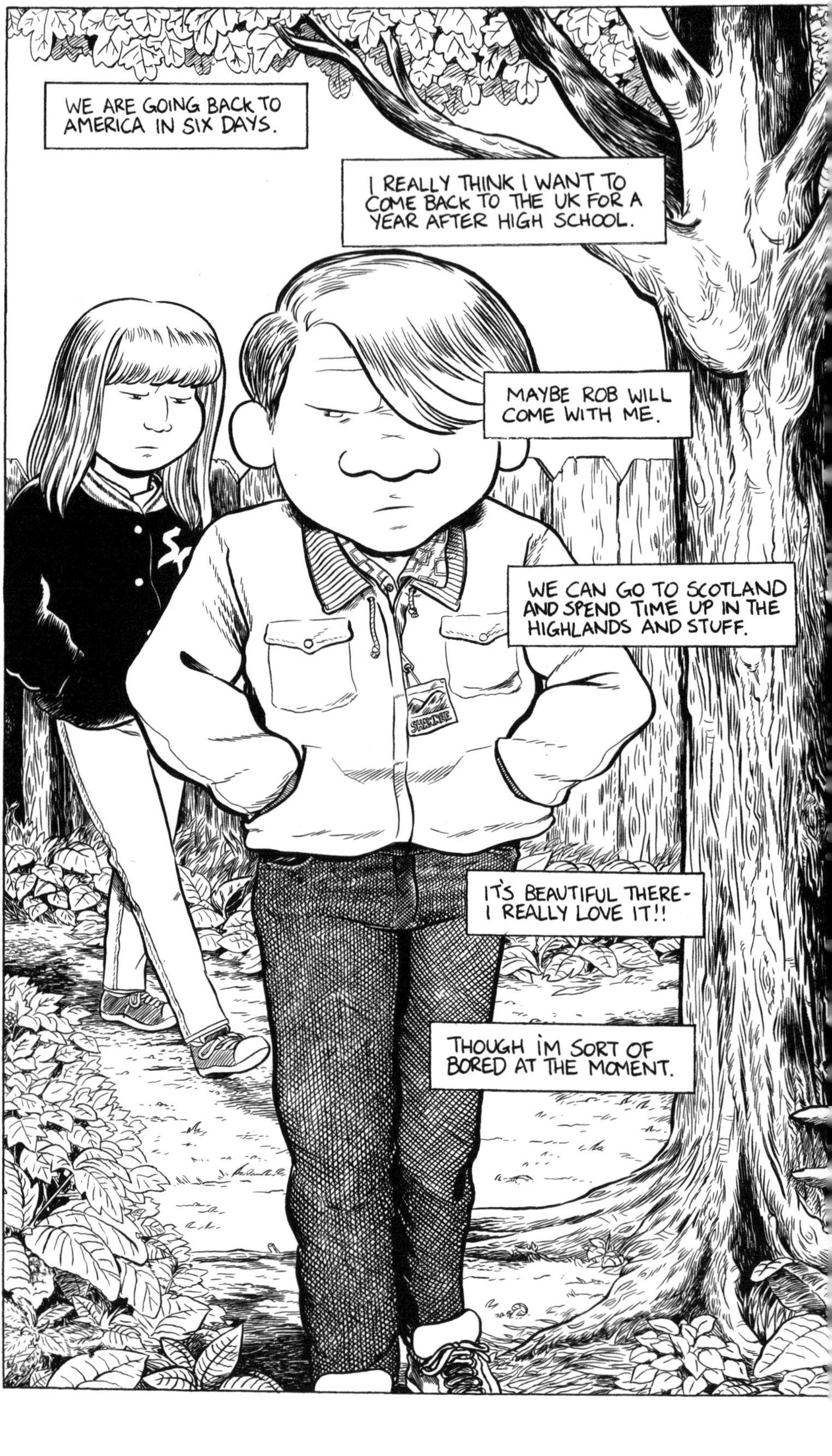
WE ARE GOING BACK TO AMERICA IN SIX DAYS.
I REALLY THINK I WANT TO COME BACK TO THE UK FOR A YEAR AFTER HIGH SCHOOL.
MAYBE ROB WILL COME WITH ME.
WE CAN GO TO SCOTLAND AND SPEND TIME UP IN THE HIGHLANDS AND STUFF.
IT'S BEAUTIFUL THERE- I REALLY LOVE IT!!
THOUGH I'M SORT OF BORED AT THE MOMENT.

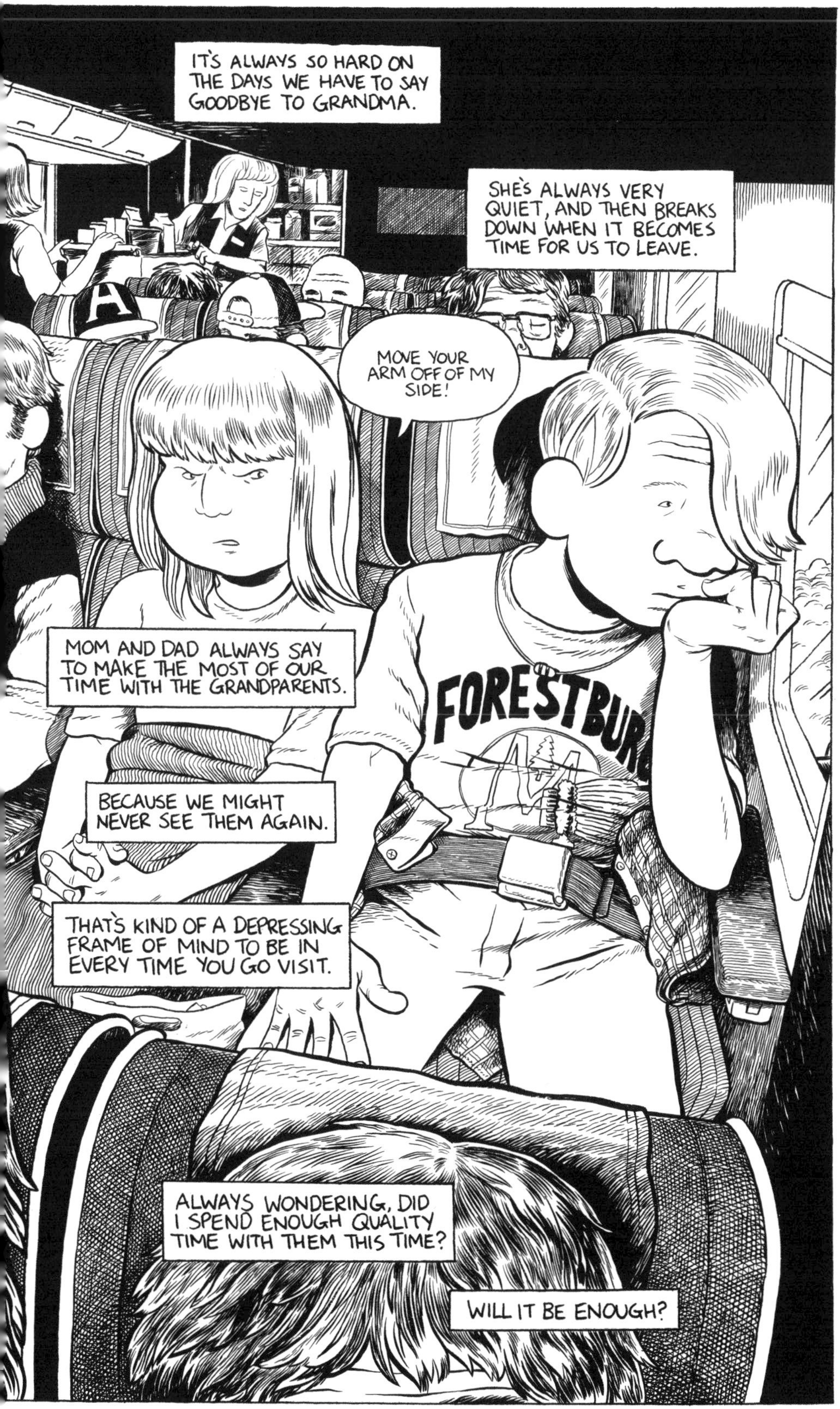
IT'S ALWAYS SO HARD ON THE DAYS WE HAVE TO SAY GOODBYE TO GRANDMA.
SHE'S ALWAYS VERY QUIET, AND THEN BREAKS DOWN WHEN IT BECOMES TIME FOR US TO LEAVE.
MOVE YOUR ARM OFF OF MY SIDE!
MOM AND DAD ALWAYS SAY TO MAKE THE MOST OF OUR TIME WITH THE GRANDPARENTS.
BECAUSE WE MIGHT NEVER SEE THEM AGAIN.
THAT'S KIND OF A DEPRESSING FRAME OF MIND TO BE IN EVERY TIME YOU GO VISIT.
ALWAYS WONDERING, DID I SPEND ENOUGH QUALITY TIME WITH THEM THIS TIME?
WILL IT BE ENOUGH?

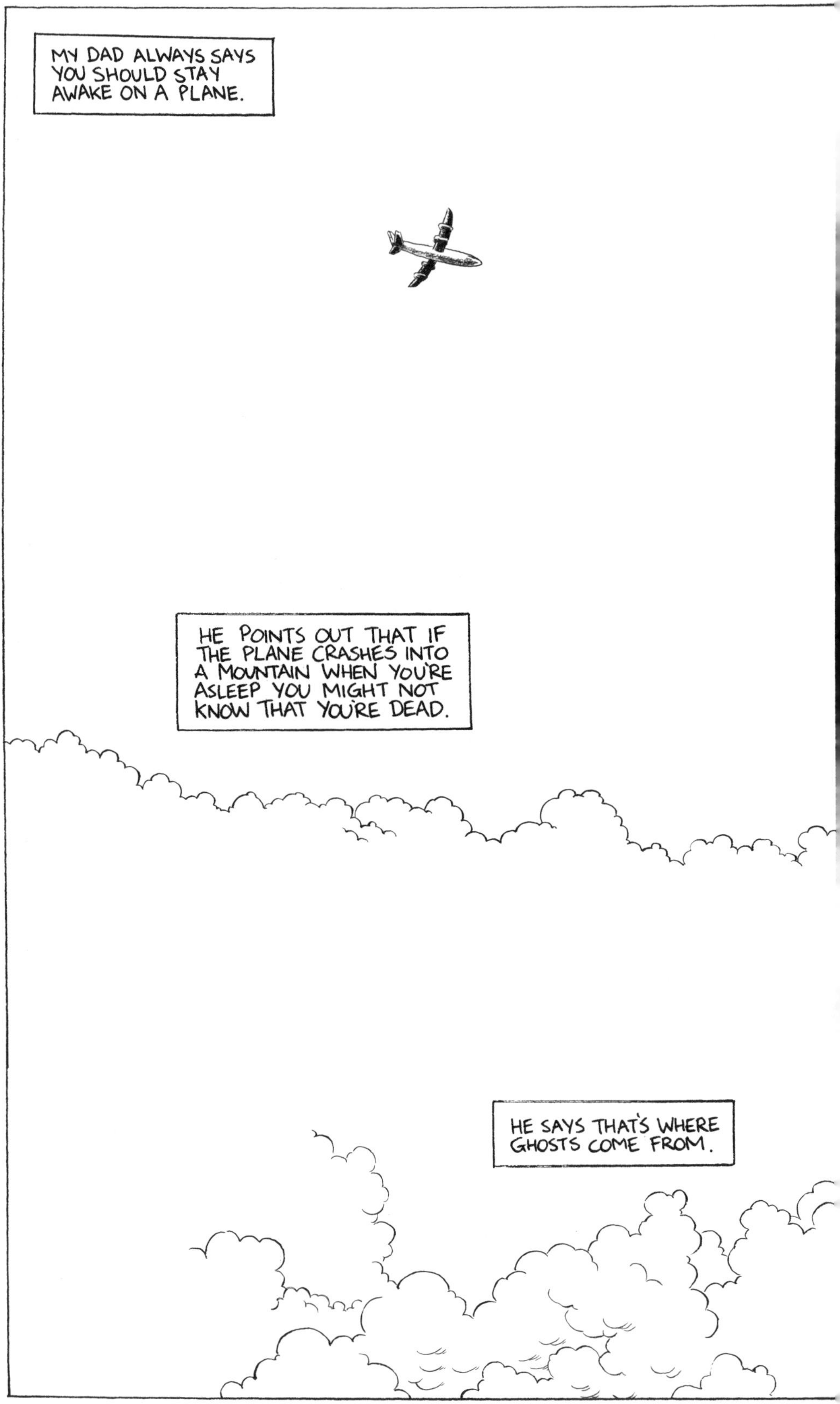
MY DAD ALWAYS SAYS YOU SHOULD STAY AWAKE ON A PLANE.
HE POINTS OUT THAT IF THE PLANE CRASHES INTO A MOUNTAIN WHEN YOU'RE ASLEEP YOU MIGHT NOT KNOW THAT YOU'RE DEAD.
HE SAYS THAT'S WHERE GHOSTS COME FROM.

NOVEMBER 30, 1992

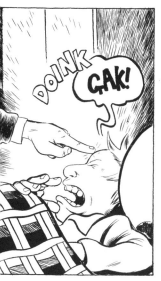
DOINK GAK!

WAKE UP, MICHAEL, IT'S TIME FOR SCHOOL.

YEAHHH- MANFRED MANN, THOSE GUYS WERE THE BEST, MAN... STICK AROUND AFTER THESE MESSAGES... WE'VE GOT... **LAYLA!**

AND REMEMBER AT TEN TONIGHT WE'RE OPENING THE PHONE LINES... THE 102ND CALLER IS GOING TO WIN TICKETS TO SEE QUEEN GUITARIST BRIAN MAY ON HIS SOLO TOUR NEXT YEAR...

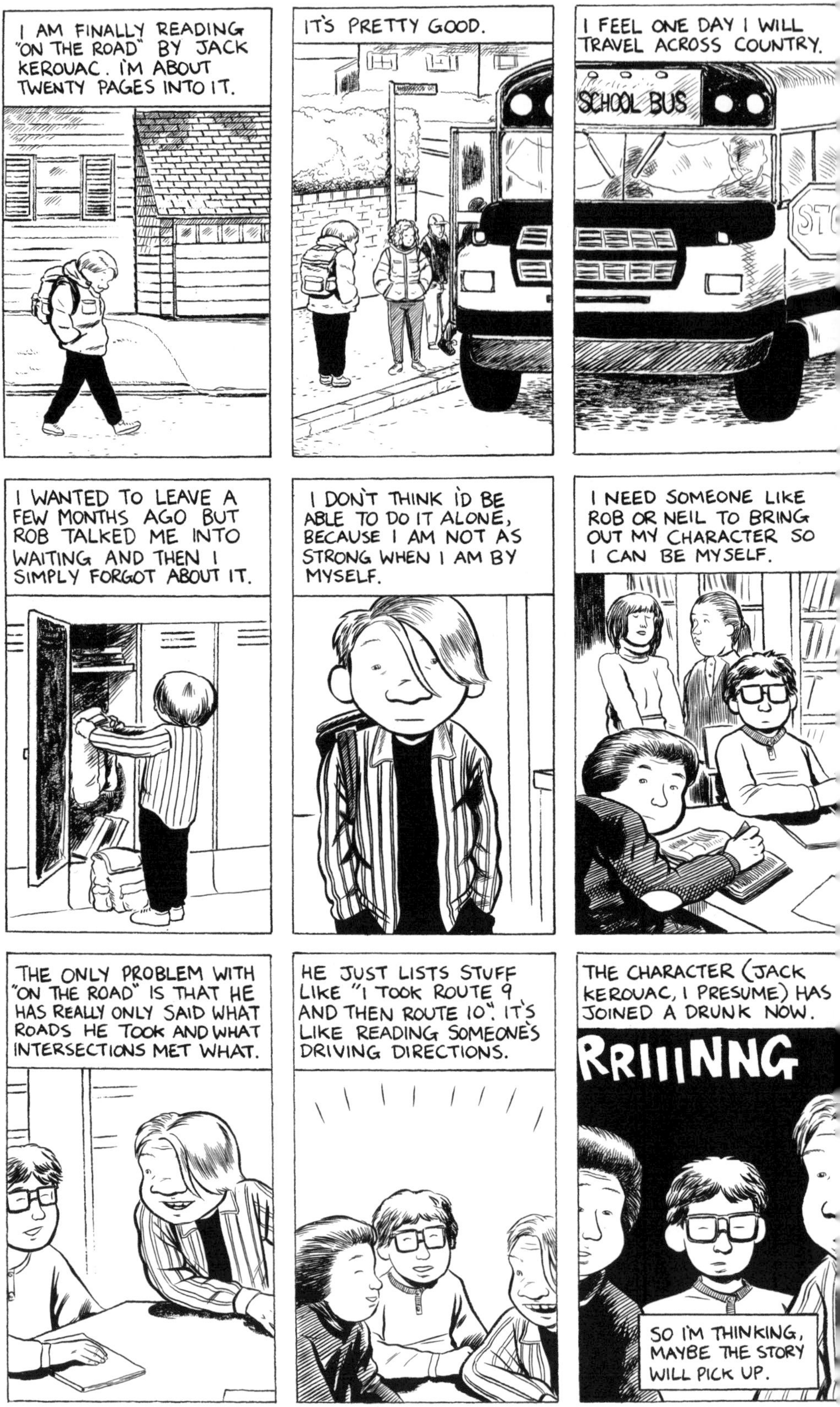
I AM FINALLY READING "ON THE ROAD" BY JACK KEROUAC. I'M ABOUT TWENTY PAGES INTO IT.
IT'S PRETTY GOOD.
I FEEL ONE DAY I WILL TRAVEL ACROSS COUNTRY.
SCHOOL BUS
I WANTED TO LEAVE A FEW MONTHS AGO BUT ROB TALKED ME INTO WAITING AND THEN I SIMPLY FORGOT ABOUT IT.
I DON'T THINK I'D BE ABLE TO DO IT ALONE, BECAUSE I AM NOT AS STRONG WHEN I AM BY MYSELF.
I NEED SOMEONE LIKE ROB OR NEIL TO BRING OUT MY CHARACTER SO I CAN BE MYSELF.
THE ONLY PROBLEM WITH "ON THE ROAD" IS THAT HE HAS REALLY ONLY SAID WHAT ROADS HE TOOK AND WHAT INTERSECTIONS MET WHAT.
HE JUST LISTS STUFF LIKE "I TOOK ROUTE 9 AND THEN ROUTE 10". IT'S LIKE READING SOMEONE'S DRIVING DIRECTIONS.
THE CHARACTER (JACK KEROUAC, I PRESUME) HAS JOINED A DRUNK NOW.
RRIIINNG
SO I'M THINKING, MAYBE THE STORY WILL PICK UP.

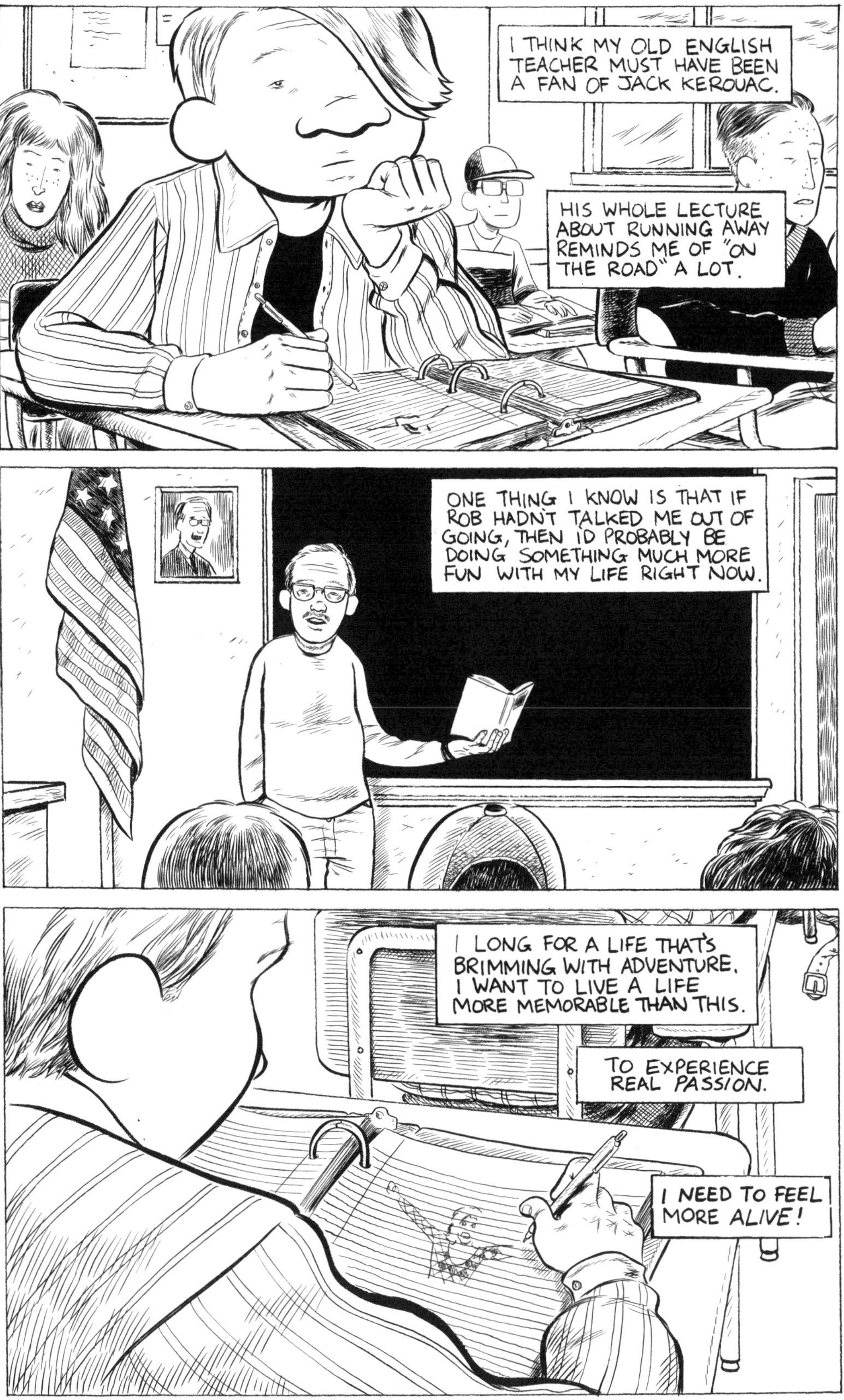

I THINK MY OLD ENGLISH TEACHER MUST HAVE BEEN A FAN OF JACK KEROUAC.
HIS WHOLE LECTURE ABOUT RUNNING AWAY REMINDS ME OF "ON THE ROAD" A LOT.
ONE THING I KNOW IS THAT IF ROB HADN'T TALKED ME OUT OF GOING, THEN I'D PROBABLY BE DOING SOMETHING MUCH MORE FUN WITH MY LIFE RIGHT NOW.
I LONG FOR A LIFE THAT'S BRIMMING WITH ADVENTURE. I WANT TO LIVE A LIFE MORE MEMORABLE THAN THIS.
TO EXPERIENCE REAL *PASSION*.
I NEED TO FEEL MORE *ALIVE*!

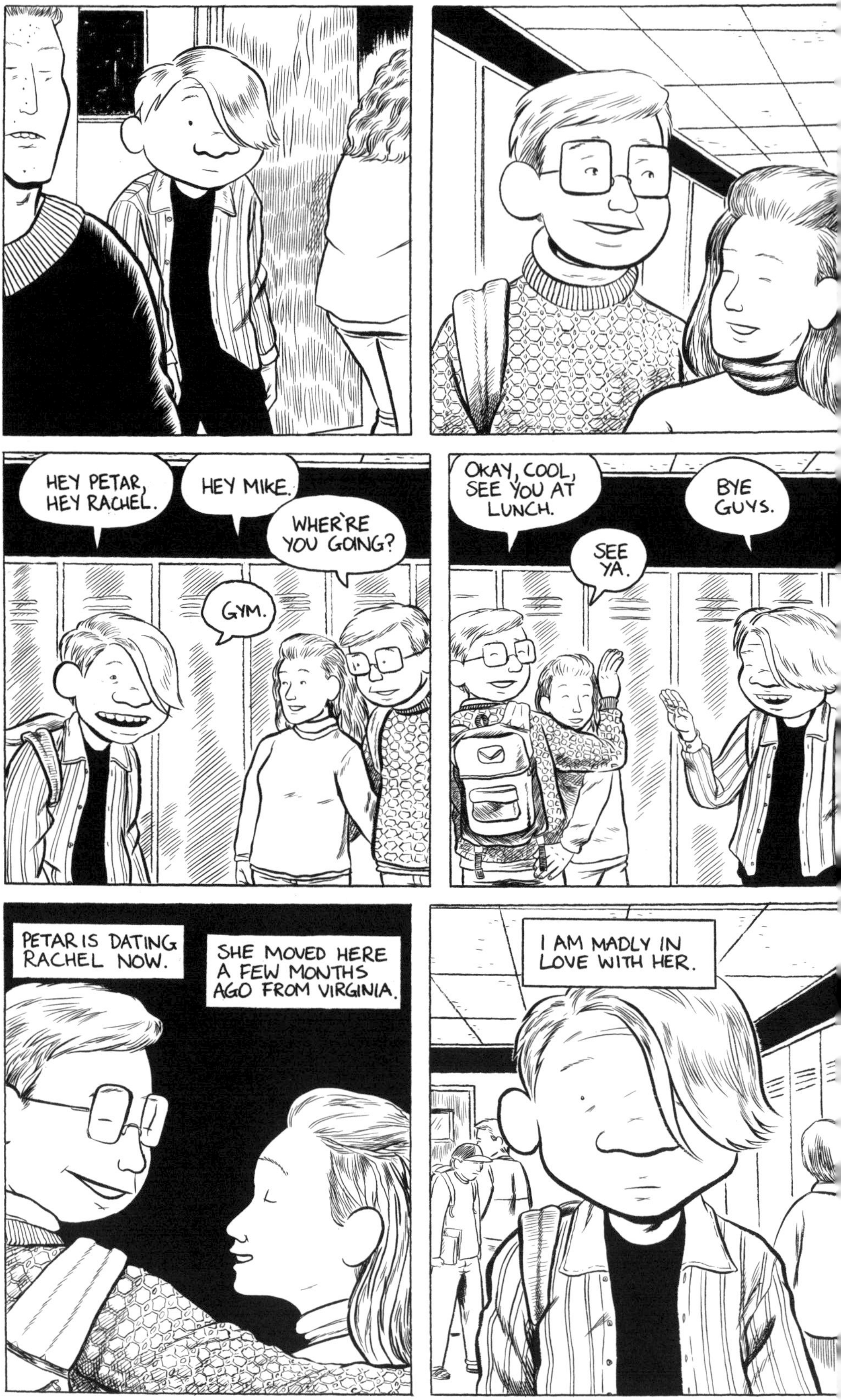
HEY PETAR, HEY RACHEL.
HEY MIKE.
WHER'RE YOU GOING?
GYM.
OKAY, COOL, SEE YOU AT LUNCH.
SEE YA.
BYE GUYS.
PETAR IS DATING RACHEL NOW.
SHE MOVED HERE A FEW MONTHS AGO FROM VIRGINIA.
I AM MADLY IN LOVE WITH HER.

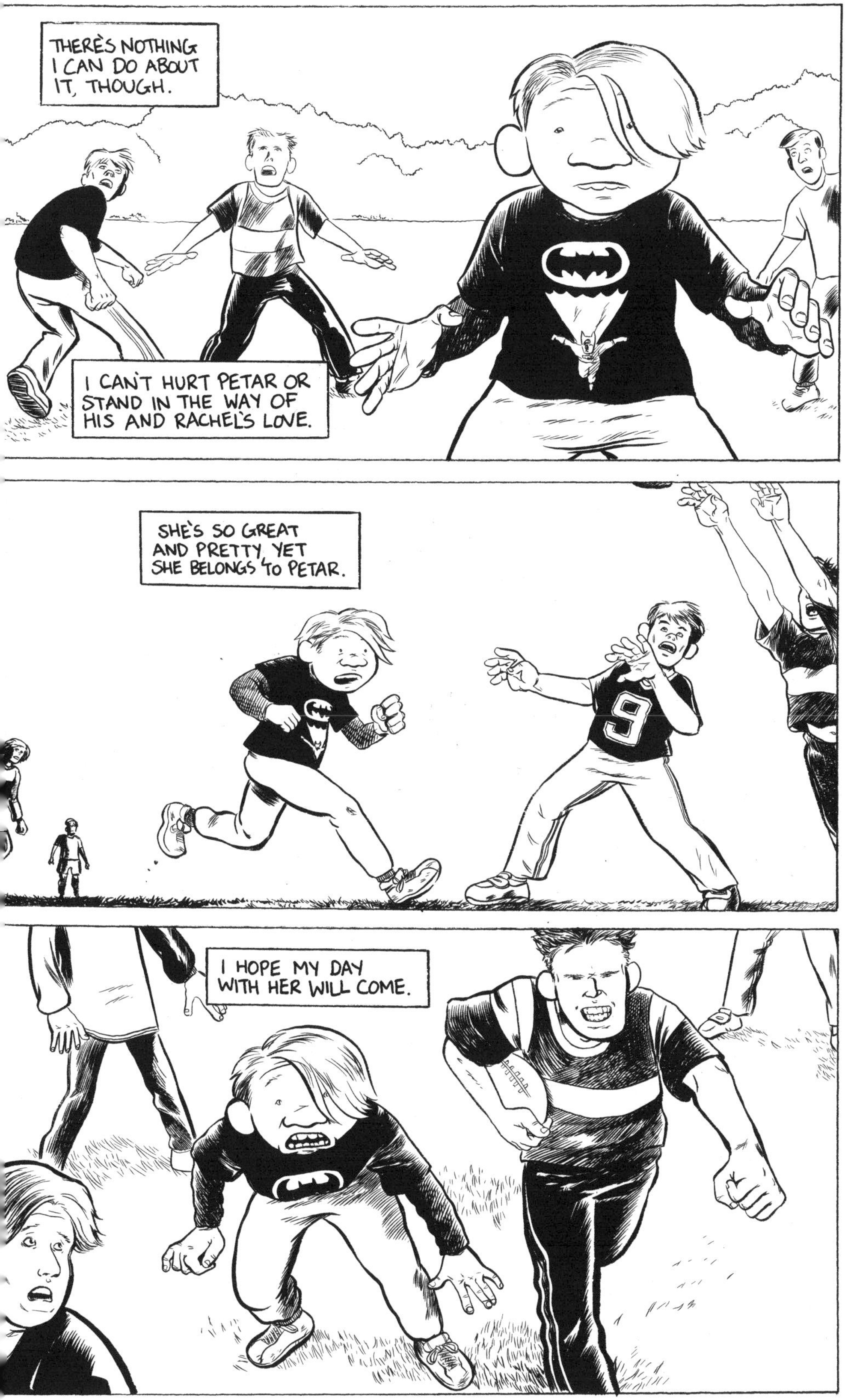
THERE'S NOTHING I CAN DO ABOUT IT, THOUGH.
I CAN'T HURT PETAR OR STAND IN THE WAY OF HIS AND RACHEL'S LOVE.
SHE'S SO GREAT AND PRETTY, YET SHE BELONGS TO PETAR.
I HOPE MY DAY WITH HER WILL COME.

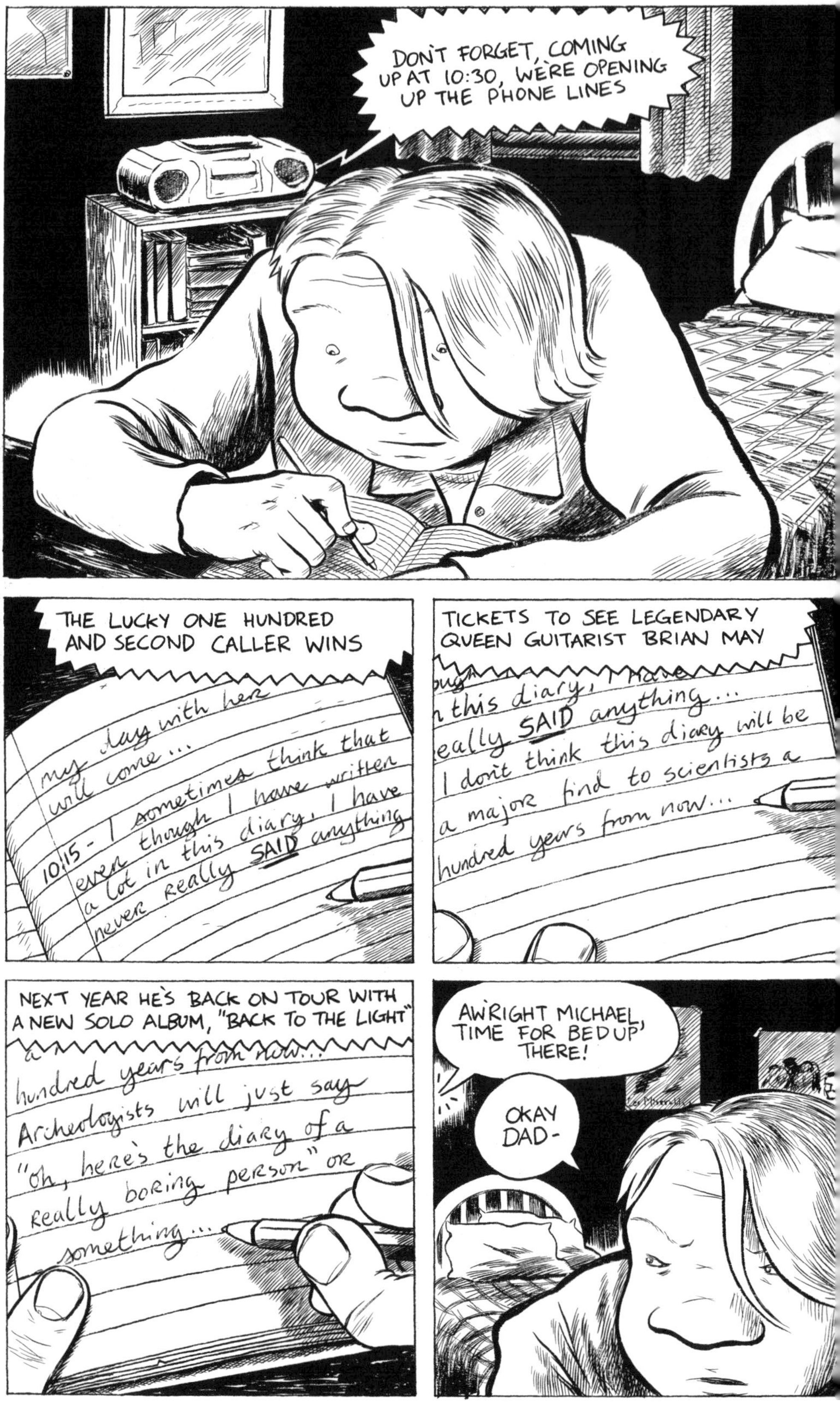
DON'T FORGET, COMING UP AT 10:30, WE'RE OPENING UP THE PHONE LINES
THE LUCKY ONE HUNDRED AND SECOND CALLER WINS
my day with her
will come...
10:15 - I sometimes think that
even though I have written
a lot in this diary, I have
never really SAID anything
TICKETS TO SEE LEGENDARY QUEEN GUITARIST BRIAN MAY
this diary, I have
eally SAID anything...
I don't think this diary will be
a major find to scientists a
hundred years from now...
NEXT YEAR HE'S BACK ON TOUR WITH A NEW SOLO ALBUM, "BACK TO THE LIGHT"
a
hundred years from now...
Archeologists will just say
"Oh, here's the diary of a
really boring person" or
something...
AWRIGHT MICHAEL, TIME FOR BED UP THERE!
OKAY DAD-

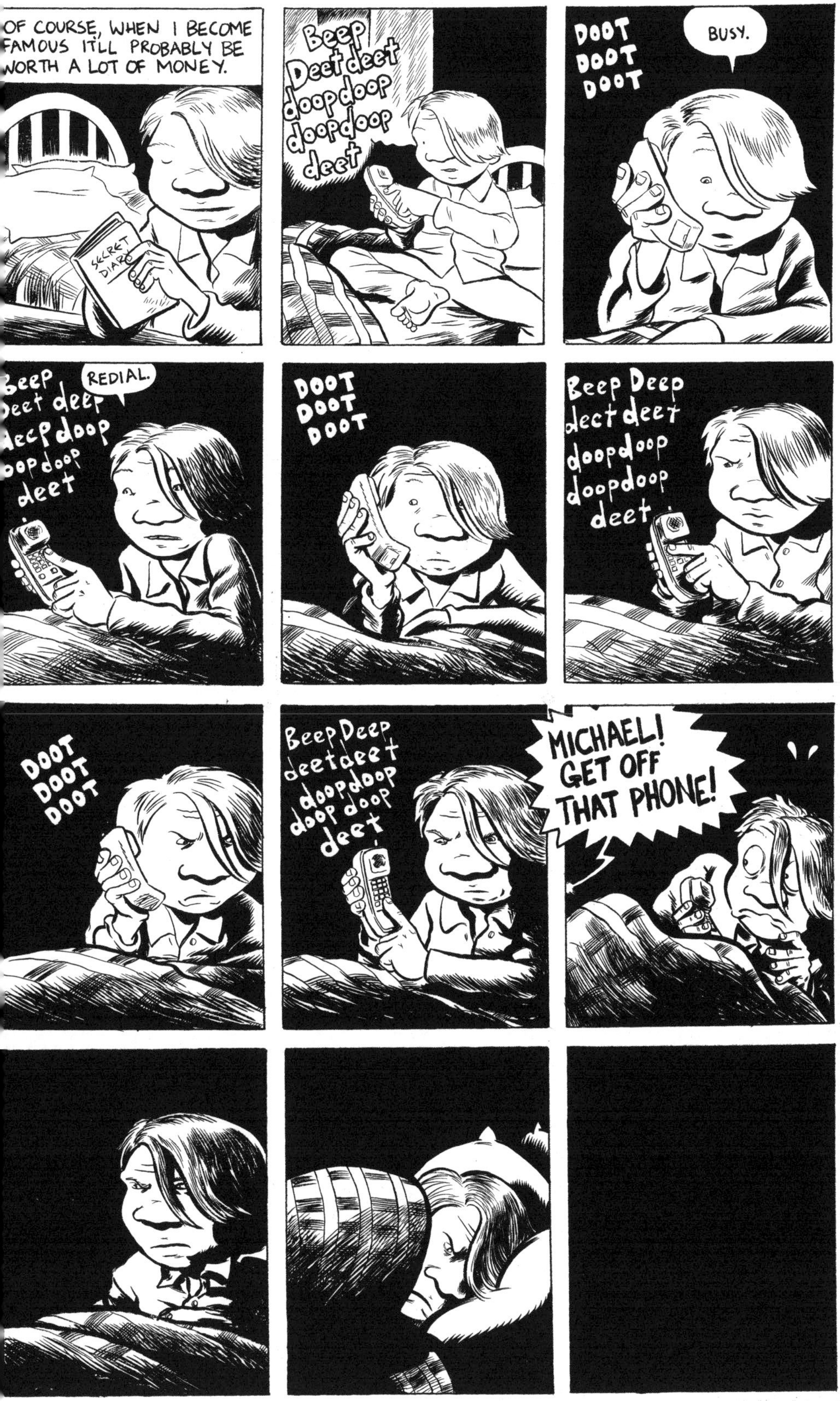
OF COURSE, WHEN I BECOME FAMOUS IT'LL PROBABLY BE WORTH A LOT OF MONEY.
Beep Deet deet doopdoop doopdoop deet
DOOT DOOT DOOT
BUSY.
REDIAL.
deep doop deet
DOOT DOOT DOOT
Beep Deep deet deet doopdoop doopdoop deet
DOOT DOOT DOOT
Beep Deep deet deet doopdoop doop doop deet
MICHAEL! GET OFF THAT PHONE!

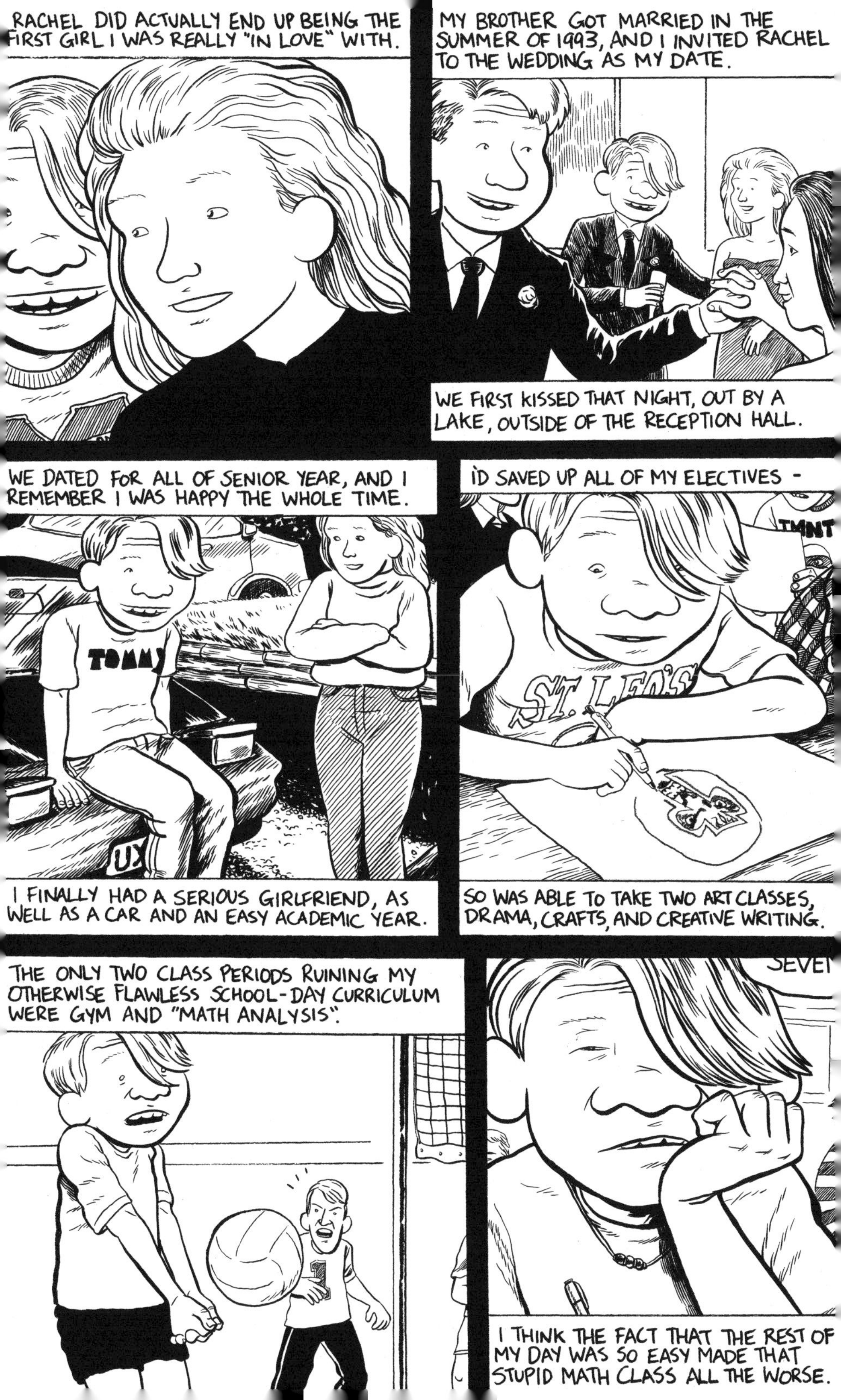
RACHEL DID ACTUALLY END UP BEING THE FIRST GIRL I WAS REALLY "IN LOVE" WITH.
MY BROTHER GOT MARRIED IN THE SUMMER OF 1993, AND I INVITED RACHEL TO THE WEDDING AS MY DATE.
WE FIRST KISSED THAT NIGHT, OUT BY A LAKE, OUTSIDE OF THE RECEPTION HALL.
WE DATED FOR ALL OF SENIOR YEAR, AND I REMEMBER I WAS HAPPY THE WHOLE TIME.
TOMMY
I FINALLY HAD A SERIOUS GIRLFRIEND, AS WELL AS A CAR AND AN EASY ACADEMIC YEAR.
I'D SAVED UP ALL OF MY ELECTIVES -
TMNT
ST. LEO'S
SO WAS ABLE TO TAKE TWO ART CLASSES, DRAMA, CRAFTS, AND CREATIVE WRITING.
THE ONLY TWO CLASS PERIODS RUINING MY OTHERWISE FLAWLESS SCHOOL-DAY CURRICULUM WERE GYM AND "MATH ANALYSIS".
I THINK THE FACT THAT THE REST OF MY DAY WAS SO EASY MADE THAT STUPID MATH CLASS ALL THE WORSE.

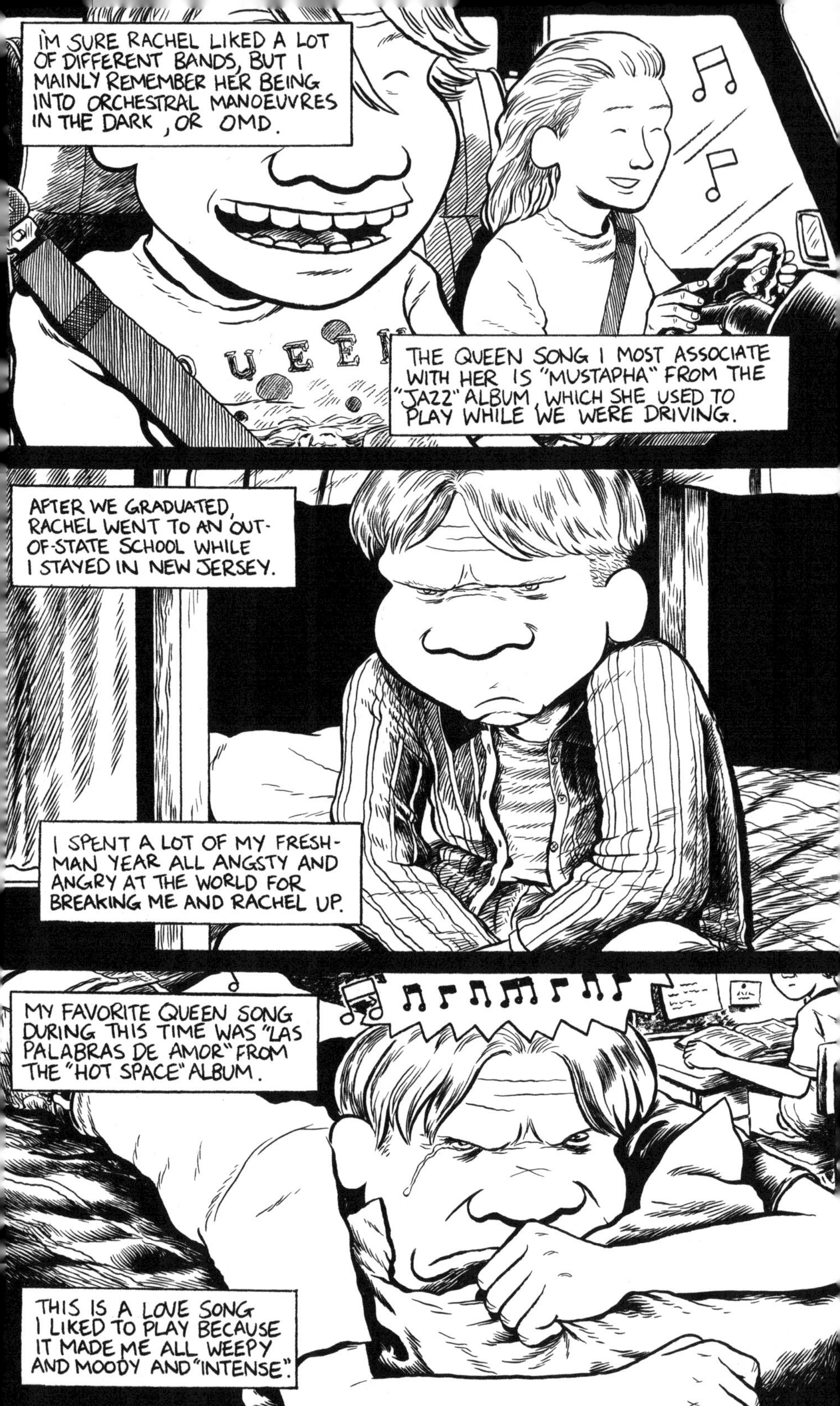
I'M SURE RACHEL LIKED A LOT OF DIFFERENT BANDS, BUT I MAINLY REMEMBER HER BEING INTO ORCHESTRAL MANOEUVRES IN THE DARK, OR OMD.
QUEEN
THE QUEEN SONG I MOST ASSOCIATE WITH HER IS "MUSTAPHA" FROM THE "JAZZ" ALBUM, WHICH SHE USED TO PLAY WHILE WE WERE DRIVING.
AFTER WE GRADUATED, RACHEL WENT TO AN OUT-OF-STATE SCHOOL WHILE I STAYED IN NEW JERSEY.
I SPENT A LOT OF MY FRESHMAN YEAR ALL ANGSTY AND ANGRY AT THE WORLD FOR BREAKING ME AND RACHEL UP.
MY FAVORITE QUEEN SONG DURING THIS TIME WAS "LAS PALABRAS DE AMOR" FROM THE "HOT SPACE" ALBUM.
THIS IS A LOVE SONG I LIKED TO PLAY BECAUSE IT MADE ME ALL WEEPY AND MOODY AND "INTENSE".

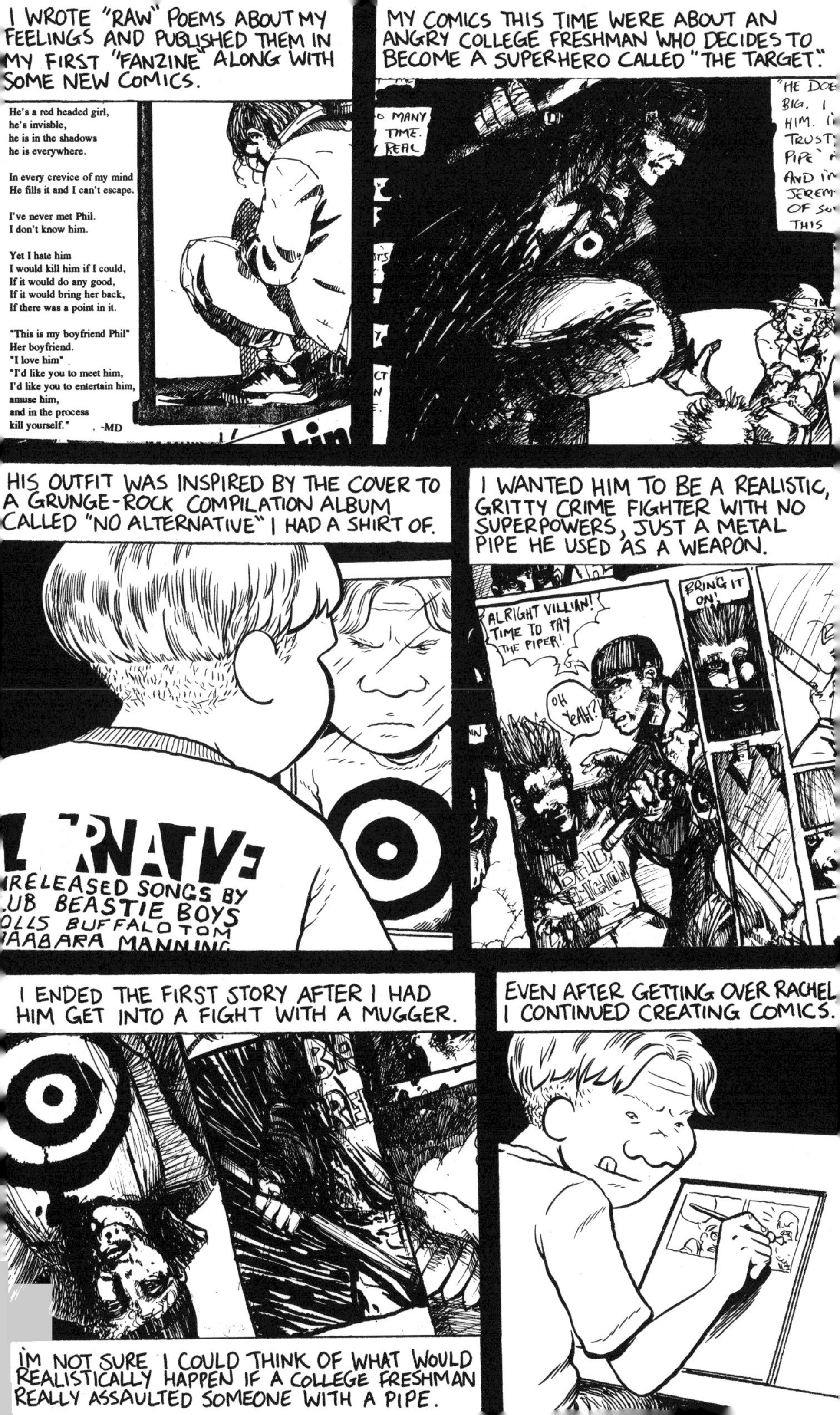
I WROTE "RAW" POEMS ABOUT MY FEELINGS AND PUBLISHED THEM IN MY FIRST "FANZINE" ALONG WITH SOME NEW COMICS.
He's a red headed girl,
he's invisble,
he is in the shadows
he is everywhere.
In every crevice of my mind
He fills it and I can't escape.
I've never met Phil.
I don't know him.
Yet I hate him
I would kill him if I could,
If it would do any good,
If it would bring her back,
If there was a point in it.
"This is my boyfriend Phil"
Her boyfriend.
"I love him"
"I'd like you to meet him,
I'd like you to entertain him,
amuse him,
and in the process
kill yourself." -MD
MY COMICS THIS TIME WERE ABOUT AN ANGRY COLLEGE FRESHMAN WHO DECIDES TO BECOME A SUPERHERO CALLED "THE TARGET."
HIS OUTFIT WAS INSPIRED BY THE COVER TO A GRUNGE-ROCK COMPILATION ALBUM CALLED "NO ALTERNATIVE" I HAD A SHIRT OF.
RNATIVE
RELEASED SONGS BY
BEASTIE BOYS
BUFFALO TOM
I WANTED HIM TO BE A REALISTIC, GRITTY CRIME FIGHTER WITH NO SUPERPOWERS, JUST A METAL PIPE HE USED AS A WEAPON.
ALRIGHT VILLIAN! TIME TO PAY THE PIPER!
BRING IT ON!
OH YEAH?
I ENDED THE FIRST STORY AFTER I HAD HIM GET INTO A FIGHT WITH A MUGGER.
I'M NOT SURE I COULD THINK OF WHAT WOULD REALISTICALLY HAPPEN IF A COLLEGE FRESHMAN REALLY ASSAULTED SOMEONE WITH A PIPE.
EVEN AFTER GETTING OVER RACHEL I CONTINUED CREATING COMICS.

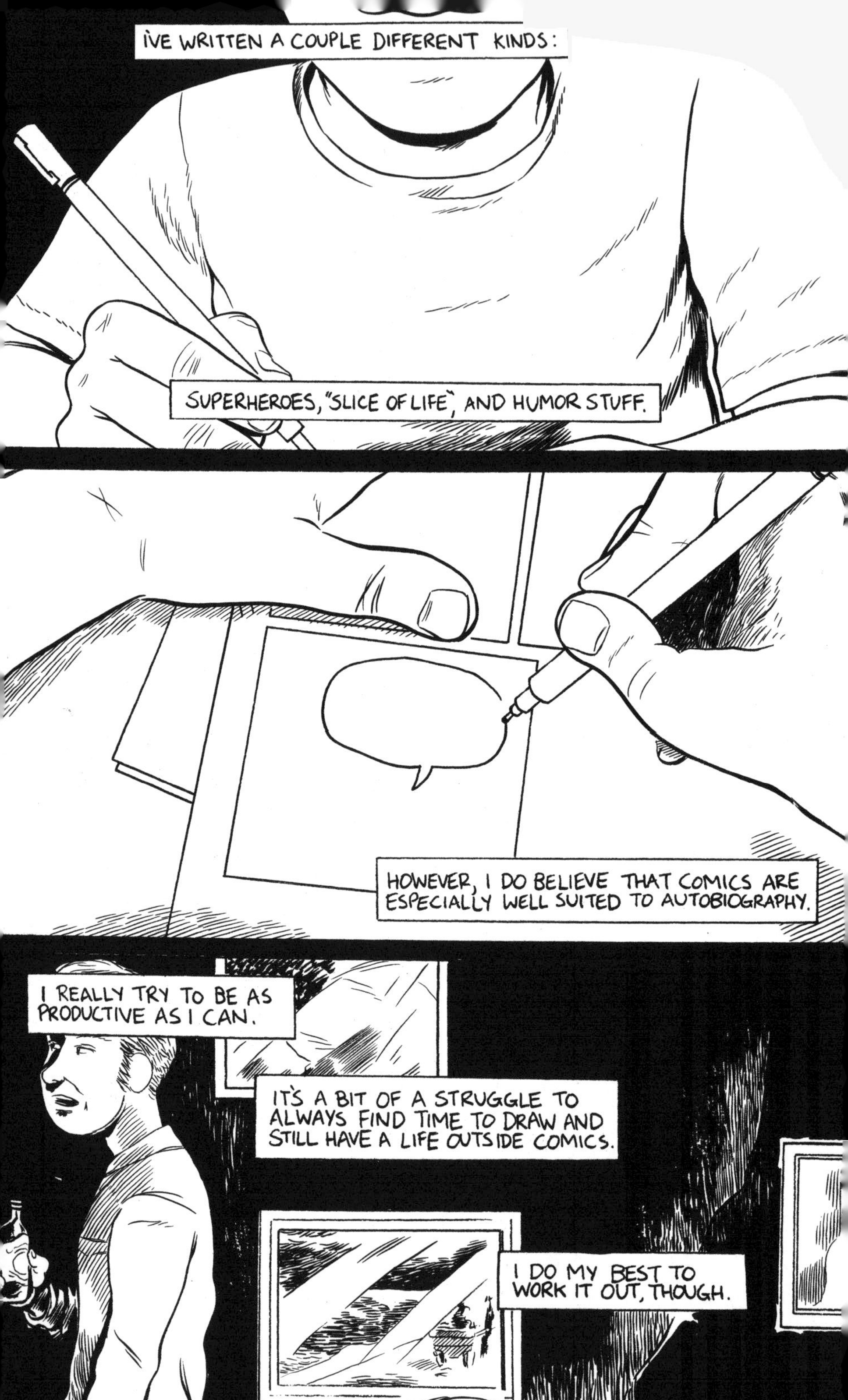
I'VE WRITTEN A COUPLE DIFFERENT KINDS:
SUPERHEROES, "SLICE OF LIFE", AND HUMOR STUFF.
HOWEVER, I DO BELIEVE THAT COMICS ARE ESPECIALLY WELL SUITED TO AUTOBIOGRAPHY.
I REALLY TRY TO BE AS PRODUCTIVE AS I CAN.
IT'S A BIT OF A STRUGGLE TO ALWAYS FIND TIME TO DRAW AND STILL HAVE A LIFE OUTSIDE COMICS.
I DO MY BEST TO WORK IT OUT, THOUGH.

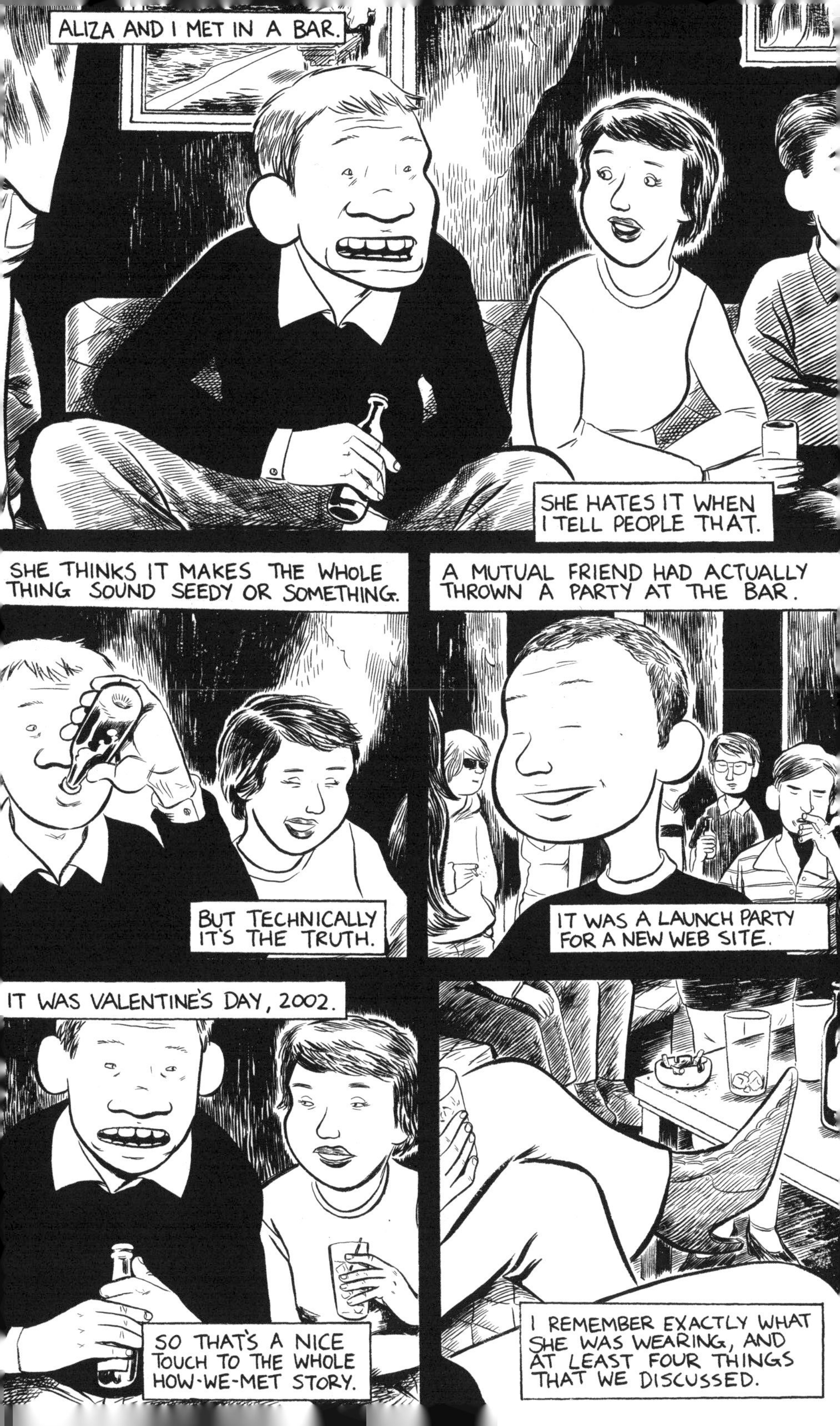
ALIZA AND I MET IN A BAR.
SHE HATES IT WHEN I TELL PEOPLE THAT.
SHE THINKS IT MAKES THE WHOLE THING SOUND SEEDY OR SOMETHING.
BUT TECHNICALLY IT'S THE TRUTH.
A MUTUAL FRIEND HAD ACTUALLY THROWN A PARTY AT THE BAR.
IT WAS A LAUNCH PARTY FOR A NEW WEB SITE.
IT WAS VALENTINE'S DAY, 2002.
SO THAT'S A NICE TOUCH TO THE WHOLE HOW-WE-MET STORY.
I REMEMBER EXACTLY WHAT SHE WAS WEARING, AND AT LEAST FOUR THINGS THAT WE DISCUSSED.

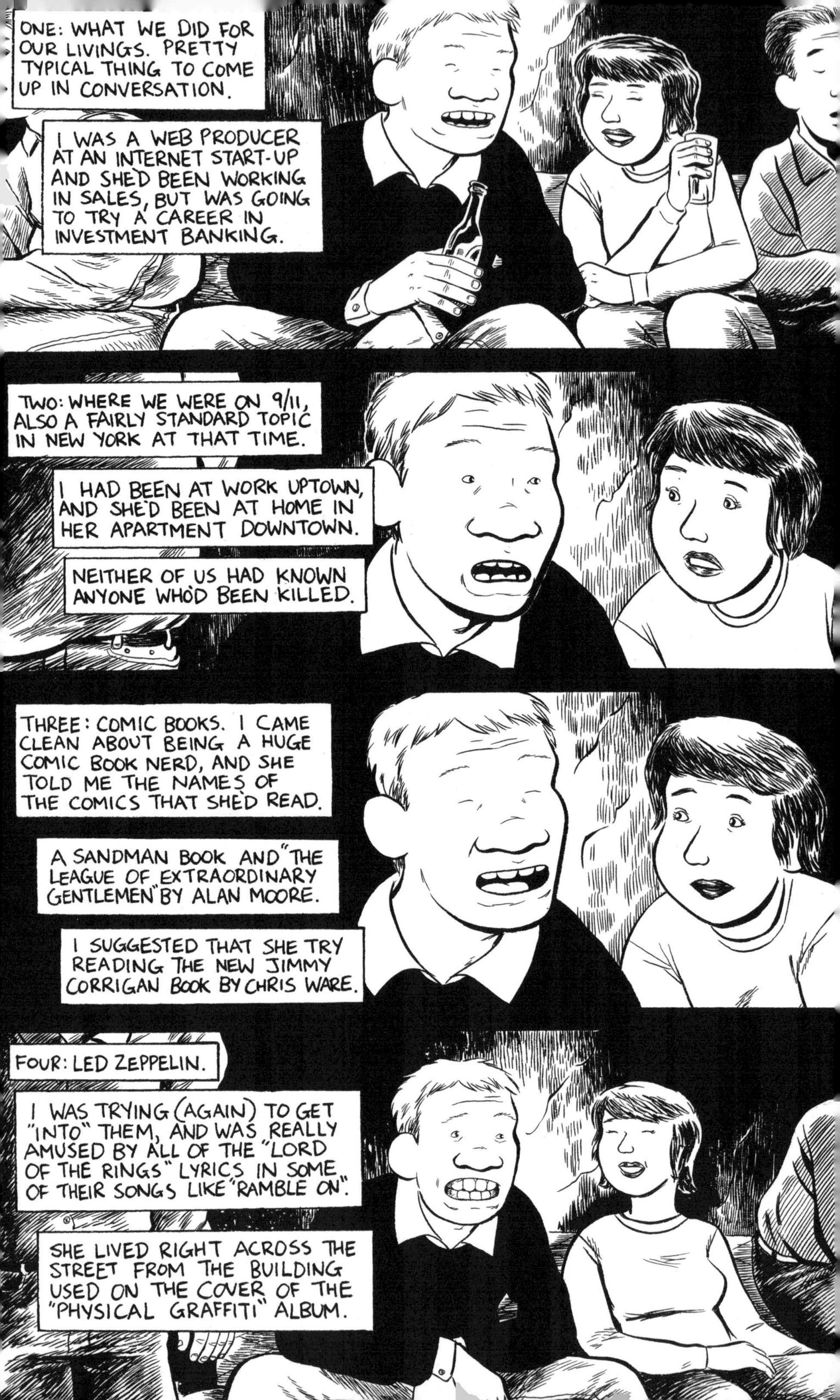
ONE: WHAT WE DID FOR OUR LIVINGS. PRETTY TYPICAL THING TO COME UP IN CONVERSATION.
I WAS A WEB PRODUCER AT AN INTERNET START-UP AND SHE'D BEEN WORKING IN SALES, BUT WAS GOING TO TRY A CAREER IN INVESTMENT BANKING.
TWO: WHERE WE WERE ON 9/11, ALSO A FAIRLY STANDARD TOPIC IN NEW YORK AT THAT TIME.
I HAD BEEN AT WORK UPTOWN, AND SHE'D BEEN AT HOME IN HER APARTMENT DOWNTOWN.
NEITHER OF US HAD KNOWN ANYONE WHO'D BEEN KILLED.
THREE: COMIC BOOKS. I CAME CLEAN ABOUT BEING A HUGE COMIC BOOK NERD, AND SHE TOLD ME THE NAMES OF THE COMICS THAT SHE'D READ.
A SANDMAN BOOK AND "THE LEAGUE OF EXTRAORDINARY GENTLEMEN" BY ALAN MOORE.
I SUGGESTED THAT SHE TRY READING THE NEW JIMMY CORRIGAN BOOK BY CHRIS WARE.
FOUR: LED ZEPPELIN.
I WAS TRYING (AGAIN) TO GET "INTO" THEM, AND WAS REALLY AMUSED BY ALL OF THE "LORD OF THE RINGS" LYRICS IN SOME OF THEIR SONGS LIKE "RAMBLE ON".
SHE LIVED RIGHT ACROSS THE STREET FROM THE BUILDING USED ON THE COVER OF THE "PHYSICAL GRAFFITI" ALBUM.

I DUNNO, IT KIND OF SOUNDS A BIT LAME WHEN I DESCRIBE IT LIKE THAT - IT'S NOT LIKE WE TALKED ABOUT ALL THESE PROFOUND TOPICS OR ANYTHING.

BUT IT WAS REALLY AN EASY AND FUN CONVERSATION, YOU KNOW? WE JUST STARTED TALKING AND WENT ALL NIGHT.

ACTUALLY, BEFORE ALIZA SHOWED UP, I'D BEEN TALKING TO ANOTHER GIRL WHO WAS SOMEHOW INVOLVED IN FILM.

I'D BROUGHT UP THAT I WAS A CARTOONIST, AND WE ALL OF A SUDDEN GOT INTO THIS HEAVY CONVERSATION ABOUT "HIGH ART."

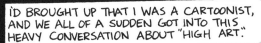

IT WASN'T EASY AT ALL - I GUESS BECAUSE WE WERE STRANGERS AND MAYBE BOTH FELT LIKE WE DIDN'T WANT TO SOUND DUMB AS WE TALKED ALL "HIGH-BROW."

IT WAS JUST SO DIFFERENT WITH ALIZA.

WE STARTED TALKING ON THAT COUCH, AND I GUESS WE'VE NEVER STOPPED SINCE.

OH YEAH, MY FRIEND ROB, WHOM I KNEW FROM HIGH SCHOOL, WAS ALSO THERE.

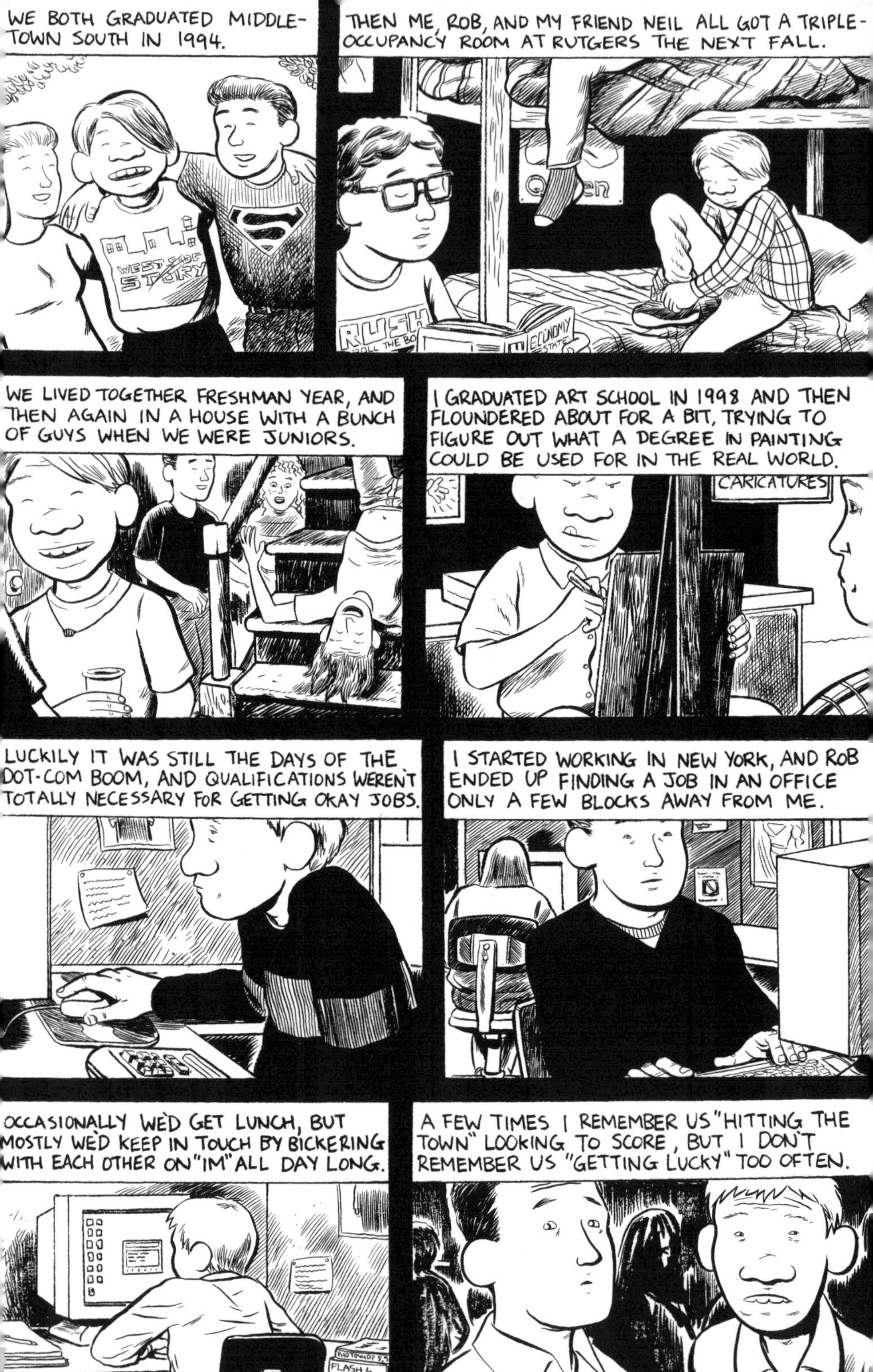
WE BOTH GRADUATED MIDDLETOWN SOUTH IN 1994.
WEST SIDE STORY
THEN ME, ROB, AND MY FRIEND NEIL ALL GOT A TRIPLE-OCCUPANCY ROOM AT RUTGERS THE NEXT FALL.
RUSH
ECONOMY
WE LIVED TOGETHER FRESHMAN YEAR, AND THEN AGAIN IN A HOUSE WITH A BUNCH OF GUYS WHEN WE WERE JUNIORS.
I GRADUATED ART SCHOOL IN 1998 AND THEN FLOUNDERED ABOUT FOR A BIT, TRYING TO FIGURE OUT WHAT A DEGREE IN PAINTING COULD BE USED FOR IN THE REAL WORLD.
CARICATURES
LUCKILY IT WAS STILL THE DAYS OF THE DOT-COM BOOM, AND QUALIFICATIONS WEREN'T TOTALLY NECESSARY FOR GETTING OKAY JOBS.
I STARTED WORKING IN NEW YORK, AND ROB ENDED UP FINDING A JOB IN AN OFFICE ONLY A FEW BLOCKS AWAY FROM ME.
OCCASIONALLY WE'D GET LUNCH, BUT MOSTLY WE'D KEEP IN TOUCH BY BICKERING WITH EACH OTHER ON "IM" ALL DAY LONG.
FLASH 4
A FEW TIMES I REMEMBER US "HITTING THE TOWN" LOOKING TO SCORE, BUT I DON'T REMEMBER US "GETTING LUCKY" TOO OFTEN.

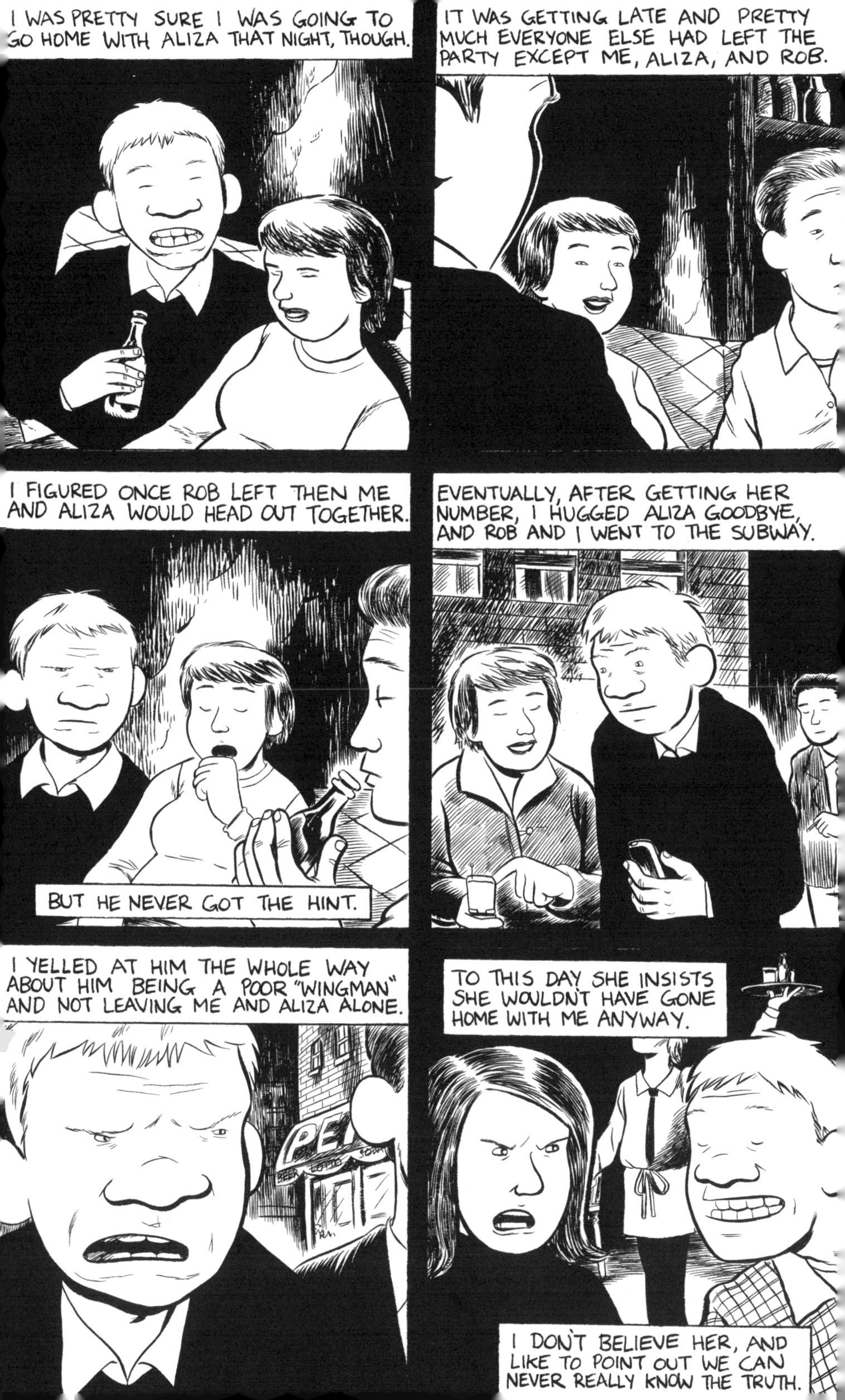
I WAS PRETTY SURE I WAS GOING TO GO HOME WITH ALIZA THAT NIGHT, THOUGH.
IT WAS GETTING LATE AND PRETTY MUCH EVERYONE ELSE HAD LEFT THE PARTY EXCEPT ME, ALIZA, AND ROB.
I FIGURED ONCE ROB LEFT THEN ME AND ALIZA WOULD HEAD OUT TOGETHER.
BUT HE NEVER GOT THE HINT.
EVENTUALLY, AFTER GETTING HER NUMBER, I HUGGED ALIZA GOODBYE, AND ROB AND I WENT TO THE SUBWAY.
I YELLED AT HIM THE WHOLE WAY ABOUT HIM BEING A POOR "WINGMAN" AND NOT LEAVING ME AND ALIZA ALONE.
TO THIS DAY SHE INSISTS SHE WOULDN'T HAVE GONE HOME WITH ME ANYWAY.
I DON'T BELIEVE HER, AND LIKE TO POINT OUT WE CAN NEVER REALLY KNOW THE TRUTH.

Hard Rock

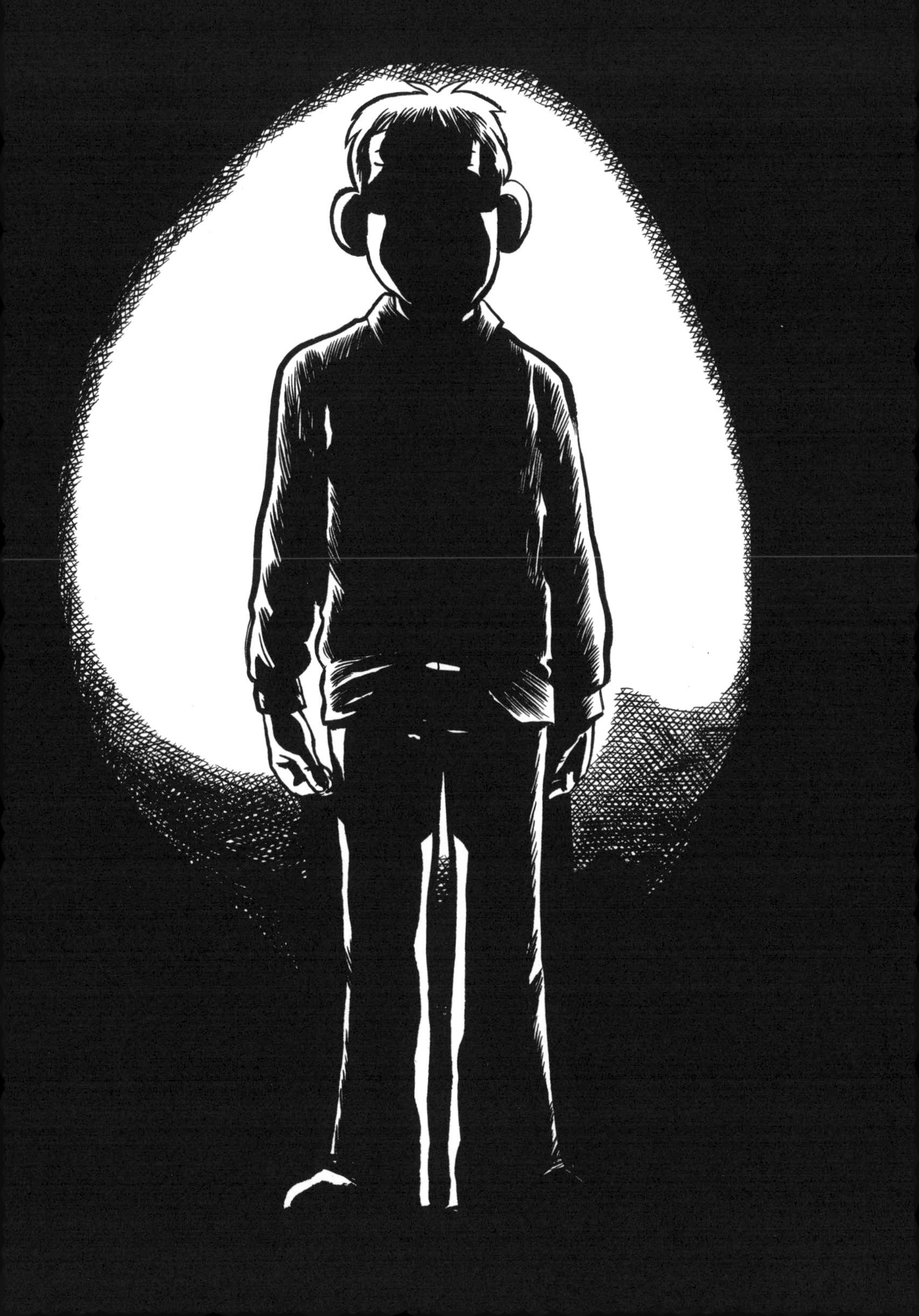

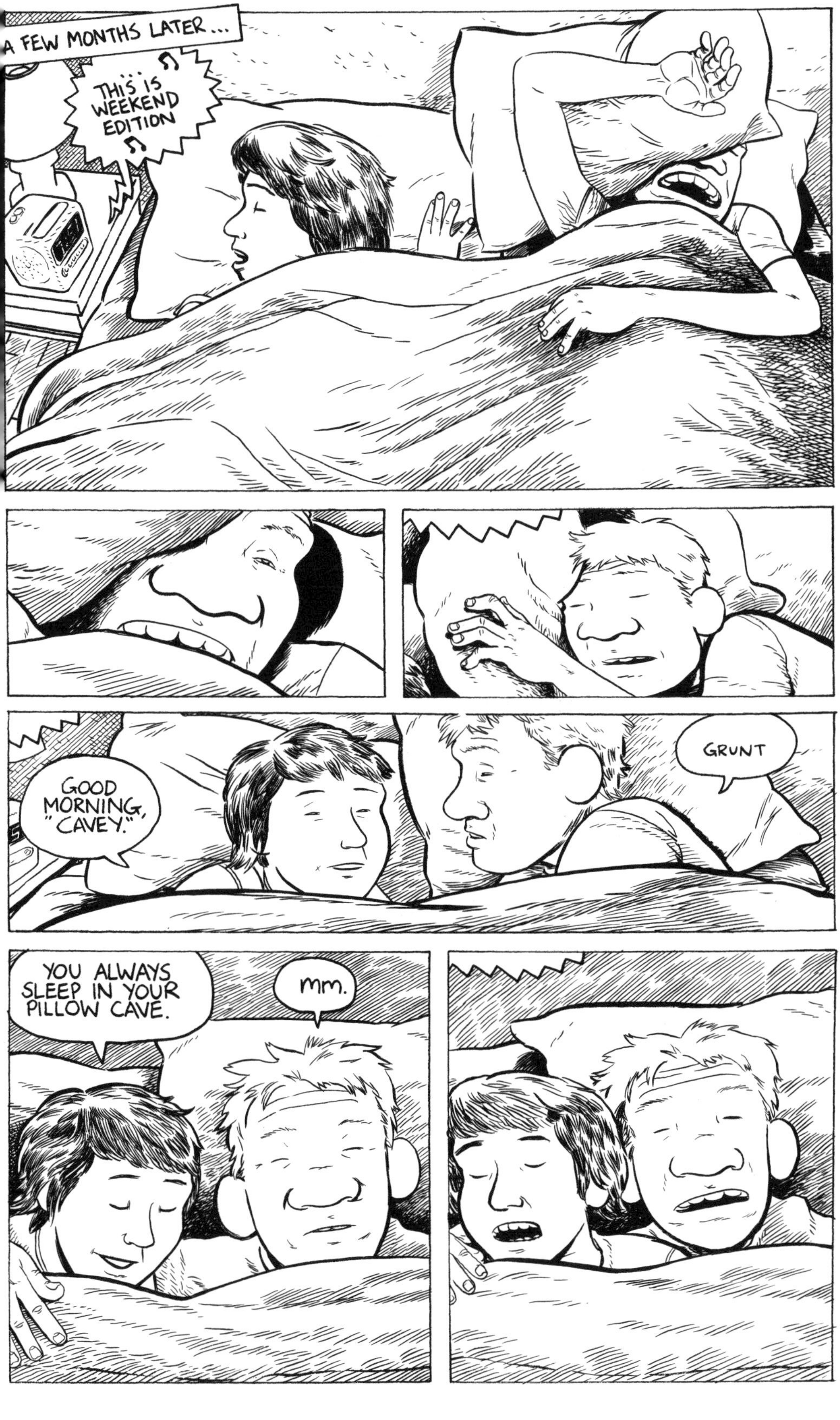
A FEW MONTHS LATER...
... THIS IS WEEKEND EDITION
GOOD MORNING, "CAVEY."
GRUNT
YOU ALWAYS SLEEP IN YOUR PILLOW CAVE.
mm.

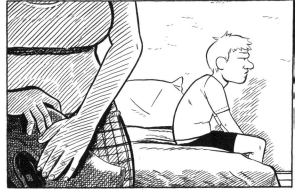

DO YOU WANT TO GO IN THE SHOWER FIRST?

I DEFINITELY NEED TO STAY AT MY OWN APARTMENT TONIGHT.

I FEEL LIKE I HAVEN'T DONE ANY DRAWING LATELY...

UM, OKAAY...

DON'T ACT LIKE IT'S MY FAULT YOU'VE NOT BEEN WORKING.

IT'S NOT...

I JUST FEEL LIKE I HAVEN'T DONE ANYTHING ALL WEEK...

AND NOW WE'RE GOING TO BE IN NEW JERSEY ALL DAY.

WELL, THAT'S NOT MY FAULT EITHER - IT'S YOUR PARENTS WE'RE GOING TO SEE, NOT MINE.

NO, I KNOW...

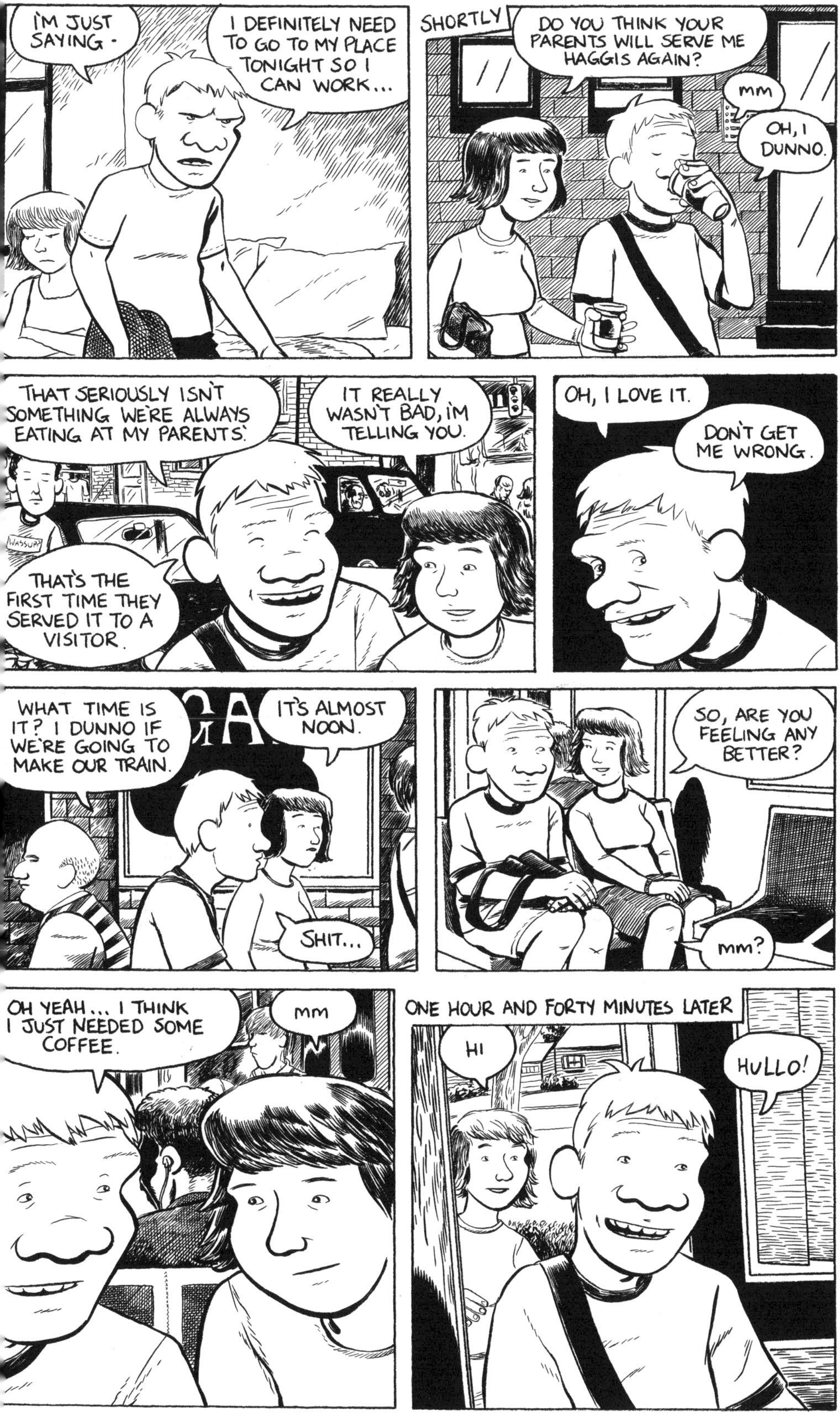
I'M JUST SAYING -
I DEFINITELY NEED TO GO TO MY PLACE TONIGHT SO I CAN WORK...
SHORTLY
DO YOU THINK YOUR PARENTS WILL SERVE ME HAGGIS AGAIN?
mm
OH, I DUNNO.
THAT SERIOUSLY ISN'T SOMETHING WE'RE ALWAYS EATING AT MY PARENTS'.
THAT'S THE FIRST TIME THEY SERVED IT TO A VISITOR.
WASSUP?
IT REALLY WASN'T BAD, I'M TELLING YOU.
OH, I LOVE IT.
DON'T GET ME WRONG.
WHAT TIME IS IT? I DUNNO IF WE'RE GOING TO MAKE OUR TRAIN.
IT'S ALMOST NOON.
SHIT...
SO, ARE YOU FEELING ANY BETTER?
mm?
OH YEAH... I THINK I JUST NEEDED SOME COFFEE.
mm
ONE HOUR AND FORTY MINUTES LATER
HI
HULLO!

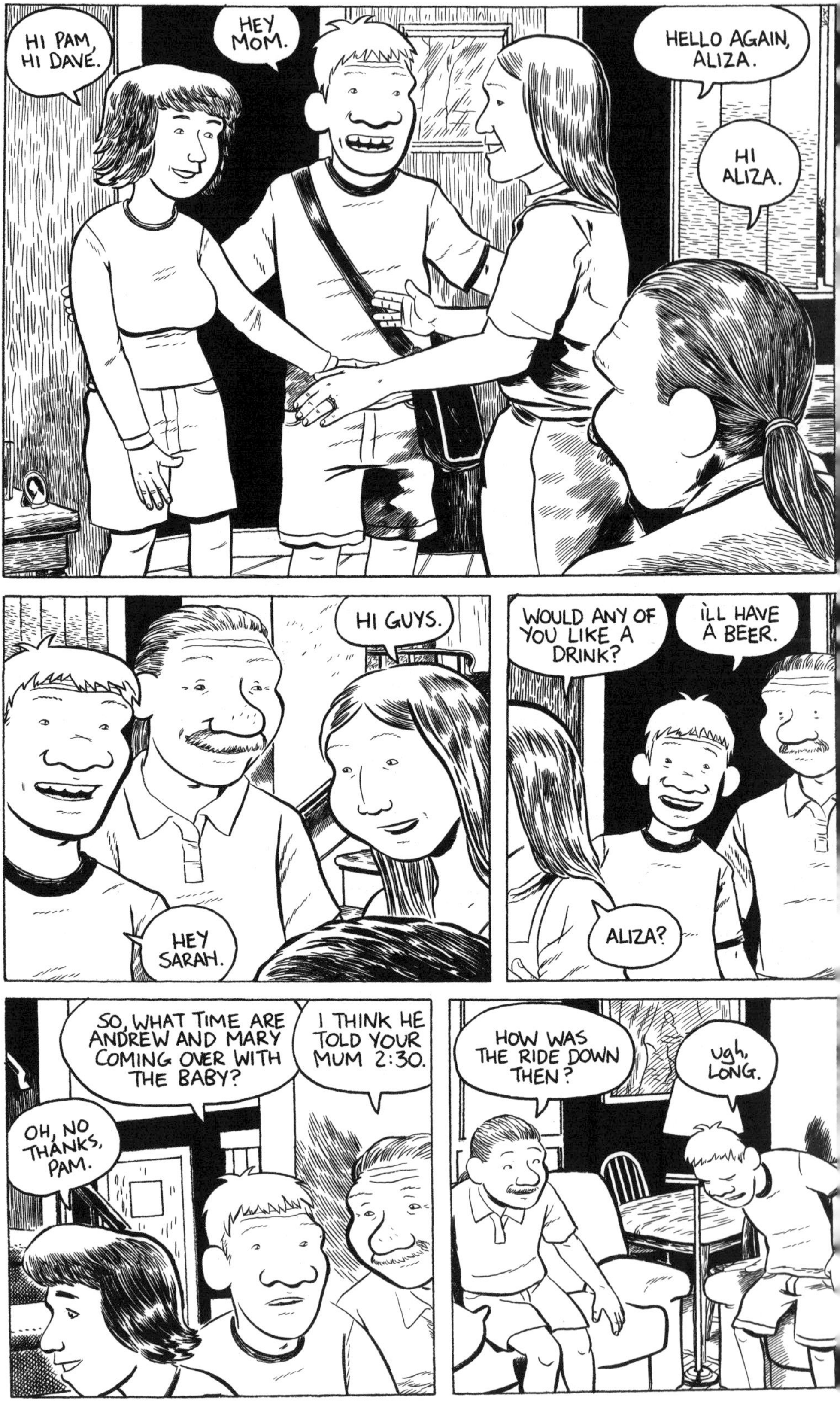
HI PAM, HI DAVE.
HEY MOM.
HELLO AGAIN, ALIZA.
HI ALIZA.
HI GUYS.
HEY SARAH.
WOULD ANY OF YOU LIKE A DRINK?
I'LL HAVE A BEER.
ALIZA?
SO, WHAT TIME ARE ANDREW AND MARY COMING OVER WITH THE BABY?
I THINK HE TOLD YOUR MUM 2:30.
OH, NO THANKS, PAM.
HOW WAS THE RIDE DOWN THEN?
ugh, LONG.

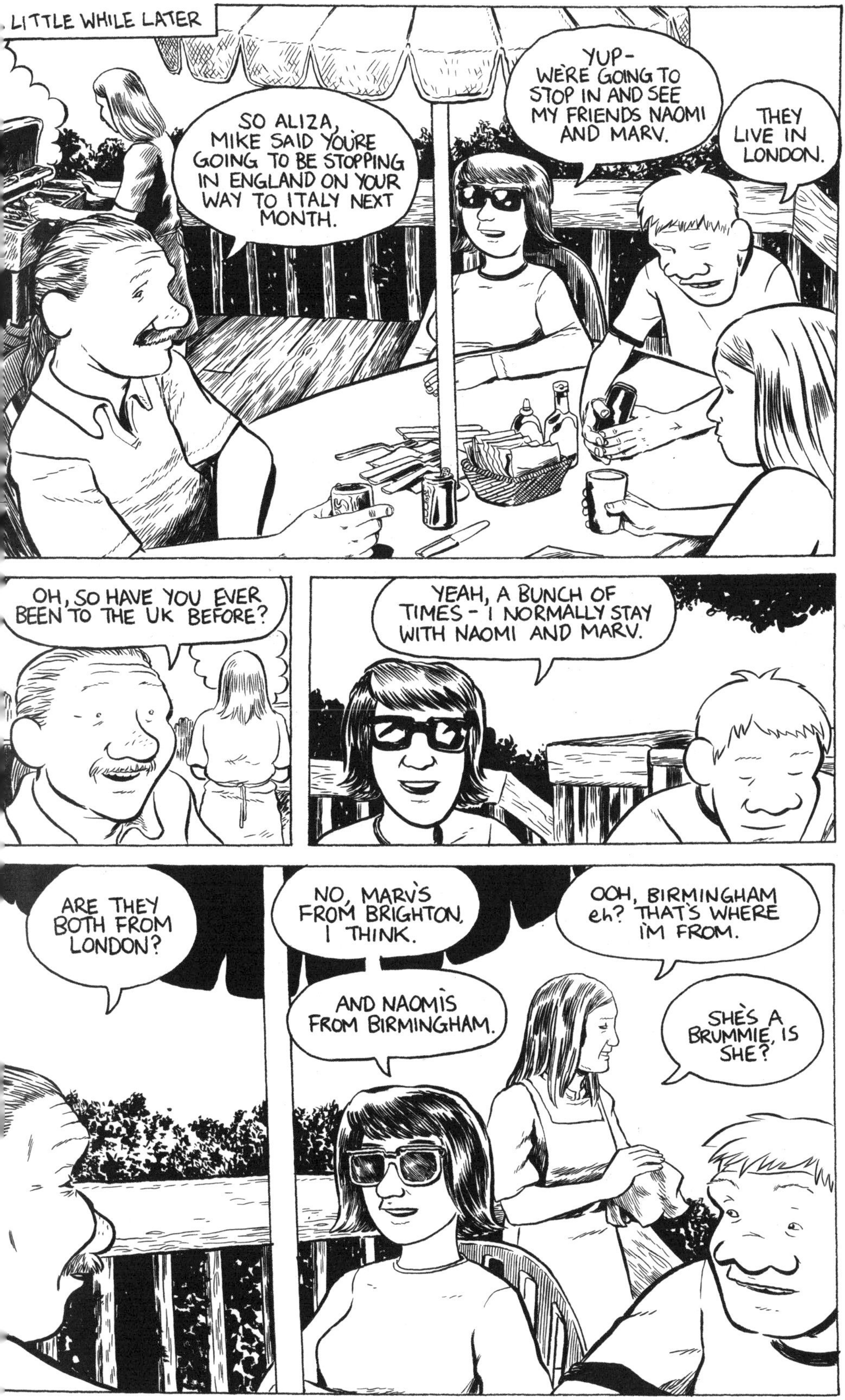
LITTLE WHILE LATER
SO ALIZA, MIKE SAID YOU'RE GOING TO BE STOPPING IN ENGLAND ON YOUR WAY TO ITALY NEXT MONTH.
YUP- WE'RE GOING TO STOP IN AND SEE MY FRIENDS NAOMI AND MARV.
THEY LIVE IN LONDON.
OH, SO HAVE YOU EVER BEEN TO THE UK BEFORE?
YEAH, A BUNCH OF TIMES - I NORMALLY STAY WITH NAOMI AND MARV.
ARE THEY BOTH FROM LONDON?
NO, MARV'S FROM BRIGHTON, I THINK.
AND NAOMI'S FROM BIRMINGHAM.
OOH, BIRMINGHAM eh? THAT'S WHERE I'M FROM.
SHE'S A BRUMMIE, IS SHE?

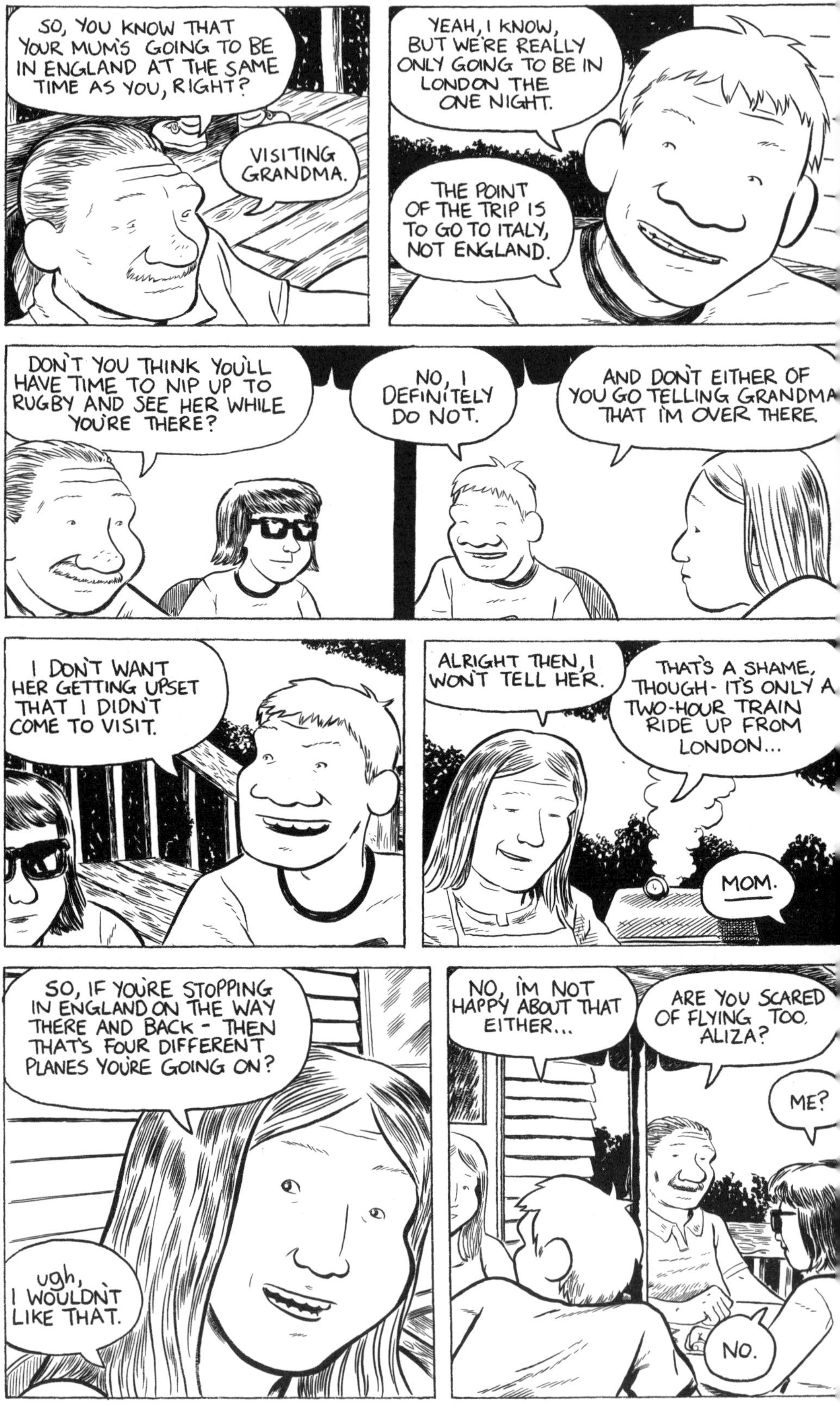
SO, YOU KNOW THAT YOUR MUM'S GOING TO BE IN ENGLAND AT THE SAME TIME AS YOU, RIGHT?
VISITING GRANDMA.
YEAH, I KNOW, BUT WE'RE REALLY ONLY GOING TO BE IN LONDON THE ONE NIGHT.
THE POINT OF THE TRIP IS TO GO TO ITALY, NOT ENGLAND.
DON'T YOU THINK YOU'LL HAVE TIME TO NIP UP TO RUGBY AND SEE HER WHILE YOU'RE THERE?
NO, I DEFINITELY DO NOT.
AND DON'T EITHER OF YOU GO TELLING GRANDMA THAT I'M OVER THERE.
I DON'T WANT HER GETTING UPSET THAT I DIDN'T COME TO VISIT.
ALRIGHT THEN, I WON'T TELL HER.
THAT'S A SHAME, THOUGH- IT'S ONLY A TWO-HOUR TRAIN RIDE UP FROM LONDON...
MOM.
SO, IF YOU'RE STOPPING IN ENGLAND ON THE WAY THERE AND BACK - THEN THAT'S FOUR DIFFERENT PLANES YOU'RE GOING ON?
ugh, I WOULDN'T LIKE THAT.
NO, I'M NOT HAPPY ABOUT THAT EITHER...
ARE YOU SCARED OF FLYING TOO, ALIZA?
ME?
NO.

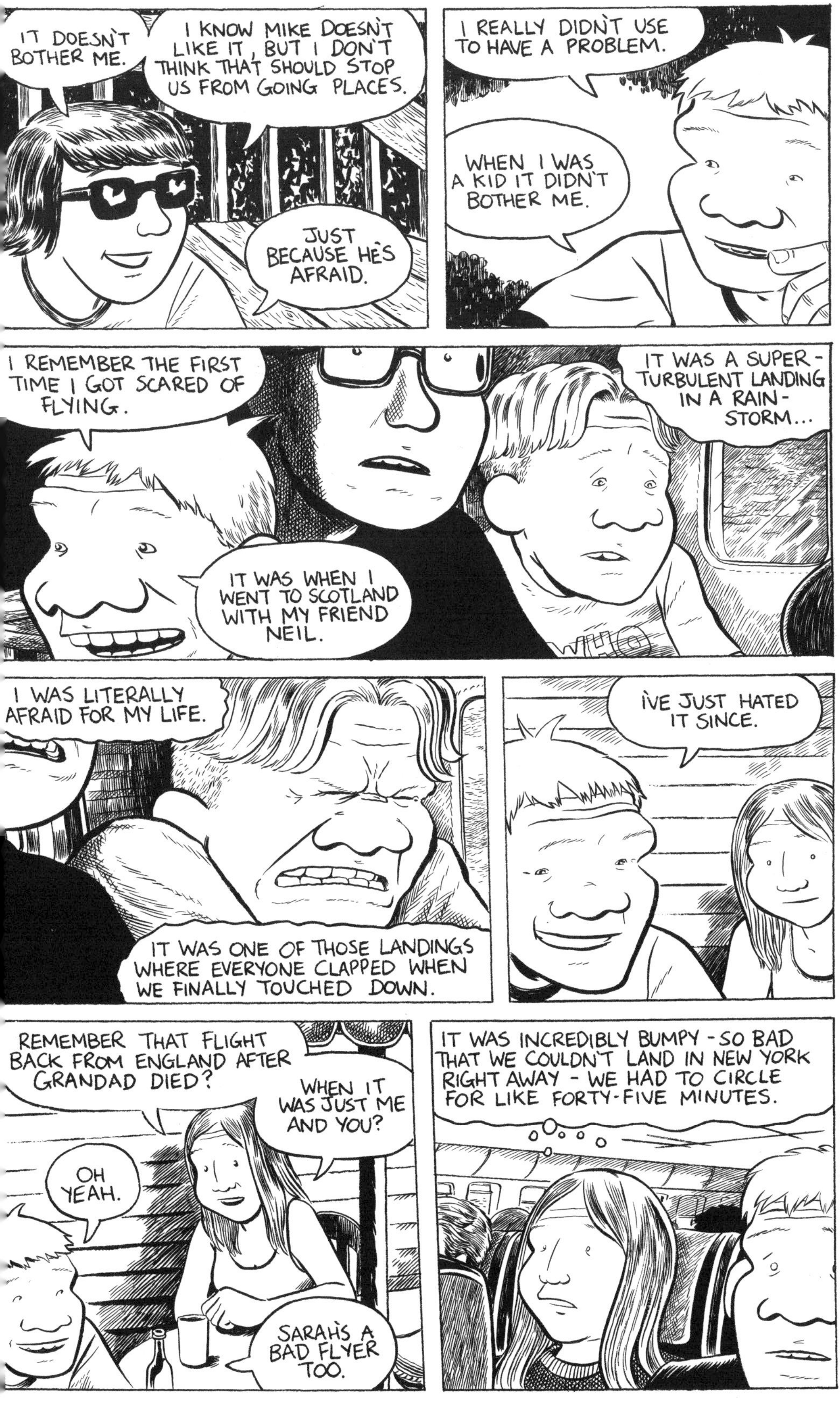
IT DOESN'T BOTHER ME.
I KNOW MIKE DOESN'T LIKE IT, BUT I DON'T THINK THAT SHOULD STOP US FROM GOING PLACES.
JUST BECAUSE HE'S AFRAID.
I REALLY DIDN'T USE TO HAVE A PROBLEM.
WHEN I WAS A KID IT DIDN'T BOTHER ME.
I REMEMBER THE FIRST TIME I GOT SCARED OF FLYING.
IT WAS WHEN I WENT TO SCOTLAND WITH MY FRIEND NEIL.
IT WAS A SUPER-TURBULENT LANDING IN A RAIN-STORM...
WHO
I WAS LITERALLY AFRAID FOR MY LIFE.
IT WAS ONE OF THOSE LANDINGS WHERE EVERYONE CLAPPED WHEN WE FINALLY TOUCHED DOWN.
I'VE JUST HATED IT SINCE.
REMEMBER THAT FLIGHT BACK FROM ENGLAND AFTER GRANDAD DIED?
WHEN IT WAS JUST ME AND YOU?
OH YEAH.
SARAH'S A BAD FLYER TOO.
IT WAS INCREDIBLY BUMPY - SO BAD THAT WE COULDN'T LAND IN NEW YORK RIGHT AWAY - WE HAD TO CIRCLE FOR LIKE FORTY-FIVE MINUTES.

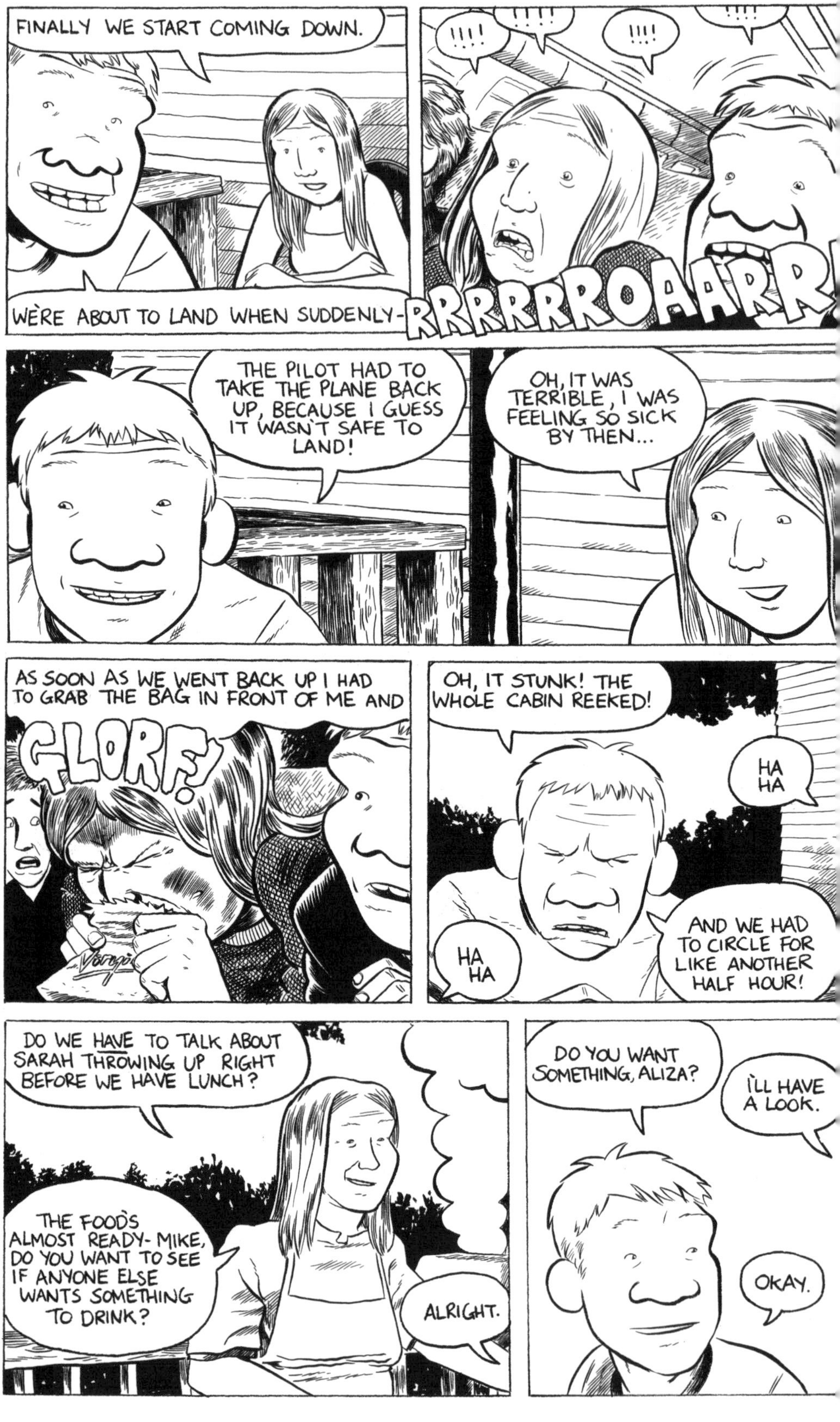

FINALLY WE START COMING DOWN.
WE'RE ABOUT TO LAND WHEN SUDDENLY-
!!!!
!!!!
!!!!
!!!!
RRRRRROAARR
THE PILOT HAD TO TAKE THE PLANE BACK UP, BECAUSE I GUESS IT WASN'T SAFE TO LAND!
OH, IT WAS TERRIBLE, I WAS FEELING SO SICK BY THEN...
AS SOON AS WE WENT BACK UP I HAD TO GRAB THE BAG IN FRONT OF ME AND
GLORF!
OH, IT STUNK! THE WHOLE CABIN REEKED!
HA HA
HA HA
AND WE HAD TO CIRCLE FOR LIKE ANOTHER HALF HOUR!
DO WE HAVE TO TALK ABOUT SARAH THROWING UP RIGHT BEFORE WE HAVE LUNCH?
THE FOOD'S ALMOST READY- MIKE, DO YOU WANT TO SEE IF ANYONE ELSE WANTS SOMETHING TO DRINK?
ALRIGHT.
DO YOU WANT SOMETHING, ALIZA?
I'LL HAVE A LOOK.
OKAY.

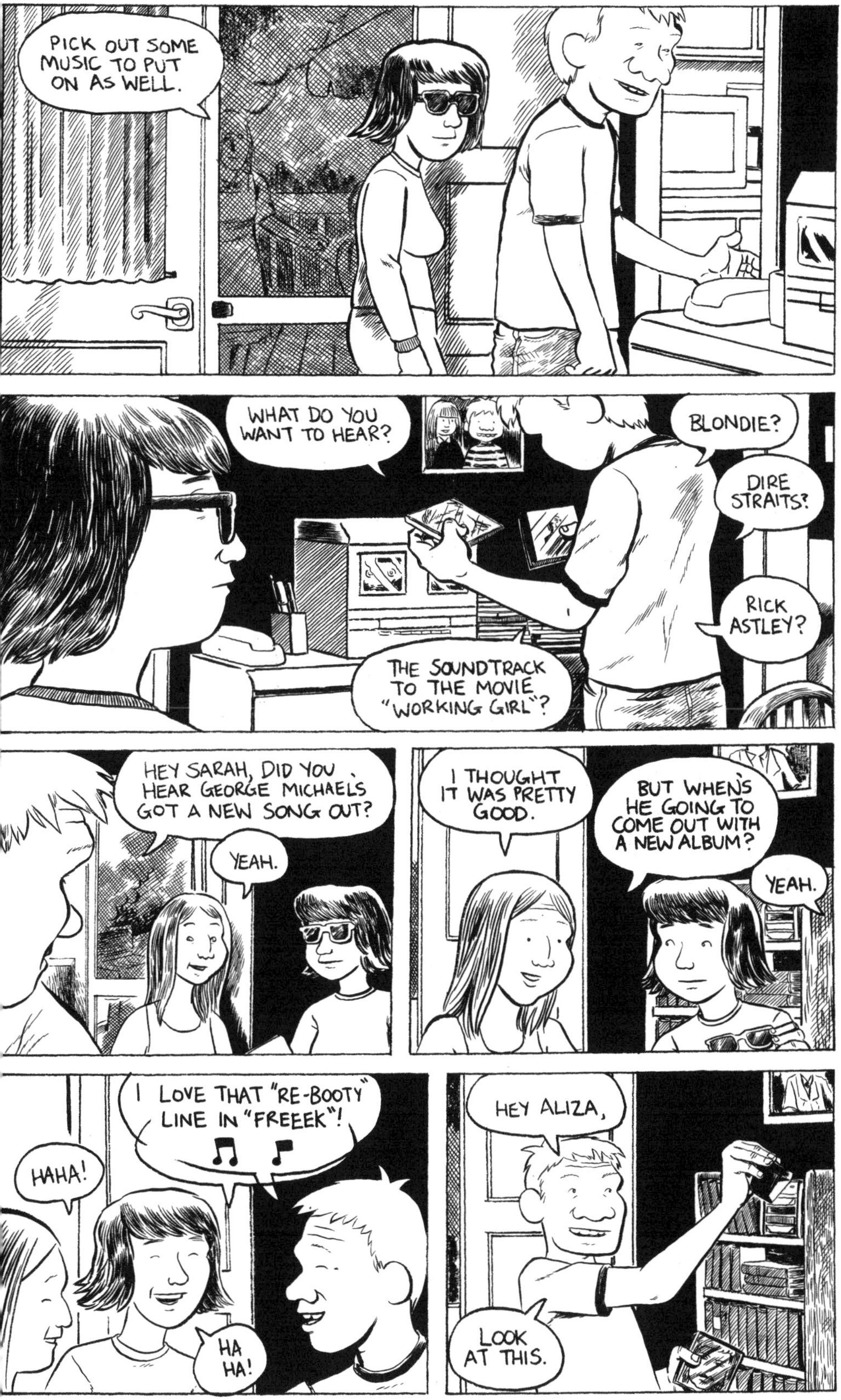
PICK OUT SOME MUSIC TO PUT ON AS WELL.
WHAT DO YOU WANT TO HEAR?
BLONDIE?
DIRE STRAITS?
RICK ASTLEY?
THE SOUNDTRACK TO THE MOVIE "WORKING GIRL"?
HEY SARAH, DID YOU HEAR GEORGE MICHAEL'S GOT A NEW SONG OUT?
YEAH.
I THOUGHT IT WAS PRETTY GOOD.
BUT WHEN'S HE GOING TO COME OUT WITH A NEW ALBUM?
YEAH.
I LOVE THAT "RE-BOOTY" LINE IN "FREEEK"!
HAHA!
HA HA!
HEY ALIZA,
LOOK AT THIS.

MY PARENTS STILL HAVE THIS...

Queen
A Night At The Opera

Queen
A Night At The Opera

IT'S THE FIRST ALBUM I EVER OWNED.

I'M GOING TO TAKE THIS.

WHEN I WAS A KID MY FAVORITE SONGS ON THIS WERE MOSTLY THE "DEEP CUTS"...

"DEATH ON TWO LEGS"...

"THE PROPHET'S SONG"...

"SEASIDE RENDEZVOUS"...

IT'S INTERESTING, AT THE TIME I HAD NO IDEA THAT ONLY SOME SONGS FROM AN ALBUM GOT ANY RADIO PLAY.

SEE— THAT'S WHAT'S SO SUCKY ABOUT CLASSIC ROCK RADIO STATIONS.

AS MUCH AS I LIKE CLASSIC ROCK— MOST OF THE STATIONS JUST PLAY ALL OF THE SAME SONGS OVER AND OVER.

mm

THEY MAKE IT SEEM LIKE THE ONLY SONGS ON THE RADIO IN THE SEVENTIES WERE "LAYLA" AND THAT MONEY SONG BY PINK FLOYD.

ALRIGHT, ANDREW'S NOT HERE YET, SO WE'RE GOING TO START WITHOUT HIM.

WHO WANTS HOT DOGS?

I'LL HAVE ONE.

THEY PROBABLY ONLY PROGRAM THE STATIONS LIKE THAT SO MORE LISTENERS HAVE A CHANCE OF BEING ABLE TO SING ALONG.

I BET THAT'S WHY THEY DO IT.

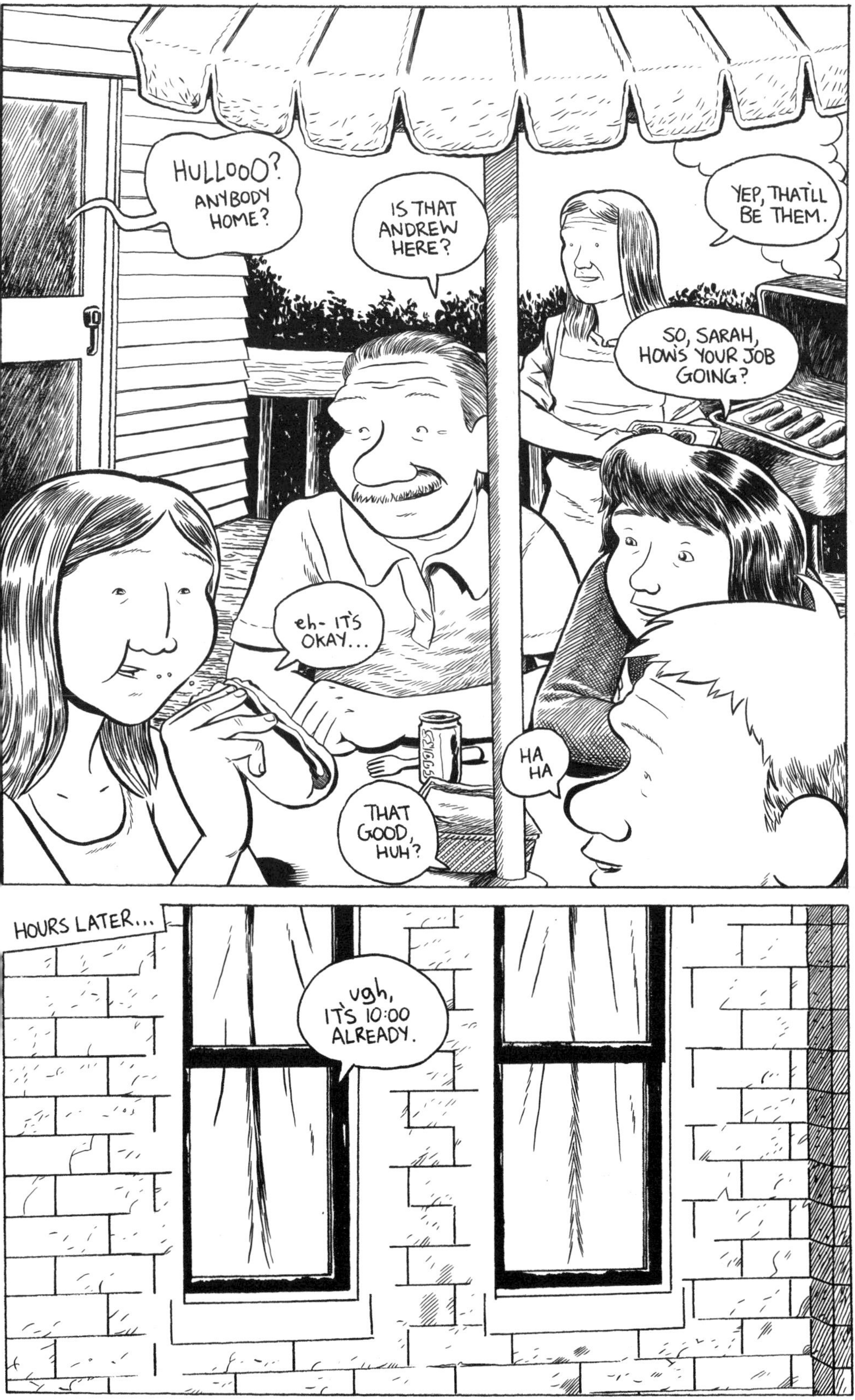
HULLOOO? ANYBODY HOME?
IS THAT ANDREW HERE?
YEP, THAT'LL BE THEM.
SO, SARAH, HOW'S YOUR JOB GOING?
eh- IT'S OKAY...
HA HA
THAT GOOD, HUH?
HOURS LATER...
ugh, IT'S 10:00 ALREADY.

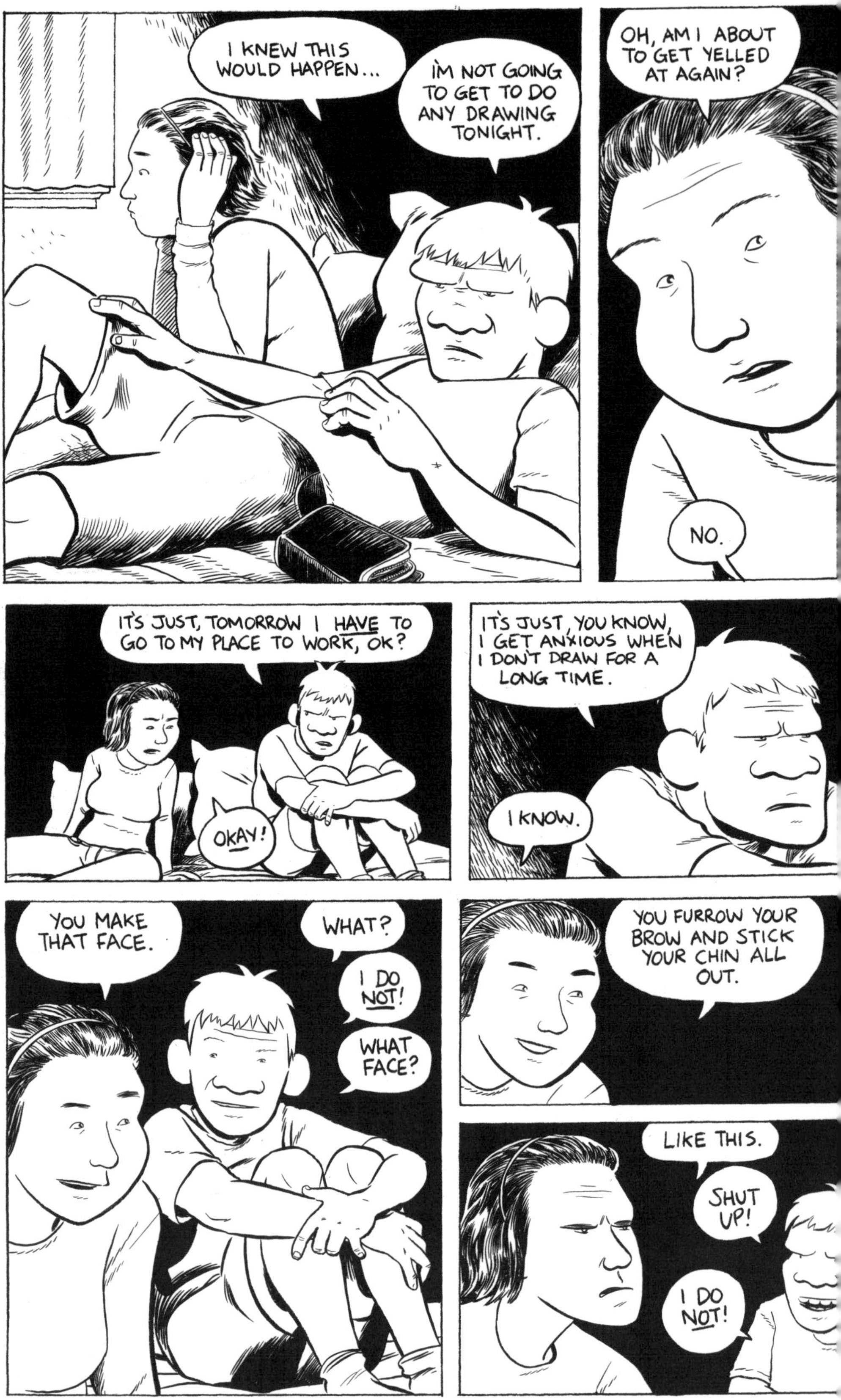
I KNEW THIS WOULD HAPPEN...
I'M NOT GOING TO GET TO DO ANY DRAWING TONIGHT.
OH, AM I ABOUT TO GET YELLED AT AGAIN?
NO.
IT'S JUST, TOMORROW I HAVE TO GO TO MY PLACE TO WORK, OK?
OKAY!
IT'S JUST, YOU KNOW, I GET ANXIOUS WHEN I DON'T DRAW FOR A LONG TIME.
I KNOW.
YOU MAKE THAT FACE.
WHAT?
I DO NOT!
WHAT FACE?
YOU FURROW YOUR BROW AND STICK YOUR CHIN ALL OUT.
LIKE THIS.
SHUT UP!
I DO NOT!

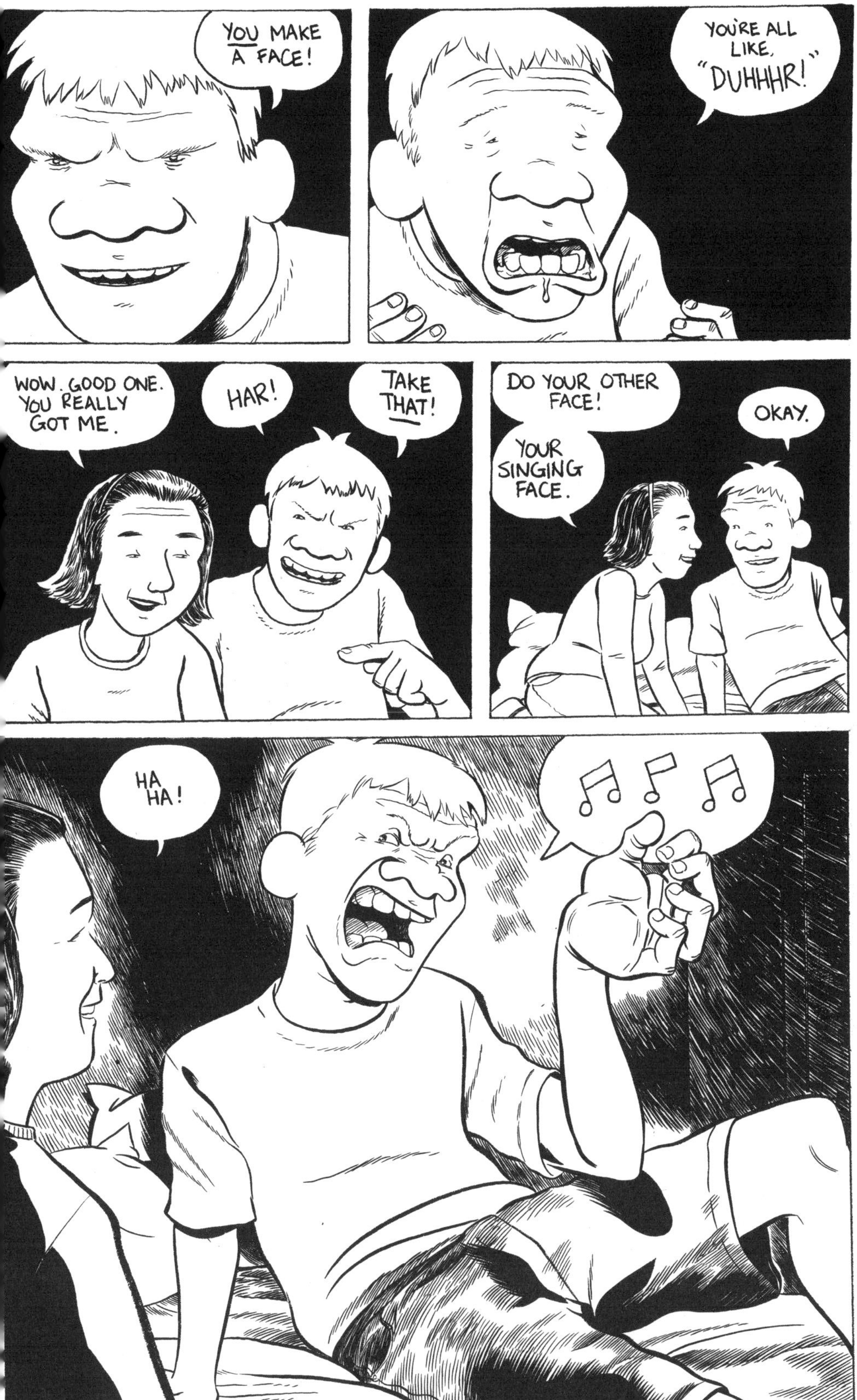
YOU MAKE A FACE!
YOU'RE ALL LIKE, "DUHHHR!"
WOW. GOOD ONE. YOU REALLY GOT ME.
HAR!
TAKE THAT!
DO YOUR OTHER FACE!
YOUR SINGING FACE.
OKAY.
HA HA!

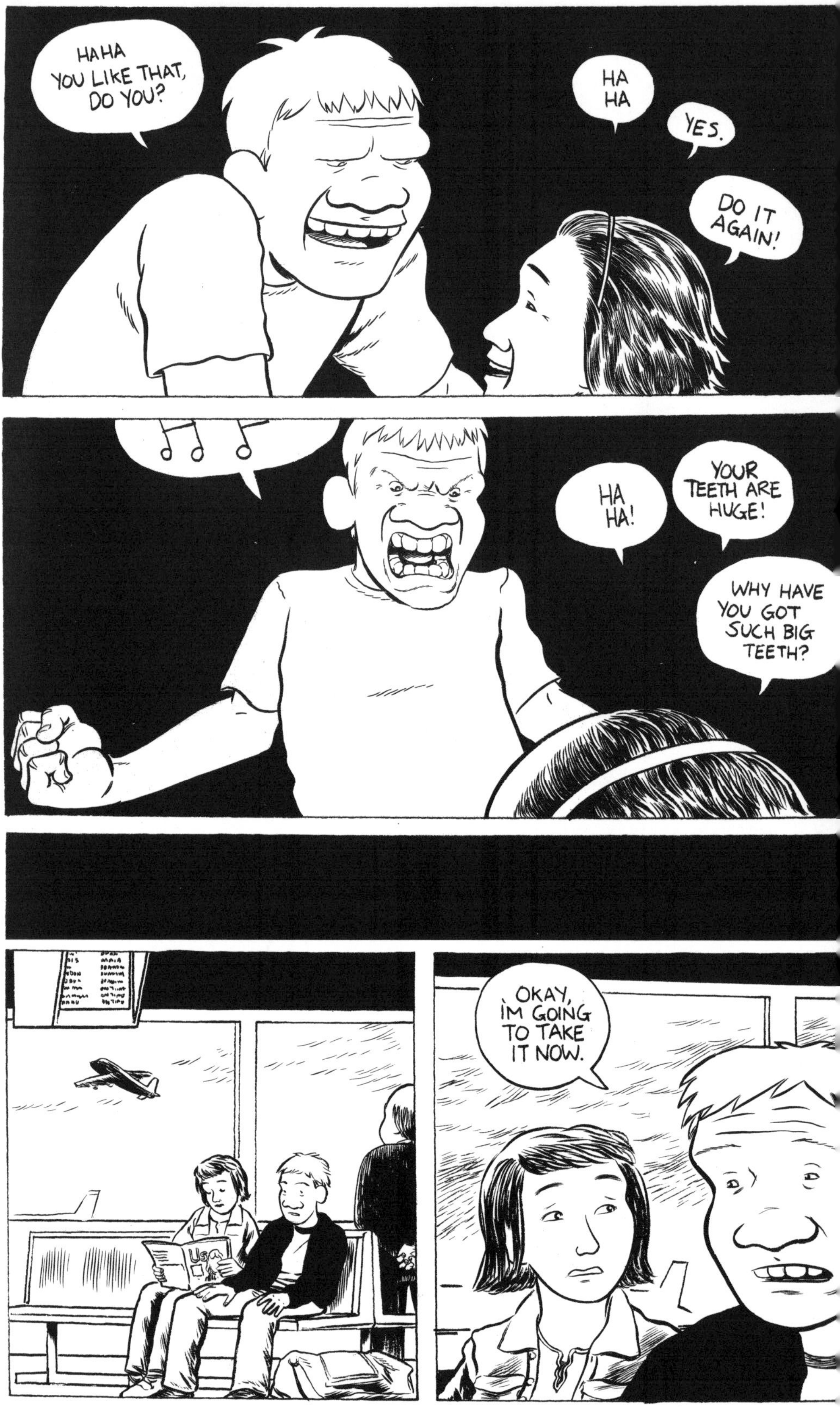
HAHA YOU LIKE THAT, DO YOU?
HA HA
YES.
DO IT AGAIN!
HA HA!
YOUR TEETH ARE HUGE!
WHY HAVE YOU GOT SUCH BIG TEETH?
OKAY, IM GOING TO TAKE IT NOW.

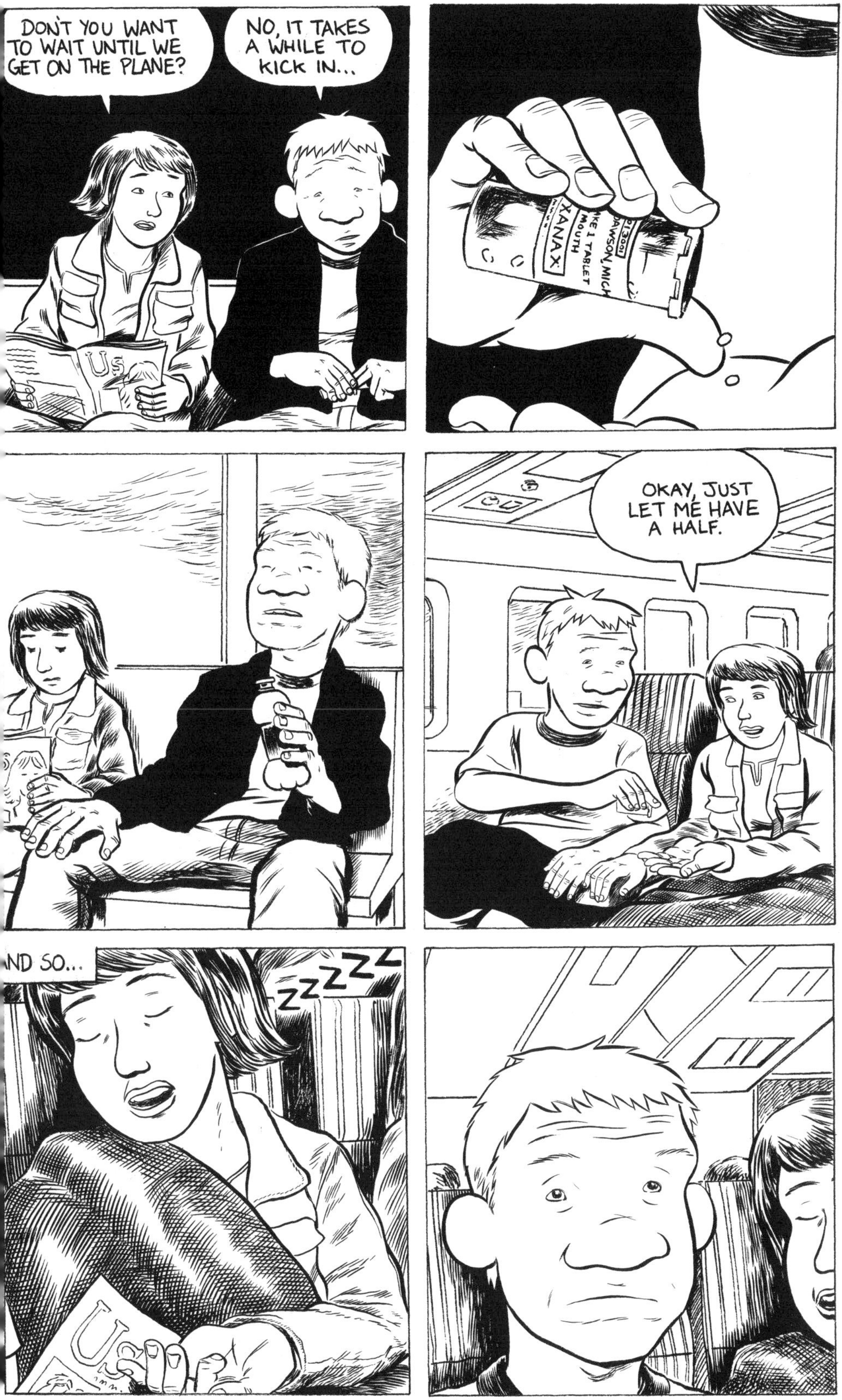
DON'T YOU WANT TO WAIT UNTIL WE GET ON THE PLANE?
NO, IT TAKES A WHILE TO KICK IN...
Us
XANAX
OKAY, JUST LET ME HAVE A HALF.
ND SO...
ZZZZZ

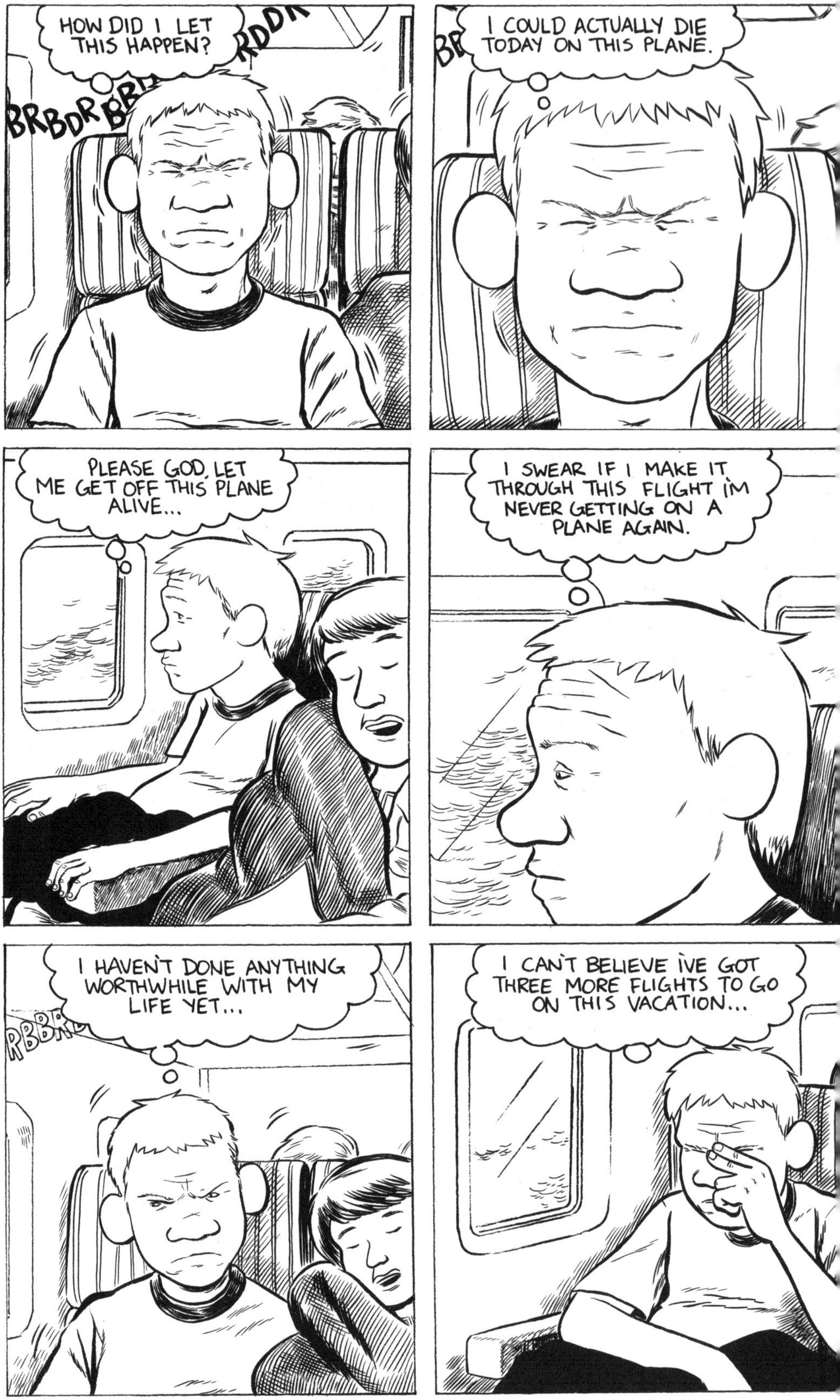
HOW DID I LET THIS HAPPEN?
BRBDRBRBRDDR
I COULD ACTUALLY DIE TODAY ON THIS PLANE.
PLEASE GOD, LET ME GET OFF THIS PLANE ALIVE...
I SWEAR IF I MAKE IT THROUGH THIS FLIGHT I'M NEVER GETTING ON A PLANE AGAIN.
I HAVEN'T DONE ANYTHING WORTHWHILE WITH MY LIFE YET...
RBBR
I CAN'T BELIEVE I'VE GOT THREE MORE FLIGHTS TO GO ON THIS VACATION...

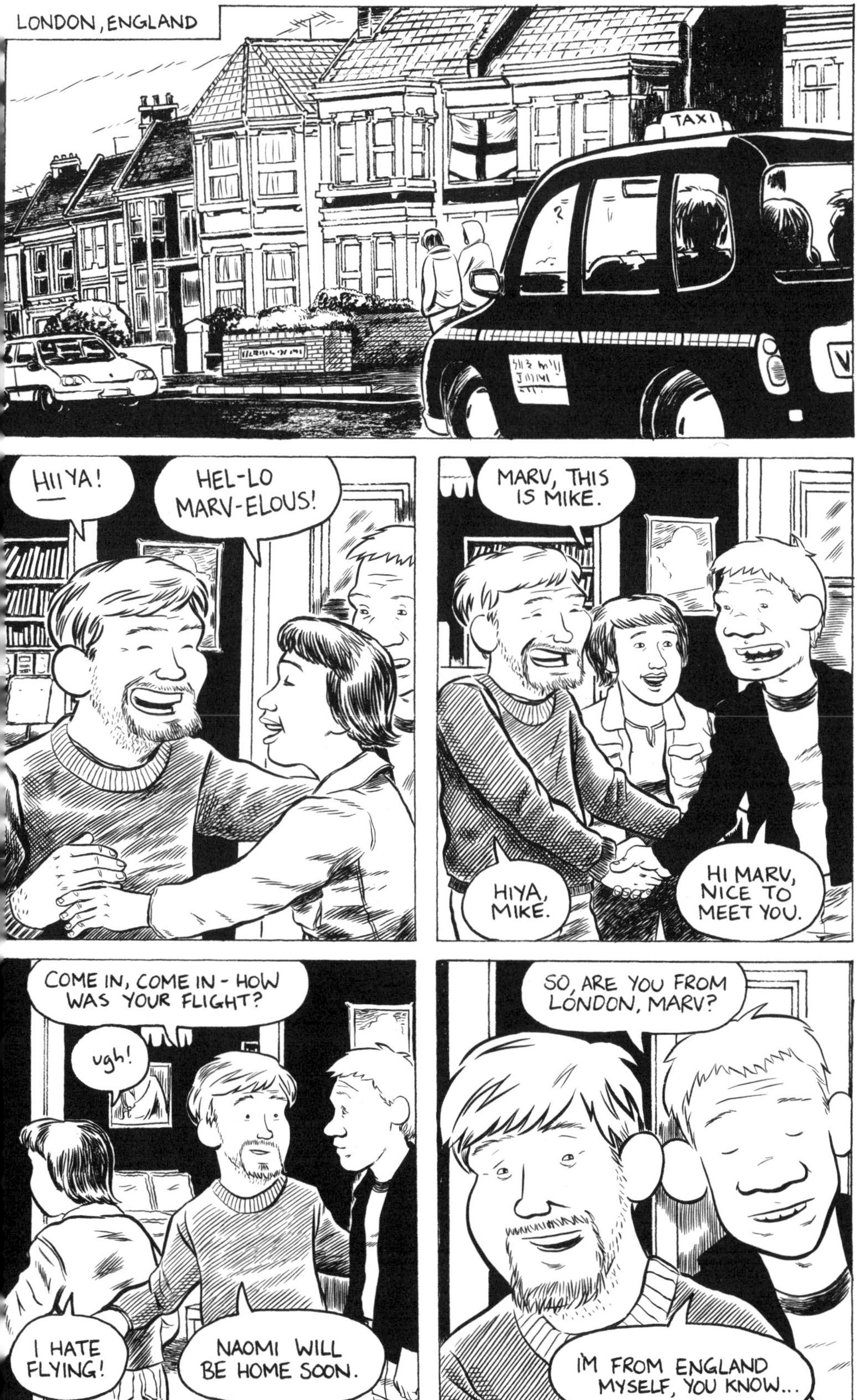

LONDON, ENGLAND
TAXI
HIIYA!
HEL-LO MARV-ELOUS!
MARV, THIS IS MIKE.
HIYA, MIKE.
HI MARV, NICE TO MEET YOU.
COME IN, COME IN - HOW WAS YOUR FLIGHT?
ugh!
I HATE FLYING!
NAOMI WILL BE HOME SOON.
SO, ARE YOU FROM LONDON, MARV?
I'M FROM ENGLAND MYSELF, YOU KNOW...

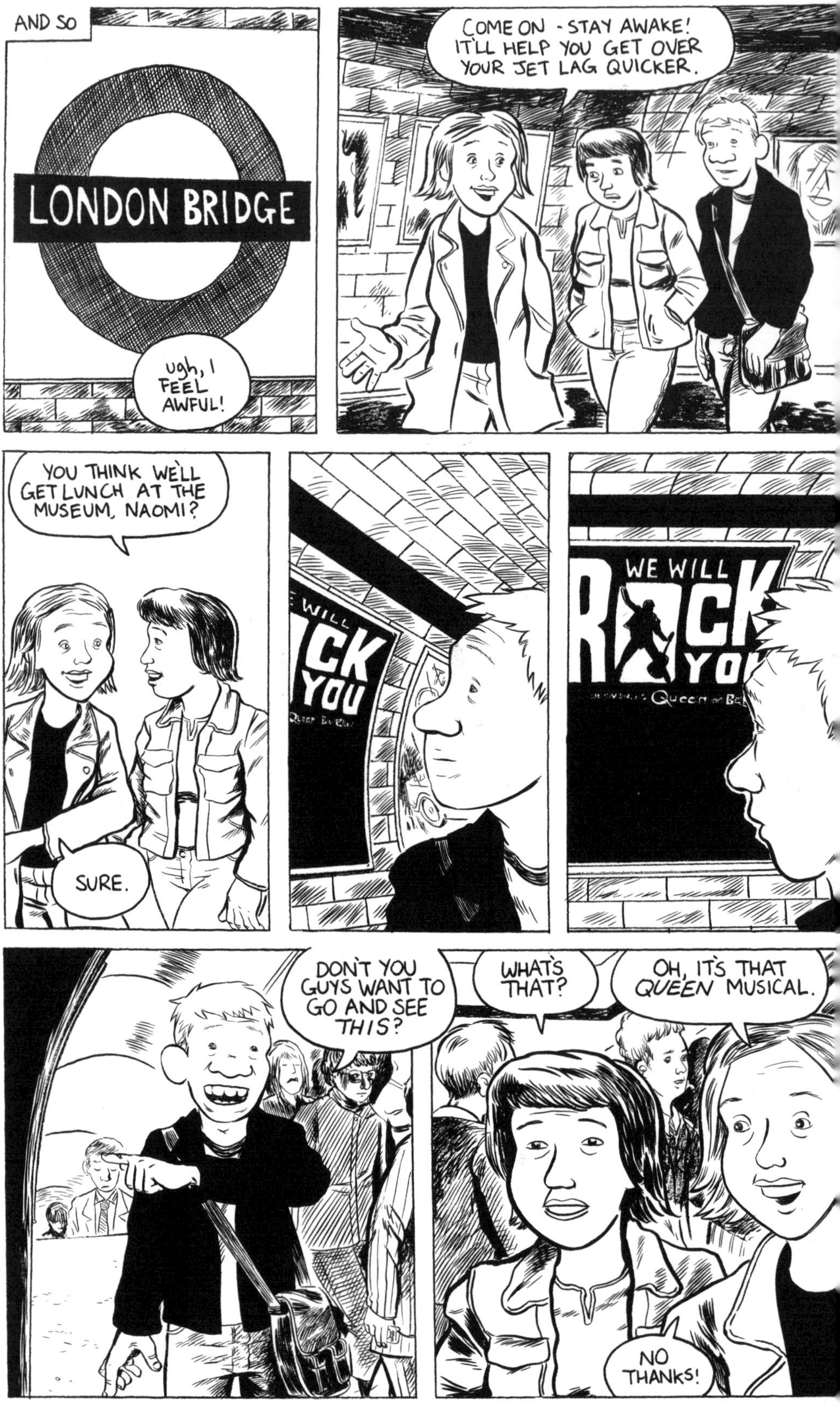
AND SO
LONDON BRIDGE
ugh, I FEEL AWFUL!
COME ON - STAY AWAKE! IT'LL HELP YOU GET OVER YOUR JET LAG QUICKER.
YOU THINK WE'LL GET LUNCH AT THE MUSEUM, NAOMI?
SURE.
WE WILL
CK
YOU
WE WILL
R CK
YOU
Queen
DON'T YOU GUYS WANT TO GO AND SEE THIS?
WHAT'S THAT?
OH, IT'S THAT QUEEN MUSICAL.
NO THANKS!

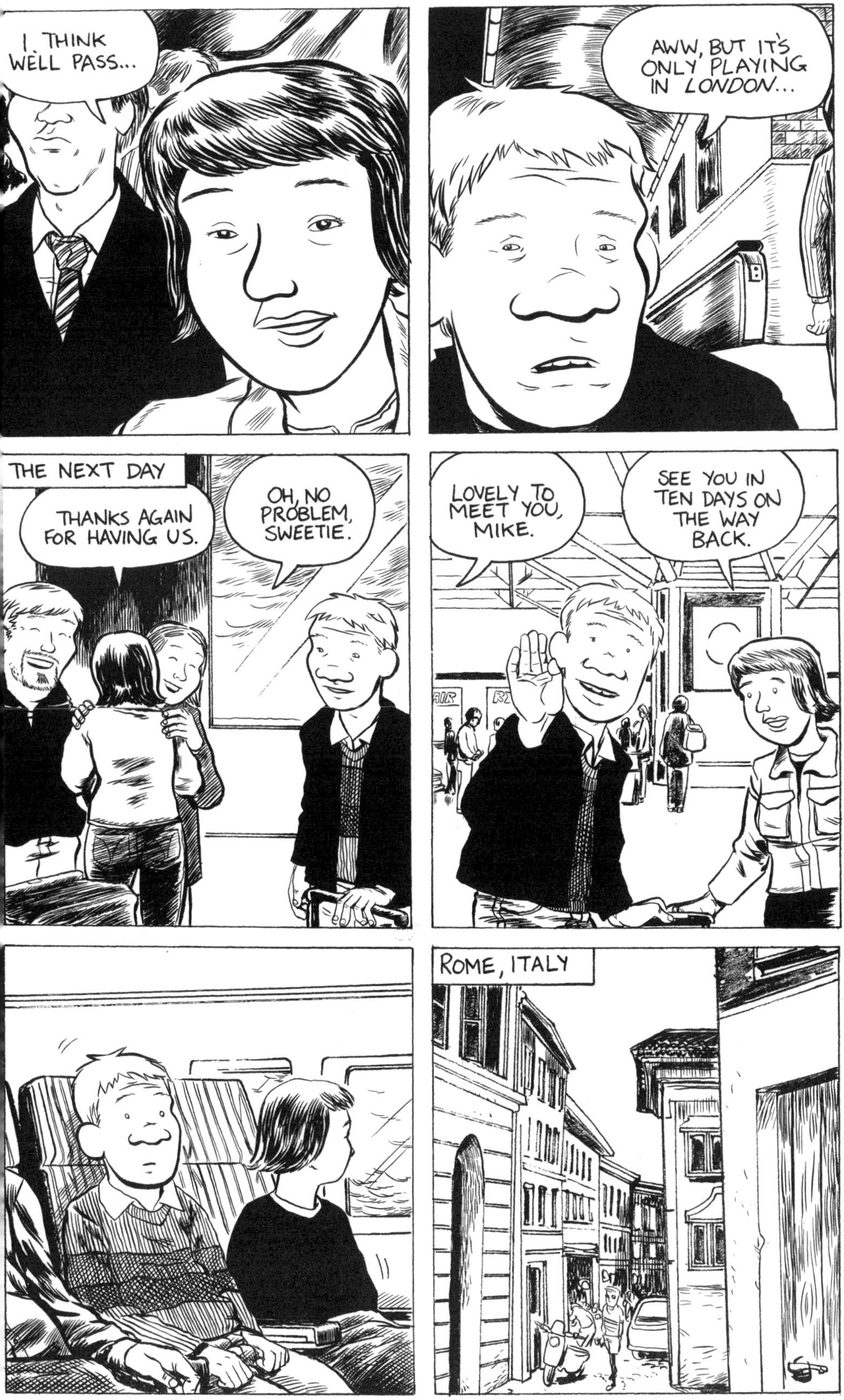
I THINK WE'LL PASS...
AWW, BUT IT'S ONLY PLAYING IN *LONDON*...
THE NEXT DAY
THANKS AGAIN FOR HAVING US.
OH, NO PROBLEM, SWEETIE.
LOVELY TO MEET YOU, MIKE.
SEE YOU IN TEN DAYS ON THE WAY BACK.
ROME, ITALY

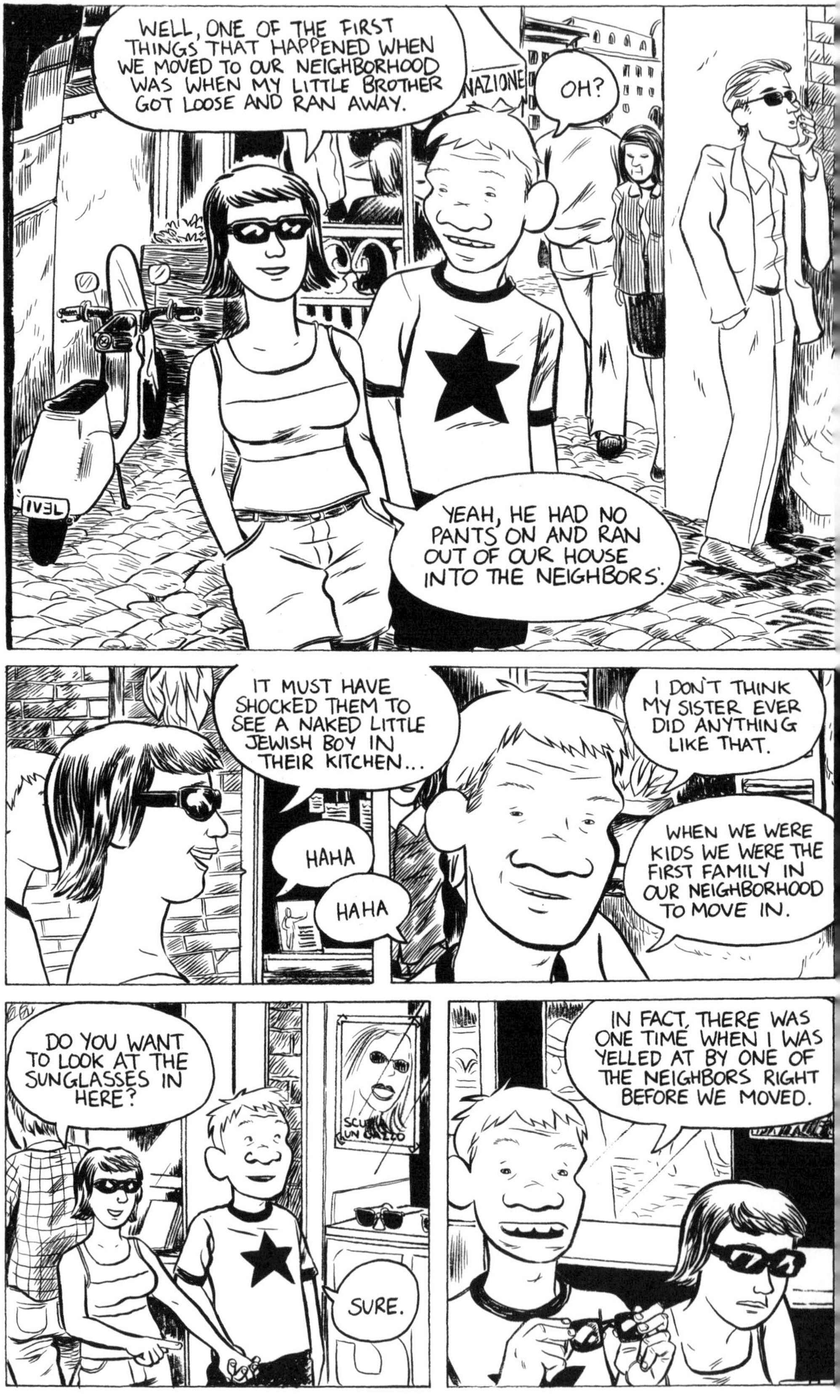
WELL, ONE OF THE FIRST THINGS THAT HAPPENED WHEN WE MOVED TO OUR NEIGHBORHOOD WAS WHEN MY LITTLE BROTHER GOT LOOSE AND RAN AWAY.
NAZIONE
OH?
YEAH, HE HAD NO PANTS ON AND RAN OUT OF OUR HOUSE INTO THE NEIGHBORS'.
IT MUST HAVE SHOCKED THEM TO SEE A NAKED LITTLE JEWISH BOY IN THEIR KITCHEN...
HAHA
HAHA
I DON'T THINK MY SISTER EVER DID ANYTHING LIKE THAT.
WHEN WE WERE KIDS WE WERE THE FIRST FAMILY IN OUR NEIGHBORHOOD TO MOVE IN.
DO YOU WANT TO LOOK AT THE SUNGLASSES IN HERE?
SURE.
IN FACT, THERE WAS ONE TIME WHEN I WAS YELLED AT BY ONE OF THE NEIGHBORS RIGHT BEFORE WE MOVED.

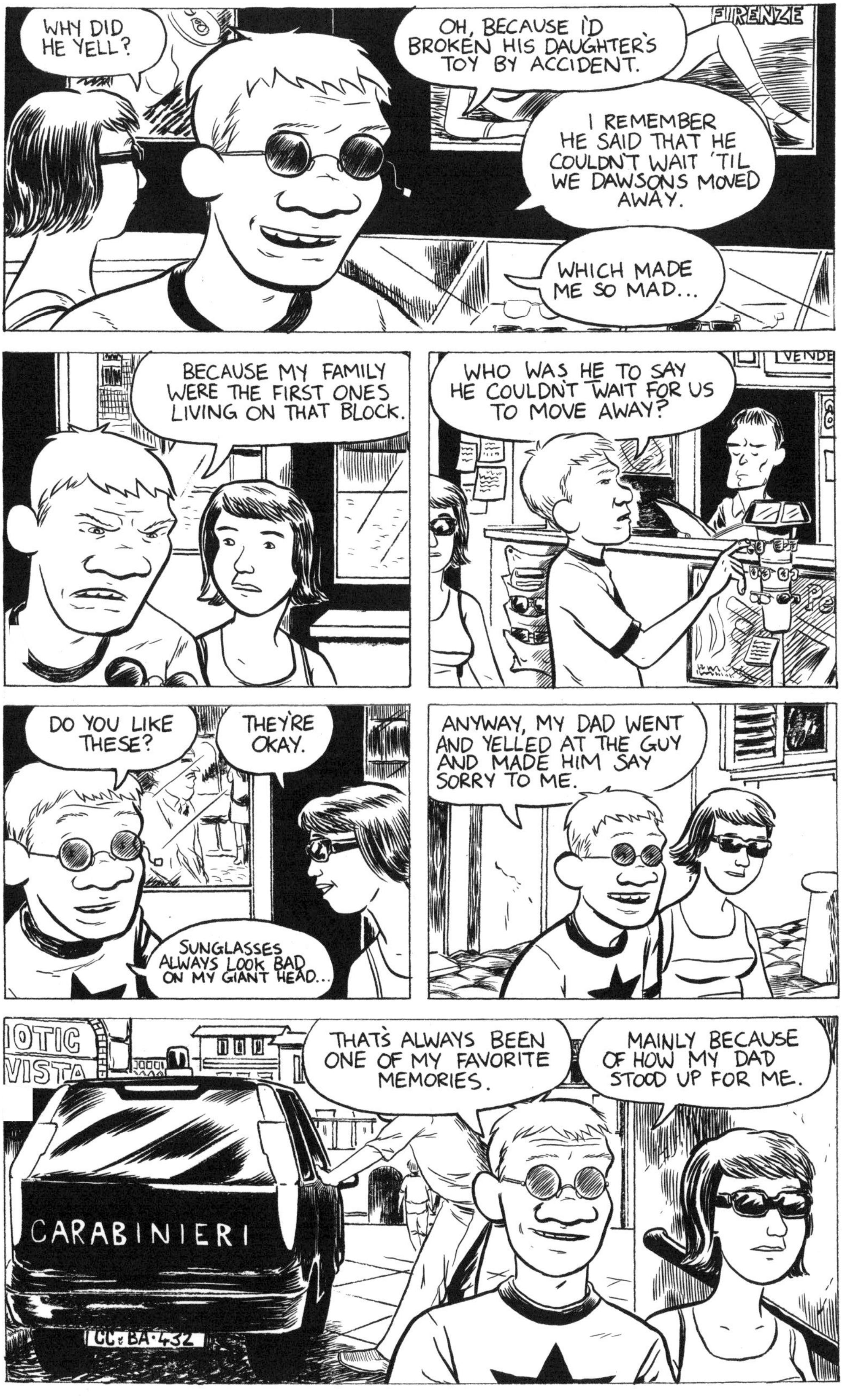
FIRENZE
WHY DID HE YELL?
OH, BECAUSE I'D BROKEN HIS DAUGHTER'S TOY BY ACCIDENT.
I REMEMBER HE SAID THAT HE COULDN'T WAIT 'TIL WE DAWSONS MOVED AWAY.
WHICH MADE ME SO MAD...
BECAUSE MY FAMILY WERE THE FIRST ONES LIVING ON THAT BLOCK.
WHO WAS HE TO SAY HE COULDN'T WAIT FOR US TO MOVE AWAY?
DO YOU LIKE THESE?
THEY'RE OKAY.
SUNGLASSES ALWAYS LOOK BAD ON MY GIANT HEAD...
ANYWAY, MY DAD WENT AND YELLED AT THE GUY AND MADE HIM SAY SORRY TO ME.
CARABINIERI
CC BA·432
THAT'S ALWAYS BEEN ONE OF MY FAVORITE MEMORIES.
MAINLY BECAUSE OF HOW MY DAD STOOD UP FOR ME.

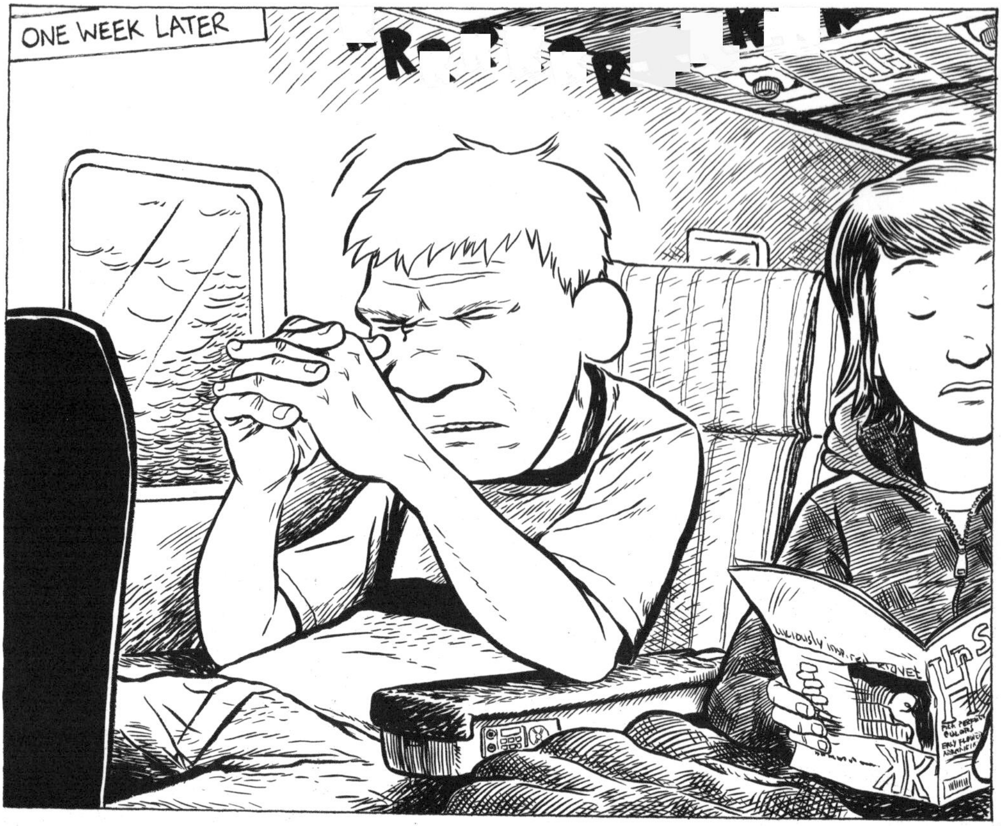
ONE WEEK LATER

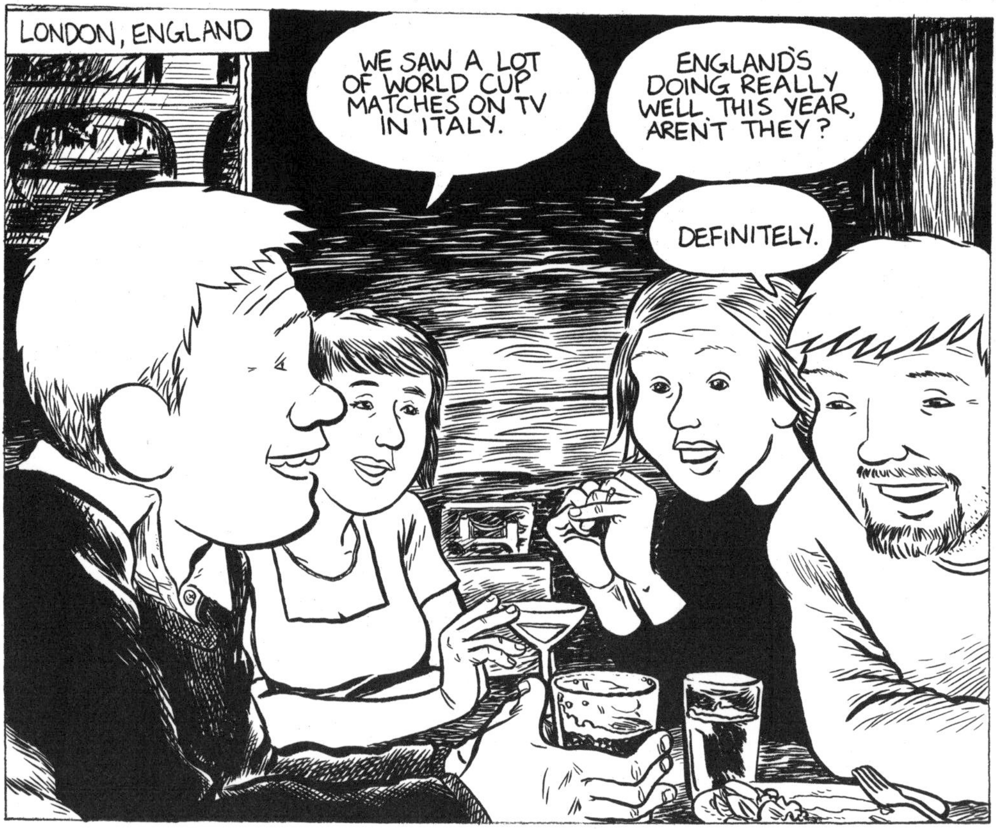
LONDON, ENGLAND
WE SAW A LOT OF WORLD CUP MATCHES ON TV IN ITALY.
ENGLAND'S DOING REALLY WELL THIS YEAR, AREN'T THEY?
DEFINITELY.

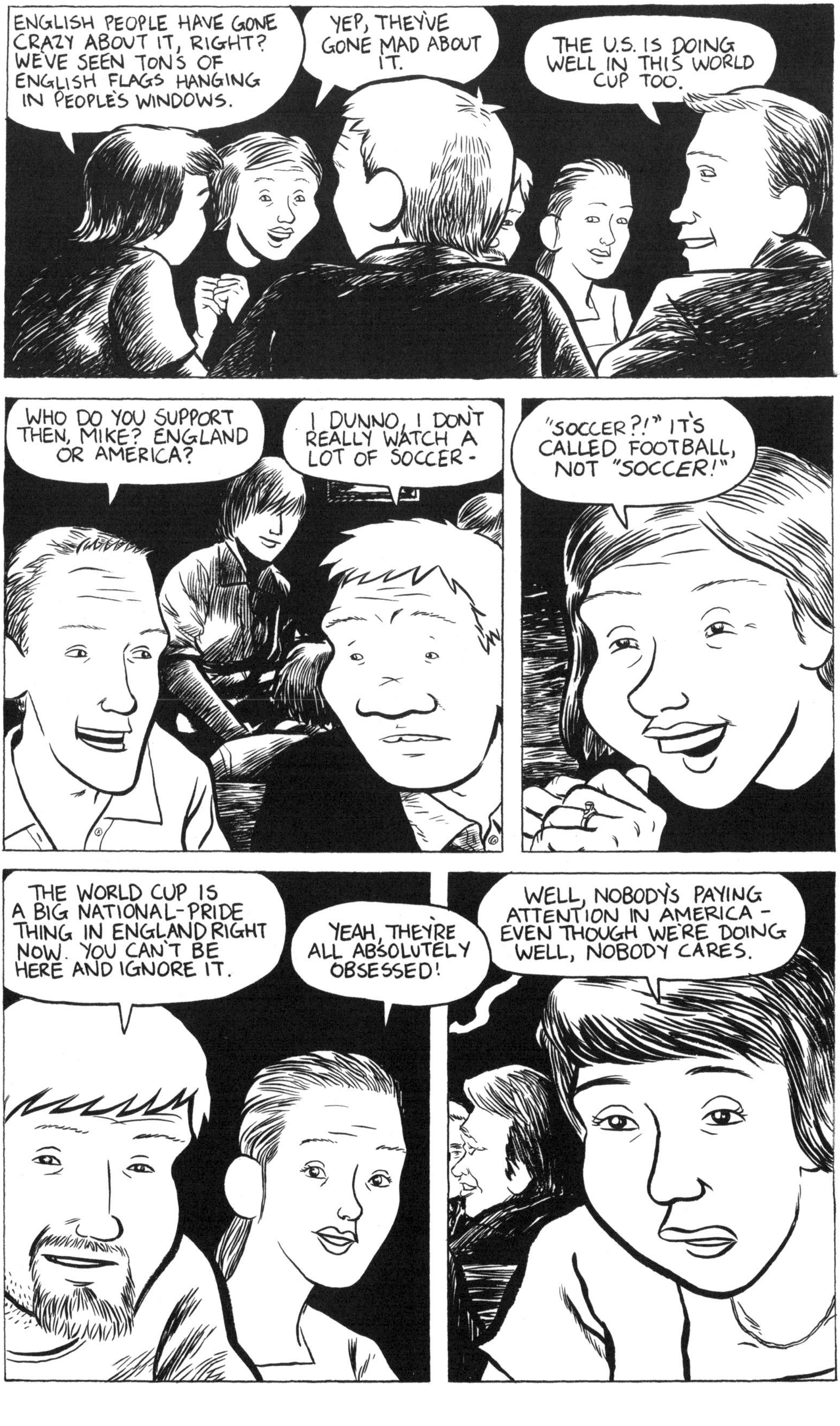
ENGLISH PEOPLE HAVE GONE CRAZY ABOUT IT, RIGHT? WE'VE SEEN TONS OF ENGLISH FLAGS HANGING IN PEOPLE'S WINDOWS.
YEP, THEY'VE GONE MAD ABOUT IT.
THE U.S. IS DOING WELL IN THIS WORLD CUP TOO.
WHO DO YOU SUPPORT THEN, MIKE? ENGLAND OR AMERICA?
I DUNNO, I DON'T REALLY WATCH A LOT OF SOCCER-
"SOCCER?!" IT'S CALLED FOOTBALL, NOT "SOCCER!"
THE WORLD CUP IS A BIG NATIONAL-PRIDE THING IN ENGLAND RIGHT NOW. YOU CAN'T BE HERE AND IGNORE IT.
YEAH, THEY'RE ALL ABSOLUTELY OBSESSED!
WELL, NOBODY'S PAYING ATTENTION IN AMERICA - EVEN THOUGH WE'RE DOING WELL, NOBODY CARES.

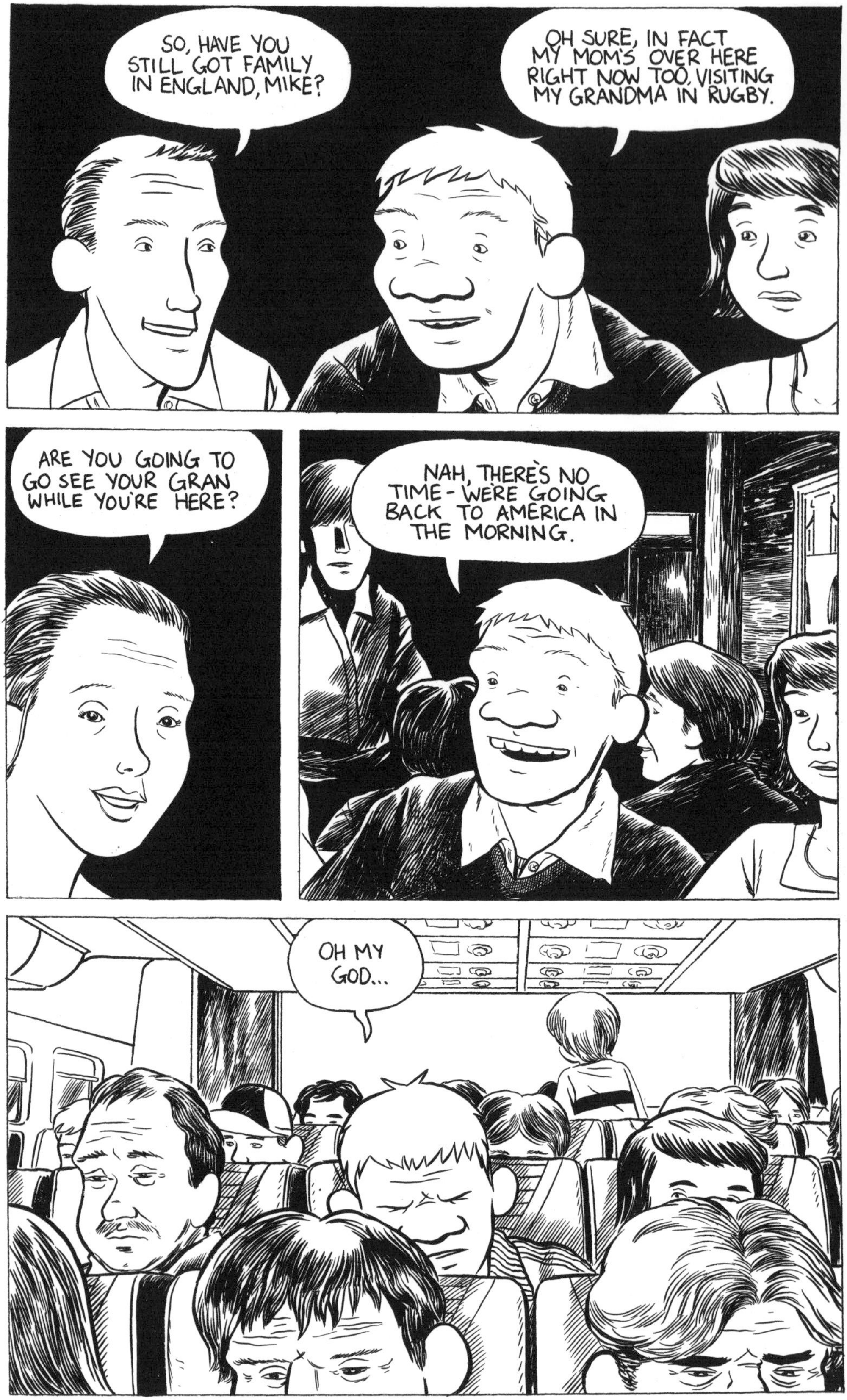
SO, HAVE YOU STILL GOT FAMILY IN ENGLAND, MIKE?
OH SURE, IN FACT MY MOM'S OVER HERE RIGHT NOW TOO, VISITING MY GRANDMA IN RUGBY.
ARE YOU GOING TO GO SEE YOUR GRAN WHILE YOU'RE HERE?
NAH, THERE'S NO TIME - WE'RE GOING BACK TO AMERICA IN THE MORNING.
OH MY GOD...

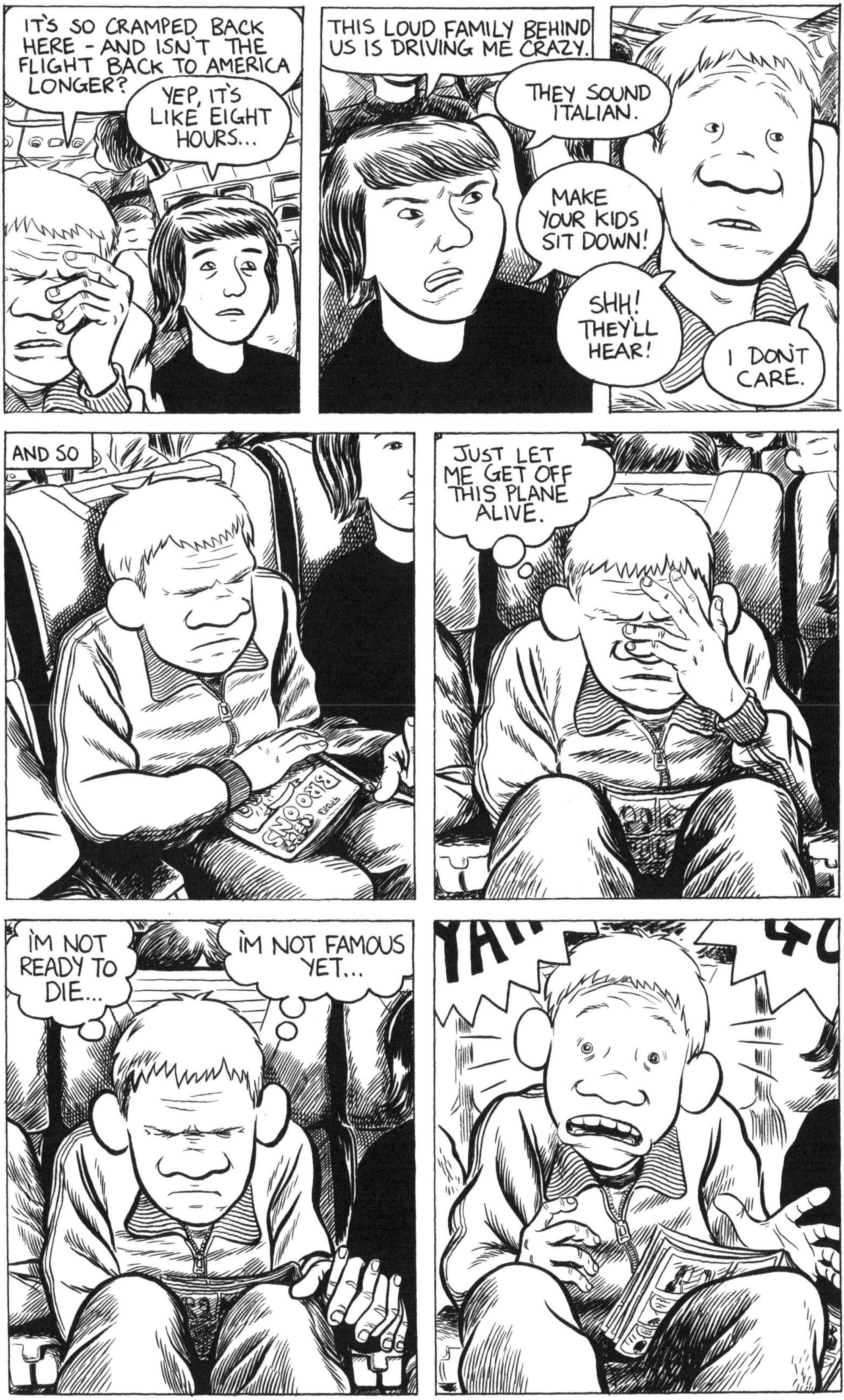
IT'S SO CRAMPED BACK HERE - AND ISN'T THE FLIGHT BACK TO AMERICA LONGER?
YEP, IT'S LIKE EIGHT HOURS...
THIS LOUD FAMILY BEHIND US IS DRIVING ME CRAZY.
THEY SOUND ITALIAN.
MAKE YOUR KIDS SIT DOWN!
SHH! THEY'LL HEAR!
I DON'T CARE.
AND SO
JUST LET ME GET OFF THIS PLANE ALIVE.
I'M NOT READY TO DIE...
I'M NOT FAMOUS YET...

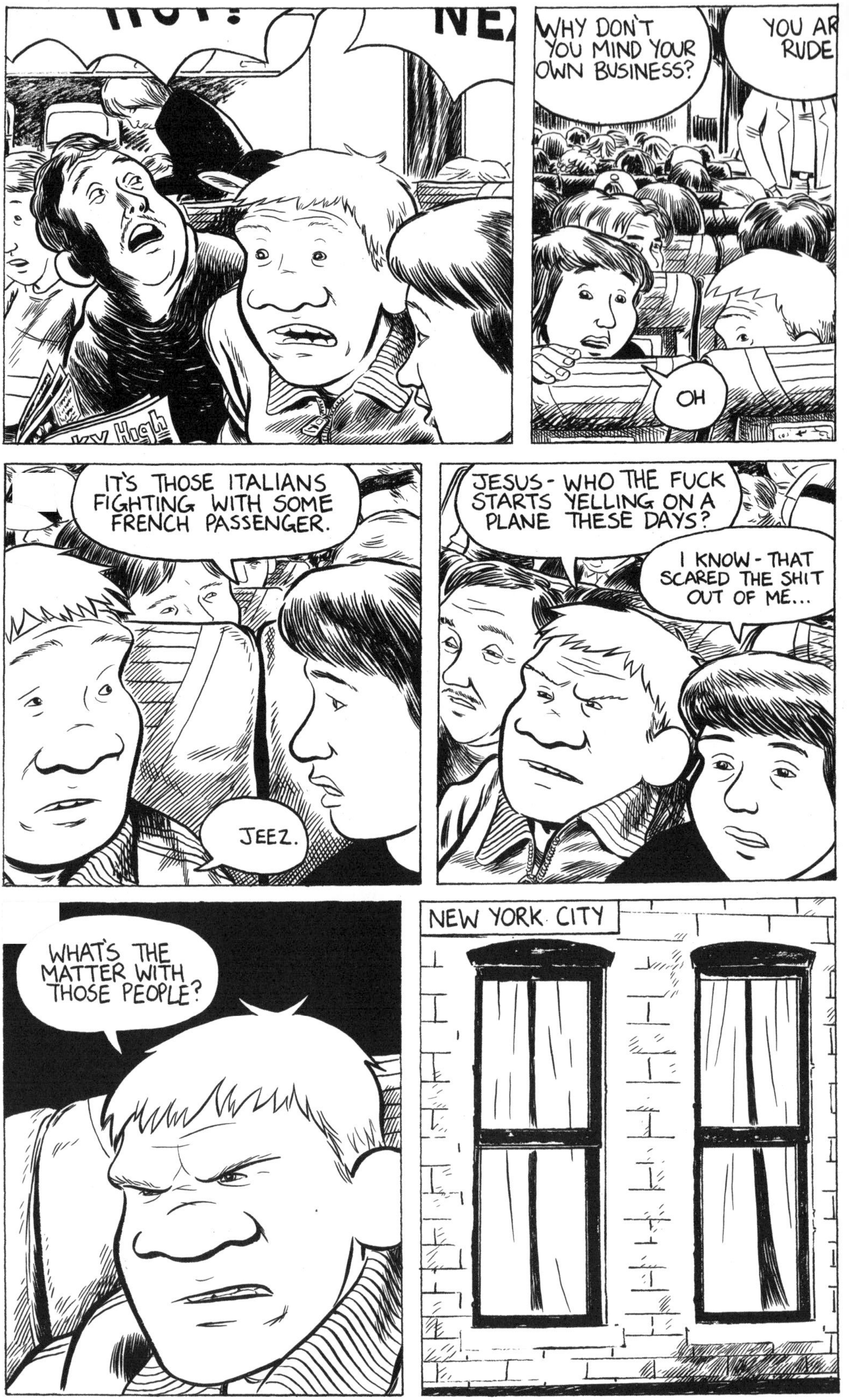
WHY DON'T YOU MIND YOUR OWN BUSINESS?
OH
IT'S THOSE ITALIANS FIGHTING WITH SOME FRENCH PASSENGER.
JEEZ.
JESUS- WHO THE FUCK STARTS YELLING ON A PLANE THESE DAYS?
I KNOW - THAT SCARED THE SHIT OUT OF ME...
WHAT'S THE MATTER WITH THOSE PEOPLE?
NEW YORK CITY

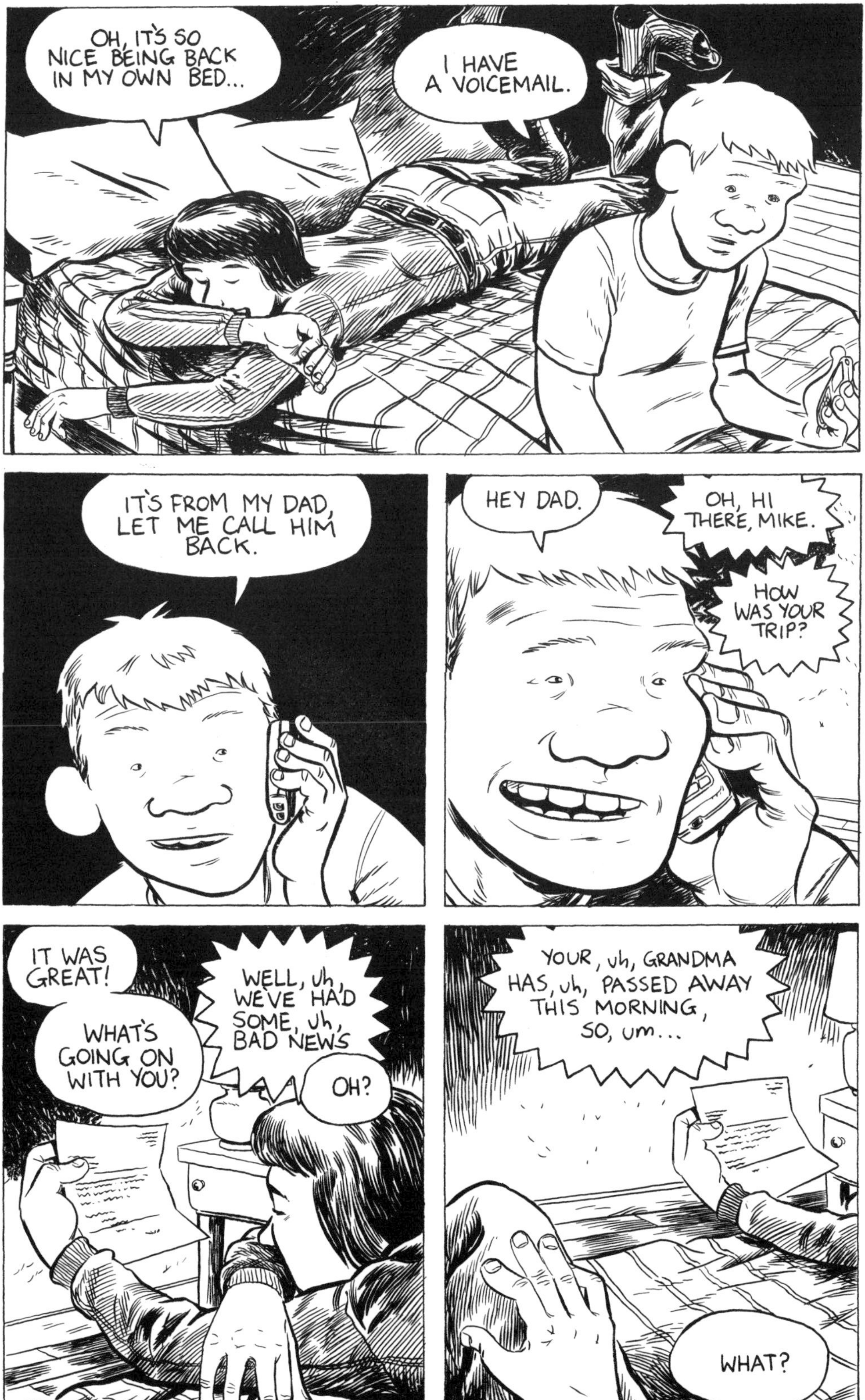
OH, IT'S SO NICE BEING BACK IN MY OWN BED...
I HAVE A VOICEMAIL.
IT'S FROM MY DAD, LET ME CALL HIM BACK.
HEY DAD.
OH, HI THERE, MIKE.
HOW WAS YOUR TRIP?
IT WAS GREAT!
WHAT'S GOING ON WITH YOU?
WELL, uh, WE'VE HAD SOME, uh, BAD NEWS
OH?
YOUR, uh, GRANDMA HAS, uh, PASSED AWAY THIS MORNING, SO, um...
WHAT?

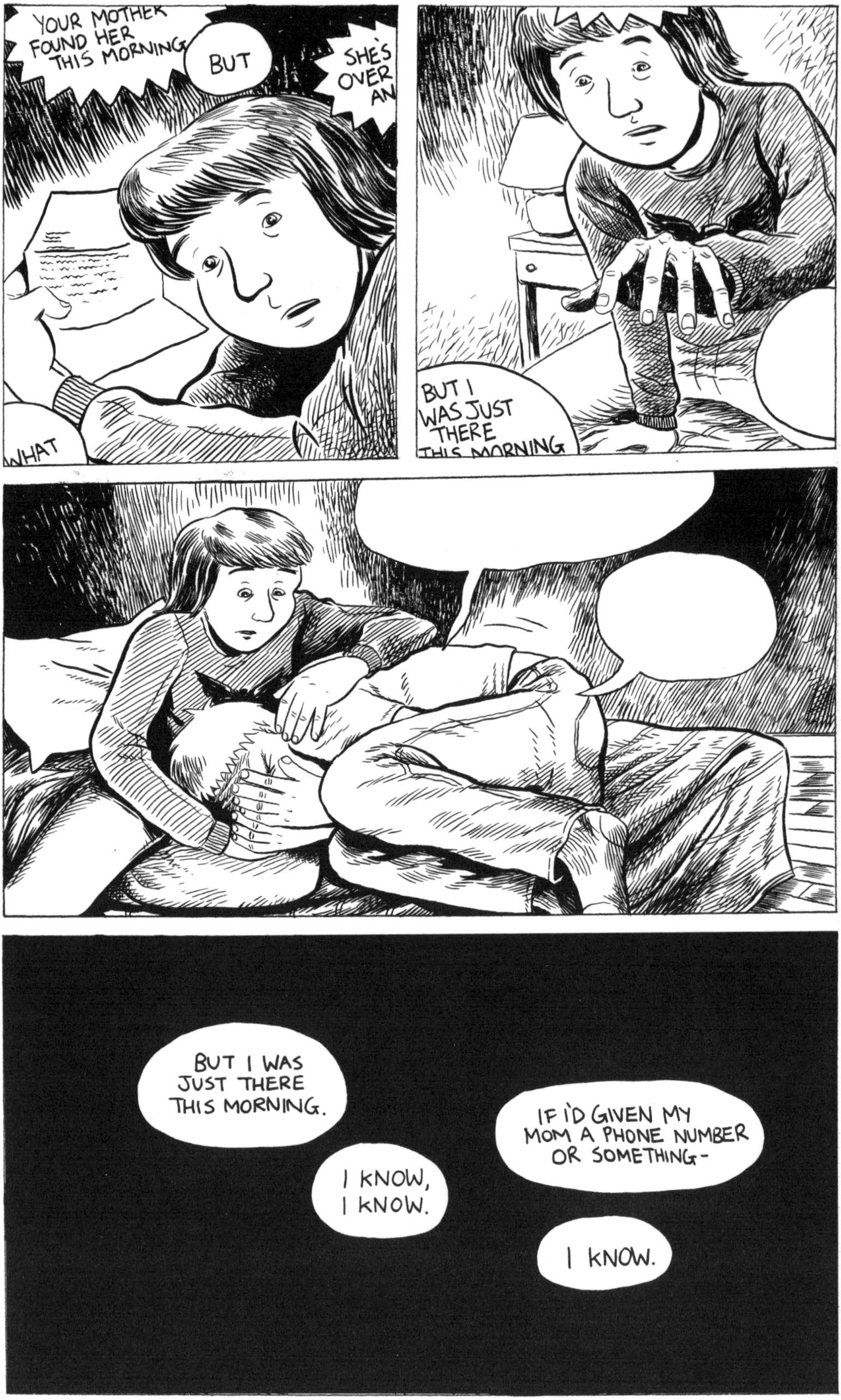
YOUR MOTHER FOUND HER THIS MORNING
BUT
SHE'S OVER AN
WHAT
BUT I WAS JUST THERE THIS MORNING
BUT I WAS JUST THERE THIS MORNING.
I KNOW, I KNOW.
IF I'D GIVEN MY MOM A PHONE NUMBER OR SOMETHING-
I KNOW.

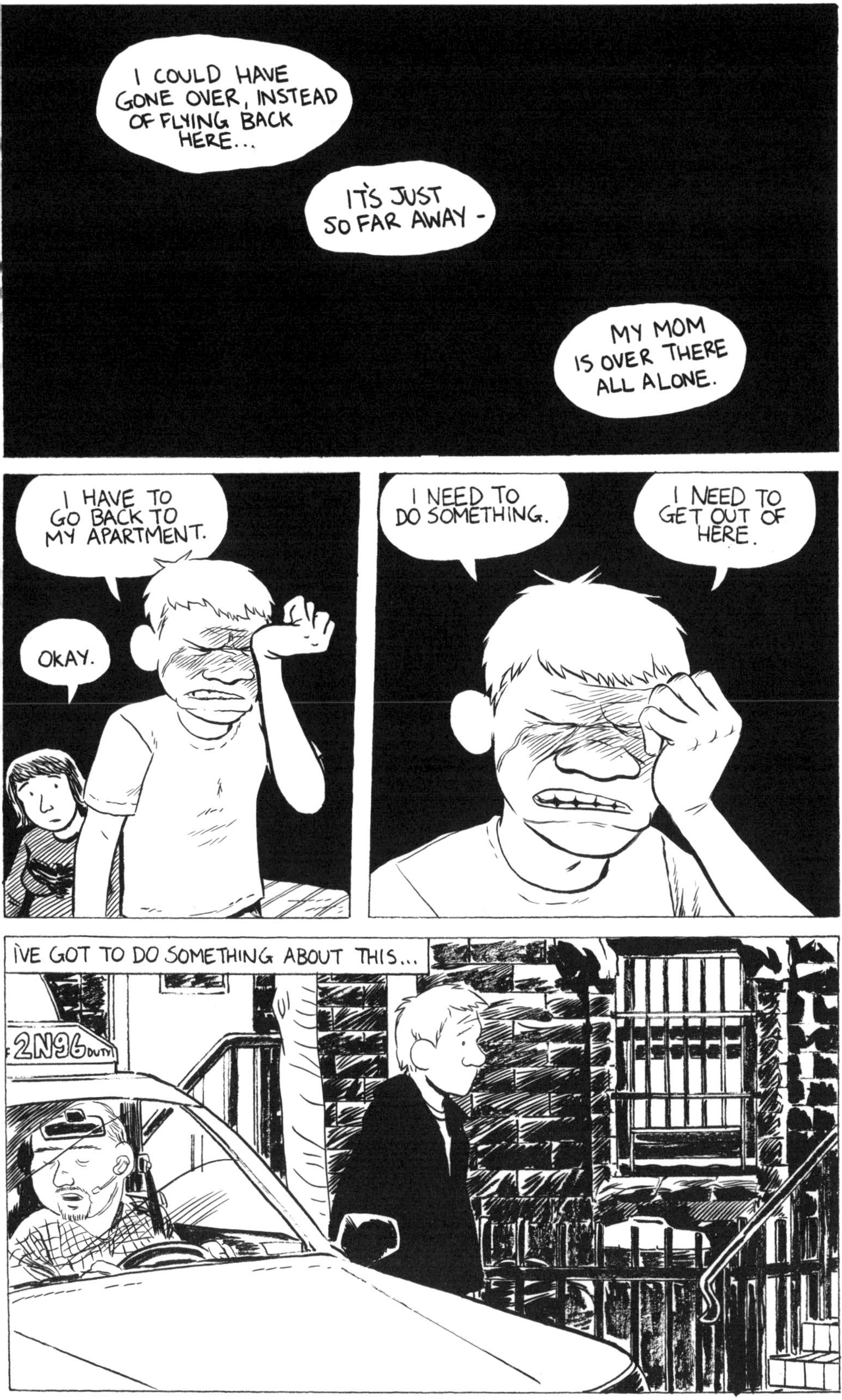
I COULD HAVE GONE OVER, INSTEAD OF FLYING BACK HERE...
IT'S JUST SO FAR AWAY -
MY MOM IS OVER THERE ALL ALONE.
I HAVE TO GO BACK TO MY APARTMENT.
OKAY.
I NEED TO DO SOMETHING.
I NEED TO GET OUT OF HERE.
I'VE GOT TO DO SOMETHING ABOUT THIS...
2N96

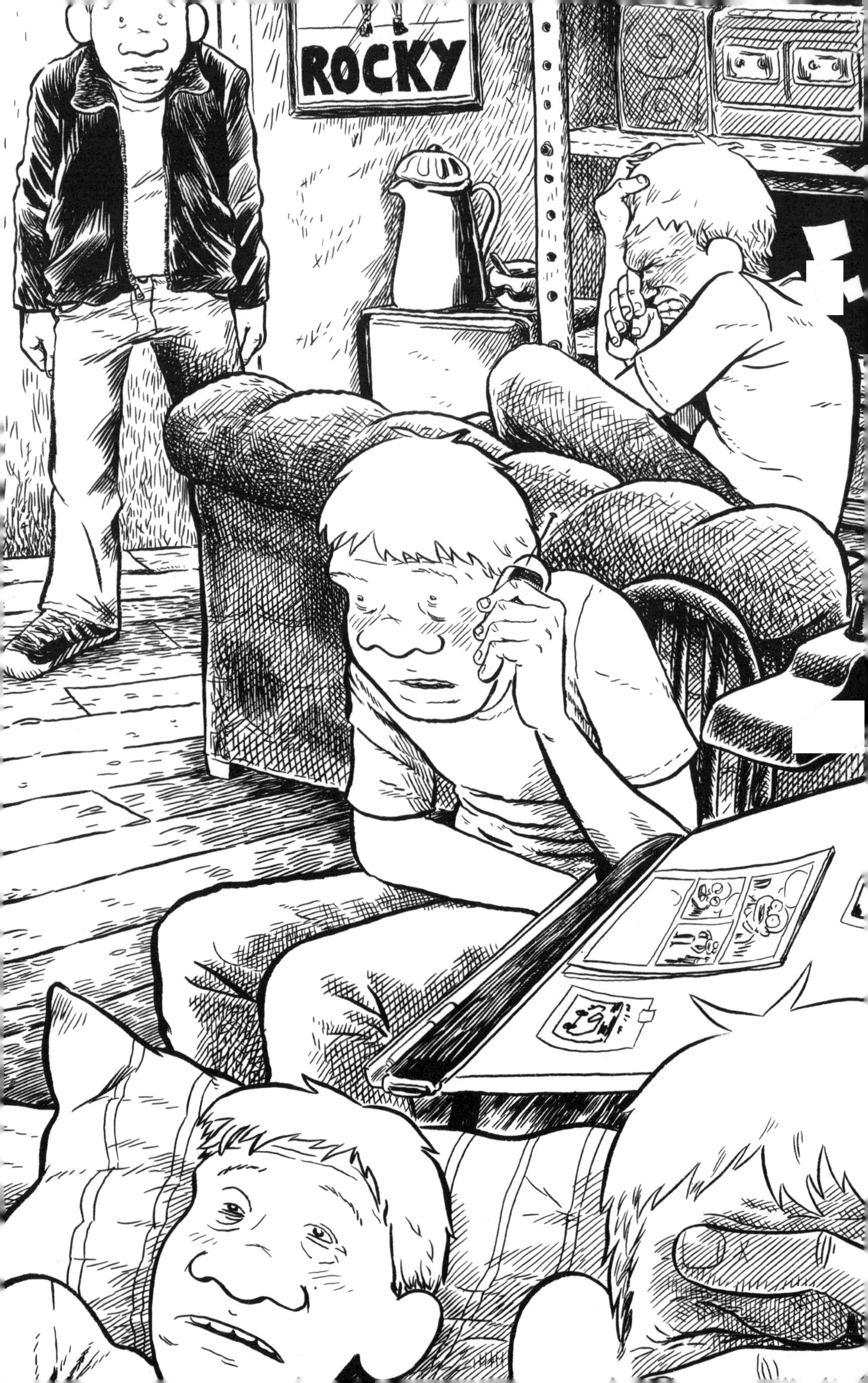
ROCKY

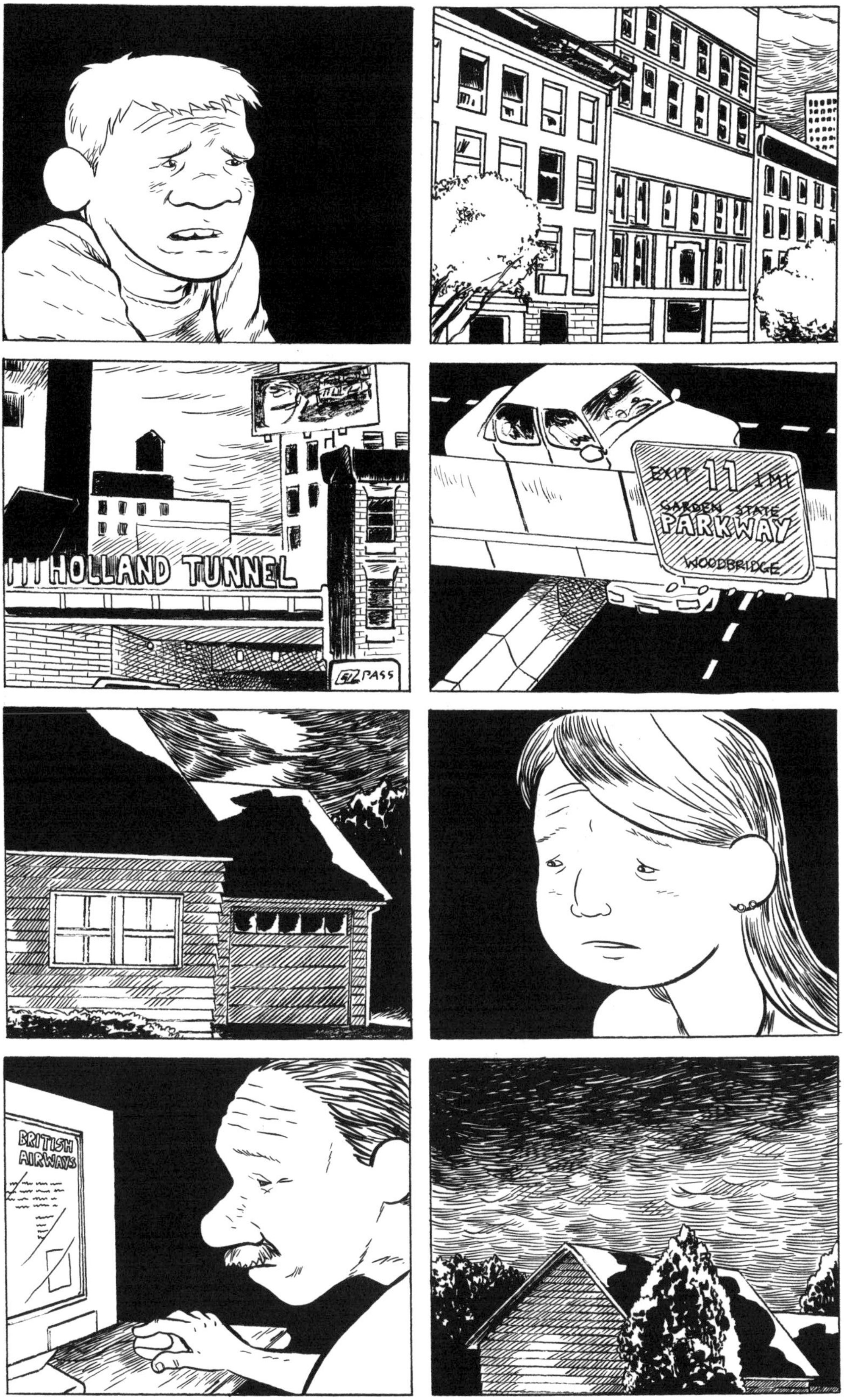
HOLLAND TUNNEL
PASS
EXIT 11 1 MI
GARDEN STATE
PARKWAY
WOODBRIDGE
BRITISH AIRWAYS

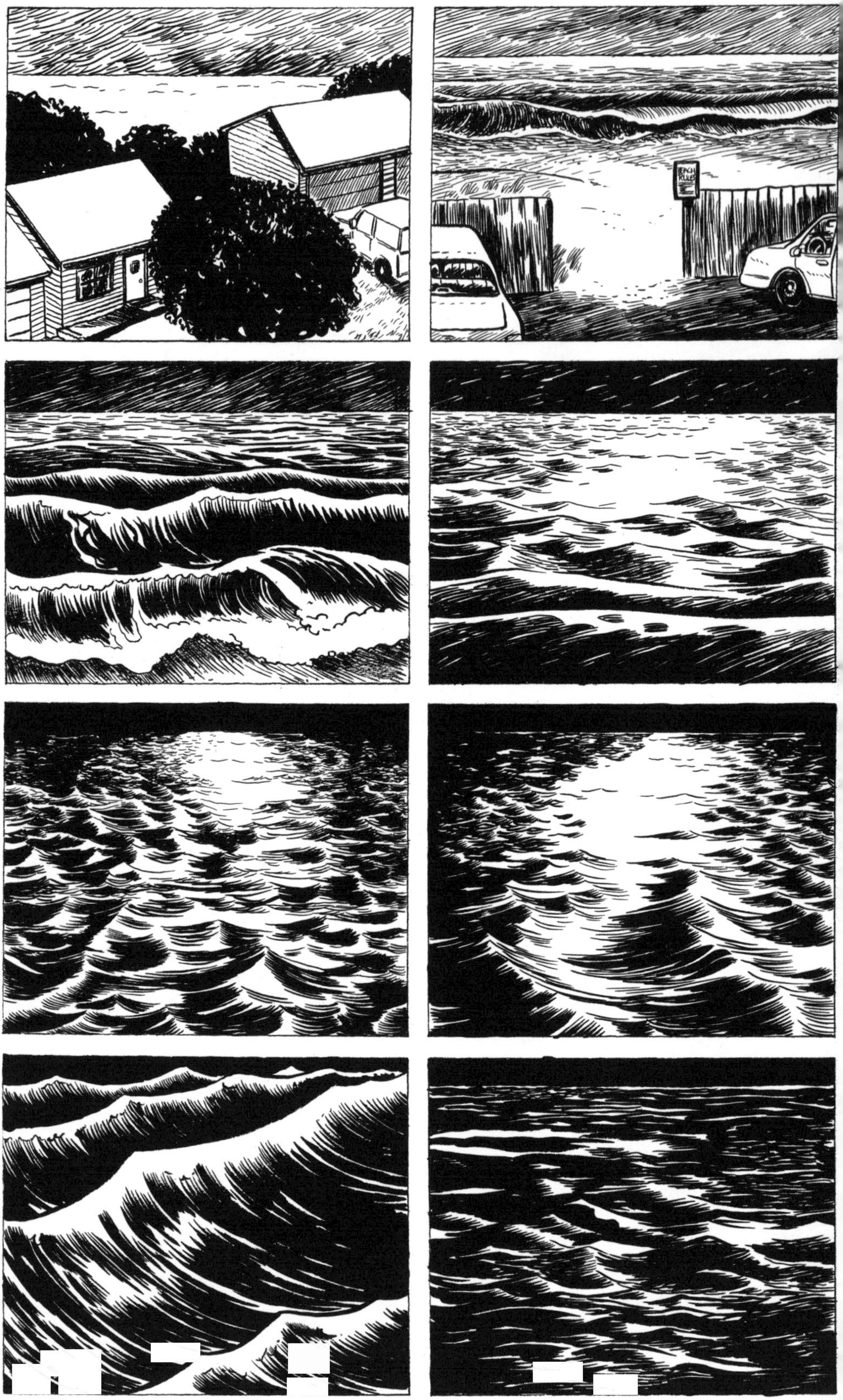

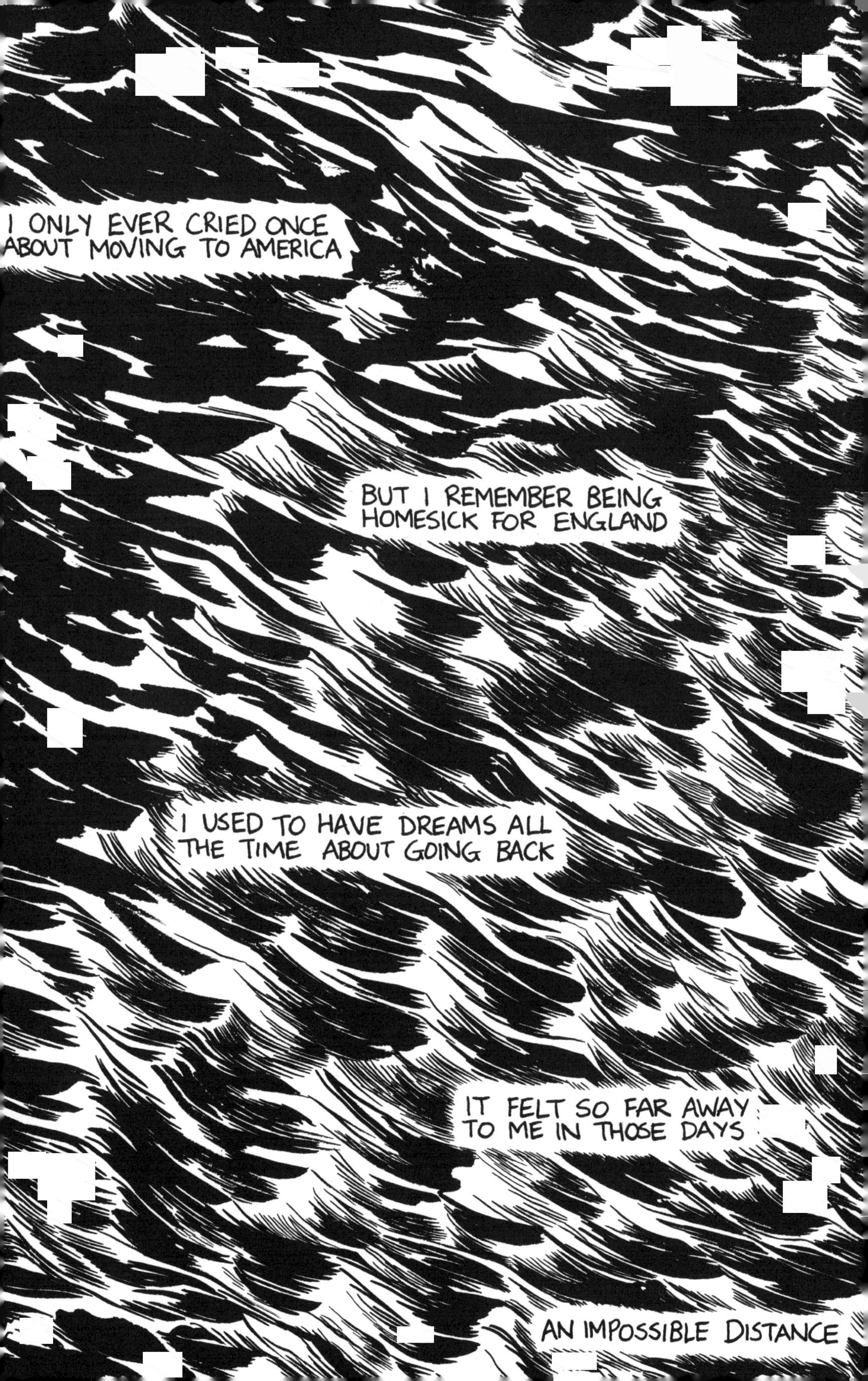
I ONLY EVER CRIED ONCE ABOUT MOVING TO AMERICA
BUT I REMEMBER BEING HOMESICK FOR ENGLAND
I USED TO HAVE DREAMS ALL THE TIME ABOUT GOING BACK
IT FELT SO FAR AWAY TO ME IN THOSE DAYS
AN IMPOSSIBLE DISTANCE

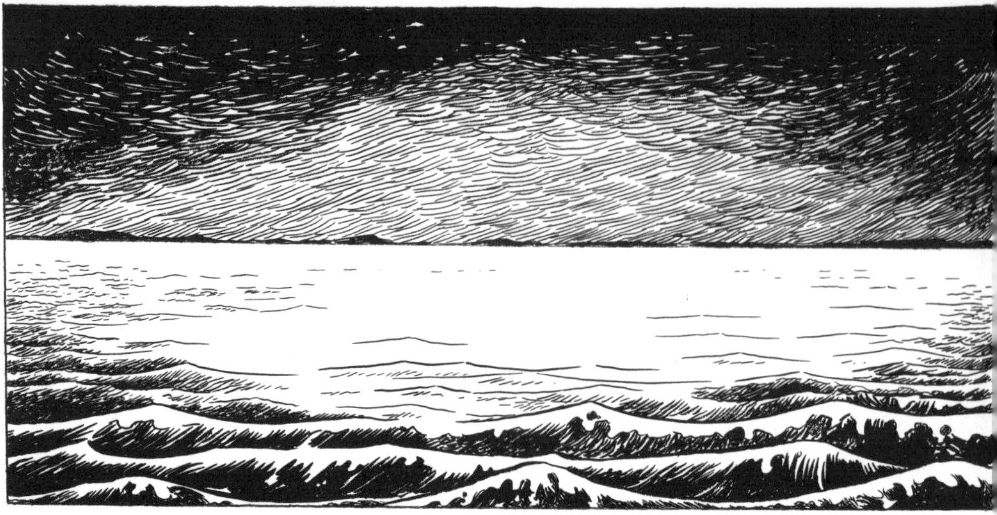

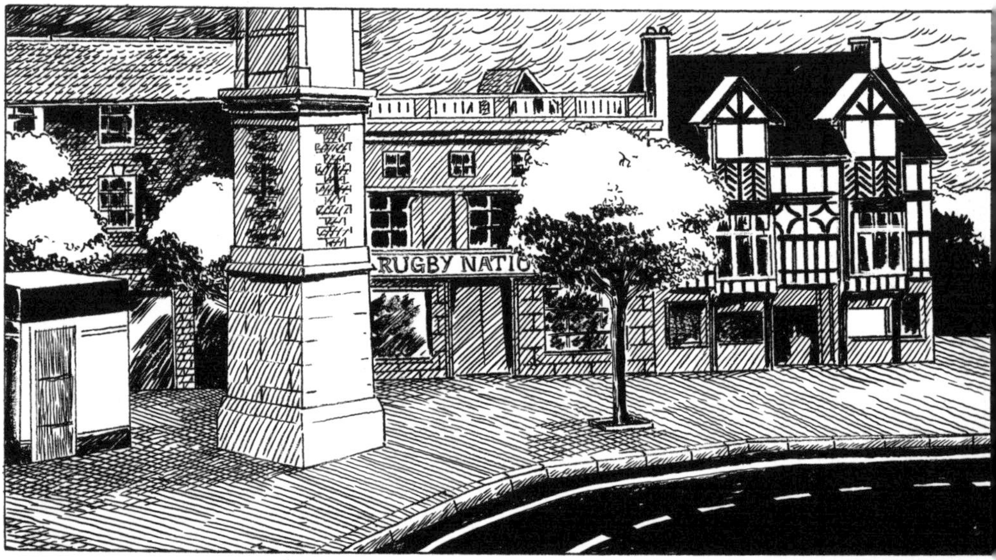
RUGBY NATIO

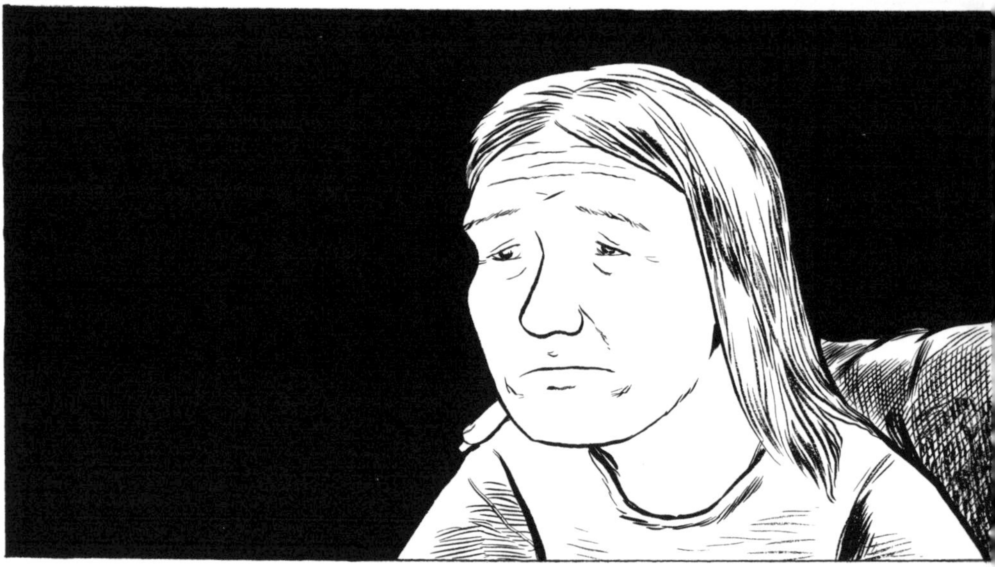

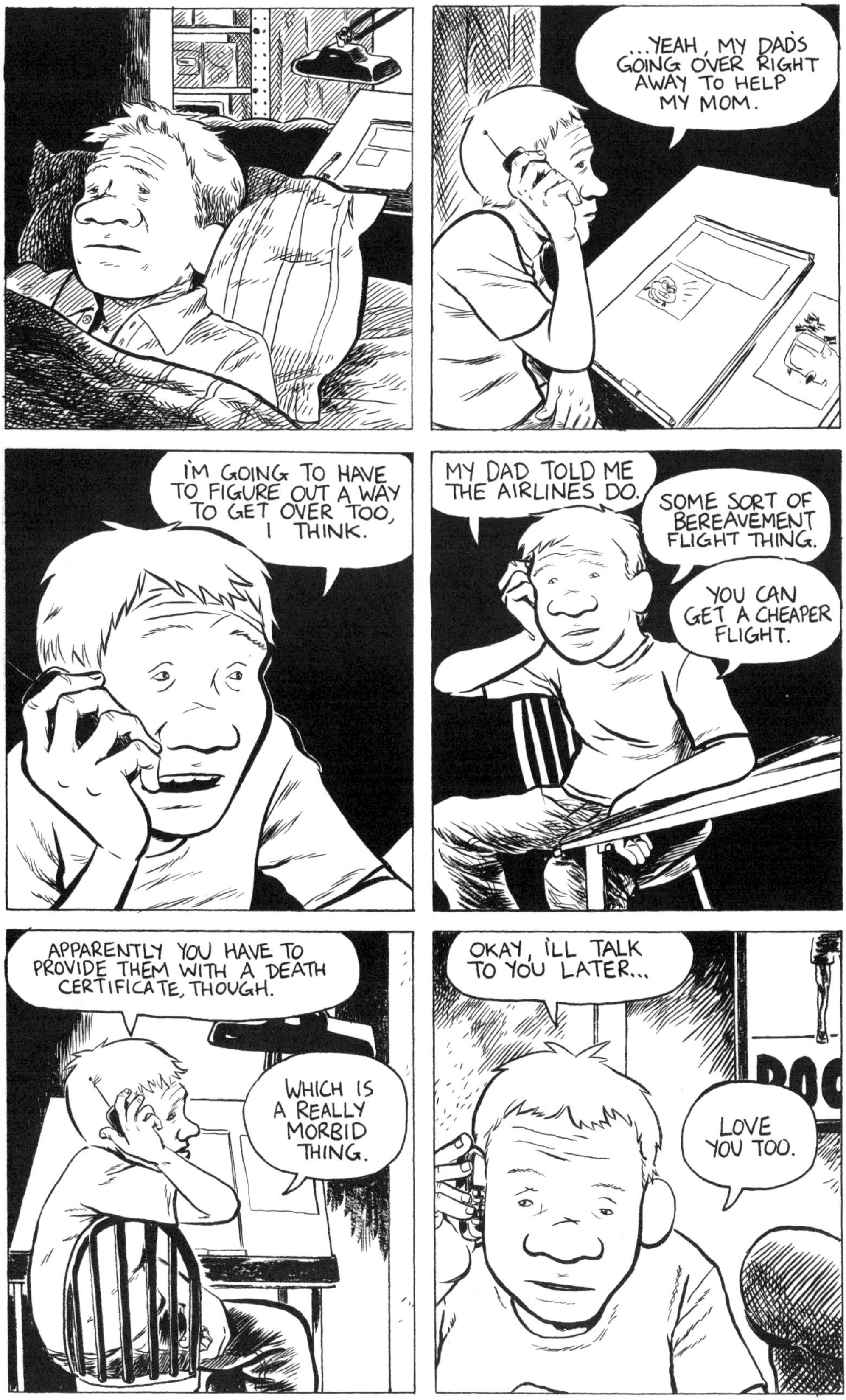
...YEAH, MY DAD'S GOING OVER RIGHT AWAY TO HELP MY MOM.
I'M GOING TO HAVE TO FIGURE OUT A WAY TO GET OVER TOO, I THINK.
MY DAD TOLD ME THE AIRLINES DO.
SOME SORT OF BEREAVEMENT FLIGHT THING.
YOU CAN GET A CHEAPER FLIGHT.
APPARENTLY YOU HAVE TO PROVIDE THEM WITH A DEATH CERTIFICATE, THOUGH.
WHICH IS A REALLY MORBID THING.
OKAY, I'LL TALK TO YOU LATER...
LOVE YOU TOO.

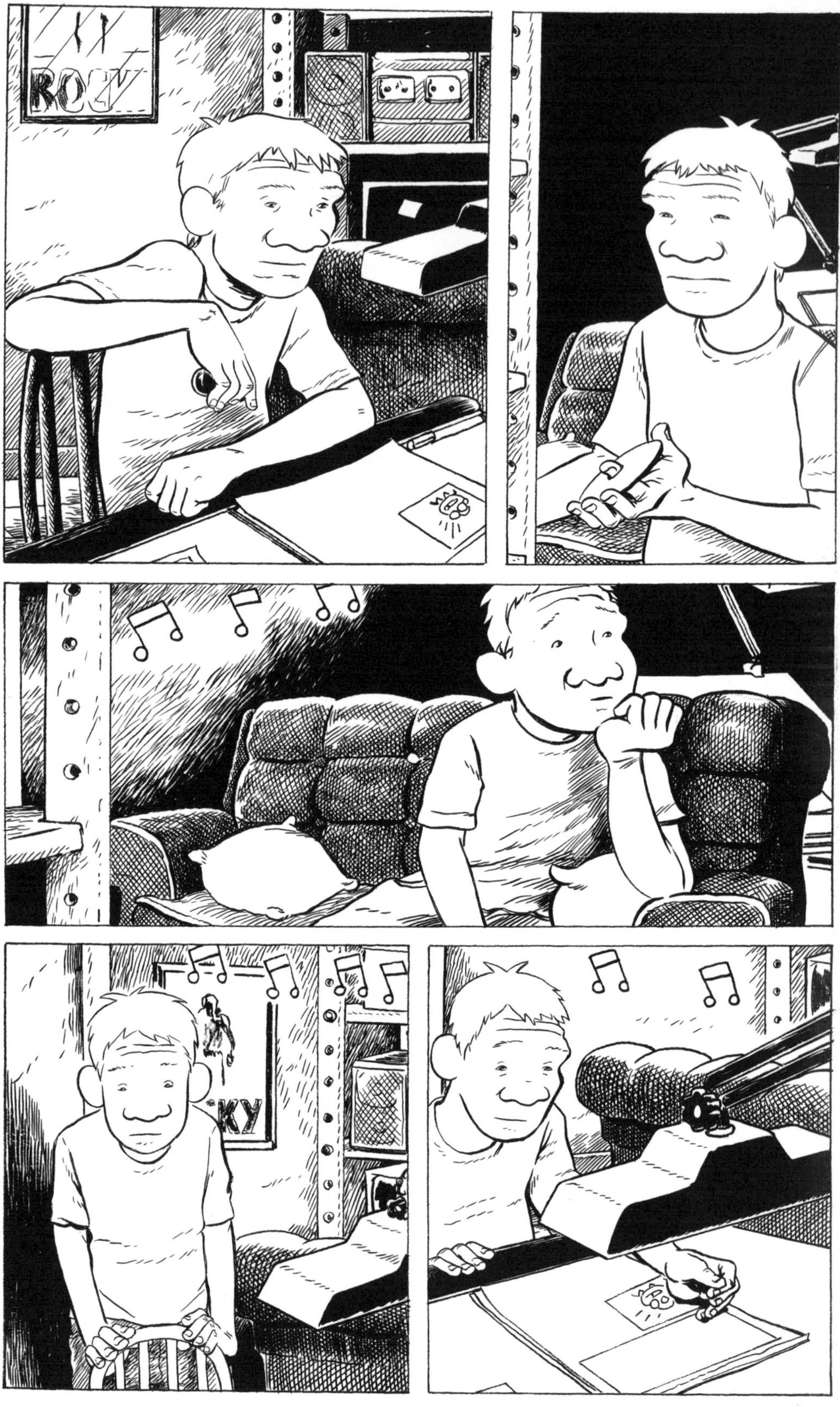

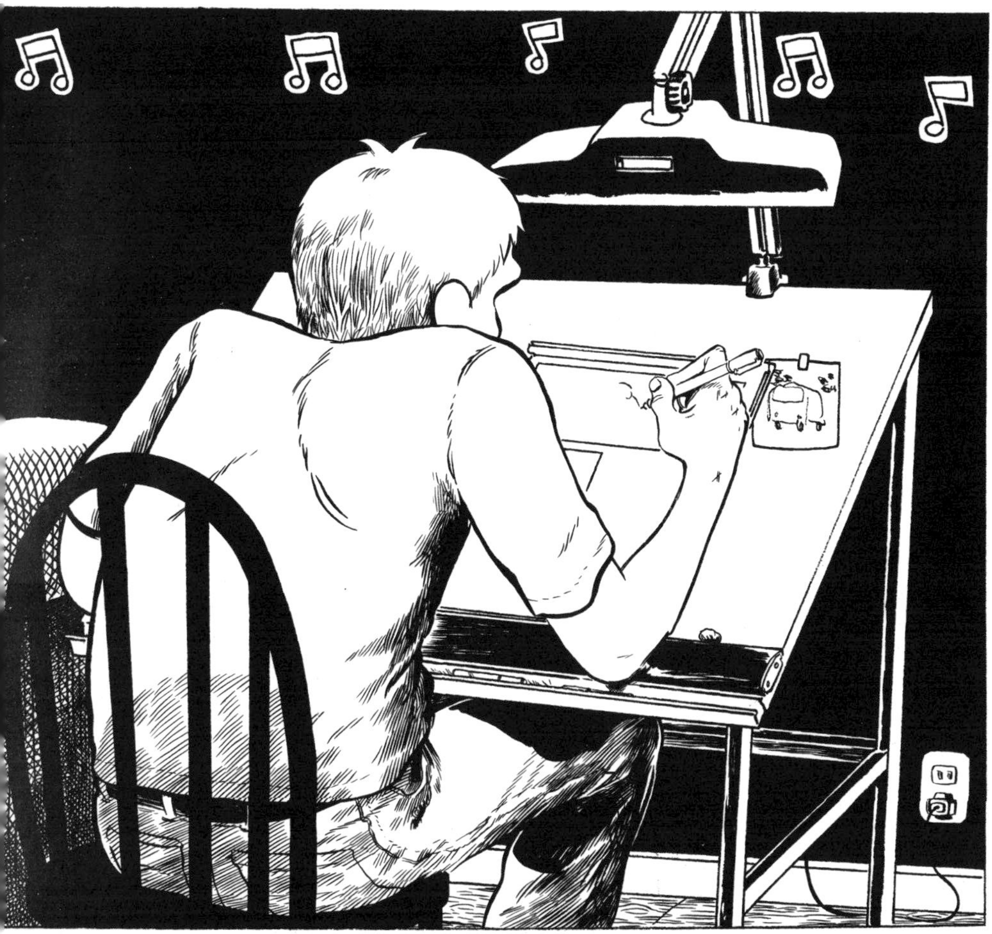
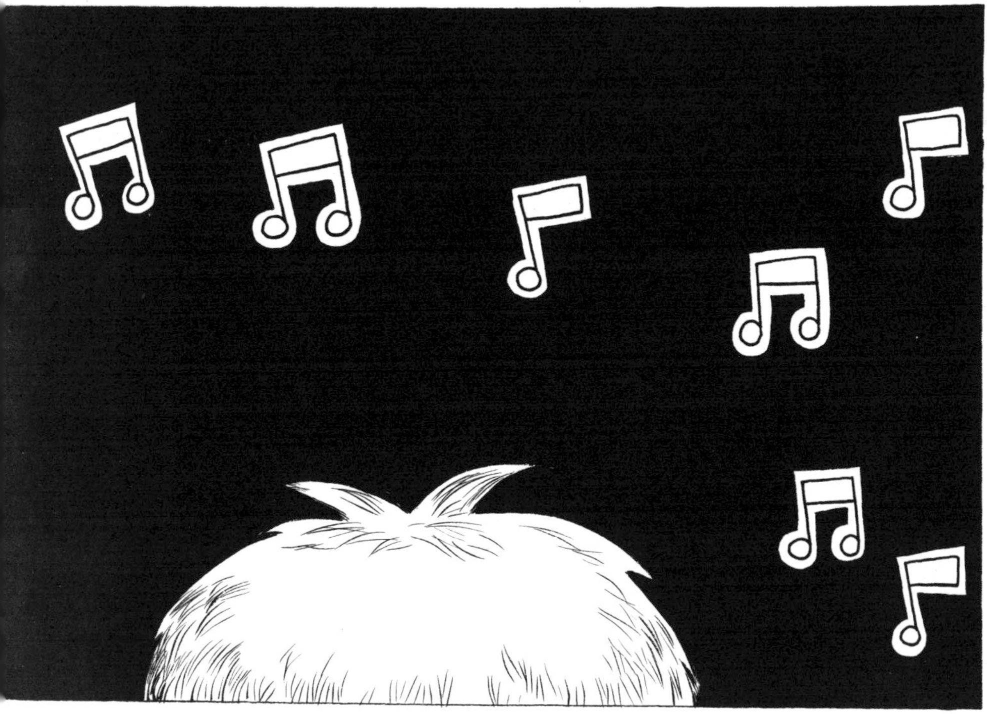

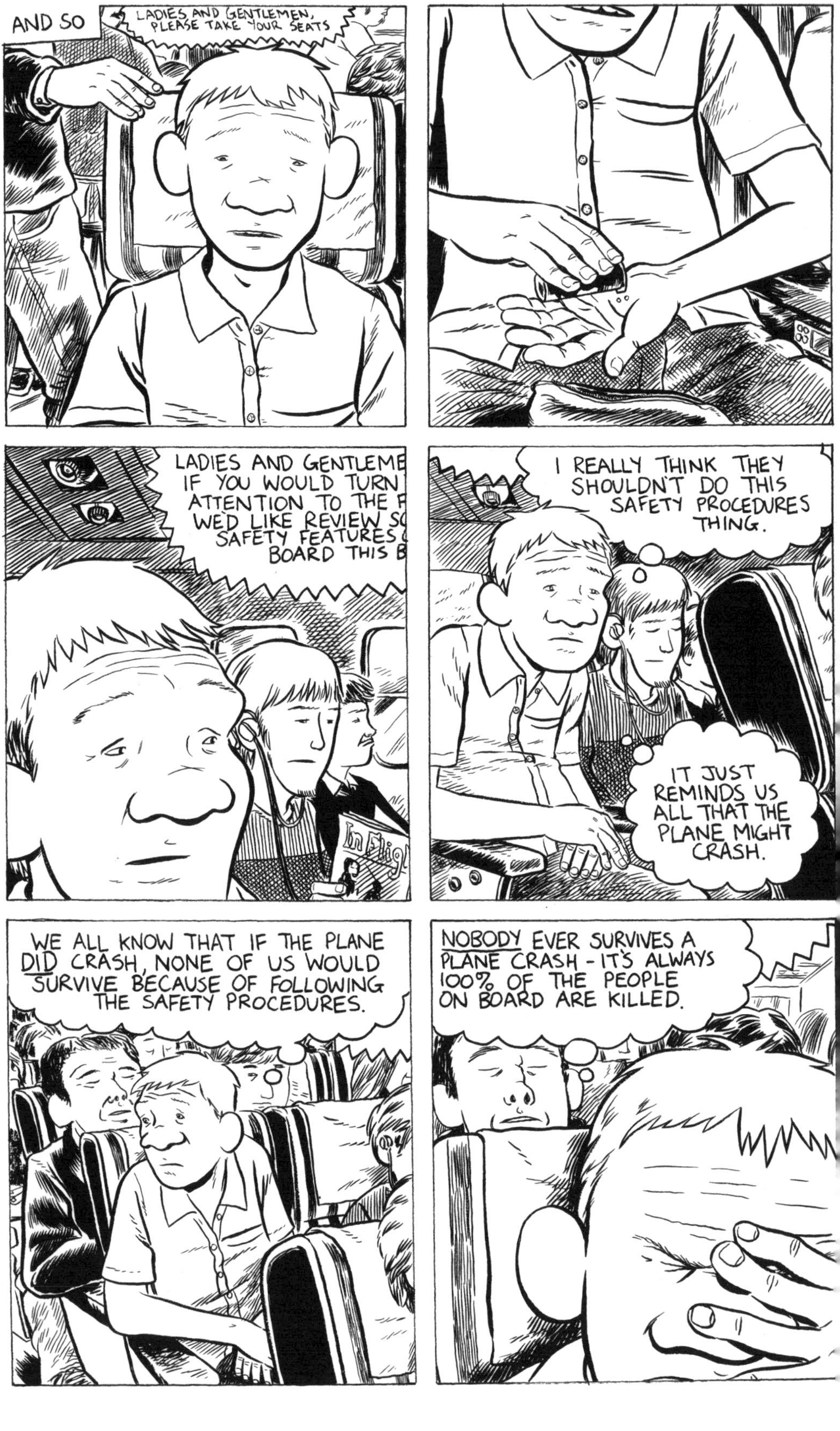
AND SO
LADIES AND GENTLEMEN, PLEASE TAKE YOUR SEATS
LADIES AND GENTLEME IF YOU WOULD TURN ATTENTION TO THE F WE'D LIKE REVIEW SO SAFETY FEATURES BOARD THIS B
In Fligh
I REALLY THINK THEY SHOULDN'T DO THIS SAFETY PROCEDURES THING.
IT JUST REMINDS US ALL THAT THE PLANE MIGHT CRASH.
WE ALL KNOW THAT IF THE PLANE DID CRASH, NONE OF US WOULD SURVIVE BECAUSE OF FOLLOWING THE SAFETY PROCEDURES.
NOBODY EVER SURVIVES A PLANE CRASH - IT'S ALWAYS 100% OF THE PEOPLE ON BOARD ARE KILLED.

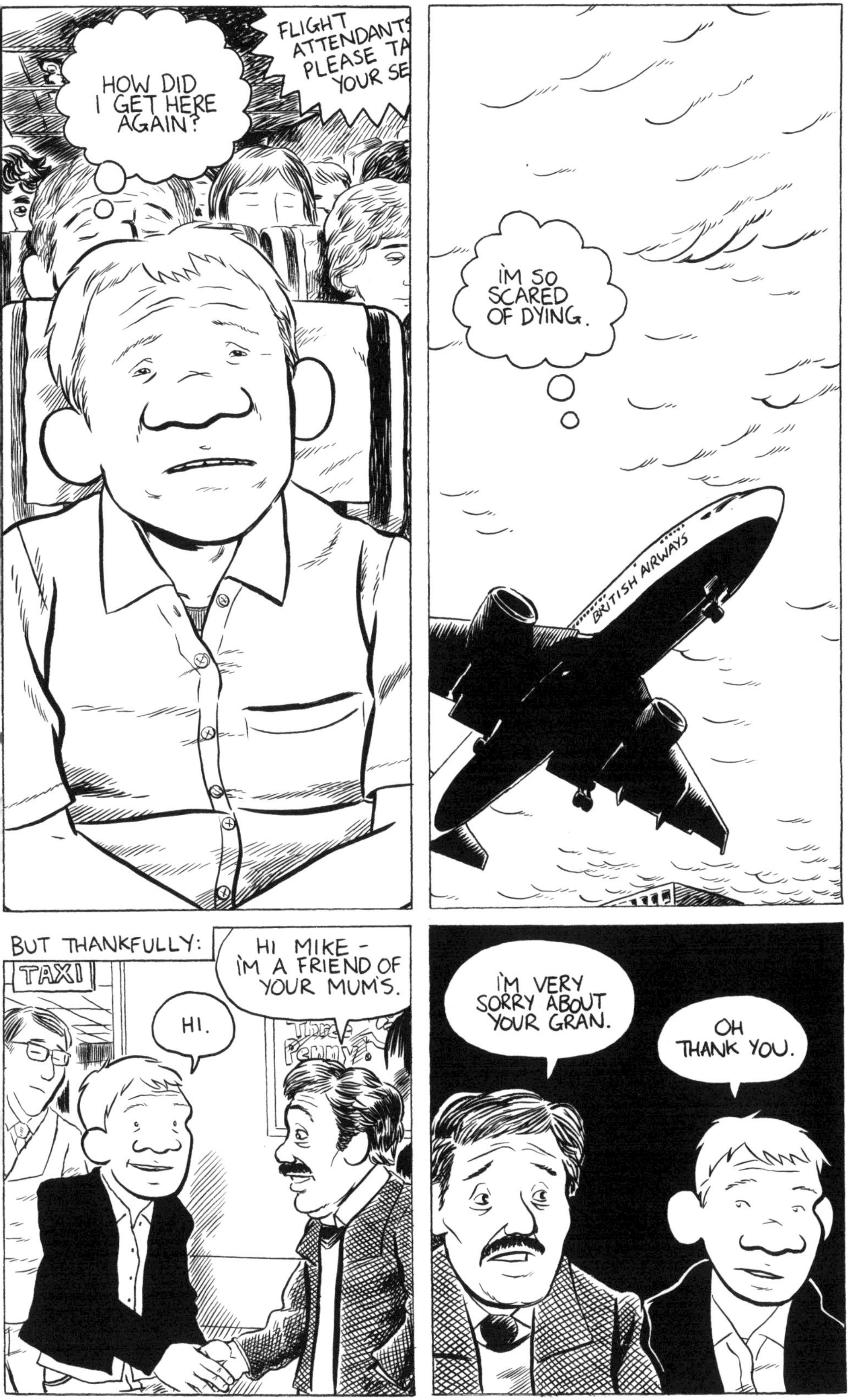
FLIGHT ATTENDANTS PLEASE TA YOUR SE
HOW DID I GET HERE AGAIN?
I'M SO SCARED OF DYING.
BRITISH AIRWAYS
BUT THANKFULLY:
TAXI
HI MIKE - I'M A FRIEND OF YOUR MUM'S.
HI.
I'M VERY SORRY ABOUT YOUR GRAN.
OH THANK YOU.

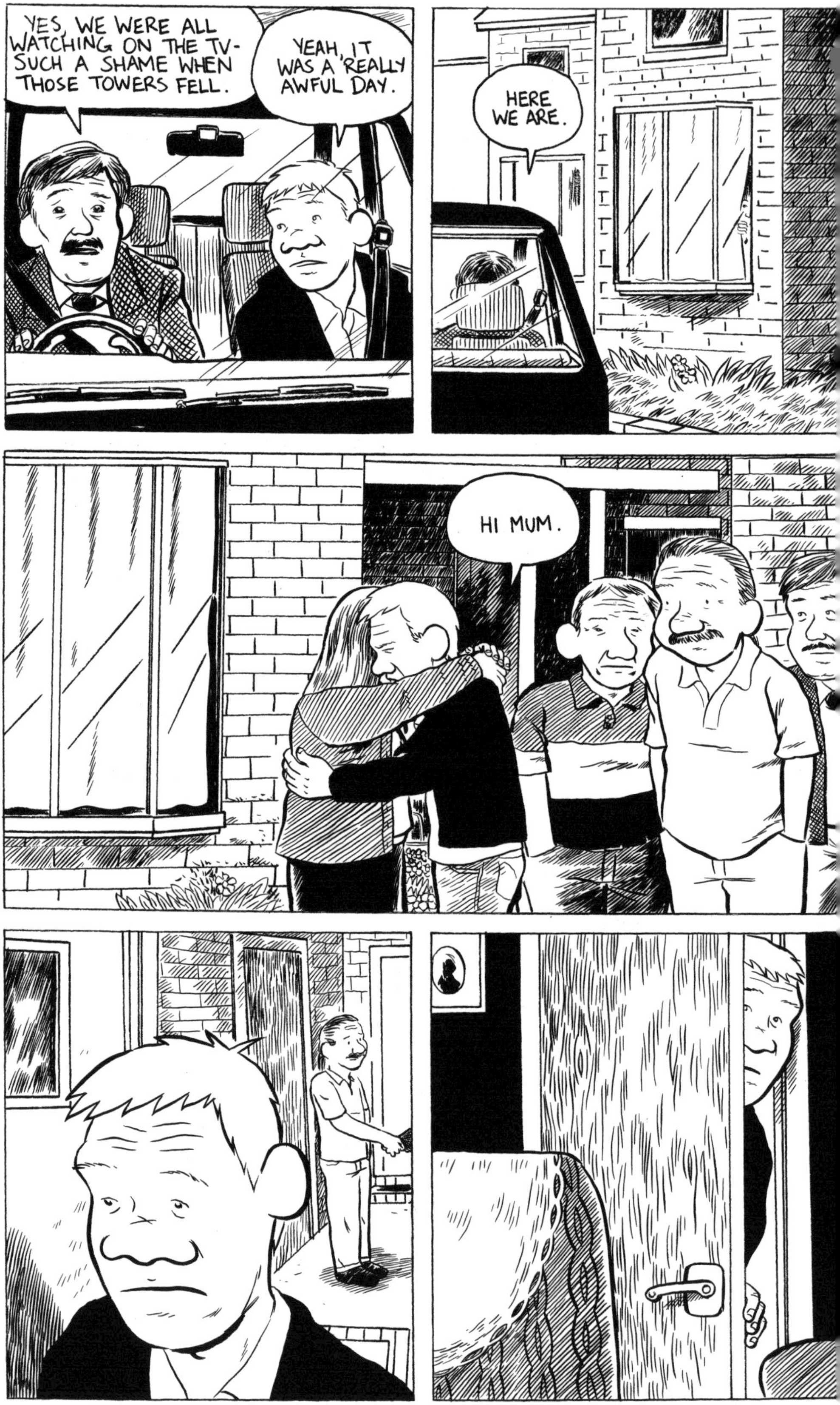
YES, WE WERE ALL WATCHING ON THE TV- SUCH A SHAME WHEN THOSE TOWERS FELL.
YEAH, IT WAS A REALLY AWFUL DAY.
HERE WE ARE.
HI MUM.

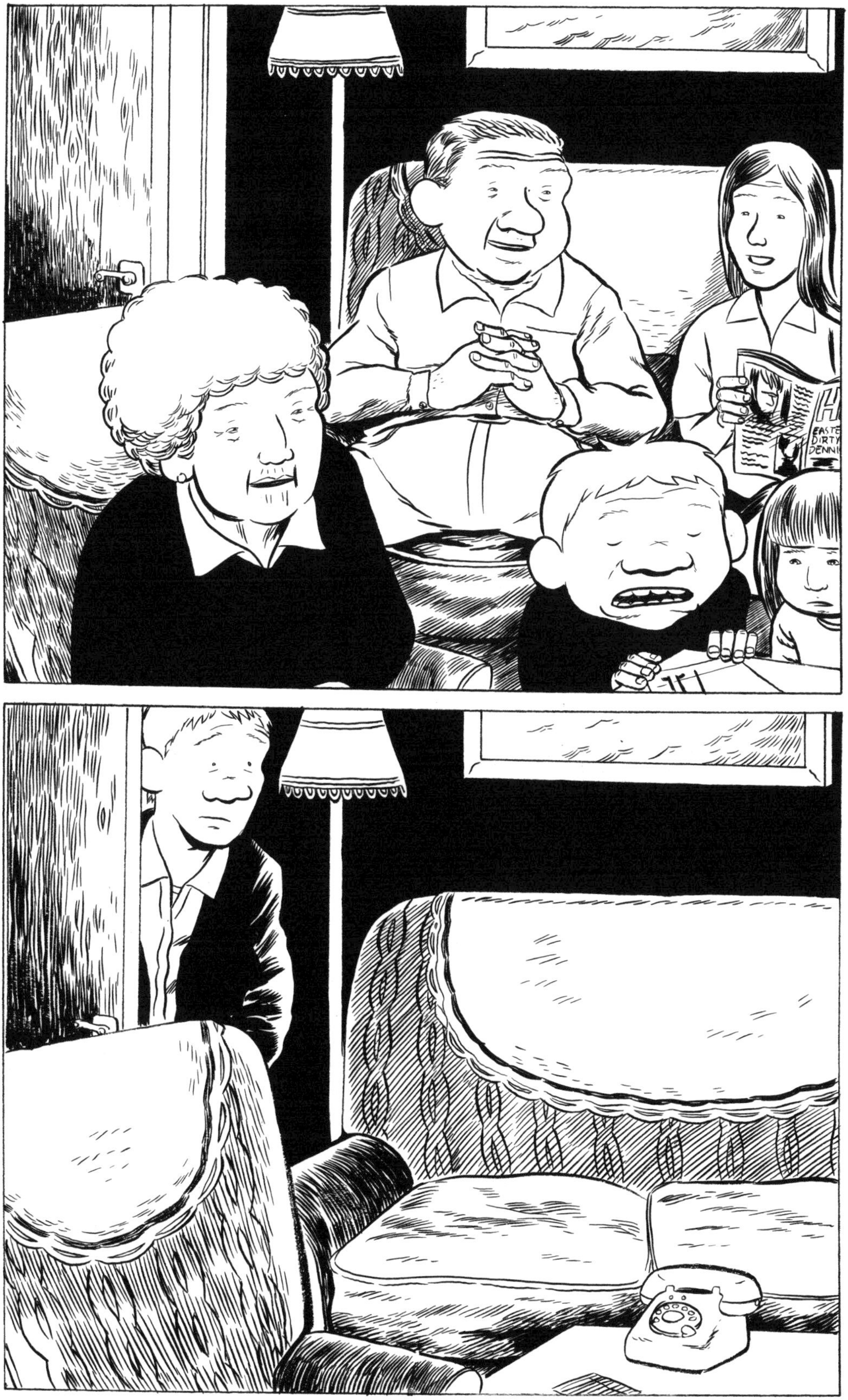
DIRTY

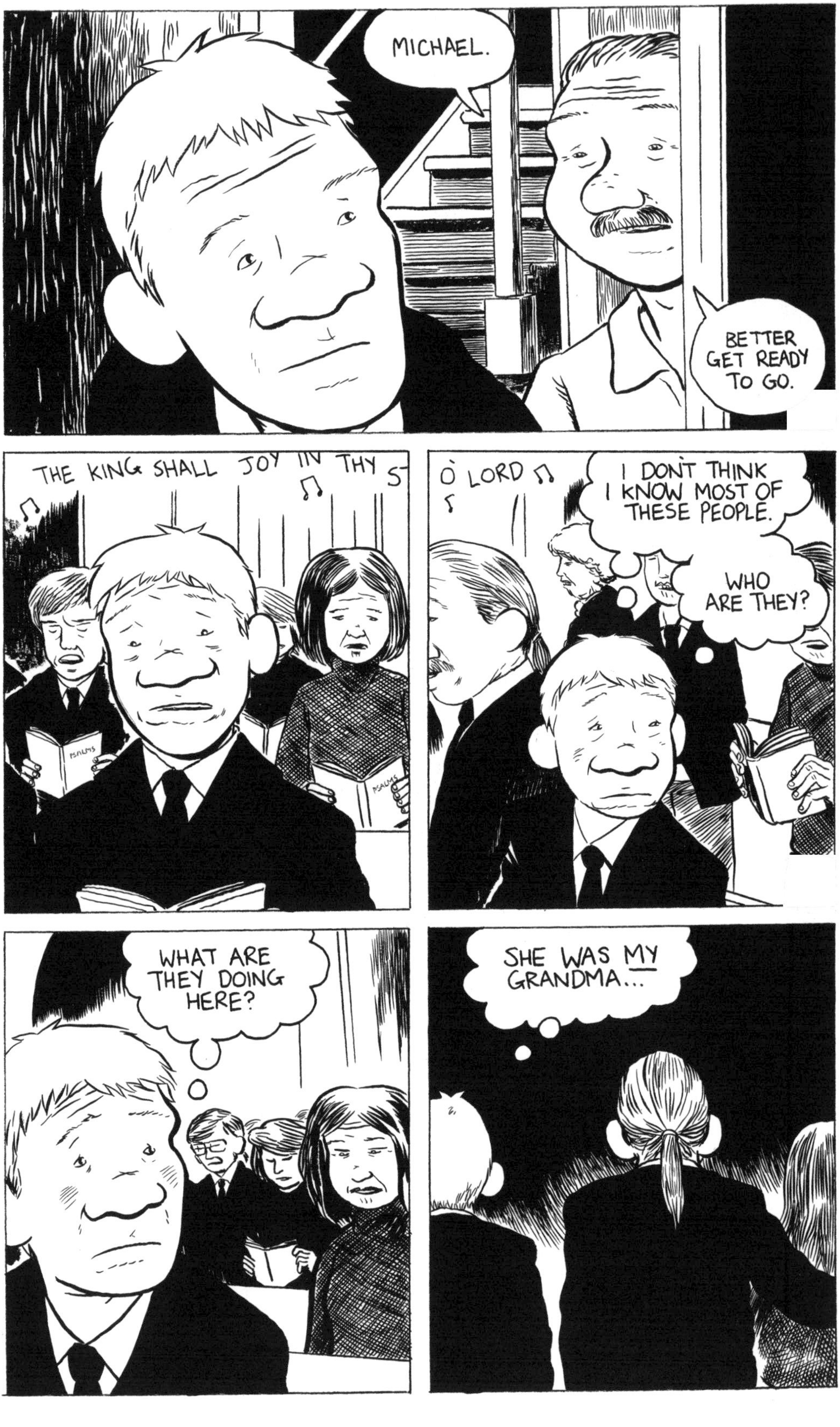
MICHAEL.
BETTER GET READY TO GO.
THE KING SHALL JOY IN THY S
O LORD
I DON'T THINK I KNOW MOST OF THESE PEOPLE.
WHO ARE THEY?
PSALMS
PSALMS
WHAT ARE THEY DOING HERE?
SHE WAS MY GRANDMA...

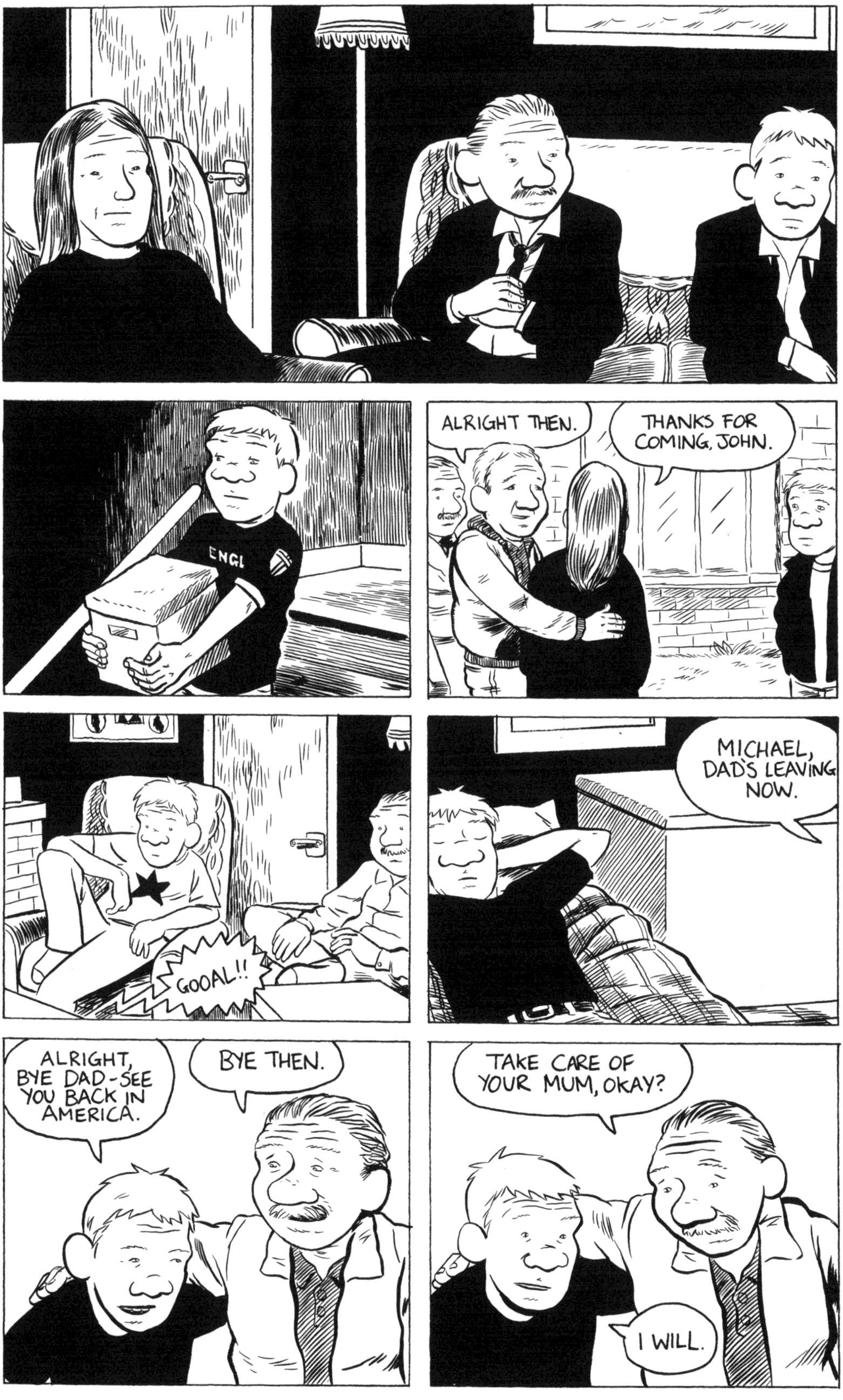
ENGL
ALRIGHT THEN.
THANKS FOR COMING, JOHN.
GOOAL!!
MICHAEL, DAD'S LEAVING NOW.
ALRIGHT, BYE DAD - SEE YOU BACK IN AMERICA.
BYE THEN.
TAKE CARE OF YOUR MUM, OKAY?
I WILL.

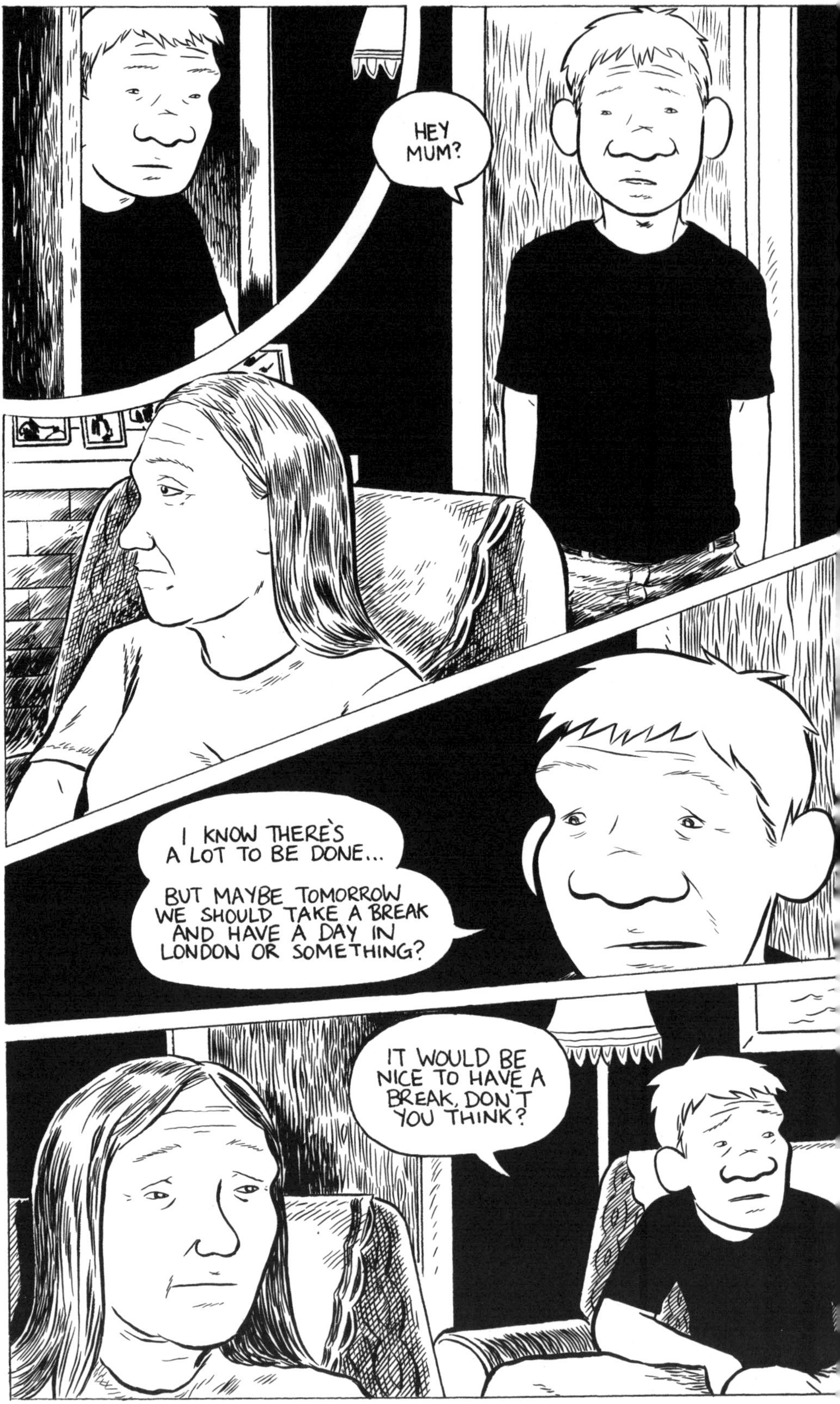
HEY MUM?
I KNOW THERE'S A LOT TO BE DONE...
BUT MAYBE TOMORROW WE SHOULD TAKE A BREAK AND HAVE A DAY IN LONDON OR SOMETHING?
IT WOULD BE NICE TO HAVE A BREAK, DON'T YOU THINK?

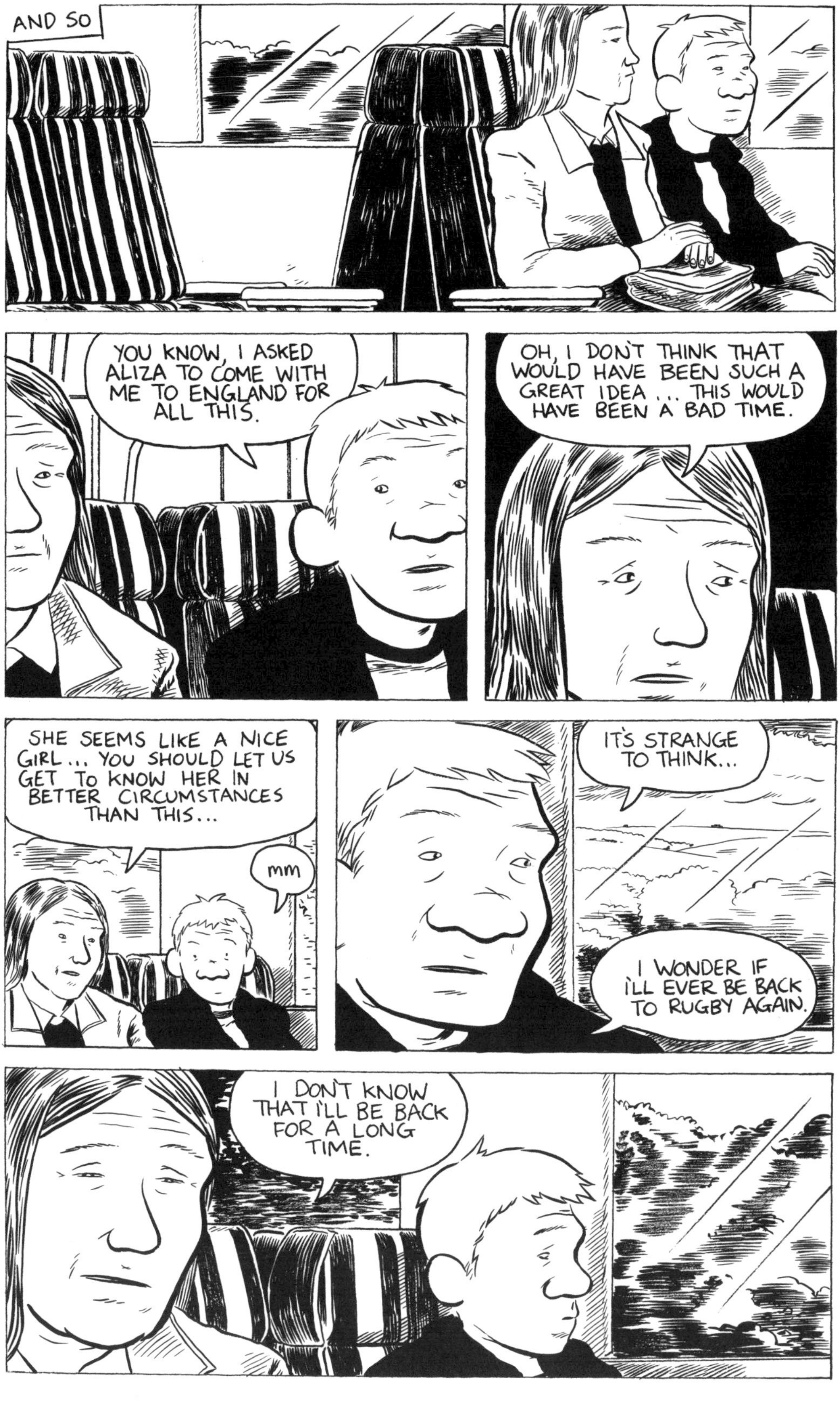
AND SO
YOU KNOW, I ASKED ALIZA TO COME WITH ME TO ENGLAND FOR ALL THIS.
OH, I DON'T THINK THAT WOULD HAVE BEEN SUCH A GREAT IDEA ... THIS WOULD HAVE BEEN A BAD TIME.
SHE SEEMS LIKE A NICE GIRL... YOU SHOULD LET US GET TO KNOW HER IN BETTER CIRCUMSTANCES THAN THIS...
mm
IT'S STRANGE TO THINK...
I WONDER IF I'LL EVER BE BACK TO RUGBY AGAIN.
I DON'T KNOW THAT I'LL BE BACK FOR A LONG TIME.

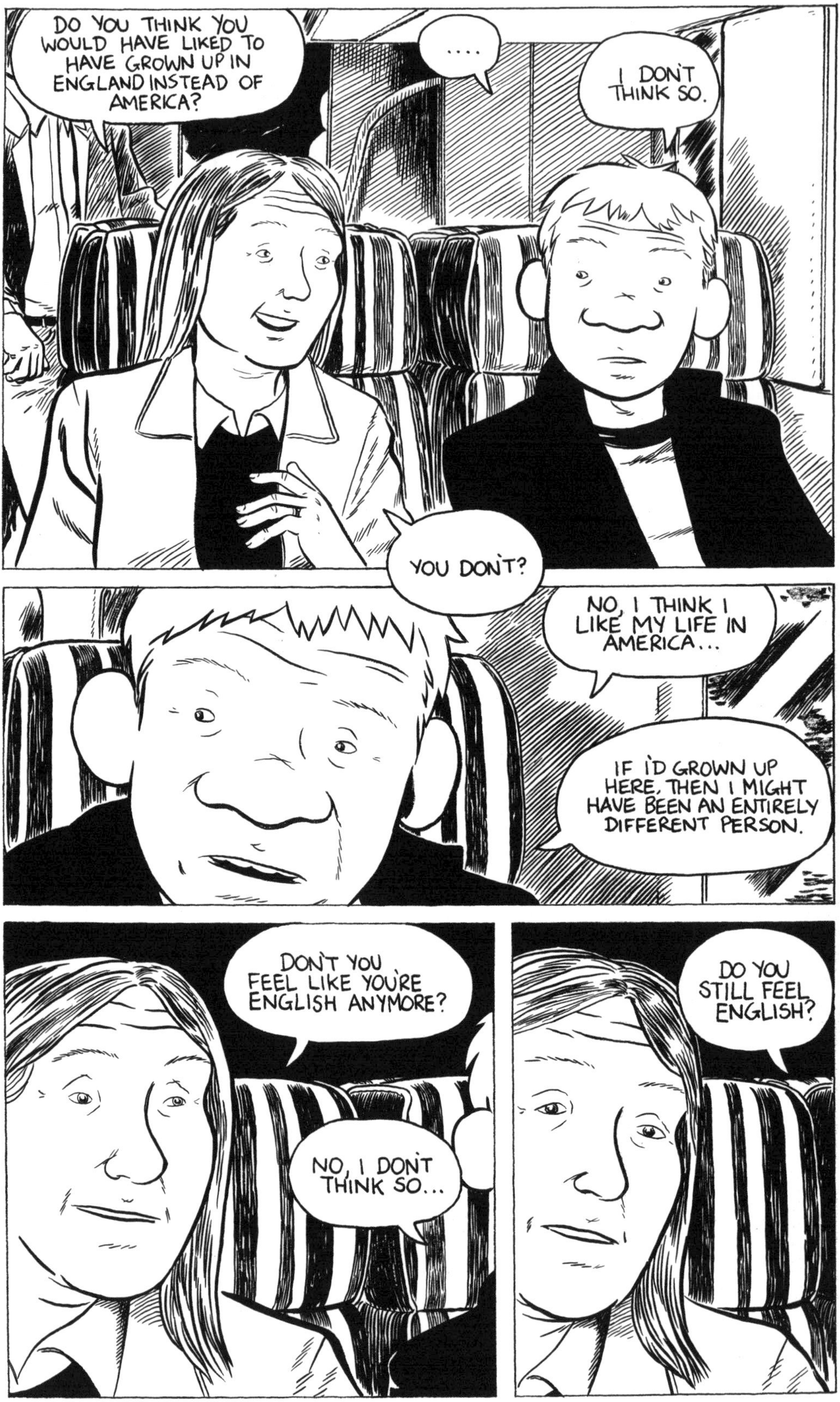
DO YOU THINK YOU WOULD HAVE LIKED TO HAVE GROWN UP IN ENGLAND INSTEAD OF AMERICA?
....
I DON'T THINK SO.
YOU DON'T?
NO, I THINK I LIKE MY LIFE IN AMERICA...
IF I'D GROWN UP HERE, THEN I MIGHT HAVE BEEN AN ENTIRELY DIFFERENT PERSON.
DON'T YOU FEEL LIKE YOU'RE ENGLISH ANYMORE?
NO, I DON'T THINK SO...
DO YOU STILL FEEL ENGLISH?

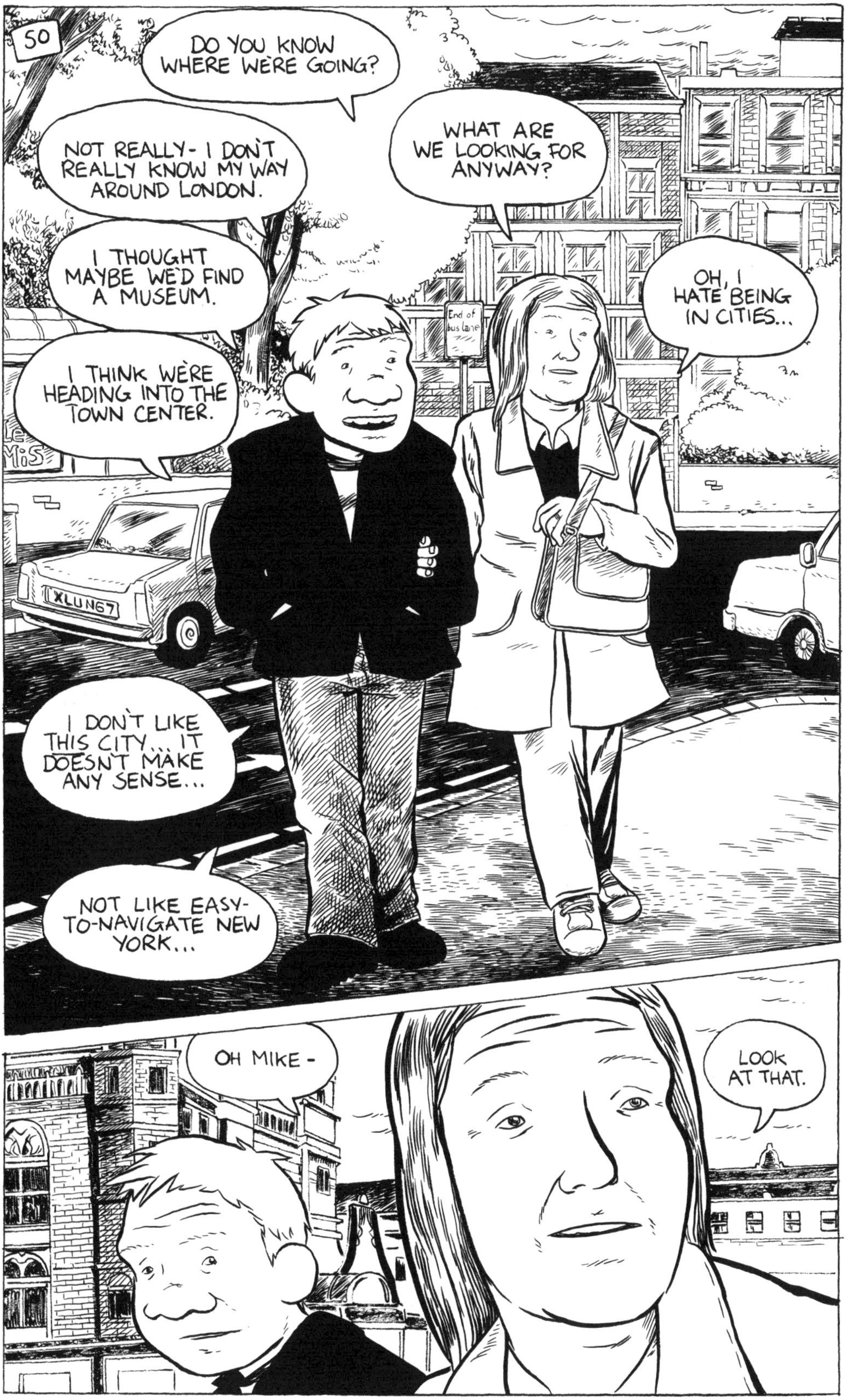
DO YOU KNOW WHERE WE'RE GOING?
NOT REALLY- I DON'T REALLY KNOW MY WAY AROUND LONDON.
WHAT ARE WE LOOKING FOR ANYWAY?
I THOUGHT MAYBE WE'D FIND A MUSEUM.
OH, I HATE BEING IN CITIES...
I THINK WE'RE HEADING INTO THE TOWN CENTER.
End of bus lane
XLUN67
I DON'T LIKE THIS CITY... IT DOESN'T MAKE ANY SENSE...
NOT LIKE EASY-TO-NAVIGATE NEW YORK...
OH MIKE-
LOOK AT THAT.

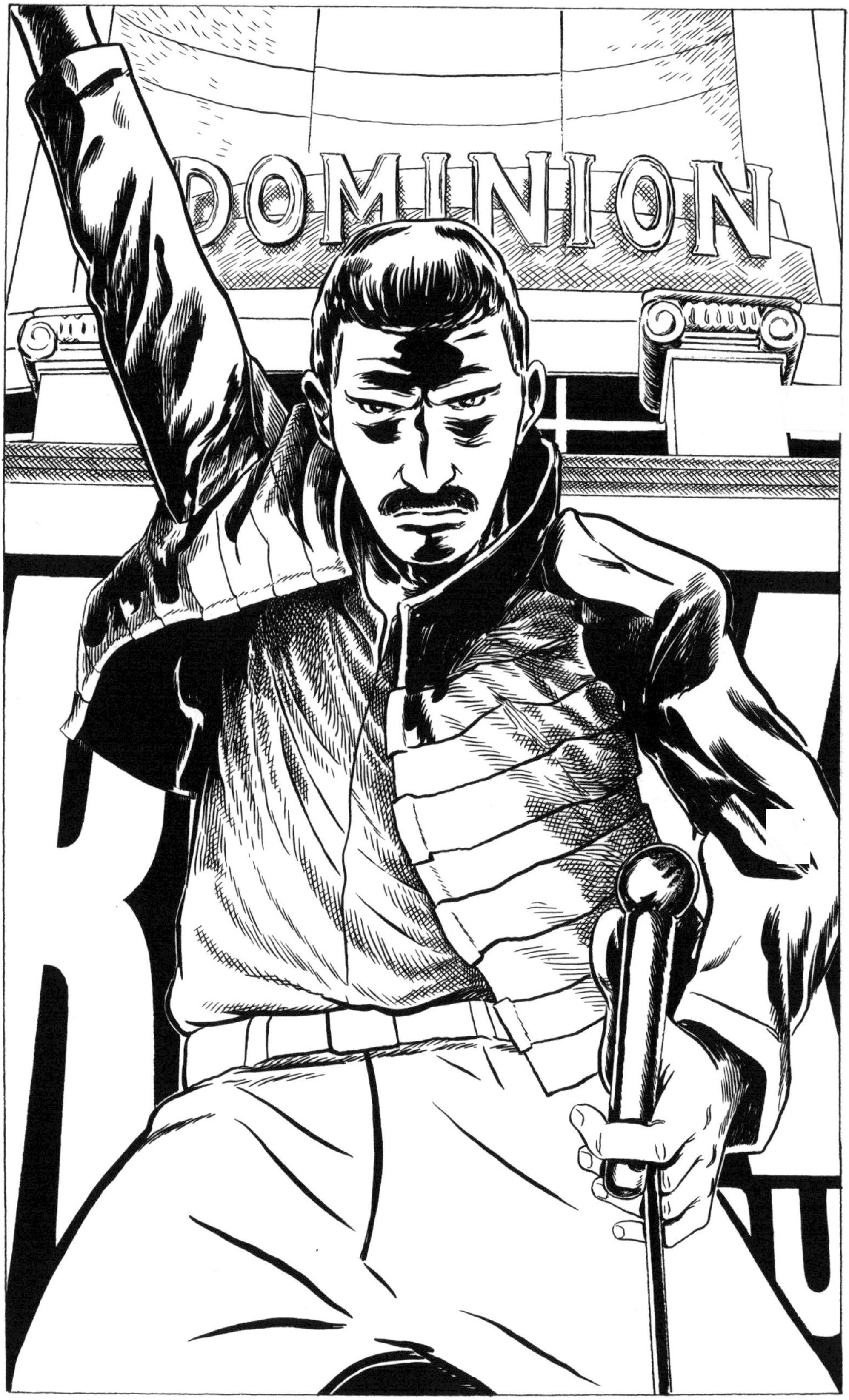
DOMINION

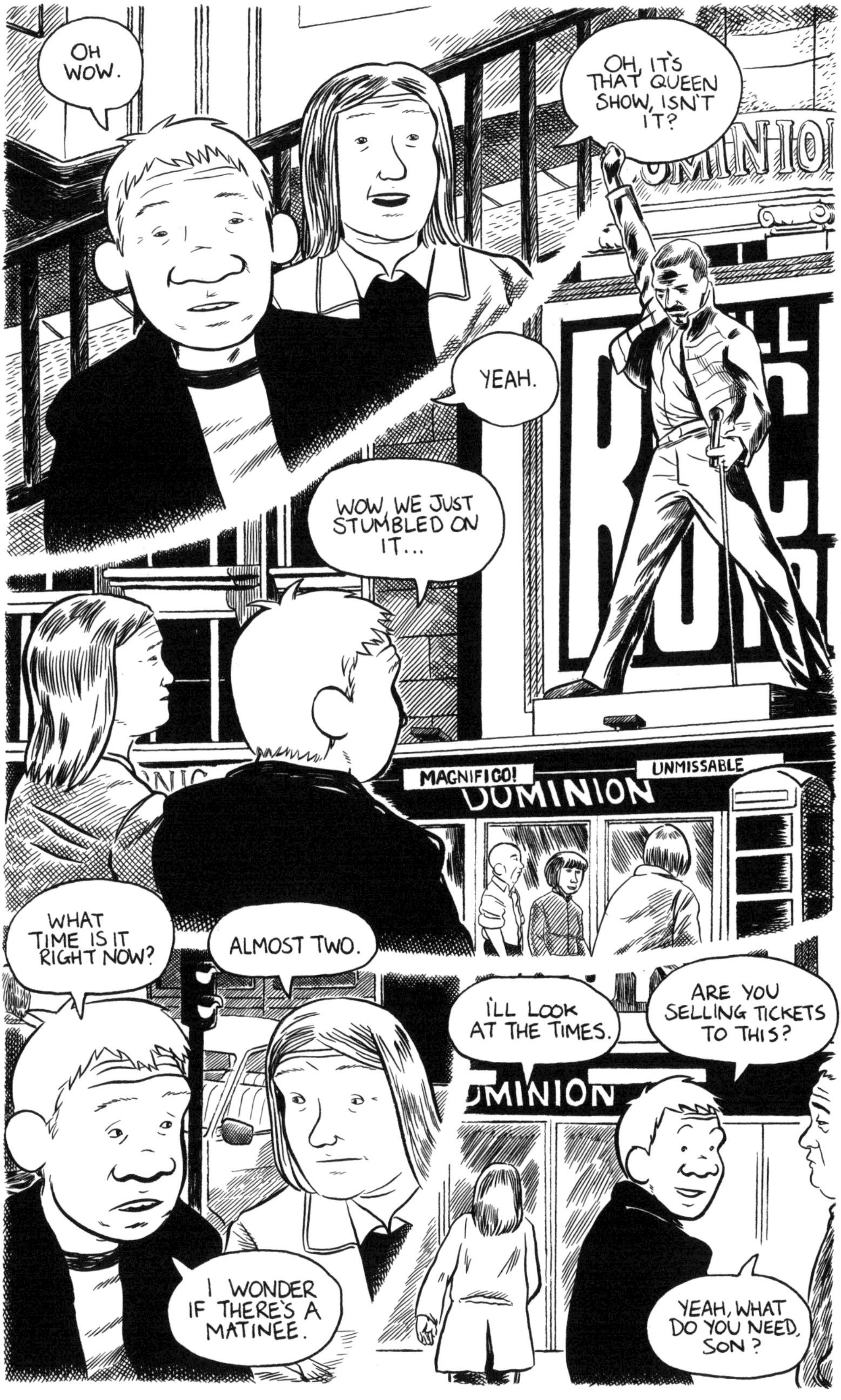
OH WOW.
OH, IT'S THAT QUEEN SHOW, ISN'T IT?
YEAH.
WOW, WE JUST STUMBLED ON IT...
MAGNIFICO!
UNMISSABLE
DOMINION
WHAT TIME IS IT RIGHT NOW?
ALMOST TWO.
I WONDER IF THERE'S A MATINEE.
I'LL LOOK AT THE TIMES.
ARE YOU SELLING TICKETS TO THIS?
YEAH, WHAT DO YOU NEED, SON?

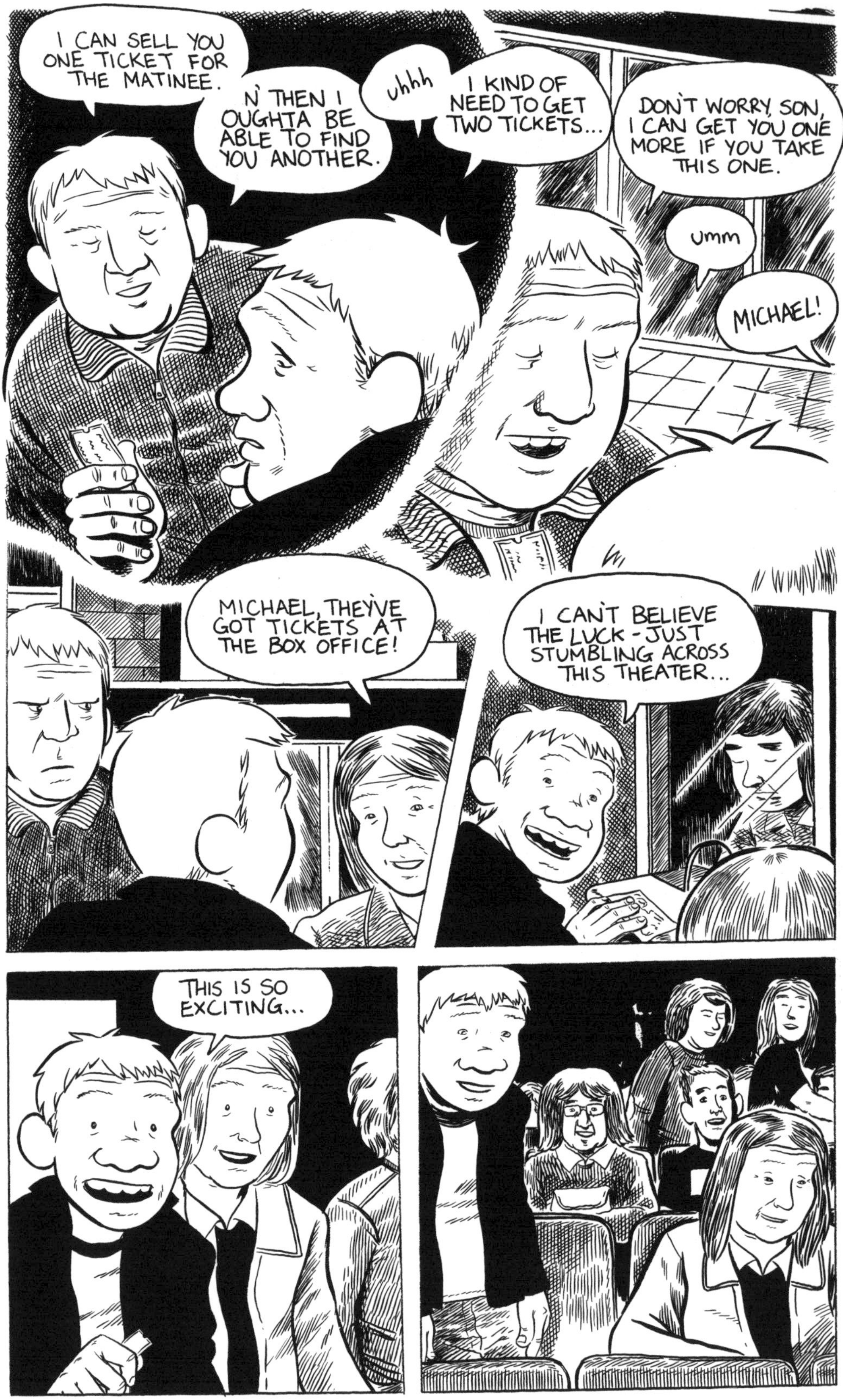
I CAN SELL YOU ONE TICKET FOR THE MATINEE.
N' THEN I OUGHTA BE ABLE TO FIND YOU ANOTHER.
uhhh
I KIND OF NEED TO GET TWO TICKETS...
DON'T WORRY, SON, I CAN GET YOU ONE MORE IF YOU TAKE THIS ONE.
umm
MICHAEL!
MICHAEL, THEY'VE GOT TICKETS AT THE BOX OFFICE!
I CAN'T BELIEVE THE LUCK - JUST STUMBLING ACROSS THIS THEATER...
THIS IS SO EXCITING...

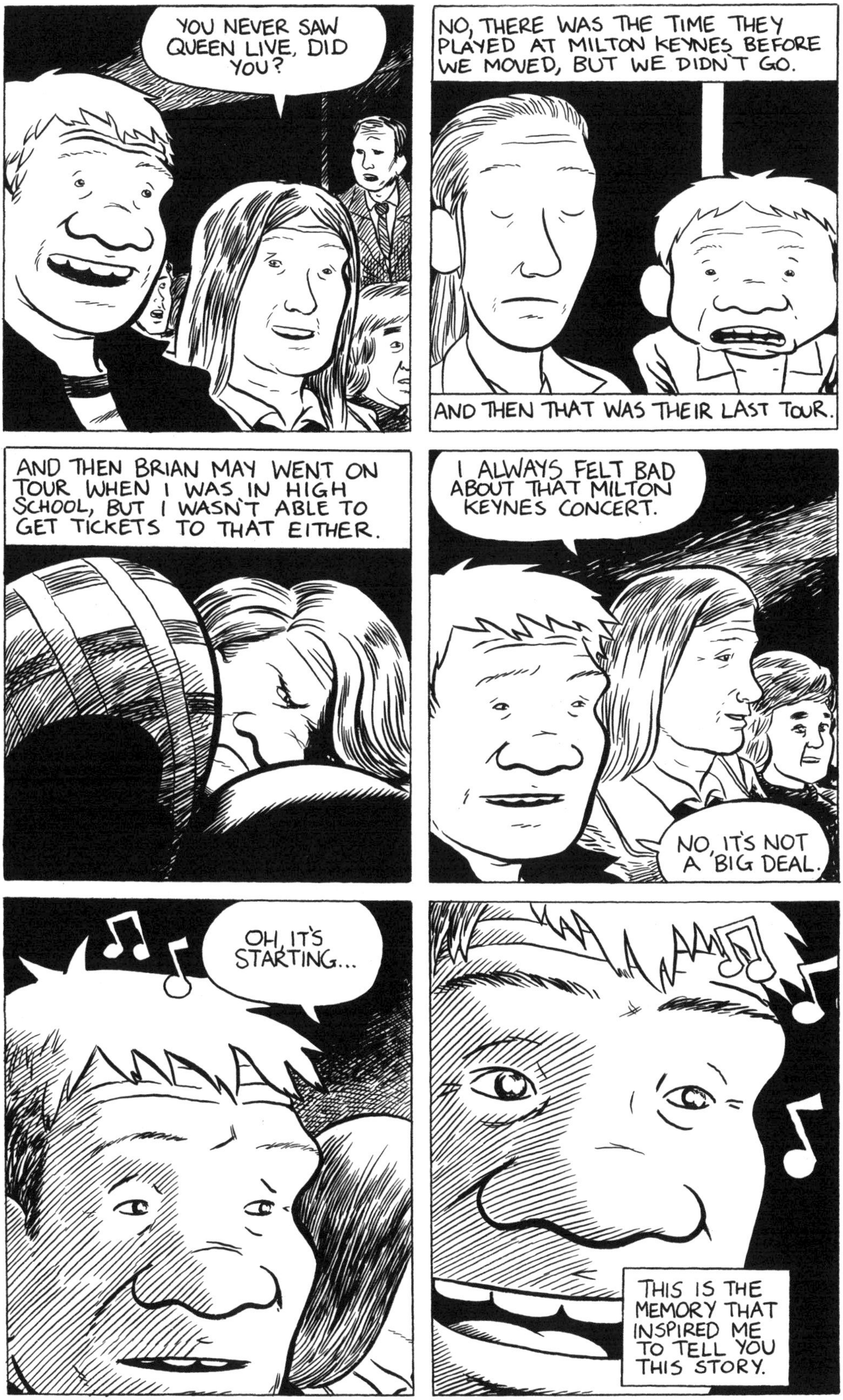
YOU NEVER SAW QUEEN LIVE, DID YOU?
NO, THERE WAS THE TIME THEY PLAYED AT MILTON KEYNES BEFORE WE MOVED, BUT WE DIDN'T GO.
AND THEN THAT WAS THEIR LAST TOUR.
AND THEN BRIAN MAY WENT ON TOUR WHEN I WAS IN HIGH SCHOOL, BUT I WASN'T ABLE TO GET TICKETS TO THAT EITHER.
I ALWAYS FELT BAD ABOUT THAT MILTON KEYNES CONCERT.
NO, IT'S NOT A BIG DEAL.
OH, IT'S STARTING...
THIS IS THE MEMORY THAT INSPIRED ME TO TELL YOU THIS STORY.

"WE WILL ROCK YOU" IS A MUSICAL BASED ON THE SONGS OF QUEEN. IT'S SET IN A FAR-OFF DYSTOPIAN FUTURE WHERE THE CULTURE IS HOMOGENOUS AND THERE IS NO ROCK MUSIC.

GALILEO AND SCARAMOUCHE ARE TWO YOUNG DREAMERS WHO YEARN FOR SOMETHING MORE VIBRANT THAN THE BLAND WORLD THAT THEY KNOW.

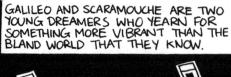

THE TWO OF THEM TEAM UP WITH A BAND OF OUTLAWS CALLED "THE BOHEMIANS".

THEY QUEST FOR A LOST GUITAR THAT WILL BRING ROCK BACK TO THE WORLD.

IT'S A LITTLE BIT LIKE THE PLOT TO RUSH'S CONCEPT ALBUM "2112".

IT'S ACTUALLY A PRETTY FUNNY SHOW, BUT OF COURSE THE THING I LIKED BEST ABOUT IT WAS THE MUSIC.

I ALWAYS REMEMBER MY FRIEND ORION REMARKING THAT QUEEN HAD SONGS FOR ALL OCCASIONS - WHICH IS WHY I THINK IT WORKED WELL TO WRITE A PLAY STRUCTURED AROUND THEM.

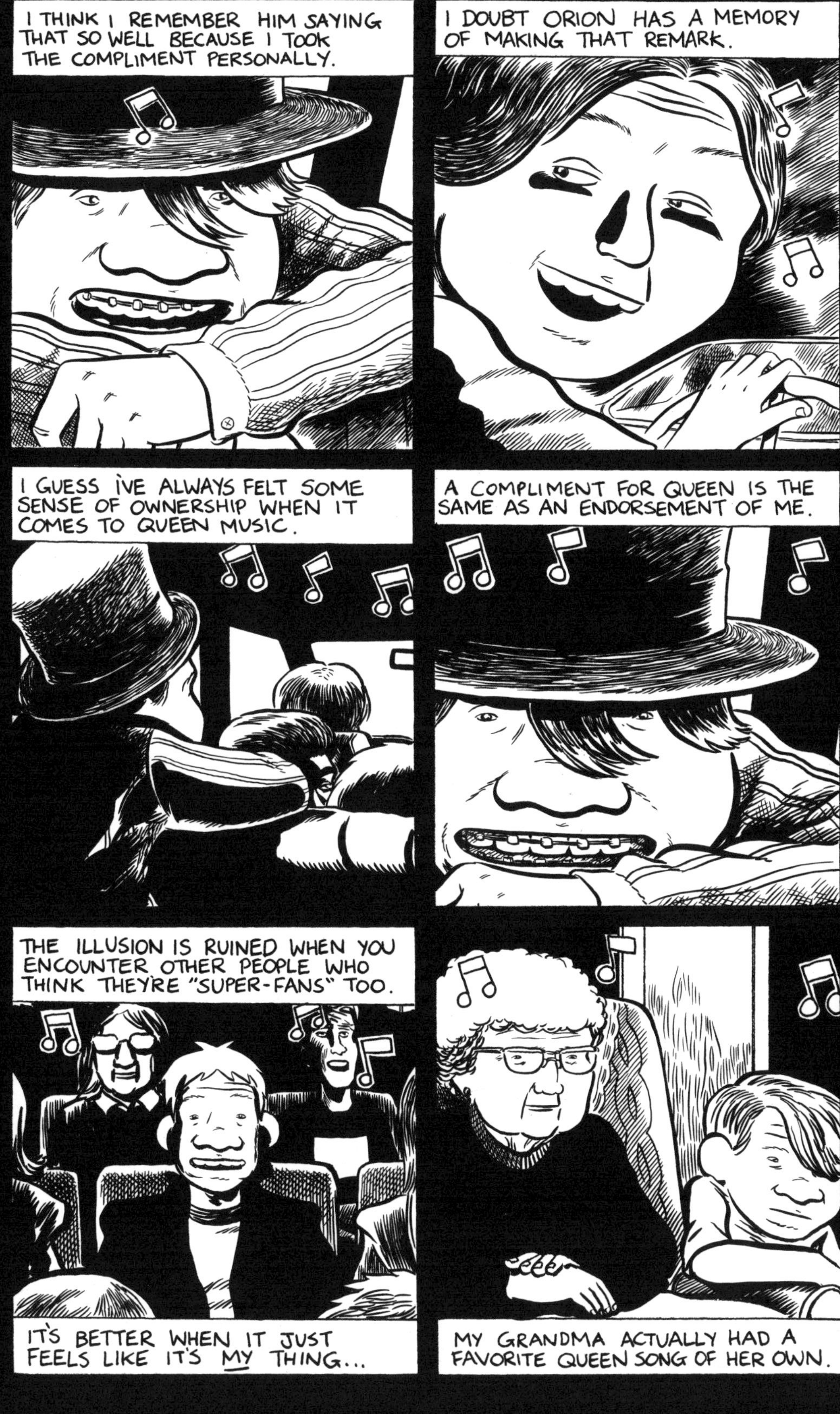
I THINK I REMEMBER HIM SAYING THAT SO WELL BECAUSE I TOOK THE COMPLIMENT PERSONALLY.
I DOUBT ORION HAS A MEMORY OF MAKING THAT REMARK.
I GUESS I'VE ALWAYS FELT SOME SENSE OF OWNERSHIP WHEN IT COMES TO QUEEN MUSIC.
A COMPLIMENT FOR QUEEN IS THE SAME AS AN ENDORSEMENT OF ME.
THE ILLUSION IS RUINED WHEN YOU ENCOUNTER OTHER PEOPLE WHO THINK THEY'RE "SUPER-FANS" TOO.
IT'S BETTER WHEN IT JUST FEELS LIKE IT'S MY THING...
MY GRANDMA ACTUALLY HAD A FAVORITE QUEEN SONG OF HER OWN.

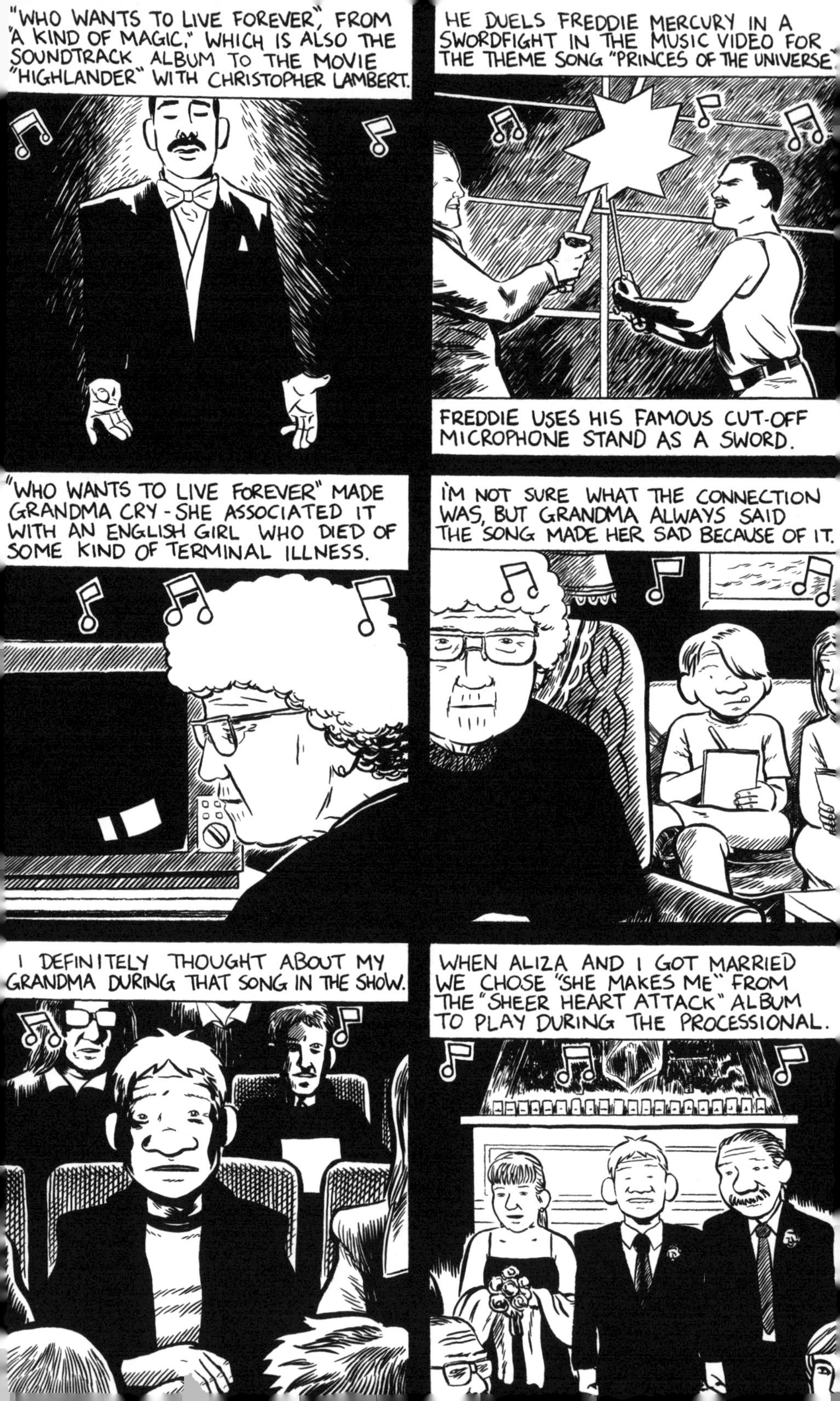
"WHO WANTS TO LIVE FOREVER", FROM "A KIND OF MAGIC," WHICH IS ALSO THE SOUNDTRACK ALBUM TO THE MOVIE "HIGHLANDER" WITH CHRISTOPHER LAMBERT.
HE DUELS FREDDIE MERCURY IN A SWORDFIGHT IN THE MUSIC VIDEO FOR THE THEME SONG "PRINCES OF THE UNIVERSE."
FREDDIE USES HIS FAMOUS CUT-OFF MICROPHONE STAND AS A SWORD.
"WHO WANTS TO LIVE FOREVER" MADE GRANDMA CRY - SHE ASSOCIATED IT WITH AN ENGLISH GIRL WHO DIED OF SOME KIND OF TERMINAL ILLNESS.
I'M NOT SURE WHAT THE CONNECTION WAS, BUT GRANDMA ALWAYS SAID THE SONG MADE HER SAD BECAUSE OF IT.
I DEFINITELY THOUGHT ABOUT MY GRANDMA DURING THAT SONG IN THE SHOW.
WHEN ALIZA AND I GOT MARRIED WE CHOSE "SHE MAKES ME" FROM THE "SHEER HEART ATTACK" ALBUM TO PLAY DURING THE PROCESSIONAL.

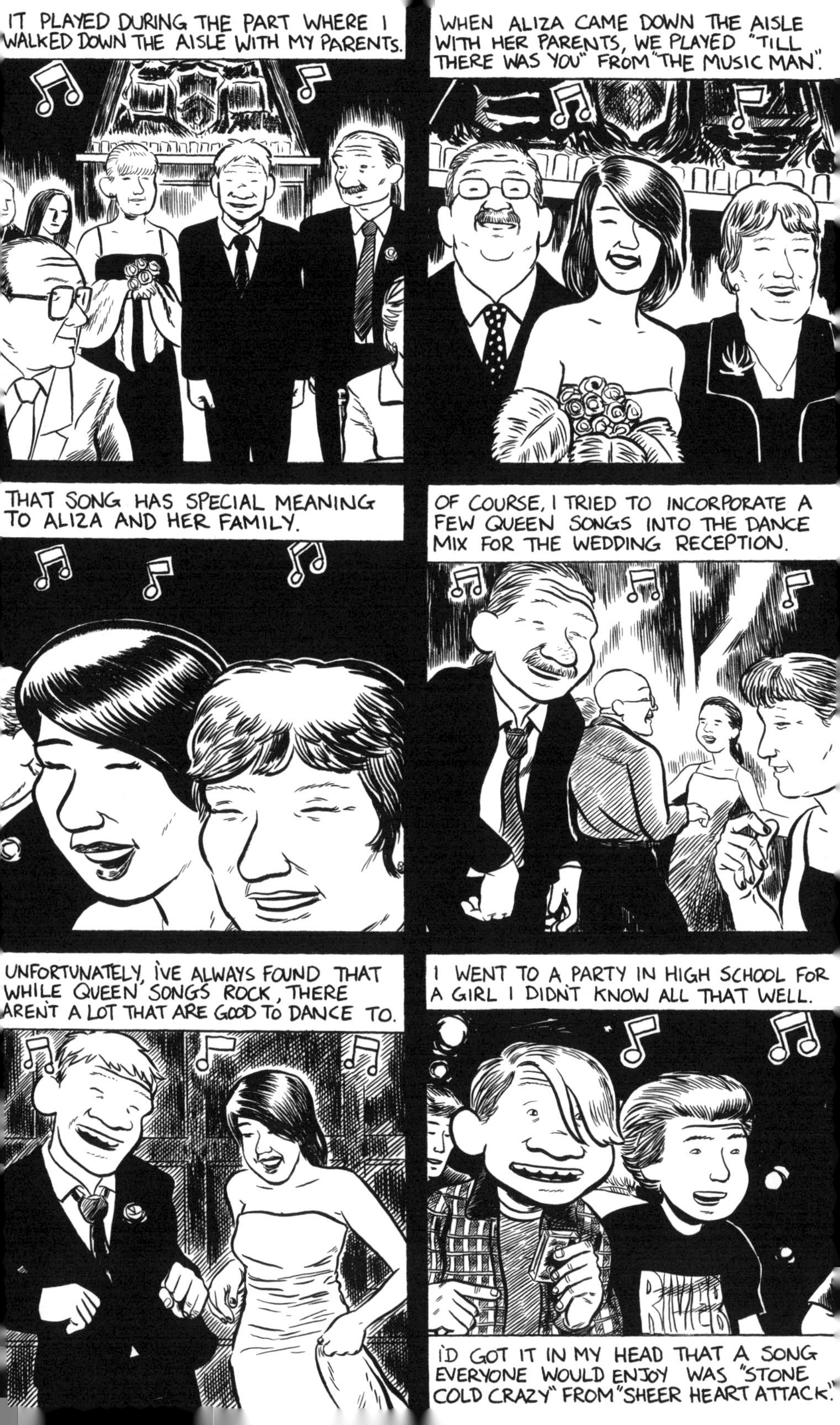
IT PLAYED DURING THE PART WHERE I WALKED DOWN THE AISLE WITH MY PARENTS.
WHEN ALIZA CAME DOWN THE AISLE WITH HER PARENTS, WE PLAYED "TILL THERE WAS YOU" FROM "THE MUSIC MAN".
THAT SONG HAS SPECIAL MEANING TO ALIZA AND HER FAMILY.
OF COURSE, I TRIED TO INCORPORATE A FEW QUEEN SONGS INTO THE DANCE MIX FOR THE WEDDING RECEPTION.
UNFORTUNATELY, I'VE ALWAYS FOUND THAT WHILE QUEEN SONGS ROCK, THERE AREN'T A LOT THAT ARE GOOD TO DANCE TO.
I WENT TO A PARTY IN HIGH SCHOOL FOR A GIRL I DIDN'T KNOW ALL THAT WELL.
I'D GOT IT IN MY HEAD THAT A SONG EVERYONE WOULD ENJOY WAS "STONE COLD CRAZY" FROM "SHEER HEART ATTACK".

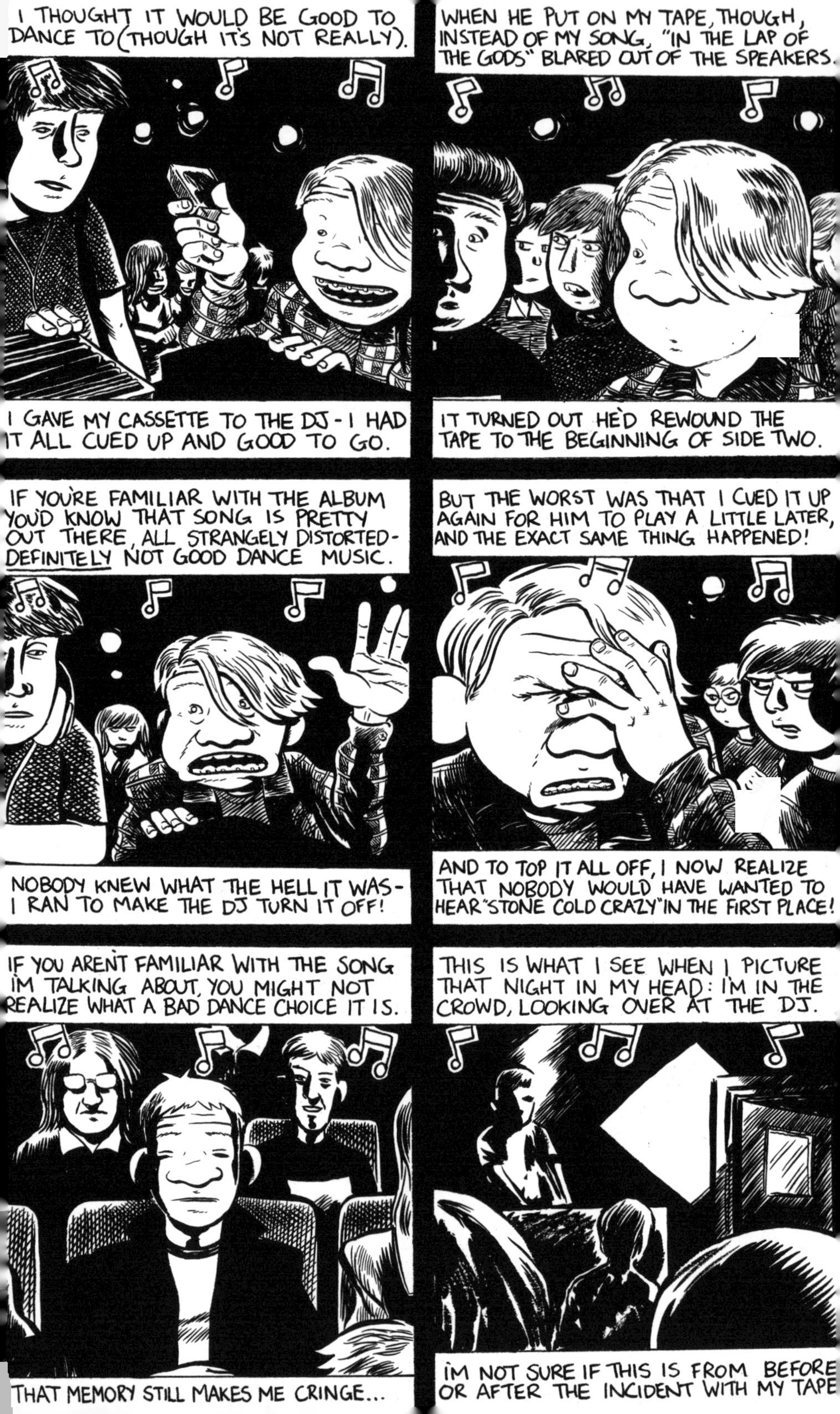
I THOUGHT IT WOULD BE GOOD TO DANCE TO (THOUGH IT'S NOT REALLY).
I GAVE MY CASSETTE TO THE DJ - I HAD IT ALL CUED UP AND GOOD TO GO.
WHEN HE PUT ON MY TAPE, THOUGH, INSTEAD OF MY SONG, "IN THE LAP OF THE GODS" BLARED OUT OF THE SPEAKERS.
IT TURNED OUT HE'D REWOUND THE TAPE TO THE BEGINNING OF SIDE TWO.
IF YOU'RE FAMILIAR WITH THE ALBUM YOU'D KNOW THAT SONG IS PRETTY OUT THERE, ALL STRANGELY DISTORTED- DEFINITELY NOT GOOD DANCE MUSIC.
NOBODY KNEW WHAT THE HELL IT WAS- I RAN TO MAKE THE DJ TURN IT OFF!
BUT THE WORST WAS THAT I CUED IT UP AGAIN FOR HIM TO PLAY A LITTLE LATER, AND THE EXACT SAME THING HAPPENED!
AND TO TOP IT ALL OFF, I NOW REALIZE THAT NOBODY WOULD HAVE WANTED TO HEAR "STONE COLD CRAZY" IN THE FIRST PLACE!
IF YOU AREN'T FAMILIAR WITH THE SONG I'M TALKING ABOUT, YOU MIGHT NOT REALIZE WHAT A BAD DANCE CHOICE IT IS.
THAT MEMORY STILL MAKES ME CRINGE...
THIS IS WHAT I SEE WHEN I PICTURE THAT NIGHT IN MY HEAD: I'M IN THE CROWD, LOOKING OVER AT THE DJ.
I'M NOT SURE IF THIS IS FROM BEFORE OR AFTER THE INCIDENT WITH MY TAPE

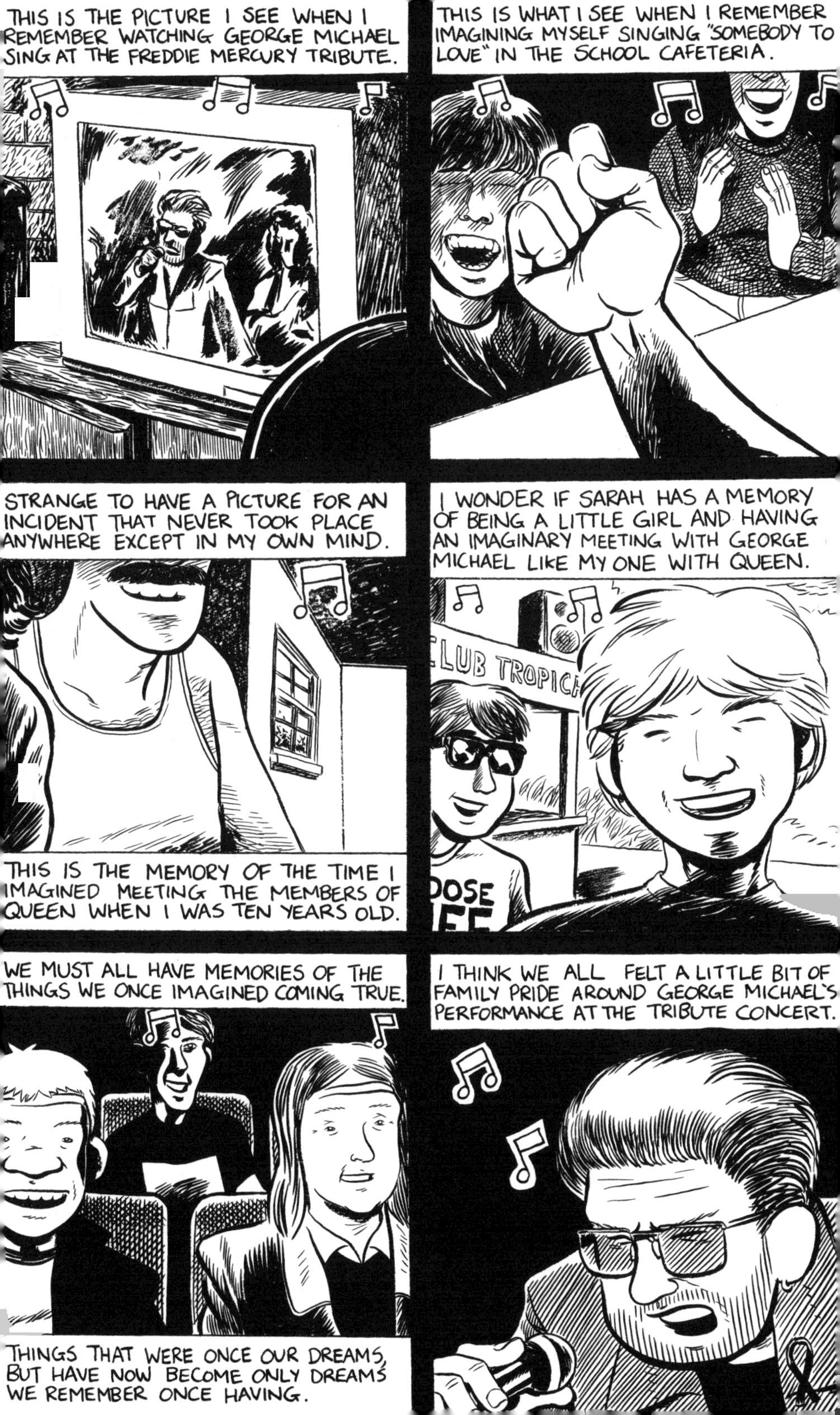
THIS IS THE PICTURE I SEE WHEN I REMEMBER WATCHING GEORGE MICHAEL SING AT THE FREDDIE MERCURY TRIBUTE.
THIS IS WHAT I SEE WHEN I REMEMBER IMAGINING MYSELF SINGING "SOMEBODY TO LOVE" IN THE SCHOOL CAFETERIA.
STRANGE TO HAVE A PICTURE FOR AN INCIDENT THAT NEVER TOOK PLACE ANYWHERE EXCEPT IN MY OWN MIND.
THIS IS THE MEMORY OF THE TIME I IMAGINED MEETING THE MEMBERS OF QUEEN WHEN I WAS TEN YEARS OLD.
I WONDER IF SARAH HAS A MEMORY OF BEING A LITTLE GIRL AND HAVING AN IMAGINARY MEETING WITH GEORGE MICHAEL LIKE MY ONE WITH QUEEN.
WE MUST ALL HAVE MEMORIES OF THE THINGS WE ONCE IMAGINED COMING TRUE.
THINGS THAT WERE ONCE OUR DREAMS, BUT HAVE NOW BECOME ONLY DREAMS WE REMEMBER ONCE HAVING.
I THINK WE ALL FELT A LITTLE BIT OF FAMILY PRIDE AROUND GEORGE MICHAEL'S PERFORMANCE AT THE TRIBUTE CONCERT.

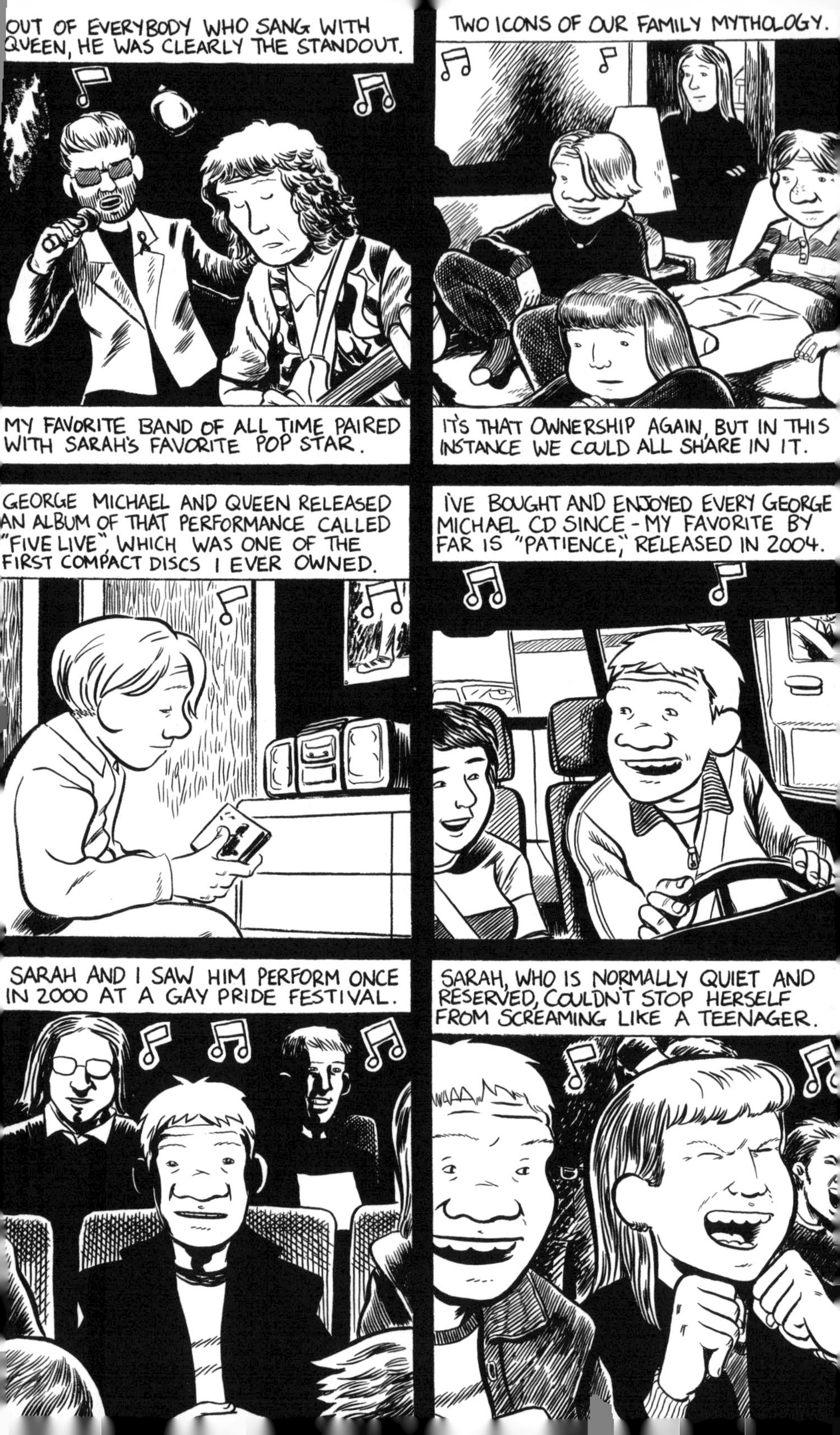
OUT OF EVERYBODY WHO SANG WITH QUEEN, HE WAS CLEARLY THE STANDOUT.
MY FAVORITE BAND OF ALL TIME PAIRED WITH SARAH'S FAVORITE POP STAR.
TWO ICONS OF OUR FAMILY MYTHOLOGY.
IT'S THAT OWNERSHIP AGAIN, BUT IN THIS INSTANCE WE COULD ALL SHARE IN IT.
GEORGE MICHAEL AND QUEEN RELEASED AN ALBUM OF THAT PERFORMANCE CALLED "FIVE LIVE", WHICH WAS ONE OF THE FIRST COMPACT DISCS I EVER OWNED.
I'VE BOUGHT AND ENJOYED EVERY GEORGE MICHAEL CD SINCE - MY FAVORITE BY FAR IS "PATIENCE," RELEASED IN 2004.
SARAH AND I SAW HIM PERFORM ONCE IN 2000 AT A GAY PRIDE FESTIVAL.
SARAH, WHO IS NORMALLY QUIET AND RESERVED, COULDN'T STOP HERSELF FROM SCREAMING LIKE A TEENAGER.

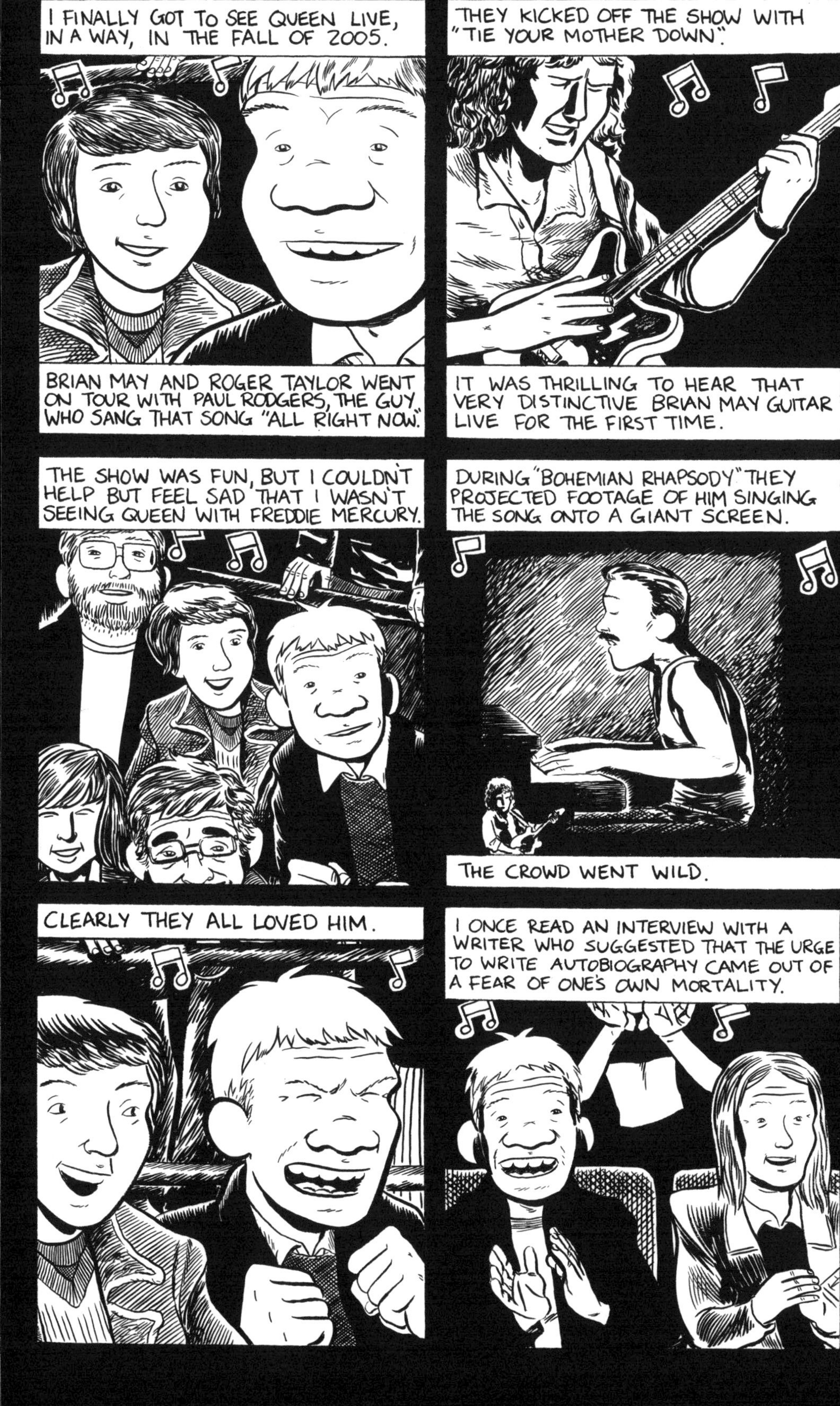
I FINALLY GOT TO SEE QUEEN LIVE, IN A WAY, IN THE FALL OF 2005.
BRIAN MAY AND ROGER TAYLOR WENT ON TOUR WITH PAUL RODGERS, THE GUY WHO SANG THAT SONG "ALL RIGHT NOW."
THEY KICKED OFF THE SHOW WITH "TIE YOUR MOTHER DOWN."
IT WAS THRILLING TO HEAR THAT VERY DISTINCTIVE BRIAN MAY GUITAR LIVE FOR THE FIRST TIME.
THE SHOW WAS FUN, BUT I COULDN'T HELP BUT FEEL SAD THAT I WASN'T SEEING QUEEN WITH FREDDIE MERCURY.
DURING "BOHEMIAN RHAPSODY" THEY PROJECTED FOOTAGE OF HIM SINGING THE SONG ONTO A GIANT SCREEN.
THE CROWD WENT WILD.
CLEARLY THEY ALL LOVED HIM.
I ONCE READ AN INTERVIEW WITH A WRITER WHO SUGGESTED THAT THE URGE TO WRITE AUTOBIOGRAPHY CAME OUT OF A FEAR OF ONE'S OWN MORTALITY.

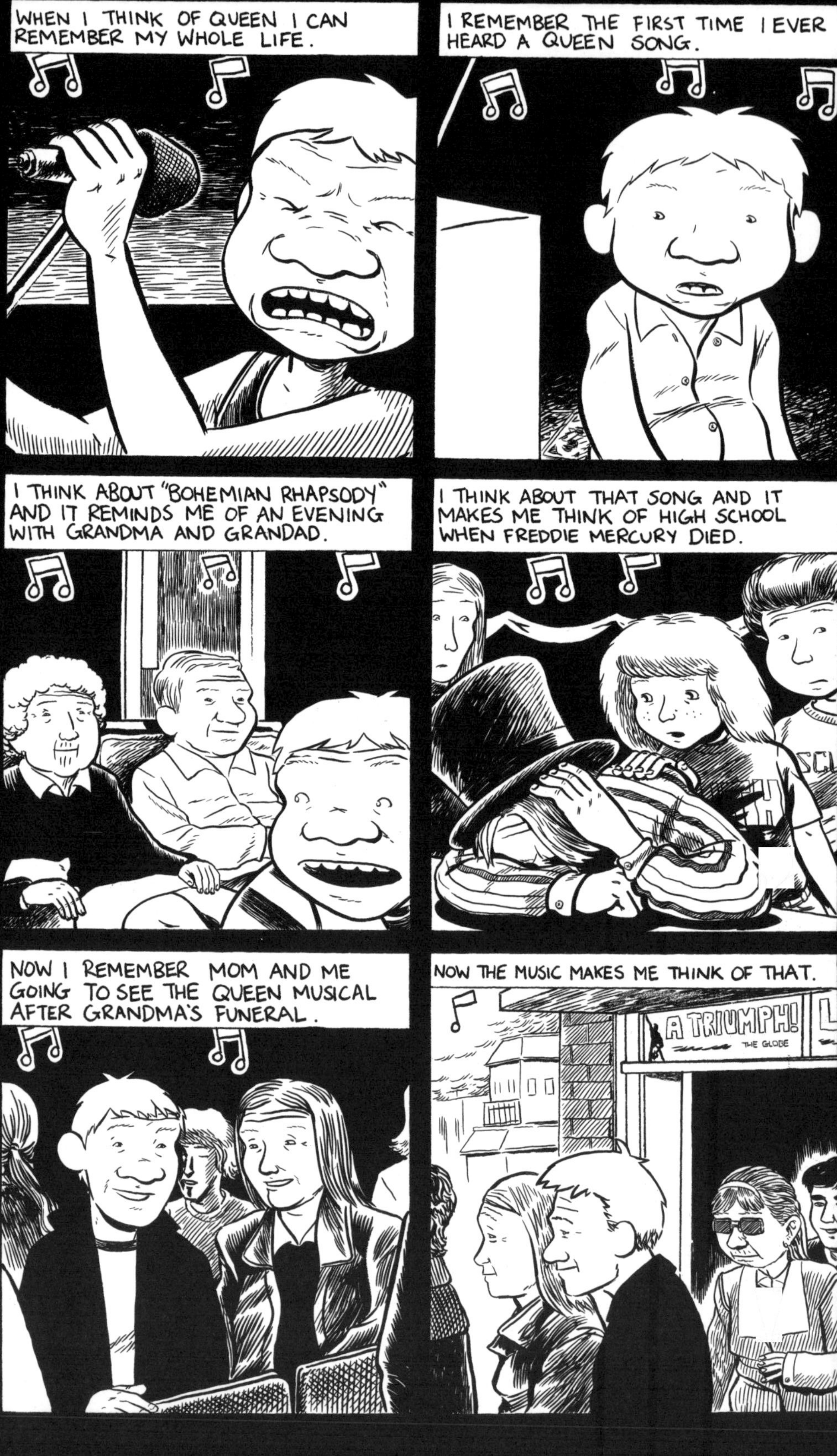

WHEN I THINK OF QUEEN I CAN REMEMBER MY WHOLE LIFE.
I REMEMBER THE FIRST TIME I EVER HEARD A QUEEN SONG.
I THINK ABOUT "BOHEMIAN RHAPSODY" AND IT REMINDS ME OF AN EVENING WITH GRANDMA AND GRANDAD.
I THINK ABOUT THAT SONG AND IT MAKES ME THINK OF HIGH SCHOOL WHEN FREDDIE MERCURY DIED.
NOW I REMEMBER MOM AND ME GOING TO SEE THE QUEEN MUSICAL AFTER GRANDMA'S FUNERAL.
NOW THE MUSIC MAKES ME THINK OF THAT.
A TRIUMPH!
THE GLOBE

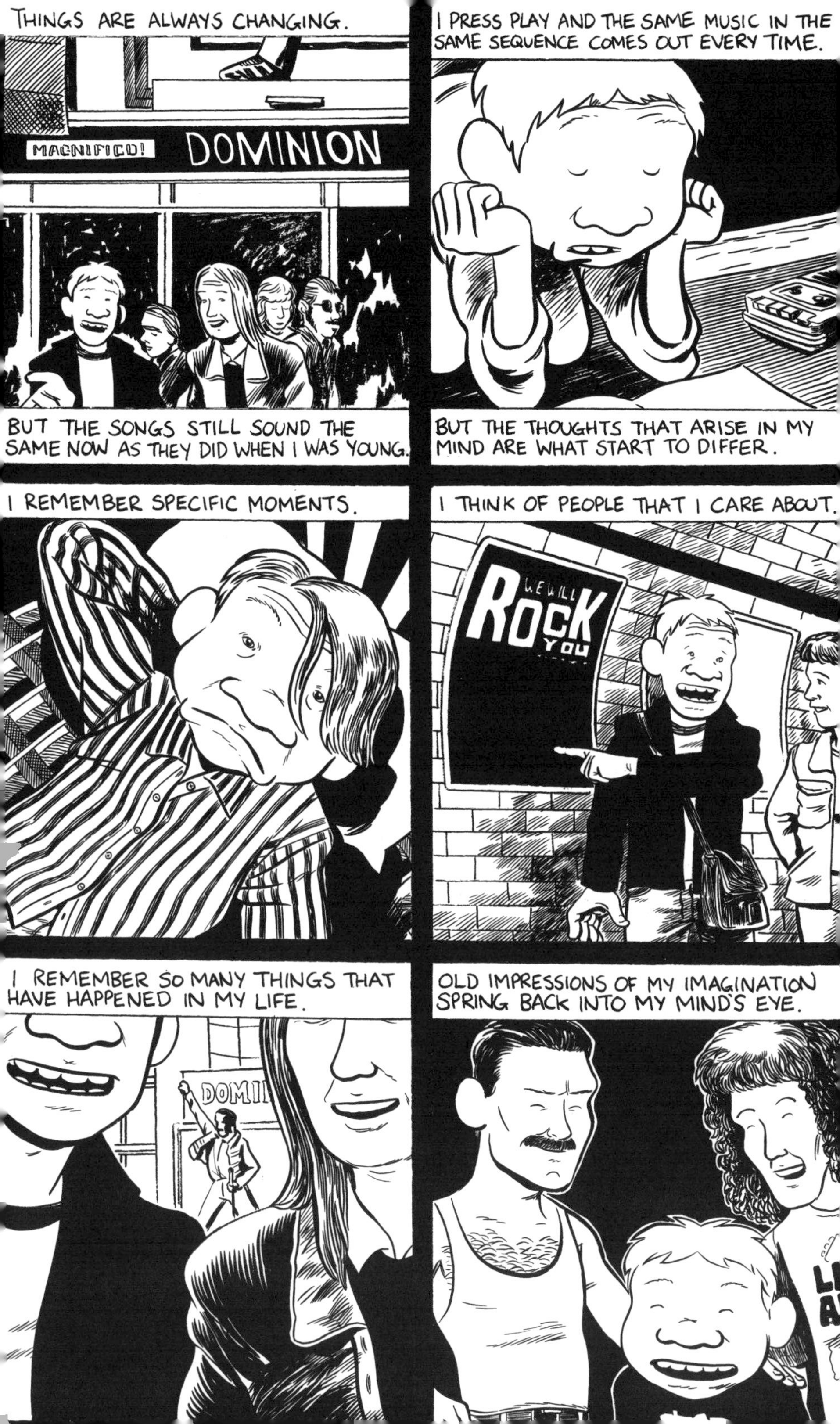
THINGS ARE ALWAYS CHANGING.
MAGNIFICO!
DOMINION
BUT THE SONGS STILL SOUND THE SAME NOW AS THEY DID WHEN I WAS YOUNG.
I PRESS PLAY AND THE SAME MUSIC IN THE SAME SEQUENCE COMES OUT EVERY TIME.
BUT THE THOUGHTS THAT ARISE IN MY MIND ARE WHAT START TO DIFFER.
I REMEMBER SPECIFIC MOMENTS.
I THINK OF PEOPLE THAT I CARE ABOUT.
WE WILL ROCK YOU
I REMEMBER SO MANY THINGS THAT HAVE HAPPENED IN MY LIFE.
OLD IMPRESSIONS OF MY IMAGINATION SPRING BACK INTO MY MIND'S EYE.

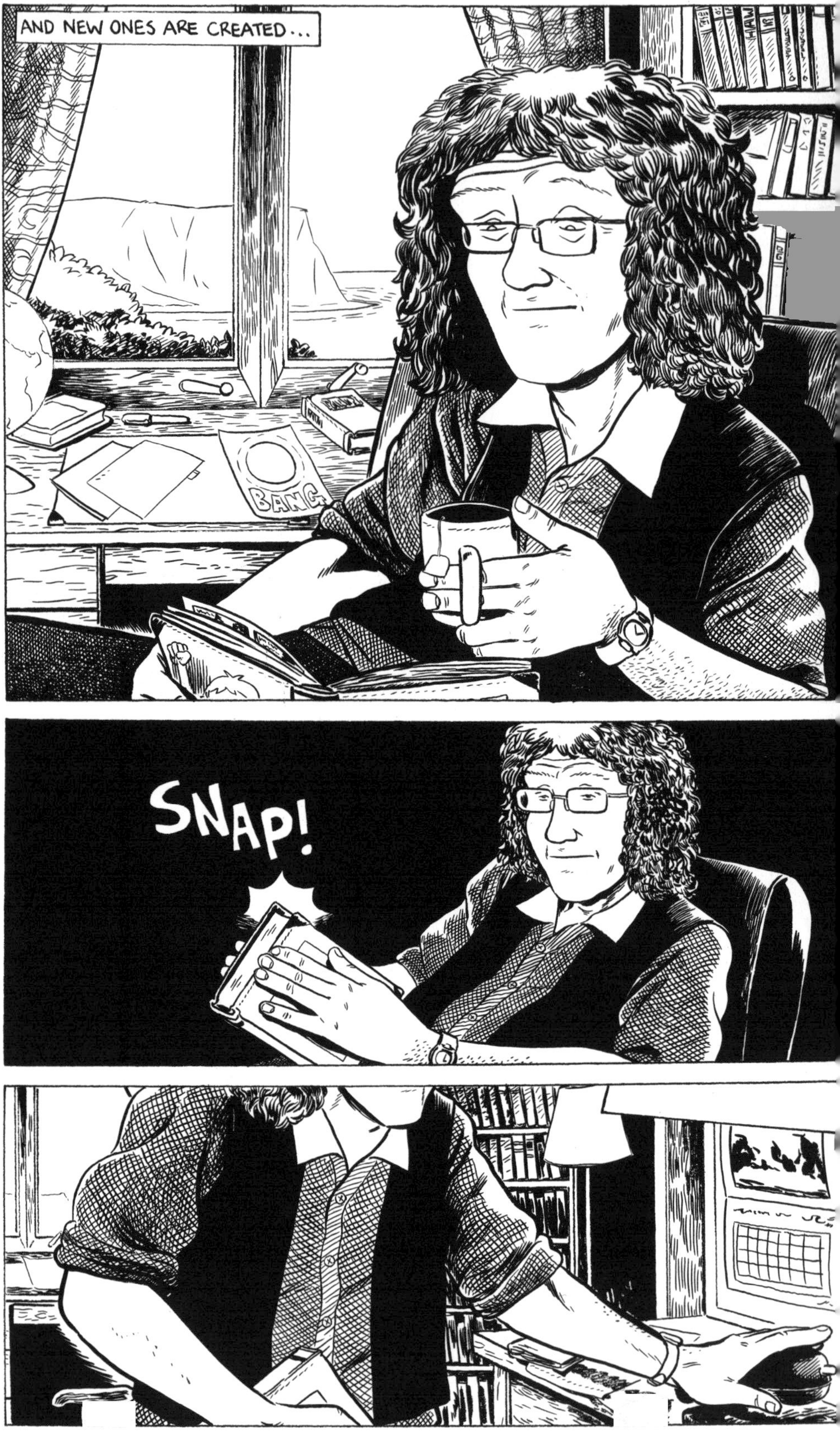
AND NEW ONES ARE CREATED...
BANG
SNAP!

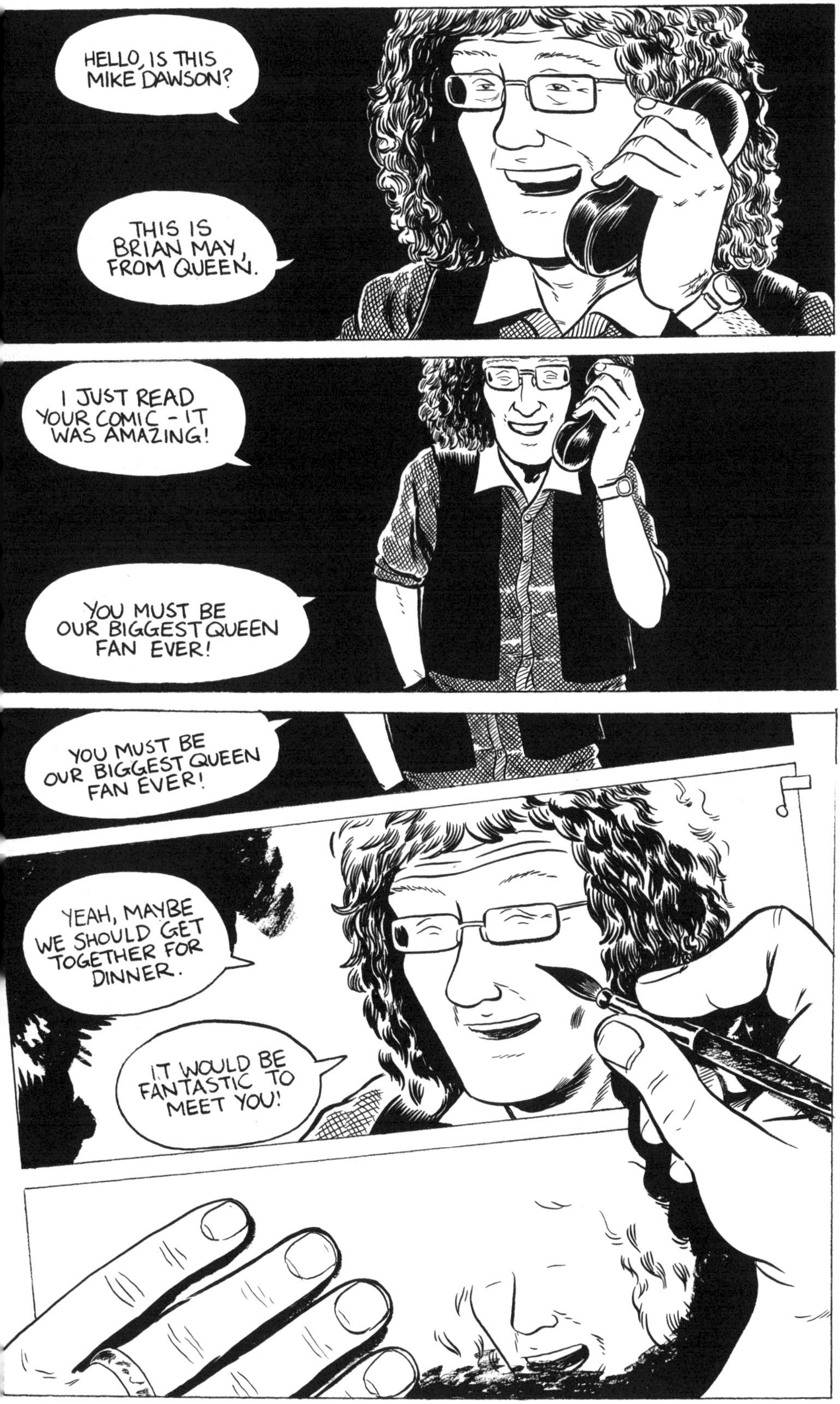
HELLO, IS THIS MIKE DAWSON?
THIS IS BRIAN MAY, FROM QUEEN.
I JUST READ YOUR COMIC - IT WAS AMAZING!
YOU MUST BE OUR BIGGEST QUEEN FAN EVER!
YOU MUST BE OUR BIGGEST QUEEN FAN EVER!
YEAH, MAYBE WE SHOULD GET TOGETHER FOR DINNER.
IT WOULD BE FANTASTIC TO MEET YOU!

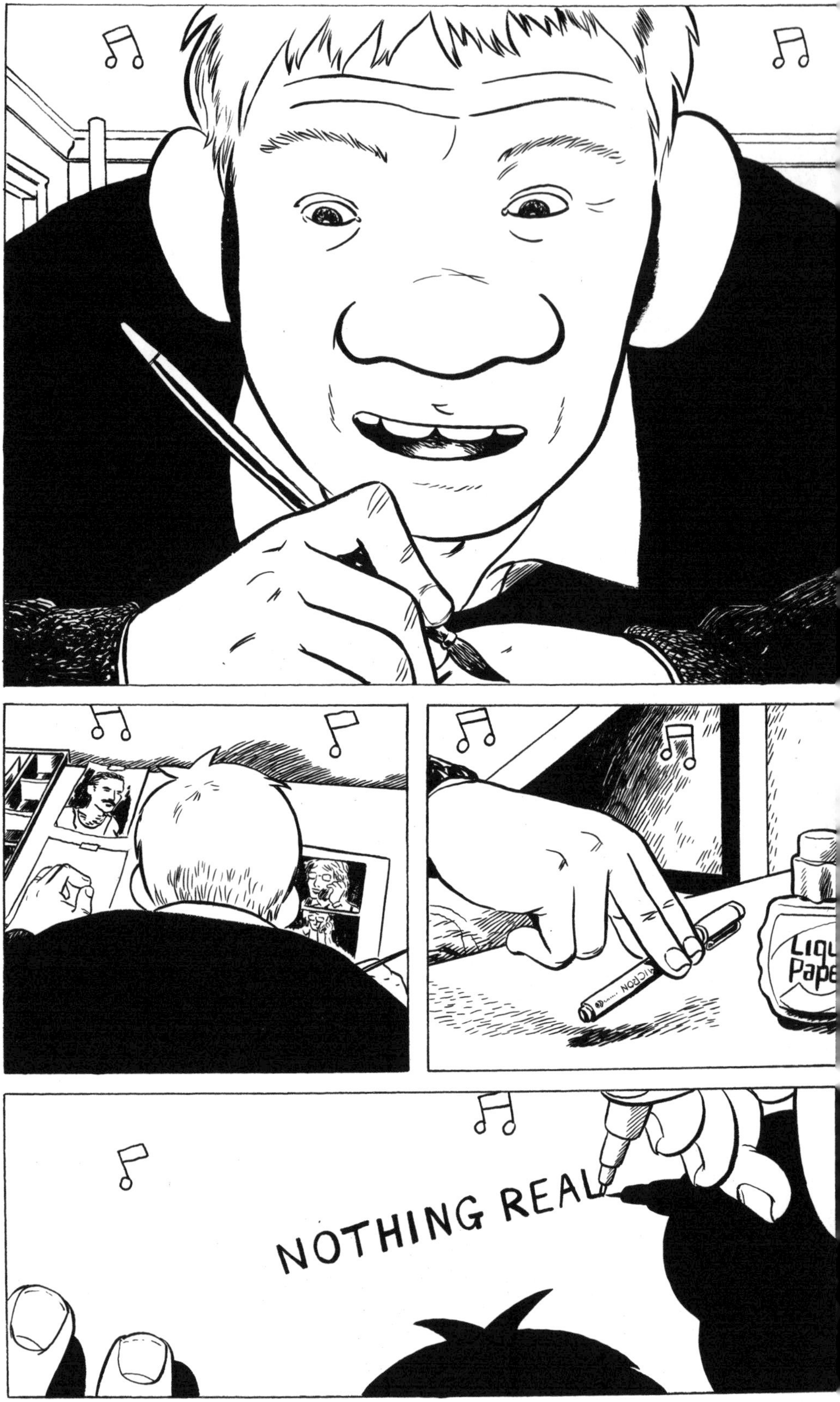
NOTHING REAL

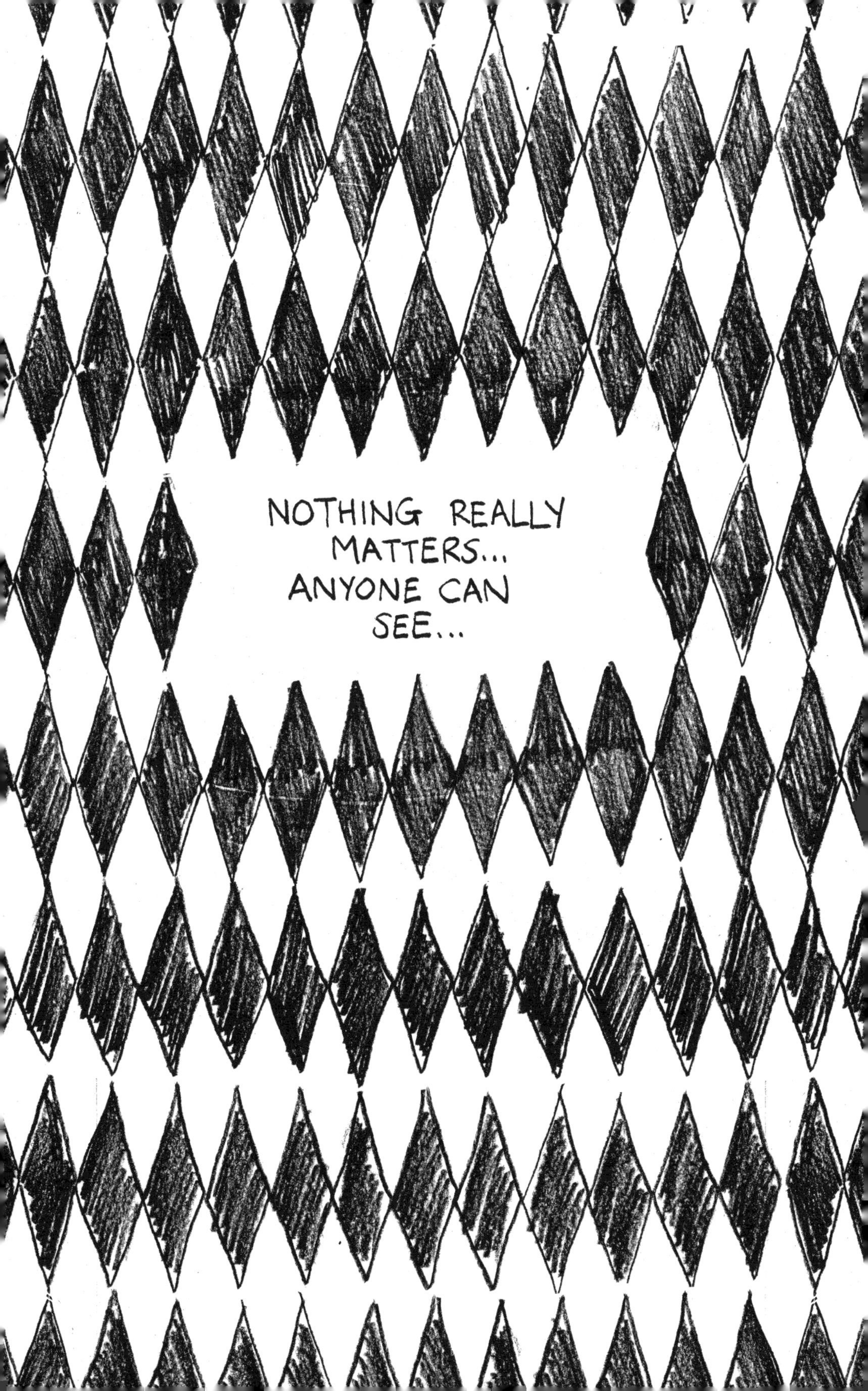
NOTHING REALLY MATTERS...
ANYONE CAN SEE...

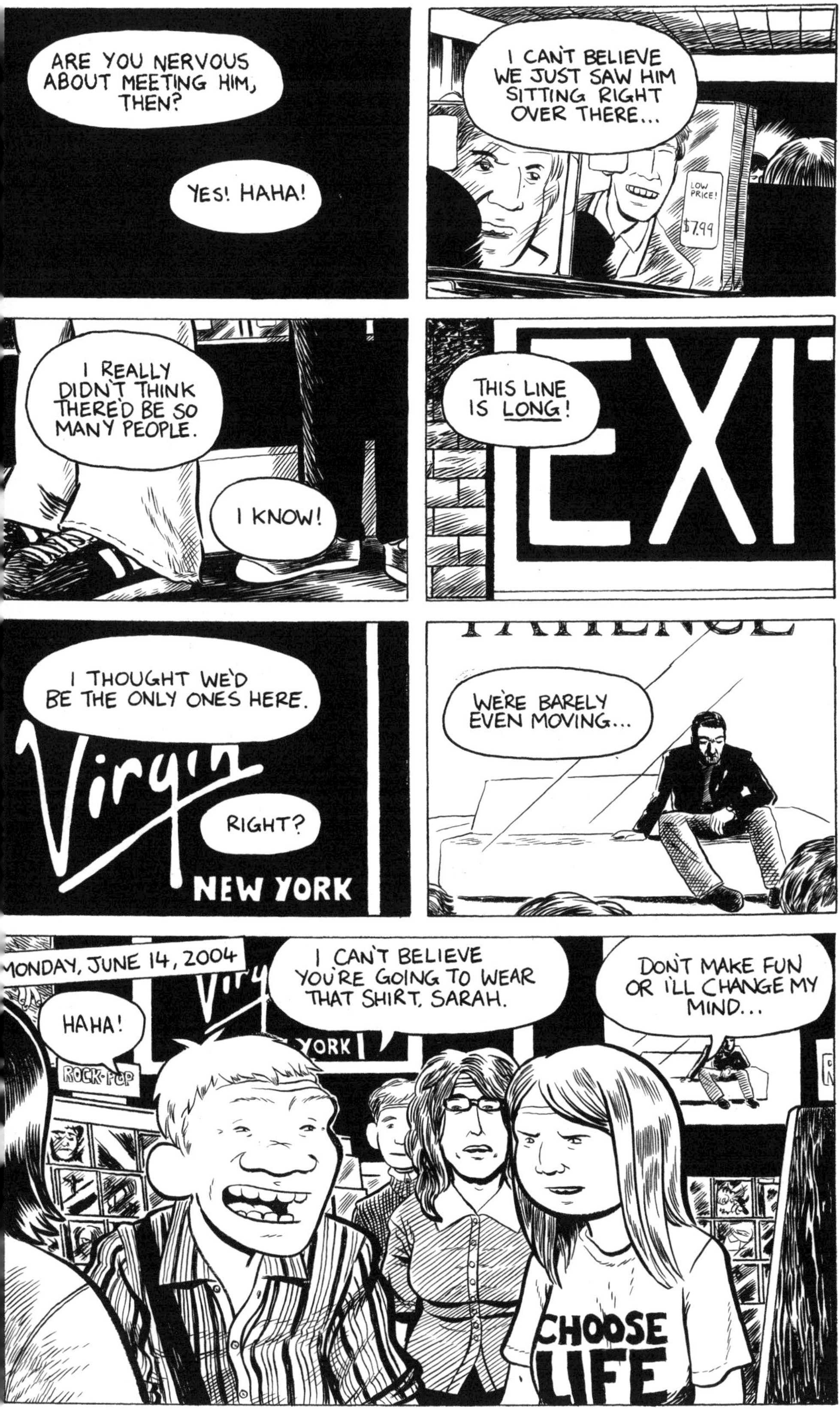
ARE YOU NERVOUS ABOUT MEETING HIM, THEN?
YES! HAHA!
I CAN'T BELIEVE WE JUST SAW HIM SITTING RIGHT OVER THERE...
LOW PRICE!
$7.99
I REALLY DIDN'T THINK THERE'D BE SO MANY PEOPLE.
I KNOW!
THIS LINE IS LONG!
EXI
I THOUGHT WE'D BE THE ONLY ONES HERE.
Virgin
RIGHT?
NEW YORK
WE'RE BARELY EVEN MOVING...
MONDAY, JUNE 14, 2004
HAHA!
ROCK-POP
I CAN'T BELIEVE YOU'RE GOING TO WEAR THAT SHIRT, SARAH.
YORK
DON'T MAKE FUN OR I'LL CHANGE MY MIND...
CHOOSE LIFE

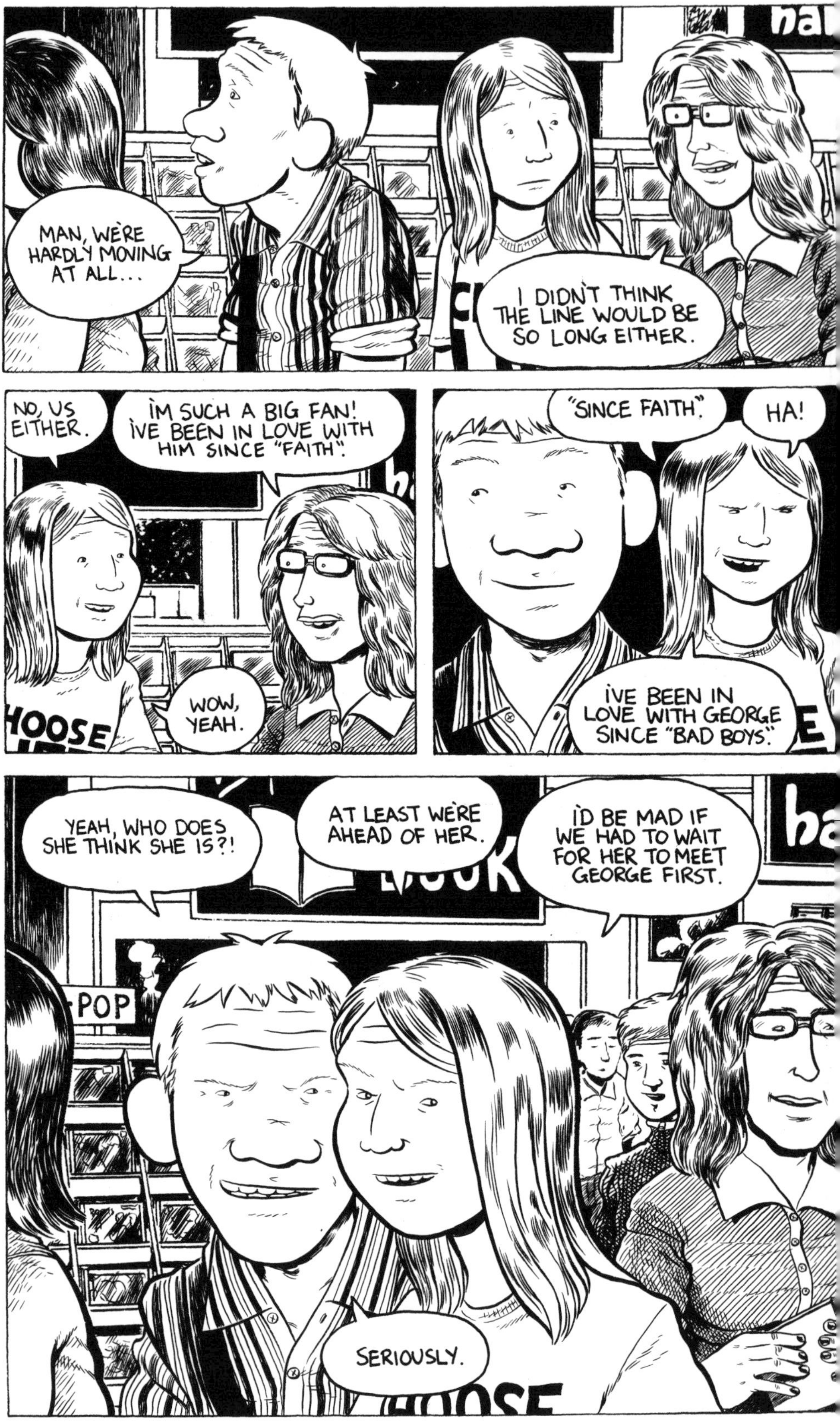
MAN, WE'RE HARDLY MOVING AT ALL...
I DIDN'T THINK THE LINE WOULD BE SO LONG EITHER.
NO, US EITHER.
I'M SUCH A BIG FAN! I'VE BEEN IN LOVE WITH HIM SINCE "FAITH".
WOW, YEAH.
"SINCE FAITH".
HA!
I'VE BEEN IN LOVE WITH GEORGE SINCE "BAD BOYS."
YEAH, WHO DOES SHE THINK SHE IS?!
AT LEAST WE'RE AHEAD OF HER.
I'D BE MAD IF WE HAD TO WAIT FOR HER TO MEET GEORGE FIRST.
SERIOUSLY.

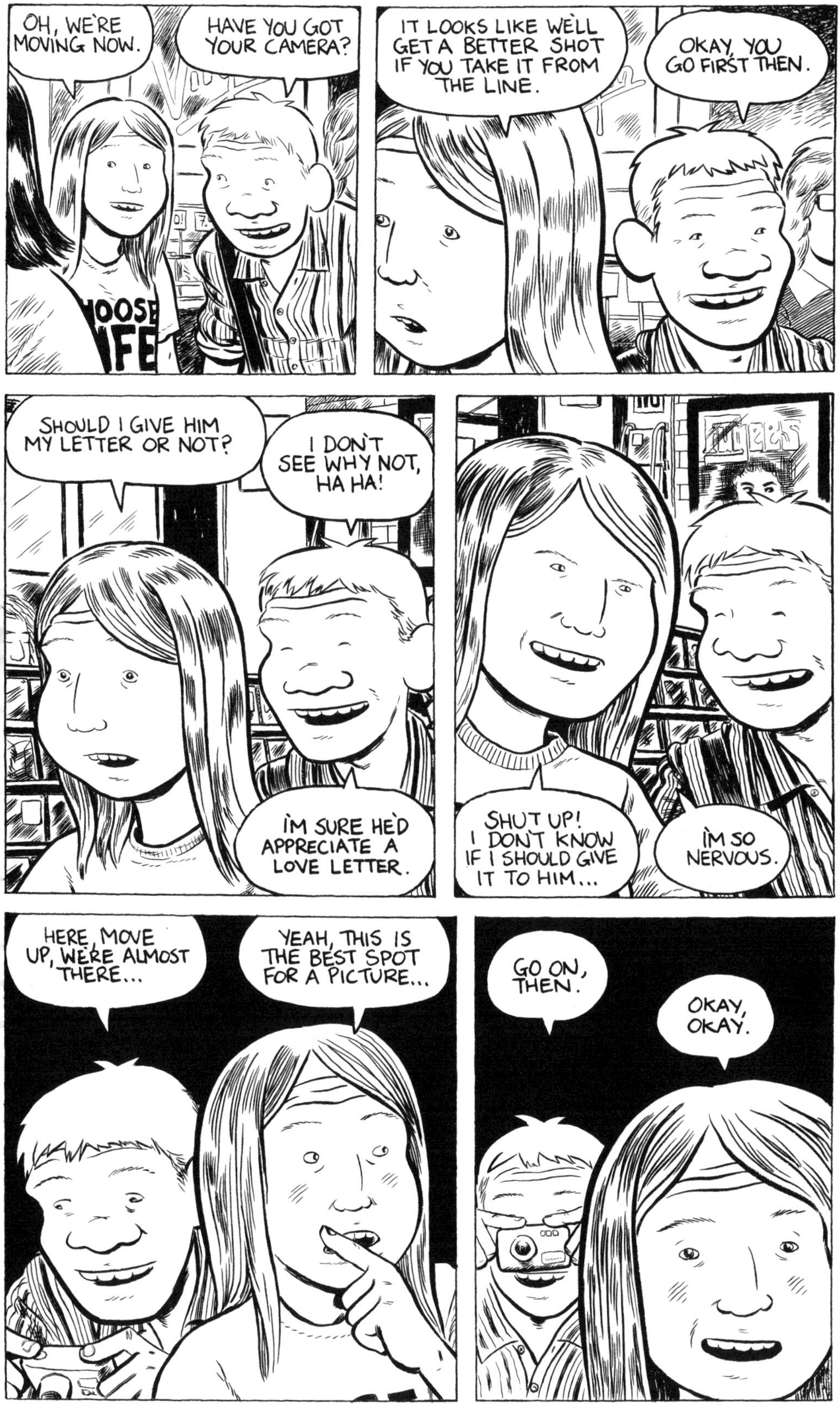
OH, WE'RE MOVING NOW.
HAVE YOU GOT YOUR CAMERA?
IT LOOKS LIKE WE'LL GET A BETTER SHOT IF YOU TAKE IT FROM THE LINE.
OKAY, YOU GO FIRST THEN.
SHOULD I GIVE HIM MY LETTER OR NOT?
I DON'T SEE WHY NOT, HA HA!
I'M SURE HE'D APPRECIATE A LOVE LETTER.
SHUT UP! I DON'T KNOW IF I SHOULD GIVE IT TO HIM...
I'M SO NERVOUS.
HERE, MOVE UP, WE'RE ALMOST THERE...
YEAH, THIS IS THE BEST SPOT FOR A PICTURE...
GO ON, THEN.
OKAY, OKAY.

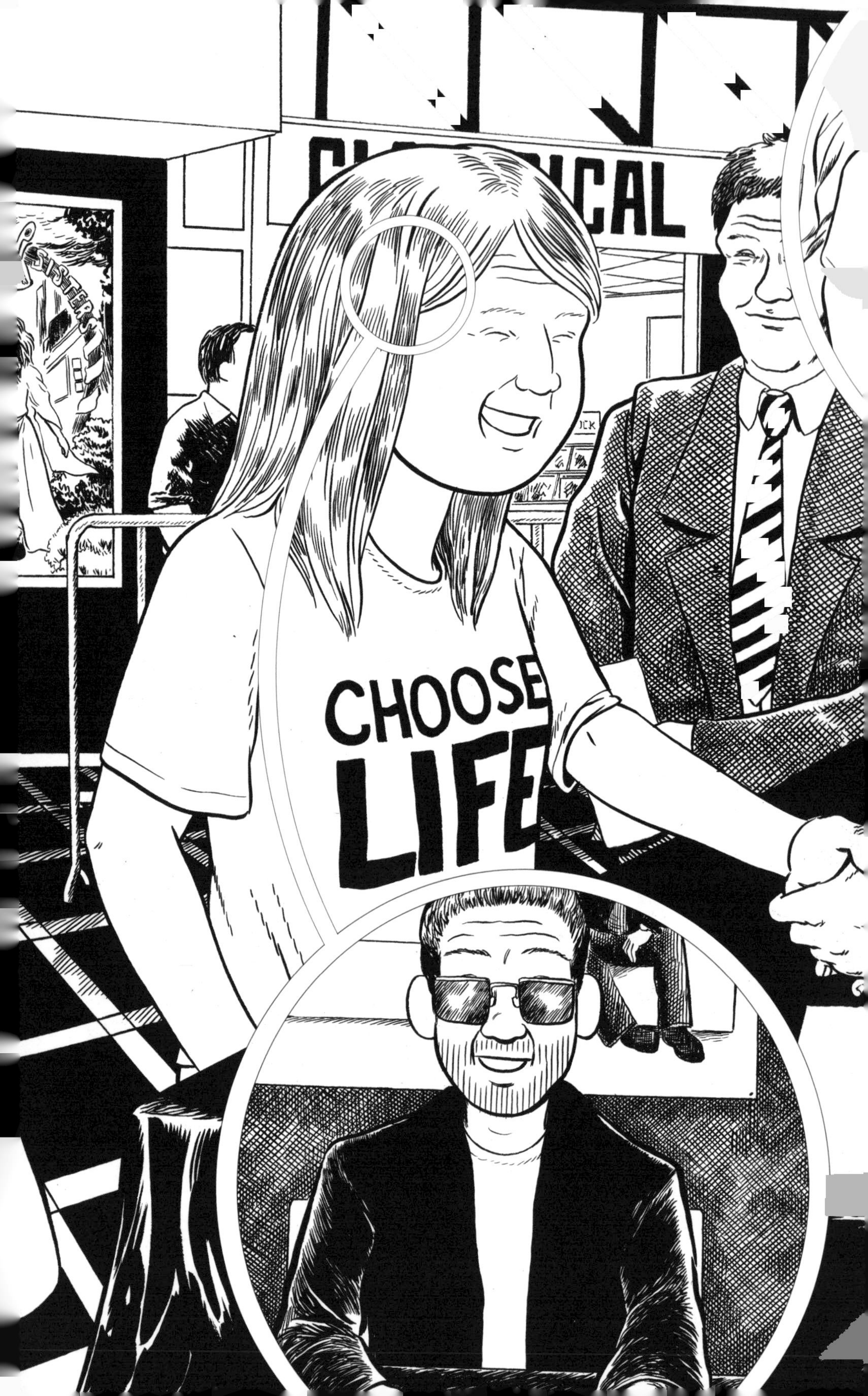
CHOOSE
LIFE

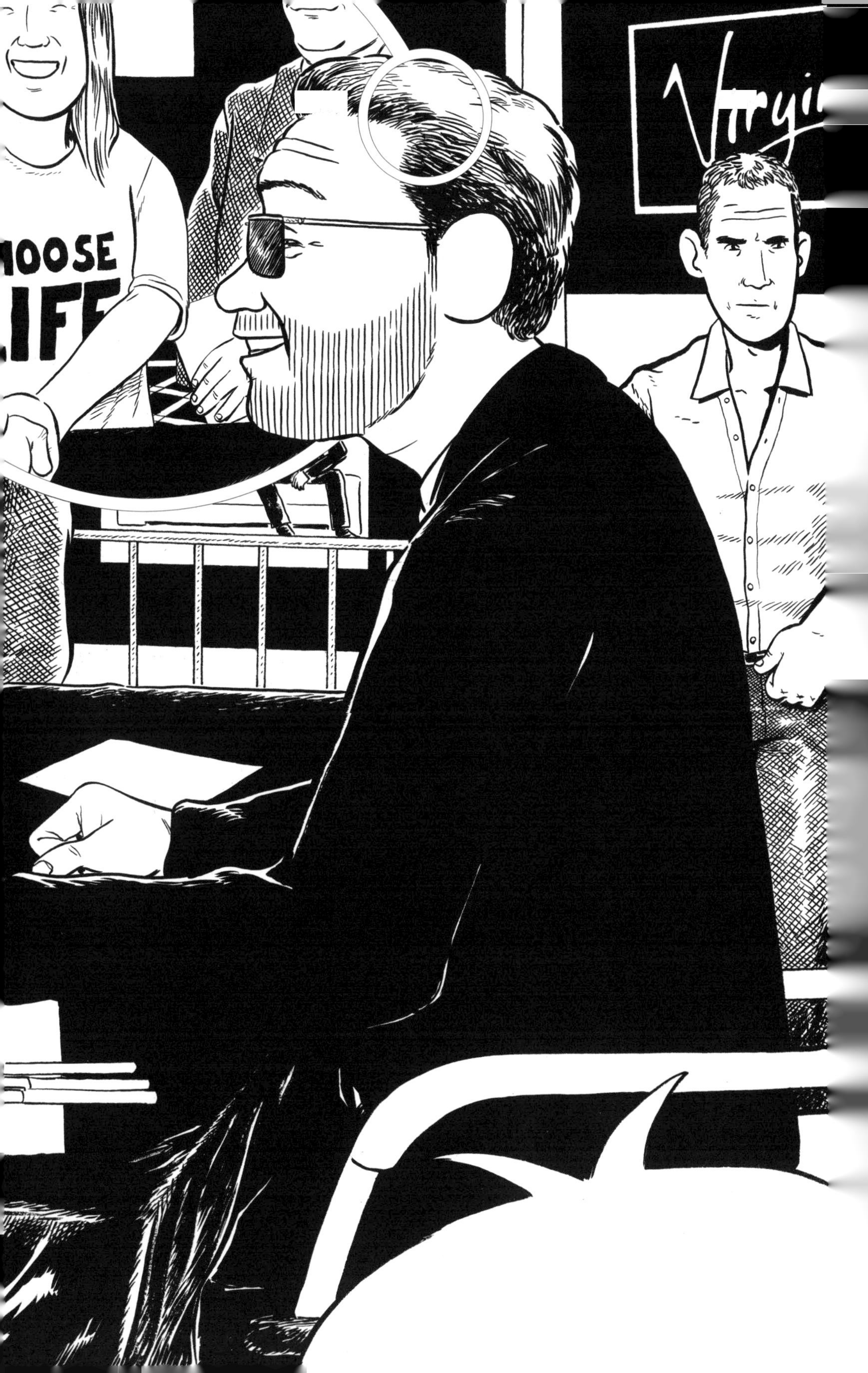
HOOSE
LIF

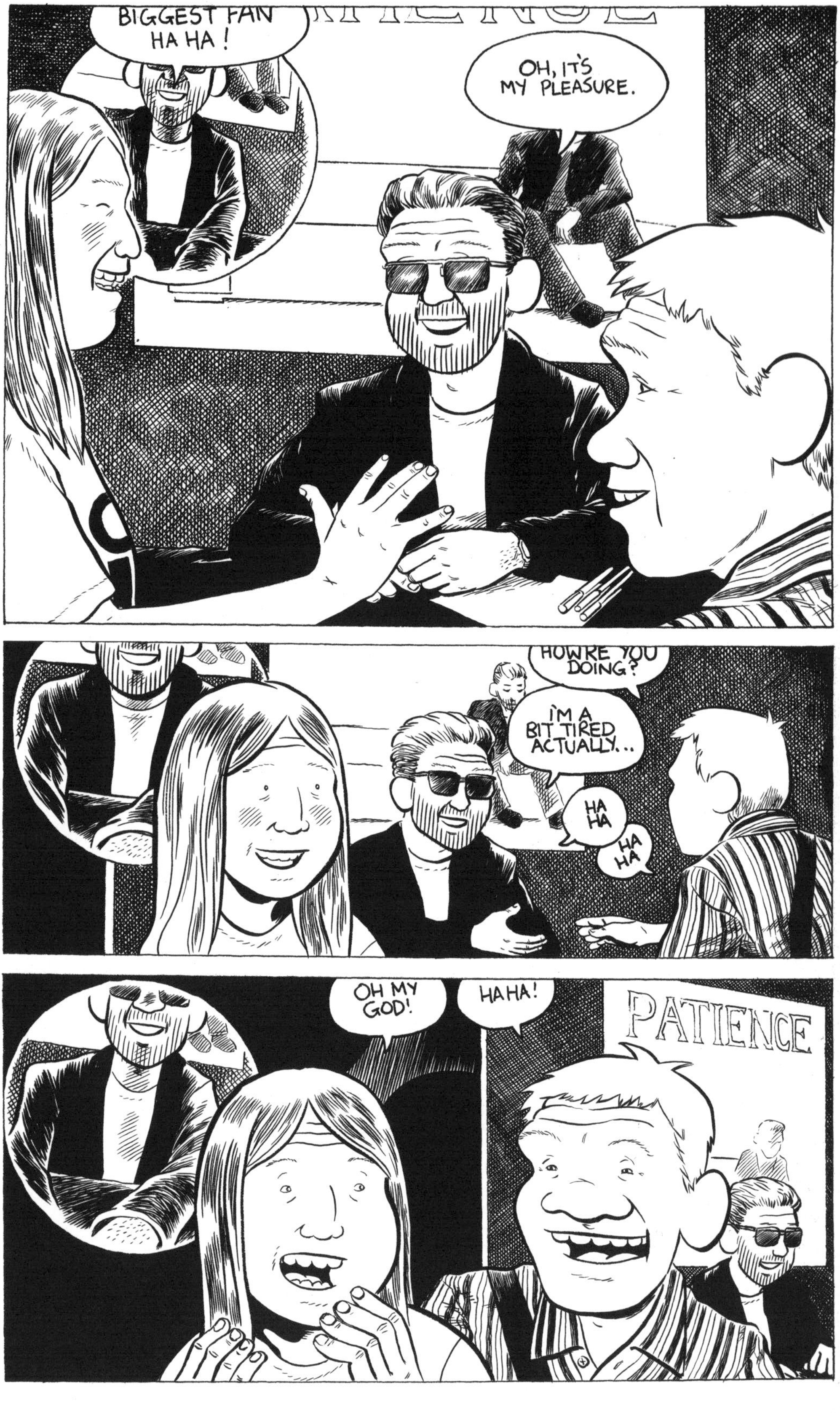
BIGGEST FAN HA HA!
OH, IT'S MY PLEASURE.
HOW'RE YOU DOING?
I'M A BIT TIRED ACTUALLY...
HA HA
HA HA
OH MY GOD!
HA HA!
PATIENCE

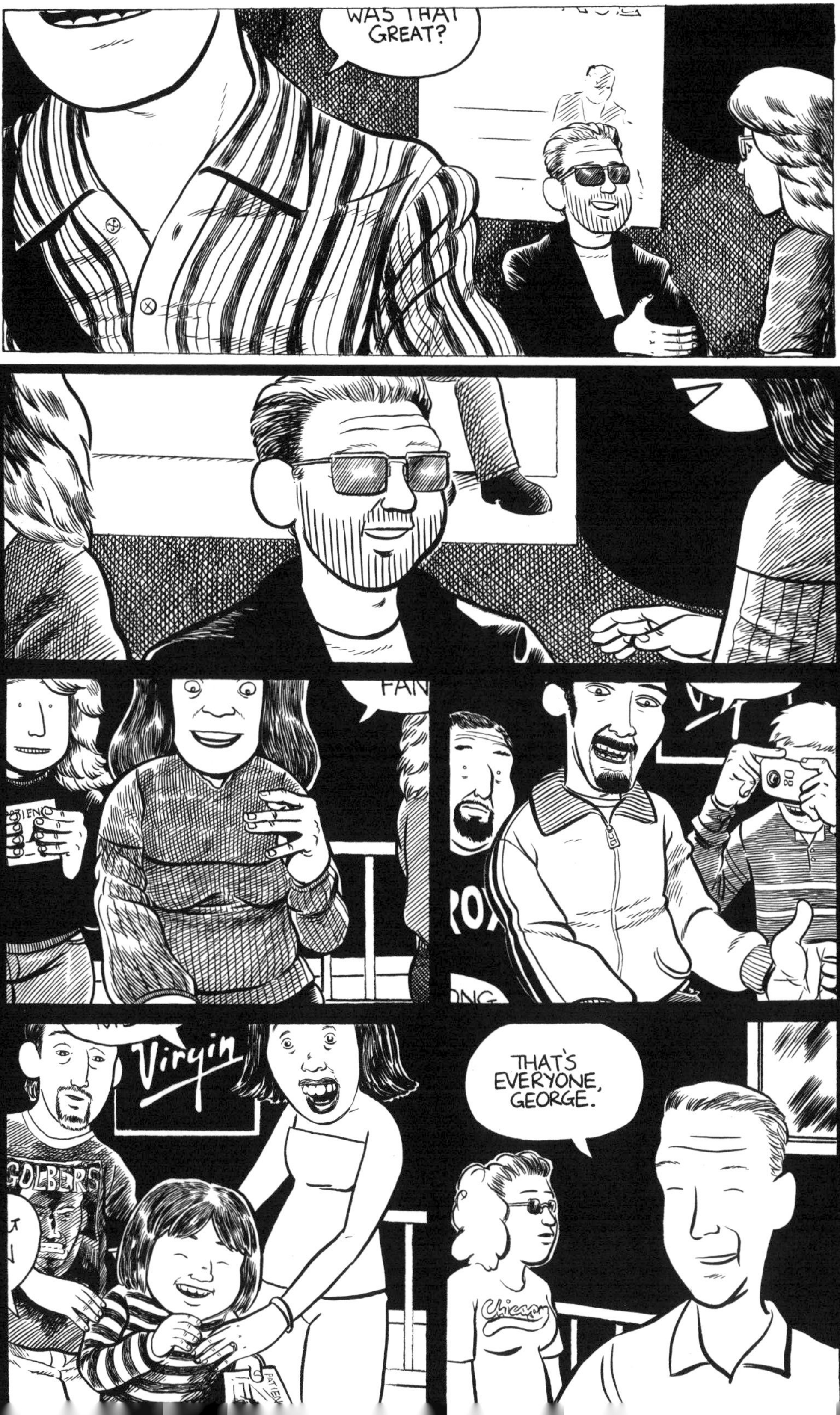
WAS THAT GREAT?
Virgin
THAT'S EVERYONE, GEORGE.

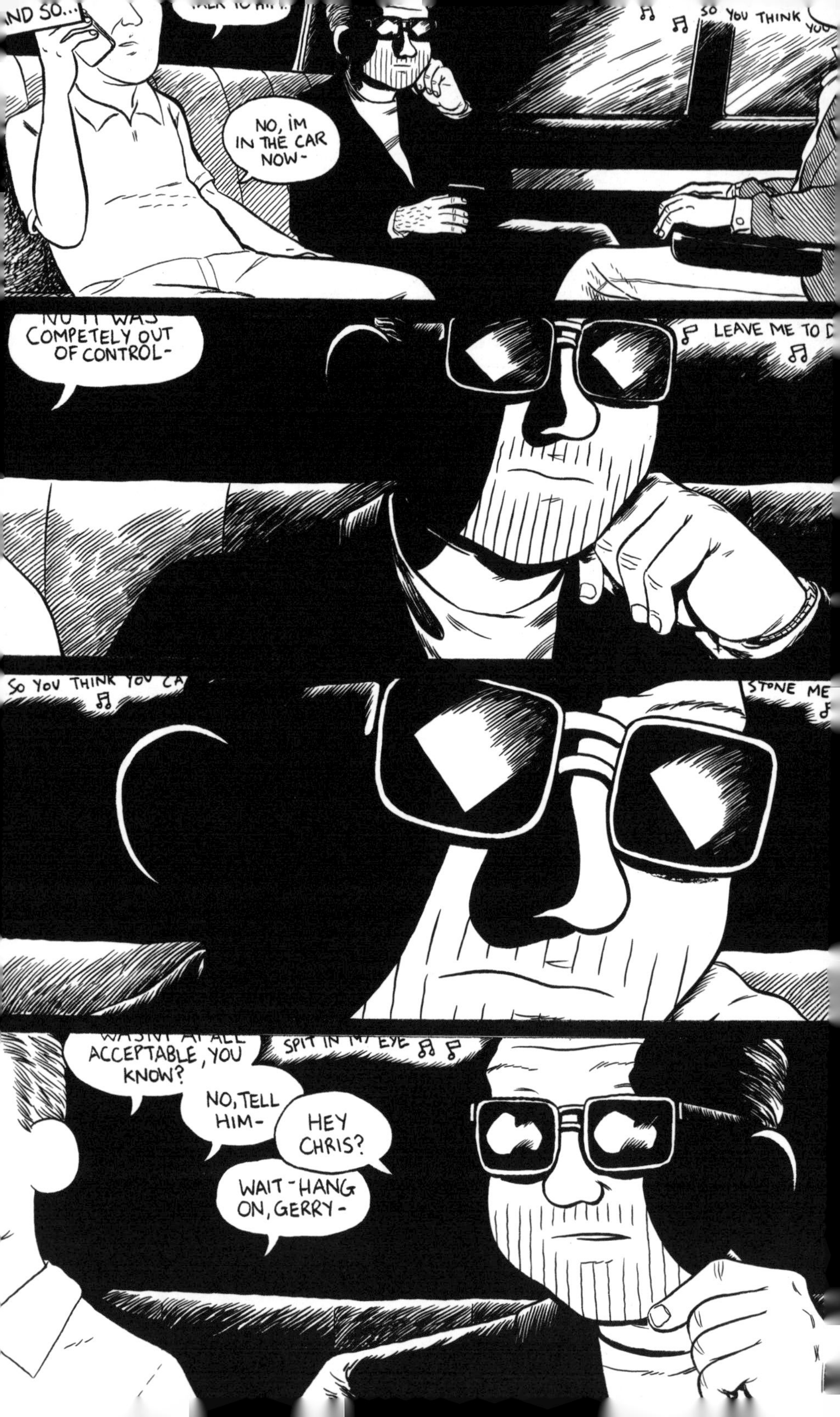
AND SO...
SO YOU THINK
NO, IM IN THE CAR NOW-
COMPETELY OUT OF CONTROL-
LEAVE ME TO
SO YOU THINK YOU
STONE ME
ACCEPTABLE, YOU KNOW?
SPIT IN
NO, TELL HIM-
HEY CHRIS?
WAIT-HANG ON, GERRY-

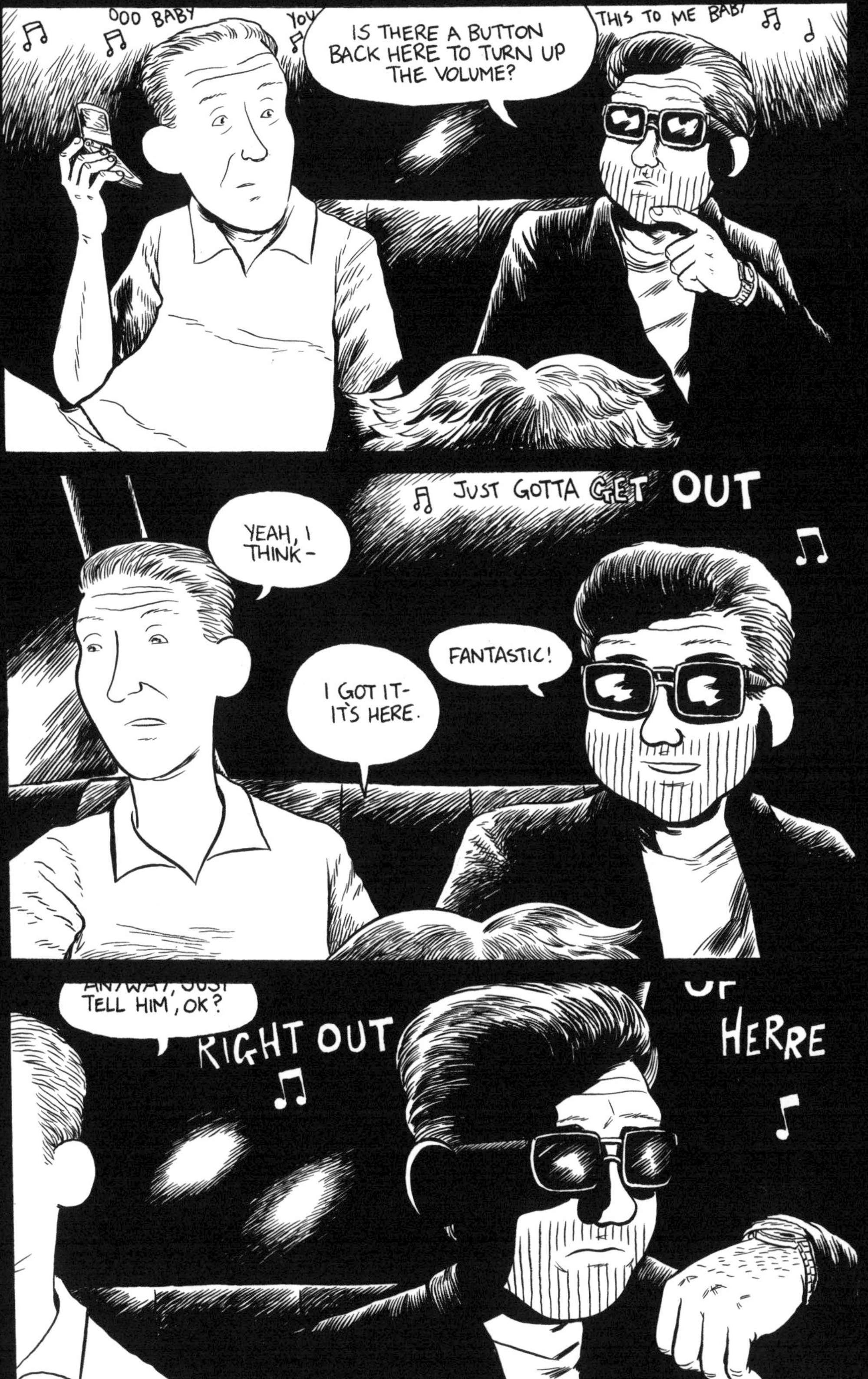
OOO BABY
IS THERE A BUTTON BACK HERE TO TURN UP THE VOLUME?
THIS TO ME BABY
JUST GOTTA GET OUT
YEAH, I THINK-
FANTASTIC!
I GOT IT- IT'S HERE.
TELL HIM', OK?
RIGHT OUT
HERRE

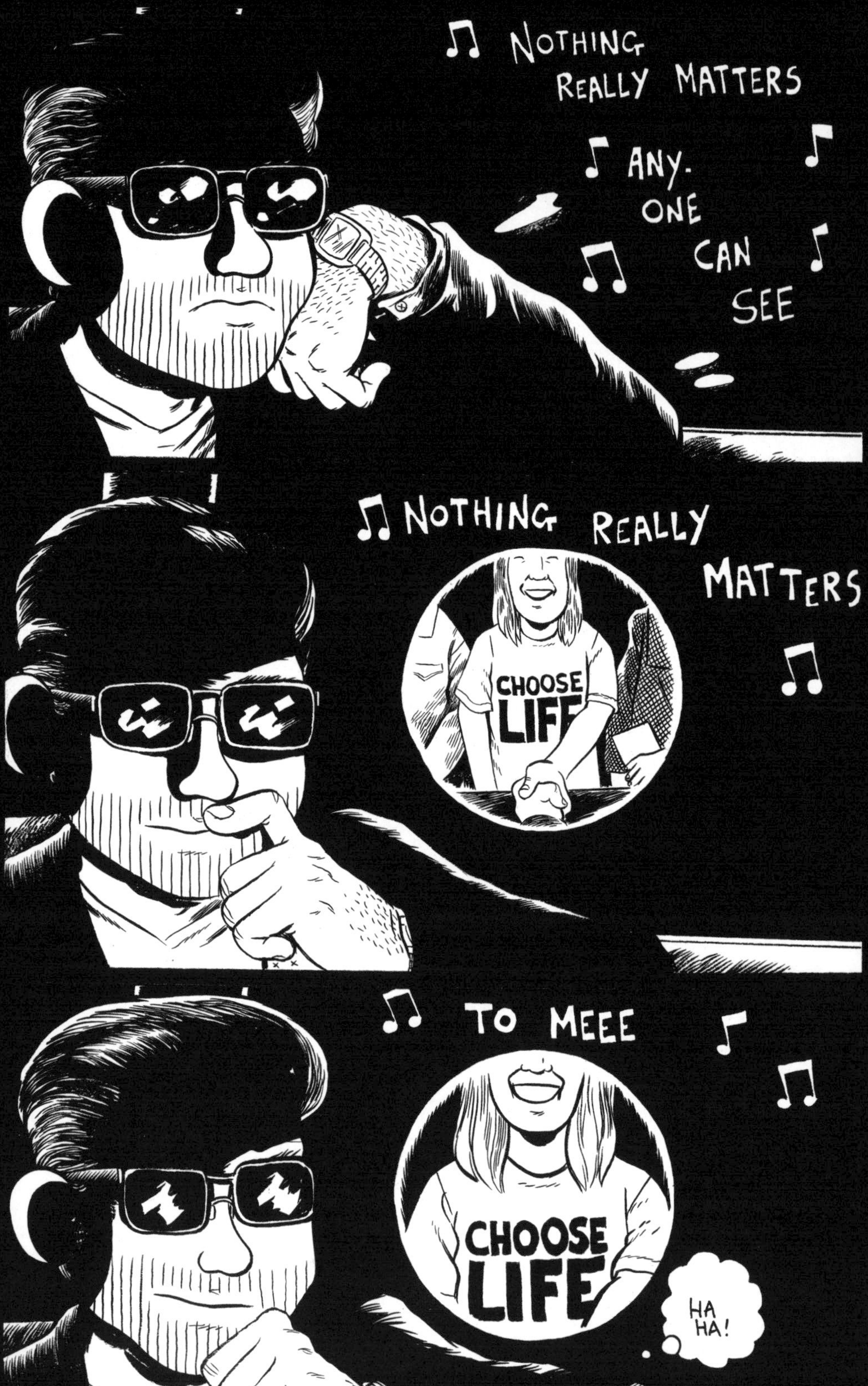
♫ NOTHING REALLY MATTERS
♪ ANY- ONE CAN SEE ♪
♫ NOTHING REALLY MATTERS ♫
CHOOSE LIFE
♫ TO MEEE ♪
CHOOSE LIFE
HA HA!

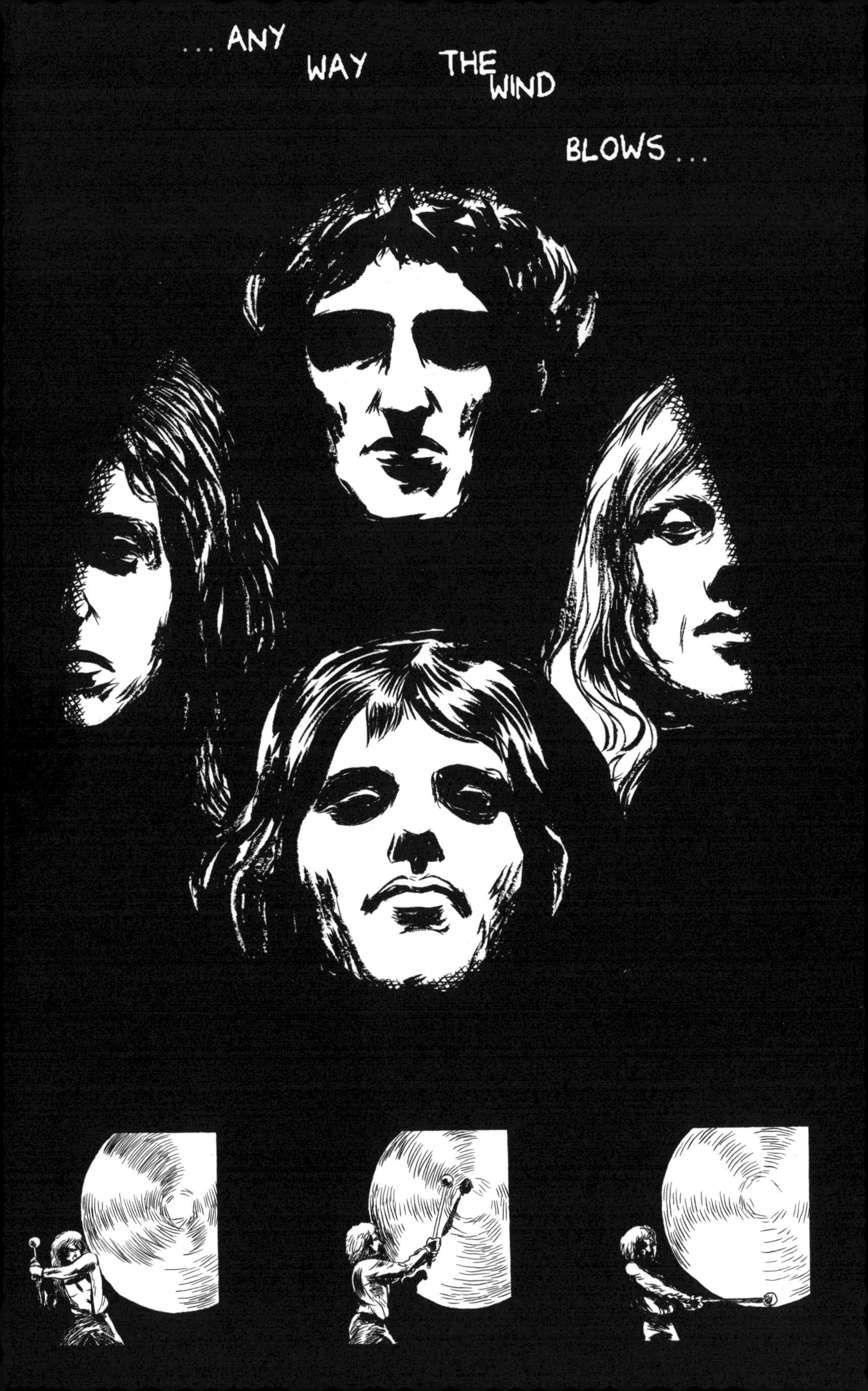
... ANY WAY THE WIND BLOWS ...

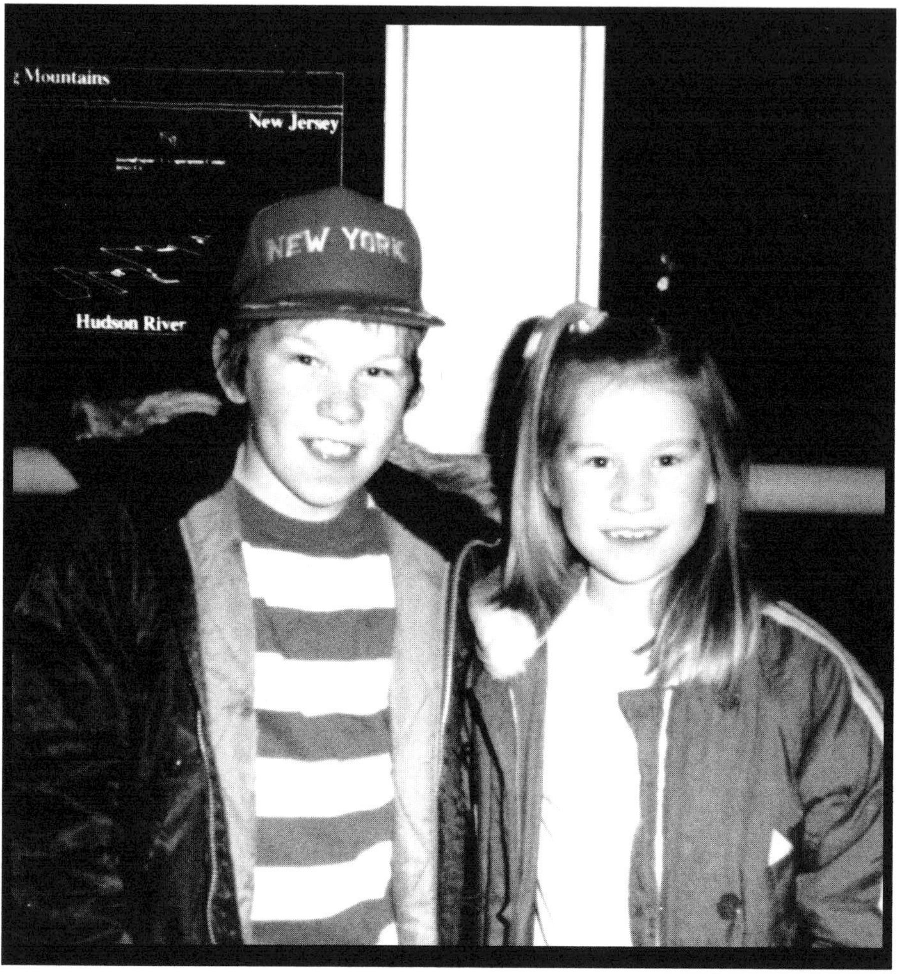
Mountains
New Jersey
NEW YORK
Hudson River

MIKE AND SARAH DAWSON, NEW YORK CITY, CIRCA 1987